I0796999

TRIUMPH

AN AMERICAN GIRL'S JOURNEY OUT OF SAUDI ARABIA

ELISE EVANS MARTIN

Triumph: An American Girl's Story out of Saudi Arabia

Published by Clovercroft Publishing, Franklin, Tennessee
ClovercroftPublishingGroup.com

Cover Design by Will von Bolton

Cover photography by Noel Marcantel Photography

Interior Design by Suzanne Lawing

Edited by Nancy Fraze

Printed in the PRC

ISBN: (print) 978-1-956370-86-7

Women are to be subservient
to their husbands in all things

A husband can beat his wife as long as
he does not leave a mark on her face

Sex out of wedlock is punishable by death ...
for the woman

Saudis are the superior race

Religious police are necessary

Jews are the devil, Israel is the enemy

9/11 was a victory to be celebrated

There is only one religion—Islam.

All non-Muslims are infidels

That is what I was taught ...that is what I believed

Until I went on the journey on which
I am now going to take you

Dedication

I dedicate this book to two strong, kind, heroic men:
Daren Martin, Ph.D., for giving me the strength
and courage to write this book,
and

An anonymous patriot who provided the environment
for writing this book and the encouragement to finish it.
Without you both, this book might never have been published.

In addition, and most especially, I dedicate this to
my adopted mom for too many reasons to list here,
but most of all, for her love and support.

Emma, may you keep your dreams on
your horizon and always know, they are reachable.

Writing this book is the hardest thing I have ever done,
but it also might very well be the most important.

CONTENTS

On a personal note, one of the most baffling parts of writing my story is the beginning. I do not want to blather on, and you do not want to read the opening line from David Copperfield, "I am born." So, here goes... I have read almost all the major books that supposedly give an inside look at Saudi Arabia and all I have to say is this:

I am going to tell the truth about everything, and I do not give a shit how that looks to Saudi Arabia or America.

SIX MONTHS IN THE HOLE

When we first came to this place, I was grateful and excited about the six couch pieces that my grandmother had removed from her ladies' sitting room and pushed together for me, creating a kind of corner-like bed for me facing the TV. My brother and I used to push the cushions together like this when we were young to play spaceship, pretending it was a castle or a secret hideout. This type of couch that was commonly seen in most homes I think is called a divan which is a long seat formed of a mattress like cushion which was measured, and custom made for the *Majlis* (sitting room). It sat against the side of the room, upon the floor or upon a raised structure or frame, with cushions to lean against. I only ever thought I would come into this room to sleep or watch TV but here I sat day after day waiting and wondering what was in store for me. The wallpaper was white and contemporary. The texture was raised up a bit making it soft to the touch, but the patterns just seemed to blend together. In my boredom I looked for things to ponder, patterns to count but sadly the wallpaper did not have enough of a distinguishable pattern on it for me to count. Like all the houses and apartment buildings the walls were of cement, making it cool in the summer but utterly soundproof. It felt like a prison I was completely cut off from the outside world. With the exception of the mattress on the other side of the room where my mother and my siblings slept, they were the only way I received any update on the comings and goings on the other side of the door. There were only six VHS movies to watch: *Swan Princess in Arabic, Man in the Iron Mask, The Blob, Casper the Friendly Ghost, Indiana Jones and The Temple of Doom* and some weird Doris Day movie that was so badly censored it was really hard to follow the plot. Little did I know that the sum of my entertainment for the next six months would be these six movies.

During my solitary confinement, I memorized every line. No matter how hard I tried to forget the plots – as if to see the movie for the first time – it never worked. And yet, I continued watching them. I started to watch the backgrounds of the movies hoping to see something new. In many ways, during those six months they were my best friends. *Casper the Friendly Ghost* felt like a very real companion. *The Swan Princess* felt like the story of how my betrothed and I came together every summer as children, the family had hopes we would fall in love one day and marry, thereby further uniting the tribe. I hoped we would have the same happy ending but now nothing was for certain.

I learned to nap on a whim. I had my mother, brother, and sisters in the room with me – they slept on the other side. But what does one talk about with three small children under the age of seven and what would I want to talk about with the woman who caused my imprisonment? Unlike me, my siblings and mother were allowed to come and go as they pleased. I thought about the boy I was betrothed to at the age of six – my Uncle Fahad – who was somewhere on the other side of the house coming to rescue me by proposing marriage. I thought about my life. I thought about outside, the rain, how the wallpaper in the hallway felt against my fingertips. I wondered what it would be like to be surrounded by people again. But as the days stretched on what I thought about the most was how I got here. I never knew when I boarded that plane at the age of three that this would be my destiny. I never contemplated having just six movies and my schoolbooks to bide the time. I never knew that sleeping and dreaming are the only true escape when you are trapped. To explain how I got here let me take you back to when it all started…

CHILDHOOD

Where we start in life affects our future, our choices, and ultimately who we become. I was born to two loving parents in San Diego in Southern California in the United States. My parents divorced when I was young – I was too young to remember my father. My mother, Jennifer, took me and my older brother to visit Saudi Arabia when I was three. It was an odd location for a woman with two small children to travel in the 1980s but at the time my mother's parents were living and working there. My mother's father, Charles, after retiring from the U.S. Navy, got a job as a technician in the King Faisal Specialist Hospital and had moved to Saudi Arabia in the 1970s with his wife, my maternal grandmother. My mother took a job in the hospital laboratory, which altered her visiting visa into a residency. We all lived together. Grandma stayed at home but slept most of the time, and my mother worked the night shift. We were looked after by a maid in the daytime and Grandpa would cook us dinner at night. I lived a life most little girls dream of at that age. I had everything I could have ever wished for – lots of toys, a custom-painted pink room, tailored dresses, and a playmate for life in my brother, Chris. I was described as a quiet, endlessly happy, and content child who never complained much and was often content with whatever I was given.

We grew up in the heart of Riyadh, the capital of Saudi Arabia. Despite the law of the land being such that all non-Islamic gatherings and holidays were considered illegal at the time, we still managed to celebrate Thanksgiving, Christmas, and go to church like any other American family. There are two major types of expats in the Kingdom of Saudi Arabia – those who lived as they would have in their country behind tall compound walls, and those who married into the local population and integrated into the Saudi culture. We were of the first kind. Behind the high walls of the compound that kept us separate from the local population we were free to embrace our own traditions, provided we did not advertise the fact – The Religious Police tended to turn a blind eye.

It is at this point that I must introduce the enforcement arms of the Saudi State. Saudi Arabia has two kinds of police. The first is the police, similar to the type of police you see in any country – the ones who deal with the real criminals. They handle traffic violations, robbery, murder, speeding tickets, and so on. The second kind is the religious police that enforce the laws and moral traditions of the Saudi interpretation of Islam and *Wahhabism*. *Wahhabism* is embedded in society in an institutional manner in both Saudi Arabia and Qatar. In Saudi Arabia, the state adopts *Wahhabism* in its political system and regards the Wahhabi establishment as part of the state. Qatar on the other hand, does not. In Qatar, women are not required to cover technically (although it would be advisable), and alcohol can be found in a hotel bar. *Wahhabism* in Saudi Arabia is a strict interpretation with roots in Saudi Arabia that is propagated by the regime and clerics. I will explain its origin in greater detail later.

The religious police, or the *Hiya* and *Mutawa*, as they are often called, made sure that all the men on the street observed the call to prayer five times a day, set up checkpoints to stop men and women from dating or engaging in what was considered immoral behavior, and many other infractions. They police almost all aspects of daily civic life to ensure compliance with the will of Allah as they see it. *Hiya* are the actual religious police that have the right to tell you to cover your face and enforce any Sharia Law they see you breaking. The less official *Mutawa* is a self-given title referring to a religious man that grows a long beard and wear a white thobe that only comes to his ankles. Since often it is so hard to tell them apart, we would just do our best to avoid any man who looked this way. Typically, you could tell them apart by the sticks the *Hiya* carried; these cane-like sticks were used to beat anyone that they decided was breaking Sharia Law. However, some of them did not carry sticks, they wore no badges and had no other indicators of who they were except their very religious demeanor and appearance. Therefore, more often they were called *Mutawa*, and if we saw a *Mutawa* we stayed as far away as possible.

The *Hiya* are the present-day manifestation and militarization of an ancient Muslim duty. Historically, it was considered the duty of every Muslim to lookout for his/her fellow brother or sister and bring them back into the fold of the righteous. When Islam was still in its infancy and Muslims were being persecuted, it may have made sense. Many of those early converts found themselves slipping back into the ways of their parents and grandparents who were idol worshipers. Perhaps it was necessary to issue reminders to the flock to not stray. Some version of this is practiced in most religions. The punishment for leaving Islam is death. This law has not been altered in Saudi Arabia. In fact it might surprise you to learn that according to a Muslim opinion survey published in 2013 by the *Pew Research Center* in the section entitled *Penalty for Converting to Another Faith,* "Taking the life of those who abandon Islam is most widely supported in Egypt (86%) and Jordan (82%). Roughly two-thirds who want sharia to be the law of the land also back this penalty in the Palestinian territories (66%). In the other countries surveyed in the Middle East-North Africa region, fewer than half take this view."

Fast forward to present times, as more and more expats arrived at the Kingdom, the religious police grew restless and stopped distinguishing between Muslims and Non-Muslims. Everyone on Saudi Arabian soil is subject to Sharia/ Islamic Law, without exception. I mentioned the high walls of the compound, but the truth is that every home in Saudi has high walls, all windows are barred, and the curtains are almost always drawn.

One of the many reasons for the curtains and blacked out windows comes from Sharia. In Islam, a woman's beauty is required to be hidden from men other than her husband or a male relative that she cannot marry. During the 1980s – and in a way, even today – this law is still enforced. Punishment for violating this law can end with something as simple as being taken against one's will to a holding center until a male member of the family comes and signs a paper stating that the woman was caught in an immoral act, and she agrees that it will never happen again. In some extreme cases however, a girl can receive lashes in the public square as an example to discourage others from doing the same, or long-term imprisonment. Therefore, the women would not have the chance to enjoy the warmth of the sun and the feeling of a beautiful breeze flowing through their hair if not for these very high walls. For if they were to go out, they must wear an Abaya and a head scarf – both of which are black.

Seasons in Saudi Arabia are not as discernable as they are in the US since it's warm year-round. In winter, all we ever needed was a good sweater, the palm trees never seemed to change color, and rain is so rare that there is a special rain prayer. Its arrival is always considered a blessing from *Allah* (God). Sandstorms were the only sudden weather I remember. My mom would panic and run around the house shouting, "Close the windows, a sandstorm is coming!" We would even have to place a wet towel under the door to make sure no sand got in. If you forgot even one window the house would get covered in a thick layer of red dust, even though the storm would only last about 15 minutes.

Snow never fell during Christmas time in the capital. We only knew Christmas was coming when my grandma would pull out the JCPenney catalog. We loved that catalog. We couldn't order from it because even today the mail is not delivered to houses, but rather only to your place of work. This system was contrived as "making things easier." I believe the real purpose was so that husbands could screen all mail and determine what made it home and what didn't.

In Islam, men are the custodians of women, and every woman is required to be obedient to her male guardian. For young women this is often their fathers, and for wives their husband. Back in those days, many things were not allowed to enter the country. For example, the first Disney movie we ever saw, *The Little Mermaid*, was a used VHS tape given to us by a Christian family who was leaving the country. They had smuggled it in as a wedding gift wrapped in silver paper. The scanner flagged it, but when the customs officer asked them to unwrap it, they pleaded that it was a gift for a wedding. The customs officer decided to let it pass and I'll bet some money exchanged hands. It was very dangerous for the family to try and take it out of the country again. They were lucky the first time and a second success would not be guaranteed. You might ask why a simple children's movie was banned back then? The reason is that *The Little Mermaid* was considered very indecent; nudity (which could be as simple as a girl in a short skirt) was never tolerated, since women should be covered at all times. *The Little Mermaid* fell under the category of pornography, and possession of such things carried a punishment no one wanted to risk. Likewise, any other religious items such as Christmas decorations, were also banned. So, our tree had to be smuggled in as well. *Barbie* dolls fell under the same category.

BUYING A BARBIE IN RIYADH.

My grandpa took me to buy a *Barbie* one day. It was always an exciting time. It's important to mention that in Saudi Arabia all Muslims are required to pray five times a day. All businesses and stores must stop what they are doing and shut their doors in order for the men to go to the mosque and observe prayer. Women are not required to go to the mosque and instead pray in their office, prayer room or home. It seems harsh but the Muslims believe that a man who prays in the mosque five times a day and never misses a prayer will have a place reserved for him in Heaven. If we think that every Muslim is responsible for helping his or her brother in Islam to follow the righteous path, the burden on the King to answer for his flock was greater, just as it is the duty of a father to make sure his family was pious or answer to Allah later.

The religious police always traveled in packs of three or more, carrying sticks and looking for stores that did not abide by the law. I will elaborate on them more in a moment. Now, what if you're not Muslim are you still required to close your store and go to prayer? The answer is yes. It is the law of the country, and you might have employees who need to go to prayer. If you are not required to go to prayer because you're a non-Muslim, you still must observe the prayer times with respect by closing your shop and sitting quietly. If you leave your house to go shopping and arrive at a store one minute after the prayer call sounds, you will have to wait 20 minutes for the shop to open again. For this reason and because of the extreme heat, most of the population shops after the final prayer of the day, *Isha*. The prayer times are dependent on the sun and include a dawn prayer called *Fajr*, a mid-day prayer called *Duhar*, a mid-afternoon prayer called *Asr*, a sunset prayer called

Magrib, and the last prayer, *Isha*. In the winter, *Isha* can be around 7:00 p.m., and in the summer it can be as late as 9:00 p.m.

I recall an example of a Christian man on the street one day who was ordered to go to prayer by a *Mutawa* but respectfully said he was Christian. The Mutawa ordered him to go sit in the Mosque regardless so that he might be able to hear the word of the one true God, *Allah*, and save his soul. Like in any religion, you can find religious liberals who will converse intelligently and fundamentalists who will accept no discussion on what they believe to be the correct interpretation of Islam. Make no mistake, the *Mutawa* are fundamentalists – if you ever meet one, do not argue – just get out of their way, bow your head, and avoid their radars. Suspected wrongdoers have been taken, tortured, locked up, and even killed at the hands of the *Mutawa*, and the people have no recourse.

Now back to the *Barbie*. My grandpa took me that day to a toy store near our compound in an area called *As-Sulaymaniyah.* As we reached the store, the prayer call sounded, and the shopkeeper was turning off the lights. We stepped inside and waited while he pulled down the metal security bars over his shop. He looked at my grandpa and said nothing. Because my grandpa was obviously a foreigner the shopkeeper knew he would not tell the *Mutawa* that he had not gone to prayer, and so he continued his routine of shutting down the shop. This happened often to us, while the locals were asked to stand outside restaurants or finish and leave while prayer was going on, we were always allowed to sit quietly inside and wait out the prayer, finish eating or continue grocery shopping in the dark. This always brought with it great risk to the shop owners, but we knew that as well should we be discovered by the *Mutawa*, we too would face their wrath.

When the shopkeeper was done closing up, he looked at my grandpa without saying anything, lifted his head back slightly and made a head gesture that seemed to say, "What are you looking for?" My grandpa quietly whispered, "We came for a *Barbie*." The man nodded, pulled a set of keys out from under the counter and started to walk down the dark middle aisle of the toy store. We followed. Like anyone can imagine a toy store looks different in the dark. All the lights were off and the teddy bears and dolls sitting on the high shelves seemed to glare down at us as we passed through the aisle. To a young girl it was quite eerie.

Once we reached the back of the store, we came upon a small door, which seemed to be a storage closet. The man unlocked the door, went inside, and reached up to pull a string that turned on one hanging lightbulb that barely lit the room. He then pointed to the shelf on the right. My grandpa nodded his head in thanks and then turned to me, crouched down to my eye level, and whispered "Pick one and let's go." I felt stressed, as I knew from past experience that a decision needed to be made quickly. Which *Barbie* to choose. I knew I really wanted a *Barbie* in a gown this time. I looked at each box intently and tried my best to guess what the *Barbies* might be wearing based on their hairstyle, since the rest of the plastic box had been blacked out with a permanent marker. This was done to everything – even books. In the event they were discovered by the religious police, the shopkeeper could claim he had covered the indecent *Barbies*, or better yet, he received them that way and had no idea that they were indecent. I finally reached up and grabbed one. My grandpa handed the man a $100 Riyal note, which is the equivalent of about $30 US Dollars, placed the *Barbie* in a black plastic bag to conceal what it was, and we headed for the door. By this time prayer was finishing, the shopkeeper opened the door slowly to check that the coast was clear so that it would not look like we were in the store during the prayer, and we went home. When I got home, I opened the *Barbie* box only to discover that, like every other time, I had ended up with a *Barbie* in a bikini. Rather than be disappointed, I said to myself, "Next time, I'll pick the right one and get a *Barbie* in a gown."

JENNIFER

My mother was the youngest of five girls. The story goes that my grandpa wanted a son to help on the farm but had five girls. Instead of despairing, he put his youngest daughter to work on the farm as his honorary boy. While her sisters learned how to be good homemakers inside the house, she was learning how to kill chickens and work the land. Being brought up in the United States where women experience independence in such a different way than in Saudi Arabia, the adjustment for her from a life of simple pleasures (like driving or going out alone) proved to be challenging to her – both in the short-term and the long-term.

Being brought up as a boy, beloved by her father and spoiled because she was the youngest, this created a superiority complex as well as a sense that… *daddy will take care of it.* These circumstances hindered her ability to hold a job long-term, commit to anything, or have the patience required to assimilate and adapt to a new culture. She didn't consider that a divorced or single woman in Saudi will find dating to be a challenge since it is illegal for a man and woman to be alone without an appropriate male chaperone.

There were very few places in Saudi Arabia that were off limits to the *Mutawa* except compounds that had guards, who were instructed to not allow any man dressed in traditional Saudi attire to enter. Compounds included the Diplomatic Quarter (DQ), which housed all the embassies, consulates, and the King's Hospital, where my mother worked. Some of the larger compounds had an onsite restaurant, (sometimes more than one) and even a golf course. The compound in which we lived was much smaller. It was located right off a major road in Riyadh called Takhassusi. There was no GPS back then and even today you still need to navigate based on landmarks. In fact, the only places that have mailing addresses are some businesses. Most people's mail had to be addressed to a P.O. Box in their local post office. There are no mailboxes for residential buildings, which meant there were no house numbers most of the time.

I was told that the palace that was across the street from our compound belonged to Prince Bandar bin Sultan Al Saud. He was born of a mother who was a Sudanese concubine. The thing that concerns me about this fact is not that he was born of a Sudanese concubine but that the country routinely imprisons, whips and stones to death its citizens for adultery. Yet the royal family seems to be placed above the very same Sharia Law it claims is at the heart and soul of its society. One cannot hope to gain the respect of one's subjects if it places themselves above the very law it enforces. If the rules don't apply to you, then how can you hope to be seen as more than a modern-day dictatorship?

He would hold court in Ramadan and the people would line up outside his palace on the street. Just like in old medieval times, this is very common in Saudi Arabia – if you were lucky enough to be granted an audience you would very possibly get anything you asked for – a plot of land, money for a marriage dowry, a pardon, anything. When I say our compound was small, it really consisted of only 23 villas – 10 on each side creating a square and three in the middle. Larger compounds could

have 100 or more villas. When you entered the compound there was one middle villa facing a small pool and the one on the other side of the pool in the middle was ours with one villa behind us. All the balconies faced the pool, not the other walls of the compound.

We all learned early that the *Mutawa* believed that most indecent behavior must take place at night so the checkpoints at almost every highway entrance and exit were extra vigilant. As a result, everyone had sex and dated in the daytime, while the *Mutawa* slept. Any car with a woman beside a man in the front, or in some cases in the back seat, was suspect. If the driver did not look like your regular Indian or Pakistani driver, the car and its passengers would be detained and subject to a request for what is called your *family document.* This document is a small passport-like book that was carried at all times, since even a husband with his wife grocery shopping might be asked to produce it. I always found it interesting that the card listed every family member under the man's guardianship. The man, however, had a picture of him in it while the women were only listed by name. In those days, and very much still today, no self-respecting Saudi man would allow a picture of his wife without her face cover to be placed on an ID card that other men would see. This also meant he could take any woman in his car and pretend she was his wife. Deeply rooted in old values and the protection of their women (one could also say "property"), Saudi men have killed each other over less. Still, today instead of a woman showing her driver's license, her fingerprint is just scanned so that her veil need never be raised.

Why didn't people just take separate cars, you might ask? They did, and in my mother's case, it was not a problem. But if, for example, a Muslim girl wanted to meet a male friend, she would often need to do so without her family knowing so using the driver was not an option.

Our family was Mormon, and my grandparents, before their arrival to Riyadh, were put in touch with a contact that would help them find out when and where church services or other gatherings were held. Gatherings and services were often held on Fridays so they would blend in with the local population and go unnoticed by the *Mutawa.* Friday in Saudi was like Sunday everywhere else, a day of rest and family gatherings. Being caught observing a different religion or soliciting non-Christians to attend services brought with it the hefty punishment of deportation, lashes, permanent banishment from the Kingdom or all three. We didn't talk about the gatherings to people outside the circle for the safety of all involved – it was a world of *better safe than sorry* – but to us that was normal.

My mother found many suitors eager to get to know her. They came and went so often for many reasons, but one of which was that my brother considered it a fun game to make them as uncomfortable as possible. The vision of my mother in her youth dressing up to go on a date or to a party always stayed with me. As she would don her yellow dress, put on her makeup and twirl around so full of light before donning her black Abaya and leaving us with the maid or my grandparents.

In the Kingdom, men are forbidden the company of any women to whom they are not related to by marriage or blood. In a country where pornography is unavailable, there were no advertisements that featured women. There were no female news anchors back then and all books and magazines that showed women uncovered were blacked out with a black marker before they could be sold – just as my *Barbie* box had been.

As you can imagine, if men have no access to see the one thing they crave, the single sight of a woman's hands, eyes, face or a naked foot in a sandal could drive them quite wild. This caused them to often follow cars with girls inside to find out where they live. Car crashes were very common, as male drivers became reckless just to look at some girl a moment longer. Men would call random phone numbers just to hear a woman say hello and all kinds of chaos which still goes on today.

My grandmother had a habit of testing the limits of the Kingdom's laws, especially that women should wear an Abaya. When my grandma was told she needed to wear this black garment for her modesty and protection, her great pride erupted. She was a stylish woman who believed that she was modest, even if she was not dressed in black. So, she rebelled and had the tailor make her an abaya in red from the finest fabric she could find. She insisted it be knee-length since in her mind a woman is still modest as long as her knees are covered. The story goes that my grandmother, wore this Abaya every time she went out and for the most part, being obviously American, she had no trouble. Everyone however stared at her in complete shock wherever she went. The *Mutawa* are too few to be everywhere at once and, somehow, she had managed to avoid them – until one day in the market the prayer call sounded.

The shops started to lock up and while walking around she did not notice the arrival of the *Mutawa* on the scene. They noticed her immediately since she was the only woman dressed in red. She stood out like a sore thumb. They approached her from behind and yelled, "Woman, cover yourself!" in Arabic. She ignored them since she didn't understand what they were saying and found them to be very rude to address her by shouting at her. Sadly, as she walked away a quick blow with a stick hit her exposed legs. She fell to the ground and my mother gently helped her up, bowed her head to the *Mutawa* and helped my grandma into a taxi home. They were fortunate that the *Mutawa* didn't decide to take any further steps that night. I suspect because of my grandmother's age – the culture has a great respect for the elderly –they let her go. One might think that such an incident would have discouraged my grandma but, alas, it was one of many occasions when she deliberately disobeyed the rules of the country, and with each incident, she became more set on the idea that they were all brutish barbarians, uneducated, uncultured and behind the rest of the world. She believed it was her role to teach them how to be civilized.

Everything continued as it did until the day I met the man who would eventually change the trajectory of my life forever.

ABDUL RASHEED AL-TURKISTANI (RASHAD)

Rashad was born in a house that was built on top of one of the mountains in the Holy City of Mecca. His father traveled from what was then Turkistan to Saudi Arabia, on foot with his infant son from his first marriage – a trip that would have taken him more than 40 days to complete if he didn't stop for anything.

Rashad's father left because at the time Turkistan was (and I believe still is) under the rule of China and so the one-child law was in place. When his wife got pregnant with their second son and gave birth in secret, he knew he had to leave for the safety of his newborn. He tried to convince his wife to come with him, but as it often is, especially back then, she felt afraid to leave behind everything she had ever known, including her family support system and way of life, to take such a dangerous trip. She agreed, to avoid suspicion, he should go and then later she might follow.

He arrived in Saudi during a time period when nationality was granted by the more traditional laws of the tribes. All one needed to do was build a sustainable perimeter around a piece of land that no one had yet claimed, and keep it maintained and taken care of for a long period of about ten years. He did this, and finally built a small house on the mountain. He raised his son happily – working and living a simple life until his son, Ghafour, was old enough to marry. One of the neighbors told him of a family known for their religious values, manners, and proper way of bringing up their children.

He went there to ask for one of the daughters' hand in marriage for his son. After a lengthy conversation with the father, it was pointed out to him that he had now been more than sixteen years without a wife himself, and the father, because he loved and respected him, offered that they do a double wedding: his older daughter to Rashad's father and his younger daughter to his son. This sort of arrangement was commonplace, as was the fact that Rashad's father was now taking a second wife. Many families in that time – and still today – only wanted to see their daughter married and protected by honest, kind men as soon as possible to ensure the continuation of the line and to strengthen the family through new ties.

Rashad's father was now forty and the older of the two girls named Fatima, who is known to me and everyone in the family as *Omi* (meaning mother) was 12 years old. From what I have heard, they had a long and happy marriage, although it was very hard at first. She was Saudi and only spoke Arabic, while he only spoke a language no longer in use today, called *Bukhari*. They spent the first few years of their marriage teaching each other their respective languages. Luckily for Fatima, her sister-in-law (and daughter-in-law) was her actual sister, so she was never alone in her struggle. They had four sons and one daughter, the first of which was born when she was 13 and the last was born when she was 46, an unexpected joy. His name was Fahad.

They lived in Mecca and raised their children. There were times when the only thing available for the children to eat was tea and some *Kaakah*, a thin hard bread that would keep for a while. They all worked hard but, with the times, feeding all the children was hard. Rashad, the second son being too young to be useful, was sent to live with his maternal grandfather. This is where he learned to read books. Sadly, most of the books his grandfather had were not in Arabic but Turkish, and so he found a Turkish to Arabic dictionary, and taught himself with great difficulty to read Turkish. In a time before TV, video games, or even mandatory school – and when it was too dangerous to let your children run around the neighborhood alone – books were his only solace to pass the hours, so learning to read was paramount.

Once his family was doing better, Rashad returned home and grew up with his brothers and sister. He attended high school and lived a typical life of a young boy in Saudi in the 1970's. His father eventually was able to travel back to Turkistan to visit his firstborn son and first wife. Rashad went along often and stayed with his mother in the hotel, while his father visited his other family. Rashad, being a teenager, went out exploring and as is often the case, ended up meeting a girl. She was Turkish and, because he had learned to read Turkish, he was able to communicate with her in writing. He was only there for a short while, so they communicated through letters when they were apart. He returned a few years later, but sadly after asking around, he discovered that she had been told she was to marry someone other than Rashad and threw herself from a balcony and died. Rashad never forgave himself, for he believed that his letters caused her to kill herself.

His life was a hard one, but he thrived. He did well in school and made his plans to get more out of life and see more of the world. As tradition would have it, he was matched with a girl from a suitable family. They got engaged, and the family planned to have them married following his graduation from college. In Saudi Arabia, as is the case in many Arab countries, it is very normal for children – male and female – to live with their parents until they are married and, in some cases, even after marriage. As soon as he graduated, he knew he wanted more than to just get married and work in the area he grew up in, so he applied and accepted a position in the King's Hospital in the capital, Riyadh, which is a ten-hour drive from Mecca. As often happens, his fiancé refused to leave her family behind and move to a new and scary place. Girls often turn down proposals that involve leaving their families behind because they fear that if something should go wrong, they would have no support system. So, the engagement was broken off, and he moved alone to the capital. His family wasn't pleased, as is so often the case; they wanted to keep everyone together and close by, but Rashad had bigger dreams.

He worked in the laboratory and enjoyed his work. His weekends were spent swimming, bowling, and hanging out with his new friends, and dating as many beautiful expats as he could – in secret. Now that he was away from his family, he could find some sense of freedom from the traditions, rules, and the constant matchmaking. Single men living alone can only mean trouble and scandal, so families try to get their sons married as soon as they can – as to avoid mistakes and the chance that their son might choose an unsuitable bride. Many tribes prefer to marry from their own, simply because it would guarantee the continuance of their traditions, food, and language onto the next generation. And as *Omi* would later say, "It helps for the couple to have a foundation in common to start their life on, since they would hardly know each other when they marry."

My mother met Rashad one afternoon at work. Although they had seen each other many times, they had never really spoken. Rashad, at the time, was dating a Russian nurse and my mother was smitten, but she held back showing her feelings. She thought he was handsome and smart, but since her ex-husband had been handsome, suave, and smart, she didn't trust that those were good reasons to consider him as a potential suitor. Once she noticed his brown teeth and his obviously cheap shoes however, she believed that it was a sign that under all that handsome, debonair, intelligent exterior was a humble and kind soul. So, she set out to get his attention. Her opportunity arrived when one of the ladies in the laboratory baked a cheesecake. Rashad, upon tasting it said, "It's the best cheesecake I have ever had." My mother, standing by, said, "Mine is better, and I don't even bake mine." Rashad noted a twinge of jealousy in my mother's voice and replied, "You can't make a cheesecake without baking it." She took his words as a challenge and said, "I will bring you my cheesecake tomorrow." And with that, she left and went home. She spent all night trying to make the best cheesecake in the world. I still recall seeing her in the kitchen making a massive mess and stressing about each cheesecake failure. The next day she took it into work, carrying it on one hand like a waitress serving something spectacular. She placed it down before him and said, "There you go." She walked away, leaving him to enjoy it. With a sense of fear of what it might taste like, he took the leap, and had a bite – followed by another bite – until he had found that he had consumed the entire cheesecake. She intrigued him, so he asked if she would like to go out sometime – to which she attributed to the magic of her cheesecake.

He took her to a Chinese restaurant. In Saudi, in order for the women to be able to eat out comfortably without being seen by other men, all the booths have curtains, and the waiter does not enter without announcing himself first, thus making it easy enough to eat dinner without being seen by the *Mutawa*. After they finished dinner, Rashad decided that it was too late to try and take her home – so, he told her, "It's too late and the *Mutawa* will catch us for sure. Would you like to come back to my place, stay the night, and then I'll take you home in the morning?" She didn't know what to do, if they tried to get her to her home, they would surely be caught. If she went to his place, who knows what would happen. And a single white female taking a taxi in Saudi Arabia back then, so late at night, was never a good idea. They arrived at his little apartment, and then ended up making love all night.

In the morning my Mother woke up so ashamed of what she had done she began to cry. He looked over, and his first thought was, "Geez." After further consideration, he realized what a gem he had found. To Rashad, like many Saudis from his time, American women were seen as women of loose morals who exposed their naked flesh and were willing to jump into bed with anyone like common prostitutes. Thus far, he had never slept with a woman who felt remorse about sleeping with someone who wasn't her husband. After comforting her, he took her home. She crept into the house – shoes in hand – and saw her father standing in the hall. He stared her down until she exclaimed, "I wasn't doing anything!" Without saying a word, he headed off to work.

After a few close calls with the *Mutawa*, my mom had the great idea that perhaps if she brought her children along, the *Mutawa* might be reluctant to think they were dating and stop them. So, she invited Rashad home to meet her children and her parents for the first time.

My mother ordered my brother to behave and be nice to her guest, but upon his arrival my brother had a different idea. He looked at me and said, "When he arrives, call him Daddy. It will be really funny." I, being the good younger sister, always said, "Okay." The time came, and the man walked in the door. Our mother introduced him, "Children, this is Rashad – a friend of mine." The two of us placed our hands behind our backs, looked up, and said in a very evil tone, "Hi, Daddy." The man's face of course turned yellow as his thoughts raced about the expectations – about whether or not this was our doing – or perhaps our mother had said something in front of us. He soon brushed it off and tried his best to engage us.

He picked me up and swung me between his legs. My brother, of course, was not interested in knowing anything about him. I was curious about this stranger since he was the first real *Barbarian*, as my grandma called them, that my mother had brought home. As our mother walked with us to the door, we encountered Grandma sitting in her chair reading. Rashed would later point out that she sat in such a way that she conveyed an air like the Queen of England. We got into the car. My mother insisted that I ride in the front seat. I was horrified by the idea that I would have to sit next to someone in the same group of people my grandma talked about every day. Ah! It was horrifying. I got in, folded my arms, and gave him a dirty look. I was busy sulking and making a face, looking out the window, and scrolling my silver letter E back and forth on its chain – a gift from my grandmother.

Soon enough, my mother said, "Elise, Rashad is from Saudi Arabia. Isn't that nice?" I turned my head slowly, looked at my mother through the crack between the seats, and then looked at Rashad with a scowl. I crossed my arms, made a face, and proclaimed in a petulant way, "I don't like Arabs." My mom was mortified that such words just came out of her precious baby girl of only five years of age. During this first meeting, she was about to scold me, when Rashad started laughing. So, my mom let it go, and the date continued. They had many more such dates, until one day, as is expected, the topic of religion came up.

Rashad had already decided that he wanted to marry her but knew he could never take a Christian bride home – since it would be bad enough that she was divorced and had two small children. In the eyes of his family, it would seem as though he had married beneath him – since a young, accomplished man could secure a match with a good virgin girl from a "known" family. As crude as this metaphor may sound, it's like getting a used car for your graduation versus a brand new one. To dilute the criticism that he was sure to face from everyone, she would have to convert. This way, at least no one could say she was a woman of loose morals.

He knew this would not be easy since my mother was stubborn and loved her religion – therefore, asking her outright would never work. So, he approached her with a question, "Why don't you cover your hair?" She looked at him with a mixture of anger, shock, and surprise, answering very confidently, "Because my religion does not require me to cover my hair." He calmly replied, "Are you sure about that?" Just like the cheesecake, she took up the challenge and said, "I will prove it to you." It took a month for her to read both the Book of Mormon and Quran, cover-to-cover, before she finally approached the subject again.

She arrived at work with everyone staring at her, shocked and surprised. When she reached her station in the laboratory, Rashad came up to her and asked, "Why are you covering your hair?" She looked down at the floor, and then slowly gazed into his eyes and said, "Because I could find nothing in my religion that said that I have to cover my hair, but I also found nothing that said I don't have to cover my hair." With that, the decision was made.

It would be a long, drawn-out battle before they could marry. During the reign of King Fahad (May God Rest His Soul), it was illegal for a Saudi national to marry a foreigner. They first married in secret in India, and then they had to wait two years to try to get a royal exception for the marriage to be accepted in Saudi Arabia. For these reasons, the newly married couple moved in with my grandparents – since it was a family home in a compound. I suppose people would just assume that the young man was renting a room and look the other way. My mom and our new stepdad did everything in their power to get the exception, which would allow their marriage to be recognized, before my mother became pregnant – or they were discovered. If she was pregnant and not married, she was at risk of being stoned to death, or at least deported. Only a Prince or the King could grant such an exception and getting a moment of their time while they were in a good mood was difficult.

It was my grandpa who finally solved the problem. While making his equipment repair rounds, he was called to a patient's hospital room. Normally, another technician would go, but in this case because of the patient's high rank, only the department head could be trusted with the task. He walked in – and in his very casual way – made small talk, was kind, helped the man obtain the channels he wanted on the TV, and fixed some odd thing or other as needed. When the work was completed, the man was so grateful that he asked if there was anything he could do for my grandpa. My grandpa already knew he was talking to a member of the Royal family, so he very calmly said, "I wonder if you could advise me on a situation? Since I know nothing of the culture here, perhaps you, as a national, would be able to help me?" The man said, "Of course," and asked him to sit and offered him some tea.

My grandpa relayed the story of how his youngest daughter had fallen in love with a national, and he wanted to see them married as would be proper to avoid shame on the family, should something happen between them. The man, hearing the situation and being a father himself, sympathized with my grandpa, and said, "Send the man who your daughter wants to marry to see me, and I'll take care of it." My grandfather had done what so many were unable to do. My grandpa learned early on that even people who speak many languages forget that you can speak the same language, but if you cannot speak the culture, or understand and respect it, you will never really be able to speak that language. After all, without the culture the language originated from, there is no language. My grandpa taught me I must first seek to understand before I could hope to be understood.

In September of the year that I turned six, their wedding took place. It was a small wedding by Saudi standards, since it was done in my grandparents' home and not at a wedding hall, as was typical in Saudi tradition. The only guests were family members and very close friends. I was given a new pink dress adorned with bows and fine lace. Because of my young age, I did not completely understand what was going on, except in the context of a fairytale happy ending. The wedding had all of the normal customs upheld, so the bride and groom were separated in the beginning and then joined the women's section of the party together. This was so that the covered ladies could dance and celebrate to their hearts' content inside the house, without fear of being seen by the men who were not their Mahrams – while the men got to sit in the tent outside the house, congratulating Rashad on his marriage. It's tradition to say something in Arabic along the lines of "May *Allah* grant you happiness, and many children." But in this case, what they really meant was, "Congratulations on marrying a very white, American woman." White skin is seen as very rare and beautiful in the Middle East. Because my stepdad was about to marry such a woman he was very revered among the male guests but of course they could not say that aloud. If a Saudi man even hinted that he noticed another man's wife was beautiful it could cause them to physically fight.

The women finished their dancing and one of the older ladies walked around telling everyone that the groom was about to enter so they needed to cover up. All the Muslim women covered up with their Abayas, head covers, and veils. Soon after, the father of the bride took the groom by the hand and led Rashad into the ladies' section, where he saw his bride for the first time that night. She was wearing a traditional sky-blue Pakistani outfit with a silver trim that she had made especially for the occasion. We had taken many trips to Pakistan before my mother met my stepdad. I don't know why we went to Pakistan so often, but I recall my mother always yelling at me saying, "Don't pick the flowers in Saudi, they don't grow naturally. When we go to Pakistan you can pick as many as you want." As a result, I looked forward to our trips to Pakistan every time she had vacation time. She would always have dresses made there. His family found the whole idea of her wearing an outfit from a country that supplies them with a steady flow of drivers and maids beneath their station, but the deed was done. They were now going to be husband and wife, and there was nothing more to be done about it.

He saw her as a vision of loveliness, and happiness beamed from them both. He took her by the arm and led her into the living room where they sat side by side in front of everyone. His mother brought out the set of gold jewelry, which is a gift for the bride from the husband, arranged on a beautiful tray, as was customary. This was to be her *Maher*, which is the gift that he gives to her, in essence, to purchase her virginity/chastity, and by receiving it in front of everyone at the wedding, the marriage becomes complete. More traditionally, she would have received this set of gold, along with a sum of money, before the wedding, which is meant to help her prepare herself for marriage. This is called *Milkia*, or *Kitabah*, and refers to the ceremony at which they sign the marriage contract, making the bride his wife legally, but not yet completely. This is done in advance of the wedding to give the couple a chance to see each other without the possibility of scandal, but they could not consummate the marriage until the wedding took place – giving them both the opportunity to change their minds before it was too late, and the girl has lost her most precious asset – her *Eadhariat Alfata* (a girl's virginity). In my mother's case, since she was divorced and American, many of the regular traditions were seen as unimportant – meaning he got off easily.

Among the golden gifts on the tray, there was a ring – a gift from her new mother-in-law, who liked to be called *Omi* by everyone which meant "mother" in Arabic. Unfortunately, it was too small for my mother's finger. *Omi* had a great idea: she took her youngest son, Fahad, in one hand, and me in the other. She then raised our hands up with the ring and said, "This girl will be for my son." She then placed the ring on my finger.

I looked at the ring, raised my little hand to my mouth to cover up my shy smile, and then I looked upon my future husband. When Fahad saw the way I gazed at him, he immediately jumped up and ran away. I know what you are thinking… since my mother was now married to Rashad, it made Fahad my uncle! But, just as *Omi* and her sister had been married to a father and a son, so too could two brothers marry a mother and a daughter.

The easiest way to explain how it would work would be to use Omi – Rashad and *Omi's* sister's daughter as an example. *Omi* was married to the father, her sister to the son, making *Omi's* children first cousins of her sisters' children. Stay with me… *Omi's* children were also the aunts and uncles to her sister's children. Although it's not uncommon at all for first cousins to marry because Rashad was also Omi's sister's daughter's uncle, uncle would therefore trump cousin and marriage, therefore, would not be allowed.

Fahad, my uncle by marriage, was two years older than me – the same age as my older brother. He grew up in Mecca, living with his mother and father. Because of the distance between Riyadh and Mecca, it would be many months before we would meet again. When summer came, Omi had a great idea that Fahad should spend his summer in Riyadh with his brother Rashad and his two children, and me and my older brother, Chris – in the hopes that he would learn English. It was suspected that it was also intended to give us a chance to grow up together, in the hopes that one day we might fall in love and further unite the family. We would spend many summers together over the years, and my mother used my love for him as a tool to keep me in line, often issuing the phrase, "What would Fahad think if he saw you ________?" – filling in the blank with "sitting that way," "eating that way," "acting that way," etc.

With the marriage – just like that – we were no longer Mormons, but now Muslim with a Muslim head of the household. Everything would change, including the holidays we would celebrate, the customs and regulations we would adopt, the religious traditions we would practice, and much more. Little did I know that much more significant and damaging changes were coming.

THE TWO EID'S

In Islam, there are two *Eid* holidays, *Eid al-Fitr* and *Eid al-Adha. Eid* means feast, festival, or holiday. The word is often added to other holidays in Arabic – for example, *Eid Al-Hub* (Valentine's Day) *Eid Al-Um* (Mother's Day), and so on. The first marks the end of Ramadan, a holy month of fasting, reflection, and charity. For us, the significance was that we got money and candy as gifts from everyone we greeted. We called this the *Eid of Money.* The second *Eid* holiday honors the willingness of Ibrahim to sacrifice his son, Ismael, as an act of obedience to God's command. On this *Eid*, we visit family and every family slaughters something – be it a ram like Ibrahim, or a goat, but mostly lamb. In Saudi, my stepdad would go to the butcher and ask him to slaughter a lamb on our behalf. He would then take some of the meat for us, and the rest was distributed to those in need. As children, this *Eid* was way less exciting, and we referred to it as the *Eid of Candy.*

There was only one holiday that had really mattered to us as children, before my mother's marriage – and that was Christmas. Now that my mom was married to a Saudi, Christmas had to go. My stepdad suggested a quick break moving us from one holiday to the other. Since we were young enough, all we would notice was that now we had two new Christmases instead of one. My mother protested since Christmas had actually been more important to her than it was to us. While we looked forward to the candy, cookies and presents, my mother had always enjoyed the feeling of the season – the tree, the Christmas songs, reading us the stories and all our lovely Mormon-approved religious movies. This change was symbolic of all the changes to everything that was familiar to her – and Christmas wasn't the first, or last, thing to go.

They agreed to phase Christmas out by dressing *Eid* up as Christmas by another name, complete with an *Eid* tree and dates wrapped in Christmas wrapping paper. We got fewer presents and more money, which was spent in the toy store the next day. We didn't know then that this was all preparation for when we would head to Mecca to spend our first Eid with our new Saudi relatives.

Let me beg your indulgence to explain why dates were in Christmas wrapping paper. Dates are enjoyed throughout the year, across the Middle East, but they are especially linked to *Ramadan* and *Eid*. This was because it was recorded that the Prophet Muhammad (ﷺ) would break his fast with dates before anything else and emulating the Prophet (ﷺ) is something all Muslims strive to do. My parents combined the two holidays by wrapping the dates in Christmas paper. The Prophet (ﷺ)'s life was documented in what is called the *Hadeeth*, which is a collection of stories about the Prophet (ﷺ), his deeds, his actions, and everything right down to how he peed. Although the first written appearance of a collection of accounts of the prophet was written more than a hundred years after his death by Muhammad al-Bukhari, his books are still considered the most accurate because he was so meticulous about the chain and origin of every story. When you read the Hadeeth by al-Bukhari, it may seem tedious when a given story starts with Muhammad ibn Ibrahim said that he heard from Yahya ibn … who was told by al-Humaydi that the Prophet (ﷺ) said … but that is one of the reasons his work is still considered the most accurate.

Omi would tell us the story about a man who was collecting stories of the Prophet Muhammad (ﷺ). He heard about a man who was known for his stories of the Prophet (ﷺ), so he went to him and asked him to relay the stories. While the man was relaying the story, he called an animal over by pretending he had food in his hand, and therefore his stories were considered unreliable because he lied to the animal.

It was now time to phase in *Ramadan* as a way for us to earn our *Eid* gifts. My brother and I found it odd since we had never had to work for Christmas. Children do not normally do fasting since it is not required in Islam for us to fast until we become old enough, which is when we hit puberty. Note that Shaykh Abdul Nasir, who earned his

Imam Certificate in Makkah, Saudi Arabia, said that even if a child does not start puberty by 15 years of age, fasting still becomes mandatory at that age. Most families start teaching children to fast as early as the age of seven. Children are often taught to fast by being asked to forgo a meal during the day – or in our case – fast for half a day in order to prepare for the full-day fast that would soon be required. My brother and I stockpiled snacks in our room and took great care not to get caught drinking the tap water from the bathroom sink. It's important to point out that the water in Saudi Arabia is not drinkable water so as a result, we both got very sick that year, and our mother would not know the cause until many years later.

MAKKAH AL-MUKARRAMAH

The time finally came for us to travel to Mecca – officially the name is *Makkah al-Mukarramah.* Meaning "Makkah, the Noble" – to see the family for the last night of *Ramadan* and the *Eid* days that followed. I was so excited. After so long I was finally going to see Fahad again. We got in the car and drove for ten hours to get there. Stopping on the road was less than safe back then, and every pit stop bathroom was swarming with flies, cockroaches big as houses (well, you know what I mean), and all the bathrooms were of the traditional hole-in-the-floor style with places to put your feet on either side and squat. If someone missed the mark and left some remnants behind, you had to take the large water hose on the side and spray the bathroom down, while covering your nose. We learned quickly to completely remove all our clothes below the waist before trying to squat down over the floor toilet, but with the floors being completely soaked by the low sinks installed for people to wash for prayer, it proved very challenging.

The ritual of washing with water for prayer, in Islam, is called *Wudu*. If you are in a place where water is scarce, or the water is not clean, you can perform the same acts of washing I am about to describe using sand or dirt. Your *Wudu*, once performed, will last as long as you don't urinate, defecate, flatulate, sleep – since you won't know if you farted while sleeping – found light bleeding, got your period, or had sexual intercourse. Sexual intercourse, however, will require you to preform *Ghusl*, which is to wash the entire body and make *Wudu* with the intention of becoming clean again. All restrooms near a mosque, or on the road, will have these low sinks since it makes performing *Wudu* easier – especially for the elderly who will find it difficult to lift their whole foot into a standing sink. You start with the silent or aloud intention to perform *Wudu* for prayer. If your intention is to perform *Wudu* to pray for show, then your *Wudu* will not count. After you have made your intention, you come to the sink, roll up your sleeves and pant legs or your skirt. You will wash the hands to the wrists three times, rinse out your mouth and snuff water into the nostrils three times, wash your face from the hairline to the neck, the chin, and the openings of your nostrils. Then your hands and arms are washed up to the elbows three times. Your head from the forehead to the nape of your neck, including your ears are then rubbed with both hands, followed by your feet – particularly the tops and the ankles – rubbed with water. Finally, you will say the *Shahada* (Islamic Oath) "*la ilaha illa llah* (There is no God but *Allah*), *wa muhammadun rasulu llah* (and Muhammad is the messenger of *Allah*)." I was taught that if you preform *Wudu* properly your sins will come out of your body, thereby making you clean for prayer. If you wear makeup, it will be a hard task to wash off and reapply your makeup five times a day. Nail polish will have to come off too, since the water must reach the nail beds. For these reasons, in Saudi, all our weddings and big parties take place after the last prayer in the evening.

When we did stop for a longer rest, my stepdad would rent a single room by the hour. These were normally attached to a gas station that had a small hall that only sold *Kabsa*, a rice and meat dish, and water. In the rural areas, it was usually made with lamb or whatever meat the caretaker had at his disposal. It was sold to people piping hot in a plastic bag, which was then dumped on a platter to be eaten communally with spoons or with your hands. I do not know how to describe its taste except that it was the smell and taste of my childhood. The meat was always tender, and the rice was as greasy as it could be. The red saffron and diced tomatoes created a red stain on the rice and meat – and even the steam rising from the platter. You would hear your stomach begging you to have a bite. Everything about my world was changing – even the food I craved.

The rest stop would of course belong to a Saudi but be manned by an Indian or another member of the expat working class in Saudi. Often you would find him asleep in a plastic lawn chair, his head tilted back, his mouth open as the flies made a meal of his saliva. My stepdad would shout at him to wake up as if he was a servant – sometimes even kicking the man's chair shouting, "You, up! Up!" "I'm sorry, sir," the man would say as he ran to pump gas into our Chevy Suburban. Almost everyone drove large six-seater cars if they could afford them because they were the most comfortable for the long drive for large families, and also because many of the roads were covered in red sand; if you had to go off-road for any reason, having four-wheel drive came in handy. This was a time before cell phones and getting stranded on the road in the desert was dangerous. This is why we stopped at every rest stop we could, to check the car, fill up with gas and so my stepdad could rest up.

The by-the-hour rooms did not get cleaned between guests. Guests were asked not to leave any trash and the next traveler would enter after the other one left. The room only had an old wooden single bed in the corner with what my 7-year-old-self thought were icky sheets – just to be used for a quick nap. I recall standing in the corner, with no place to sit except an old dusty rug on the floor, as my stepdad napped. We always did the journey in one large stretch, and I recall once the air conditioner broke, but we continued driving in the excruciating 125-degree heat. The road to Mecca from Riyadh was safe enough in that time but there was no predicting the desert tribes once you left the safety of the city. I heard many stories growing up about raiders plundering, kidnapping, and raping women if the car stopped in one place for too long. I did not know then that we would undertake this trip twice a year from now on.

At the road entrance to the city of Mecca there was always a checkpoint. At the last stop we made on the road, my stepdad would don his *Ihram*, which was two white towels – one wrapped around his waist, and one to cover his chest – hanging over his left shoulder and exposing his right. It looks like a toga. This was the traditional attire for making the pilgrimage to Mecca for *Umrah* and *Hajj. Umrah,* which means visiting a popular place, is a shorter version of the *Hajj* pilgrimage. Unlike *Hajj*, which can only be undertaken during the month of *Dhul Hijjah, Umrah* can be done any day of the year. While it is not one of the required pillars in Islam, it is considered something you should do if you are going to Mecca. To perform *Umrah*, you must enter the city in a state of Ihram. This means that you will have made *Wudu*, the ritual washing performed by Muslims before prayer, and wear the proper attire.

There are three major parts of performing *Umrah*: *Tawaf*, *Sa'i* and *Halq* or *taqsir*. *Tawaf* is when you circle the *Kaaba*, the black box in the holy mosque, in a counterclockwise fashion, seven times. The counter-clockwise direction, I think, was decided so people do not bump into each other, since many people will perform *Tawaf* at the same time. *Sa'i* is when you walk seven times back and forth between the hills of *Safa* and *Marwah*. And finally, *halq* (for men) or *taqsir* (for women) is a ritual hair cutting. For men, *halq* is to shave their entire head and, for women, *taqsir* is cutting about an inch of hair. It is meant to glorify *Allah* over our vain worldly appearance.

At the checkpoint to the entrance of the holy city of Mecca, national guards would check your documentation to make sure you were Muslim. They know if you are Muslim because if you arrived in the country on a visit visa, your visa would state your religion. If you are a local Saudi, they will wave you by. Foreigners would need an Imam to sign off, certifying the individual's conversion to Muslim was indeed genuine. Even if you got past the first check point and into the city, the guards do have the authority at any time when you are entering or just walking in the mosque, to ask for your proof that you are Muslim. If you fail to provide it there are many possible outcomes from simply being asked to leave, to deportation, imprisonment, and lashes. If you were caught as a non-Muslim foreigner taking pictures, filming, or anything else they deem to be malicious – well, let's just say it's not worth the risk. The only way to get in safely would be to convince an Imam that you genuinely converted, obtain the proper documentation, and learn how to behave in the Holy Mosque.

The Holy Mosque or *Masjid al-Haram* (meaning the sacred mosque) is the largest mosque in the world, and in 2021, it was the most expensive single building in the world – valued at 100 billion U.S. dollars. There was a time, pre-oil, when Saudi Arabia was very dependent on the money that came from pilgrims visiting the Holy Mosque for *Hajj* and *Umrah*. The King of Saudi Arabia is referred to as the custodian, or

"Guardian of the Two Holy Mosques" – *Khādim al-Haramayn aš-Šarīfayn* in Arabic. The Mosque is a marvel to behold. Pictures can never do it justice, and it is sad that you have to convert to Islam to see it. It is a great piece of Middle Eastern history, but it also is a part of Christian and Jewish history since Abraham (known in Islam as *Ibrahim*) and his son, Ismail, in Islam, are said to have constructed the *Kaaba*. In my mind, like any religious site, it should be open to all who are respectful when they visit.

The first time I saw the Holy Mosque. As I removed my little shoes and entered, I saw the *Kaaba*. I saw the people praying their personal prayers all around it. I saw women clutching the Black Stone *(Hajar al-Aswad)* and crying out to *Allah*. The stone is set in the eastern side of the *Kaaba*, and no one really knows what it is made of. Some say it came from heaven, and others say it is a meteorite. I have never touched the stone since getting close enough is very difficult. Once someone makes their way to the inner circle of pilgrims circling the *Kaaba*, they tend to linger for a long while. I recall sitting on the floor on my knees as my mother prayed beside me. I stared at the *Kaaba*. To a little girl, it was so big. It is about 42 feet in length, 36 feet in width, and 43 feet high. It is made of limestone, rock, and marble, but you won't see it without its gold thread-embroidered black cover, unless you were there on a day when they changed the cover. It does not wear the same cover twice, they say, and the old covers are cut up and sold on the market as relics. I have seen framed pieces of old *Kaaba* cloth in many homes. As I sat, I saw that the sparrows flying around were emulating the people circling the *Kaaba*. They circled from above but never landed or pooped on the black cover that adorned it, which baffled my little mind. My mother said it was because it was *Allah's* box, so he kept it clean. I wondered why God needed a box? Was it to keep his toys in? What was inside it?

I killed a grasshopper once in the Holy Mosque and *Omi* scolded me saying, "Every creature here is here to praise *Allah*. You should not touch them." I felt so bad for sending a creature that was praying to his death, but the good news is that death on the road to Mecca, with the intention of a pilgrimage (be it *Umrah* or *Hajj*) means you go straight to Heaven – so I figured I did the grasshopper a favor. I learned this rule on the day that we heard that a Western family, which had recently converted to Islam, died on the road to Mecca with the intention of doing *Umrah*. Their car apparently slid off the treacherous roads in the mountains of Taif. The two young girls and I had played *Barbies* once. When my mother heard the news she said, "Oh that's too bad, but at least they're going straight to Heaven, so no need to be sad." Even at that young age, I thought it was an odd response to a whole family falling to their deaths – unlike my cartoon characters who were able to survive anything. I felt sad that I would never play *Barbies* with them again.

Then there is the *Zam Zam Well,* which is Islam's version of holy water. People believe that drinking from the well can cure sickness, heartache, and all manner of things. Pilgrims bottle it and take some with them. Locals tend to have at least one bottle of it in their house. All I remember about drinking it was that it tasted funny. A BBC London investigation in May 2011 stated that water taken from taps connected to the *Zam Zam Well* contained elevated levels of nitrate, and arsenic at levels three times the legal limit. But this was later contradicted by The Council of British Hajjis after the Saudi government insisted it was safe and evaluated daily.

I looked at this strange city I had never seen before. It was congested even back then. Because of the season, everyone was making the trip to pray and ask for forgiveness at the Holy Mosque. Our new grandparents had a house on one of the mountains in Mecca. I remember that we had to park the car at the bottom because it would not go up the steep hill, and then we climbed all the way up. I recall looking up at the beginning of the journey, wondering if it was even possible to climb such a steep road and feeling frightened that I would fall.

Once at the top, it was a beautiful little house – the same house my stepdad's father had built when they arrived in Saudi Arabia. We greeted everyone who had come to spend *Eid*. We had new uncles, cousins and of course, Fahad. As my grandmother squeezed me between her boobs with joy – a hug dreaded by all the children – my eyes scanned left and right until I saw him. I blushed and looked away. Fahad and my brother started playing, and as much as I tried, I could not get Fahad's attention. He ignored me almost the whole trip. At night, all the children got to sleep in the formal living room together. It's normal for Arabic homes to have a family living room for everyday use, and, in most cases, two fancy living rooms for guests – one for men and one for women, which were always clean and ready.

We slept on the floor on thin mats with blankets. My mother said goodnight and went to bed. The boys started roughhousing and laughing. Suddenly the door swung open, and the shadow of our large new grandma Omi held her pose, saying something in Arabic that I could not understand but by the thwarted movements of all the other children. I froze to see what would happen. She came in with an *Agal* swinging in her hand. An *Agal* is the black strap or cord that holds the red and white *Ghutrah* on a Saudi man's head. She swung it and hit both Fahad and my brother. Then to my surprise, she sat down next to me and started to brush my hair until I fell asleep. She spoke to me softly, saying "Never mind those boys, you're a good girl, sleep now *ya mama* sleep" (*Ya mama* is a term of endearment used for little girls. It would be hard to translate but it is a very sweet term).

I loved my new grandma in that moment. My mom's mom, on the other hand, was obsessed with teaching me proper things like why I should wear stockings, learn cursive and how to cross stitch, but there was always a distance – a coldness. My new grandma Omi just loved me, hugged me, and told me how beautiful I was. It spawned a loyalty in me that would last many, many years to come.

There are four days of *Eid* – the most exciting being the first. People dressed in their finest clothes for this holiday. Everyone purchased new *Eid* outfits for each day. To be seen in something worn before would signal financial hardship and cause gossip. If a girl is known to have grown up poorer than a potential suitor, for example, it would affect her bride price or, *maher*, later on. After all, if you can bargain to pay less, why wouldn't you? I got new shoes for Eid with pink fabric and a big bow. I was so excited about them! The tradition the morning of Eid was to wake up for the morning prayer around 5:00 a.m. and walk to the Holy Mosque for the Eid prayer, along with half the city.

I'm not sure how far it was from my new grandparents' house, but I remember it being a long way away for my little feet. By the time we arrived, my bright pink shoes were black and when my mom pointed it out, my stepdad said it was because of the way I dragged my feet. I didn't mean to drag my feet and his tone cut me to the core. I was afraid of being punished and stayed silent as he told my mom how much those shoes cost and how she should have never bought them for me. As a result, I cannot remember my first Eid prayer. I only remember thinking I just wanted to go home and hide my shoes that seemed to have made everyone mad. I walked home with what seemed like a cloud of shame hovering above me. This would be an early signal of just what a monster my stepdad could be.

As a little girl, I had no idea how important it was for me to be perfect. Consideration for marriage starts early. Betrothed or not, plans can change, and better offers could be made. People would look upon my shoes and not say "there is a little girl who drags her feet" – they would say "here is a girl whose family cannot afford to buy her new shoes for *Eid*." During *Eid*, it's traditional that cousins, aunts, distant relations, neighbors, and everyone travel house to house, paying calls for about 15-30 minutes each, depending on how much you like them. People you might not see for a year would show up on Eid, so the coffee was always brewing, and the sweets were always on the table. That year, I believe our stepdad's father was ill, so we received everyone but did not make the rounds ourselves. The best thing that we discovered that year was that all we had to do was greet them and say, "*Happy Eid*," and out came the money. Each child was in competition to collect more than the others, and if we found someone who was especially generous, we would alert the other kids of their location in the house. I was not required to cover my hair until my first period, but it was frowned upon by my stepdad for me to enter the men's section. I was to start learning how to be a lady and stay with the women since, in a short time, I would no longer be able to be in the men's section.

I didn't mind, at first, and I liked being with the girls. But when my brother came to the door to tell me that a man in the men's section, an uncle named Uncle Shakour, was giving out 500-riyal notes to each child that greeted him, suddenly the disobedience was worth it. I ran into the men's section. As I entered, I looked over at my stepdad who glanced at me, and then I saw Uncle Shakoor and ran over to greet him, and as was reported, he pulled out a beautiful 500 riyal note (around $133) and handed it to me. I was overjoyed and ran out of the men's section paying no mind to anyone else, which in Arabic society is very rude. When you enter a room, you start from the right and greet everyone by taking their hand and placing your cheek next to theirs and making a kissing sound first on the right once, and then on the left twice. Every Arab country and tribe will do this differently. Some with only one kiss on either side, and some with one on the right and three on the left – but you get the idea. I returned to the women's section and ate as much candy as I could manage – all the while counting my money. The day was looking up. In the end, my stepdad was not happy with my being in the men's section. I don't know if it was because I didn't greet everyone, or that I was a girl, but I knew from his tone that it would be the last year I would be allowed to wander between the sides. Two more days of *Eid* and then we headed back on the road to Riyadh since school would start again soon.

I was sad to leave Fahad but secure in the fact that he was meant for me. And, his mother loved me, so she would never choose someone else. The drive back was long – my brother playing with his new toys and me writing away in my diary about anything and everything that came to mind.

I was a very obedient child, even a trouble-free child if there is such a thing. When my mother said, "Sit here," I sat. When she said, "Listen to your older brother," I listened without question. If my brother said, "Let's steal candy from the corner store," I followed. If he said, "Build a fire in his bedroom hideout," I would help. If he said, "Let's go out at night and rescue the neighbors' bunnies from slaughter," I went along. I even recall once being beaten with a belt and my mom saying, "Why did you listen to your brother?" after I helped him get into something, I recall thinking, "Because you told me to."

My brother got into so much trouble as a child that I became even more obedient. Just like the way the Saudis behead people in public to set an example for others, so too beating a child in front of another child can have a big impact. At the age of eight or so, my stepdad woke us up and pulled my brother into their bedroom. My brother's only crime that night was that he wet his bed. My stepdad made him stand in the corner, with his nose touching the wall all night, and I was told to watch. Each time he passed out from exhaustion and fell to the floor, my stepdad woke him up and told him to stand again. He peed on himself that night, standing against the corner of the wall. He was being punished for something he couldn't control, and I was there to watch the beheading, so to speak. That night, as I sat on the floor watching my brother suffer, I wondered, "Where was my mother? Why would she let this man be this cruel?"

I bristle at using the word *brainwashing*, because a part of my brain still says this was perfectly normal. Just one more indicator of the emotional and intellectual civil war that is constantly raging in my heart and in my mind even today. I was always there, but they painted me over like a wall that was once one color and but was now another. All I needed was a little paint remover, but there was none to be found for many years.

The year I turned ten, during a trip to the bookstore, we ran into the cousins of a girl who had lived in one of the compounds we lived in with us, we moved around many times before settling in the compound mentioned above. It was so nice to see some familiar faces after so long. After bumping into them, their mother came to visit my mom with the two girls, Hiyfa and Zulfa, and we talked and reminisced about our days in the compound. My mom knew the family well and that they were very conservative, like us, and felt relaxed enough to let me go spend time at their house. I liked hanging out with them, but always found their sense of adventure a bit reckless. When they got bored, they would call for the driver to take us all to buy candy or go to the mall. On the way, we would sit in the station wagon in the back seat facing the car behind us – this way we could flirt with all the single boys driving past, and as we did, the boys posted their telephone numbers on their windows in the hopes one of us would write it down and call. We giggled and held our face covers down exposing our eyes to get more attention. One man even had a giant piece of cardboard held out his window as he drove to make sure his number was clear. We found it all too hilarious. Telephone relationships were all the rage and while Hiyfa and Zulfa enjoyed flirting, their other cousin, Najlah, who came with us on occasion, had a habit of collecting numbers. She had a whole little black book of names and numbers of boys. I recall thinking when she showed it to me how wrong it was to have such a thing. What if it had fallen into the wrong hands? People would think the worst of her.

In Saudi, it was not about what you did but what it looked like you were doing, and that was enough to ruin your marriage prospects forever. One day, I went over to see them again – tired and fearful of what my mother and stepdad would say if they found out what they were doing. I ended the friendship. My stepdad finally asked me what happened during a grocery shopping trip, which was our custom. We would go grocery shopping alone, and I would talk to him about life, and he would talk to me about my mom – what she did that annoyed him that week, and how I should not be that way when I get married. I listened attentively since I very much wanted to be a good wife to Fahad. I told him about the boys. He went silent and said, "I understand that being your age, you want that kind of attention. Remember, however, that if you do that, one day someone in one of those cars will be a prince and will have the authority to remove you from your car, and there will be nothing we could do to stop them." My mind flashed with fear – so, I agreed.

In Saudi Arabia, especially in the capital, the King will have four wives, each one of them will have ten children (at a minimum), and when his sons come of age, they will have four wives each and ten children from each of those wives. The daughters will be married and have at least ten children each. King Abdulaziz, it was said, kept only three wives at a time so that he could always keep one spot open – in case this girl or that took his fancy, or if he needed to temporarily marry a woman from another tribe to create an alliance between them. It was considered an honor to marry a king even if it was just for a few nights. He was said to have had 75 wives during his lifetime, and just as many children. With all of this exponential royal lineage, there are a great deal of princes and princesses running around the city – with power that we knew not of, and a reach that meant they got what they wanted

– regardless of if it was right or wrong. I nodded my head and heeded his warning vowing never again to align myself with such girls or take part in such an adventure.

We left for Leicester, England that year so my stepdad could complete his PhD. In Leicester, my mom was pregnant again and spent a lot of her time on the online e-card company that my stepdad had built for her to make a little extra money.

We had lived in Leeds previously for a year as my stepdad completed his Masters. I was in the 4th grade and enjoyed fitting in, making friends, and experiencing the whole school experience. School, this time around, was a vastly different experience. I was older now and my stepdad and mom insisted that I cover up when I went to school. In Leicester, I stuck out like a nun in a brothel. Kids mocked me, shamed me, ignored me, and made me feel like I was a useless piece of trash. To make matters worse, my stepdad insisted I dress like a boy to hide my emerging figure. This included a large jacket, big pants, loose shirts, and my gray head cover. Try as I might to make friends, I always ended up being drawn in and then subsequently beaten up. Girls would say, "let's be friends," and then ask me to come with them to hangout during break, but then someone would be dared to try and rip off my head cover to see if I had hair. The safety pin that held my head cover in place tended to pop open and poke me in the neck when the scarf was pulled from behind. The teachers were not much different. Some did their best to ignore that I was different, but my English teacher, Mr. Evans, took every opportunity to call out my mistakes in front of the entire class. On my first day, he asked me to spell Leicester for everyone, and when I was unable to do so, everyone laughed. This was pre-9/11 and despite the fact that the media drummed up a lot of hostile feelings towards every Arab after 9/11, there was still a great deal of hostility towards Muslims long before.

I spent most of my school days alone and doing my best to avoid people. After the first year, I was able to gain the minor acquaintance of another outcast whose name was Hannah. She was the only 6-foot fat girl in our class, and she understood what it felt like to be ridiculed and picked on constantly. My brother, on the other hand, looked like everyone else and since he was American and very handsome with his blondish hair, he was popular.

Money was tight again like it always was when we lived in England. *Ramadan* was here and our meager means showed. We had leek soup so often that we just stopped asking what was for dinner. Mad Cow Disease arrived ruling out beef. Bird Flu followed, adding chicken to the "Do Not Eat" list, which helped bring down the grocery bill for our ever-growing family.

That was the year my leg hair started to grow out, but because of my long pants, my mom didn't notice. Once it got too long to handle, I went and asked her to teach me how to shave. Her hands, busy at the computer, paused as she slowly looked up at me and said, "You're too young to shave. No way you have hair. Go on, I have things to do." Disappointed, I left her room. I was embarrassed, itchy and desperate. I turned to my brother and asked him how he shaved. He took pity on me and demonstrated how to shave using his own leg as an example. I was overjoyed. I took a long shower and shaved every hair on my body I could find. A few weeks later , I got my period. I went to my mom once again and said, "Mom, I got my period." She said, "You're bleeding?" To which I replied, "Gross, Mom, don't call it that!" She got up, took me into the bathroom, handed me the sanitary pad instructions and left me to it. When I came out of the bathroom, she was sitting on the stairs crying about how I was all grown up. She then went on to relay the dangers of pregnancy, while I wondered how I could ever end up pregnant from kissing. My period lasted three days, during which time I was overjoyed to learn that I was not allowed to fast those days in *Ramadan*.

In Islam, a woman may not pray, nor touch the holy book, the *Quran*, nor fast when she has her period. The reason she is not required to fast is simply explained by the fact that her body will need nourishment since she is losing so much blood. The others are up for debate as some say prayer is not accepted during that time even after performing *Wudu*, which is the washing that is performed before prayer. *Wudu* is said not to be accepted since the woman is considered not clean enough to pray. Others say that a woman can pray if she wishes – for *Allah* is always listening. Likewise, touching the holy book is also not allowed since to touch the holy book you must perform *Wudu*, just like you want to pray, which is not possible for women on their period. Some women think there is no harm if a clean blanket or cloth is used as a barrier between the woman on her period and the holy book. I ran around the house poking fun at my brother who still had to fast. He yelled, "Mom! Elise is not fasting!" – to which my mom replied, "She's sick." He said, "She's not sick. Look at her, she's faking." My mom ignored him.

My breasts started to grow in, and at first, I was so scared. I thought for sure they were some kind of strange disease, struggling every morning to push them back in. At first, I thought it's working – they are getting smaller! – until I realized that they were not, in any way, going away. I talked to the other girls at school, and they said I needed a bra. I mustered up the courage and asked my mom for a bra – to which she replied, "You don't have any boobs. You don't need a bra." What was I to do in PE class? All the jumping hurt, so I took one of my pajama tops that was too small and used it during PE under my gym clothes to help stop the pain.

A month later, it was time for my next period to arrive, but it never showed. My mom had made it her mission to track it and every day that it was late she would fling open my bedroom and say, "Are you bleeding?" I would say no, and she would close the door. The third day after I said no, she came in to ask me if I was pregnant – to which I was, not just mortified, I felt distrusted – like she didn't know me at all. She offered me another lecture about men, which I zoned out. In all, her lectures never explained how I could actually get pregnant. She would always say, "Beware, men only want one thing." But what was that one thing, I thought? Holding hands? Kissing? After all, my entire experience with boys was Fahad and the small kisses he would steal here and there, or when he would touch my hand when my brother wasn't looking. She was always vague and confusing. "What was the one thing?" I thought but dared not ask – since I feared it would cause her to act even more oddly than she already was. I thought if it was kissing, how could she think I would want to kiss anyone but Fahad? And since we are to be married, it couldn't be wrong to kiss him, since she kissed my stepdad all the time? There is a great deal of control that comes when you keep children under-educated and innocent, and there is a great deal of danger, too.

A month later my period arrived, and she thanked God that she was wrong. She never apologized for accusing me so wrongly. In her mind, if I had crushes, I must be having sex. Perhaps she forgot that her rules actually made me the most unattractive girl in school – barely even recognizable as a girl – dressed in baggy boy clothes and a head cover among modern Western kids. Underneath the layers of extreme modesty – the layers that my peers and teachers would never see – I was a very pretty girl.

She never asked my brother if he was having sex, but then again, he was the boy my mom always favored and adored. The boys in our family were always favored since, she herself, had been raised as a boy and beloved by her father.

My brother got into more and more trouble with my stepdad pushing curfews and going out without permission. He was constantly getting the belt for his disobedience while I hid in my room knowing full-well that I wanted no part in his punishment. My stepdad was an expert spanker, and unlike my mom, offered no alternative punishment. Our mom would go into the room after my stepdad was done with my brother and tell him things like "He's not your dad, so you need to mind him or else he will leave us, and we won't have a home." Of course, my stepdad overheard one day and was livid, creating one more thing for them to fight about. He shouted back, "How could you tell them I'm going to leave them without a home, that I'm not their father? I love them and I'm raising them, blood, or no blood." It would be many years before I would understand that a Saudi man adopting two children that were not his own was very uncommon. The scenario was often that once his children arrived, we would become extra weight and a possible bad influence on the proper upbringing of his Saudi children and sent to live with our biological father after the age of seven. Instead of embracing the common scenario my stepdad, adopted us and decided that we too would be brought up as Saudis. I had embraced our new religion, new traditions, and new extended family. While my brother, however, held tight to the past and fought tooth-and-nail to keep his American red blood from turning Saudi green.

One night, just before my mother's delivery, the house was asleep and I, being a great sleeper, slept deeply. I awoke to the feeling of someone lifting up my pajama top. I lifted my eye lids just enough that my lashes concealed that I had awoken. In cases of extreme fear, I always resorted to freezing until I figured out what to do. Seeing my stepdad lift my shirt that night sent me into a fright. What did he want, did he think I had a rash and just wanted to check on me? "Yes," my mind replied, he is in the medical profession and probably just wanted to make sure I was okay. A short while later he put my top down, all the while thinking I was sleeping, and left.

The next morning, I wasn't my usual bubbly self. I looked at my stepdad across the breakfast table and justified the incident to myself again. I decided to forget about it and go on with my day. The next night when the house was asleep, he came again – this time pulling back my pants, then my panties. He seemed just to be looking, but looking for what? I'm not sick. I dared not move, for fear that he would get mad and beat me like he did my brother. So, I stayed still until he left. This went on for a while. I tried to sleep in a onesie to put him off but one night he resorted to pulling his penis out and touching it to my face. I was beyond frightened and stayed very still until he left again. I heard him head downstairs. I felt angrier than I had ever been. Normally when I was angry, I knew exactly what it was about. In this case, I was confused about what was happening and had no context for understanding. Is this okay? Is this normal? I did not know, but at some level it felt like the ultimate violation, which produced a nebulous – but powerful – rage in me that I had never experienced before. I clenched my fists together, got up from my bed, and went to the stairs. I told myself, "I'm going to tell him if he doesn't stop, I'm going to tell my mom." I crept down the stairs and saw him bent over in a prayer position. I stared at him for a little while and thought, "He's sorry. That's why he's praying. He won't do it again." I forgave him at that moment and went back to bed. Looking back now, I'm not even sure he was praying, because the only time he ever prayed was when he was in front of other people, in other words, for show.

I stopped sleeping as soundly as I used to, since I knew once everyone was asleep, he would come. I hated him and thought about telling my mom, but every day my mom would remind me in some way or other, that she didn't believe anything I ever said. She loved my stepdad, and I didn't want to break them up. What child would want to see their parents break up? He was the only father I had ever known. This is the dilemma faced by many children of abuse. Do I tell and run the risk of disrupting everything, or keep things intact and bear the horror?

The one thing my mom worried about every day was losing him. She spoke of it often and I didn't want to be the cause. I felt alone and had no idea what to do. My bedroom faced the bathroom in the hall and my brother's faced the wall next to the bathroom. One night my brother woke up to go downstairs for his blanket, which he had forgotten, and while passing the bathroom saw my stepdad touching himself and masturbating in my room near my bed. I knew he was in there but could not see what he was doing because my bed was raised up with a desk underneath. My brother froze, and when my stepdad saw him, he ran back into his room. My stepdad went in pursuit of him, closed the door and had a chat about how my brother must have been having a bad dream. My brother fought back saying, "If I ever see you in there again, I'm going to tell my mom." My stepdad returned with fire, saying that if he ever said anything he would cut his penis off. My brother, afraid of a beating, conceded for the moment until he thought of a better plan, and went to bed. It was only a few years ago that my brother told me about the subsequent threats he received after catching my stepdad masturbating in my room.

The next morning, my brother told me that our stepdad was bad and that he had seen him in my room at night. I asked, "What was he doing?" He said ,"I can't tell you, but it's bad." I said, "What should we do?" He said, "We have to tell mom." I answered him, "Okay."

He was always more courageous than me, and he went and told our mom, who cried and confronted our stepdad, who denied the incident and called my brother a liar. He then brought up incident after incident of times when my brother had lied in the past. My mom cried and my stepdad started to belt my brother harder than he had ever done before, while my mom stood by paralyzed like a rabbit caught in the trance of a snake. I hid in my room.

I heard the screams and went out of my room worried about my brother. My stepdad stopped beating my brother when he saw me and looked at me. I shrunk back and moved back into my room where I sat and listened to the screams and thought, "I should tell mom." But if she didn't believe her golden child, why would she believe me? She never believed me. Would I just end up getting beaten as well? Or worse, will my interaction get my brother an even worse beating? Scared and alone, I stayed silent.

The night visits stopped for a while, but the impact and feelings lingered on. I never slept as well as I used to. My grades dropped. My creative writing stopped. I walked home from school slower than I used to. Before these incidents, walking home took 20 minutes. After, I made it last an hour and a half.

Walking home from school was the only time I was allowed to be out of the house without supervision. It was my solace. I was, after all, the only one I could talk to about all of this. I literally talked to myself out loud, since I rarely encountered anyone on my path home. If I could speak to 12-year-old-me today, I would tell her to speak to someone. But then I also think… who? Who was I supposed to tell? A school counselor probably would have told my parents. I would have definitely gotten a beating like my brother, and my stepdad would likely pack us up and take us back to Saudi before anyone had time to even get a social worker involved. In Saudi, accusations of sexual abuse or sexual misconduct are kept in the family and ruled on, only, by the family. They are covered up even if that means marrying off the girl in question to avoid scandal whether the girl was "intact" or not. The girl alone will carry all the shame for something a man did, even if that man was her father. It's always the woman's fault. They brought it on themselves in some fashion.

I didn't know what the right answer was, and with no one to confide in that could be trusted, it was left to me to navigate this alone. I wondered if being without fear and without pain was worth the destruction of my family and I pondered the consequences that might befall me if my family broke. Twelve-year-old me carried the weight of the world that year with no one to help shoulder its heavy burden. The *Eid* pictures from that year say so much.

My repressed anger kept popping up in different ways. Our allowance for lunch at school was one pound. It was enough to eat lunch but not to get anything fancy like a soda or bag of crisps. In the morning, every day our stepdad would reach into the pocket of his worn dark-

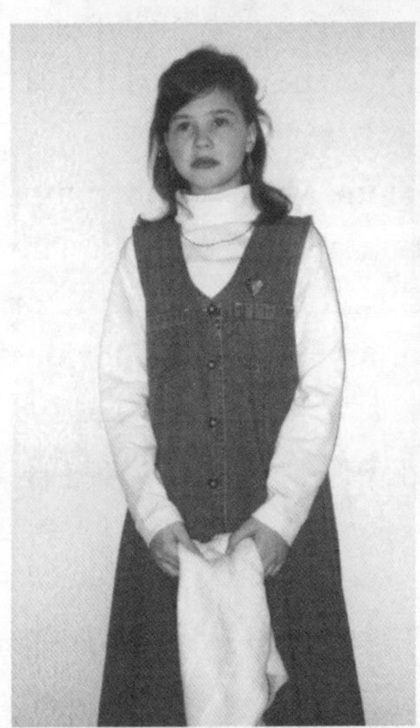

blue jacket that hung next to the front door, jingle around the coins, pull out a pound for each of us and off we went.

One morning when I came down for breakfast before my parents. I put my hand into the pocket and pulled out two pounds. I had decided in my mind that he had plenty of coins and wouldn't miss a few. As we were leaving as usual, he reached in and handed us each a pound and off we went. That day I had three pounds to spend on lunch. I bought everything my little heart desired and told my friends that my parents raised my allowance. I took great pleasure in also treating the other kids, which resulted in temporary friends. It was nice to not be bullied for a change now that I could buy them stuff. This went on for a few weeks. It was so out of character for me but hurting him felt really good every morning. He stole from me, and for damn sure, it felt good stealing from him.

One morning when my stepdad reached into his pocket to jingle his coins, it didn't jingle as much as it usually did. He moved his hand around checking for pounds. His face was flustered, he pulled all his coins out, found two pounds and we started out the door. My heart left my chest and slid up to my throat because I knew where the missing coins had gone. As we headed out, I looked back and saw him checking his jacket pocket vigorously for holes. I felt bad. I talked to myself on the way to school, "Why do I feel bad, he had it coming, right?" But to no avail, my mind could not justify what I had been doing. Stealing was wrong, and even if he was a bad person, I knew better.

I took the long way home from school alone with my thoughts. When I got home that afternoon, my parents were sitting down with my brother who had a history of stealing silly things like candy or taking other kids' toys and bringing them home. He was the obvious scapegoat, but I couldn't let him take the fall. He's already suffered too much at the hand of my stepdad. I took a deep breath and walked into the room. I told my mom I did it. She asked me why I would do such a thing. I looked at my stepdad and the room became silent. My stepdad looked shocked since it was so out of character for me. He stood up and told my mom he would take me for a walk.

I thought for sure I was in deep trouble. Who knows what he had planned, and my brother looked at me and I knew that he knew, at that moment, that I knew he was telling the truth. As it has always been with us, we understood each other so simply through our silence. I grabbed my jacket and headed for the door, and off we went down the street, mom watching the whole time as we walked away, as if she was left out of a secret.

During that walk, I knew he knew that I knew and didn't tell. He told me he forgave me for taking the money and then he explained (like any good father would) that taking that money took food from my brothers' and sisters' mouths. He explained why money was tight and told me he knew I was old enough to understand. We walked all the way to the little store, which was a tiny convenience store at the end of the street beside a fish-and-chip shop that always smelled of grease. He bought me some candy, which I agreed to keep to myself, and we walked back home. I thought, "It's over. He's sorry even if he didn't say it." I went to sleep happier than I had been in so long.

My mom had worried and warned me about the men outside the house, taught me how to handle myself, and what to look out for – but she never mentioned what to do if it happened inside the house. She never made me feel like I could really talk to her. How could I break her heart and tell her that the love of her life was no Prince Charming, but just a man – like all the other ones she warned me about.

Time passed and everything seemed like it was back to normal. I forgave him and decided to be happy again. I don't remember what day of the week my mother gave birth to my sister, Yasmin, but I remember being home from school.

I had decided to take a hot shower on that cold October day. When I was almost done, the bathroom door opened. I held very still thinking if it was my brother or little sister that they would make themselves known, but the curtain opened, and it was my stepdad standing there. I didn't know what to do. I was scared. My mom was not home. Chris was out. Who should I call out to? There was no one.

He took the soap and started to help me wash. Then he rinsed me. All the while I was trying to figure out what he wanted? Was it to make sure I bathed well? Then he got the towel and carried me to my parent's bedroom. Everything else is a blur that I wish I couldn't remember. Because I was a virgin, he would never risk leaving proof and taking my virginity, but sadly, there are many other ways for a young girl to be violated without running that risk.

Mentally I was still a very small child. I was not a typical American 12-year-old with all of the exposure and knowledge. I was a girl raised in a repressed country that values virginity over knowledge. I was never taught about sex – it was not the subject of conversation among friends at that age.

The entire experience was wrapped in dark shadows of confusion, pain, and anger. It was the loss of innocence to a girl who didn't even know what innocence was. I spent the rest of my day curled up in a ball in my bedroom closet trying not to show any weakness at all, not shedding a single tear. I would not give HIM the satisfaction.

As a victim, the tendency to put on a strong face is normal but can also create lasting damages. Like an open wound that won't heal, you relive and try to understand something that goes beyond the pale of human understanding. Telling yourself that you're strong while actually feeling so weak creates a schism in your psyche that is either addressed at some point or lasts a lifetime, keeping you from being everything you can be. There is a proverb, "The beginning of wisdom is calling things by the right name." At some point, you face it and address it, or spend your life raging against everything that meets your gaze.

My mom came home from the hospital weak and tired. I looked at my newborn sister and when I looked at all my brothers and sisters gathered around, I thought about what happened to me. I swore to myself I would be the vigilant eye who would believe them if the need ever arose. They would never be alone like me, with no one to confide in.

Nothing happened for a while and again things went back to "normal."

Now I had a secret that could destroy him, so I used what influence I had for myself and my siblings to get them what they needed. I took on the role of mother at a very young age, not by choice, but out of necessity.

I loved my mother, but she had no interest in us. She watched TV all day, and when she did come around, it was to play with the children for a bit and then just head back to her bedroom. I wish I could give her the excuse of being an alcoholic, but she never drank – she simply lived in a vegetative state, almost like she was always escaping from something. In this way, you could say that she was like many Saudi wives who hand everything off to their maids and spend their days doing almost nothing.

That same year, my school decided to give us sex education and I brought home a paper for my parents to sign. My mom refused, saying that there was no need for her children to learn this.

She said, "The British are notoriously promiscuous, and I don't want my children learning from them." She also said that the British never wipe their asses, never showered and so many more accusations along these lines.

My stepdad said, "Just let them attend. They will hear about it from their friends afterwards, so they might as well know all the facts." She reluctantly signed the paper, and I went.

I was shocked, like so many in my class. For many kids their innocence was lost that day, unfortunately for me mine had already been painfully ripped from me. We knew, but we didn't know – it's hard to explain.

When I got home that day, my mom sat me down and asked me to relay every wrenching detail of that disgusting class, so I did. I say "disgusting" because now I knew that I understood. She listened intensely disputing facts at every turn to make sex seem as dangerous as possible. The irony was palpable.

The next morning when I came down before school, to my surprise, my mom said I didn't have to go. I never really enjoyed school, so I went back to my room to play. That day, she sent a letter saying she was keeping me home for a bit. The next day we stayed home again. After that, the school sent a letter stating that if we did not return to school, they would need to send a social worker to see what was wrong.

My mom asked me and my brother to get dressed as she put on her brown baggy raincoat, which was her British version of an abaya, and off we went to school. She stood like a cobra ready to strike as she waited for the principal.

My mother informed the principal that she would be removing us from the school. The principal informed her that they would need to alert social services per procedure. My mom in her haste said, "That won't be necessary."

"I'm sorry but it's procedure."

While the mention of the word "social worker" is often concerning to most parents, it was of particular concern to my mother…

Background here: when my mother left my biological father, and I was just a baby – my brother barely two years old – she struggled to make ends meet. So, she took to waiting outside supermarkets to collect the old vegetables and expired canned goods that they would throw away to see if there was anything salvageable for us to eat.

When the Mormon church heard how she was struggling, like most good communal religions, the bishop called her in and offered for my brother and I to be placed temporarily with one of the church families until she was back on her feet. My mother, of course, stormed out of the bishop's office saying, "You'll never take my children away from me!" The bishop let her keep trying to take care of us and offered as much support as the church could offer, until he felt he was obliged to contact social services. When my mother was contacted by a social worker, she feared the worst and fled. The principal had struck a deep nerve, and my mother instinctively reacted.

My mom had us collect everything from our lockers to show the principal that she had no power to tell my mom what to do with her children, and we went home. When we got home, mom called the American Embassy and asked for their advice. Their advice was simple: "Take your children and go home to the United States. We cannot help you with this."

My mom freaked out and told my stepdad what happened and after fighting over why she couldn't for once escalate a situation, the next thing I knew, we were all on a flight back to Saudi Arabia.

I recall thinking, "Thank goodness. Now I can see my Fahad again, and we'll be married, and my life will be beautiful." I look back now and realize my stepdad had to be greatly relieved to be out of the risky England and back into the safety of a country where his authority ruled, greatly limiting his risk of exposure.

The hospital that my stepdad worked for paid for our housing, schooling, plane tickets and many other things within reason. But they would not agree to fund the house in England while my stepdad finished his PhD. and rent another home for us in Saudi. Therefore, we stayed in Saudi with my grandparents on my mother's side who were now living in a flat owned by the Hospital.

It was shotgun-like, but L-shaped with two formal living rooms, a large dining room, kitchen, three bedrooms and a large master suite. Mom and the little ones took the guest room. I got grandma's craft room, which had cabinets built to run from the floor to the top of the 10-foot ceiling. The cabinets all had clear drawers, and you could see that they were filled with every kind of fabric, button, zipper, or thread you could have imagined – all organized by color, make and style. There was nothing you couldn't make in that room.

My brother got to sleep in my grandpa's computer room, which was right across from my grandma's craft room. It had every new computer gadget imaginable, and back then, it was a marvel to behold! Prior to our arrival, Grandpa was always tinkering away in there, trying to invent something new by taking something apart.

My stepdad stayed as long as he could, but then left back to England promising it would only be about six months. My mom mourned his departure and then quietly departed to her room where she continued her lifestyle of watching TV constantly. Secretly, I was thrilled. My brothers and sisters and I had a lot of fun – dancing and filling the day with excitement in the vast apartment.

It was decided that Chris and I would continue our education through correspondence, since the international schools were far too pricey for us, and neither of us spoke, read, or could write Arabic, a local school was out of the question. All of our books for the year arrived at once in a large box, and our exams were multiple choice at home with mom as the monitor and mailed to the United States for grading. Naturally, we left most of our schoolwork to the last minute when mom finally asked how far we were. Both of our grades were terrible, and I recall my brother even coming up with a multiple-choice cheating system, which he swore by, that had no logic to it whatsoever, and hardly ever worked.

My brother – now a full-on teenager – heeded only my grandma who doted on him and brought him everything he asked for, despite my mother's protestations, which caused them to argue over everything.

My brother had the freedom to go and come from the house as he pleased. He slept most of the day and was out most of the night. The little kids and I spent the day coming up with ways to entertain ourselves in the house. If we got too bored, we would beg mom to take us to the bookstore or the supermarket. Otherwise, there really wasn't much else for us to do except waste time waiting for life to begin.

It may seem odd, but for the women of Saudi Arabia back then, a trip to walk around Ikea was an exciting adventure. Back then, it was not really acceptable for a girl of any age to be out without a chaperone and since my brother had no interest in the duty at the time, my grandpa had work and my stepdad was out of the country, I was pretty much stuck indoors unless it was a family outing.

While many American girls that lived in the same apartment building as my grandparents did come and go as they pleased, I could not – if I ever wanted to have the chance at getting married. I needed to be beyond possible gossip. Sadly, my mother, having been divorced, and the fact that American girls are considered to have loose morals, my entry into the Saudi world would be filled with skepticism. After all, how could a prostitute raise a princess?

Days turned to weeks and weeks turned to months and still my stepdad did not return. I eventually saved enough money to buy a pair of roller blades. My mom agreed that I could skate in the parking garage on the bottom of the building, which was never used. I could skate only for an hour each day, and only if I told her when I left. If I should see anyone, I should come upstairs at once. I agreed with so much happiness!

My Walkman had been replaced a few years earlier with a CD player. I did not have many CDs, but it didn't matter: this was my escape, music, and rollerblading alone. It's funny when you grow up in a big family, you long for your time and silence, but when you grow up and move away you long for the pitter patter, the annoying chatter, and the random arguments. I would rollerblade every day in a space no bigger than 1500 sq feet wearing my head scarf, jeans, and a very long baggy shirt. It was my favorite time of day. Gloria Estefan blared in my ears as I pondered about life. I missed my walks to school in England and the freedom I had to go out and see a park, a city center, or just other children at school. I felt so alone and isolated on the inside, even though I spent 95% of my day surrounded by my family. I spent the greater part of my life with no one to confide in or really talk to, as many Saudi girls my age did during that time.

Time passed and my brother found himself hanging around with a group of boys that were up to no good. In the U.S., you might think it was drugs, drinking, stealing or vandalizing but in Saudi, with the laws in place, all they would need to be doing is calling random numbers, hoping to hear a girl on the phone or following cars that had girls in them to see where they lived.

My brother only got more and more defiant of my mother's rules and Grandma continued giving in to his every demand. Since Chris was born on Grandma's birthday, he was therefore, in her mind, meant to be her son – born of her daughter simply because she could not have a son of her own. Crazy, I know, but that was how it was.

One day Grandma and my mom got into a huge argument about my brother because my brother the night before had made it clear that when my stepdad got back, he would not be living with us. He said that he intended to stay on with Grandma and Grandpa. My mom was livid at the idea that her own mother wanted to steal her first-born son from her, and they went at it. She knew, however, that for them to debate the issue was useless, since my stepdad would have the final say upon his return.

Feeling a little bit of cabin fever and wanting to do something different, the little ones and I convinced mom to take us to the bookstore, so we called a taxi, and we went. It was like a modern-day *Barnes & Noble* with toys, books, and gadgets for sale. We walked around until the *Maghrib* prayer (Mid evening prayer) sounded, which meant the store would be closing until after the prayer was completed. Everyone was being asked to leave since the religious police might come see if anyone is hiding from the prayer, so we headed home. When we came in, the lights were out, indicating that no one was home, so we started to take the kids' shoes off.

Chris appeared standing in the doorway. He told my mom that he wanted her to sign over his guardianship to Grandma and Grandpa.

She sternly replied that she would not. Enraged, he reached up for the Saúdi sword that had decorated my grandparents' living room wall, took it down, and asked her again.

My mind worked extra quick that night, knowing my mom's stubbornness and my brother's temper. With no one home, I quickly grabbed all three children in haste and hid us behind the couch near a window using the curtain on the window to hide our shadows, a trick learned while playing hide and seek so often as a child. I leaned down and placed one finger on my lips and whispered, "Quiet."

As I listened to my mother screaming, I held the children close so they would not make a peep. My brother, having no luck scaring my mom into submission, said the thing I knew he would: "If you won't let me go, I'll kill Mohammed. He is, after all, your husband's son and not my brother. Where is he?" He started to search the house and went into the bedrooms, calling for him. Just as I was seeing if we could make it to the front door without being spotted, Grandma came out. She had been napping in her bedroom and just like that, the incident ended. After all, if Grandma knew how violent my brother had been toward his mom that night, she might change her mind. My mother cried and held onto my grandma, as my brother insisted she was exaggerating. My grandma didn't know who was telling the truth and decided that everyone should go to bed and put it behind us. Even my mom locked her door with the kids that night.

Following the incident with the sword, my mom called my stepdad and told him what had happened, explaining that it was no longer safe for us there. Two days later, my stepdad arrived on the scene. He packed us up, left my brother, and we climbed into a car to go to Mecca and live with his mother, *Omi*, and Fahad. Naturally, I was overjoyed! The drive was long, but I smiled the whole way, wondering what it was going to be like to live in the same house with him, without my brother to distract him. Would he remember me?

We arrived in the middle of the night to the apartment building that they now lived in, which was built by my Aunt Zakia. She asked her mother to move into her building since my stepdad's father died. It was getting harder and harder for Omi to be up on the mountain alone.

Fahad came down and unloaded the luggage. We had to wait in the car until it was time to go up – my face entirely covered now because of my colored eyes, which made me a prime target for kidnapping. (I tended to draw a bit of attention whenever I was on the street, so everything had to be covered.) I stared at him through my veil. My heart was beating so fast feeling things I had not felt in years.

We went upstairs, unloaded, and went to sleep. Grandma had set up her fancy guest room for us, clearing out all the furniture except six couches pieces, which were pushed together to create a pit-like corner which was to be my corner of the room. The next morning, we awoke to have breakfast. In Saudi households – not all, mind you – it's not uncommon for the whole family to eat together when there are no guests, so I put on my head cover and headed to the kitchen to help out with the preparation for breakfast, not forgetting to kiss my grandma in the traditional way once on her hand – once on her forehead and once on either cheek before beginning my work in the kitchen.

Since we were all family, and me and Fahad were betrothed, I could be seen by him in modest attire and a head cover without my veil. When I was young, all the women in the house helped with the serving and preparation of every meal. When I think about it, Omi spent almost the entire day in the kitchen and the evening seemed to be when she rested. If you were staying in someone's house as a form of rent, or simply for gratitude for letting you stay, you would help out. It is very common for the host to insist you don't trouble yourself, and it is the duty of the guest to insist on helping while grabbing something and start working. The host must treat her guests as royalty and the guests must honor the host. But, at the same time, there is a kind of dance, the host although always needing help, cannot appear to require it since she would not want to appear as if she was incapable of taking care of her guests – and the guest does not want to appear lazy, implying in its own way that they consider themselves above the host.

I learned this lesson the first time I avoided the kitchen – when my aunts were making the *Shishbarak* in bulk for freezing, which was done once a month. *Shishbarak* are a kind of very small dumpling; in Arabic. They have a bit of beef mixed with spices and parsley in the center, and only as big as the tip of your finger and took HOURS to make. They would go into a soup made with a tomato broth that we ate regularly. Up until that day, I only ever knew one tribe that made or ate this particular soup, and that was ours – *The Bukhari's.*

One morning when we were visiting Mecca years ago, I walked past the kitchen in the morning looking for my cousins and Fahad to play, only to have Omi drop her apron and walk straight to my stepdad to give him a lecture about how I was being raised wrong and that I should be in the kitchen with the other girls. My stepdad looked at me as if I had gotten him into trouble, and said, "Go to the kitchen and help." I resented being there that day, but today I am glad I did, because many of my fondest memories and much of the Arabic I acquired early came from those hours spent in the kitchen with the women talking about anything and everything.

That day, my mother (of course) was still sleeping, and had no interest in taking part in traditions she was not accustomed to. Being back here in Mecca reminded me how much Arabic I actually understood – growing up around the language and never wanting to speak for fear of being laughed at by the other children, but now conversing daily with my aunt and my grandmother, the words started to come naturally and the smile my grandmother would give me that seemed to say how proud she was to watch me embrace my Saudi traditions and language was all the encouragement I needed to practice my Arabic. I saw Fahad as he entered the kitchen that morning, he looked me in the eyes, which was not done. Women and men would lower their gaze out of respect, so to stare is very bold. Afterall, to look upon a woman who is not yours is not only an actual sin, but very disrespectful. I blushed and lowered my gaze as I continued to cut the parsley and get breakfast ready. It seemed no one noticed, and I assumed it was a sign that he loved me too. It's amazing how much we, as humans, infer throughout our lives; we become like the Sherlock Holms of every encounter we have, assuming we are able to interpret every glance and every action while only seeing what we want to see.

The main living room was large and, as is common, the couches were custom made to fit the room out of bright pink and gold fabric. Piece by piece, they sat up against the walls creating the illusion that they were simply one large room shaped couch reaching from door to door. The seating left a large empty space in the middle of the room where the *Suffrah* was laid for everyone to sit upon the floor and eat. As we ate breakfast, I tried not to look at him too much but could not help myself. Every time I looked, he glanced away from me. Everyone was talking and laughing. My mom was the only one who could not understand anything that was being said, sitting in silence just eating, and wishing she didn't have to stay here when stepdad left again.

PROPOSALS

That afternoon, while my Aunt Zakia and my Uncle Shakour were visiting, there was a knock at the door. My stepdad, my Uncle Shakoor, and Fahad suddenly all retired to the men's sitting room while the women stayed in the main living room. The nicer of the two rooms was always reserved for the men, unless it was an all-ladies event. When my aunt heard the doorbell, she leaned over and relayed a secret to me in Arabic: "Your Cousin Muhammad, the son of your Uncle Ghafour, has heard about you and came to ask for your hand in marriage." I turned to my mother beside me, and translated to her what was said to me, since she was dying to know what was transpiring around her. My mother only understood marriage proposals in the sense that it happens once in your life, giggled proudly and over excitedly.

Why did he come to propose to me? I was already betrothed, marrying my sweet Fahad soon. Could it be that my stepdad thought Fahad was too long to wait for? I lowered my head in fear. We were very close in age – perhaps Fahad would take four more years to be ready to be my husband. I lowered my head, remembering the times of playing soccer with my cousins, yet not ever interacting with him – Muhammad, the man I might be now supposed to marry. From my distant childhood memory of him, he was a tall, well-dressed Saudi boy in a white thobe, walking as if his feet never touched the ground.

My mom and I were the only ones who hadn't seen my cousin by marriage in a very long time, since my Uncle Ghafour had never come to Riyadh when I was young. Muhammad was at least seven years older than me, and therefore was never in the women's section during my visits to Mecca. I only saw him on family trips to the desert while I was just a young girl who was veiled.

I asked my aunt, "What does he look like, Auntie?" She answered, "Peek through the crack in the door to see him arriving."

I cringed at the sight of him and put my hand over my face. He arrived wearing baggy jeans, a black bandana around his head and a chain connecting his wallet to his belt loop. *What?!* He was so awful looking that I cringed and turned to my mother who held both her hands up to her face to help hold back her giggles.

"NO!," I said very assertively. "Why not marry him?" My mother continued, "He's a good-looking boy." Boldly, I said, "Is that a reason to marry him?! Because he is good looking?!"

I was only 15 years old, but even then, if he felt the need to change who he was, thinking that would impress me, I knew he was all wrong.

I loved my culture and the thobes the men wore all looked so dashing, strong, honorable and most of all – Saudi. I hated when I saw one of our men dress up like an American when we were obviously so much more superior to them. There is a kind of self-importance instilled in every Saudi child from their infancy – that we are the chosen people.

We are the land and people chosen by *Allah*, the birthplace of Islam, and the land of the Prophet Muhammad (ﷺ).

We were not only raised believing that we were better than westerners because they were inferior infidels, but we were also better than any other Arab nation. I was not born a Saudi child, but I was raised to be one and as time went on I agreed and absorbed everything they taught me. I had become a Saudi girl with all the arrogance, self-importance, superiority complexes and superimposed views on the western world. I agreed constantly with *Omi* that Westerners are infidels, how their ways are sinful, and I often said that I wished I could burn my American passport and become a real Saudi girl and never have to think about going to that horrid country again.

I could hear the men talking in the other room, but their voices were clouded by the doors that separated us. This was the usual case when men talked in the house. You hear them talking, but without knowing any of the details of the negotiations. I knew, this time, it was certainly about me and my *shepkah* – in other words, my dowry, the agreed payment that a groom will pay the 'guardian' of a bride for her virginity. My stepdad wished his brother a good night, and that was that. I went to sleep that night, happy that I was still betrothed to Fahad.

Saying someone's child is not a good match for yours is – of course, naturally – an insult, which can end long-term friendships. Families that have known each other for generations have vowed to never speak again over much less, and it could most definitely cause a rift between brothers, like my stepdad and his brother.

Often the excuses used are: she's too young, she's still studying, her mother has her mind set on marrying her daughter to ______, and the list goes on.

Excuses for men are: he's not financially stable yet, he's still studying, we want him to see more of the world/travel, and enjoy having sex before settling down, he's still establishing himself and, so on.

It is very uncommon, though, for a Saudi man to offer his daughter in marriage since it would be considered equal to "pimping out" your daughter and basically saying you need to marry her off to hide something (like, she's ugly, she's fat and an entire range of reasons why there is something wrong with the girl).

It can happen that two fathers, who already know each other, agree that their children should marry, but even then, the man must always come and ask for the girl's hand. There is a delicate balance to these negotiations that must be observed, and the smallest of accidental insults can put a halt to everything. What my stepdad took into consideration that day were factors I would not know until years later when we drove to the outskirts of the city to visit my cousin Muhammad's family home.

Unlike my grandmother's house, where my uncles and their wives often sat together with their head covers, this house was strict – meaning no women were allowed to be seen by any man, unless it was their *Mahram*. They lived a lifestyle that, they thought, put them as close to the Prophet (ﷺ)'s lifestyle as they could. All of the furniture was floor-level, and everything was plain. Compared to my grandmother's house, which was decorated with bright colors and floral designs, here I sat in a room that was as barren as the desert surrounding us — beige and silent. There was no TV, no music, nothing Western at all, electricity was used sparingly.

Women, when they sat with their husbands, were seen, and not heard. All prayers were observed rigorously along with eating only the food that the Prophet (ﷺ) might have eaten. Similar to the Amish in America today, a great lifestyle for some, but not for us. My stepdad knew that with my unconventional upbringing I would very soon find myself at the end of my husband's stick.

Had I married my cousin Muhammed – and since we were considered among many to be more liberal – my life with my cousin would have been too dark for me to handle. You need to understand, that it was almost like I was living in two parallel and wildly divergent universes – where my stepdad was the monster who assaulted me, but also the person who had the final say on every outcome in my life.

It was as if he had my best interest at heart on one hand, and absolutely not my best interest on the other hand. I would come to discover that he never had my best interest in mind later in life. It was as if he had two faces, but I would discover later one face was barbaric and the other was cold and calculating.

We were taught by my stepdad to pray anytime we visited the family, but it was all just for show – in our house, prayer was not enforced. So much of the culture involves "a show." Just like in olden times, when people would take note that you didn't attend church, likewise if the men in our house didn't go to the mosque on Friday, people would talk.

You might say, let them talk! That's not something you want in Saudi Arabia. I'll try to elaborate: Let's say my stepdad stopped going to the mosque on Friday. First a member of the men who goes to the mosque with him would visit and ask why. If that didn't work then the Imam, the head of the congregation would come to check. If that didn't work, then the whispers would start, one rumor after another until one of them reached the *Muttawa* | *Hiya* (the Religious Police) through an anonymous source of course usually a "Concerned Neighbor." No one wants a visit from the *Muttawa*. When that happens there is no chance that they leave your house without finding proof that you're guilty of turning your back on your religion. At that point something as simple as a picture in a picture frame, a cassette tape with music on it or your child's doll that has a face can be used to prove your guilt. Graven images are strictly forbidden and are said to scare the Angels. Once found guilty there is no official court process, just a nice lineup of integration rooms, fines, followed by lashes. Think of it like the Arab variety of "Repent and return to the fold!" The *Muttawa* as I mentioned before are above your regular justice system because they are entrusted with intervening when they witness another Muslim straying from the rightful path, and it is still the job of every member of the community to report on their fellow Muslims. For this reason, my stepdad always attended Friday prayer and when asked by anyone we all prayed all of our prayers, fasted Ramadan and read from the Quran regularly.

A few days later, my grandma hosted for dinner her sister and her two daughters, Ahud and Abeer – these were Fahad and my stepdad's first cousins from *Omi's* other sister. When they arrived, they were completely covered. Not even their hands were visible but upon entry all that changed. Ahud walked in, her back arched pushing her hip bones into the air. She was tall and tan with long black hair that reached the lower of her back. She had brown eyes and wore a pantsuit of metallic gray which was fitted to reveal every single curve. She didn't wear her head cover like I had too, covering every single hair on my head. She simply draped her head cover starting from the middle of her head and crossed it under her neck leaving her beautiful long black hair to hang from the back like a fox tail swinging back and forth. I recall thinking she looked like princess Jasmin from the Disney movie Aladdin.

They all sat for tea, and she very boldly sat next to Fahad. My eyes glared as he whispered to her, and she laughed at his few words – it was clear they were flirting. I felt hurt, and stupid for thinking he was pining for me all these years.

I wondered how her mother would permit her to be so forward with her cousin, someone she could marry. "*How could it be, I thought? He is betrothed to me!... Could he have fallen in love with her while I was away?*"

I went back into the bedroom and cried.

My mom found me and told me not to worry – she seemed sure that their flirtations were nothing. She tried to comfort me by saying, "They're cousins, they grew up together."

I still had hope, and I went out again into the living room. The next night, we celebrated Fahad's birthday party. All the family was invited, everyone dressing up to the nines. Ahud was wearing makeup – something still forbidden to me.

I watched her flaunting her beautiful slender torso and walking around with her head scarf draping from her head as an accessory, instead of its actual purpose – coverage.

I felt ugly and out of my league.

I returned to my room, cried, and wrote in my diary this line: "I love him, but my Aladdin has found his Jasmin and I must be happy for him."

It is apparent to me now that my relationship intelligence was that of a dreamy 5–6-year-old.

My mom came in, looked at me and said, "This won't do."

She let me borrow her jewels to make myself feel pretty, so I could go and join the party. I entered the room, feeling slightly more grand, but all I heard were the words from the women the room that Fahad and Ahud should be married.

I wished I was her.

Why didn't I have brown eyes, long, black hair and pretty clothes? I was crushed. I had waited four years to see him again so faithfully. There it was, right in front of me: the truth that he had forgotten me.

I could not sleep that night, thinking of ways to bring him back to me.

In the main living room, there was a small door covered by a beautiful curtain concealing its existence.

The apartment layout was flat. The men's guest room and Fahad's room were on the far-left side of the front door. To the right, down the hall, was the kitchen on the left – followed by the main living room, our room on the left (where me, my mom and my three siblings lived), a small bathroom on the right and my grandma's room at the end of the house. There was a back room where the maid slept which also connected to the back of the kitchen so that the maid could get to the kitchen and the living area quickly and efficiently without needing to walk in front of the guests constantly.

The next day, it was time for my stepdad to leave back to England. Mom said her goodbye, while I stayed in the room until he left. We then just started our new daily routines.

Unlike in my other grandmother's house, instead of being bored, I had the chore of helping the maid make meals, and the whole morning was spent in anticipation of when Fahad would return from school. Each day at 3 p.m., the doorbell rang to alert us to cover up before he came in from school. Fahad came home hungry, like usual, for lunch before his nap. We put down the food for him on a Suffrah, which is a disposable plastic sheet for eating on the floor, and I pretended to read my schoolwork just to glance over the book to watch him eat. It was in that same room, many years ago, that we had been asked to race to see who could finish their food the fastest by Omi, the winner getting a five riyal note.

All the summers we had spent playing as children, how could it all be for not?

I stared as he touched his dreamy, smooth, black hair and a smile took over my face immediately, like watching a prince from a Disney movie. The sight of him warmed my heart and alleviated all my doubts – he must be for me.

After his nap, I managed to accidentally end up in the men's sitting room, which was next to his bedroom on the other side of the house. When he woke up, he saw me.

I'm going to speak to him!

He said "Hello," standing up but without approaching me, as was customary. It was the first time we had spoken alone in 4 years.

Looking at the floor and clasping my two hands together, I said, "Congratulations on Ahud."

He smirked at my obviously jealous comment and said, "My aunt wants us to marry, that doesn't mean we will."

My eyes lit up. I smiled and he left to use the restroom before we were seen speaking alone. It was like warm water had been poured over my butter heart that had been frozen the night before.

There was hope that I would finally marry my prince, and we would live happily ever after. As I mentioned earlier, it's so common to hear only what you want. I never for one second thought about his words more carefully.

Just because he said that it doesn't mean that they would marry, it also didn't necessarily mean they wouldn't.

The days wandered on as beautifully as can be. Every day, after his nap we would watch TV with grandma chaperoning us. We spoke in English so that she could not understand us with the occasional hand touch when she was not looking. We ate dinner together in the kitchen some nights, always with my grandma in attendance.

One night he brought me a silver diary that he had bought just for me. He wrote on the inside cover, "I know you love writing; I thought you might write in this for me."

I held the notebook close to my heart and felt so loved.

Occasionally on the weekend, we would pay a visit to family – like *Omi's* sister or Ahud's family. We would all hang out together. I began to feel that Ahud hated me. She glanced at me from the corner of her eye and when I turned to look her way she would reposition her head with her nose facing upward which seemed to indicate she was better than me. I thought myself to be less-than, or not as beautiful as she was, but I understand now that I was a major threat to her. An American passport, beautiful white skin, colored eyes and younger than Fahad while she was older than him. I was everything any Saudi mother would have wanted for her son and more. I spent so much time trying so hard not to be different all the while not realizing that my greatest assets and qualities were what made me so special and priceless.

If *Omi* was feeling up for it, we would all drive down to Jungle Land – a theme park in Jeddah for kids to play on Thursdays – since in Saudi Arabia at that time, the weekend was actually Thursday and Friday. It was family day, so Fahad acted as our *Mahram* and was allowed to enter with us. All theme parks had separate days for people to visit: ladies days, men's days, and family days. These differentiations are in place so that women can enjoy the park with their friends and family without the need of a cover, since all the operators that day would be women. Any boys over the age of ten were no longer allowed to come with their mothers or sisters on ladies days and had to come on a family day or a men's day.

On one such occasion Fahad secretly signaled to me by saying to his mom he wanted to go try this ride. The kids were too small to go on. She agreed and said I could go too. My mom looked nervous, letting me out of her sight but agreed. He grabbed my hand and led me through the crowd. Since technically he was my uncle, no one would stop us and give us any trouble. We walked for a while then finding the right spot, he kissed me in a dark corner. It was the first time he had kissed me in four years since our summers as children. It was the year of the Titanic movie. Everyone was playing Celine Dion's song, *"My Heart Will Go On"* and as it happens, that was the song playing. He whispered this will be our song, I blushed and looked down as he took my hand, and we kept walking. I was nervous being alone with him outside in a public place. I had never experienced that before. What if we got lost? But one look at those beautiful brown eyes and I forgot what I was worried about.

We went to the café on the edge of the park, and he ordered me a juice. I was so timid not knowing if I should order something or not. At the age of 15 I had never been in a restaurant alone with a boy, it was foreign territory for me. He ordered a *shisha* (a molasses-based tobacco product heated in a water pipe that Westerners call hookah but is known in other parts of the world as *Argila*). My eyes grew at least two sizes as he offered for me to try it. Declining and judging him for smoking since I knew it was wrong.

Eventually finishing his *shisha*, we returned to the family. My mom looked relieved to see me like I was wandering the streets with a rapist.

I recall once while driving back from Jeddah on a similar occasion we had to stop on the road to pray at a small mosque. There was no women's side so my mother stayed in the car because she had her period. We entered a small waiting room and my grandma saw the Indian drivers sitting there. She would wave her hand around as she entered the room and say, "*Atlah! Atlah!* (Get out! Get out!)." I looked around the room and said, "*Omi*, there is no rug to pray on, maybe we should just wait until we get home," as I glanced at the dirty floor and all the cockroaches crawling about. "Nonsense, is that how you think prayer should be performed, when it's convenient? No, prayers should be performed on time." She pulled out a plastic supermarket bag she had in her purse and placed it on the ground and began to lead the prayer. I recall cringing as I lowered my face to the floor to put my forehead against the bag. She then finished and said, "*Allah* will reward you, there is never an excuse for not praying on time. You remember that," I nodded, and we continued on our way.

My mother would tell me the next day that she had the worst nightmare that I came back pregnant from being in the theme park with Fahad. My eyeballs rolled in the back of my head as I thought how could I get pregnant in a crowded theme park in Saudi Arabia and why would we have sex? We weren't married yet!

One night after dinner as we sat at the kitchen table having tea Fahad asked me if I had ever taken a boyfriend while I was in England or in Riyadh? My mind went frantic, thinking he doesn't want an inexperienced girl. That's why he liked Ahud. She was older and more worldly. She smoked *shisha* with him. I had to do something so I came up with some experience as quickly as my brain could fabricate it. "Yes, of course," I said. I made up a boyfriend that wasn't serious and called him Patrick or James I really can't remember. Not knowing all the while how jealous Fahad was. He listened and asked if I loved Patrick to which I said "No." And just like that, the subject was dropped. He asked me if I had ever had *Sobia*, a traditional drink we only saw in Ramadan even though it is sold all year round. It is sold in the street in bags. I said "No, I don't really like the taste." He took another sip from his cup and said, "You know what's in it right?" I said, "Sugar?" "Ha-ha, yes, but also people buy them all up and hide them under their kitchen sinks." "Why would anyone do that? Won't it go bad?" "Or turn into something else...," he said. He looked at me for a minute while my brain tried to figure out what he was talking about, but it was no use. I had no experience in understanding much of the world outside of what I was told. "Alcohol! Everyone stores the bags all year, there is alcohol all over the city underground if you know who to ask." "In the holy city!" I exclaimed, utterly horrified. "Yes, of course," he said. I sat back in shock. I was appalled that such a thing could be happening in the most holy city in the world. Scared to ask any more questions, I dropped the subject. The Saudi Food and Drug Administration in later years would feel compelled to issue a statement saying that Sobia contains no ethyl alcohol or is full of fungi. If it was all a rumor, why bother to give it any notice?

Saudi's made wine from dates in the old days so there is no reason to assume they ever stopped. If you go to Winemakingtalk.com you can find full threads of conversations on how to make wine in Saudi Arabia and beer along with a full list of the equipment you would need. Instructions on how to cross the border to Bahrain to obtain supplies. Of course, all of the people used aliases. If you don't and you get caught you would end up like the Australian Peter Mutty in 2014. He was arrested for possession of homemade alcohol. He was sentenced to six months in jail and 75 lashes. True he only received 25 of those lashes and he was released but then banned from travel out of the country. In a Daily Mail article, he said, "My own embassy didn't stand up for me and finally we went to the Australian media and the embassy has now decided to do something" he said. Another example is the Briton Karl Andree in 2015; he served 1 year in prison and was sentenced to 350 lashes. His daughter said in a BBC article, "He's an old man, he's 74, he's survived three types of cancer with very strong cancer treatments, he's asthmatic, he has gout - he's not very well," she said. His government stuck up for him and he was lucky never to receive any lashes.

A few days later Fahad had an intercom installed so we could talk after hours at night, me in my room with my mom and him in his. Anyone could see that we were becoming close. My mom decided to keep an extra close watch on us. One day after he came home from school, he rang the doorbell, and I ran to open the door. He took me to the corner, and we started to kiss and kiss as he lifted me up and rested me on the sink so that I could reach his height. Sadly, my mom walked in on us. I jumped down and ran for the other side of the house while she ran after Fahad to tell him he was not to take advantage of her daughter. I went from pure ecstasy to terror?

Following that incident my mom decided the living room door leading to the kitchen and the side of the house where Fahad's room was should be locked at night. I spent a great part of my evening after dinner near the living room door watching TV and waiting for him to stick his fingertips under the door so I could touch them or so he could pass a note under the door saying how much he loved me.

One night my mom saw him talking to me under the door and started explaining that this is why she needed to lock the door at night. My mind started calculating and looking around. I looked at her and said, "If I wanted to go to his room I could easily hop through the maid's room over there, go through the kitchen and be on the other side of the locked living room door, locking this door would not stop me, be serious." My mom's eyes opened wide, and she got up and went to bed. There is a kind of safety in getting to know your betrothed within the family when all parties have given their blessing. If Fahad was not my uncle or cousin, our relationship would not have been possible without much greater risk. I will elaborate more on this later.

There was safety in the fact that normally two mothers are vigilant enough while still understanding how the new generation might require a little more connection in order to marry. My grandma and mother knew that if things went too far, we would be married right away which was why they were allowing us to see each other in the first place. Afterall, no one inside the family would dare risk the reputation of the family. This is yet another reason why marriages in the family are so common. If love in the romantic sense is what you seek you have to look to what is safe and nothing is safer than your own tribe.

If, for example, two mothers agree to let their children get to know each other from different tribes their loyalties will always be to their own child or their own tribe making this kind of courtship dangerous! For example, let's say one day the boy changed his mind after things went too far. The same mother who had agreed that her son should marry the other's daughter would always side with her son and not pressure the marriage to go ahead, leaving the daughter of the other mother to deal with the loss of reputation. If Fahad decided to back out of marrying his own brother's daughter after taking things too far the entire tribe would force the marriage forward. What happened next no one could have foreseen.

The next day my grandma hosted a ladies' luncheon. All the women sat in the ladies' section gossiping as they did, pretending each one of their marriages was perfect to save face while secretly listening for advice on how to manage their husbands. I always liked to hide in the kitchen with the maids to hear all the real gossip and avoid the old ladies' conversations in the other room. The maids were always so funny and normal while in the other room I was forced to behave a certain way and sit quietly while translating for my mother every little detail. Here we just laughed, talked, and listened. This day, however, my grandma came into the kitchen in a whirlwind, looked at me, and said,

"Is it true?"

I said, "What?"

"That you're going through the maid's room at night to visit Fahad?"

I said, "No, I would never," As I stood up, she said,

"That's what your mother is saying."

I went into the living room to see my mom talking to my Aunt Iptihag, the only lady in the room that spoke a little English. The next thing I knew everyone was leaving and I was asked to stay in our room. Just as I sat down the phone rang. It was my stepdad. Until this day how the news of my mother talking to my aunt had reached him across the sea so fast, I will never know, perhaps it was just a coincidence. He talked to *Omi* first. Her voice carried throughout the house. His displeasure was obvious. She then rose from her bed where she had been sitting and marched over to call my mother to talk to my stepdad. I was then ushered upstairs to my Aunt Zakia's apartment. They had the penthouse. She had the maid serve me some tea as I kept asking, "Auntie what happened, what's going on"? "Your mother relayed the story of your conversation with her the night before to your Aunt Iptihag and your Aunt Iptihag not understanding all of it in shock turned to *Omi* and asked her if it was true. We could not be sure who in the lunch party heard so we made an excuse that *Omi* was unwell and asked everyone to leave. Even if it is untrue no one would believe a mother would say such a thing about her daughter unless it was true. After all mothers normally protect their daughter's reputation above all. I broke down in tears, saying in my mind, "How stupid can my American mother get."

I knew what this meant, and I asked my aunt to excuse me while I went to the roof to spend some time alone. I laid on the concrete looking at the sky while hating my mom. All these years being married to an Arab and a Saudi and she could not grasp one of the most fundamental ideas that if a mother thinks her child is doing something and shares it then it must be happening. In one swoop she damaged if not ruined my reputation and told everyone in that room that I was a prostitute.

When it was decided I could finally return to my grandma's house, I was ushered into our room. Then I was told that the decision was made by *Omi* and my stepdad that since this was Fahad's house and he was a man he could not be told not to go about freely but I would stay in my room until my stepdad returned. You might say how unfair, just because he was a man? But based on my Saudi conditioning to that point, it seemed reasonable at the time. He was the man of the house to which respect was due and I, a woman, was raised to respect and obey. I stayed day after day looking at the same four walls and I was only allowed out to go to the bathroom which sat directly in front of our room with my grandma's room on the left and a locked door on the right which led to the main living room and the rest of the house. Every time I walked past the door that led to the ladies' sitting room, I wished to hear his voice, but I did not. The window in our room that I had never noticed before now became my only eyes to the outside. My only entertainment was six VHS movies and my schoolbooks to keep me company. The world seemed a sad place now. Now I understand the cruelty of it all, at the time it just seemed like what needed to be done for my own good and I bore it with as much grace as I was capable of, respecting that my elders knew best. You might ask if there was suspicion of us going too far, why did they not just marry us? But my stepdad refused to allow it until his return. At the same time my grandma now questioned if I really was an American girl of loose morals just like she had suspected my mother of being in her past. How could she marry her son to someone like the woman she had disapproved of her other son marrying?

I didn't know then how long I would be in that room alone in my head with my thoughts. My stepdad could be arriving next weekend, or he could be coming back a year from now. It all depended on when he finished his Ph.D. Here started my six months in the hole, as I called it.

I learned to nap at whim. Bathroom breaks seemed like the most exciting part of the day. It was another room. To make it exciting when I was finished going to the bathroom, I would pour small amounts of each one of my grandma's colorful shampoos and lotions into the toilet pretending it was a caldron. Pretending I was a witch casting a spell that would get me out of here. The end magic was always flushing the toilet and watching all the colors as they swirled down. This shows the creativity or insanity that comes from being isolated.

I knew it was a grave sin to even play at practicing witchcraft, but what they didn't know wouldn't hurt them. If they did find out I would have probably ended up like Amina bint Abdul Halim bin Salem Nasser. According to a BBC article, she was beheaded for witchcraft and sorcery in 2011. Then there is Mustafa Ibrahim. According to a Reuters article, he was an Egyptian man who was arrested because another person accused him of casting spells to separate the accuser from his wife. Of course, that was the reason they picked him up, they also added the charges of desecrating the Quran (because he put it in a bathroom) and adultery. He was beheaded in 2007. The Wahhabi clerics who serve as judges do not kid around. Sometimes the harshest of punishments are given out for witchcraft. Saudis and Arabs by nature are a superstitious people and the clerics fear the disruption it could cause. The degree to which you are sentenced will depend on how much disruption they think you are going to cause.

Here would be my advice if you ever got caught… drop to your knees, praise *Allah*, and say the Devil possessed you and made you do it. Then thank them for helping you and start praying. There was a story about a woman who was caught in bed with a man who was not her husband. That's what she did, and they set her free. There was a line from Apple TV+'s show *Foundation* that I think the Wahhabis are working off of now, *"The maturing of dissidents in a dangerous business."* Hence, Loujain Al-Hathloul was kept in prison for driving in 2014 even though women were allowed to drive in 2018. She created a great deal of disruption and for them it's safer to keep her locked away or kept under their noses then to behead her…

Days, weeks, and months had blended together. It was a time before your smartphone told you the date and time every morning. Now the only way I could tell what day it was required looking at the little flip calendar on the table in the corner. Unfortunately, with three children under the age of seven in the room, that calendar was played with far too often and my mother never bothered to fix it.

After five months *Omi* took pity on me and invited me to her bedroom. She asked me to sit on the edge of her bed. As I did, I started to cry.

"*Omi* I did nothing *Wallahi*." (*Wallahi* meaning 'I swear by God' which in the Middle East is always taken as assurance that someone is telling the truth. This is because saying it in a lie would result in the speaker getting a one-way ticket to hell). "It was all my mother; I don't know why she did it." She wiped my eyes and handed me a blue card with two silver hearts on the front.

"Fahad got it for you for *Eid Al Hub* (which is Valentine's day)" she said. In Saudi Arabia Valentine's Day had to be renamed so that the more liberal Muslims could claim they were not celebrating a heathen holiday. If you did celebrate it, you did so privately. Why would it be considered a heathen holiday you might ask since it's not a Christian holiday? Well, I'm sure the first conservative Muslim who heard that it was created because of a Saint named Valentine declared it so. Not to mention it was a Western holiday and everything Western had to be bad. On Valentine's day in Riyadh for example everything red including cakes and flowers was forbidden for sale by the *Muttawa* (Religious police). Everything shaped like a heart was also forbidden and shops selling these items under the counter were quickly shut down. Every year we would watch as the large trucks were piled up with everything Valentines items for disposal. Whether intended it or not, if you were a man on the street wearing red that day, you could look forward to being carried off to one of their lovely facilities to await whatever punishment they saw fit. If you must go to prison, you don't want to go to prison in Saudi Arabia. What's worse is you're more likely not to even go there for long since lashes and losing a limb is more likely to be prescribed. Unless you are deemed dangerous to public order.

In the all-girl schools if you were caught wearing anything red on your person, a pendent, a brooch, a string, a hair ribbon, or a sweater that day even if you had been wearing it all year you would be taken to the principal's office for a sound beating with a nice stick. As I looked inside the card, I noticed the message which was glued in had been ripped out. I held the card up to my heart and asked, "What did it say *Omi*?" She said "It doesn't matter now but I had to rip it out in case your mother saw it. There is no trusting her with anything sensitive now. She doesn't think." I nodded, hugged her, thanked her, and went back to our room. I look back now and see how brilliant this plan was. Brainwashing 101. They first isolated me. Then they offered me a little bit of what I craved. Then they made sure I knew it was my mom's fault because she was American. What was next?

WIFE TRAINING

Another month or so passed. I started to mime the movie characters in the six movies we had as a form of entertainment, getting better and better at doing the voices of characters in Casper, Man in the Iron Mask and Swan Princess. I would copy out song lyrics as a way to avoid my mother reading any actual poetry written about Fahad. Since she had a tendency to snoop when I went to the bathroom or fell asleep which I did as often as I could.

Finally, one day my aunt invited me up to her home for tea alone. I remember walking through the locked door to the living room and pausing for a moment to take in the feeling of being free from the four walls I had been living in. I took a breath and drank in the living room and the smell of the kitchen. I sighed as I saw the kitchen table where Fahad and I had taken all our meals. I ran my fingers across the hallway wallpaper leading to the door. I stood for a moment in the apartment building hallway and never knew how enjoyable it could be to ride in the tiny elevator that was barely big enough for two people and always moved like it was about to break down.

It's amazing how simple things become so precious when everything is taken away from you. Just you. Just the freedom to breathe different air can become a pleasure. I thought for sure Fahad had convinced her to help us. When I got to my aunt's house my aunt asked me to sit at her table in the kitchen where she poured the tea. We never spoke about Fahad directly, but we did speak about marriage. "*Omi* has pointed out that since your mother is unable to teach you the proper ways and since you will undoubtedly marry an Arab, you need to be prepared," She said.

She took me under her wing. This would be my new routine. Every day after I finished my school studies in my room, I would go up to my aunt's house for training. I was grateful for the newfound freedom and determined not to lose it by displeasing her or my grandmother in any way.

LESSON 1 – THE DUTIES OF A WIFE

The first day we started by discussing the duties of a wife to her husband. The duties included to always look her best, to never refuse him his rights: be it sex, obedience, honoring his family and so on. In Islam if a wife refuses her husband his rights the angels will curse her all night long. In essence never say no to anything and if being cursed by the angels isn't enough, a husband is allowed to beat his wife if she disobeys *Allah's* commandments or is not obedient to her husband. My aunt said, "But, don't worry too much my dear, nowadays it's not as common and as long as you are good you will never have cause to worry." My mind flashed to my Uncle Shakour's second wife. She was a meek little thing who would have never done anything to deserve a beating (I came to understand on my journey that there is nothing anybody can do to "deserve a beating" but at the time I truly believed that there could be a good reason to beat your wife), nonetheless even if we all never talked about it, we all knew he beat her regularly. The whispers among the maids made it obvious since they saw and heard everything in the house. My aunt continued, "And, if you do displease your husband not to worry, he is not allowed to strike you on the face and he can only use a stick that isn't thicker than his thumb so as to not cause serious injury or harm." I sipped my tea and tried to remember how thick Fahad's thumbs were and then I recalled my mother talking about how if her grandma beat her for something she did she would pray the switch was thick since the skinny ones hurt more. I had heard tales of the Prophet Muhammad (ﷺ)'s wife Aisha saying that he never beat a single slave or wife his entire life, but I also knew that he did not say it was not allowed if the husband deemed it necessary. I nodded and said, "I understand, Auntie, I would never do anything to displease my husband."

LESSON 2 – MULTIPLE WIVES

We went on to discuss the acceptance that one day I too would get old, and should my husband feel a need to take a second wife, I should accept it with dignity. “For the winner will always be the understanding one not the one whose emotions are not under her control” She said.

In Saudi Arabia then and very much still today the values and ideologies remain very much the same as in the Bedouin before the cities and the oil wealth arrived. When we discussed a second wife, how she would be younger, more beautiful, and perhaps even more accomplished than me my heart sank. I had never considered such a thing for myself since I had an American mother who certainly would have never considered the notion.

She relayed the reason the law came into being in the first place. “During the time of the Prophet Muhammed (ﷺ) tribal warfare was common. Lots of men died and as a result many women were left with no one to care for them, so the men were encouraged to take multiple wives. The female slaves could not be denied to any man unless they were married and so this law although seen in the west as an abomination was actually intended as a kindness to protect women from rape and destitution. When we think about it, it seems like a great solution during the time in which it was invented, but I wonder if the Prophet Muhammed (ﷺ) ever intended for it to continue into the 21st century.

My Aunt went on “Now, let’s say it turns out you can’t have children? Would you not want your husband to be happy and have children by marrying a second wife?” I replied, “Of course, he will want to have sons to continue his family line.” “*Shatoora!* (meaning: “good girl”), now you’re thinking like a good wife.” She went on to ask a series of questions.

“If your husband was having an affair without being married would that be better than him taking a second wife?”

“No,” I said.

“Would it be better than if he was tired of you that he divorce you so he can marry someone new?”

“No,” I said.

She continued,

"You see in America men have affairs because they cannot take a second wife, they conceal their relationships and bring home diseases to their wives. When concealing the affair is too much, they simply divorce their wife and leave her for another woman. Luckily in America if divorced, a woman is left with something. In some cases, half of everything but here you leave with what you came with. Nothing is yours, not your home, not your children and not any money. In some cases, they even have children with their mistress, leaving those poor children illegitimate, even though it wasn't the man's fault. He was forced into sin by being denied his natural instinct."

I felt sad for the illegitimate children and thought for a moment. She continued, "Now one of the most important things is that you are the first wife. You will allow him to take a second and he will be grateful to you. You will be safe, and you will teach yourself to pretend that he is on a business trip when he is with his other family. You never need to see her or cross her path."

"But my stepdad's uncle has four wives, and they all live in the same building, " I replied. "He built it for them years ago with the purpose of easing the fact that they all needed to be treated equally so he divided the nights among them. If he bought one a lamp, he had to buy the other a lamp of equal value so having them all in one place helped. He also wanted the children to know each other and play together."

"This could happen but even so my dear, you still would not be required to see any of them. As you recall each wife had her own floor completely separate from the other."

I nodded as she continued,

"This is one of the makings of a great wife, do you understand?"

"Yes," I said softly.

"You will never inquire about her, unless he brings her up and when he does you will offer no advice, only your attentive ear. Nor will you show any displeasure whatsoever. You are his safe haven, his kind landing ground, and his loving wife. You are the master of your emotions and so you will learn how to make him happy even when you're sad, how to smile when you're angry and dance when you're heartbroken. Happiness is a choice that you will choose every day and you will make yourself indispensable to your husband everyday by making this choice," she said.

It might seem cruel too many to talk to a young girl who dreamed of fairy tales about second wives, but I came to see it later for what it was, a great kindness. I was probably going to marry a Saudi and my aunt was preparing me for the reality of that relationship. If a young girl getting married is not prepared, then that is where all kinds of bad things happen. In Islam we have no right as wives to say, "No, you may not take a second wife." We have the right only to be informed according to Islamic law that our husband plans to take a second, third or fourth wife. Why not then teach us patience and how to find happiness in all things? To compartmentalize so to speak, when he is with us, he is with us, and when he is not, he is not.

We all knew the story of the man who took a second wife in Jeddah, the city by the sea. His first wife did not agree and raged against him. When she found out where his wedding would be held, on the night of his wedding she set the wedding tent on fire, killing many including her husband and his new bride. Arab blood runs hot and my aunt over the years has seen many homes destroyed by jealousy.

"Your husband will be jealous and possessive of you and this is good because it means he loves you greatly. But if you're jealous, it will not feel to him like you love him greatly. It will appear that you don't care about his happiness, and he will tire of you. Do you understand? *Allah* made us different, gave us different roles and different burdens to bear. The best of us are those who bear them with dignity and grace," my aunt said.

I nodded silently.

Every night I would lay in my little couch bed and contemplate all that she had said. It saddened me to think perhaps, I might never be Fahad's wife. I swore I would be the best wife to the man Allah intended for me to marry and make my family, my tribe, and my land a happier and better place because of it. Little did I know that I would find myself without any aspiration except to be someone's wife, have children and be cared for. What my aunt was teaching me I would have very little time to master since most girls my age would have received all this information early and in small consistent doses over the course of their lives starting from the time, they could talk, and I had not been taught any of it at all.

LESSON 3 – MOVEMENT

Since I was already a good cook and had spent many hours in the kitchen with the women in the past my aunt next turned to teaching me posture and movement.

"Every movement you make, from sipping your tea to rising and sitting will be noted and you will learn to do it as seamlessly as water," she began.

We started with how to walk in high heels which was done by walking in circles around the dining room table until I got it right. Even if my feet began to blister, the lesson would continue.

My Aunt would say, "The lesson is even more important when you're in pain. Strength will come from being in extreme pain and yet you still move as gracefully as a tree slowly moving in a light breeze displaying a beautiful and pleasing disposition at all times."

I nodded and continued.

At night I would apply ice to my feet and barely want to move, my mom leaning over me saying, "What are they doing to you?" I would snap back at her saying,

"Stay out of it, mother, they know what is best, this is my home and I need to learn how to live here."

"But you're American, you don't need to learn their ways."

"I'm not American, I'm Saudi, and I love my home, I never want to live in America where the women walk around half-naked and sleep with everyone they meet."

"Not everyone walks around half-naked, and you could drive one day think about the freedom of that?"

"I hate to tell you this, but I never want to learn to drive. That doesn't sound like freedom, it sounds dangerous for a woman. A woman alone on the street? You must be mad! Who will protect her if something happens and why would I want to drive when we have a driver for that?

Oh, go to bed mother, you will never understand our customs. Their way is not our way. Goodnight."

With that I rolled over to fall asleep.

I'd like to say that I hated America because of the reasons I said but I think truthfully looking back now. I hated America because it frightened me. A world where you were free, but life was hard compared to a world where I would be safe and cared for my entire life just the way my grandmother was loved and cared for in her old age. A world of slow and consistent traditions that one could rely on instead of a world where anything was possible. A world where your children grow up, move away, and see you only on holidays versus a world where the family sees each other every single weekend and sometimes more. Even though I was locked in a room and only allowed out to meet my aunt for lessons, I felt safe and loved and America sounded like a lonely place where everything was about the individual. I was determined to stay with my people.

LESSON 4 – BALANCE, GRACE, APPEARANCE & SERVING

I learned how to serve tea, coffee, juice, and such by balancing six goblets on a tray filled to the rim with juice. Let me just say that being nervous and bending down to each guest to serve the juice is not as easy as my Saudi cousins made it look. I recall breaking so many glasses before mastering it that my aunt made a special trip to the Bi Riyalain Store (two Riyal store, which was the equivalent to a Dollar Store in the States but two Riyals which was equal to fifty cents) to purchase cheap glasses for me to practice with. There was a long spreading of the fingers as if your fingers could stretch to hold the tray entirely, along with an extremely calm walk. Your back had to be as straight as possible when you bent so as to not spill and you would need to hold your position until the guest had chosen their glass. There should be a minimum of two cold drink options but preferably three to show how well-off you were. One might ask if you had maids or housekeepers, why would you need to serve? The answer is that to serve one's guest with your own hands honors them and if you were receiving a prince, would you want to give that honor to your housekeeper? Every guest is as honored as royalty; this is a basic rule.

Elderly people, like my grandmother, were not capable of serving so it was not considered a slight when she had her maid do it but as a young potential bride, I would be judged for not attending to my guests myself. "What came first when a guest arrived? "Juice?" I said. "Yes, but if it's nighttime or Eid, then Saudi coffee. If it's a very hot summer day then start with ice water, every refreshment should come with something to eat, whether it's cake, nuts, or biscuits. Not to do so implies you don't wish them to stay long, which is an insult. This is similar to asking someone how long they will be staying. It automatically means you are looking forward to their departure and it is an insult to even ask.

All cups should always be filled to the brim as much as possible, otherwise they might say you're poor, lazy, or stingy. Guarding your reputation does not end after marriage for then everything around you will be scrutinized. The cleanliness of your home even inside the cupboards, the crease in your shirt, a chipped nail, everything. Don't think that because only ladies will see you or be in your kitchen you will be safe from gossip, your husband will hear of it, causing his displeasure. As you have already guessed a lot of life is governed by what people thought about you and what they said about you to others. To avoid gossip I was taught to always put my best self forward. I was to wake and get dressed for the day even if I had nowhere to go. This was so I did not get caught off guard by an unexpected visitor. Everything in every room in the house was to be kept spotless and tidy as guests often tended to wander about opening cupboards and the like to find evidence for gossip.

We moved on to what to do when your husband arrives home. For this I learned how to give foot massages to my grandma so that when my husband returned from a long day, I could rub his feet.

"Lay out his night clothes or the clothes he may wish to wear to visit his friends in the evening. Dinner should be on the table and hot when he walks in the door."

The trick is to know when he would be home, even if he got off work at five or six, he might meet a friend or go visit his mother and he is under no obligation to call, say where he was going or when he was coming back. You should avoid asking as much as possible so that you do not seem jealous or suspicious. "We are the ones who make sure things happen." I learned that I should be dressed either in something erotic or as splendidly as possible. He was never to arrive finding me in my PJ's or without makeup. Likewise, in the morning I was to rise as early as needed before him to dress and put on my makeup.

The lessons went on and on. When one was assimilated, we went to the next one. We moved on to Islam, how to pray and why it was important. "What is the first thing you do before praying?" "I perform *Wudu* (The washing of your hands, feet, noise, face, mouth, ears and so on three times each with water)" "Wrong, everything starts with the intention." "Intention?" "Yes, if you are intending to pray so people will say she is good, then your prayer is not valid whether you washed or not." Although my family was Muslim, I had never seen an Islamic book in my life in the house. When I asked my mom and stepdad what a Shiite was, I was told it was not important, we were Sunni and that was that. When I asked why we only prayed when we went to visit family the response was because they will talk about us, or they will keep pushing the idea that we had to until it got annoying so let's just pray when we see them.

The difference between a Sunni and a Shiite is actually a difficult question to answer at least it feels like it is. I asked a Sunni friend of mine in Saudi Arabia years later to help me work out a simple way to describe the difference, but this is what she had to say "First of all the Shiites don't say *La Ila ha Il-Allah Muhammad Al Rasoul Allah* (ﷺ) (There is no God but God and Muhammad is his messenger). They say substitute Muhammad (ﷺ) for Ali. They believe that Ali was the prophet of *Allah*, they believe that something went wrong, and Ali was meant to be the Prophet. May God forgive me for saying so. The way they pray is so much different from us Sunnis, they are strange they hit themselves, they are weirdos, honey. They beat themselves and dance in a weird way to Islamic music. But in the end, we are all Muslims, so I don't know what else to say." The question stressed her out, but the answer shows how little we really know about each other.

The major differences between Sunnis and Shiites to put it simply is that the Shiites emerged after a dispute over who would succeed the Prophet Muhammad (ﷺ). Abu Baker was chosen for merit, but one group wanted Ali because he was a blood relation to the Prophet (ﷺ) and married to the Prophet's daughter Fatima. Both Sunnis and Shiites believe that Muhammad (ﷺ) was the messenger of God, both follow the same five pillars of Islam: Shahada (Profession of faith), Salah (Praying), Zakat (Almsgiving), Sawm (Fasting), and Hajj (Pilgrimage to Mecca called the Hajj at least once in their lifetime).

In Saudi they are the minority (They are also the minority throughout the world representing only 10% of the Muslim population) and most of the Shiites in Saudi are poor laborers since most of the Sunni Saudis until very recently considered manual labor beneath them. In fact, most of the first workers in the old refineries in Saudi Arabia during the reign of King Abdulah were Shiites making them at the time an important minority group. They are considered extreme but, then again if you look at Saddam Hussein who was a Sunni and Osama Bin Laden and all they did I don't know for sure how different we really are. The Wahhabi clerics in Saudi Arabia were opposed to women getting an education and many still are today. Shiites think Sunnis are all sinners who have strayed from the right path and Sunnis think Shiites are all weirdos. To me the answer is simple: a Muslim is a Muslim. It is not religion that makes people good or bad, it is how they choose to be. Belief can often cause the death of rationality.

I had no idea there was so much to learn, but I was determined to make my aunt and *Omi* proud. After all, why else would they be teaching me if I was not to marry Fahad: I felt sure they wanted me to be able to integrate and further unite the family, not sit in a corner like my mother did. My mother suspected all the while that they were just helping me meet Fahad in secret to seal the deal. After what she had done, any feedback she had was taken as irrelevant by me. She had no understanding of the people or the place we lived, and I would need to rely on wiser counsel. So, I thought. In my mind my grandma and my aunt knew best and wanted the best for me, while my mother lived oblivious to everything around her. The only thing worse than not having a mother was thinking you had a mother when you really didn't. I was constantly craving and looking for a mother, a father, and some sense that I belonged.

I call this period in my life my wife training. There was so much I learned that influenced my life later on. How to treat every guest as if you were receiving royalty. The patience to deal with people in general. The kindness to really genuinely care for your elders no matter who they are. How to walk, talk, sit, insult someone without words, dancing, religion, cooking, etiquette and most importantly how to take care of my future husband whoever he might turn out to be.

I learned about the tribal hierarchy. In Saudi Arabian culture like so many around the world the oldest family member is the wisest and the de facto head of the family. When we lived in Riyadh Uncle Shakour was the oldest in town, so we always had lunch at his house on Fridays and when Grandma came to visit, she would always stay with him. When we were in Mecca with the passing of her husband, *Omi* was now the family head, so the family naturally flocked to her house. It was why she had a special greeting every morning which was different from everyone else to demonstrate an extra level of respect.

When our elderly became unable to take care of themselves, they were cared for by the family at home. This duty would fall on her son's wives and if they were lucky a maid was hired or a nurse to help. The cost for her care would be split between the children evenly, everyone chipped in and took care of *Omi*.

I learned how to tie a tie, so that I could help my husband dress in the morning. Great emphasis was placed on how I should always remove all my bodily hair in a way that kept me smooth. By using *Halowa* (a type of homemade wax commonly used in the Middle East), traditional wax or plucking. The importance of taking care of my skin. I was taught never to use cheap makeup products that came from a drug store. How to moisturize and wear sunscreen while always avoiding the sun which was deemed the killer of youth. My aunt pointed out my mom's wrinkled freckled shoulders one day and said, "There is the proof." The proof is in the pudding you might say. Since my mom had forehead wrinkles at the age of 25, while I, now 35, have no single line on my face, yes, I'm grateful.

At the same time, I see now that my time in that room alone was meant to make sure I was more than willing to learn and accept what they taught me. Afterall if the only other option was to stay in my room, who wouldn't be grateful for a short break from one's own mind.

I would read in a book years later where after some extremists had taken over the holy mosque, the leaders of the group who called for the overthrow of the Royal family were executed and the rest were sent off for 'reeducation'. If you ask me what I think that means I would say it means torture until their suffering sends the right message to prevent others from committing a similar crime by questioning Saudi and Wahabi law or until they are dead. Either way people were reeducated. My time in that room and the conversations with my aunt was my 'reeducation.'

I was finally ready; it was time to attend my first wedding in Mecca. My aunt had a dress made for me. My stepdad would have never approved of because it was an off the shoulder white dress, with a red sash, that only came to my knees. Although all the other girls could wear whatever they wanted in all female company, my stepdad had decided that since I was technically American and already prejudged as a loose woman because of my nationality, I should be dressed even in all female company as modestly as possible to give no oxygen to any fiery gossip someone might make up. Therefore, all my dresses were full length, half sleeves at least and modest.

My aunt helped me dress, examining my dress and examining everything I had on. "Why are you wearing stockings?" she asked. "My American grandmother taught me to." "Hmm, do you have hairy legs?" "No, Auntie." "Only women with unsmooth legs wear stockings. Show me your legs.' I took off my stockings and showed her my legs. She nodded and said, "Your legs look good, no need for the stockings." My American grandmother had been so adamant about how proper ladies wear stockings that I felt a little uncomfortable wearing a short dress and not wearing stockings. I asked my aunt if I could please wear them to which she let out a "Hmmm," accompanied by a short stare before saying, "I'm sure she is a lovely woman, but are her customs our customs?" I lowered my head and said, "No, Auntie." "There, my good girl, of course you can wear them but remember that THEIR WAYS are not OUR WAYS."

I was relieved, feeling so naked without them.

The dress was made for me by a tailor and even though my aunt had measured me for it, it was slightly too big on one side since I was not allowed to leave the apartment for fittings. "Well, it's not too bad, you'll just have to remember to stand up straight, so it won't fall down. Now, shoes. Here I got these for you. They were the smallest I could find anywhere." Excited to have my first pair of fancy heels I put them on, but they were a size 8 and I was a size 6.5. "They are too big, Auntie!" "Nonsense, you can stuff some tissue in the front, and you'll be fine. Besides you only need to wear them from the entry to the table and then you can dance without them. All the girls will take off their shoes to dance and the rest of the time you will be sitting at the table. It will teach you balance."

It did teach me balance. It is very hard to walk in shoes that are too big for your feet. I nodded and put on my abaya and headcover.

It would be the first time I had left the apartment in who knows how long. As the car moved along, I recall there was so much sensory information to take in that everything felt like a blur. Mecca back then and perhaps today was so different from the capital. It still had so many dirt roads. You would always see little boys playing in the street with a half-deflated soccer ball in nothing but their undergarments from their thobes so they would not get their thobes dirty.

I saw the little shop where my mom and I used to walk sometimes to get snacks and ask the shop keeper if he could ask around for some American cereal. When we finally did get some, it was so precious to me that I refused to share. I remembered that was the first thing my aunt taught me, to share. She did so by coming purposefully into the kitchen and stuffing her hand into the box of cereal to grab a handful. When I turned and said "No, that's mine," she slowly removed her hand and stared at me for a moment then left the kitchen. I never said those three words again and I never forgot the look of disappointment on her face. These are the moments that change us forever.

My mom naturally accompanied us in one of her old dresses. She entered the ball room very somberly. Since she was not very social and did not speak the language, she did not get invited to many weddings. She greeted no one thinking since she knew no one she should greet no one but that was not the proper way as it only alienated her further. My grandma and aunt entered and greeted every single woman that they saw by grabbing their hand and kissing them two times on each cheek. Always remembering to ask about their health, their children and so on whether they knew them or not. This was the way. Even in smaller social settings when you enter a room you walk from right to left and greet every woman. If they are sitting, they rise to greet you. My mother always entered and sat right away, and they forgave her what would have been considered a grave insult had she not been American. It was almost like saying, I'm better or I don't care to meet you, but she never cared to watch and learn.

What I was going through that night was the equivalent of an American coming out ball. I was being presented to society as a young woman old enough for marriage. *"Here is a young beautiful girl, ladies! Who will make the best offer?"* The hall was vast with at least 400 women, all at tables facing the stage which was a raised platform where the bride and groom sat on thrones. The raised platform is called a *Kosha.*

In the beginning of the wedding the bride arrived first, alone, this is called a *Zaffa* (Wedding March). When the bride is escorted to the stage, usually by her mother and sometimes also her grandmother, she sits and watches the girls dance while everyone one lines up to congratulate her. Married women dance but mostly the young single girls dance, and the mothers sit back in their chairs examining the merchandise so to speak. I got over excited and stood to dance in front of our table, forgetting that the side of my dress was loose. All the shaking caused it to fall down revealing my right breast. My aunt jumped from her chair to cover me while my grandma almost fell over laughing. "You need to watch out for your dress if you get up to dance again" "Sorry, Auntie, I'll be more careful." I was mortified but the evening went on.

The songs played and the mothers watched. As the girls tired and came down from the stage a mother would politely approach the girl of her choice, greet them, and say, “My dear, from what house are you?” meaning what is your last name. Last names in the Arab world can tell you a lot about where a person comes from including if their family migrated from somewhere and became Saudi, or if they were Bedouins or of Syrian descent and so on. The next question normally went to things like age and where is your mother and do you go to school.

For me especially since I looked so American, they always included the question, “What passport do you have?”

The reason for this question is that if I had an American passport, I could pass it to their son through marriage making me twice as valuable as most girls in the room. I was approached 6 or 7 times that night. It’s not uncommon to be handed a nut by a mother and be asked to crack it with your teeth, have a mother come up to you and touch your hair then give it a nice tug to see if it was your real hair or were you wearing extensions. The oddest encounter was when a mother sniffed me very obviously. As odd as it sounds, I really can’t blame them. Mothers in the States run background checks on their future daughter in laws all the time. It’s just a different way of knowing what they’re getting.

When the groom was about to enter, the groom’s mother escorted the bride from the hall to meet him. The women were alerted to cover up. Then the bride and groom walked in together. When it was time to go, my aunt signaled, and we left the wedding. It was such a wonderful night. I went to sleep happier than I had been in a while.

We went to a couple more weddings that season. All the while if I wasn’t learning from my aunt I was locked back in my room. When my grandma would have the ladies over, I would pretend I was heading to the bathroom so I could place a small pocket mirror under the door so I could watch everyone laughing and drinking tea hoping I would hear some news about Fahad. One day one of the ladies saw the small mirror and asked if it was a little boy spying. My grandmother jumped up and swung open the door saying, “What are you doing?” I had no explanation for myself and returned to my room head down, closing the door behind me. I felt lonely. I missed sitting in the kitchen giggling with the maids, but this was the way my life would be until my stepdad came back and decided otherwise. For five months I stayed in that room before being allowed to visit my aunt for training. For six months I pondered all manner of outcomes for when my stepdad returned. None of them was what happened.

One day the doorbell rang, and we heard my grandma leap from her chair to run to the door, something she had never done before. It was my stepdad. Suddenly my room was unlocked, and I was free to roam the house again, but Fahad was nowhere to be found. My grandma, talking to my stepdad, mentioned that he was given a new car for graduation and was trying it out by driving to Jeddah. I spent the first night walking the halls crying and listening to *I will always love you* by Whitney Houston. My stepdad finally sat me down to talk to me about Fahad. I told him what happened and what my mom did, and he agreed with me that she was wrong to talk to my aunt as she did and said that if Fahad did ask for my hand, he would not say no. I was relieved to know he would say yes and calmed myself waiting for Fahad to return from Jeddah. Fahad returned two days later but he never asked for my hand. He stayed on the men's side of the apartment, and I tried so hard to see him, but he stayed away.

MAIDS

We finally left back to Riyadh, I slept the whole ride back trying to figure out what happened "Why didn't he ask for me, was he scared, did he think he wasn't ready? No matter what, he will come for me." I told myself. We got to Riyadh and rented a villa we called the purple house because it was painted a terrible shade of purple on the outside. It was really dirty. I recall it needed a lot of fixing. We could not afford to hire people to do the repairs, so we got to work.

It was a large house compared to many American homes but very average in comparison to many of the homes around us. I never asked the square footage since it was not a question I was taught to be concerned with back then, but it had three guest sitting rooms, one living room all big enough to seat at least fifteen people. Five bedrooms and a large office upstairs. There was a main gate which led to a small front yard that wrapped around the house. The main iron front door which locked by pulling a metal rod across from the inside led to a small entryway which had one door on the right which was the ladie's sitting room and on the left was the men's sitting room, which was always the better of the two. The small entry had two double doors that led to the main living space of the house. The ladie's sitting room had a door that led to the kitchen so that in the case of having both men and women over for lunch the women would set up lunch for the men in the ladie's sitting room and then retire to the kitchen or the other small guest sitting room across from the kitchen. Through the double doors was the kitchen on the right was the main living room on the left which had the stairs and the other small sitting room across from the kitchen. Upstairs we had 5 bedrooms, one no bigger than a walk-in closet. That would be the maid's room. Most houses were built with already planned maids' rooms, but they are normally on the first floor near the kitchen so that she is kept separate from the rest of the family.

It might seem sad to many in the States but very often many maids sleep in the kitchen on a mattress they must roll up every morning whether there was a preplanned room or not. Maids generally worked all day, every day. If there were guests, they didn't sleep until the house was all in order again and clean. They were still required to wake up early to prepare the children's breakfast. If they needed clothes, it came out of their pay. If they wanted some kind of special food, it came out of their pay. That might sound reasonable if their pay was more than 700 Riyals which was about $189 US Dollars at the time.

Indonesians were some of the cheapest because they often came with no ability to speak Arabic or English. They were sent by their families to make money and send it home. They would enter the country under an employment contract and the man of the house held on to their passport. After two years they could choose to renew their contract or return home. If the family was displeased with them, they could be denied the right to return to Saudi Arabia to work ever again.

If they ran away which many did and still do, they were reported as runaways and could only work for cash with families who knew their circumstances. As a result of their desperation, they were taken advantage of and paid less. I met a runaway maid once and my heart ached for her stories of sleeping on the kitchen floor, or beatings for not getting something right. She shared with me some worse stories from other maids about rape by the young men in the family and even the father. She could never leave the country again after being so long past her visa expiration date and reported as a runaway or even a thief out of spite. Meaning that if she was caught, she not only faced deportation but also the loss of a hand (the penalty for stealing).

Why doesn't she go to her embassy or the company that contracted her to her host family? Everyone knew that the embassy would not want to make a fuss with the Saudi Government over a maid and if she was labeled as a thief, they would have to hand her over. The company that contracted her would do the same. Unlike so many households where the norm was to treat maids as servants that were beneath us, we were taught to treat maids just like everyone else. There was no such thing as a Saudi maid. They all came from Indonesia, the Philippines, Eritrea, and other poor countries not just because they were cheap but because having a maid from the local population would be tantamount to having a gossiping spy in your house. A Saudi would have also considered it beneath their dignity to work as a maid. Many Saudis still consider any job that involves physical labor beneath their dignity. I'll never forget the look of eternal gratitude in our maid's eyes every time I told her not to work on the weekend, to go to bed and finish the dishes in the morning, to not give me any of her money for all her needs are for us to take care of. I don't know why we treated our maids differently, but I suppose it was because our tribe were once expats before we were Saudis and maybe that gave us a degree of compassion for someone who had traveled to another country alone and without a support system of their own.

Anytime she asked my stepdad would drive her to Western Union to send money home or take her to make a phone call to her family. She stayed with us for two years and after that she went home, had a baby, and decided not to return. There were some maids who stayed their entire lives with their Saudi family, whether out of love, the protection of a child (maybe their child passed off as the wife's sired by the husband or a son of the household) or just because they had raised them from infants. Some of them are happy, I hope. They were still always my favorite company because with them in the kitchen when guests came over no one was judging how I stood, walked, dressed, spoke, or ate. We all just laughed and shared stories.

It was now the 1990's and sad R&B love songs were popular. I spent a great part of my day listening to songs that reminded me of Fahad and writing the lyrics down in my diaries all the while hoping one day to share them with him. I knew he would come when he was ready. I discovered Mariah Carey, and her music would become the soundtrack to my life story. The first song that stood out to me was a song called *Close My Eyes*. The lyrics said,

"The weight of the world that I held deep inside, life was a winding road and learned many things little ones shouldn't know. So, I closed my eyes. Steadied my feet on the ground, held my head to the sky and time's rolled by, still I feel like a child when I look at the moon. Maybe I grew up a little too soon."

That was me. I was forced to grow up so fast but when I looked at the moon I felt like a child and missed knowing nothing and playing with my *Barbies*. There was too much to think about now. I needed to watch out for my stepdad, watch out for my reputation, control my mother's gossiping habits, take care of my brother and sisters and so much more. There was no going back for me, only forward and I intended to do it with my feet steady on the ground with both eyes looking to the future and the day I might be free.

After we were settled into the house, my stepdad began "accidentally" opening the bedroom or bathroom door as soon as I got out of the shower. Always swearing it was by mistake. I feared a repeat of England, so I started to lock the bathroom door and my bedroom door. He would get mad and bang on the door saying, "We don't lock doors in this house," to which I would say, "I'm dressing!" really loud so everyone in the house could hear. Then I would dress as quickly as possible and open the door. I'd like to say he never succeeded and that I managed to avoid him at every turn but that would not be the truth. There were occasions when I would be taking a nap and he would manage to give my mother some money to take the children to the playground in the hospital. When she would say, "Let me just let *Maha* know," he would reply, "She already said she didn't want to go," or "She's sleeping I'm sure she doesn't want to go," to which my mother would reply, "Oh, all right. Well children, let's go."

One might think to lock the door when you sleep but when my mother was not at home it would do no good since there was a spare. Locks in Saudi are not like in the States. There are no deadbolts, only keys. Meaning if someone locks you in a room and you don't have a key there is no way of getting out. If you had a key, if someone else also had one there was no way of keeping them out. Even if I did manage to leave the key in the door he would bang until I opened it and if I didn't there would be hell to pay. I would have not been surprised if he took the entire door off its hinges to get to me.

I'd like to say screaming would bring someone to help. But it's my stepdad who would answer the door even if the police did come. They would take his word and remember it's not against the law to beat a child or a wife for disciplinary reasons. What about running away? Where would I run to? The American Embassy? They would not want to create an incident and would send me straight back. A neighbor? They would not want to get involved and would send me straight back. What about telling *Omi,* his mother, she was the head of the family after all? She would side with me for a moment and then consider me spoiled goods and no longer suitable for a good marriage, especially to her other son, Fahad.

So, my stepdad would "pay visits" to my room as often as he could. Like so many young girls being sexually abused by a "loved one" I felt helpless to stop it and so I had to come up with other ways to cope. I learned to detach myself and dream about happier things all the while feeling angry and helplessly violated.

I would like to say I planned to run away on our next visit to America. I had that option since I am American, but being disconnected from my tribe in a strange land, I really knew nothing about, scared me more than bending over for my stepdad. In my mind I had no skills; I knew nothing about working or how to do anything on my own. No, the only freedom I had on my horizon that was possible in my mind was marriage. That was the only way I was ever getting out. At least when I did marry, I would have my country, my lifestyle, my family, my tribe, and my people so I just needed to be patient.

I like so many women, wished I had tried harder and that I fought more. After a while and with no options in sight I did what many did and simply went to another place in my head and hoped that he would finish quickly so I could be left alone. Forgive me if I do not elaborate on each incident or go into greater detail but some things need not be dwelled on, and some things are better left in the past.

FIRST GRADE AT THE AGE OF 16

The education system in Saudi, especially for women, is greatly lacking with so many religious topics tossed in that there is hardly enough time to teach you anything else.

Memorization is how you pass your exams, not through thinking or questioning. It is considered a great accomplishment to memorize the entire Quran and at a minimum most of us memorize parts of it, many by choice. Since one cannot pray without memorizing at least a minimum of Surah Al Fatiha and one other Surah (a chapter in the Quran). This was because in order to pray every prayer must start with reciting Surah Al Fatiha followed by any other Surah of your choice. Although there is debate that this can also be done in one's native language instead of just Arabic it is very uncommon. But for me and my brother Chris it was always a grueling process. My stepdad would offer us 100 Riyals to memorize a Surah which was about $20 dollars. A great incentive for a young child but until we memorized it, we remained locked in a room with the Surah playing over and over on a cassette tape that would be rewound and restarted when it stopped. Naturally we sought to memorize the shortest Surah's we could find. If you memorized it, you got out and got the money. If you didn't, you stayed until you did. A child would have no cause to complain since eventually to get out you would memorize the Surah and get the money and forget that you sat on the floor of that room listening to that Surah sometimes for more than nine hours.

The religious leaders barely agreed to allow women to go to school in the 1960s and when they did their education was restricted to those subjects which they thought appropriate. In the 1950s no girls attended school and 92% - 95% of the population was illiterate. In Saudi Arabia it is staggering the levels the kingdom and its religious leaders go to keep its people docile and silent through fear of arrest, brutal punishment, and 'reeducation' in particular when it comes to women.

I am reminded of a quote by Sir Thomas More from his book *Utopia* first published in 1516. "If you suffer your people to be ill-educated and their manners corrupted from infancy, what more is to be concluded except that you first make thieves and then punish them." The religious leaders forget that the soul needs more and that if the women were given equal opportunity to learn and help the country they love grow, they would find them standing beside them as the Prophets wives did, leading their nation into the modern world as King Abdul Aziz (God Rest His Soul) would have wanted. Instead, we find the women are often divided into categories: those who openly oppose the laws and restrictions thereby facing the consequences and those who have given up and submit to their lot in life. We will need a third category if anything is going to change. A friend of mine recently said something that stuck with me, "If the TV show, Hand Maidens Tale, had been a true one it would have been about Saudi Arabia."

Because of my confinement for six months in Mecca I managed to finish all my high school work by the time I was sixteen. Completing my high school through old school mailed correspondence is no easy task because you had no teacher back then to answer questions and no Google to refer to. You had to rationalize and figure things out for yourself. This is not to say I was smart, just lucky. My grades were terrible, but I managed to make it through.

After a while of diving into my sadness, spending my free time sitting alone in my room day after day with my sad music waiting for Fahad to arrive and take me away from my stepdad. I went to my parents one evening when they were watching TV. I said, "I would like to expand my Arabic." I had learned a great deal as a child from here and there. Being in Mecca with my aunt and *Omi* helped a lot. But while I could understand a lot, I was nervous to speak out loud too much when around company. "This is going to be my home for the rest of my life, so

I want to fully understand the language." My stepdad said, "I'll consider it."

The next day he called Sarh Al Islamia, the private Arabic girls' school where my little sisters were going and asked to speak with the principal. He spoke to her for a while and told her my story. How I was American, but I loved Saudi Arabia and wanted to finish learning Arabic, but he didn't want to send me to the university because in the universities they teach traditional Arabic and never touch much on spoken Arabic. My mother had gone to the university to take an Arabic class many years ago but instead of what she learned helping her it just made her sound more like a foreigner when she tried to speak.

Every Arab country and for that matter every tribe in any country has its own spoken dialect called *Ammiya* (colloquial Arabic). But we all read and write the same way. Traditional Arabic/Classical Arabic, or *Fusshah*, is the Arabic the Quran was written in, so everyone knew it regardless of their tribe or country of origin. The Quran is not allowed to be altered in Arabic in any way since this is a point they like to make about how many times the Bible has been changed thereby making the Quran superior. It might seem right to teach people traditional Arabic first since that is the root of all the dialects but when it's spoken it can only be described in my mind as if someone came up to you and spoke in pure Shakespearian English, you would think they were strange.

The principal thought for a moment and said, "Why don't we put her in the first grade, so she can learn Arabic like the children learn it." My stepdad agreed but mentioned that if I was dressed in the uniform like the children, it might cause them to tease me for being the only sixteen-year-old in first grade. Since the school catered to all grades including high school there were bound to be girls my age there as well. So, she suggested that I be dressed in the teachers uniform and then I could sit in the back of the class and pose as a teacher's assistant. My stepdad agreed and paid the tuition for a child in 1st grade and the next week I joined the class.

The teacher's uniform consisted of a full-length black skirt and a white shirt. All the teachers tried their best to add a bit of color to their outfits by wearing pins or little scarfs. The day I arrived the Principal was tickled pink about her new social experiment. It had never been done before.

The school building was large and painted green, the national color. There were no windows to be seen from the outer walls. Entering through the outer gate, you entered an open-air courtyard surrounded by the tall outer walls. Directly in front of you upon entry was a large gate made of metal bars which would be locked once each girl entered to prevent them from leaving before their guardian or driver could be confirmed. Roll was taken as each girl entered so an accurate account of their arrival could be kept.

The Principal walked toward me and greeted me. We walked through the metal gate, across the vast courtyard which was paved with marble tile towards the actual school building that stood like a green tower with 5 stories. She described the building's layout: one floor for each school group. The first floor was Pre-k and Kindergarten. The second was 1st through 5th grade called *Iptidaaei*. The 3rd floor was 6th through 9th grade called *Mutawasat*. The 4th floor was 10 and 12th grade called *Thanwiya*. The 5th floor was storage and where a teacher who had no one to care for her lived, at least that was what people said. We walked in through the doors of the school building that had some small windows in the halls but none otherwise to protect the girls from being seen anywhere outside the vast courtyard.

I recall feeling safe that we were all secure from anyone who might think to try and access the girls' school. Later years would prove that although we were indeed pretty safe from rape, we were also unable to leave. No one would think that in 2002 there would be a fire in a girls' school like this one. Because of all the locked doors and the fact that the religious police stopped the firemen from entering because the girls were not covered, 15 girls died and 50 were injured. Think about trying to find the person with the key during a panicked emergency. It would prove almost impossible. Not to mention that if you are running from a fire, you're not thinking about grabbing your head cover or abaya and even though the safest place would be the parking lot, the teachers could never allow the daughters of some powerful Saudi men to be seen without their headcovers in the street, fire or not. The religious police felt the same about any girl, despite her rank. So, despite the flames growing closer to the gate, they would have been held back from leaving until their guardians/*Mahram's* arrived to take them home or they found something to cover with. In the Arab world, honor and reputation held more power than life itself.

The Principal walked me to my teacher, Ablah Amal. I was so scared of being discovered and picked on by the other girls but also so excited to learn my language properly. Only the principal and my first-grade teacher knew I was really a student. I walked as I had been taught, back straight with a great calm so as not to reveal how nervous I was to everyone who looked at me. I was different and obviously not Arabic, so as we passed everyone stared and wondered about the beautiful young White girl who was walking with the principal. I recalled something my stepdad told me when I was young. "If you ever find yourself in a tight spot, stand up straight, puff out my chest and say, "Do you know who my father is?" It was meant to be used if ever a time came when someone harassed me in the street. Since there were so many members of the royal family, for all they knew I was one of them and no one wanted to take the risk of messing with the honor of the royal family. Feeling so out of place I channeled my proud self. I knew, of course, that I was in no danger here, but knew that people in Saudi Arabia will treat you based on "the air you bring to a room." If you look scared, then you will be prey and if you stand like a lion, you will be treated like royalty.

Ablah Amal was a short, dark haired Syrian woman who was very kind. The word *Ablah* is an old word which means "wise older sister" or "aunt," a term of great respect and I had learned to always use it when speaking to any woman who was my superior in years, even if only by a few years, to let them know I respect them and I am eager to learn from their wisdom. It was a class of ten girls they all referred to me as "Ablah Maha" which was my Muslim name chosen by my stepdad years earlier. I sat in the back of the class, my notebook ready as we discussed what day and month it was, in Arabic. Then we moved on to mathematics, then science, then Quran, Islamic practices like how to pray, wash and worship, and finally, grammar. I learned so many new words. At the time it seemed completely normal how the teacher managed to integrate every subject into being good wives one day, since my upbringing had very much been the same. We were never encouraged to aspire to be more than a good wife since all of us were destined to be married. Even if we did dream of being doctors or teachers or any other vocation, it would be up to our husbands as it was up to our fathers now whether we should go to college or have any kind of employment. So, to avoid false hopes, a more realistic aspiration was integrated into every subject. It was also not surprising how every subject integrated Wahabbi Islam. Any first grader can tell you what an infidel is. We learned it like we learned grammar.

In 2001 after the 9/11 attacks, it was revealed that 19 of the hijackers were Saudis. Saudi Arabia had to throw a bone to the Western media to prove they were not in fact creating little Jihadists. Even though their own education system reinforced it, the Saudi government announced it would amend the school textbooks, so they no longer taught an ideology of hatred toward non-believers. This indoctrination typically began in the first grade textbooks and was reinforced and expanded every year following. When a student reached 12th-grade, they learned their religious obligation included waging jihad against the infidel to spread the word of Islam.

Unfortunately, their promises to reform the education system were just like most things reported by the media. Bread, circuses, and diversion for the Western world. Do not be fooled by the money, the flash, and the glamor. The Saudi Royal family are politicians, I'll give you a moment to think of an honest politician... The next time you see a news story about a great stride Saudi Arabia made, I would encourage you to remember that what they say they do, and what they actually do, are not always aligned. If you're busy celebrating women being allowed to drive, then you're not questioning the female guardianship system. If you're celebrating changes to the education system, you will more than likely miss all the news of the arrests of free-thinking teachers ...

The textbooks, although probably less direct than they used to be, still teach an ideology of fear and hatred toward non-Muslims and most especially the Jews. The Saudi Government did not want to be associated with the 9/11 attacks directly and the American government needed them to throw out a bone so that they could keep their long-term ally. A Wall Street Journal article written in 2006 managed to obtain copies of the school textbooks and published their content.

FIRST GRADE: " Every religion other than Islam is false." "Fill in the blanks with the appropriate words (Islam, hellfire): Every religion other than ______________ is false. Whoever dies outside of Islam enters ____________."

FOURTH GRADE: "True belief means . . . that you hate the polytheists and infidels but do not treat them unjustly."

TWELFTH GRADE: "Jihad in the path of God -- which consists of battling against unbelief, oppression, injustice, and those who perpetrate it -- is the summit of Islam. This religion arose through jihad and through jihad was its banner raised high. It is one of the noblest acts, which brings one closer to God, and one of the most magnificent acts of obedience to God."

In 2005, four years after they said they had reformed the education system, any teacher caught discussing Christianity, Judaism, the causes of terrorism or expressing their views in general was to be immediately imprisoned on charges such as endorsing allegedly un-Islamic sexual, social, and religious practices, being an apostate, and seeking to disrupt the country.

A teacher whose students were boys between the ages of 13-15 only wanted to help them navigate their sexuality in a country that provides them with truly little options. Also, in response to the 2002 bombings in Saudi Arabia, he wanted to discuss with them the dangers of terrorism. Most of these teachers are picked up and thrown in prison long before the government can come up with some formal charges. This is not a system where an officer needs to obtain a warrant to enter your home, nor is it a country where due process is observed unless it is observed by the media, and they are forced to do so. Muhammad al-Harbi, a Chemistry teacher, was charged with blasphemy charges for just discussing his views on current events and religion. He was sentenced to 750 lashes, 40 months in prison, and he was banned from teaching. In 2004, Muhammad al-Sahimi, a middle school and high school teacher was also banned from teaching for expressing his views in a classroom. He was sentenced to three years in prison and 300 lashes.

The list goes on and on. As stated before in the quote by Sir Thomas, you first make thieves and then you punish them. In Saudi we make religious extremists and then deny any involvement in their education. A change in the ideology of hatred towards those who are different can only come about by changing what we teach the next generation and sadly the reverse is also true. By allowing and encouraging people to discuss and openly debate EVERYTHING. Especially how the old Islamic ways fit or do not fit in the modern world. Blind allegiance only breeds fundamentalists.

On the first break I went hand in hand with the 1st graders and helped Ablah Amal keep them in line. As the break ended and the second bell rang, the high school girls started to come down as we were heading up. I recall looking at them and wishing in part that I was among them holding hands and giggling. I would have to point out that while the British are known for their emotional restraint Arabs are not. It is never thought uncommon for friends to hold hands at any age, men or women. I had missed out on being in a real school for my high school years and seeing all the girls my own age, I longed for a friend or two. My stepdad discouraged me from having friends. He said it was because he feared bad influences. But I see it now for what it was. If I had no one to confide in there was no risk of anyone ever knowing what he really was.

As the day went on, my first instinct was to write each new word and its translation. I soon realized that once I wrote the translation, every time I looked at the page my eyes would first gravitate to the English, not the Arabic. So, I decided to take a lesson from the first-grade textbook and draw a picture of what it meant instead. The words came easier that way and I raced through the syllabus so fast my teacher took to teaching me in the teacher break room on her breaks to help me go further. The other teachers noticed and took a keen interest in helping me as well. The grammar was the hardest, it was so different from the English I had learned. There is a word in Arabic for everything so the addition of the qualifier word "small" before the word "dog" is not needed in Arabic when there is a different word for small, medium, and large dogs.

Everything was backwards. *"White milk"* in English is *"Milk white"* in Arabic. Learning which nouns were masculine or feminine took memorization more than anything. It was like I had always known how the words formed; I knew how to pronounce everything instinctively but seeing them on paper was a whole different story. The Arabic text was written and read from right to left, instead of left to right. Arabic was also written like English cursive. Each letter on its own was different from when it was formed into a word. I had to do away with the letters "P" and "V" since they did not exist in the Arabic alphabet. I learned to read quickly since I already knew many words. It was not hard for me once I had a grasp of the alphabet.

I took to immersing myself at home as much as I could by placing post it notes on everything in the house with the items Arabic name so I could see the name and practice. I even took to making the grocery list for my stepdad in Arabic, forcing myself to use it when I could even if I spelled everything wrong. My mother disliked it when I tried to practice by speaking Arabic to my stepdad since she felt excluded from the conversation and hated that, so I had to limit my verbal practice to the school.

In three months, I had devoured and assimilated the entire first grade syllabus. So, it was decided that I would jump from grade to grade taking only the classes that furthered my Arabic. My schedule which I still have today says 1st period Quran 3rd grade, 2nd period grammar 2nd grade and 3rd period reading 4th grade. Designing and changing my schedule as I learned enabled me to learn as much as I could. The principal signed off on it every week and praised me for my progress.

When I finally made it to the upper grades on the 3rd level of the school, a rumor began that I was a "teacher inspector" as it is said in Arabic. Since I went from class to class asking questions about the lesson and only staying for one lesson, the students suspected that I was analyzing how the teachers measured up and reporting back to the principal since I was often seen going to her office. Just like in today's school system, it was not uncommon for the principal and other representatives to sit in on classes to see how the teacher was doing and so it was I was deemed a spy, making me even less endearing to my own age group.

I made a friend with one of the girls in the 11th grade. Her name was Safa. She was dark skinned, fat, and exceedingly expressive. She had just returned from America on a trip with family. She was half-Saudi and her mother allowed her a great deal of freedom when they traveled to the States on vacation. I was very reserved and cautious. I worried a lot about how she openly stated to me that she didn't cover when she was in America, even though I was a stranger. I took her arm and said, "You should be careful about saying things like that." She asked, "Why?" "Because it will ruin your reputation and that of your sisters. I don't care what you do but you need to keep it quiet." "Okay, sorry. Hey, let's go down to the basement. I have something to show you." I agreed to sneak her past the teachers to the basement. Since I was thought to be a teacher, no one questioned us skipping a class as long as she was with me, she was viewed as being with a teacher. When we got to the basement, she walked to the storage area and crouched down behind some old stage props. "Here, look at this," she said, handing me a novel that was banned in Saudi Arabia for its erotic content. The types of books still banned in Saudi Arabia today include books that express anti-government or anti-Layanrchy sentiments, books that are anti-religion or are critical of religion (especially Islam), pornographic magazines or those that feature nudity, any books that talk about homosexuality, the Bible, the Torah, and erotic novels like this one that featured graphically described sex scenes.

I stared at the book but dared not touch it. It felt like just handling it would get me into trouble. I said, "What is in it?" "Well, it talks about all sorts of things we learn after marriage. You can borrow it if you want. " "No, I think I am good. What makes you interested in all that?"

"Well, I kissed a boy when I was in the States last time and I just wanted to know more."

I leaned in and said, "How was it?" I pretended I had never been kissed because I felt that if she was no good at keeping her own secrets, there was no way she would keep mine. "It was amazing," she answered enthusiastically. "Will you marry him?" I asked. "Oh no," she responded, "it was just for fun."

I found her attitude very cavalier and inappropriate. I smiled and said I needed to head back to class.

The next day, Ablah Layla, the English teacher, pulled me aside to ask if I was friends with Safa.

"Not really, she just talked to me because she visited the U.S. recently. Why do you ask?" I answered her.

"Well, there is a rumor that she is a lesbian, so I didn't want you to be accused of being a lesbian with her when I know you're a pious and good girl."

"Oh my! Thank you for telling me. I will make sure not to talk to her again." A few times I had witnessed a few girls who would enter the bathroom handicapped stall together, but I had thought nothing of it. The slightest whisper of me being a lesbian could have grave consequences.

In Saudi Arabia, male and female courtship is illegal outside of marriage and segregation is rigorously enforced. Since the gender segregation is so rigid, one can anticipate and even expect that since all one sees every day is their own sex, that often there is resulting love, affection, and even sex in that segregated arena. This is not to say I think it is a bad thing today, but rather to reference the way I was brought up. I believe everyone has a right to choose who they love and what they do with their own body. But because the country and culture was so appalled by it, it definitely encouraged it to flourish underground.

I met a Saudi man a long time ago named Majid. He asked me if I had ever had sex with a girl, naturally partly out of his own fantasies but also out of curiosity. I said no and asked him if he had ever had sex with a man. He said no, but added, "I can understand why some over here do. Once I was swimming with my cousin in the backyard and his smooth leg brushed up against me. I had never felt another person's flesh against my skin before and I got very aroused. Unfortunately, there are not many outlets for us without very great risk." I felt badly for him.

The penalty for same sex sexual activity in Saudi Arabia is death, usually by stoning. This is because in Islam, sodomy is a crime of the highest magnitude. Technically however, in Islam there is a requirement to have four witnesses of good character to prove such a thing, as you similarly would for a case of accused adultery. I believe the Prophet created that law because the likelihood that four people watched you have sex would be low, if not completely impossible, therefore he would not need to pass judgement on it. As a ruler and religious leader, he knew it was important to appease the fundamentalists by saying it was punishable and then he simply made it almost impossible to prove. Saudi Arabia is not the only country that punishes same sex activity. It is the same in Iran, Afghanistan, and even in 2019, the Sultan of Brunei enacted an Islamic law making it legal to flog to death someone who was LGBTQ.

This is not an issue of the past. A Yemeni blogger named Mohamad al-Bokari was imprisoned in 2020 for simply stating in an online video, "Everyone has rights and should be able to practice them freely, including gay people." He was charged with violating public morality and what will happen to him next, no one knows. Suhail al-Jameel posted a picture of himself in shorts wearing makeup and he was arrested for *sharing nudity online,* even though technically in Islam, a man is not considered nude as long as his shorts reach his knees - that is all a man is required to wear. I know his shorts only reached his thighs but unless they try to arrest every male swimmer in the Red Sea … we all knew that the real charge was because of his sexual orientation.

In a country where the religious and regular police rely highly on the conservative people to rat out their neighbors and friends, it is no wonder few people have the courage to stand up, since the risk is too high. You don't even need to be gay; you only need to be associated with someone who is to find yourself locked behind bars without any actual charges.

The worst things that happen to same sex people in Saudi actually doesn't come from the government but rather the community, the tribe, and the family. Just like how young girls are locked up for being caught talking to boys in a chat room or over the phone until the family decides to marry her off or kill her, so too a gay child can be locked away until the family decides if he or she will change, marry, and repent in the best-case scenario or, in the worst-case scenario, be suffocated, poisoned or who knows what. The police do not regularly arrest families for upholding and protecting their family honor. Instead, it is ruled as an accident and swept under the rug. Respect, honor, the tribe, and bloodlines trump all.

For me, the risk was higher than most. I was an American, I was a girl, and I was just seen going into a dark basement with a girl rumored to be a lesbian. While my Saudi stepdad might argue that the girl was at fault and nothing happened, I would have been viewed not as an innocent Saudi girl who was corrupted like the half-American girl who was drummed up on immoral behavior charges after visiting America. I would simply be thrown into the same bucket reputationally, and that was too dangerous. I distanced myself from Safa and prayed no one made any association between me and her or made any anonymous phone calls to report the rumor. Unfortunately, homosexuals will have a longer battle to fight for rights than the women in Saudi Arabia.

I spoke to a friend of mine in Riyadh recently about the lesbians we heard about in our school days and her reply was, "I used to think they were not normal, Honey, but now I see that they are normal. Look at me, I'm married and I'm miserable with my husband. At least they might have found some happiness in an equally balanced relationship."

Love, among many things in Saudi, is hard to find for many reasons but mostly because we marry who our tribe wants us to marry. As a virgin, you need your guardian's permission to marry, therefore, he will have a big say in who an acceptable person is. Courtship of the kind you find in Saudi online in a chat room or over the phone is pretty much what we have, and it often never bears fruit since as much as you may love each other, there are so many other factors that come into play when you are a Saudi.

For girls, the questions that come into play are does he come from a good well-known family, how much is his income, is he educated, and is his family respectable? However, even if all these are perfectly in line on paper, how do you introduce the idea to your family if you can't prove that the idea came about through the proper respectable channels, such as a mother saw you at a wedding, a lady saw you at a lunch, a cousin suggested you to his friend when he heard your parents were seeking a husband for you to marry, and so on.

Often, we would just flirt and fall in love until one or both end up receiving a good marriage proposal backed by their families. I have witnessed many a sad bride nursing a broken heart for thc one they could not have because of outdated traditions that do not suit most of the younger generations. The saddest was the wedding of an Emirati princess in Dubai, she was thirteen-year-old and as she stood on her Kosha next to her fifteen-year-old husband, she wept tears stained black from all the eyeliner she wore. At least a lesbian will never lose her lover even if she is pushed to get married by her family, as long as they were careful. If a girl fell in love with a man, there is a greater than 90% chance he would not become her husband.

NOOR

I took a particular liking to the third graders. They were so much fun and when I had a free period the third-grade teacher, always in need of a break because she was a smoker I suspect, would ask if I could watch them so I did. We had a good old time laughing, drawing, and sharing stories which was in sharp contrast to the third-grade teacher who was known for being scary and yelling at students to push them into obedience. I took a page from another book and chose instead to earn their trust and to be liked. When they made fun of their teacher, I just gave them a half smile meaning I can't condone but I won't say anything. When she came close to the door, and I signaled they all settled as if we had shared a great secret together. The girls would often give me notes saying, *I love you Ablah Maha.*

One of the girls in their class was named Sara. She was a bright, happy girl with porcelain skin and beautiful brown hair. She was Palestinian and like so many, her family had immigrated from Palestine in search of a better life. First to Egypt and then the Saudi government, due to the unrest in Palestine, agreed for them to enter the country and gave them a residency but not the right to obtain nationality. With their travel document they could travel around certain Arab countries but not beyond since they had no passports. Their country was torn by war and while I will not go into much detail, I will say that if they tried to leave there weren't many countries that would take them on a permanent basis. In Saudi they were seen and treated by the local population as charity cases and lower-class citizens. Sara and I became close. She was inquisitive and very conversational for one so young, and I enjoyed her company.

One day her sister, a very tall girl with a boyish haircut, came downstairs to see her. I stepped aside as she and her sister greeted each other. The next day she came downstairs again this time with her girl posse. They stood in the hall and made fun of me. As much as I loved Sara, I hated her sister and her sister's friends. On the second floor I was the respected and dearly loved Ablah but on the third floor I was the enemy, just another teacher here to tell them what to do. The days went on and I moved more and more around the school than ever.

One day the English teacher named Ablah Laila from the third floor came to me and said there was a problem. "What is it, Ablah, how can I help," I said. "Sweet girl, I have been requested to put on a play, but I don't have enough girls who can speak good English and who are willing to be in the play. It is only a few days away. Would you be willing to take the leading role as the devil?" "The devil has the leading role? What is the play about?" I asked, "Well, I wrote it myself and everyone just loves the idea. The play is about a family that moved to America and while they were there the devil whispered in their ears. The devil made them forget to pray, praise Allah, and respect their elders, thus ruining the family because they went to such a misguided land. The children stop praying and start listening to music. I have seen it happen and I am sure so many mothers will identify." If that moment were a movie scene you would have one camera shot of my blank face and one camera shot of her utter excitement and the sound of crickets in the background. I wondered for a moment if she was serious but one look at her giddy expression, and I knew she was dead serious. This is what many mothers believe that if you indulge in Western habits and customs, you're bound to lose your way. I smiled and said, "Sure, I'm happy to help."

While I found the play utterly comical, I agreed to take the role and met them the next day for rehearsal. As I walked into the hall where the girls were rehearsing, I froze for a second as my eyes gravitated to one of the girls. Lo and behold, there was Saras' older sister playing the boy in the play. Our eyes met and with one look we conveyed to each other how much each of us disliked the other.

As the days went on and we practiced together we realized that we were not so different after all. Her name was Noor. Maybe it was her going home and Sara defending me. Maybe it was because we were spending so much time together or that we were the two best English speakers in the school but whatever it was, we started to call each other on the telephone almost daily. Which seemed to make my stepdad feel a bit uneasy. I had been friendless for so long and the friends I did have would fall off gradually since my mother was not very social and my stepdad always made excuses for why he could not take me to visit them. You see, after everything I had been through the last few years, my stepdad feared the day I would find a confidant. In the past he never had much concern I suppose since I was an outcast in England and in Saudi, I was raised to be always on my guard to avoid gossip. I, on the other hand, was overjoyed to have someone to really talk to about almost everything and nothing.

We talked for hours about life, our families, and looking back now, I see why my stepdad would have been uneasy about her. I now had a close friend. How long would it be until I told her what had happened to me? How long would it take her to tell her mom, who would tell her friend, who would tell someone else that knew my stepdad's family. How long until his reputation was ruined along with mine and that of my sisters? How long until my mother was told by someone, and she put together a plan to take the children and leave him (although that was the most unlikely concern since she would need his permission to do anything). After all, he could not have worried about jail time or social services. Such things didn't happen in cases like mine.

The school was run like a tight ship, and only the teachers were allowed to move freely between the floors at any given time. The gates on each stairwell were locked to ensure the girls didn't get into any mischief. If there was a fire on the lower floor and you were on the fourth floor, you would need to find the person who held the keys to five barred gates before you could exit the school. An elderly lady who lived on the top floor held all the keys. She opened and shut the gates when needed daily. Her name was Ablah Naamaat.

Ablah Naamaat was a sight to behold: she was of average height, she had very strangely dyed orange hair and was a little plump around the middle. There were lots of rumors about her around school. That she was crazy, that her husband had left her which is why she was miserable, that she was a witch, or that she was hiding from something or someone. But all I ever knew for sure was that she was strict, angry, and mean. Looking back now her story, whatever it was, must have been very sad and I regret not making more of an effort to learn the real sadness that must have resided behind the mask she showed all of us.

She didn't know if I was really a teacher but my close and obvious friendship with Noor made her concerned about the sharing of power. As my friendship with Noor grew, I did what any teenager would do and that was to use my power when I had a free class to remove Noor from class so that we could hide in some odd place and discuss the secrets of the world. She would talk about the boy she had met that summer in Egypt, and we would eat candy we had saved up. I always returned her to the class saying thank you, Ablah so-and-so, for letting me speak with Noor before departing the classroom as if I was a teacher.

Noor's family were what my family would call liberal Muslims. They prayed five times a day, but the girls only covered their hair in Saudi. When they went to Egypt in the summer, they wore bikinis and went to nightclubs, things I only secretly dreamed of being able to do. It was so much fun to listen to her stories. In my family, although we secretly didn't pray five times a day, the women covered all the time even when we were abroad and most of my traveling clothes were like my clothes in England, baggy and unattractive. She had three sisters close in age, so they had a closet full of cute things and I was dying to get over to her house to try them on.

Noor was the fourth born of five children and as much as I might try, I could never do her inner and outer beauty justice. She was a girl who was teased constantly because of her height, her short boy haircut, and because she was considered by the Saudi girls to be a low-born Palestinian. Like me, before my aunt took me under her wing, she was a little tomboyish. We both had a long journey ahead of us before we knew our real beauty did not come from comparing ourselves to others but rather from within us. We were two shining stars who had no mirror to remind us of our beautiful light.

One night I asked my mom and stepdad if I could go the next day to visit my friend. My stepdad replied, "Do we know her family?" "No," I said, "but you could." My stepdad replied, "Call your friend and have her mom speak to your mom as they should meet if you're going over there." Turning to my mom he said, "She should come visit you here for the first visit, since they are Palestinian, and you are the wife of a Saudi." Typical class and origin intimidation, I found it annoying, since I had never seen my aunt make such distinctions. I wanted to be able to visit my friend, so I did as he asked and introduced her mother to my mother over the phone. Then, as requested, Noor's mom agreed to come and visit my mother for tea. It was a very short visit since it was only a formality. I recall Noor telling me at school the next day that her mother found my mother to be extremely odd. I giggled saying, "You have no idea."

Finally, now that the first visit was over, I would be allowed to visit Noor's house with my mother in attendance for the first visit. As was the case with any teenager, I felt like it was so lame for my mother to be there, but it was better than not going at all. My mother, being my mother, was not there to help appease my stepdad but rather, as his spy, to find evidence to uphold the reason why I should no longer associate with Noor. I hoped my mother would only see a nice Muslim home so it would be decided that she didn't need to come back with me the next time. I had prepared Noor by telling her what to hide from my mother, like pictures of them in Egypt on the beach without their headcovers. I also informed her what topics her mother should avoid talking to my mother about.

We only had 30 minutes at Noor's house before my stepdad began telephoning saying we must return home where I picked up the phone and immediately called Noor to find out what her mother thought about my mother now. As expected, she didn't like her but for Noor's sake, she put up with her. After my mother gave her report on Noor's family, their values that she could surmise and their living conditions, I was allowed to visit again on my own.

For the next visit, I went over for lunch. My mother, at the request of my stepdad to make sure we didn't leave the house and go to the mall, called every 30 minutes to make sure "I was okay." We were busy having a photoshoot in her room with her sister's cute clothes. Noor had three sisters, Sara, the youngest, Hala, who was my age, and Layan. Layan was a classic beauty that we both aspired to be like. A real beauty inside and out, soft spoken, endlessly kind, and fair in complexion with flowing red curls. We took pictures and had a good time until my mother finally called and said Baba had arrived and it was time to go. We sulked as I rubbed off my lipstick and headed down to the car. Baba asked, "So, how did it go?" and thinking if I had too much fun, he would not let me go again, I told him, "Well, I had to eat a small pigeon for lunch, it had so many little bones. They eat very strange food." I knew if I seemed like I liked them too much he would fear I was forgetting who I was and who they were. For him, real influence can be most dangerous, i.e., "when the lion forgets he is a lion." I told Baba what he wanted to hear, hoping it would stop him from thinking my friend and I were too close.

No doubt he had already made inquiries of his own, but as long as I appeared to uphold our ways and disdain their ways, everything in his mind would balance out as fine. I dared not think of what would happen if he found out that we were trying on bikinis and taking pictures! Trying on such a garment was bad, but documenting it was terrible. My stepdad believed in never documenting things he didn't want anyone to know, like that he still smoked or that he had once made an image of a nude lady out of sand on a beach. These seem like trivial things to most people but in my stepdad's family, they could be extremely damaging. I diverted his attention knowing full well that he was a master at catching me in a lie. I learned early on that the best way to avoid suspicion was to talk a lot as if I had nothing to hide. If he thought I had exhausted the conversation, he would have no more questions. My secrets would be safe, and I would be safe from his wrath. He knew that I detested bones in my food because it reminded me that the animal was alive but when served as a visitor it would have been rude not to eat so I ate a little and said I was full. He laughed and agreed that pigeon was gross, and we went home. Saved by the pigeon lunch that I hated, I was able to relax.

One day at school it began to rain, which was a rare event in Saudi. Saudi rain is a warm rain that barely hits at all without drying up immediately most of the time. We received an average of 58 mm of rainfall annually and the temperature could rise to 54 °C (129 °F) in a day. The teachers, being warned that rain was coming, moved all the girls inside and locked the doors and windows to make sure none of us got wet and sick they said, but really it was so the parents didn't complain that we came home wet. Luckily, I heard the teachers talking and already had Noor outside. We both loved the rain as many of the girls did because it was such a relief from the extreme heat that we experienced day in and day out. We danced in the rain in the courtyard for all the school to see from the small hall windows. The girls cheered us on as the teachers tried to figure out how to pull us inside. We ran off and took a back stairwell we knew was open to return into the school, both soaking wet, out of breath, and laughing about how Ablah Naamaat looked like she was about to burst a blood vessel. Eventually when we were cornered I explained, "Oh, so sorry, Ablah Naamat, but we got locked out when we were getting something from downstairs." She stared me down, but knowing the principal was bound to believe me, she let us go. I will always remember that day, I loved the rain so much for it was always a blessing. I loved it in England on my walks to school, but you realize how much more you really love something when it is rare, making it feel all the more precious, and when you find someone who shares that love with you … it was pure joy.

I started taking my recess with the middle schoolers instead of the primary schoolers so that Noor and I could spend the time together. We sat on the stairs as she drank non-alcoholic beer. The whole school was up in arms saying it must have alcohol in it, but it didn't. It was the taboo of drinking something called beer since alcohol was illegal in the country because it was against the religion. People were afraid of anything that resembled alcohol as they might be associated with such a horrid practice as drinking. It wasn't always illegal. I recall my aunt telling me the story of when it became illegal. The announcement was made that behold; liquor has been declared unlawful. Then all the liquor was poured on the ground and flowed through the lanes of the city of Medina. Consuming it was such a grave sin that one drink could mean your prayers would not be accepted for forty days.

One day while I was having lunch with Noor in the courtyard, a group of girls asked about me and I went to greet them. Wajdaan was my age whereas Noor was 3 years younger. Her friend Amal was interesting and spoke perfect English. Amal had spent some time in America and so she was very popular among the high school girls. I enjoyed speaking with them, but they loved America whereas I had been raised to believe that it was a place where people who did not respect our traditions, religion, and way of life lived. Where people were shot in the street without reason, where all the girls had loose morals and had sex with everyone. It was a place I never wanted to go or see. I was however curious why they liked to dream about it so much and I enjoyed having my harsh Saudi upbringing that everything American must be bad worn down by the beautiful things they would describe. Amal talked about how she was permitted to drive a car while she was in the States and the other girls listened in awe. These are the dreams of the young girls of Saudi Arabia who did not know that there was so much more for us to be interested in pursuing. The typical average older women saw driving as nothing of great importance since they had chauffeurs, and the average Saudi driver runs almost every red light making it very dangerous to drive. Actually, if you had asked an average Saudi woman if driving was important to us, you would find that the reply would be something along the lines of, "We have bigger issues that need attending. The guardianship law for example that keeps us from doing anything without a man's permission. The child custody laws in cases of divorce and the lack of educational options and job opportunities for women. These are the much bigger issues. A man may come and go as he pleases while we must have permission, a man may study what he pleases while we must have permission, a man keeps the children and the property, and we get to keep only our jewels and our marriage dowry in a divorce. Our judges and religious clerics are men and they take the husband's side in most domestic court cases, leaving us with no female representation."

While the West celebrates reforms like women driving, they miss the major issues Saudi women face daily that do not change. Saudi women would have gladly never driven if these other reforms were addressed, but sometimes you need to take what you're given and save your ammunition for another day.

I divided the time during recesses between Noor and this other group of girls. But after a while, Noor began to be upset by this since we had been inseparable. "Why are you spending so much time with them?" she asked. I said, "They are my friends just like you." Noor huffed off, angry. Deep down I think she was afraid that since they were my age, and they were Saudi and more like me, that I would soon choose them over her. We started passing notes back and forth in a notebook that still exists today since we could not bear to fight out loud. My other friends noticed her reaction to their arrival and started asking why she was being so childish. I refused to comment and decided it best since the high schoolers had a separate lunch break then the middle schoolers, I would just take both breaks so this way they would not fight over my time. The tension grew until eventually Wajdaan did something I thought was very wrong. She, being a Bedouin, was of pure Saudi blood, whereas my grandfather became Saudi after migrating to Mecca. If my stepdad had a superiority complex Wejdaan had it worse. Wajdaan tolerated Noor but deep down she did not consider Noor her equal as a Palestinian. Almost anyone on the school ground who was not Saudi in one way, or another would get bullied at some point in some way. It was because our parents and grandparents spoke freely at home about how low they believed the other nationalities were on compared to, how great our nationality was. Naturally, we absorbed these comments and remarks and began to say and treat people like they did. One day, while passing Noor in the courtyard, Wajdaan silently reached her hand to her face and using her thumb and index finger, she touched them to her face from mid cheek and ran them down until the two fingers touched together on her chin while looking at Noor as we walked past. It was a signal that meant "I'll show/get you or just you wait." It was so disrespectful and although I had wished for them to get along, I could not allow Noor to be insulted just because she was not Saudi. It wasn't right. I said, "Wajdaan, that was unkind." "Pshaw, she had it coming, the stupid Palestinian acting like a big baby." "Wajdaan, she is my dearest friend and who cares where she is from," I replied. Wajdaan's face registered her puzzlement. I realized then there would be no changing the way she was raised. As my stepdad would have said, Noor is not fit to even clean my shoes. That day I stopped seeing my group of Saudi friends and apologized to Noor for how rude they were.

We spent many great days at that school. Once we even had a competition to see who could save the most candy and hide away in a storage closet on the fifth floor during the 5th period to eat it all. Ablah Naamat opened the storage room door, but we hidden behind a bunch of chairs giggling to ourselves at how we had outsmarted her once again. When we finally emerged Ablah Naamat came up to me and said,

"Where have you been?"

I calmly replied, "Around, why?"

"Because your father was here asking for you."

My heart almost stopped beating as I asked, "When?"

"He just left but he was waiting an hour. You didn't hear your name over the speaker?" "No, Ablah, sorry I didn't."

With that she turned on her heels and went to let everyone know I was found. No doubt they called my stepdad to assure him of my safe recovery. My mind however began doing extreme calculations. Why did he come? Why did he need me to come out early? Surely if it was a family emergency, he would have told the school and he would have asked to pick-up my sisters, Noura, and Yasmin, as well.

I had spent the last few years working on the perfect plan of never being alone at home with my stepdad, but it never occurred to me that he could pick me up from school if the house was empty and there would be nothing I could do about it. Scared at the thought, I knew this was not the time to worry about making a new plan but rather to plan an explanation for my absence. I knew he would think I was up to no good and that Noor was the bad influence. We heard stories all the time of girls who would fake a doctor's note, have their driver pick them up, take them to see their boyfriends, and bring them back to the school to be picked up by their families later on. The idea that he could come and take me out of school when the house was empty was horrifying.

I knew since he didn't get his way and I never appeared, he would be angry more than if I just made some excuse that I had a class or an exam. He would turn the whole thing around now. Now it wasn't him who did wrong but I who was up to something, and I had better have a good reason for being missing. I picked up my two sisters when it was time for school to let out and walked through the gate when our last name was called.

My two sisters climbed into the back of the car, and I got in the front as usual. My stepdad was obviously angry, clinching the steering wheel and staring straight ahead. As the car started moving, he asked the question, "Where were you?" I resisted the urge to ask him what he was doing there trying to take me out of school early for no reason, since I knew by now that nothing would convince him that he was wrong, ever. I swallowed my saliva and looked down as I decided there would be no excuse better formed with so little time as the truth.

"Noor and I were hanging out in the storage room, we were eating candy."

"You expect me to believe that you were in a storage room eating candy?"

"We had saved up for weeks to share that candy. we had a competition to see who could save the most, she won, of course, she has more siblings who are older and give her candy."

He stayed quiet as I added, "Well, there are no loudspeakers on the fifth floor since it's not used for anything except storage, and although Ablah Naamat told me you came after I came down, I could have easily not planned to be with Noor up there if I had known you were coming."

He paused in a deep silence and when we arrived home everything seemed normal. Knowing my stepdad, he had accepted my story, and this was the sign of it, otherwise there would have been a great storm in the house. I had no doubt about that. A week passed before he finally decided to try his hand again, arriving unannounced at the school to call for me. When the teacher told me, I turned pale as I gathered my things, but an idea came to my head. I walked calmly down to my sister's classrooms. I knocked on the doors softly and calmly said, "I'm so sorry, Ablah so-and-so, but our father is here to collect us early." "Oh, no problem," she said. My sisters collected their things and we all headed to the car together. My stepdad frowned and, with nothing to say, drove us home in silence, dropped us off, and left. When my mother asked him why he picked us up early that day his reply was that he heard there might be a sandstorm so he thought he would bring them back early, just in case.

I don't give myself much credit for outsmarting my stepdad so often, but I will say this, if you put a child in any environment, they will adapt, and I knew there was no escape from my stepdad except by marriage. I had to survive until then. Even the worst hide and seek player will become an expert when frightened.

Time at school flew by and finally I was taking grammar in the 12th grade. I recall feeling out of place, since half the 12th grade class was engaged, married, or married and already pregnant. I thought of Fahad and wondered why he had not even tried to contact me. I asked myself, he could if he wanted to? The Internet was fairly new in 2001 and I didn't know if he had an email account. He couldn't call on the telephone or send a letter both which would be intercepted by my stepdad, and I presumed, highly unwelcome. So, I waited. I felt glad to have Noor. I finally had someone to confide in, not about everything, but at least about Fahad. The other topic was too taboo. She might think it was all my fault and fear for her reputation if anyone found out. She might stop talking to me, so I left that where it needed to be, buried.

One day on the last day of school for Eid break we both went down to the basement to a place where there was a hole in the ceiling that led up to the courtyard. You could see the sky. We laid on our backs, our heads back-to-back on the old green carpet. I told her about my love for Fahad and she told me about her love for an Egyptian boy she had met while in Egypt for the summer. We giggled and dreamed of our weddings, having our own homes, making our own rules and pledged that one day we would go to Egypt together and dance in night clubs in pretty dresses. We giggled again because such a thing for me would have been a big no-no, but I was sure marriage would bring me all the freedom I had dreamed of having.

Before you ponder about why we were so naive to think that one cage would prove better than the one we were in, let me point out that it was not because we were young, rather it was because we all received the same saying from our parents, aunts, teachers, and really, everyone. If we asked for something that they didn't approve of, in my case, for example, perfume, a sleeveless dress like the other girls had, to go to college, travel, or go to the mall alone, the answer was always the same. "I understand, but one day you will be married and then if your husband wants you to go to college you will go."

The request I remember most vividly was when I asked to cut my very long beautiful hair so I could look like the girls in the music videos. I was told by my stepdad, "One day you will be married and if your husband wants long hair, you already have it but if he wants short hair then you can cut it, but if it was already short and he wanted long hair, you will have a problem so we will just wait and your husband can decide."

Life often seemed like we were just wasting time until marriage. Some of us worried, since everyone knew there was only a short window for a good marriage before the age of twenty. Why twenty? Perhaps because it was two years after high school and if you weren't going to college, you probably got into mischief, or you were waiting for someone. Families liked to marry their children young to get grandchildren and keep the children busy and out of trouble.

If you weren't at least engaged by the age of twenty the rumors would start. Why isn't she married? What's wrong with her? Is she ugly? Has she done something bad, like talk to boys? Is her family not respectable? Unfounded gossip was commonplace. But if a boy wasn't married at twenty, or any age, he was advancing his career, working hard, or making himself ready for marriage. Most of us knew it was a big possibility that we would marry older men who were stable and ready to care for a family. Many of us dreamed of someone our own age and had a crush on someone we grew up with, be it a cousin or a son of a close family friend we had seen for only a moment through a door that was partially cracked open. This was, and still very much is, a world where love stories can start and end, with a glance through a cracked open door.

There were many stories. We knew of a family who had a daughter who was seen holding a boy's hand in a mall. Once spotted, the story went from woman to woman until everyone talked about her and now, because she had a stain on her character, everyone assumed the family let all their children do as they pleased and so her sisters were stained as well, making it very hard for the family to find husbands for them until the rumors died down.

We all tiptoed and chose our friends wisely because if word got out that we had even just spoken to a boy on the telephone, there would be no way of cleaning the stain from our households. Being the oldest girl and the de facto oldest child since my brother left, made me responsible not just for myself but for my sisters' marriage prospects as well. I took this responsibility seriously and watched out for anything I did that might be misinterpreted. Instead of just asking myself if what I'm doing is right or wrong, I also stepped back and asked myself what does it look like to others? It was like playing chess every time we left the house. Each move, each glance measured, and each possible outcome had to be considered.

Marriage were all any of the girls talked about in the 12th grade class. I recall my friend Wajdaan was in love with her cousin. She wore his initials on a gold chain around her neck. She was like me, waiting for him to come ask for her. They used to play together as children, but since she became of age, she was no longer allowed to see him and settled for glances of him through a partially opened door or by looking out the upstairs windows, hoping he would see her and remember she was waiting.

The summer arrived and Noor planned to visit me for the day. I was very excited. My stepdad insisted that her mother should come with her to see the house and get to know my mother a little better. Since I knew it's really only customary for the first visit, I assumed he was trying to find a way for Noor's mom to say no, so he could pretend to be insulted on behalf of my mother and end our friendship. Friendship, after all in most of the Middle East, typically revolved around the family. If I was friends with someone my family must be friends with their family, or at least appear to be. A night was chosen, and they were about to arrive. I rang up Noor on the telephone in the kitchen stretching the long telephone cord as far in the corner as I could so I wouldn't be overheard. I reminded her that my stepdad would open the gate, and to cover her face since I knew she didn't normally, knowing full well that if he knew that she didn't cover abroad, or cover her face in public, I might not be allowed to be friends with her anymore for fear that she would damage my reputation. She did as I asked, and all went well. They stayed for about an hour and left.

Noor came to visit again a week later, and we took over the fancy guest room. My mother tried to make us the traditional Bukhari soup called *Shishbarrah*. We played music and used the camcorder to record us singing along to our favorite songs. We forget to turn it off when my mom served the soup and I recall it being so gross we spit it out back into our bowls. And then checking if the coast was clear we dumped it back into the pot so she would think we had eaten it. Watching it years later we laughed so much our sides hurt. We were kindred spirits, and she was always able to make me laugh, which was something I had lost touch with along the road. That happy little girl who found everything around her wonderful and could breathe again.

Another time when Noor came over she brought the prints from our photo shoot at her house. We laughed and giggled and divided up the pictures and placed them in small photo albums. That same day she had brought her camera and did my makeup. Her sister was a makeup artist and had taught her a few things, so she enjoyed putting makeup on me. We snapped some more photos, and the film went with her to be developed.

The Internet arrived with dial-up in every home. My stepdad gave me a computer for my room on the condition that my mother could use it if needed to talk to her sisters in America. I will never forget the sound of the Internet connecting through dial-up. At night, I would wrap my blanket around it so no one would hear me connecting. I would spend hours waiting for one high resolution picture of Mariah Carey to load. Finding them was hard, as most sites were blocked for being indecent content, but eventually I found them. I would not be surprised one day when I read that Saudi Arabia is second only to China when it comes to censoring and blocking certain websites. They are good at it, but we all found our ways around them. Why Mariah Carey photos? Well so I could cut them out and place myself next to her, having learned how to use a digital art program. I enjoyed being able to dream about meeting her one day so I could tell her how her music comforted me.

The following week, Noor came over with the new pictures so we pulled out the first album that was hidden under my bedroom mattress for fear that my parents would find it and started to add to it laughing and talking. Noor pointed out one of the old pictures and said that when her mom saw it, she said that Noor looked like a gorilla standing next to Cinderella. It hurt her deeply and I recall thinking that doesn't make any sense. She looks nothing like a Gorilla. We were opposites. Yes, she was tan, I was very white, she had short hair, I had long hair, and she was tall, and I was short. She never forgot that comment to this day. It's these memories that remind me to choose my words wisely, for a word said in jest can have long term effects on a person. We never know how much we can hurt a friend, a family member, or a stranger … until we do.

It's funny the things that people say that can stick with you forever in a positive or teaching way. Every time I put on mascara to this day, I recall Noor saying, "You look like the mascara is trying to attack you. Ugh! let me do it for you!"

We sat on the floor of my room as we always did, since in Saudi, it's normal to sit on the floor for meals, with guests, or whatever was the case. We were laughing and talking when my mother called us for lunch. We jumped up and went downstairs and following lunch, we flipped through the TV channels.

My stepdad had recently found a man who sold him the codes to unlock the paid German satellite channels so that we could watch movies and cartoons in English with German subtitles, but it would not be long before the codes changed, and we lost the channels. I was in charge of recording "each and every good movie that came on in English" I told her. When I was little, the only TV stations available were Saudi Channel 1, which was all in Arabic and mostly featured religious clerics giving sermons or a very controlled news broadcast, which Donald Trump would have called "fake news." Saudi Channel 2 broadcasted religious sermons as well as news in English, along with cartoons that were deemed appropriate like *Tom and Jerry* and a few TV shows like

The Waltons, which were censored so much you needed to guess if the girl and the boy ever held hands. When satellite dishes arrived people everywhere began installing them but when the religious clerics saw what was being broadcasted, with women news anchors and TV shows depicting men and women sitting in rooms alone, they decided to issue a hefty fine to anyone caught with a satellite dish on their roof. People started building water towers to hide them from sight and the religious clerics lost the battle for control of all the media.

We watched TV and stayed downstairs and then her driver arrived, so it was time to go. She left just as my stepdad was coming back from work. All of a sudden, they sat me down and my mom pulled out the photo album. My mind raced. How did I forget to put it away before we left my bedroom, but it was too late now. My mom started the interrogation obviously because she had been the one who found it by going into my room while Noor and I were occupied by the TV.

"What do you need these kinds of pictures for? Were you two giving them to boys or were you planning to give them to boys?"

"We didn't do anything wrong! We are not planning for anyone to see them."

My stepdad chimed in, "What about the man who developed them, did you think about how often they make copies and sell them in the black market?"

"They are just for us, it's fun to get dressed up," I protested, to which my mom replied, "It's fun to get dressed up like a street walker…?"

I sat down on the couch and folded my arms once she used the word whore. I knew that once it was time for the whore lecture, there would be no leaving. I waited until it was all over, and I was told I should never take any photo without my head cover again and these pictures will be burned along with the negatives. I nodded, concealing the fact that Noor had half of the prints at her house. My mom called her mom and told her how shocking it was that we were taking pictures like this. Noor's mom said, "Girls will be girls and they just wanted to feel pretty." My mom let it go, but I knew Noor was now on the extreme watch list as a bad influence, and we needed to be extra careful.

The next morning was the weekend, and my stepdad went out into the yard where we had an old tin barrel where we burned things. Before you ask why anyone would need to burn things the answer is everyone burned things. You see, if a Quran is severely damaged or tattered, it is not allowed to be thrown into the trash or recycled, out of respect for the word of God. Much like the American flag, it must be burned. So, we all had some place for burning things.

On this day, my stepdad was going to burn my photos so there would be no evidence left for anyone to find, ever. I was so upset about it, but I went out to watch him, as he placed the entire album on the fire, and I watched the photo paper curl up and melt when he started to talk.

"I ask you to think beyond just the fact that it's fun to get dressed up and take pictures."

I said, "Like what?"

He said, "Well, let's say Noor had a copy of the photos, and she kept them safe because she cares for you and never showed them to anyone but one day her brother, while looking for a book or something in her closet while she is at school, accidentally comes across the album, looks at all the pictures, and puts it back. Then one day he has his friend over to the house and says to his friend, "Hey, you want to see something cool?" and shows his friend your pictures, who turns out to be the brother of a man who was asking for your hand, or better yet, his friend is the man you're going to marry, and he shows him a picture of you covered and his friend says, "I've seen her before in a photo." What do you think would happen? Would you still be a suitable match, or would they assume that your pictures must be everywhere?"

I felt like I was listening to my Aunt Zakia's voice as he continued, "Remember, as innocent as it might be to you or I, if they fell into the wrong hands they won't look that innocent, remember that."

I pondered over it and realized I never considered the possibility of them falling into the wrong hands, so I called Noor and told her she had to burn the pictures she had. She protested and I told her it was too dangerous and to get rid of them. She reluctantly agreed and burned the remaining photos.

From then on, we took great care not to take any photos that could be misinterpreted in any way and if we did, we destroyed them right away. Noor thought the whole possible scenario was idiotic and that my stepdad was an ass, she might have been right, but I had decided it was for the best and would not budge.

The summer was a great time for movies and visiting the King's Hospital grounds. The hospital grounds were a sanctuary all their own and created to make the lives of the many employees who were brought from overseas more comfortable. Especially the single nurses who lived on the grounds for their safety. There was a bowling alley, a small grocery store, a large gift shop, a music store, a jewelry store, a large restaurant that could seat 300 people easily, and a formal dining restaurant in the main building, which was only for doctors and royalty, of course. There were endless gardens, trees, and flowers you do not see anywhere else in Riyadh. When the flowers died, which they often did due to the heat, they were pulled out and replaced. I never saw the flowers die but I always noticed how often they were replaced. There were tennis courts, swimming pools, and everything else anyone would need to never have to leave the grounds.

I cannot tell you how vast it is, but I will say that it was an island of expatriate life in the heart of a conservative Riyadh. Women could walk around without abayas and head covers, and the only entry was through the main gate with an official hospital badge. All of this was for the employees and although the hospital was exclusively created for the care of the royal family, the majority of the staff's time was spent caring for the medical needs of the employees and their families. Free medical care was one of the perks every employee and their immediate families enjoyed, since it wouldn't be good for any of them not to be in their best health.

When you think about a hospital that has more than 14,000 employees, you can see that they kept very busy indeed. There were sixty different nationalities working there but instead of a pay scale based on the job you did; you were paid based on what country you came from. I would see the salary list years later and ponder how this could be. When a member of the royal family did arrive, everyone was immediately aware because of the royal guard armed to the teeth with machine guns who would line the long hallway which we called Hospital Road. The guards lined every exit. I remember seeing them once as a child and my mother telling me not to make any sudden movements.

There was a video shop on the hospital grounds that pirated movies for the expats. It was still hard back then to get many movie titles that hadn't been censored and chopped beyond recognition. Even when Casper the Friendly Ghost kissed Kat, the scene was cut. It didn't bother me as much, since if you never knew there was a make-out scene in a movie, you wouldn't care but for many people like my mother it was very annoying.

Since it was the King's Hospital, the religious police didn't go there. We had rented movies so much since we came back to Riyadh but all of them were pirated and of really poor quality, filmed by a small camera in the back of a movie theater in Bahrain or another country close by, since movie theaters were illegal in Saudi Arabia. I can still recall seeing the man who would get up in the movie theater to go somewhere, passing right in front of the screen making his shadow forever a part of the movie scene. After my stepdad obtained the codes to the German channels from the illegal he suggested we could record the movies that came on and we would then have a nice library. The German channels had been banned for just this reason: unedited movies meant all the kissing scenes were included.

One night, there was to be a good movie coming on one of the German Channels after my bedtime. My stepdad had put a rule in place that no one was allowed to turn on the TV after 8:00 p.m. So, I crept downstairs, pushed in the VHS tape, checked the channel, turned the TV off, and went to bed. The next day when I woke up and I went to make sure the tape did not run out before the movie ended since there was nothing worse than half of a great movie.

I was pleased when I saw it all there, then I wondered if there was another great movie after it. Maybe I was lucky and recorded two! I hit the fast forward button and then noticed that something very strange had come on after the movie. My eyes grew three sizes as I leaned into the screen giving my brain a moment to realize what I was looking at.

Then I suddenly stopped the tape, ejected it, and ran to the telephone. Noor picked up and I said, "You have to come over right now!" She said, "Why? What happened?" I said, "Come now! Hurry! My parents are out!" She hopped in the car with the driver and hurried over. As soon as she arrived, I dragged her upstairs to my parents' room, closed the door, and told her about recording the movie the previous night. Then I pushed the VHS tape into the machine, and as I did I said, "But this got recorded too …." We didn't know what it was, we had no idea that people made sex movies, or what they could be used for, but as we watched, we saw the man onscreen entered the hair salon, remove his pants, and we leaned toward the TV, wondering how something so big could be attached to a man? It was a frightening thing to behold as the movie went on and Noor pulled back from the screen. Noor said, "Oh, my God, honey, he's hurting her! Look, she's screaming!" I tilted my head a little bit and said, "Is he?" We both decided to turn it off and get rid of it before it was found. We didn't speak any more about it and Noor went home. I realize now that my stepdad's rule of no TV after 8:00 p.m. had nothing to do with bedtimes, but more to do with what he knew would show up on the TV. I remember thinking maybe the Saudi government was right to ban such things, what purpose could they possibly serve? Was this what my aunt was talking about when she said all the women in America were loose and immoral? I was shocked beyond reason.

The first day of the new school year arrived, and we were all sad to discover that our beloved principal had retired, and with great sadness, they hired a replacement. A short, sassy old woman who insisted I wear the uniform like all the other girls. When I heard this, I went to see her hoping to renew the arrangement I had enjoyed with the former principal. "Ablah, how could I go to school in the uniform, the other girls would pick on me?" She answered me, "You're a student and so you should be dressed as a student and there will be no more moving about the classes, you're in second grade and there you should stay all day like any student." I lowered my head and went to pick up my first uniform. Suddenly all my privileges were revoked. I could no longer pass between the building levels without convincing a teacher why I had to go up or down floors. I was trapped and could not spend time with Noor. That school year the discovery was made that there was a secret door to the boy's school next door, and all the havoc that caused. Girls were sneaking through hoping to catch glimpses of the boys on the other side, but they were caught, and the new principal had no problem punishing them: three hits each with a long wooden ruler on each hand. Although we all thought they were reckless, we admired and pitied them at the same time.

I finished the school year and, with not much left to learn, I decided not to go for a third year but to finish out this one. Noor was sad, but most of my days there with nothing new to learn had become very boring. I needed more mental stimulation but had no idea what I would do now.

9/11

One day after school I returned home to see a large explosion on the TV. My mother very oddly was on the phone with a friend of hers and oddly cheering its destruction. I asked, "Mom, what is it? What happened?" She replied, "The Jews are dead! Praise be to *Allah*." I puzzled at what I saw on the TV. "But people are dying and so many, are you sure they are all Jews?" "Yes! My friend just told me."

We were all raised to believe that Jews were bad, but from the sight of the destruction of the Twin Towers it seemed rather extreme to me, after all, I had never met a Jew. I went upstairs to change my clothes and the day continued almost as normal. The next day at school nobody talked about it, like it didn't happen or was unimportant.

I thought about my brother whom I was told was now in the US. I would learn years later that they were not really away in the States but rather, my stepdad had refused for my brother to visit unaccompanied and apparently there was a day my brother showed up at the house on his bike, sorry and wanting to see us but my mother turned him away, refusing to open the gate. I can see both sides, but I still feel it was unreasonably harsh on a young boy who was so confused for so long. We lived in the same city but barely saw each other more than once or twice a year.

In American culture that seems to be very common but in Arabic culture it is far from normal. We ate Friday lunch with Uncle Shakour and his family every week. The men would barbecue fish or lamb that was then placed over a bed of rice and served with yogurt. The men and women ate separately since my uncle Shakour was a very jealous man who didn't want any man, even his own brother, looking upon his wife. Sometimes, after lunch, all the kids played together. The boys and the girls could play as long as I was covered. My stepdad had decided that since I was obviously still obsessed with Fahad and since my two small male cousins were so much younger than me, they were deemed unsuitable for marriage.

No one had any concern that there would be talk or mischief. I could walk around the house as long as I had my headcover on, which felt like a great freedom. My cousins, Faisal and Sultan, played basketball with me in the inner hall since it was too hot to play outside. My Uncle Shakour's sons were from his first marriage to a girl he met when he was in school. I never saw her my entire life, but I heard she was beautiful. The story goes that they fell in love. When I say they fell in love I don't mean they ever really met or spoke before they got married. They probably stole glances when they entered and left their respective schools, since it was not uncommon to build a girls school and a boys school in adjacent buildings. After a while he would have asked *Omi* to go inquire after her.

One might ask how in the heck did *Omi* know who her family was, but back then in Mecca, everyone knew who everyone was and still does very much today. A good simple example as to why is because, unlike in other parts of the world, families didn't typically move around as much so a family home was known to all as it passed from generation to the next. This is true for many Middle Eastern countries.

My Uncle and the girl married very young, but she came from a more liberal family than ours and by that, I mean she didn't cover her face as we did, and her family believed girls should continue on with their education after high school. Naturally, she wanted to go to college and have a career outside the home. My grandma told the story as if she thought of herself before her sons and left them to pursue her dreams. After gathering pieces of the story over the years, I found that the story closer to the truth was that my Uncle Shakour beat her often for being too strong willed and independent minded. He wanted his wife to stay at home and take care of the house and the children as we were all raised to do, and she wanted both. Since it is not a woman's choice but a husband's, she had two options: ask for a divorce and go to school or stay at home with her kids. I suppose the beatings got to be too much since with two boys it's obvious she gave it a try. In the end she asked for a divorce, and he gave her one. *Omi* encouraged him to do so to avoid problems with her family who lived in the same community. It would make it easier for him to marry another more obedient woman from the same community if he let the first one go as she wished peacefully. He did however take her children as punishment. They were convinced at the age of seven when the time came for them to choose that their mother was not fit and so they stayed with their father. I know she called the boys sometimes. I would often hear them on the kitchen telephone, but I dared not ask too much.

My Uncle Shakour's daughters were all from his new wife; they were just a little older than my brother, Muhammed, who is about ten years younger than me.

After lunch I was walking around and overheard a strange conversation my stepdad and my uncle were having. My stepdad said, "My brother, listen he is too young for her." Uncle Shakour said, "Let me explain how that is not true, they are the same age." You see, according to the Arabic Calendar, I was born in 1405 and because it's based on moon cycles my uncle was arguing with my stepdad that perhaps I and my cousin Faisal were closer in age than he thought, making him a good match for me. My stepdad fought back saying that Faisal was too young for me, and I dared not weigh in, but I definitely didn't want to marry Faisal. He was a super quiet introvert at the times when we all did sit together. He never spoke to me and stared at me all day long like a freak. I would consider his brother the horny inappropriate Sultan before I would consider Faisal -- at least he liked to play games and was fun.

I walked around their old home a lot remembering the days when, as children, I, Fahad, and the boys, had spent there together on Fridays in the summer playing cards in the back bedrooms. Fahad always winning. I enjoyed my brother's defeat. The days on the roof playing soccer and the boys so afraid to touch me that I always won. Following the games, Fahad, being the uncle, would order my brother, Faisal, and Sultan, to leave us alone on the roof where he would walk around talking to me in his broken English and then kissing me before I went downstairs. Those days seemed so far away to me now because I had not heard any news about him in more than two years. I suppose the family thought not to mention him in front of me in hopes that it might ease things. The saying 'absence makes the heart grow fonder' is not how things are done in Saudi. Quite the opposite: if something is done or uncomfortable, we just forget it ever happened and move on. Moving on was what they wanted me to do and the only way to achieve that was to make sure I forgot that he existed.

The moment that I had been dreading arrived that year. My parents began to talk to me about how they thought I should no longer be friends with Noor. My stepdad started by saying, "We think that Noor is really not the kind of friend you should have." "Why is that?" I said, and my mom chimed in, "Well, she's a nice enough girl but we feel like she's teaching you things like make-up and hair styling, and you're too young for all that." "I'm not too young to get married so I should be learning to put on makeup and do my hair to please my future husband," I replied. My stepdad weighed in on my mom's pathetic excuse, "Princess, her family seems all too liberal for us, and I just worry that if you're not careful she might ruin your reputation by association." I nodded, showing that I had heard their concerns and went to bed. I refused to give up the only real friend I had ever had, without school or any means of making another friend making me all the more determined to keep her. I told Noor what happened and as a precaution, we began using code words when we spoke on the telephone, as my mom was set to the task of finding evidence for a stern decision on our friendship. Whenever we discussed Fahad, we talked about a girl named Farhana, when we talked about boys in general, we talked about all the cute cats we saw outside the school today and my mom was none the wiser. Over time, we switched to something a little more complex. Since her family could not speak English, she spoke in English, and I replied in Arabic since my mom could not speak Arabic. This way no one could understand us and even if they listened in, they only got half the conversation.

My mother took a part time job at my sister's school and so when she went, I came along to see Noor. One day at school a mother was picking up her children as Noor and I were walking in the courtyard. She asked me for my name and what family I came from. When I replied in my perfect Saudi accent her whole body moved backwards in shock. "Is she Saudi?" the woman asked Noor. Most Arabs can tell where you are from by your accent and mine did not match my appearance at all. This was because it would seem impossible; my accent, tone, and mannerisms would lead any Arab to the conclusion that I was Saudi, but I was a small, Caucasian, green-eyed girl. My speaking in Saudi with the harsh nature of the accent was never expected to come out of me.

My first-grade teacher had offered to teach me Syrian Arabic two years earlier but I insisted I must learn Saudi Arabic so I could fit in with my family, and in my mind, make Fahad proud. When Noor saw how the woman reacted to my pure Saudi accent she came over to my house and said, "It's time, woman! You must speak something softer. It's not nice on you that you speak Saudi. You should speak Lebanese or Syrian, trust me, it will be really cute on you." I said, "Okay, so teach me something softer." But going from a very harsh accent, the only one I had grown up with, to something softer was very hard. I struggled through my lessons with her and eventually what happened is what someone noted as my 'international Arabic.' I began to say one word in Saudi, and another in Syrian, and another in Lebanese, depending on whichever came first to mind. It was utterly confusing to everyone. Eventually I managed to send most of my Saudi accent into submission to my newer softer speaking tone.

We hired a maid that year since I had to keep up with the house and the children. It became too much for me. My stepdad tried to make my life easier since managing the housework and caring for the children was a lot for a young girl even though I never complained, convinced that as the eldest girl it was my duty to care for my family. I was, however, thankful he finally agreed to hire a maid. She was from Indonesia and her name was Janeen. My stepdad's one condition was that the maid would never cook food for the children. It was considered the mother's job to feed the children and if people knew the maid was feeding them, it would look like the children were being raised by the maid. My mom agreed wholeheartedly, excited that she would have a maid to brag about, but in the daytime the maid cooked for the children at my mother's request, and the children and I were sworn to secrecy. I could have cooked for them but seeing as it was the only job she was asked to do, I let her dig her own hole. I helped the children with their homework after school. I translated every mother-teacher call or meeting for my mom, not to mention taking on my siblings' constant supervision while she lounged in her bedroom.

One night my mom was in the guest bathroom throwing up nonstop, with my stepdad and I standing outside the bathroom. I asked my stepdad, "How sick is she?" but when my mom opened the door and came out, she said, "I'm pregnant." My mind thought of one more diaper to change and I said, "Haven't you ever heard of protection?" and stormed to my room. Nine months later, my little sister Lina arrived; a joy for sure, and a small, fussy baby like my little brother, Mohammed, had been.

One night my stepdad came home. We laid the *suffra* (a disposable plastic mat) for dinner on the living room floor and placed dinner on it. The food, being too good to be my mother's cooking, made my stepdad look at me and ask, "Did you cook this?" I remained silent and looked at my mother. He looked at her and said, "Did you?" She did not reply, so he repeated his question. My sister Noura answered, "Janeen did." My stepdad put down his spoon and asked to have it cleared. He looked at my mom and started yelling, "I gave specific instructions that the maid was not to cook for the family ever! There have been many children poisoned by maids. If she gets upset, she could just poison the food and we would all be sick or worse. Why don't you listen to me, woman!" My mom fought back, saying, "We treat her well, it's really no big deal." My stepdad clenched his teeth as he did when he was really angry, looked at me and said, "Make something for dinner. Now!"

I went into the kitchen and began making a simple tomato soup that was ready within the hour. As I was cooking, Janeen came in frightened, asking in broken Arabic she had learned whether the food was bad. Had she done anything wrong, or if Baba was mad at her? I sat her down and said, "No, Janeen, nothing is your fault, this is Madam's fault; she is in trouble, not you." We ate in silence and went to bed. My stepdad and mom yelled and fought all night long about everything under the sun, as if the maid cooking had drummed up years of past fights and this was the final straw.

The next morning, I awoke to my stepdad saying, "Make sure you look after the baby. Your mother has gone missing somewhere." I knew if she would go anywhere, she would go to the hospital grounds. It was a familiar place and safe for women on their own. I nodded my head and went to tend to little Lina. She was crying since she was still nursing. She finally settled and went to sleep, and I slept beside her on the bed from utter exhaustion, asking Mohammed to wake me if they needed anything and not to get into trouble. My stepdad looked everywhere for my mom to no avail. He returned home and I had already made dinner. We sat and ate in silence again. After dinner, he asked each child individually to come see him in the small guest room so he could ask if anyone had any information about where she might have gone. No one knew. Then he asked me, and I said I thought she might have gone to the hospital grounds, that's where she would be the most safe. He said he had searched the grounds but not found her there. We cleaned up the dinner dishes and the children went to bed. I helped the maid clean up to help soothe her nerves, assuring her that it was not her fault and went to make sure the main door in the hall was bolted. When I entered the guest hall, I saw something move in the guest room. I'd like to say I thought it was a robber but part of me already knew that it was mom.

This behavior was all too common for her. She had a great knack for pretending she ran away and hiding in some odd place. The guest room, the laundry room, a closet, the car, etc. I always wondered what her logic was, after all, if it didn't fix things the first time why did she continue with it? She put her finger to her lips and called me over. I came into the guest room and said, "Where have you been?" She said "I was in the trunk of the car. I wanted to see where he went and when he went to the hospital, I followed him and got back into the car to go home." I thought she was crazy. "Why?" I asked. She did not say but made me promise not to tell him where she was. I said "Okay" reluctantly, because I knew I could never keep such a promise, he would know I knew something, and I was not getting the belt for her. I went to my stepdad as he was sitting in the main living room and stood right in front of him. I did not tell him anything, I only looked at him, took Lina from his arms and pointed to the guest room. Thereby keeping my promise to my mom and avoiding the belt from my stepdad and getting this ridiculous drama over with.

He stayed in the guest room with her for what seemed like hours. Lina screamed because she would not take the bottle. Then he emerged, saying he would be taking mom to a furnished apartment for a little while. These were the original Airbnb rentals. A flat that was furnished but had no service. He took her and did not return until morning. Lina cried all night. I tried everything, even offering her my breast to suck on hoping it would ease her, but it was no use. I tried changing her, rocking her, shushing her, burping her, and feeding her again and again, but she hated that bottle. Finally, with no success and at the end of my nerves, I put her down on the floor and sat in the corner and cried with her for an hour. Finally, she took the bottle and slept, but I will never forget that night. The screaming and the frustration. Loving her too much to ever hurt her. I had to put her down. In retrospect, I know I made the right choice, but as I cried that night, I felt like such a failure.

The morning came and I got the kids off to school while I stayed with Lina. My stepdad returned in the evening for dinner without mom. The kids asked where she was, but my stepdad replied she was praying and taking some time. Apparently, my mom had told him she wanted to seek God to help her decide what she should do. She was right to really think about things if she was going to divorce him. In Saudi Arabia, boys at the age of seven could choose to stay with their mother, or father, or both. She only had one boy. Any girls over the age of seven must stay with their father because he is their guardian. It was a hard decision to give up her children and still be stuck here if she wanted to see them. All I could think of was how could she love us if she could leave us so easily, especially with poor Lina being so young? I thought this would mean I would have to leave everything I knew and go with my mom since I wasn't Saudi. Even if it meant not dealing with my stepdad, it would also mean never seeing my siblings again if she decided to return to the States. I begged my stepdad after dinner to please fix it. It was hard on the kids. They didn't understand because they were all so young. He said nothing and went to bed. Lina was with me in my bed all night. Of all the children, it was hardest on her.

Three days passed before my mom finally picked up the phone and called the house. I let her talk to the kids, hoping they could convince her to come home. That night Baba stayed out all night again, we assumed with her. The next day she returned. We were all so happy, but I was angry. She had left me with the burden of taking care of the children and not even a thank-you was offered upon her return. I knew then that I would undoubtedly be caring for them the rest of my life and, if she would not love them as they needed to be, I would.

Soon enough my stepdad announced that he would be going to spend six months in Kansas City, Missouri, in the United States, and we would all be going. The hospital was sending him to inspect some new lab equipment. I look back now at the timing after such a big fight and wonder if he asked for the assignment on purpose to appease my mom. He had promised her when they were first married that he would take her to see her family in America every three years. We had gone twice when I was little but not at all since then. I greeted the happy announcement with a sharp turn, and I went to my room angry. My brain puddled around. How could I live six months without my friends in that strange country with those people who hated Arabs? I thought about how Fahad might come to ask for me when I was gone. What if we missed him?

Omi came to visit us the next week and stayed with us, since my Uncle Shakoor was away on vacation with his family. Now was my chance. I thought if I called the Mecca house, he would surely be alone now whereas in the past, she would have answered. I waited until everyone was napping and I went to the small guest sitting room, which had been turned into the study, picked up the phone and called. He answered the phone just as expected and I spoke to him in perfect Arabic, something I had never been able to do in the past. He said something flirty, and I told him, "Sorry, I don't know that word." He asked, "Who is this?" I said "Maha." A long pause happened before he said, "Oh, how are you?" My reply reflected how long I had waited to hear his voice.

"I love you, how are you? We leave for Kansas soon. Why haven't you come to ask for me?"

There was a sigh and a silence then he said,

"Maha, I'm getting married."

"How! When? Who? No one said anything."

"Her name is Reem, and I met her when I was in college."

"Is there anything I can do to change your mind?"

"Maha, I love her."

"Thank you and congratulations," I said, and hung up the phone.

I walked calmly and quietly to the maid's bathroom, knowing I would not be discovered there, and cried for the good part of an hour, until the idea hit me … I could be his second wife! He could have four, why not have us both? I came out, went back to the phone, and called him again. "I could be your second wife if you would have me." He sighed again and said, "You should go." I hung up the phone and returned to the maid's bathroom to compose myself. I then returned to my room to pack my things and try to let go of the love I'd held so dear for 10 years.

To me it wasn't in my mind it was real, I was his and he was mine, but looking back for me, it had been so real while for him, it was just another cute girl his mom tried to set him up with. For ten years it was a lie - how could it be? All our days together in Mecca circled in my head and it was hard to let the memories of him go. I would go back and forth. Maybe he would change his mind now that he heard my voice, but no such thing was to happen. I left for Kansas solemn as the grave telling no one what had happened.

After landing in the United States, I looked around and hated everything around me except my brothers and sisters. I took long walks in the only place I was allowed to go alone, a trail located behind the apartment that the Hospital had rented for us to use during our stay. It had a great big green walking trail, and I would take the video camera and the kids and film them running around. I would find the highest peak and talk to God, making grand gestures like, "I will give up this if you will just bring him back." Soon enough, we heard the news that he had married Reem, and it was all over. The days were long so my stepdad thought it would be good if I had something to do, so I completed a correspondence course to become a teacher's aide.

I recall reading about abuse and thinking how much I wanted to become a teacher so that other girls like me would not have to go through what I did, alone. Maybe I could make the world better by becoming a teacher. It's no surprise why this course was chosen, since in my time in Saudi, good girls either became teachers, nurses, or homemakers, and since in my mind homemaker was out of the picture now, I had to move on. We never went anywhere in Kansas except when my mom needed her fix of McDonalds fast food or felt a need to take us to the local amusement park.

We had to go to California to attend our Aunt Connie's wedding. She was venturing into her second marriage at the age of fifty and my mom wanted to be there to support her older sister who she had so admired as a girl. My stepdad had to work, so mom, the kids and I flew to California and checked into a hotel room. When my Aunt Angela asked if she could see us in the hotel, mom refused to disclose the location, saying that Aunt Angela might try to convert us back to the Mormon faith if we spent too much time with her. The wedding day finally arrived, and Chris and my grandparents were there. I recall my mom trying to show off by calling the kids in Arabic, but they did not understand and would not come. I rolled my eyes at her Arabic attempts and called them in English, and they fell into line. My mother would spend all her time making up stories about how rich we were, how awesome her life was, and bragging and pretending we owned land, riches and so on. I remained silent, letting her enjoy her time pretending we had money to burn. I looked after the children. My ever-watchful eye on them. Always knowing every second where each one of them was without even seeing them. It's funny how, at the age of 16, I knew they were more like my children than my mother's since I was always with them. They would disobey my mother but with me there was a mutual respect. They knew that I always knew best.

The wedding was the first American wedding I had ever attended, and I recall it being so much different than Arab weddings, in fact, in a way, even peasant-like through my Saudi eyes. Instead of a prepared meal of lamb marinated with spices for the couple's good luck and served over a bed of rice, there was a buffet of ready-prepared Mexican food that everyone gathered around. There was no respect for the fact that the elders should go first. The boys and girls danced together, and I stood back like a wallflower, thinking it was all very inappropriate. My mom hugged her brother-in-laws and nephews, while I stayed silent, taking note of her behavior as an American woman hugging men. A man 10 years older than me approached. He was my cousin Aaron. I hardly remembered him from our youth when we would go on vacation to the US and stay with my Aunt Connie. He was her eldest son and when I was seven, he was already married and living on his own. He had a daughter now and was again single and attended the wedding without her. He was blind in one eye, thanks to his brother who shot a BB gun at him when they were children, but he looked completely normal. He was my height, with red hair and blue eyes. He asked me if I remembered him and I said yes, he then asked me for a hug, which I refused while standing up straight as a sign of try it and you'll be in trouble. He looked at my mom and my mom said, "It is okay because he's your cousin," to which I replied, "In Saudi we can marry our cousins so it would not be proper."

The happy wedding continued, and my brother danced with cousin after cousin while I stood back and pondered whether I was wrong. Maybe I was meant to marry him. Maybe he was the one. Maybe I just messed it all up by refusing to give him a hug. I mean I was covered. What was the big deal when mom said it was okay? But wait, what if I hug him and then everyone else wants a hug? I can't hug that many men! So, I wandered around the church and then the moment arrived. Everyone was leaving. My mom was in the kitchen and there was Aaron bidding my mom farewell. I walked up behind him and said, "Did you want a hug?" and opened my arms. He hugged me. I had not been hugged in so long and I savored every second until it was over, and we left.

The next few days while we were in California, we met up with Aaron again. We walked with the family and talked about life and the world. He was kind. When we returned to the hotel that night my mom asked me if I liked him. Seeing the sparkle in her eyes like she acted like she approved, I confided in her but said, "How would it work? He's American and Mormon, and in America, cousins don't marry their cousins." She said, "Leave it to me." We saw him one last time before we left to return to Kansas, and he asked me if I would write to him, which I agreed to do.

When we returned to Kansas there was a letter from Aaron waiting for me. It was three pages long. He wrote about his day, life, and his feelings, that he loved me and his hopes for what might be. My stepdad, seeing the letter, asked my mom and she explained, "What is the big deal? It's her cousin and in Saudi they marry cousins. Maybe he would convert and move to Saudi, besides what harm can some letters do?" My stepdad allowed the letters and so I wrote back. We corresponded right up until we left to go back to Saudi. When we got there it became harder and harder to get letters through, so we began emailing. I would email as often as I could, almost every day, and he would email me about once a month when he could find time to sit at his computer.

Things started to get serious and my mom, now thinking she had made a mistake, started encouraging me to end the relationship. Thus, leaving my side in the battle. Once he called out of the blue to hear my voice and tell me that he was going to speak to his dad about us and how we could get married with the American laws being what they were. It was the greatest day of my life, I smiled for a week nonstop but then all of a sudden, the emails stopped coming. I emailed but received no reply. I waited and waited but nothing happened. One day my stepdad caught me crying and I told him I just wanted to know what happened. Was he all right, was he dead, or was it something I said? So, like he had done with his own sister years earlier, he took me to a phone booth to call him, his number written on a small piece of paper I carried with me, I dialed his number and with each ring before he picked up my heartbeat got faster and faster. What would I say, what if I cried, what if he had found someone else? He said hello and my mind remembered the phone call with Fahad. I told him "It's me, Maha," and he sighed. "How are you?" I said "Good." He asked, "How's your mom?" I said, "What happened, why did you not reply to my emails, are you okay?"

He sighed again and said, "I spoke to my dad and then my minister, and it's just not possible. What kind of life we would have? You're there and I can't come there. I like it here and if I bring you here I won't be able to marry you in the church. We wouldn't be able to be sealed for all eternity and I would want you with me in heaven. I'm sorry," he said while I struggled to hold back my tears. I bid him goodbye saying the telephone card was running out, so I had to go. I hung up the phone and sat down, weak and trembling. Feeling like the tears were being pushed out from my heart directly, thinking I would never be married or find true love.

My stepdad took me home and told my mom I wasn't feeling well. I stayed in bed for two days. I had given up. How could I now marry someone I didn't know like my friends had? Someone I had never met after knowing real love? Most of the girls I knew went through arranged marriages and were very happy as I might have been, just like my Aunt Zakia, my stepdad's only sister.

The story was told that she once fell in love with a boy over the phone. They never met but she loved him, and he promised he would come and ask for her hand soon. When her parents found out her older brother, my Uncle Shakoor, said they should stone her for bringing such shame to the family. The family decided to cover it all up. They would marry her off immediately. So, a man who was from a noble and well-respected family was selected, and plans were made. As one would expect, she despaired as I did over Aaron. So, my stepdad, being the younger and more liberal brother, took her to a pay phone. The day before her engagement he asked her to call the boy and tell him if he came to ask for her hand all would be well. She called him and he said he could not. So, she married the man her parents had chosen for her. Their first years were hard as she loved another but over time, they became widely known as a well-matched couple. He was so devoted and so understanding. She grew to love him. Everyone could see how he was able to communicate with her with one glance. They had five children and lived happily ever after.

Of course, even this story could not convince me such happiness would be possible for me. After all, she had not been kissed or been in love with him for ten years as I had been with Fahad. I ate, drank, and slept with Fahad on my mind. If I heard he liked silver, I liked silver, and if he liked eggs, then I liked eggs, but the truth lingered. I did not choose Fahad. But I did choose Aaron and I loved him as he was, and I thought he loved me as I was. It was so easy to just be myself. How could I marry a stranger now?

I watched TV and despaired about the world for weeks. My stepdad tried to find a college that would take me, as a distraction, but in those days expatriate women were not accepted anywhere except for Arabic studies. They considered sending me to Bahrain, a neighboring country, to study but they could not send me alone because it would be sure to invite scandal. My mom could not go with me since the children would need someone. He asked his mom *Omi* whether, since Fahad was now married, perhaps she could go with me, but she said she could not leave her newlyweds. It was decided that college would have to come later.

Our residential contract, which was like a lease on the house, was expiring so we moved to a brand-new house far away from the city. We could no longer go to the bookstore or the new Ikea retail store, or the Hospital bowling alley as often as we wanted, which had always been a treat. Now we live an hour outside the city, completely isolated except for our very conservative Bedouin next-door neighbor.

The house was a tan sand-like color with small windows covered with vine shaped bars. No house outside a very secure compound was built without bars on the windows. I was told this was meant to protect the women inside from men who would try and climb in. The main entrance led to two large guest sitting rooms and the side door, which was the door we used on a daily basis. It led into the main sitting area where there was a grand staircase leading to the second floor which had four bedrooms. I was very pleased that my room was equipped with its own inner bathroom. The third floor had a sitting area and a very nice bedroom with its own bathroom. Even though there was a small room downstairs near the kitchen that was meant for the maid, we decided she should have the third-floor room since it was bigger and offered her more privacy. In an effort to make the house more like a refuge than a prison my stepdad had a basketball hoop installed so we could play in the backyard. This house, like any other Saudi home, had high walls so no one could see in from the street.

Being so far from the city meant Noor could not visit as much, meaning we had to spend more time talking on the phone catching up since while I was in Kansas it was too expensive to call her long distance. It was like I missed six months of my life in Kansas and then suddenly had my world uprooted again. *Omi* visited from Mecca and stayed with us. She slept downstairs since her knees would not allow her to get up the large flight of stairs.

Of course, the first thing she remarked on was why the maid needed such nice accommodations. After my stepdad told her that the maid was given the room upstairs so her maid could sleep in the room near the kitchen or with our maid on the third floor. My grandma leaned back, looked at my stepdad and said, "My *Techronia* here has only ever had the small room by the kitchen and she's perfectly happy. Aren't you, Nyala?" looking over at her maid from Ethiopia who naturally had to agree that she was very happy even though the word my grandma had just used to describe her, "*Techronia*" was equal to the N-word in English.

Omi, since getting her maid from Ethiopia, used the word often and without thought. I suppose in her mind it was just a word. She had after all been alive when slavery was legal in Saudi Arabia. I would not be surprised to learn that her family had a slave or two when she was growing up. If it wasn't for the international pressure the Saudi Government was under in 1962, I think they would still have slavery today. "Oh, Rashad, my son, you should put her in the small room near the kitchen. She will only get too used to being in that big room that later, she will be unhappy if you move to a smaller house. Not to mention she will unsettle all the other maids if they hear how grand her life is here." My stepdad let out one of his, "I'm about to disobey you, *Omi*" laughs and said, "I disagree and we're not using the room so she can have it." *Omi* clasped her hands together and said, "Well it's your house, have it your way. But now that I have said it, don't cry to me when a revolution of maids starts asking their [employers] for better accommodations and more money. It will be your fault if it happens." My stepdad changed the subject as I looked at our maid, Janeen, and gave her a slight smile to send her a message that she should not worry nothing will change no matter what *Omi* says.

My mother spent as much time as she could in her room brooding over how much my grandmother hated her. How she had been so rude to her in the past when she first married my stepdad. It's a great insult not to sit at least for tea with the head of the family when they visit. No matter whether you like them or not or if you could speak the language or not. I knew it was my duty to tend to my grandmother. She was my elder and had never given me reason not to love her. It was strange how an old wound from years ago was suddenly summoned up by my mother's memory, since in Mecca they seemed to get along just fine. Then again that was *Omi's* house, her playing field, and my stepdad had probably told my mom when he left us there that if she upset *Omi* and she decided she didn't want us staying with her, we would have had nowhere to go.

Omi loved the children and would bring them gifts. My mother turned her nose up at everything she gave the children, finding any reason to speak ill of her in the presence of the children. As children often do, they started to act out towards *Omi* since they noticed how angry their mother was at her. After three days, I finally went upstairs and laid it out for my mother. "No one is asking you to love her or even like her but poisoning the children against her is unacceptable. That is their grandmother, and they are entitled to the right to choose on their own whether they like her or not. When you act this way, you decide for them and that is not fair to them or to *Omi*. Suck it up, go downstairs, smile, and be an adult. She will not be here forever, just a few days. Will you continue to give her a reason to talk badly about you to the rest of the family?" My mother, being the amiable that she is, nodded her head and went down the stairs to sit with *Omi* as was expected of her as a daughter-in-law. After that, the children stopped mimicking their mother's childish behavior.

When it was possible to get into the city, we went to the Hospital pool on women's days which were the two days a week that the pool was open for women only. My stepdad would drive us in the morning, and we would come back with a Hospital car in the afternoon. On one such occasion I was swimming laps in my Islamic bathing suit, which is a bathing suit that was loose fitting and covered my arms to my elbows and my legs to my knees almost like a romper. It was an awful bathing suit because when I jumped in the water it puffed out like a balloon. I felt someone was staring at me, so as I swam, I turned my head a little to my left and right until I saw a mature woman about my mom's age. I thought it was odd that she should be staring but I kept swimming, thinking she would be gone when I swam back the other way.

When I got to the end of the pool and came back around, I slightly glanced at her position and found that she had now pulled up a chair so that she could have a better view of me. I ignored this and proceeded to get out of the pool and head to the shower and to change out of my wet bathing suit. All clean and dressed, I walked up the steps from the basement showers and saw that she was gone. I let out a sigh of relief, thinking how strange she was and went to help get the children ready to go. I started to put on my abaya and when I turned around and saw her, like a vampire moving so quietly out of nowhere, directly in front of me. I looked at her, wondering what she wanted. I waited for her to speak first since she had approached me.

She took my right hand into both her hands and said, "What passport do you have, my dear?" My mind flashed at how that could be the first question burning in her mind, not perhaps my name? I said, "American," not wanting to be rude. She smiled and asked, "And how old are you? Are you in school?" I answered the latter and then seeing my mother, grabbed her by the shoulders and said to the woman in Arabic, "Thank you, *Khali* (which is another polite way to address an elder woman meaning Auntie)." Bowing my head a bit, and moving my mom in front of her saying, "This is my mother," and then I walked away. I was content with the idea that my mother could speak no Arabic and this woman clearly spoke no English and therefore it would be over before it began. You can imagine my utter disappointment when they found a way to chat through sign language.

When we got home, I happened to pass by my parent's room and overheard a discussion about me and, in my good old Saudi girl fashion, I stopped to crouch down by the door to listen in on the conversation. My mom said,

"There was a woman today who asked about Maha."

"Yes, what about?" my stepfather asked her.

"Well, it's rather exciting! She wants her to marry her son. I'm not sure but I believe he is going to be a doctor."

"What was she like?" he asked as I sat by the door thinking she was something weird like a passport creeper. "Oh, she was so nice, I think we should have her over to discuss the prospect."

My brain screamed at the thought of pursuing someone who obviously only wanted me for my passport. My stepdad let out a deep breath and said,

"Well, we must entertain all suitors. I suppose there is no knowing where we will find the best match for her." Being the American that she was, the idea of engagement excited my mom, so she encouraged my stepdad to consider the match.

"Just think of our daughter marrying a doctor, what a catch!" she said.

I cringed and pushed the door open, and said to my stepdad, "The first thing she asked me about was my passport, she just wants an American! She will marry me to her son and send me to America and while he is studying, he will take the nationality from me and then dump me off all alone in that scary place. No! I won't marry him. He's Palestinian, all of them are well known passport hunters. I don't blame them, but I don't want someone to marry me for my passport."

My stepdad said, "Maybe you misunderstood the woman, I think you should at least meet her again."

I folded my arms and replied, "Fine!"

My mom clapped her hands with joy and ran to place the call inviting the woman for tea to discuss it further, which was the custom. The men do not meet until the women agree that the two children and the family are suited.

My mom was scared she would not be able to communicate with the woman, so she invited a woman who worked with my stepdad and was close to our family, to help her. We called her *Khali Jan*. Khali Jan had worked in the hospital for as long as my stepdad. Unbeknownst to my mom, my stepdad had a big crush on Khali Jan years earlier, but she sought a better match. She married a rich Lebanese man who ended up being a disappointment but gave her two girls close in age to me. The date was settled, and Khali Jan arrived with her two daughters. I, being the good older daughter, knew that I would sit in the room only when the guest of honor arrived, and my entrance would be accompanied by the serving of the juice. The girls and I hung out in the kitchen while waiting and laughed and giggled about the prospects of marriage. My stepdad and mom had decided I should wear my purple Eid outfit, which was a suede purple jacket and a shimmering purple and blue skirt, for this meeting, and I obliged them.

Upon the woman's arrival she was ushered into the women's sitting room. As I poured the juice, but before I entered, I overheard the mother telling my Khali Jan in Arabic that she had singled me out at the pool when she saw me put on my Abaya as we were getting ready to leave, because she knew I must be a pious and well-raised Muslim girl, not one of those girls who wears pants like the boys. I turned quickly and handed the tray to one of Khali Jan's daughters and said, "Wait here, I have an idea." I ran upstairs and changed into my pink princess T-shirt, my tightest blue jeans, and a pink low-slung hip belt and returned downstairs again. I took the juice from Khali Jan's daughter and walked into the women's sitting room to serve it with pride. Everyone looked at each other as the woman said, "Oh, how pretty she looks in her jeans, it suits her," sipping her juice ever so slowly. My Khali Jan looked at me and smirked while my mom scowled, but my point was made. At least my Khali Jan got the point. The woman was only interested in me as a match for her son because of my American passport, and she was prepared to do anything to close the deal.

I sat with the ladies after the coffee was served, which normally happened at the end of the visiting time. We would bring out one course of drinks after the next, so if the guest tried to leave, we could say, "Wait, you have not taken some tea, or you did not have some coffee." In so doing, even if they left early, they knew how hospitable we were as a family.

The woman showed us pictures of her son and mentioned how he was away in England studying to be a doctor. My eyes rolled back in my head as I thought, who cares if he is a doctor? But then I remembered: my mom cared. For her it meant I would marry well. Money and a good life were very alluring to my mother. How many times does a woman receive offers of marriage during her lifetime? The woman departed with a promise that my mom would speak to my stepdad, and we would see her again. I folded my arms and said to my Khali Jan, "Why do we have to see them again?" She replied with all the grace in the world, "She seems like a nice lady from a good family, it couldn't hurt to just meet the family and give them a chance" I sighed and said, "Maybe you're right."

A few weeks passed and it was time for us to return the visit of the woman by visiting her house. We entered the house and a girl my age hurried toward me and grabbed me. She was so excited that I might be her new sister-in-law and she guided me to her bedroom where she handed me a note she had written in the best English she could muster. I was moved and thought how fun it would be to have a sister my own age to laugh with like Noor. The visit went well, and the girl and I became fast friends. I knew, however, that I could never confide in her as I did Noor, knowing how extremely conservative this girl's family was. She didn't even listen to music since many Muslims consider it sinful, so I avoided topics like the latest songs and other music related topics.

After a few months of back and forth we moved back into the city into a compound owned by the Hospital that was only for doctors and their families. It had been some time since we lived in a compound, but this was not like the ones we had lived in before where everyone was an expatriate. On the contrary, most of them were Saudi and we were to be on guard since one wrong discussion with a neighbor about how we don't pray, and the religious police might be summoned to inspect our way of life. The house was smaller, having only three bedrooms upstairs but I didn't mind sharing it with my sisters. It could only mean more safety for us all. Looking back now I am stunned by the fact that safety and not being abused were such an overarching factor that it governed every decision I made and everything I did. My stepdad had reduced me all the way down Maslow's hierarchy, to where self-actualization was irrelevant. Life was 100% about survival. Dream crushers come in many forms but there is no bigger dream crusher than stealing a child's innocence.

My mom went to my stepdad and told him the woman's son who was studying to be a doctor would be on leave soon and at home to visit his family. She said it was time for the men to meet. My stepdad turned to me and said, "What do you think?" I said, "They seem nice, I guess why not." He nodded, and my mom made the phone call to tell them that their whole family should come for tea when their son arrives, including the men, signaling that things were serious and the men should meet to discuss my *Maher*, or marriage dowry, which was always a heated topic.

The night they arrived everyone was nervous; I had recently gotten my very first mobile cell phone. Noor and I texted back and forth about each detail of the night, since there was a chance I was getting engaged. As was customary, the women sat in their own sitting room unable to hear the men talking. They chatted quietly as the men discussed the arrangement in their own sitting room. None of us were able to hear what was going on in there. Until this day I dare say I have no idea how they come about discussing such things as how much my daughter's worth is. It wasn't until we heard the men's voices rise that we women all fell silent.

I stopped serving the tea and sat down on the couch next to the daughter who'd written me the sweet note when my cell phone beeped. It was my stepdad, instructing me to put on my head cover and bring the juice into the dining room which was adjacent to the men's sitting room. The dining room was arranged outside of the men's and women's sitting rooms so if there was to be a lunch, the women could set up the lunch service without being seen and exit the room before the men entered to eat. I nervously put on my head cover. All eyes were on me as I lifted the tray with the four glasses of juice and made my way to the dining room. I placed the tray down as my stepdad came into the dining room and whispered, "You will not serve the juice just yet. He is seated in the far-left corner, just peek in the room and look at him before we go any further. If you don't like him, then that will be that." I nodded, took a deep breath, and peaked through the door.

A boy with glasses, completely bald, scowled at me as if he were very upset. Frightened, I pulled back in shock. I looked at my stepdad and shook my head no. My stepdad said to them, "So sorry, but she said no." The men, insulted that their son, the doctor, was rejected in such a manner, called for the women to leave and everyone left in haste. Because they were Palestinians, the polite social graces I discussed earlier were not deemed necessary by my Saudi dad. We were after all, the superior race. We never heard from them again and my fast friend never contacted me. One more friend lost in the casualty of war that was my life. To this day, I long for deep connections with girlfriends but find it is exceedingly difficult to actually attain.

I always thought if he had just smiled at the poor little girl who was already nervous, perhaps she (me!) might have entered the room to serve the juice. Later my stepdad told me that the young man was angry because my stepdad had asked him to change seats so that I could peek before I came in and he was unhappy that I would not be serving the juice and joining them.

BABY BLUE

My stepdad, who had finally found a diploma school that taught computer and web design, asked me if I would like to attend the course, and I agreed happily, eager to learn more about this field. I was excited to take the entry exam. I passed with flying colors but wondered how so many girls had trouble learning how to use a computer mouse. There was even a whole class built around how to use a mouse, which utterly surprised me since I had been using one at home since its creation. I felt fortunate to have known my grandfather when I was young. He was a lover of all innovations in the tech world. Later my stepdad would continue my grandfather's role of teaching us about the advances in technology.

I went to class every day and made many friends. All the classes seemed easy except JavaScript. My teachers loved me. They called me a very polite student who they could point to as an example of success as if they had taught me how to use a mouse. We took keyboard typing and learned how to search on Yahoo, which was very exciting. We were given a lunch/nap break in the afternoon from Noon until 3:00 p.m. Each day I would go home for lunch and a nap and then return to school. Most days I preferred to stay at the school since my mom was sometimes out. I dared not be home alone just in case. "Home" was a remarkably interesting word to use, given the context, because in so many ways it felt more like a massive danger zone than a place to go to let your hair down and relax. A place to bask in the love and affection of your family members? Nothing could be further from the truth for me.

It was the age of the MSN Messenger platform, and all the girls communicated by chatting on what we called The Messenger. One day in an Internet class they introduced us to a new concept called a chat room. The teacher directed us to sign into an Arab chat room called Maktoob. I entered under the pseudonym *Real_Princess* and thought how dizzying it was to see hundreds of people conversing all at once on a single screen. How do you talk to anyone I thought, so I typed "Hello" and watched it scroll off the screen and disappear because so many boys kept asking anyone with a girl's name for a picture or their name or their email. I ignored the boys since I knew better than to talk to them and watched as an Arabic girl named *Baby_Blue* wrote to me, "Hello *Real_Princess*, how are you today?" I felt relieved that it wasn't one of those boys talking to me, so I replied to her chat. We chatted for about two minutes before the bell rang for the next class. I typed, "I need to go, but it was nice meeting you." She asked, "Are you on MSN Messenger?" I typed, "Yes, of course," and gave her my email to add me as a contact.

When I got to the next class, I had a few minutes to spare so I signed in and there was the request from *Baby_Blue,* along with a bunch of boys who had been in the chat room. I deleted all the requests, accepted *Baby_Blue's,* and we started chatting. It was so nice to have an online pen pal who lived in another land. I had never seen Canada! What an idea to be writing to someone who didn't know my real name or who I was or I her, but we spent the next few weeks finding we had so much in common. She was funny and fun to talk to, smart and helpful when I couldn't figure something out in my textbooks. She always seemed to be online. When I had nothing to occupy me, I would jump on the dial up, waiting patiently through the loud and abrasive sound to finish, and for the connection to be made. When I wasn't online, she would leave me messages. I was glad to know her. I had decided not to tell my parents about her since they would say it was not proper to talk to strangers, but I thought what harm could there be, as she lives in Canada.

One day late at night when everyone went to bed, I was up working on one of my class projects when she popped up online. We started one of our random conversations and then she typed, "Can I ask you something personal?"

I typed, "Sure!"

She asked, "Do you cover your hair?"

I replied, "Yes, of course, don't you?"

She paused for a moment and then said, "I'm not a girl, I'm a boy."

I gasped and then froze in shock thinking for two weeks I had been communicating with a boy! I immediately blocked and deleted him without saying goodbye, in fear of what my parents would do if they knew. I disconnected the Internet and went straight to my bed, texting Noor to tell her what happened. She texted back, "Good thing you blocked him, good for you, honey."

In Arabic it is very common to use terms of endearment when you speak to dear friends, like honey, sweetheart, darling, and more complex ones like *Hiyate*, which means "my life." Hiyate was my nickname for Noor for in many ways she was my life, my joy, my confidante, and my anchor to sanity.

The Arab culture and the language is very warm in its usage. I laid in bed thinking of all the privileges my parents would surely take away if they found out. The school that introduced me to a chat room, my computer, my ability to visit Noor, my whole world! I decided I did the right thing. Noor was right and I went to sleep.

The next day I went to school as usual. I met my friends for lunch and went to my classes, but something was missing. I missed my Canadian friend who was always online. There was a void. I got home, got online, and stared at my blocked list. I went back and forth with my brain and my heart. Right, wrong, good, bad … until I was about to hit the unblock button. I got up from my chair and paced in my room. Back and forth my mind raced, thinking about the competing thoughts of threat and loss.

"Should I unblock him? I mean he is in Canada; he doesn't know anyone I know, right?

"What harm could it do to just talk to him online?"

"He can't see me, and I could avoid telling him anything that might give away who I was, it should be safe, right?"

"But it's wrong, what if he does know someone who knows me …. Arabs talk…"

"He's Syrian. I know some Syrian's in my school, maybe he was sent to trick me by someone who hates me."

The risk was high, but I took a deep breath and clicked the unblock button.

He was online. I messaged him to explain that I was sorry for being offline, but I didn't know he was a boy, and I made it a practice not to talk to boys. He explained that he assumed I knew he was a boy and I replied sorry, I did not. I explained that it was not acceptable for us to converse with boys in any way; it was very dangerous to our reputations. He understood and told me about how he was very liberal, but his family was very conservative like mine. His mother covered and was very involved in the religious community. His family prayed religiously, read the Quran in the evening and he had been raised in a very similar way. I loved that he understood my life, but a part of me was excited about a boy who was liberal and had a Canadian passport. At least if he ever did propose it would not be to marry me for my passport. "Finally!" I thought.

We talked every day, sometimes for hours and one day he sent me his picture. I thought he was handsome, so I decided to send him a picture of me wearing my head cover but showing my face. He thanked me and said I looked very pretty, and I blushed. We exchanged love songs without ever saying we loved each other.

During that year I had many suitors come and go, but all of them were rejected. So frequent and unoriginal were the gifts these suitors sent to precede the suitor's mother's arrival that I would often awaken, come downstairs, pass the kitchen island, and say, "Mom, what's that?" pointing at a vase filled with red roses and a tray of expensive chocolates. My mother would clasp her hands together and bend forward, saying giddily, "Aren't they beautiful! This one is a (insert occupation, such as lawyer, doctor, or businessman)," etc. I took a deep breath and said, "Let me know when someone bothers to put in an effort to find out what I like." I hate chocolate. I know that makes me weird, but for some reason chocolate makes my mouth dry. "I tell you what, Mom, the first one that sends pink roses and a tray full of Gummi bears I'll marry."

THE PLANE, THE PLANE

One suitor of note was an older man around 45-years-old who had a wife and three children. He was both wealthy and was a distant relation of the royal family. He had seen me once while I was walking around the hospital on my way to the laboratory to let my stepdad know we were here to take the children to the hospital park. I stress he had seen me because I most assuredly did not see him. I had been trained to walk at least two steps behind a man. The way it was explained to me was that a man walks ahead to make sure the path is clear and safe, and I am to follow. This also includes never looking at any man in the eyes. Eye contact was dangerous, since as I have mentioned before with so little female stimuli around, one glance in the eyes could stop a man and make him explode in his pants and cause him to then run up and propose marriage. You think I'm exaggerating but I'm really not.

Much of what I saw when I walked was my feet. So much so that even now if I am in public, I feel more comfortable looking down than looking at people in the eye. Looking down, in the Middle East, is a sign of a very shy, properly brought up girl. Shyness was one of the most cherished traits young women should have. In the West, looking down as you walk through a crowded room is seen as a sign that you have something to hide, perhaps … but it was not the case in Saudi Arabia.

I recall I was not covering my face that day as I normally did, since it was decided perhaps the hospital grounds were safe enough for me to go without covering. Since there were so many young nurses running around without any abayas at all, going without my face cover would have hardly made me a target.

My stepdad came home that day and told my mother that a woman had an offer of marriage for me and that she should be prepared to receive her tomorrow evening. Naturally we were curious who this mystery woman was and how did my stepdad know her. My stepdad said, "If you must know, her husband came into my office today." My mom squirmed in her seat and said, "Her husband?" "Yes, he is allowed four wives and he apparently accidentally saw Maha as she was leaving the laboratory. He asked around and came to my office to ask for her hand. I told him I could not possibly marry her to him if his wife did not agree." (Too often we hear of the awful things first wives do to second wives.) "He swore she was completely in agreement and offered to send her to start the process as is properly done. I agreed and so she will be here tomorrow night."

I had no interest in an old man with a wife but my mother on the other hand sat for a moment to decide if she could accept me being a second wife to someone. A few moments later she was back with another question, "What does he do?" "I believe he is working in the ministry of finance since he is a distant royal blood relation." I have to say any girl would be intrigued at the idea of being married off to any member of the royal family, but I took in this information and considered it very carefully. My mother heard the words 'royal family' and started getting very excited. Just like that her thoughts of my being a second wife no longer bothered her.

The doorbell rang at around 6:00 p.m. My mother opened the door, always remembering to stand behind the door until the guest entered so that the man dropping her off would not see her. Once the door was closed my mother greeted her warmly. She took her abaya and called for the maid to hang it up. She followed my mother through the dining room and into the small living room. I listened at the kitchen door where I was hiding, waiting to be called to serve the tea. It was customary for me to make an entrance so that a potential suitor could judge the way I entered a room, the way I served the tea, and how gracefully I sat down. When you go to a show the star is never sitting on the stage waiting for the audience to take their seats.

The woman said, "Thank you so much for having me, my husband told me that he heard about your daughter and since he has no sister and his mother is dead, it falls to me to come and start this process." There was something in her voice. A kind of timid trembling, almost like she didn't want to be there, like her heart was aching. My mother called for me, "Maha!" I picked up the tray and entered the room. The woman was old, around my mother's age, and yet still very beautiful. This surprised me, because I assumed that she would be very ugly if her husband was looking for a second wife. I greeted her and started to serve the tea. She looked at me the whole time I poured the tea. I did my best to look away so as not to cause her any embarrassment for staring at me. It was after all what she was here for, to see me as much as she could and report back about what she had seen. She timidly pulled a photograph of him from her purse and said, "This is my husband, Ahmed." He was fat around the middle as most Saudi men his age. He had white hair, and I thought he had an authoritarian looking personality like my stepdad.

His wife felt the need to explain why he was looking for a second wife. "You see, I have three children and cannot travel anymore with him when he goes on business trips. He travels so much, and it would be nice for him not to be lonely." My mental translation of her story was … he wanted a pretty little thing to travel with him everywhere he went. I continued to listen all the while taking note of how the sight of me seemed to be making her sad. She went on at some length about all the wonderful places I would go until she said the words, "private plane" that sent my mother into a tizzy. My mother clasped her hands together tightly yet ever so slowly and said, "He has a private plane! How wonderful." I wanted to roll my eyes but dared not be seen doing so even though my mother's behavior was ridiculous. The woman said, "Yes, oh, you should all come and see it. It's very beautiful and it has a pink interior. I chose it myself when we were first married."

Later I would come to realize that my mom was not trying to find a perfect match or partner for me but someone of prestige and power so that she could live vicariously through me and be honored to brag about the good match she made for her daughter. "Maybe that's why I have never been impressed by a suitor's wealth or status until today. If I like him, I like him. If I don't, I don't.

My mother looked like she wanted to jump out of her seat and dance a jig but instead she said, "Yes, I'll tell my husband to arrange it with yours." She nodded and said that it was time for her to go. She bid us farewell, which is just like hello, by kissing us on our cheeks. I brought her the abaya and she departed. As soon as the door was closed, my mother threw out her arms and grabbed me in a hug. My response was to leave my arms at my sides and have no reaction to her over-excited response. She ran to the men's sitting room where my stepdad had been reading and talked and talked about how wonderful a match this could be. "Just think, she will be married to a royal! We'll be taken care of! She would even travel on a private plane, no less!" My stepdad looked over at me slowly, "What do you think?" he asked. I took a deep breath and said, "I don't know." He nodded his head and continued to listen to my mother's excitement. I also realized that my dad wasn't really that interested in my finding a great partner because that would be an end to his dominion over me. I retired to my room to call Noor.

"What do you think, honey?" I asked.

"Oh, I don't know, honey, he sounds nice, but how strange that his wife should come. I mean it's not unheard of, but most wives would refuse."

She got quiet for a minute and said, "Honey, maybe he threatened her or beat her? If she seemed as scared as you said."

"I don't know, but we're going to see the plane, so we will see what happens. Goodnight, honey."

"Goodnight, sweetheart."

That weekend my stepdad drove us out to the airport to see the plane. Since the man would undoubtedly be there, I was fully veiled that day. Normally if it wasn't a crowded market or a place where many men would be I could go without a veil, but my stepdad wanted the man to understand that just because he was related to the royal family and had a plane, didn't mean he would let him look upon his daughter. I admit to trying to look up to get an idea of his mannerisms and way of talking. Something about him made me uneasy. The plane was indeed grand with pink interior and laid out like a very formal sitting room. After a quick look my stepdad shook his hand and told him to give him a call in a couple of days once he would have time to talk things over with my mother. Which really meant me, since it was obvious that if she had her way, I would have been married to him already.

I would be lying if I said the offer wasn't enticing but on deeper consideration, I realized what would happen. The day I got pregnant, I would be at home just like his first wife and then there would come young wife number three. While I am not against a man having more than one wife, I would like to have had the memories his first wife no doubt had of love and romance in the beginning before she aged and had children. After all, when we are sad it is often our happy memories that comfort us and if we don't get a chance to make as many as possible, the sadness could be overwhelming. In a way I think my Aunt Zakia would have been as proud of her as I was for handling the whole situation so gracefully. In the end I declined. I had no interest in being ordered around by a first wife who had Saudi blood while I was a foreigner. Besides, my aunt always said I should be a first wife not a second since I was pretty enough for it, and I had an American passport that I would not easily give to anyone.

Many girls dreamed of marrying royalty but usually it was the ones who did not know someone who did so. With so much power can come great trouble. If my mother would have a hard time taking her children and leaving my stepdad, it was certain that if he was a member of the royal family there would be no move at all without the family's permission and that frightened me a great deal.

HAIL, CANADA!

I kept my Canadian friend apprised of the suitors while hoping he might step up to the plate, so to speak, but he said he was in college and unable to marry yet. One day my stepdad said he would like to install a web camera and a set of headphones on my computer so that my mom could talk to her sisters and parents from time to time. I agreed and did my best not to look excited. I would have never asked for these items since he might suspect something. And now he had just offered them! Now I could use them to talk to my Canadian friend at night and actually see and hear him. The only problem was my stepdad would ask to be on my computer that day to load the equipment's software, so I had to continuously block and unblock my Canadian friend because, knowing my stepdad, he would undoubtedly ask me to sign into my MSN Messenger app to test the camera and microphone as an excuse to see who I was friends with in the app. Everything went smoothly and my stepdad was none the wiser.

My Canadian friend finally told me his name was Ata and I told him my name was Maha. One night I agreed to turn on the camera to talk to him, first with my head cover and then, thinking what could be the harm, I sat on camera without it. He introduced me to an add-on extension to the MSN Messenger. Once installed, when you clicked *control + space bar* it would make the Messenger and any notifications appear invisible until the correct keystroke was entered to make them reappear. As I waited for him to come online one day, I thought I would leave it on while I went to take a shower. I locked my bedroom door and the bathroom door and started taking my shower. I heard the bathroom door handle twist, but no one knocked. Then I heard someone banging on my bedroom door, which was locked, and I had the key with me in the shower. I finished, grabbed my robe, and came out. There was my stepdad. Apparently, he had tried to call home to tell my mom something important, but the phone line had been busy for hours, so he came home for lunch to find out why.

He demanded I unlock the door and asked why I had the door locked while I was in the shower? I said I forgot the Internet was connected. He moved my computer mouse to see what programs were open but found nothing. My heart raced faster than the sound of a bumble bee's wings, but my face kept its composure as I gave him a look like what are you doing? I had done nothing wrong. I knew he would be looking at me for signs of fear to tell whether I was hiding something. He said, "Well, remember that the Internet should not be connected all day tying up the phone line." I said "Okay," and he left. I closed my door, locked it, and sat down on the floor to breathe. It was a close call, too close for my own good.

I stayed offline all day until the late evening when I got on the app to tell Ata what had happened. He asked why my dad was so obsessive. I said I didn't know and changed the topic. A year later, Ata still wasn't ready for marriage as he was only two years older than me. I kept him as a friend and took more security precautions online, never talking to him except from school or late at night.

When I needed a new cassette tape my mom would take us to the music store on the Hospital grounds. There was a handsome Pakistani man who worked there. His name was Ghassan. I would speak to him through my veil and ask him to find cassette tapes for me in the market if they were not available in his store. He would always ask me to write down the name of the singer and he would find it. He was always so confident he would. I was always so happy when I came the next time and he had found the cassette for me. One day I came in to make a purchase and he checked me out and placed a small note in my bag. I saw him do it but said nothing since my mom was standing nearby. When I got home, I opened the note. It was in Arabic said, "You are the prettiest girl I have ever seen, please call me, here is my number." I kept the note and showed it to Noor on her next visit. She said, "You should not call him, *Hiyate*, he works in a tape store, and he is a Pakistani for God's sake!" I knew she was right but still I had enjoyed the slight flirtations we had shared. I kept the note hidden and put him out of my mind. Every time I saw him I would smile from under my veil, but I didn't dare to call him.

There is a strong divide between the nationalities in the Middle East. I will try to explain the way it was taught to me as I grew up. There are the working-class nationalities. Such as those who came as drivers, maids, shop keepers, construction workers, and so on. Common nationalities in these fields were Indian, Pakistani, Philippine, Eretria, Ethiopian, and Indonesian. They were considered the working-class and I was taught to consider them to be beneath us. This made them absolutely ruled out for marriage. Then there were the other Arabs, like those who came from what was called Bilad al-Sham, which comprised the area of Greater Syria, spanning the modern countries of Syria, Lebanon, Jordan, and Palestine, as well as the regions of Hatay, Gaziantep, and Diyarbakir in modern Turkey. These nationalities were considered middle ground, depending on the kind of life they could offer but often a more suitable match was preferred.

I was raised Saudi and the Saudis, in their minds anyway, are the highest-ranking Arabs in the Middle East, followed by the other members of the Gulf countries which include Bahrain, Iraq, Kuwait, Oman, Qatar, and the United Arab Emirates. The Gulf countries are considered the closest nationalities to our equals since we were the people chosen by God to give birth to the Prophet Muhammed (ﷺ) and our king was the Custodian of the Two Holy Mosques in Mecca and Medina. If I had to compare the idea of being the Custodian of the Two Holy Mosques to any other authority, I would say it would be like the Pope's position of supreme authority and head of the Catholic Church. Saudi Arabia is made powerful by not just oil, but by being the location for the two holiest Muslim locations besides Al-Aqsa Mosque in Jerusalem.

THE RIGHT TO BE INFORMED

My parents' marriage took a sharp turn that year. My stepdad stayed out late, night after night to smoke *shisha* with his friends. There was only one such place back then in Riyadh that we knew of to smoke *shisha*, and it was on the outskirts of the city. It was only for men. I asked him why he stayed out every night and he said, "When I am nice to her she lays around forgetting all her responsibilities and when I am silent at least she gets up and helps you with the children." I dared not tell my mother what he had said. It was between them, and I was already tired enough just by picking up the slack to run the house, go to my classes and help the children with their homework to even consider getting involved in that issue. My mom suspected that he had a second wife, but she could not get him to admit it. The more she pressured him the less he came home and the more silent he became.

My mom's worry and obsession about a second wife all started when *Omi* came on her last visit a while back. *Omi* had asked my mom in front of my stepdad, "Why do you have only one boy and so many girls?" I was asked to translate for my mother. My mom laughed it off at the time and then chewed on that question for months. Now she feared it was the reason for a second wife: "He wanted more sons, that is what she meant, and now he probably has a second wife who can give him more sons," my mom repeated.

Right before my stepdad had begun coming home late, she was hysterical, crying and telling him to just tell her if he was planning to take a second wife, if he was disappointed that she had not given him more sons. No amount of reassurance would help. She would calm down and accept him saying she had nothing to worry about, but then would begin to fret again. He refused for the longest time and the more she cried and looked depressed, the more he stayed out to keep away from the drama. I can't say how long it went on. Finally, one night my stepdad came home and came into the living room where my mother and I were watching a movie and said, "Okay, I'm taking a second wife, now you're informed."

My mom broke down and asked, "Why, when, how?"

He said, "None of that! The wedding is in a week."

My mom said, "You're giving her a big wedding?"

He said, "Of course. It is her day!"

My mother wailed so loud I feared the neighbors heard. Then after pausing for a moment as if madness had overtaken her, she said, "Then I get to sit beside her in a white dress on that day, just like her."

He said, "No way! You had your day."

She secretly had never forgiven him for throwing her a small family wedding when he was young and did not have enough money for a big affair, and now he was about to throw this little girl a big wedding.

He said, "You had your day, forget it!"

She refused, saying, "It is my right! It is my right! It is also my right to forbid you to take a second wife. I never agreed."

My stepdad looked at me, unable to tell her, I think. A silence fell on the room like a tornado about to arrive. I moved slowly and sat beside her, taking her hand in both of mine. I looked into her eyes and said, "No, Mama, actually it's not, your only right is to be informed." She looked at me with daggers in her eyes like I agreed with the whole situation when really I wanted to help her accept that there wasn't anything she could do about it. No one had prepared her for this truth, and she had no idea what to do, say, or what her rights were.

I had my aunt, but she had no idea what world she lived in and how things worked. She had fallen in love, married a man, and had children without really digging into the culture and its mannerisms, rules, and possible bends in the road to come.

Over the years I had studied my stepdad carefully. His mannerisms, what made him mad, when he was messing with us. I had a feeling this was all for the benefit of making my mom reach her peak of despair before letting her know how ridiculous she was for suspecting him. Afterall it was a card that could be played by him, and it might just scare her into behaving. After they threw threats back and forth like my mom saying, "I'll take the kids and leave for America," my stepdad replying, "Good luck, they go nowhere, they are Saudis." My mom sobbed for two hours until he finally laughed and said, "Oh, none of it is true." She was so relieved she ran and hugged him saying how sorry she was for ever having doubted him. I found the whole deception sickening; she was relieved but hurt.

In the following weeks the little she had done in the past for the children ceased, despite my stepdad's elaborate plan to scare her into her place. The maid had gone home to have a family of her own and my stepdad decided it was best not to get a new one. With my schoolwork I tried to keep up with cooking dinner, watching the kids, and getting them off to school but I always fell behind while she stayed in her room unless Baba was home, then she pretended she was actively participating. My stepdad made the mistake one day of saying, "Why can't you be more like your daughter? She is more a mother to these children than you!" Now she hated me, too, and spent even more time in her room.

A week or so later my stepdad came home and said, "I have a trip to Europe. I will be away for two weeks." My mom was depressed, begging him every day to let her go with him. To which he replied, "You have four children to take care of." My mom was so deep in despair and two weeks of her suspicions that he could be finding a new bride in Europe seemed like unneeded torture to all of us. So, I stepped up and one night at dinner said, "I can take time off school and stay with the kids, all of them. So, Mama can go with you." My stepdad said, "Are you sure you will be okay?" I replied, "I take care of them already, I'll take time off school and be with them all day and if I need anything like groceries or if there is an emergency, Uncle Shakoor is in town." My stepdad looked at my mom and said, "It's up to you." She jumped up and kissed me on the cheek. She was so happy with me again. I can't think of how many sacrifices I have made for my mom's happiness, but I did them willingly. She was my mom after all, and I just wanted her to be happy.

My brother always used to say, and I had never believed him before, that these kids were her children now and we were just extra, but I saw it now. Not that he was right per se, but all day she seemed to wait for my stepdad, and the more he worked the more she isolated, she felt lonely and trapped. She loved him, yet no effort was put into the kids unless it was for show when he returned home. It was my hope the trip would bring them closer together again and give her a break. After all, no one was born knowing how to take care of four children at once.

The day came for them to leave, we said our goodbyes and they left. I turned around, looked at my siblings and said, "Slumber party in the living room!" They screamed, "Yay!" and started running about. I laid out the sleeping bags in the living room and we had a slumber party/movie night every night, which they loved. It was my way of having them all in one room, making them easier to manage. The next day the kids went off to school and I had a chance to talk to Ata for the first time with no one around to eavesdrop on our conversations. When the children returned home from school I let them help me cook their favorite dinner together. We baked a cake, decorated it together, put on cosmetic make-up, put on a play, and had so much fun every day. Life seemed so happy, peaceful, and fun with the unhappy couple gone.

Friday came and my Uncle Shakoor came by to take us to spend the weekend at their house. My young girl cousins and I played house while the boys played cards. I left Mohammed to their charge, since it was good for him to spend time with other boys being the only boy at our house. I worried if he felt like he was missing out. The girls and I played wedding all night. Sara, now twelve, was old enough to dream of weddings and happily ever after. When all the girls went to sleep, we sat up talking about how she loved her cousin and how her mom's sister's daughter loved her brother, Faisal. We giggled. Noor was away in Egypt and so I showed my cousin the note from the man in the music store.

She said, "Call him."

I said, "I can't, he would know my voice."

She said, "Let me, let's send him a message, here, let me type it."

I agreed in fun, she typed out a message saying in Arabic, "You're my moon and stars." Like clockwork he called.

I freaked out and said, “We can’t answer!”

She said, “Wait, I have an idea.”

“What?” I asked.

“Give me the phone,” she said, and she wrote another message, “Ahmed, why are you calling? Don’t forget to bring the bread.”

He replied, “I know who you are. I love you.”

She said, “Ahmed bring some tomatoes, too.” We giggled and giggled.

I knew it wasn’t her first-time texting or talking to boys. He called again. I reached down, grabbed the bed sheets, and pulled them up to my mouth as she answered the phone and spoke to him in Arabic like an old woman who was married to a man named Ahmad. She shouted at him asking him if he was on his way or not? and he said, “I’m sorry, I think I have the wrong number.” She said, “Oh, I’m so sorry,” and hung up. We both laughed all night at the poor man’s expense, and I could not help but think again, did I miss my chance, was he the one, and had I treated him so badly by allowing a twelve-year-old to mess with him for her amusement?

Uncle Shakoor took us home a few days later and then my parents returned. My mom had so much to say about the trip. Not that she had an enjoyable time but rather about how all they served was raw fish and she didn’t eat well. I thought to myself, “You just saw all of Europe and stayed in hotels with no kids. How could you not come back happy? I took time off school to take care of your children, I gave up my life and you are still unhappy ….” I forgave her. I always did. She was my mother. It seemed that my stepdad had found a way to settle her nerves while they were away, so, I let it go. The next day she returned to her room and back to her old routine and we went back to ours: me cooking and caring for the kids and her missing in action.

LADIES' DAY

Sometimes we went to the theme park which was as small as a state fair on ladies' days, Tuesday and Thursday. Only women and children were allowed in on those days and all the ride operators and shopkeepers were women. This time I asked Noor to go because I wanted someone my age with me. She came and we wore heels and rode all the rides, got fake tattoos, and laughed. My mom, relaxed because there were only women in the park, left us alone.

We walked and talked, and she said something odd, "You know, honey, there are some things I could never tell you, things I can never tell anybody." I thought about a bad secret that was not mine and said, "You know, my mom once told me a story about my real Dad, that he adopted a young girl after they got divorced and he raped her." Noor became silent and said, "I can't tell you anything." I did not press her anymore; I knew what she meant. It all made sense, all the times she left my house because her mom said she had to go out and her sister would be home alone. At the time I thought why do you have to go just because your sister is alone, but there it was, staring me in the face. They had a pact between the sisters that no one stays home alone. Their plan must have been like mine. Always two, so one can help the other or call the mother. I wanted to talk to her but how, how do you talk about such things? So, we walked in silence for the rest of the night.

She came over another time and we talked some more, and I asked her if it was true. "Is your secret like my secret…?" She said "Yes," and that was all we said on the subject. I laid my head down across her lap. I had never known anyone who really understood me, but I knew now she did. God had brought us together. We never spoke about any details, but we understood each other. We were lucky, we thought, at least one day we would escape while others, might not.

In Saudi, unless the man agrees to the divorce up front it can take years for a woman to take her husband to court to prove any harm and to request a divorce. I knew a woman whose husband was so cruel that when she left him at the age of twenty-five, he refused to divorce her until she was sixty. Just to spite her so she could never remarry, have children, or live her life. When I met this older woman and pitied what had happened, she smiled and said, "No matter, my dear, I'm free now and that is all that matters." Smiling for the freedom she had fought for all those years had finally come. These women's experiences were lessons we all took to heart. When we heard their stories, we understood that it could happen to any one of us. Their stories were warnings to marry wisely.

At lunch time, the institute was full of interesting stories, gossip, and conversations. I recall once there was a debate between Ghadah, Basmah, and myself about whether women and men should study abroad. Ghadah held tightly to her opinion that women had no business studying abroad, mingling freely with men, and being taught by non-believers. "It will only fill their heads with nonsense," she added. While Basmah pointed out, "If we want the Bedouin population to give up their superstitious beliefs and its tribal urges to wage war (*Jihad*) on non-believers/infidels, we will need to broaden their minds. That can only come about if we expose them to something else. For them to see for themselves through experience that just because something is different, that does not necessarily make it bad. Every time I talk to one of those Bedouin girls in our class all I hear is, "Christians are bad, the West is bad" and oh, my favorite, death to all the Jews. Yes, Jews are bad, but I don't want them all to die, we don't get to choose if we were born Jewish; God chooses that for us." I said, "But, will that really work? Let's face it. The men will go learn, maybe have a lot of unmarried sex, then return home and marry a good Saudi girl who was chosen for them. In order to please their previous generation, they will just fall back into line upon return. America is like Disneyland for sinning, *Sin-Land,* ha-ha. They will have fun abroad, but never question their in-laws once they are back. The women who return will never question their husbands. In the end, whether they travel or not, they will be the same." Basmah said, "Perhaps, but it will come about in the next three generations. I feel it." I said, "That is a very long way away." Ghadah looked confused and wondered if anything should change. As a Saudi, she was content but Basmah, having lived abroad for a time, had brought back with her a whole bag of contemplations about the country. I liked pondering things with her, but more often than not, her words fell on deaf ears. We all had much to occupy our minds. Ghadah with her problems and me with mine. Both of us feeling powerless most of the time.

One day Basmah was talking to me about something happening in Syria. She was Syrian and always seemed to be so informed about the world. That night I told my Canadian friend online,

"Hey, my friend, Bashma said something was happening in Syria. She is Syrian like you."

He paused and said, "What is her last name?" so I told him. He laughed.

I said, "What?"

"My very best friend is her brother; my family knows her family."

"Wow, such a small world," he said, "Don't you see! She can tell her brother about you, who can tell me officially, and then I can tell my mother to call your family."

I blushed because I knew what he meant; after so long, he was ready to marry.

TIME TO TELL SOMEONE

Trying to hide my excitement from my family while we planned on how to bring this about was a difficult task for a girl who was almost 19. I went to class as normal and every night we would talk. I decided if we were to be husband and wife he should know about my stepdad if only to anticipate the hard road ahead. That night I told him, and his silence was deafening. I knew that as an Arab he would judge, and it was always the girl's fault. As we hung up that night my head hung low wondering if I should have told him. Wondering if he would ever speak to me again.

The next day he decided we would continue to press on. My friend Basmah would be the reason he knew of me and on his leave to Jeddah, he would tell his mom to call my mom. The night she was scheduled to call I waited by the phone, being banned from answering it myself, because once as an 8-year-old girl I had answered the phone and made friends with a random male crank caller. I thought he was nice, and he thought I was of marriage age. From that point on it was decided that only my mom or my stepdad could answer the phone.

It rang and my heart beat out of my chest. My mom answered and spoke to the woman on the other end of the line. "Yes," she said, "Oh, how interesting, what a small world, oh yes, let me speak to my husband," and then hung up. I asked insistently, "Who was it?" My mom relayed the message that a girl I knew from school had mentioned me to her brother, who had mentioned me to his friend, who was her son, and she would like permission to visit us when she is next in Riyadh. I said, "Wow, how interesting, we should hear the offer." This time my stepdad drew back in skepticism saying, "Well I don't know." I said, "Why not, she just wants to stop by?" He agreed, and my mother always happy about a suitor, bounced around the house. I talked to Ata that night and told him all was going well with our plan, and everything was on track. I slept like I had never slept before. Soon I would be married and far across the sea. No longer the property of my stepdad. Me, the mistress of my own home at last.

Time drew on waiting for their visit, and my stepdad tried to make excuses as to why it could not go ahead as planned.

"They are Syrian, really they are not fit to clean my shoes so why should we even bother to meet them?"

"We met the Palestinian family; this one at least has a passport. There is no harm in meeting the woman."

"I still find it hard to believe that she would come all the way from Jeddah on the word of a girl who told her brother who told her."

He looked over at me as if he smelled a rat. I realized I had miscalculated. I had been so reluctant when it came to every suitor thus far and this one had not even sent flowers and I was walking around as if on air. I told Ata that my stepdad seemed like he was going to call it off.

"That is not up to him, that asshole! I have an idea. Let's use the webcam you have to catch him. You never stay home alone, you said. There must be a day when everyone is going out and you can stay home and catch him on camera, then for sure he will behave."

I shook my head no, saying I didn't want to go on the webcam. He insisted it was the best way to get me away. I reluctantly agreed and one night, the moment arrived. My mom was going out and taking the kids to visit someone. So, that night I made it clear I was staying home. "I have schoolwork to finish" I said. My mom was surprised since I always went along. I connected to the Internet before she left, started the webcam. Ata got online and started recording from the other side as I pushed the space bar combination to hide the Messenger app on my computer. My mom said her goodbyes and my stepdad drove her to her friend's house.

Like clockwork, my stepdad drove back and came upstairs to my room. I positioned myself in the corner for the best view of the camera and pretended to be getting something from the top of the high closet. He entered and grabbed my butt, knowing we were alone. I dropped the box and started to yell at him and then unfortunately looked over at the camera. He went to my computer but found nothing. Knowing something was up he restarted it by pressing the restart button on the side. Luckily Ata had been recording from Canada and so the video was safe.

My stepdad asked me, "What is going on?! What are you up to?!" and I told him. "You're making trouble and I have been talking to this boy for more than a year, I love him and if you don't put me on a plane to Canada, I will release the recording." He said, "Release the recording, ha! you won't get any Internet forever." I said, "Sorry, I meant he will release the recording If I don't contact him within the hour and I'll finally tell mom! It's time!" He raised up his hand and struck me across my neck. It was the first time in a long time that he had hit me. I ran for the window knowing that he always parked the Suburban under my window because this house was in a compound that had no bars installed on the windows. My plan was to jump out the window onto the roof of the vehicle below and run to the neighbor's house.

As I opened the window, he grabbed me back. I screamed loudly as he pulled me to the ground. I got loose and ran out of the room as he hit me again. Trying to get away he threw me down a flight of stairs. My earring fell off. I reached to pick it up. I was shocked, shaking and hurt. I looked over at him as he smashed my little Nokia cell phone. Bringing himself back to a normal frame of mind, he put it back together and suddenly it rang.

He looked down at it and saw an unknown number . He said, "Is it him," I said, "I don't know." He said, "Did he call the police and they are trying to contact you?" I said, "I don't know!" I was hurt, beaten, and bruised. He yelled, "Answer me!" I said, "I think it's a wrong number," and then, just like that, my mom called his phone asking to be picked up. He said, "We will continue this later. I'll lock the door on my way out, so don't even think about going anywhere." He took my phone and left to go pick her up and bring her home. I began to cry as I went to my room. As soon as I heard the car leave, I connected to tell Ata I was OK. My stepdad was worried but he said the video was safe. I heard the car engine. He was back quickly, so I said, "I have to go," and got offline, dressed in my pjs, and went to bed.

In the middle of the night, I opened my eyes ever so slightly to the sound of the door opening and saw my mother doing something she had never done. She came in, looked at me, said nothing, and left. The next morning, I dared not leave my room. I didn't want to see anyone, and I felt so much like a wounded, scared bird whose wings had been so broken that flight was no longer possible. The Internet disconnected, my phone taken away, and my mother nowhere to be seen. When I did come downstairs for school the next morning, my stepdad stared at the air as he issued a harsh question, "Where do you think you're going? Not to school… You're going nowhere until you're better, back to your room." I returned to my room and stared at my neck, where the ugly bruise of the hand print he had left confirmed the ugly events hadn't been a nightmare. I wish I could say I was angry; I wish I could say I was sad; but all I thought about was the plan. What would be my stepdad's next chess move, and how would I counter?

MOVES AND COUNTER MOVES

My mom finally came to speak to me. "Baba said you were planning to commit suicide by jumping out the window in your bedroom if he didn't let you marry this boy?" I looked at her and wondered how she thought I would die by jumping half a flight with the family Suburban parked literally right under my window. Anyone with half a mind could see that I could have dropped straight from my window to the top of it. I remained silent and let her continue thinking whatever she thought. This was my stepdad's move, and I needed more information. She continued, "And, he said that you had snuck out with this boy on dates multiple times while at school." I thought for a moment and decided to go along with whatever his plan was.

I had spent years watching and listening to my stepdad and now it was time for graduation. You see, if you want to outsmart a spider you must first study his weaving techniques. I had seen him do this multiple times. Weave a story that was believable based on actual events but not what happened. Facts would support his cause and give him ammunition for whatever he did. Such as the fact that the neighbor had heard a scream that sounded like it came from my window. When my mother mentioned it my stepdad calmly said, "I was trying to pull her back in the window to save her life . . . she was trying to jump." Remember the simple rule? It doesn't matter what happened, it matters what it looks like … could look like.

This was just as he had done to my poor brother when he spoke up about what he saw when he walked in on my stepdad masturbating next to my bed that night in Leicester, England. I had lost the battle, but it was winning the Cold War I had been fighting for so long that was on my mind. I knew that arguing was useless and would bring me nothing. I could not win that way. He had the ultimate power and all I had was some small amount of leverage that I knew he was chewing on at this very moment. I knew what my mom did not. The facts. My stepdad offered up to my mother, who we all knew could never keep a secret to save her life, a story to cover his tracks. She went on, "I'm so sorry, baby." As she reached up to touch my neck I pulled back. "Does it hurt?" she asked. I said nothing. "He told me everything and I'll tell you after he did, I came in and saw you. I thought about leaving him. But, when he told me what happened, how he pulled you back and his temper just got the better of him and he started to cry, I knew that he was truly sorry. Afterall, I have only seen him cry once and that was when his father died. Now, tell me about this boy," she said. "What do you want to know?" "Well, how many times did you go out with him? How far did it go?" I knew she would bring the conversation back around to sex. The irony was, unlike her at my age, nothing sexual had happened with any boy to that point other than her husband, and he was the very one she kept protecting.

I quickly recalled a story one of the girls who used to sneak out of school to see boys told me and just used it as my own since Ata and I in fact had never met. "I met him online and after talking for a while he picked me up at school and took me to a remote donut shop on the edge of the city where no one would see us." "And nothing happened?" Once again, she stared at me with disbelief. I stood up straight and said, "Nothing happened, we just talked for a little while." There was a long pause as I waited to hear what my stepdad had decreed. She obviously had been informed, since besides getting a bit of gossip to fill her day, which was why she was here.

"Well, I have to tell you that Baba said this will mean shame on the family and so it is decided since the boy wants to marry you, we should marry you as soon as possible." I clasped my hands together and held them up to my mouth as she continued. "I'll call his mother today and get plans started." I felt like I could breathe for a moment. Even if it covered up my stepdad once again at least I would have my Ata and my freedom in return.

That night, my stepdad entered my room as everyone slept. I was still awake. He stood in the doorway, as he often did when he was angry, and did not look at me. "Come downstairs, let's talk," he said. I got up slowly and followed him downstairs where all the lights were out. We sat at the dining room table in the dark. He started talking as I looked down. "Your mother has told you my decision?" I nodded as he continued, "Now I need to tell you that it doesn't matter what you have, we're going to do this my way." "How soon can I go to Canada?" I asked. "You cannot leave this house just like that, the whole family will talk. We will do this the right way or not at all," he said. I nodded, but wondered if he was just biding time, keeping me quiet so to speak while he thought of a better plan. I knew I had to be on guard.

I stayed at home for a week, avoiding my stepdad at dinner since neither he nor I wanted to look at each other. Finally, I spoke up and said, "Can I please return to school?" My mom replied, "That is not possible your bruise has not yet gone." I said "Look, I could cover it with my hair, and no one would see it, please." I received no answer at dinner and headed to bed. The next day my mother told me that I could go back to school. I assume that my mom, knowing from her phone call with Ata's mom that he was in Canada, told my stepdad that since I was obviously in love with this boy it was unlikely I would get into any more trouble.

I pulled my hair over my neck, making sure no one saw my bruise. As I entered the green painted glass lunchroom my friend Ghadah said, "I missed you! Where have you been?" I had no answer, so I pulled back my hair to show the hand print my stepdad had left me on my neck. She covered me back up and sat me down next to her taking my hand in hers. She said, "A year ago do you remember seeing my wedding pictures?" We all saw the beautiful wedding pictures of her turquoise wedding dress, the prettiest dress I had ever seen. "Yes, of course. You looked so beautiful," I said. "Well, following my wedding I discovered that my husband was a very jealous man and an aggressive man. On our wedding night I, like many virgins, was scared and nervous and asked him to please be gentle. It's hard to say these things, you know." I nodded because I knew what she meant; we all talked to each other about sex after marriage and what it was like but if your new husband thought you knew too much it could be interpreted as you getting this information firsthand. So, it was always difficult for new brides to know how much knowledge to reveal they knew. She continued, "He said, "You're my wife now," and he laid me back and forced me to give him what he wanted. The next day I was angry and refused to serve him breakfast so as punishment he beat me and locked me in the house without a telephone. Like a prisoner there I stayed for many months." The doors in Saudi Arabia are made in a way that both sides will require a key to open so if one side is locked and you don't have a key, there would be no leaving since even the windows had bars that do not open.

I felt ashamed that I had not noticed her absence. We all assumed that after marriage an absence was only a sign of wedded bliss and setting up a new home. It was often excused by the teachers. "I tell you this to tell you that I am alright and so you will be alright. Everything will be all right. I will pray for you." I thanked her. It would be months later that I would hear the rest of Ghadah's story, how she finally borrowed a phone from the wife of her husband's friend who came for tea. Ghadah used it to text her father, who arrived the same day and took her home. I admired the woman who let her use her phone and have always wondered if her husband beat her for helping Ghadah. Most of us would not want to get involved. We all had so many of our own battles to fight that this kind of courage is not often seen.

Her father then got to the task of telling his new son-in-law that she wanted a divorce, which he refused and, so like so many, she remained married living in her father's home unable to do anything such as renew her passport, travel, and so on. In Saudi Arabia men manage such matters and the man who was entrusted with your care was the only one who could sign everything and take it to the appropriate municipality. A year later when he had calmed down her father offered him a sum of money to divorce his daughter and they were divorced the same day.

A week or so passed and things returned to normal. My stepdad had given me back my cell phone since it was the only way he could text me to come out of the institute when he arrived to pick me up. Unlike the girls' school, they did not call names over the speaker since all the girls had cell phones now. Ata's mom called to tell us that her son had returned from Canada and now that she had a chance to discuss the matter of our marriage face to face, she would like to pay a visit to see me. My mom agreed.

My stepdad left the house to spend time with his friends on the appointed night, as we prepared for Ata's mom's arrival. Ata and I had resorted to only speaking while I was at school. That night he texted me from his temporary Saudi number as they were driving to our home to say, "I am driving my mom to your house, can I see you somehow?" I thought and thought about how it would be possible, since I knew how the process would work. His mother would ring the doorbell and we would open the door while standing behind it. Once she entered, we'd close it. To risk accidentally showing myself on the other side of the door could potentially cause my new future mother-in-law to think I was very loose indeed, since Ata had told me how pious she was. Suddenly another plan came to mind.

"There is a small balcony in my parents' bedroom that is located directly above the front door. When you arrive, I'll sneak up there so you can see me before I go greet your mom. This way my mom will be distracted, and no one will think anything." I was so nervous to finally see him in real life. Once the doorbell rang, I ran upstairs to my parents' balcony. My stepdad had safety pinned a sheet, now dusty, over the balcony rail so the neighbors could not look at him smoking at night.

I lifted my head slowly to peer over the dusty sheet. I saw Ata getting back into the car. Our eyes met, and he smiled for just a moment as he started the car and poked his head out of the car window as he drove away. I sat down on the old wooden chair on the balcony and sighed deeply. I had waited so long to see him, and he was as handsome in person as he was online, only a little shorter than I thought, but that didn't matter to me.

I suddenly awoke from my momentary floating. I heard my mom calling my name. "Maha! Where are you?" I had forgotten that you can't hear anything inside the house while on the balcony. I ran down to greet our guest. "Where have you been?" my mom said. I replied simply, "I'm sorry," which she laughed off and then requested I serve the tea. His mom had brought photos of him to help me get an idea of what he looked like, because in her mind, I had neither seen nor spoken to him before. It was decided by my stepdad that since they didn't know we had been video calling and texting, there was no need to tell them. This way we could keep any potential gossip to a minimum. After all, the tighter the circle of the secret the less likely it is that it will get out quickly.

"He is a little taller than you, my dear. He has brown eyes and curly black hair," she said, and then she told us all about his accomplishments. How he memorized the Quran at a young age, which was a great accomplishment. What he was currently studying and how they had not intended to for him to marry until he was done with school but were finally convinced that it was necessary to keep him from sin. My mom said, "Well, I think it is a great idea this way they can both study safely together." I felt like I was dreaming as I listened to how his mother saying she liked girls to study as well as boys. Could it be possible for me to be able to go to college, something that had never seemed possible before, and have Ata too? The thought was dizzyingly wonderful. I recall feeling so euphoric that night. The evening ended well, with my mom seeing the goodness in the match and enjoying his mom's company. Later, she relayed all of this to my stepdad - who held back his reply.

Since the women were in agreement that the match was a good one, we moved on to the next phase, the women discussing the details. The women worked as proxies for the negotiations. This way everything could be settled before the men met. The truth was that it is more often the men negotiating through the women, since the men tended to get a little more hot-headed around negotiating. The next few weeks were filled with plans and details being worked out.

Ata's mom was a strong, empowered woman and in her house she ruled. She and my mother were discussing planning details via the MSN messenger, since calling from city to city incurred long distance charges which were very expensive. Ata's mom texted, "I think it's time we talk over the expectations of a dowry and a wedding. How much do you think?" she asked my mom. My stepdad was naturally standing over my mom's shoulder as he issued how she should respond. "Tell her 100,000.00 Riyals upfront and 200,000.00 in case of divorce," my mom typed out the message and pressed the send button. As I watched this transaction, I already knew this would go very badly. I knew they didn't have the money with two more boys to think about sending to college in Canada soon. But it was already too late. The back-and-forth negotiations began in earnest.

There is only one dowry paid by the man to the bride at the signing the marriage contract. It does not have to be money, it could actually be anything, such as a house, assets, camels, anything. The agreed upon dowry amount was to be recorded on the marriage contract. Oftentimes part is paid upfront, and part is allowed to be paid on a later date. What if all is agreed and the man decides never to pay the rest once he is married? While this could happen, I would think more often it gets paid to the bride even if it is 10 years later. Upon his death if it is not paid the families often pay the debts off so that the man does not suffer in the grave and afterlife. In any case, many families put the larger amount down as the second portion. The reason we say in case of divorce is because it just means he will need to pay that back no matter what. So even if it is two days after the wedding and he changes his mind, that money will still have to be paid back, provided one condition has been met… that the marriage was consummated. If there is no consummation, everything is returned to the groom.

I started to pace back and forth, nervous that everything was going to fall apart. If we insisted on a price that they felt was too high, his mom could walk away. I finally stopped moving. Clenched my fists together, looked at my stepdad and said, "You're being unreasonable!" to which he replied "They are Canadian, living and working here. They must have the money." I shrugged at the arrogance of it all and walked away, slamming my bedroom door. My stepdad came in after me and said, "We do not slam doors in this house, Princess." I folded my arms and looked at him like a cobra looks as it raises itself up to take on another cobra and said softly, "You're doing this on purpose, so they leave and then you think I will believe it is not your fault and forget the whole thing. Not this time. I don't care if everyone sees that video if this wedding doesn't go through." My stepdad, being reminded of the video, exhaled deeply, and departed.

He reluctantly agreed to 100,000.00 Riyals to be split 50,000.00 upfront and the second half to be saved in case of divorce. The two families agreed. I had fought an important battle and decided it was time for bed.

Day after day the families fought over everything, especially the wedding. Ata's mom said, "I think a small family wedding in the house would be good, since they are so young, and we can't afford a big wedding right now. We need to save for that since we didn't expect to marry him so soon. Maybe we throw the big wedding later once they graduate and return?" My stepdad, through my mother, said, "No, it must be an elaborate wedding of Saudi magnitude so we can make sure everyone knows she was married off properly and well." I lashed back, "I don't care about a big wedding!" but my stepdad insisted. "But you will care in the long run," he said. "Tell her not to worry about it. I'll pay for the wedding. All of it."

This sentence was meant as an insult of magnanimous proportion. In Saudi culture he was basically saying Ata's family was poor and unworthy of me, but since I loved her son, he would take care of doing things properly. Ata's family begged to pay for something, but it was game on for my stepdad now. My stepdad refused to accept, thereby giving him the means to declare them poor by asserting his right to tell everyone how cheap they were with his daughter. If they had been Saudi, and if I had not had the leverage and Ata the convincing power as the first son, this would have been the knockout punch that brought down the entire marriage discussion altogether. No Saudi that I knew of would have accepted this offer, they are such a proud people. Ata's family, however, only wanted him to be happy. To push back, they offered a compromise: my family would throw me a wedding in Riyadh for our friends and family, and they would throw me another wedding for their friends and family upon our return visit to Jeddah the following summer. So, this is what was told to anyone who asked. There would be two weddings and that was that.

All was finally agreed upon and Ata's family came down to Riyadh to do a short *Shabkah* party. This was a "promising party" where Ata would be announced as officially my intended husband. The party celebrated the announcement to everyone but didn't include the formal contract signing. Having only the *Shabkah* party without the formal contract signing meant that even if he had been in attendance, which he could not be due to his school schedule in Canada, we could still not be alone, see each other, or date. We could, however, talk with supervision. His parents made do without him. I was basically reserved for him, so people knew that a proper contract engagement was on the way and following this party our extended Saudi family could be informed.

The party was only for the family. The men in the men's sitting room nodded and agreed that all was settled while the women in the ladies' side celebrated as I received my gifts. I was given an engagement ring with a small white gold band to accompany it. "I never had a daughter, but I asked around and my friends said this ring was the style now, I hope you like it?" My future mother-in-law said. The ring had a center diamond with four baguettes on either side. It was exactly what I had wanted. "Thank you, *Khalai*!" I said, throwing out my arms to hug her. She also presented me with a book titled, *The Book of Marriage,* by Ibn Abdul Wahhab. I had never seen an Islamic book before and was so excited to read it. I figured she must have given it to me to help me become the best wife I could be. I felt so loved and cared for every time she looked at me. Something I had not felt since the last time I saw my Aunt Zakia, but perhaps even more.

My mother-in-law had grown up in a house of boys and raised a house of boys. To her at that moment I was the most precious responsibility she had ever been given. She believed that girls had just as much a right as boys to live in this world equally and safely as Aisha and Khadija had done beside the Prophet Muhammed (ﷺ) as his wives. I would have to say, looking back now, that she played a major part in my love of Islam.

The ring was too big, but I loved it so much. It represented freedom to come and everlasting love. It is interesting to note that the most important piece of jewelry his mother put on me wasn't the ring but a simple white gold chain bracelet. This is the meaning of the word shabkah. At least how it was explained to me by *Omi* and my Aunt Zakia. In the old days, a bracelet was given to hold a girl for a man before the Western idea of wedding rings was assimilated. Some people even today in the Middle East do not wear wedding rings. It is just a gift. A piece of jewelry. Over the years your husband may give you many rings and all of them can be worn as a wedding ring. It is not uncommon for some women to wear their wedding rings on the right hand, because in Islam, the left side of the body is considered unclean since that is the hand you wash your backside with. Not to mention we always did everything with the right hand, just as the language is written from right to left. Everything in our culture is done this way. So, despite popular opinion and the new changing fads, I wore my engagement rings on my right hand.

Following the *Shabkah* my stepdad made the call to *Omi* telling her that his daughter would be getting married. I always imagined it like the movies where the family is overjoyed, and the phone call goes something like,

"Oh, little Maha is getting married! We're so happy!"

But no, in Saudi it sounds kind of like this, "*Hala* (Saudi hello) *Omi* how are you? How is your health?"

She would ramble on about her knees and her back and her maid until she would ask, "How is your family?"

“Ah yes, well, Maha is getting married soon. We just did the *Shabkah* today,” my stepdad said in his most solemn tone. Like he was informing her we had a new sink installed.

Omi was in shock. “What! To whom? Do we know the family? Where did he come from? We have heard nothing!”

“Yes, well a girl saw her at school, told her brother, who told his friend, and the mother came, so it’s all agreed. They should marry in the fall; we settled on September 1st.”

“So soon? Why don’t they need time to be sure?”

“I would say yes, but the college classes start in the fall and there is no need to delay, since Maha will be attending college in Canada with him in the fall.”

“Canada!? You’re first daughter going away to Canada! I would have never agreed. You should marry her to someone closer to home or at least wait until the boy finishes college. Canada, oh my! That is very far away and it’s a heathen country for sure, it will corrupt her.”

“I understand, *Omi*, but her mind is set, so that is what it is.”

“Well, if you need me to fly down and change her mind just let me know she has no idea how cold it is there. Not just the weather, but those Westerners are not friendly to Arabs.”

After hanging up the phone with my stepdad, *Omi* informed the family one by one. This was common for her as she sat by the phone with her address book calling everyone on her little family list. Most were overjoyed but still some started to gossip, since the boy showed up out of nowhere in their minds, and they had heard nothing about him before now and my parents were willing to part with their first daughter to a foreign country so quickly and with our wedding being only four months away, some people wondered if I had gotten pregnant or had some kind of relationship with the boy.

As time went on and I still looked as skinny as ever they eventually were convinced it was not the case. My parents only wanted to make sure I got to Canada in time to start college at the beginning of the term and so the story had spun properly. Saudi Arabia is a strange mixture. It is ancient in many ways and at the same time so advanced because of the wealth.

Growing up in it was like growing up in 1950's America with all the modern technology of the 1990's but none of the liberties of the era. Much of it is still like that today, skyscrapers and technological advances, a royal family, and so much oil wealth have brought change, but traditions are still held fast, too. I don't know how else to describe it except that it's as if you took everyone from the 1950's and dropped them in the 21st century they would still act the same as if nothing had changed.

THE WEDDING

The time came for me to select my wedding dress. My stepdad drove my mom and I to almost every dress shop in Riyadh. I wanted a pink dress since in Saudi Arabia it's perfectly normal for a girl to marry in any color she likes. My mom, being American, would not accept this. We argued constantly about how it was my wedding and I wanted pink. "But a bride should be in white, it represents purity," my mom said. "It's just a dress and it's my wedding. Over here color does not represent anything." I looked at my three sisters and thought for a moment before finally saying, "I tell you what, if you promise to let them marry in whatever color they want I will agree to wear white on my wedding day." She agreed and so I selected a white dress imported by an American wedding designer. Unfortunately, it was backless and so it would need to be approved by my stepdad since he had forbidden me from wearing such things.

That night as we showed him the pictures my mother had taken of me wearing the dress he said, "No, it's backless and way too revealing." "Baba, I'm getting married, who cares if I'm backless now? What will they say that I was too revealing for my husband? I have spent the last ten years covered up at every wedding." "Fine, but the back must be covered." ""It will ruin the dress!" I said as I stormed off to my room. My mother called the tailor who looked at the dress and, not wanting to lose the sale, said, "I can do it and it will look like it came that way." Relieved, my mother told her to go ahead with the changes.

My stepdad had to be the one to take me to buy my trousseau since I needed a *Mahram* in the *Souk* (which means market) and in the mall and mom had to stay with the kids. Deciding I would be leaving soon we both agreed to put our swords away. I needed to get ready for my new life and there was no one else who could have taken me. Supposing he still had time to convince me to stay he began telling me how harsh life would be in Canada. "You know it will not be anything like you were used to here. Life is harder for women in that part of the world." I replied, "I'm aware that life will be different, and I will have much to learn, but I'm ready."

I thought about how little he knew me. None of the things in my room, nothing about my life meant as much to me as having my own life and getting out. I had given up my life long ago, to be a sister, a caregiver, a replacement for my mom, a caregiver to my mom, a house manager making things run smoothly, a politician, a referee, a translator, a house cook, and a teacher to my siblings. I was ready to see what life had in store for me and to answer only to myself. Taking care of one man sounded like a breeze after caring for four children and a mother, all the while trying to avoid my stepdad. I asked him, "Do you know me so little? Do you think I'm not up to the challenge of life in Canada?" He stayed silent and we closed the subject.

The wedding dress was ready, and the hall was booked by my stepdad. It would seat 1,000 people easily. I recall walking into the hall to see it for the first time and thinking how grand it was. The carpets were red and there was gold trim on everything. The large marble stage would be where I would sit with my husband for the first time. My mother and I selected the invitations which needed to go out as soon as possible. Unlike in America or other countries, the invitations could not be mailed, because the postal system then, and still very much today, only came to businesses. Therefore, if you were a housewife all your mail needed to go to an office. There are no mailboxes outside houses. My stepdad and my mother would need to hand deliver every single invitation which was considered the more proper approach to the task since every guest is treated as royalty and, if you were inviting the king to dine, you would invite him in person not over a call or a text but with a handshake and a statement like, "We would be honored if you could come."

The wedding cake was ordered and a second cake as well. I wanted to get married on my birthday but since the wedding would need to be on a weekend to increase the likelihood of attendance, it was decided it would be the day after my birthday. I had chosen this date because my biological parents had married on that date and then surprise, I was born on the same date about three years later, so I wanted to continue the tradition. The wedding cake was not too elaborate since my stepdad was paying for everything. It had to be grand enough for him to keep face, meaning at least five tiers and cheap enough not to break his perceived budget.

My mother tried so hard to have the experience she wanted out of my wedding plans. She wanted us to go over every detail. She worried about the trimming on the cake, the colors of the chairs on the *Kosha*, and many other things, but I had no interest in anything except getting married and leaving as soon as humanly possible. "What about the flowers, what kind do you want?" "Pink would be good but really whatever you think." "Don't you want it to be perfect? Don't you want to be involved in the details?" "Since this elaborate wedding was not my idea and only came into being so Baba could show how Saudi he is and how poor Ata's family must be for them to not pay for it, I don't really care about the flowers, the cake, or anything except that it is done in the *Bukhari* style (Which was the name of our tribe) and *Uma* (meaning aunt on my father's side) Zakia will take charge when she arrives."

Looking back, I can see how she wanted so desperately to have her fairytale movie version of her first child's wedding, but she was living in a fantasy. She had no idea what I had to go through and why at some point, the little fluffy things do not tickle the mind of someone whose only thought, day in and day out, was finally being able to breathe.

My Aunt Zakia finally arrived a few days before the wedding to help with the preparations. I felt a relief of extreme magnitude as she took over everything, issuing order after order about the proper ways things get done in a traditional Bukhari wedding. Candles were bought for my sisters to carry on the day. They had to practice carrying them but after an hour of practice because of how young they were it was decided that they would carry them unlit on the day. "I don't want to risk burning the wedding down," my aunt said. She walked about the house examining every wedding item, expressing how the trunk we had bought to display my Shabka, or wedding jewels, to the guests was too bland. Then subsequently she went out and bought pink fabric, sparkle spray and all manner of craft items to spice it up. She was a master present wrapper. I had wrapped presents with her in Mecca and when she got her hands on some cellophane, she made it sing.

Ata and his family arrived in Riyadh a few days before the wedding. I had him saved in my phone as *Hiyate2* so that no one would suspect that we were still talking without supervision since officially we had never spoken without supervision. If the phone rang and someone saw his name, they would just think it was Noor. I was so excited and nervous that on the following day I would see him for the first time so close, and maybe even talk to him.

That night, the men arrived as normal in through the men's section as the women sat by, waiting for me to be called to serve the juice. In a way, the serving of the juice is something that was done to avoid embarrassment. If the girl entered and didn't like the boy she could leave as soon as the juice was served without the need to formally reject him. Virgins are often very shy, and shyness in the Arab world is a highly admired virtue and so traditions are put in place to help. For example, in the prophet Muhammed's (ﷺ) day, his wife, Aisha, said, "I asked the Prophet, "O *Allah's* Messenger (ﷺ)! Should the women be asked for their consent to their marriage?" He said, "Yes." I said, "A virgin, if asked, feels shy and keeps quiet." He said, "Her silence means her consent." In essence I was to enter and not say anything if I sat silently long enough it would be considered as my consent to the marriage after my guardian/*Mahram* had approved the match by asking for the juice to be served.

The time came and I put on my head cover since we were not yet married. He was still not allowed to see my hair but because there was a marriage being planned, seeing my face was permissible.

I recalled one previous suitor asking my stepdad if he could see what I looked like and my stepdad called for my little sister, age four Yasmin. and said, "Like this one, just whiter." The man frowned at the obvious insult. Basically, my stepdad told him you'll never see her, I don't approve but here is an example of what you will never have.

I made my way to the men's section carrying the juice, trying my best not to shake the tray, saying to myself, "You've got this, you have been preparing for this, you can do it." I walked through the sliding door, eyes cast down at the floor, using only their shoes to guide me as I served. It would be considered very brazen if I were to look up. Being in such proximity to him made me shaky and his dad laughed saying, "Put it down and sit, my dear." I was relieved. I sat and looked at him and then, as is custom, I looked away to give him a chance to gaze at me. Our fathers talked about details and so on and we continued with our shy gazing. Then my stepdad said to me, "I think you should retire to the women's section." Nodding, I did so without saying goodbye or goodnight, only slipping away like a silent dream that had sat for a moment in the men's section. The wedding was three days away, and the morning after I'd served the juice to the men we would sign the marriage contract … and this was the first time we had sat in the same room.

The next day we all woke up early and it was time to go to the courthouse to sign the marriage contract. This can be done in some rare cases at the actual wedding, but most families like to do it before the wedding to get the formality out of the way. Once signed I would be his wife and he would be allowed to see me without my headcover, but we would not be considered really married. To make it an official marriage: the contract, the consent of the *Mahram* for the couple to be wed; the dowry to be paid, and the celebration or announcement which was meant to alert the tribe that this woman was now married to this man, and finally, the consummation of that marriage. The contract was only a layer of the engagement, so to speak, and without the celebration or announcement, technically it could be dissolved as easily as it was made. The sad thing that we all knew is that this is never as we're told. We knew so many girls who were engaged and not even court married but when they broke off the engagement, as usual, people gossiped about how it was the girl's fault, what was wrong with her, and so on.

Therefore, we were all very careful not to enter into an engagement or contract marriage lightly.

I was frustrated that day because my stepdad had refused to let me go to a professional hairdresser and I had no idea how to use a curling iron. I made a mess of my hair and got angrier by the second. No one outside the two families was invited so I had to make do without Noor who would have made me look beautiful. It's often funny to me how quickly fear and panic can turn into anger. When I asked my stepdad to go to a hairdresser he said, "No, he must see you as you are. The real you, not a made-up doll." I finally gave up on my hair and we dressed in our abayas and headed to the courthouse.

At the courthouse I sat in the woman's waiting room in my modern abaya. While the other woman wore the more traditional abaya that started on the top of their heads as to not show the shape of their shoulders and their body since doing so as I did could still be considered by some more conservative Saudis just as bad as showing one's hair.

I recall once while I was in the *Souk* (market) buying something with my stepdad the religious police showed up. I was with my *Mahram*, I was fully veiled, and yet they came over to my stepdad and asked to have a word. My stepdad didn't need to say anything to me. I knew that I needed to stand back and be silent. "Who is this woman with you?" they asked. "*Binti* (my daughter)," my stepdad replied. The man touched his beard and said, "I see, well, I noticed her abaya hangs on her shoulders and I am sure you want her to be properly covered as she should be according to Islam. I am sure you're a reasonable father." Under normal circumstances if any other man had commented on my abaya, they would have met with my stepdad's wrath for even looking at me for a second, but no one dares talk back to the religious police, their authority is absolute. My stepdad looked at him and said, "*Sheikh* (a leader in a Muslim community, organization, tribe, family, or village), I completely agree and that is why we're here to get her a proper abaya. Her mother is American and bought her this one by mistake. You understand." "Of course, well on your way then. I'm sure the next time I see you she will be properly covered." My stepdad nodded and walked over to me slowly as he whispered, "Walk slowly, we need to get out of here before he comes back."

The ladies in the courthouse spoke to me and asked in Arabic if I was here to be married. I said, "*Naam*," which means yes. One woman looked at another and then turned to me and said, "Oh, the *Sheikh* recently refused to marry a girl wearing an abaya just like yours. He said she needed to be properly covered." Panicked, I asked them, "What should I do?" She said, "Take mine and bring it back when you're done, I will be an hour at least." Quickly we switched abayas and suddenly I was called to meet the Sheikh.

I entered the room where my stepdad, Ata, and his dad sat. They had all already spoken with the *Sheikh* and now it was time for my arrival. Upon entering the room, face covered and in a strange abaya, I was afraid Ata would not recognize me. I could have been any woman that he was marrying so I discreetly revealed my hands, hoping he would see my dolphin ring I was so fond of and know it was me.

I was all covered up. They could have switched me for another girl for all he knew since women are not asked to show their faces for any reason. Even a police officer cannot tell a man to ask a woman to show her face. It would be tantamount to war and even the marriage book that we would now receive would never have my picture in it, only my name. The *Sheikh* began by asking Ata if he would take this woman to be his wife and he said, "Yes," and I responded with only a nod as was proper, since a woman, especially a virgin, is not required to speak. Just like that, in less than five minutes, it was done. The paper was signed and now we were husband and wife. Marriage and divorce is simple in Saudi Arabia once all the conditions are met.

My stepdad and I returned to the house, and Ata and his dad went to pick up his mom to bring her over for lunch at our house to celebrate the new union of our families. Now he would be allowed to sit with me uncovered as a member of the family for the very first time. I kept worrying what if he didn't like me in real life? What if I wasn't as pretty as he expected me to be? Scared and alone in my head, the doorbell rang. My husband and his family had arrived.

My mom wore a modest, loose fitting traditional *thobe* dress (an ankle-length dress with long sleeves) and covered her hair to welcome and meet her new son-in-law. Under different circumstances my mother would not be required to cover her hair in front of her son in-law but because his dad would be in attendance for lunch my mother had to cover her hair. Customs are complex but let's try and make sense of this.

I married into Ata's family so that now made Ata my *Mahram* and his father became my father and a *Mahram* to me, just like my stepdad, but his brothers did not. I, too, would need to cover in front of his brothers. It was not uncommon if something were to happen to my husband and I had children, that one of the brothers would step up and offer marriage to keep the children in the family and under the protection of the family, tribe, clan, and so on. If we think back to old Arabia, we understand why this custom would have been the best solution.

Women did not take their husband's last names since last names would have included lineage. For example, the name was given to me when my stepdad adopted me and my brother was *Maha Bint Abdul Rasheed Ibn Abdul Ahad, Ibn Abudul Saad Al Tukistani*. While Al Turkistani is our last name it would read like this: *Maha* (first name) *Bint* (meaning 'daughter of') *Abdul Rasheed* (Father's name) *Ibn* (Son of) *Abdul Ahad* (Father's name) and so on. You see, it was a great way to figure out who someone was in the historical ages past, before paperwork, ID's, facial recognition, fingerprinting, and so on, because while there can be two Maha Al Turkistanis, there would only be one "you" based on your lineage. Based on what is written in Surah Al-Ahzab 33:5 in the Quran, we were taught that if you adopt a child, it is wrong to change their name, it is their identity, and they have the right to it. So, it is the same with wives I suppose since they too are being adopted into a family through marriage, they still hail from another. Although I have never come across any text that says not to change wives' surnames specifically, it is still how things were done in the days of the Prophet (ﷺ) and striving to follow his example is what we did. It was especially ironic, since I was adopted, and my name was changed completely, but we will get into the reasons for that later.

In historical Arabia when it was nothing but warring tribes and was very unsafe. Let's say you marry a girl from another tribe. She does not change her name so that her tribe can always find her. You probably also want to keep the name for political reasons after all, if you married a woman from a well-known family, would you not mention that your wife was from that family? Saudi Arabia is well known for marrying to build familial and cultural stability. This is how it was always done and changing a new wife's name didn't help. The children however would take their father's name. In the case of the death of a husband, if the wife was not married back into the tribe, she would need to return to her family tribe and the children would probably go with her. To honor the blood of the children which was of their father's tribe, one of the other male relatives would more than likely step up and marry her.

I slowly descended the stairs dressed in a long black dress that was stepdad-approved. Ata saw me and approached with a small jump in his step, bringing me an engagement ring with a yellow diamond that had been custom made just for me. Seeing it, I lowered my gaze and blushed deeply red, trying to control my breathing. I looked up and looked away again as he placed it on my hand. This was the very first time he had touched me. My mom and his mom sounded the wedding call, and we went into the living room where I handed him a gift I had picked out for him, as was customary. When he reached to open the sealed card I had written, I touched my nose, signaling he should read it alone later. He laughed and put it aside. Lunch was ready and we all sat at the table. He was seated beside me and as we dished our food, he fed me a bite from his spoon. I giggled and turned red since I had never been fed by a man. I was overjoyed with happiness, but my mom scolded me and said, "No." I looked at her and said, "But we're married now." My stepdad looked at me as if to say stop it and then turned to Ata's dad and said, "I want to speak about custody."

In Saudi a woman of any age was the property of her father or brother or uncle, or husband. Her *Mahram*, as it is called in Arabic, is the only one who allows her to go and come from the country or do anything, for that matter. My stepdad said, "I know normally it would pass to the husband once she is married but, in this case, since he is over 21 and holds a Canadian passport, he can only ever visit the country on a visit visa through you. One day you might not live here anymore and since we don't know where he will get a job in the future, I think it would be best if her custody stays with me so that I can insure she always has a visa to come and visit her family." His dad agreed and I thought nothing of it. All my planning, all my patience had finally paid off. I was happy and married and soon I would be on my way to Canada with the love of my life.

The next day came, and his family invited me to eat with them and spend a little time with Ata, but my family refused, not trusting that his family would supervise us properly. My stepdad said, "He can stop by here later for tea if he wants to see you. He's Syrian and we are Saudi. Don't forget who comes to who and who you are. Just because you're married to a Syrian doesn't mean you forget who you are." I took a deep breath and restrained any response. It was almost over I thought so I smiled and said, "Yes, *Baba*, and thank you for letting him stop by."

Ata came by later and we sat together in the men's sitting room talking and trying to steal hand touches as my parents sent my little brother and sister to sit in and spy on us. I repeatedly sent them away but with so many siblings and cousins staying over to attend the wedding they kept coming into the room, so he eventually left.

The next day was my wedding day and I wanted it to be perfect for myself and for Ata. I was beyond nervous about the wedding night but dared not speak to anyone about such a delicate topic. I had something to bring up with my mom, but she insisted it had to be discussed in front of my stepdad. They called me upstairs to their room and closed the door. There in their large walk-in closet my mom handed me a box of condoms as a wedding gift to which I screamed "Gross! Why!" my mom said, "Until you finish college you make sure he wears one all the time." I took the box and hung my head at the weirdness of the whole conversation. Since it was already awkward, I said, "Hey, I need to go to a salon to remove my hair." My stepdad said, "What hair?" I looked at my mom and said, "You know," looking for my mom to intercede on my behalf. She stayed silent and I said again, "You know…." he said, "No, I don't." I took a deep breath and said under my breath, "Down there, I don't know how to, so can I go?" To this my stepdad replied, "If he wants you, he should take you as you are. A girl intact just as you were made. End of discussion." I felt like I was stuck in the stone age. All my friends had teams preparing them, hairdressers, make-up artists, mani-pedis, full body waxing. I just really needed this one thing. As I solemnly walked to my bedroom, I knew this was too important. I refused to have a bush on my wedding night, so I had to do it myself.

That night, from 11:00 p.m. when everyone was finally asleep to 5:00 a.m. plucking my own pubic hair with my Braun Epilator, something I had never done before because it was such a sensitive area. With every hair I stopped and cried I could not see half the hair down there, so I repeatedly snagged my skin and bled every time. I had to keep going so I felt for more hair and continued, hoping it would be over soon. I knew it had to be done, my aunt said no hair. I had to be the perfect bride. How else would he love me? So much stock was placed in perfection, and I did my best to heed the wise advice of my aunt. Now it was time for everything she taught me to be put to use.

I finally got some rest and woke up around 8:00 a.m. It was the day of my wedding and, whether I was sleepy or not, I intended to enjoy it. *Omi* was staying with us for the wedding and called me over to her bed that was brought to the living room so she could hold court there, being the patriarch of the family and unable to easily climb the stairs. "*Binti* (My daughter) come here sit beside me." I made my way over and kissed her as is the custom. She was a very fat, round woman who laughed like an Asian cartoon character, her mouth being just the right shape like a slice of an orange. She handed me a box, opened it up, and as she pulled the necklace from the set of gold jewelry that she had brought me as a gift, she put the necklace around my neck and she said, "I know you don't have anything this big. Normally young girls like small things but it is very important that when you enter the wedding you are already wearing something very amazing. We don't walk around like maids with naked necks as if we can't afford to dress our women properly. Every woman in that room will be looking at you and judging all of us, so it's important that everyone can see that you come from a good family." She adjusted the necklace, so it was centered on my neck and added, "There, it's perfect. Then your husband can remove the necklace and replace it with the one from his house, making you officially now a member of his family." I was so happy for the last-minute gift and the wise words *Omi* had to offer. I could hear my Aunt Zakia's voice in them.

I was asked not to speak to Ata that day to make it all the more exciting when I saw him at the wedding in the evening. I wondered how it could be less exciting if I was talking to him. Since he had not even been close enough to kiss me yet but tonight he would be. Since it seemed important to my mother I obliged. It was a strange morning as I looked around the breakfast table, as I had the feeling like I was looking at everything for the first and last time. Everything seemed so vividly colored, and I tried to soak up the laughter of my siblings, the sound of *Omi's* voice, the smell of the Saudi coffee. It had just dawned on me that last night was the last night in my bed with my sisters in the room. It was the last morning I would get up to the coffee my stepdad had already brewed. I was really getting married. I realized that all the trouble I had navigated had made me disconnect in so many ways and now saying goodbye suddenly seemed harder than I thought. I held back my emotions and decided to pretend as if everything was normal because I didn't want to have my hopes smashed by my stepdad knowing full well that he could still find a way not to let me go.

Everyone was gathering the last-minute things that needed to go to the hall. The center pieces, the gifts, the champagne glasses that would hold the juice we would share for the first time as husband and wife. I took all my things to the hotel room and prepared it for our wedding night. I had purchased matching toothbrushes for us, a shaving kit for him in case he forgot his, special towels, robes, flowers, and candles to make it all so perfect just as I was taught. To think of everything and always be a good caring wife. First impressions never leave, they can be mended, my aunt would say, but never forgotten, so take care. This was to be our very first night as husband and wife and I intended to make it as perfect as I could.

After I was done beautifying the room, I managed to get in a good two-hour nap before a Filipino lady arrived to do my hair and makeup. My mom had hired her to do my sisters, my grandma, and my mother's hair as well. I do not recall how the misunderstanding occurred perhaps it was my mother forgetting to mention to my mother in-law that the lady would have no time to do anyone else before the wedding started, but my mother in-law arrived thinking that she would also be getting her hair done by the same lady and the lady said she would not have time. I felt bad for her as I watched her have to try and find a way to do her own hair on the day of her first son's wedding. As all of us crowded in the little dressing room getting ready, the videographer was capturing the preparations as I danced around in my little pink robe. I was so excited that tonight I would no longer belong to my stepdad and in three days I would be in Canada in my own home seeing and experiencing life.

Noor arrived just in time for photos and helped me with everything. I stood and posed in front of three massive different backdrops. Since it would never be possible for a bride to be photographed in a public park or in some flower garden where she could be seen, they had backdrops made that looked like I was in a Roman Colosseum or in a beautiful garden. Taking instruction from the photographer, I posed for more than 200 photos until suddenly I started to feel faint. The hot lights shined down on me and I realized I had forgotten to eat. I looked at Noor, who instinctively came over to see what I needed. I told her I felt like I was going to pass out and so she asked the photographer to wait a minute and ran to grab me a piece of chocolate from her room. Even on the eve of a great victory there is always a small chance that everything could go wrong, and even though I was beyond the moon, I was also wary that at any moment my stepdad still had a chance to pull the plug. The money he had spent on this wedding would be way less important to him when it came to making a point. The pride of my stepdad and many Saudis today is more important than anything, not to mention his other motivations for keeping me around.

We finished my photos and moved on to the family photos of me and my parents, me and my sisters and any other women from the family who wanted a picture with the bride. Friends who asked for a picture with the bride were restricted to only those who were trusted by the family not to show the picture to any male relation they had.

Finally, it was time for everyone to go down to the wedding hall to greet the guests. Noor sat with me as we waited for my entrance. Giggling and holding hands, then hugging, as we knew once I left for Canada there was always a chance that I might not see her again for a very long time. The wedding started at 9:00 p.m. but I was not expected to enter until 10:00 p.m. That plan was subject to the hall being full, or at least almost so. Arab time is where everyone arrives fashionably late on purpose. Although the party may start at 9:00 p.m., no one really arrives until 10:00 p.m. and even after that, some only like to arrive when the wedding is almost ready to go. The better to make an entrance.

For Americans it is considered rude to look your best in a wedding, "Don't outshine the bride," they say. In Saudi weddings this is not the case. Weddings are the best place to find mothers hunting for brides for their sons and the competition is fierce. Everyone always dressed in their best, most glamorous, and flashiest gowns that they could respectably get away with. Their hair done and dressed to wow; they would do their best to outshine everyone else in the hall. Brides, like myself and many I knew, never felt like it was rude of them. On the contrary, I hoped they could make a match so we could all be wives at the same time. After all, I was the bride, the spotlight, and all the eyes would be on me. We were taught that no one can outshine a bride and so it was.

The girls danced and talked and had tea until about 10:30 p.m. when finally, they called me down for my entrance. Noor departed from my side to enter the hall and take her place among the guests. We did not have bridesmaids like in the West, since there would be a wedding video seen by my stepdad and my husband and my father in-law and it would be impossible to include eligible women from respected families in the procession. My mother and grandmother helped me navigate the stairs one on each side, my mother on my left and my grandmother respectfully on my right side each holding one of my arms as I clutched my bouquet.

There were two grand entrances to the hall and a separate entrance for the guests. The first was a small gold door with a descending staircase, where I would enter. The other were the two large gold double doors where I would enter again with Ata. It is done this way to give the ladies lots of time to dance and have a good time with their friends before they would need to cover up when my new husband entered. The doors opened to the Arabic *Zaffa* song I had chosen by one of my favorite Saudi singers, Rashed Al-Majed, that talked about a beautiful bride making her entrance. Out went my little sisters Noura, Yasmin, and Lina, all carrying the ceremonial candles lighting my path. A tradition that is not necessarily done in every Saudi wedding but for us, the Bukhari's, it was.

Down the steps I came, pausing at regular intervals to give everyone a chance to get a close look at me so they could store a mental picture of what I looked like and so the photographer could capture her shot. Cell phones were prohibited in many weddings back then to stop people from snapping photos of other girls and having the photos fall into the wrong hands. My wedding was no exception to this rule. On the invitation was a note saying cell phones would not be permitted in the hall, and everyone understood why when they thought of their own daughters' and wives' reputations.

I recall looking out over the vast hall. The people, the Kosha, not knowing what to think as I walked, my mind went blank. I had been so used to being behind the scenes, cooking and serving, but never really being paid attention to until someone wanted to have a look at me or ask me a question. I was happy that way. Now, I was the one everyone was looking at. All the lights and the music were so loud, I concentrated on getting to my *Kosha* so I could gather myself.

The *Kosha* is different for each wedding, colored and designed by specialty companies who knew how to create these elaborate thrones to make sure every bride's dais was special and unique. Mine had two large, tufted chairs with gold trim with a small table between them. In the right corner on display was a beautiful wooden chest where my *Shabka* (wedding jewelry) would be on display for all the guests to see until the groom's arrival. The box also doubled as the place where guests could drop envelopes with money or gifts, which traditionally were gold jewelry. It is an interesting tradition in Saudi Arabia that it is not proper to open gifts in front of the guests. This applies no matter what the occasion might be - a birthday party, an engagement party, or a get-well gift from a friend. The reason was that firstly everyone would be judged by what they bought. Arabs love to gossip. To save your guests from the embarrassment of being shown up by the others we waited to open the gifts until everyone had departed. Secondly, not everyone is good at smiling and pretending they love a certain gift, and everyone would be looking for micro expressions. To avoid hurting anyone's feelings all gifts were opened in private.

I had not seen the hall since the morning when my aunt came down to do all the finishing touches. Everything was pink and white, two of my favorite colors, and even though I was barely involved in the planning it was as lovely as I imagined it would be.

When I reached the *Kosha*, I sat on the upholstered settee as the ladies lined up to wish me congratulations, tell me how beautiful I looked, always adding the word *MashAllah* (Meaning basically *By the grace of God*) afterwards. In Saudi Arabia, although they have tried to do away with superstitions, what we called *Al-Aayoun* (The Eyes) is still very much a part of the culture. Similar to the Evil Eye in Egypt, without the wearing of an eye talisman. Instead, for protection we wear Quran verses or the word *Allah* (God) in our gold jewelry. It is a secret insult to go up to anyone and say how beautiful they are without adding the word *MashAllah*. In a way it invokes the good nature of your compliment. Not adding that phrase is like saying, "You're so beautiful and I hope you fall on your face." When you add *Mashallah*, you invoke that *Allah* granted you this gift and you wish them no ill will.

Because I was the bride it was one of those rare occasions when I was not required to stand for anyone except a very important person in the family such as my new mother-in-law, my grandma, or my mom, out of great respect. The reason for this exception was that they did not want the bride to tire early. Wearing such a heavy gown and obviously very nervous, as most virgin brides are, it was decided it was best for the bride to save her strength and avoid fainting, which can be very embarrassing.

Once the greeting was done, I walked down to the center of the hall. It is always a big moment when the bride moves in a wedding. I can't explain it, but as she stands, the ladies jostle each other in their excitement to look up and see what she is about to do. As I reached the center of the hall my mom had a big, pink birthday cake brought out and all my friends and family gathered to sing happy birthday to me, first in English and then in Arabic, as my 20th birthday had been the day before. I smiled and cut the cake as my mom distributed the pieces to the guests. I returned to the raised stage. My friends danced on the floor in front of me to celebrate my wedding. I was starving and decided I would have to wait for a really great song before I ventured down the stairs since I had only had the one piece of chocolate to eat that day. I danced a few dances with Noor before they came to tell me I would be leaving now to meet my husband, Ata.

My face went white. Suddenly it was actually happening. Noura my little sister leaned in toward my mom and asked if I would be coming home with us later, to which my mother replied no, she won't be coming home again, she is going to her husband's house now. Noura realized for the first time that I was leaving, and I would never again stay up late at night to play *Barbies*, help her make fun of little Yasmin, color together, and our sticker collecting and cooking together. I was leaving and I wasn't coming back. Her heart broke and she began to weep the kind of tears only the true broken heart of a child can shed.

My mom brought her to me and said she was sad. I held everything, even heading to the door to meet my now husband, to take time to speak with her and explain what my mom had not explained. That I would be back to visit, maybe even stay over sometimes, I just had to go for a little bit, but she could write to me. She shook her head and said, "Mama will read them." I asked her if she remembered the code we used to write in? She said, "Yes." I replied, "There, you see. Just write to me in code. This way only you or I can decipher it. I promise to call as often as I can and to never really be gone." She stopped crying and I stood up, indicating I was ready for my mother-in-law to walk me back through the hall to be handed over to my husband.

My mother-in-law took my arm and the music started again. I walked to the two double doors that led to a small corridor that eventually led to the buffet area and the men's side of the hall, where all the men had been having coffee and celebrating in their own way. The men's section in Riyadh was often seen as a rather dull side. There was hardly ever any music, just men sitting together while sipping coffee, and smoking. In Jeddah however, often the men were known to have their own music and to dance with each other celebrating, dancing with swords, and twirling prayer beads. The reason for such a difference between Riyadh and Jeddah is complex, but I will try to give you the short version.

When the Prophet Muhammad (ﷺ) was alive, he united the people, not just as a Prophet (ﷺ) and not just in religious matters, but as a judge and leader in battle. When he died in 632 A.D, many people began to fall back into superstitious practices and tribal war. Although the first four *Khalifa's* after Muhammad, Abu Bakar, Umar, Uthman, and Ali, were early followers of Muhammed and great leaders devoted to Islam, in my mind, each one lacked something that Muhammad had. They were, however, instrumental to the continuation of Islam. Without them, the Quran being recorded into the book we have today, the actions of Muhammad that were recorded in the *Hadith* by Sahih Al Bukhari might have never occurred and the lunar or *Hijrah* calendar that they use today would have never come into being. As time went on and the power shifted from one *Khalifa* (successor or leader after The Prophet Muhammad (ﷺ)) to the other, people started to return to their old ways. You see, before the Prophet Muhammad (ﷺ) the Saudis were pagans and the *Kaaba* (the black box every Muslim prays toward) was actually a place where all the idols were housed. Often, baby girls were buried alive for fear that they would someday bring shame on their family, should they be allowed to live. Following his death there were many, many, years where there was distrust, tribal wars, and each tribe tended to follow its own version of Islam. There was one man who finally brought back some religious unity and that man was named Muhammad Ibn Abdul Wahhab, which is where we get the name for *Wahhabis* [leader] today.

In 1744, Muhammad Ibn Abdul Wahhab joined forces with, Muhammad Ibn Saud. If you don't recognize the name, let's just say that Saudi Arabia might be the only country I know named after a family - Saudi Arabia. Even though the story is more complex than this and the fact that Muhammad Ibn Saud was not the first king of modern-day

Saudi Arabia, uniting the two created a kind of great stability between the strict call to return to the true path of Islam by Ibn Abdul Wahhab and the leadership of Ibn Saud.

Modern day Saudi Arabia could never exist today, in my mind, if these two had not united. They maintain this unity today by marriage. Years later stability would come, but *Wahhabism* would unfortunately hold the country back from joining the modern world. The *Wahhabis* are very strict religious people and Ibn Abdul Wahhab's call for the return to Islam turned out to be a call to stay in the past. Anyone caught questioning *Wahhabism* would be arrested for causing disruption. A world without questions becomes a world without knowledge, and a world without knowledge remains stuck in the past. If you don't move into the future, you get left behind.

When King Abdul Aziz took Jeddah in 1925 (Yes, as recent as that) the city asked that he not allow the *Ikhwan* (religious police as they are known today) force to rule with an iron fist. They liked the way their lifestyle was and didn't want to change. Abdul Aziz also knew that his country could no longer be isolated from the modern world and protecting the foreigners in the port city of Jeddah on the Red Sea from the religious *Ikhwan* was very important to that dream, so he agreed to keep them at bay as best he could. This is why in Riyadh the religious police are much more strict then in Jeddah. If you ask me how the religious police came into being I would say it was because a wise ruler wanted to give them something to do. The *Ikhwan* were *Wahabis*, and as such, are loyal to the Al Saud family. They also had 150,000 men willing to die for their religion. Let's just think about this for a moment … that is not a group of people you don't want to remain loyal. When King Abdul Aziz began to make alliances with infidel countries (as the *Ikhwan* considered them) like Great Britain, they started to get restless, and you know what they say about idle hands. They often would run off without permission from King Abdul Aziz and attack towns when they were not given some cause to occupy them.

When I was young there was a famous advertising campaign that used the slogan *Jeddah Ghaair* (Jeddah is different) and it was true. We all used to marvel at the stories of couples being allowed to sit in cafes in

Jeddah without being questioned if they were married or not. Women were allowed to sit in hookah/*shisha* cafes and of course we admired the women in Jeddah who would chase religious police down the street with their shoes held high ready to beat them for even thinking they could tell them what to do.

In Riyadh, however, no one dared. The religious police had the complete authority to pick up anyone who was not being a good Muslim. Sometimes when you absorb or take a city and unite it as part of your country or territory, you need to have the wisdom to respect their unique way of life. Otherwise, you run the risk of that city breaking off at some point in the future. The reality is that the people of Riyadh have always been more conservative than the people in Jeddah. In short, the religious police would gladly interrupt the men's side of a wedding in Riyadh, but if they heard music coming from a wedding in Jeddah, they probably would walk on by.

I arrived at the men's side and stepped through one side of the double doors. As I looked up, there he was, smiling and looking at me without looking away, even for one second. I quickly looked down at the floor, wishing in equal measure for him to stop staring and that he would never stop staring. I timidly moved closer. He put out his arm and I placed mine in his. I had never been so close to him, never smelled him, never really touched him. All I remember is feeling like I was soaring on the wings of birds. Noticing that he was as nervous as I was came as a relief. He adjusted his jacket, cleared his throat, and gave me a smile. I blushed and looked down since I was not used to making eye contact with any men.

All the while I was greeting Ata, my grandmother, and Aunt Zakiah, who were running around the hall shouting, *"Al-Aarese! Al-Aarese!* (The Groom! The Groom!)" to let all the women know that they should run and get their Abayas, headcovers, and veils on before the doors opened. Once the women were appropriately covered, the double doors were swung open to reveal us to every female guest standing by, waiting to see the wedding couple take their first steps as husband and wife. A few adjustments, a photo taken, the videographer ran to get the right angle for the double doors, and the wedding call commenced.

The wedding call (In Arabic, *Zaghrouta*) is a sound almost like a bird call. An old Bedouin tradition, it is made by pushing out an "ooooooooo" sound and moving your tongue back and forth at the same time, creating a "Lo lo lo lo lo" sound. It's origin can be traced back to the pre-Islamic era, when it was practiced collectively by women asking the idols for relief, mercy, rain, and everything else. It was also used to excite the troops on the battlefields. Some of us are better at it than others, the older ladies can often project their call very far. The calls continued as we walked to the *Kosha*, all the while making short stops for people to look at us and so the photographer could take some shots. When we reached the *Kosha* I bashfully looked down as I reached for his arm to help me up the three marble steps. All our parents came up for a quick photo before leaving us to the ceremony. The only men who were allowed in the hall at this time were the ones that I could not marry, customarily my stepdad, biological uncles (if I had any), grandfathers, brothers, and now my husband, and his father.

Ata was asked to remove the jewelry I was wearing and then to dress me with the new gold jewelry that was part of my dowry. He took a deep breath in his comic way and wrung out his hands as if he was warming up for a fight. The girls laughed. Everyone knew that this was always one of the trickiest parts of the ceremony since most men had no experience undoing clasps and clips of this nature. Luckily, all the family was there to laugh and give him verbal instruction as he struggled with my necklace. Once it was off and safely placed in the box, the wedding call started up again as he dressed me in my dowry.

As he placed the new necklace around my neck his face got as close to my face as he had ever been. Our eyes met for what seemed like an eternity. Everyone in the room faded away. Then suddenly he moved back, and I remembered who I was and where I was. I looked down, giggled, the crowd roared, and everyone clapped. Then it was on to the juice. Two glasses of pink sparkling juice were brought out for us to sip, my arm locked in his arm. It was the closest our lips had ever been. When I recall it now, it was almost like the whole wedding was designed to put us in situations, now that we were married, that were meant to build up some kind of sexual tension but all I thought of was how much love I saw in his eyes as well as how happy I was and how excited I was to start our life together.

The DJ played a famous Nancy Ajram song and we danced. The ladies were all surprised as Ata actually danced on the floor to the music. Most grooms only seem to want to bob back and forth to show that they did their duty. My love of dancing was something Ata and I had never discussed. I was so happy to see that he danced. We danced two songs as my stepdad kept signaling "enough." I purposely ignored him. I was married now so I thought, "Pshaw"... suddenly it was midnight. If we were to get the cake cut before everyone left, we would need to get a move on.

We walked towards the doors to the buffet hall and proceeded to cut the cake. This always declared the buffet open. It was an unwritten rule. We then retired upstairs to have our photographs taken as husband and wife. Now semi-alone, with only a few people around, Ata whispered to me how much he loved me and kissed me on the forehead. My stepdad then came up with my family to get a family photo for the mantle. Sadly, the sight of him standing next to Ata concerned me because I worried there might be an outburst. I was very uncomfortable, causing all the photographs to show me as displeased or unhappy. Whereas when his family took a picture with us, I smiled so as not to offend my new family.

Party over and photos done, it was now time for us to retire to our room. My stepdad and new mother-in-law noted that if we wanted to walk to the room, we would need to cross a small hallway that was visible to the hotel reception desk. The decision was made to cover me with my black head scarf. The family followed us down the small hallway to the room, which was tradition. In some cases, especially among the Bedouin tribes, they even wait outside the door for the groom to come out with a blood-stained napkin, or handkerchief. The groom would then twirl it around as the family cheered for the consummation of the marriage. Thankfully my family had done away with this tradition years ago. They wished us goodnight and Ata lifted me over the threshold into the room and shut the door.

I went directly to the bathroom to change out of my wedding dress and into my white nightgown. Ata remarked on how pretty I had made the room look. I spoke to him through the door, "Oh, thank you, do you really think so?" The hairdresser had explained how to remove the pins from my hair which would allow the curls to just fall, this way I would have a second look for my wedding night. After removing all the pins and refreshing my make up, I realized that no one had shown me how to get out of the dress … in a state of panic, I sat in the bathroom for a moment and then called Ata to help me undo my dress. He unzipped me and I darted straight back into the bathroom.

Once I was ready in my white silk nightgown I put on my pink robe and came out. He came over and kissed me. He took me back into the bathroom he used the mirror to take a selfie of him holding me. Taking me to the bed for our required activity I felt my breathing escalate, not out of excitement but out of sheer panic. He took off his pants as I looked away. Then he kissed me and tried to get himself in, but it was too tight. The pain was so extreme and thinking it might get worse, my body suddenly shut down and I collapsed.

I only recall waking up hours later with him holding me in his arms. The sight of him holding me made me feel so safe. "I'm so sorry," I said to which he said, "We have plenty of time, let's go to sleep." It felt as though it was one of the safest slumbers I had had in years. It is incredible how differently you sleep when there is not the ever-present threat of someone who is supposed to be watching out for you entering your room in the dark and abusing you.

The next morning, we received a visit from our mothers. It was traditional for the mothers to visit the morning after and bring breakfast so that they could confirm everything went well. They came, ate, and then we packed to go spend the last few days with his family since we would soon leave for Canada. Ata wanted to spend as much time with his family as possible before we left. My stepdad drove us to my new in-law's apartment and said he would like to have us for dinner the night of our departure before we left, and we agreed.

That night we ate with my in-laws. They were so different from my stepdad's family, but I enjoyed my time. They had a little swimming pool in the apartment building that they rented for the wedding. The pool was at the bottom of the building and had no windows. It could be rented by the hour so that women could enjoy the pool as well. His parents rented it for us, and we swam for the first time together. We kissed and kissed but when it came time to complete the deed, I was still too tight for entry. We decided to give it a little more time.

The next day Ata asked me what I wanted to do. The first thought that came to my mind was to visit my friend, Ghadah, at her house. I had never been allowed to just go and visit a friend without all kinds of red tape, protocols, and procedures that needed to be upheld. Ata agreed without a second thought. I got on the phone and got the directions to her house. Unfortunately, I have never been good with directions, so I got us lost. Ata asked to get the directions from Ghadah himself, but I refused to hand over the phone until I was sure she was comfortable talking to a man who was not her husband or her *Mahram*.

She laughed and said, "I don't mind as long as you don't mind. He is your husband." I handed Ata the phone and he drove me there. How wonderful it was to have someone who just wanted me to be happy. I spent a few hours with Ghadah. It was so good to see her. She was one of the kindest and most soft-spoken people I had ever known. I was sad that she had married the wrong person and ended up back in her parents' house, divorced. Marked by the community as damaged goods, there was always a hint of sadness hiding somewhere in her, but she always smiled and was grateful, humble, and content.

We returned to Ata's parents and his two brothers, Aymen and Ahmed, who, although very young, still required me to cover my hair in their presence. His brother was already considered a man at the age of twelve. In Islam, technically a boy becomes a man when he has his first wet dream, and a girl, likewise, once she gets her period. In Saudi it was not uncommon to start making a girl cover at the age of nine and to restrict the boys from entering the women's section from a similar age. Ata's family, however, did not really abide by many of the Saudi customs; they followed only what they believed was the right way, Islamically.

Their life seemed so drama-free and it made me wonder what kind of family I had been living in all those years. I watched them laughing. I took note of the stories of their family in Canada that I was about to meet. How the men and women would gather at times for a meal together. For *Eid* (the festival at the end of Ramadan) they would attend grand parties at the mosque. There was an Islamic school where my mother in-law used to teach. "*Khala Sumaya,* do women talk to men in Canada, even strangers? "Yes, why not, otherwise how would I get anything done? Here the men do most of the work outside, but in Canada, you will need to share the work with your husband sometimes. After all, the first Muslim women, like the Prophet's first wife, Khadija, did. She worked outside the house, ran her own business, made business deals, and it was no problem. "Maha, my dear, did your parents not tell you a lot about her and the women in Islam?" Out of embarrassment I gave my mother in-law a blank stare and she continued, "Well, no matter, you will learn a lot while you are there and remember that in Islam, a woman can speak to men and even make eye contact, as long as the purpose is honorable. Much of Saudi Arabian Islam is mixed with old customs and ways of doing things not the actual Islam." I nodded and thought of how glad I was that she didn't say any of this in front of my parents. My stepdad, even if he knew she was right, would have "blown a gasket" just for the fun of calling it an insult to his way of life.

I wondered why my parents never allowed or even encouraged me to read Islamic texts and interpret them for myself. I wished while I was in school learning Arabic that I had taken more Islamic classes to help with my transition into a new world and a new family lifestyle.

If I had to compare the type of Islam I grew up with to their kind of Islam, I suppose Saudi Islam in my family was like Catholicism while theirs was more like Protestantism. For us, religious doctrine, understanding, and interpretation was best left to the learned *Shakahs, Muftis, Judges,* and your *Mahram*, be it your father, uncle, grandfather, or brother. Theirs was to read, learn, debate, ask questions, and then to go spread what they had learned.

In a girl's college in Riyadh today, there is a mandatory college course called, *A Woman's Place in Society*, and I think that says it all. I was brought up to follow not lead, listen not question, learn not explore, and memorize not analyze, for in these graces I would find safety.

My mother-in-law was the most outspoken Muslim liberal woman I had ever met, and I was curious to learn from her. The next day Ata and

I wasted time in the market picking up last minute gifts for his friends in Canada, and then we headed to my parents' house to have the final dinner before we departed for Canada that night. When sex is off the table for a little bit, making out and necking is not. Ata had managed to give me my first few hickeys, which I was very proud of since, do I need to say it, I was married.

My parents, on the other hand, were less than pleased when I arrived and there was a big purple mark on my neck. My mom was shocked and asked me straight out in front of my little brothers and sisters, "What's that on your neck?!" I looked at her, wondering how she would like me to answer, because I was standing in front of the children. If I didn't answer I would get the third-degree until I did, and if I did answer, I would be asked how I could talk of such things in front of them. I thought for a second, reached up, touched my hickey, and said, "What do you mean? Oh, this… I must have left the window open, maybe it's a mosquito bite." My mother stared me down as I changed the subject. My dad interceded and said, "Where were you the last two days?" to which I answered, "With my husband and his family." He said, "You were supposed to be here every night for dinner and lunch!" I said, "We agreed that we would come for dinner the night of our departure and so we are here." He argued that that was not what was agreed upon. He asked what I had been doing the last two days. I said, "Ata took me to visit my friend Ghadah." My stepdad clinched his teeth, which always caused his upper cheek bones to flinch, invariably meaning he was very, very angry. I was not afraid anymore. I was married, I had a protector, I was untouchable now.

I said, "Well, are we going to eat?" My stepdad said, "You're late so there is no dinner." I shrugged my shoulders and said, "Okay, well then, I'll just go get my bags from upstairs." Ata said he would come and help but my stepdad answered by addressing me, insinuating that Ata was beneath him. "He can wait downstairs; husbands are not allowed upstairs." Ata not wanting to escalate things further, sat.

I went up and finished closing my bags. As I lifted them up and turned to the door, there was my stepdad. I said, "I have to go now, or we'll miss our flight." He said, "You have been so disrespectful and inconsiderate to your mom and your brothers and sisters." I said, "Okay, well I have to go now." He said, "You're not going anywhere until I say so." I said, "You can't keep me here anymore, I'm married." He laughed and said, "Ha! Do you remember when his father and I agreed not to transfer your residency and guardianship over to your husband since he was not a Saudi and could only come on a visit visa?" My mind moved fast, and I realized what was coming next.

I changed my strong stance and moved back a step. He continued, "You see, Princess, one phone call to the airport and you'll just be brought right back here. Husband or no husband you're under my guardianship." I said, "Well you know what? I'm still leaving, I'm done." I tried to pass him, and he grabbed my arm. I started to scream for Ata, but he covered my mouth. When I fought back, he threw me against the bed, my left leg banging against the sideboard, leaving a large purple mark. I sat on the floor crying as he stared at me and left the room. I picked up my bags and walked down the stairs to Ata. He asked what was wrong. I looked at my stepdad and said nothing. Ata said, "Well, I guess we should be going." My stepdad said, "Yes, let's go!"

My stepdad grabbed both my suitcases and threw them violently into the car. My whole family loaded in the car and Ata sat in the front. My stepdad sped down the highway angrier than a predator that had just had his prey stolen from him. I stayed silent; we all did. We had all seen him this way before and we all knew not to make a peep. My mom held Lina and looked down as I stared out the window. Noura and Mohammed shrugged down in their chairs so as not to be seen.

The last time he drove like this was in Ramadan. A man cut my stepdad off and as he drove past, issued a disrespectful hand gesture. You might think it was the finger, but in the Arab world we have many hand gestures that can mean many things, most of them very disrespectful. In this instance, the man leaned out his window. Palm flat, he gestured that my stepdad should get out of the way. Almost like when you shoo a fly away. My stepdad did not take insults or disrespect very well. Then again, neither does any other Saudi man I know or Arabic man for that matter. Their blood runs hot and so they are prone to outbursts. It's the women who are known for their calm tact, even with insults. We tend to always be composed and able to render the same amount of insult back but without making a scene.

That day when the man cut him off, my stepdad sped up and chased the man down, cutting him off, forcing the man to stop. He stepped from the car in the middle of the busy intersection, holding up traffic. My stepdad removed the black rope-like item called an *Igal* that would sit on the top of his *Ghatrah*, which is an Arab man's headdress. The Saudi male headdress is normally red and white checkered or just plain white. He reached into the man's car and pulled the man out and beat him right there on the side of the highway while people slowed down and gawked as they drove by. In Saudi Arabia people tend not to interfere in conflicts regarding two males, assuming it was none of their business. We were all too scared to remember what was said but when it was over, we all knew that none of us wanted to be the first to speak and we never asked why he beat the man.

In much of the Arab world, but especially in Saudi, no cop is likely to reprimand a Saudi for beating up, even ever so slightly, another man who was a Saudi, and especially not if a Saudi beat up another one of the working-class nationalities. Respect was important to everyone; fights happened and as long as the man was not related to the royal family or beaten so badly that he could not work and provide for his family, it would be an open and shut case. You can put a barbarian in a suit and give him a briefcase, but he will still be a barbarian.

That night, the night of my departure, was no different. He drove like a crazy person, he didn't get stopped for speeding. The explanation would be the same reason why if you stopped at a red light, you could always see tens of cars that kept on going. Have you ever heard the expression, "*He who has the gold makes the rules....*" Well, welcome to the Kingdom of Saudi Arabia where the more money you have, the less the rules apply to you. I'm not saying my stepdad had a lot of money, but he knew how to bluff really well. Afterall, with a royal family as big as it is, what traffic cop wants to accidently stop the wrong prince for something as trivial as speeding.

Once again, like so many things, instead of making it a happy occasion, one to remember, my stepdad found a way to rip away a piece of my happiness as he had always done. A saying he always used to say was, "You can't be happy all the time. It will put you in danger because you will not be paying attention to the world around you. Life is hard and you must be harder."

We finally arrived at the airport. My stepdad continued his huffing and puffing as I hugged my mom and brother and sisters goodbye. He carried the luggage into the terminal with Ata, and violently tossed my bags on the conveyor belt. My face was covered as I said goodbye to him. He walked away without saying a word. We were finally on our way through security. As soon as we passed passport control, I felt a huge weight lifted from my soul, I was safe now, I thought …. We sat and I put my head on Ata's shoulder. He asked me what happened, and I said, "We had a fight and he's being stupid. Let's talk about it later."

CANADA

The plane ride was long and when I went into the bathroom, I saw the purple bruise that Ata would surely see once we arrived. My mind went through all the possible scenarios about how Ata was going to react. I just wanted to put it all behind me. I knew he would threaten to kill my stepdad and would want to call him and yell at him. If I refused, then I was not allowing him his right to protect his wife. I was so tired of all the hurt. People hurting people, would it ever end? I just wanted to be happy, forget about everything, and move on but it felt like it was too much to ask for.

In Saudi Arabia women boarded the plane in traditional full black Abaya, head cover and veil, but once the plane was in the air they often changed into traveling clothes. Travel clothes normally included a long jacket of color like an abaya and a matching head scarf Women often ditched the veil. It was also common to see fully veiled women enter an airplane bathroom and come out in crop tops and shorts once they were sure no one who knew them would see them. So many Saudi women, with their husband's permission like my Uncle Fahad's new bride, would fly to a foreign country and wear bikinis. They would keep it a secret from the rest of the family. I saw a picture once by accident and let's just say a part of me was kind of envious at what it must have felt like while another part of me was appalled.

When we landed, we were greeted by Ata's dad's cousin who lived in Mississauga, located in the Ontario province, and the general area where our apartment was to be. I sat in the back seat as they jabbered about how Ata's dad was and caught us up on all the family news. I stared at all the green trees and thought how pretty but oh so different

Canada was. I had grown accustomed to the tall buildings of the city, the noise of the cars at night, the dusty sandstorms and the sound of the prayer call five times a day. I smiled and thought of my new apartment, a home of my very own! Suddenly the car stopped. "We're here," said his uncle, looking at me as I looked down out of respect.

I looked all around my new neighborhood. There were three apartment buildings close together about 10 floors high and each apartment had a small metal balcony that was rusting and the white paint on the building had started to peel. If I had to describe it today, I would say it was not a great neighborhood but back then my innocent little eyes only saw home and knew nothing about what constitutes a good neighborhood or a bad outside of Saudi Arabia. We went up the elevator and down the narrow hall and as Ata unlocked the door, he mentioned that he had not yet put together the bed before he left to which I said, "No worries, I'll help you!"

We entered the apartment and walked into the living room. The window was open and there was a smell of rot. Ata's cousin asked, "What is that smell?" and Ata said, "Oh, I must have forgotten to take out the trash!" Walking to the other side of the kitchen I saw the trash bag open and the window open. The flies had laid eggs that had turned into maggots. I had never seen a maggot before, but I immediately started to pick up the trash bag to get it out of the house. Ata's cousin took the bag from me and said, "Ata, take this out."

It was hot in the house, so I asked where the air conditioner was, and the reply was that in Canada we did not have air conditioners because the summers were mild and very short. I found the fan and used it to air out the smell. A part of me questioned how anyone could live without an air conditioner since in Saudi there would have been no surviving the summer without one. I had no idea that people lived in countries without air conditioning. The apartment was a very open layout with the living room directly to your left, the kitchen to your right and a small dining room area past the kitchen leading to the balcony door. Straight down to the right was the bathroom and to the left of the bathroom was the bedroom. The floors were linoleum that imitated wood. I recall thinking the apartment was very cute.

Before departing, Ata's cousin invited us to a big family lunch in honor of our wedding, and we happily accepted. Ata went into the bedroom to start putting together the bed. The house had no other furniture besides the bed and a desk. He avoided buying much so that we could pick out the furniture together. I watched him sweating and getting mad at the screws as he put together the bed. I thought to cheer him up by bringing him a glass of water, to which his response was, "Put it over there." I went back into the living room so I would not be in his way and noticed a pile of clothes on the floor, so I sat and began to fold them. I was happy to be able to help until the bed was ready.

Once he was done, we put the sheets on, took a shower and went to bed. The daytime in Canada is the nighttime in Saudi, so we slept most of the day and night being so tired from the wedding and the journey. I woke up around 4:30 in the morning. I slipped out of bed as I had been taught, to wash my face, brush my teeth, and put on my makeup so that when my husband woke up, he would see his beautiful wife all made up like she had fallen asleep that way. He could, after all, not see me in the daylight without my face on. He would be happier if he woke up and found me perfect as I should be. I got back in bed.

Thirty minutes later he did not wake, so I reached over and kissed him saying, "Good morning," he gowned and said, "I'm sleeping." At the time I had no idea he was not an early riser as I was. Unable to sleep, I got up and looked around the house for something to do. There was no television, no cell phone, and a computer sat in the corner, but I did not have the password for it yet.

In my little nightgown and in full makeup I decided to clean the floor but there was no mop, so I found a bottle of Windex and a roll of paper towels. Segment by segment I wiped the floor on my hands and knees until all the dust was gone, all the while thinking, when Ata sees this clean floor, he will be so happy with me.

He woke up but he did not notice the floor. He asked me why I had my makeup on so early and I could not understand what I had done wrong. I thought maybe I just needed a lesson in makeup. Noor always used to tell me how clumsy I was with mascara. The truth was we had been speaking and getting to know each other but we didn't really know each other at all since the customs and lifestyle that each of us found to be normal was foreign to the other and when you normalize something in your mind and in your life, you often forget that it could be very foreign to others. We were strangers who knew each other well and my life experience was sorely lacking in comparison to his.

Finally, the time came for us to really consummate our marriage. I could see the doubt in his eyes that I was a virgin at all, since even though I told Ata my stepdad never had me in that way, I would not be the first girl to lie about her virginity. At the institute I heard stories about Saudi girls who would travel to Lebanon to have a surgery that would revirginize them because they had made a mistake somewhere. Their parents took great care to cover it up. Why would anyone want to be a virgin again? The answer lies in the poor girls who were not virgins on their wedding night. The best possible outcome would be that her husband would quietly divorce her giving some other reason as to why. The second possible outcome was that her husband would divorce her publicly bringing with it the shame and dishonor that accompany her and her family for the rest of their lives. If she is lucky that's all that happened... If she was unlucky, she could be beaten first by her new husband and then by her family and if she was semi-lucky that would be all that would happen. Worst case scenarios involve the husband calling the religious police or just the family talking about turning her over or stoning her to death themselves. While in America they have abstinence clubs we have a lot of good reasons to protect what my grandmother called "our white dresses" from blemishes.

He tried again and I tried to relax, as he was finally entering it was too painful and still no blood came out. Finally, my brain said, "This can't go on, this thing has to break." I pulled him down onto the bed, took the KY jelly and sat down on him slowly. He helped me go up and down until finally it was all in and just as it did, the blood rushed out. He laughed and said, "Well, you're not a virgin anymore, *Habibti*" (meaning my love (feminine). The male version is *Habibi*). I thought, "Thank goodness it's over!" and "Geez, if having sex for the first time is this painful, I hope I never have kids!"

We cleaned up and I dressed for lunch with Ata's extended family. All the clothes purchased for my new life were chosen by my stepdad. They were very conservative since I would no longer be wearing my abaya. I had a long velvet violet jacket that I used to cover my tight jeans and a white headscarf that I thought was very flattering. Ata looked at me and said, "Don't you have anything else to wear? It's too conservative!" I shook my head and said, "All my clothes are like this. I was taught that I should not show my shape, my beauty is for you alone." He shrugged and said, "We will have to get you some less conservative clothes later, let's go" and we started off to lunch with his extended family.

I was a ball of nerves. New people, new place. They were Syrian Canadian, and their customs were very different from what I was used to in Saudi as my mother-in-law had made me aware of before we left Riyadh. I was determined to make a good impression since this was my new family. We arrived at a duplex where two of Ata's dad's cousins had bought houses side by side so they could live close to each other.

In every Arab culture they share a love and need for family. In old times, which were really not that long ago, the protection of the tribe was necessary to their survival but that soon turned to family, and this is why they tend to move together, migrate together, and live close to each other. Building these small little communities, just like Greeks, Jews, and Chinese, allowed them to look out for each other. This was something Ata's family and I had in common.

I didn't know much about Islam despite being raised in it. I knew enough to be able to pass as if I did and I was brought up to be a good Muslim girl and pray when they prayed. I knew my basic prayers and could lead the women's prayer if needed. Above all, I knew when Islam was discussed how to listen and agree with whoever was the eldest and the most respected in the group.

For this occasion and many to come, one house was to host the women and one the men so that the women could relax without their head covers and chat at their leisure. Likewise, the men enjoyed the ability to talk about things the women wouldn't normally discuss like the economy, housing prices, the cost of living, and the great old days when they all lived in Syria.

Some of the women had jobs and some of them were doctors when they were in Syria. They were all loud and outspoken, even shouting that lunch was ready for the men to come and collect their dishes so they could eat in the other house. I recall thinking, "Goodness, a woman shouting at a man loud enough that the people on the street could hear, how unladylike." Despite all that, it was nice to see that no one was fighting, everyone was talking and happy to be there.

They asked about my wedding and how Ata heard of me, and I stuck to the official story since his parents only knew that he had heard of me from his friend's sister. Lunch was served and it was packed with all kinds of Syrian food. I had never seen or had Syrian food before and a lot of it seemed strange. I could not believe that I missed the large platter of rice topped with lamb my Aunt Hind would serve every Friday at my uncle's house, but I was excited for the new food adventure.

The ladies remarked that everyone brings a dish to these lunches but since I was a new bride still setting up my home, they would let me off the hook and everyone chuckled. There were so many interesting new things to eat. In fact, we rarely ate hummus when I was young, but it seemed to be a staple for them. All our *Bukhari* food, with the exception of the newly adopted Saudi dishes of meat and rice, were almost reminiscent of Chinese food. We ate a dumpling dish called *Monto* which was steamed, a meat pasty pastry called *Farmoosa*, and a tomato soup with finger-sized noodles filled with meat which was a staple called *Shish Barahk*. The Syrian version of *Shish Barahk* was a large noodle filled with meat in a yogurt sauce. A lot of the food, however different, was really delicious with the exception that my grandma stopped cooking with fat years ago. It's not uncommon to ask the butcher for actual pieces of fat that could be boiled in with the food for flavor. Here, they loved cooking with fat and the sight of the pieces of fat in everything were extremely off putting to me. My stepdad had made us stop cooking with salt when he came back from getting his PhD. Needless to say, it was a fatty salty yummy feast.

I finished my first plate full and then they served me again, "You're too skinny. Eat!" they said, since I was weighing in at only 100 lbs. Not wanting to offend, I ate. I was taught never to leave a single morsel on my plate. In my family it was against the rules to take more than you can eat and waste food but when I cleaned my plate again, they filled it again. I continued to eat until they all finished, and we retired to the sitting room for tea. They served the tea and put some lemon in mine insisting it was good for me. I made no objection as I was eager to please my new in-laws. Sure enough, as soon as the tea touched my tongue, all my lunch expelled onto the floor in front of me. I was mortified that I did not make it to the bathroom in time and immediately offered to help clean it up. The ladies took me upstairs to clean up and said I should lay down.

As I laid on the bed I could hear through the paper-thin walls all the gossip… "Poor thing, it must be the long journey. Maybe she is ill." "She is a newlywed, I bet she is pregnant." I thought, Geez, can no one throw up unless they are pregnant, especially after you force them to eat three plates full of food piled high? Anyone in my position would have thrown up. No one was meant to eat that much food in one sitting. As is always the case a rushed wedding and the bride throws up in your living room … she must be pregnant - no other evidence is necessary or considered.

Why would I agree to eat so much despite being full? Well, if you don't try every dish unless you have a good reason like an allergy, then you're being rude to the woman who made it. If you don't fill your plate, then you're saying you don't like their cooking. For them, when you clean your plate, it means you're still hungry and if you say, "No, thank you, I'm full," they will insist you have more. If you refuse, they will offer again and again until you give in just to make them stop asking. If they don't offer it might be considered as a lack of hospitality and no one wants that reputation, especially the lady of the house.

In Saudi we were taught that when a guest arrives, and we offer them refreshment they will need to refuse at least seven times before we can stop worrying about asking. This was the way. I've never seen anyone refuse seven times since normally by the third or fourth time they give in and accept something. It's a delicate dance of not accepting too soon as it could be seen as being desperate or maybe you lack the means to buy the expensive juice we were about to serve and refusing entirely might seem like you did not trust the contents of the glass. In retrospect I should have taken a small bite of each dish eaten very slowly and left a small amount behind on my plate, indicating I was too full to finish, but at the time, I was an American Princess who grew up in Saudi Arabia, and while you can take the princess out of Saudi Arabia it would take many, many years to wash off the lingering red sand.

Three hours passed as I napped on the daughter's bed until Ata arrived. I wanted to go home. I could not go down without them sending me back up to rest. They said they called Ata but where was he? It seemed like it was taking forever. Finally, the doorbell rang, and I heard his voice at the door. He asked for me to come out to the car, then they told him I was ill, sleeping upstairs. He yelled, "Why didn't anyone tell me?" They said, "There was no need to disturb your lunch, she is resting." He exhaled and ran up the stairs, came into the room, picked me up and carried me to the car saying how sorry he was that he didn't come sooner, no one had told him I was unwell. I smiled at him, and we drove home. The next day he bought me a cell phone so that we would never be out of touch again.

Two days later the furniture was delivered, and I was busy setting up house and home, happy to be able to move the furniture around and not have to consult anyone. The TV arrived and I tended to leave the TV on any channel that was playing, old Star Trek reruns since a lot of them I had missed because the religious leaders in Saudi had decided that certain episodes were too indecent to import or display on TV. I left it on as I worked. I enjoyed the sounds of voices in the house as I cleaned. The daily silence was harder than I had imagined. I missed my sisters, my brother and even my mom. After nineteen years of never being physically alone it was hard to sit in silence day in and day out.

Every night before Ata arrived home from work, I would get dinner ready and dress up in one of my cute outfits, apply my make-up, and wait for him. When he arrived, I would run into his arms. He was happy to see me, and we would make love. I remember the first night he came home he asked me to stay back while he took a shower. I finally asked him why I could not just take a shower with him as we had done when we were in Saudi. He sighed deeply and said that his feet stink after a long day at work and he wanted to spare me. I thought it was sweet of him to want to spare me, but I insisted he get in the shower, and I would wash his feet. He protested as I washed them, and we finally ended up laughing about his stinky feet. After that it would become a tradition every day after work all dolled up, I would wash his feet before dinner. There is a certain charm in the old ways. I knew a woman once whose husband, from the day they were married as teenagers until they were in their late 80's, never shaved himself. She shaved him every day and washed his back in the bathtub.

One day Ata came home and gave me a debit card. He told me if I needed groceries there was a supermarket down the road where I could go and pick up a few things in the daytime. This would save him from picking things up on the way home. I looked at the debit card. I had never had a card before. To me they were like strange plastic cards that my stepdad kept in his wallet. My mom was always given cash for fear she would overspend, and she never knew how much money was in the bank account for fear that she would ask for more than he wanted to give.

It was very normal in Saudi families that the wife knew nothing about the family finances and was given a household budget that she would stick to. If she needed to make a big purchase, she would ask her husband and he would let her know if they could afford it or not. It's also not uncommon for a man to have two bank accounts. The one his wife can see and the one he keeps private where he would keep the bulk of his money. I was brought up that the finances of the house were not for me to worry about, it was my job to follow the wisdom of my husband.

Ata explained to me how much he made, how much we had in the bank account, and told me that if I needed anything to just let him know. I felt so trusted and returned that trust a hundred-fold. That night as I thought about walking to the grocery store alone, I got scared. I asked Ata, "What if I get kidnapped or what if something happens to me going alone to the store, I have never done it before?" He laughed and said, "We're not in Saudi Arabia, this is Canada. Just keep your cell phone on you and you'll be fine."

The next morning, I stood on my balcony for the longest time looking at the world below and wondering if it would be okay. Recalling that the last time I was ever left on my own was the time my family and I went to Walt Disney World in Florida. The kids were too young for all the rollercoasters I wanted to go on. I was fifteen or sixteen and since my brother Chris was long gone and there was no one my own age to go with me, my stepdad allowed an exception that I could ride whatever I wanted to, alone. I was so excited that I was going to be able to walk around the park on my own. He told me, "On the condition that when it was time for the parade, we would all meet at the clock tower," I agreed and ran off.

I bought candy, rode the rides I wanted over and over and had a great day. I met the Little Mermaid and Belle, two of my favorite Disney characters at the time. Finally, it got dark, and it was time for the parade. I went to the clock tower, but they weren't there. I climbed up on a lamp post to look over the crowd for my mom's head cover. I knew it would be the most distinctive thing to look for, but more and more people arrived, and they were nowhere to be found.

The fear started to sink in that I was lost. I was going to be stuck here, did they leave me behind? The tears started to fall, and I started to shake as the announcement came over the speaker that the park was closing, and everyone should leave. I had looked everywhere but they were nowhere to be found. I finally sat down on a large planter box in front of the exit gate to the train hoping as they left, I would see them, or they would see me, but they were nowhere. I started to despair. What should I do? No one ever told me what to do if I got lost except to sit still and stay put, so I stayed put, crying.

Finally, a few park attendants approached me. I backed away, wondering what they wanted, they asked "Are you okay?" I didn't answer. "Are you lost?" they asked, and I started to cry saying, "I can't find them, they said to meet them at the clock tower, but they are not here." They asked me my name and said to come with them and that they would help me find them. I protested and said, "I need to stay here. They will find me if I stay put." They said they would help me find my family and not to worry about coming with them. I noticed the last few people leaving the park and they were still nowhere in sight, so I went with them to a room. It was full of lost children who had been separated from their parents in the park. At that point the fear that had overtaken me was real. I could hardly think of anything. They asked what my parents' names were, where they were staying, and the name of the hotel they were in. I said, "We're in the RV park. We came on the train." They said okay and asked me to take a seat. I looked around at all the crying children and noticed that I was the only teenager, everyone was under the age of six. I felt so ashamed that I was lost at my age. I stopped crying and tried to think, what was the name of the RV park? Will they find me here?

After an hour or so I calmed down and suddenly remembered that my stepdad had a cell phone. I crunched my brain and remembered his phone number. I ran to the attendant and said, "My stepdad has a cell phone!" She said, "What's his number?" I gave her the number I remembered, and they made the call.

A little while later my stepdad arrived. I cried and ran into his arms saying how sorry I was that I could not find them. I was so grateful that he came back for me. His face was as unemotional as it normally was. Calm and reserved. The attendants asked if this was his daughter to which he answered, "Yes." Then they asked me if this was my dad and I said, "Yes." We left, got on the train, and returned to the RV park where my mom and brother and sisters were waiting. My mom sobbed uncontrollably as she held me for the longest time. I never wanted to get lost again. I promised happily not to go off alone ever again.

Is it learned helplessness, or should I call it taught helplessness? When I look back now at how good my stepdad was at making me submit, I wonder if he left me there on purpose and planned this event all along. After all, if you have a teenager who might start to question your rule of law, what safer place to put the fear of separation from the tribe into that teen than one of the safest places on earth? Afterall, what parent leaves the park when their child is still there? We were not taught independence; we were taught that we can only be dependent. You grew up never thinking you will support yourself so that you would never think of trying. You felt trapped, stuck, scared. Even today I still struggle with it. It's like they break you down slowly. Mental games and psychological manipulation are just as impactful as physical torture, perhaps even more so. Their effects are long lasting. My stepdad was an expert.

Breaking away from the awful memory, I came back to where I was, standing on the balcony. I realized I could see the supermarket in the distance and thought to myself if I could make note of the route and remember my way, I should be okay. I had my own cell phone now and if I got lost, Ata will surely come and get me. I nodded to myself, took a deep breath, got dressed, and headed for the door. I was extra vigilant. Growing up in Saudi we were taught to watch out for people following us. We actively listened to footsteps behind us and if we thought they had bad intentions we would slow our pace to allow them to pass or watch what they were up to. I watched everyone on that walk, suspicious that everyone was dangerous. I kept my head down as I would have in Saudi and walked through the three inches of snow to the store. I took in the cool air with a sense of freedom I had never felt.

When I arrived at the store, I got a cart and walked around the store buying anything and everything that caught my eye, cake mix, icing, candy. I bought everything I would not have been allowed to buy in Saudi as it was considered a waste of money. Over excited I filled the cart and when I went to check out, I looked and realized I would never be able to carry all this home. Then I saw a small shopping cart with wheels in the corner for sale and asked to buy it as well. Joyfully I extended my hand straight out, proud of my very own debit card! I piled up my groceries in the cart and pushed it all the way home in the snow. I was so proud of myself, I had done it all by myself, I didn't get lost, I felt like a real grown up now. I could buy groceries ALONE.

Looking back now I would bet I looked super suspicious to everyone who looked at me or was going the same way. I would turn away, change sidewalks, or leave the grocery aisle when someone looked my way for too long. When Ata got home, I told him all about my shopping adventure and he said, "That's nice, good." His tone was as if it was odd, how could an American girl not have ever been to the grocery store alone? We changed the subject and talked about his work. He said he would take me on the weekend to meet his team and see where he worked. I was very excited.

Saturday came and we got in the car, and he drove me to the mall. We went in, and he introduced me to the team. There were three boys and a girl. Alex from Afghanistan, Omta, who was half Afghani half Persian, Omar from Pakistan and a tall Sikh man who was from India. They were a fun lively bunch. I said hello and Omta said she wanted to go pee, so she grabbed my arm and in typical girl fashion we went to the bathroom. She peed and asked me how I liked Canada. Then she talked and talked about how much she was in love with Alex. I said, "That's great! When will you two get married?" She laughed and said, "I hope really fucking soon." Her profanity appalled me but in typical Arabic fashion, I kept my feelings about her bad language and un-ladylike behavior to myself. I smiled and nodded she continued, "It will take some time I think, I don't know if he wants to marry me," to which my brain replied, I can see why he would not want to marry someone so inappropriate but as I was raised to do, replied "Oh, I'm so sorry we should get back. Ata will be worried about where I am." She laughed and said "Okay," and took me back to Ata.

Ata said he needed to do a few things at work and that I would be bored waiting around. "Why don't you go shopping?" he suggested to which I replied, "Shopping! Me? Alone?" My mind thought the supermarket was different. This was a busy mall with multiple dark places where someone could grab me. There was a girl my mom said once who was raped in a mall bathroom in Texas. I said, "Maybe I'll just stay with you, I don't mind." He said, "You'll be fine, you need to get some more liberal attire, your clothes are too conservative for Canada." Taking my hand and leading me to the escalator he pointed and said, "You just go down this escalator and go to that store down there. I have a friend who works there, and she will take good care of you." I gripped my hands together as he kissed me on the cheek, I said, "Wait, how much can I spend?" He said, "Get whatever you want, we just got paid."

He walked away as I stood in front of the escalator, my heart racing, alone in a mall. Person after person passed me as I stared at the escalator saying, "No, I can't walk around a mall alone, it's dangerous. I can't." In

Saudi the malls are one of those places I would never have gone alone. The religious police were so diligent about watching the malls and the boys would always follow the girls into the underwear stores to get a glimpse of the girls touching the lace panties so they could imagine what they might look like wearing such things under their black abayas. It was finally decided that all underwear stores would need to be in the women's sections and attended by women. Years later this law would lax and lingerie stores would be allowed in the main malls but would also still be attended only by women. The Kingdom Tower in Riyadh once had a women's only section. The upper floor was where ladies could go shopping without the worry of being seen by men. It had most of the lingerie stores in the mall and a Debenhams and a café in its time. It was a wonderful place to go. I stood at the top of the escalator for the greater part of maybe twenty minutes watching the people until I finally decided if my husband said it was okay then it must be safe. I gripped the rail and took the step and went down the escalator.

It was a life changing moment, something so simple like going shopping on my own seemed impossible until that day as it feels to many who grew up as I did. Granted there were many girls brought up in Saudi Arabia that had more freedom to have the driver simply drop them off at a mall, a *souk* or a friend's house, and then bring them back, but not me. When we think of how they teach elephants in Thailand not to run away they start with a very heavy metal chain one they could never break no matter how hard they tried. Then a thick rope once they calmed down, then a rope so thin all the elephant need do was pull to break it, but they don't because all they remembered was that the last time they tried to run it was no use and so the illusion of the heavy chain lasts a lifetime and at some point, even if the rope was removed completely, they would not even try to leave the side of their masters. It was as if I had been under lock and key for so long and now someone says, "You're free to go," and I froze because I had learned to only feel safe in my cage.

The shops were so foreign to me. We had none of these brands in Saudi and the sight of all the crop tops in the store windows on manikins seemed distasteful to me. If a mall in Saudi had mixed company walking around, a female manikin wearing a crop top would have never been allowed in the window. The religious police would have shut the store down and beaten the shop owner without a doubt. These things should be in the back I thought, since they should only be worn for one's husband and certainly never in public.

I entered the store and found the nice salesgirl Ata sent me to. She grabbed me by the arm and helped me select a few sweaters suggesting primarily short sweaters. I looked her over and wondered if it was good for Ata to have friends who were girls. Afterall, where I came from, that would never be allowed. People have gotten divorced over less. Then I realized that his mom had male friends. Perhaps in this new life it was normal since as his mom said, "As long as there was no impure intention." I smiled at her sweater suggestions thinking, "Of course you would suggest that, you walk around half naked." I insisted that they must come down over my butt so as not to show my shape if I was to go without my abaya-like purple velvet jacket. "My beauty is for my husband alone and not to be flaunted in the street," I said proudly. She thought I was strange.

I bought a few things and headed back to Ata right away. I worried that he would worry if I took too long. When I got up the stairs Ata said he was almost done so I waited. I noticed a customer asking Ata if he could unlock his phone for him. Ata looked around as if someone had asked him for something illegal and told him it would cost fifty dollars to which the man agreed. The man handed him the cash and Ata typed the code into the phone and it was unlocked. I had never heard of a locked phone before. In Saudi everyone always bought their phone then got their line from whatever service they chose. If they were not happy with their service, they would just pay their last bill and change service providers. In Canada, however, there were plans and contracts for people who could not afford to buy the phone outright, so people signed 2-, 3- and sometimes even 4-year contracts with cell phone companies. Agreeing to pay for that service for 3 years, the phone was then included in their monthly payments and the phone of course was locked so that they could not leave and go to another service so easily. It felt so wrong to me, to bind people and take away their right to choose. If people weren't happy with the service, they were still stuck paying off the phone that could not be transferred. That seemed wrong to me but I understood that this is how things were done in Canada and so I watched.

After we got in the car, I asked why it was such an odd transaction to unlock the phone, I mean it was the man's phone right? Ata said, "Yes, it's his phone but we're not allowed to unlock the phones. We are supposed to sell them another phone and if our boss finds out we're unlocking phones we could all be fired." My ears rang. "What!" I said. Ata said, "Yes, but if I can't sell the man a new phone why shouldn't I just unlock it? Besides, it gives us a lot of extra income." I took a deep breath and said, "We don't need it, your salary is enough. It's too dangerous. What if you get caught? What will happen to us if you're not working? How will we pay the rent? Ata, listen to me, you must stop this and follow the rules, it's safer." He rolled his eyes and said he would not, and we were silent the whole ride home. When we arrived home, he sat on the couch, and I went to bed. By the time he came to bed I had decided it was not my place and after all it was the man's phone. I urged him to be careful to which he agreed, and we made up.

I spent the next few weeks waking up and deciding we were out of something so I could justify to myself why I needed to walk to the supermarket every day. Even if I only bought one thing, I enjoyed the freedom I felt in that walk. Even if the temperatures were very low and the snow was up to my knees, I still pushed my little cart down to the supermarket and skipped back kicking the snow up and listening to my little USB MP3 player. Day by day my confidence grew, and I started to see the world outside Saudi Arabia with new eyes.

One day Ata called to say his friends from work would be coming over to play cards. He said there was no need to make dinner as they will have eaten before they arrived. I was so excited to finally entertain for the first time as a wife. Eager to make a great first impression. I walked to the grocery store with a skip in my step to buy cookies, juice, extra tea, snacks, and everything I was taught was right to serve on such an occasion. No beverage should be offered without something to eat even if they had already eaten. It would be very impolite not to offer them proper refreshment.

When they arrived, I opened the door and Ata's friend Alex handed me a bottle of strawberry flavored rosé wine. I looked at it and my face was screaming, "What is this?" Ata took it from me and said, "It's ok it's just wine." I whispered, "Alcohol in our home?" to which he replied, "Yes, it's no big deal, it's only once in a while." One of the other boys brought vodka and someone else brought a hookah. I was intrigued, curious, and appalled all at the same time. I thought smoking was especially appalling and had already asked Ata to quit as soon as he was able. I hated the taste of tobacco on his lips and always requested that he brush his teeth after smoking before he kissed me. He considered the hookah to be a compromise since it was apple flavored. It was not as disagreeable to me.

I offered them juice, tea, coffee, snacks, but there were no takers. I offered and offered as I was taught. Sitting down for a moment and then making the rounds again offering them more refreshment but still they just drank, smoked, and played cards. I was confused. "Did I do it wrong?" I asked myself. Finally, Ata said, "Don't worry about us, go sit and relax." As the men played cards, Omta and I sat on the couch. I watched them all drinking and then I thought well, if it's okay for my husband ... I want to try some of this alcohol. After all, if my husband is doing it then it must be okay.

I walked into the kitchen, hoping Ata would not notice with his back turned, since I had not asked for his permission to try this alcohol stuff. I reached for the wine since it had the word strawberry on it, and I liked strawberry flavored things. I grabbed one of the red Solo cups and was about to pour when his friend Alex leaned over and said, "The wine is not very good, better add some of the vodka to it." I nodded and smiled, trying not to give away my lack of experience. I thought okay, if that's what you're supposed to do. I guessed they were both the same, just one being better than the other? That's what he must have meant. I filled the cup with half vodka and half strawberry wine. I remember thinking it smelled so bad, the vodka smelled like the alcohol swabs my mom had used on my cuts when I was little. The wine smelled rotten but if everyone was drinking it then it must be good. They all seemed like they were having a good time.

I took my cup, sat on the couch, and smelled it again. Telling Omta, "It smells bad," she said, "Try it!" I took a sip and said, "Yuck, it's gross," and she said, "Have a little more you'll get used to it." Not wanting to bear the awful flavor for too long like you do with cough medicine, I chugged it down, swallowed and let out a shriek, "YAAAK!" Omta said, "You drank it all?!!!!" I said, "It was awful I wanted to get it over with." We sat for a few minutes watching the TV, when all of a sudden, the TV before me split into two TV's. I got scared so I laid down on Omtas' lap for a minute. Omta asked, "Are you okay?" I could not answer. I didn't know what was happening to me. They had told me alcohol was bad, from the devil, my whole life but no one prepared me for its effects. No one explained the difference between wine and liquor. How much was too much, it was just all thrown into one big pot of bad stuff never to touch.

Omta told Ata what had happened, and he took me to bed and went out to the living room to let the guests know the game was over. Everyone left and as I laid in bed, I felt hot, so hot that I began to take all my clothes off. When Ata finally arrived back in the room to check on me, I was naked sitting on the floor asking him what was wrong with me. Then it happened … I threw up. Ata cleaned me up, put me back into bed and placed a bucket at my side in case I needed to throw up again and then he went to bed next to me. I spent most of the night vomiting and woke up the next morning feeling awful.

That evening when Ata got home, I asked all about alcohol. "Why do you drink when you know it is bad?" He explained, "Even though I know it's bad, if you drink a little it's not that big a deal," he paused for a second before continuing. "You must never tell anyone in my family about the drinking." I lowered my head and promised. I asked what his favorite was, and he replied, "Vodka and orange juice." I asked, "Why?" to which he replied, "Because it covers up the flavor of the vodka and I really like orange juice." Even though I was raised very conservative, I was eager to taste, try, flavor, and see everything I had never tasted, flavored, tried, and seen. We became very close that first year like real best friends. It was a relationship so different from the one I had observed between my mom and stepdad or any couple really.

One day while on my usual trip to the grocery store, I noticed another store I had never gone in. It was odd because all the windows were covered in bars, which was something I had not seen since I left Saudi. I looked at the sign and it was a liquor store. I went inside and walked around. I did not see myself as out of place buying liquor as a covered woman since in my mind if Ata was Muslim and he could buy it what would be the difference I thought if I bought it. I found a pretty bottle of vodka and took it to the cashier and bought it. The man wrapped it in a brown paper bag looking at me oddly as I looked down thinking he was judging me. I added it to my grocery cart where I had already purchased orange juice.

When Ata got home, he asked for some juice which I normally served to him in a tall glass but this night I put a little bit of vodka in. Thinking he would be so happy that I had gone to the trouble of buying and preparing his favorite drink. He drank the first glass and asked for a second. He had not noticed that there was vodka in the juice, so I figured I needed to put more so I added a little more. I made myself one to try and sat beside him. He drank some and turned his head slowly, looked at me and said, "What's in this?" I smiled and said "Vodka!" He put down the glass and asked, "Where did you get it?" I said, "From the liquor store." His face turned red as he said, "Are you crazy! A covered woman in a liquor store! What will people say! They have cameras. You don't think someone saw you. What if my parents found out? Put down your glass, you're not to have any!" "Why!" I protested "If you can drink, I can drink. It's only a little bit and why can't I buy liquor for you? What is the big deal? No one saw me, none of your family live around here." He lowered his head and shook it side to side and said, "Because you're my wife, you're pure and perfect and I don't want you to have the same bad habits I have." I stood up and all my wife training crumbled around my thirst for more freedom and my stubborn soul. I said, "That's not fair! I want you to be my guide. I just want to try things. Why do you get to do whatever you want while I must be the perfect little Muslim wife?" He said, "I said no, that's it." I heard my stepdad's orders in that statement. I stood up and said, "Fine!"

I walked to the kitchen, and something snapped. I thought he was going to show me the world and let me explore and be with me, but I felt as though he was just like all the rest intent on keeping me as I was while he did whatever he pleased. I went to the fridge and grabbed the bottle of Vodka. As I walked to the balcony door I said, "You don't want any liquor in the house, fine!" He said, "Don't be crazy, you're not going to throw it" to which I replied, "Here it goes!" and then I chucked it off the balcony. It landed on a car below smashing into pieces. Ata got up and said, "What the fuck did you just do!" I grabbed the glass he was drinking and said, "Better get rid of that as well" and chucked it off the balcony. He said, "What are you doing?!" and placed his fist in his mouth, biting down as if hoping to suppress whatever it was he wanted to say. I went to the bedroom and slammed the door, telling him he could sleep on the couch.

I was so mad it was almost impossible to sleep but finally I did. When I awoke, Ata had already gone to work. It was the first time he had left, and I wasn't already awake, fully dressed getting him breakfast, kissing him, and grabbing his tie for one last quickie before he left, making him late more often than not. That afternoon as I began my chores in my little booty shorts that were supposed to be only for Ata's eyes, I decided the balcony windows needed a good cleaning. Instead of changing and putting on my head cover, I got a bucket filled with soapy water and washed the windows. In plain sight of all the other apartments. Stubbornness was in my blood, and it was all too apparent that it was in Ata's blood as well. When he said no, I would move to the extreme and when I said no, he would do the same. When he arrived home that night, we both had had time to calm down. Realizing that we both had acted rashly we made up. I promised not to throw things off the balcony. He promised to try and let me experience things as long as I followed his lead.

His friends would come over and we would go out to dinner with them. We visited his family every Sunday for lunch. It was like we lived two different lives all at the same time. When his friends came over Ata would drink. I realized that I had no taste for any kind of alcohol thus far, so I didn't drink. When we went to his family's home we prayed and upheld his mother's well-known reputation as a leader in the Muslim community.

The story goes that Ata and his brother were born in Canada after his parents left Hallab, a city in Syria. The previous Syrian president had started killing off their family members after his uncle who was a preacher said something the regime didn't like. The government started systematically killing anyone with the last name *Hallak* (which means Barber). Many family names in the Sham countries Jordan, Syria, Lebanon and so on came from the profession their ancestors had many, many years ago. While my last name for example was Al-Turkistani (Meant from Turkistan and given to my stepdad's father when he arrived in Saudi). Out of fear Ata's mom and dad migrated to Canada and started over. I always found it odd that I was sworn never to share this information with anyone since it seemed very reasonable. I was never told what his preacher uncle really did to cause the entire family to be singled out. While they had lived in Canada Ata's mom worked a lot with the religious community. She was very religious. Yet so laid back and fun to be around. Adored by all who knew her.

Once Ata started going to college his dad got a good job offer in Jeddah, so Ata's family moved, leaving Ata behind. The plan was that he would study and once his younger brother was old enough, they would send him to Canada for college as well. Once Ata finished college he would move to Jeddah and work with his father and help to support his family, once his dad retired. Unfortunately, this was not to be, since upon my arrival in Canada Ata revealed to me that he had quit college. In order to be able to stay in Canada he was forging his grade reports so that his dad would continue to send him money for school. At first, I was worried, but Ata explained that if he returned to college he would lose his chance to move up at his job in the telephone store. At the rate he was going he was going to be managing his own store in a year, he said. He was already making good money and I did not question since I had no knowledge of these things. There it was, one more secret I was forbidden to share with his family.

My parents would call once a week despite the tensions when I left. My mom urged me at the behest of my stepdad to find a college course near my home to get my teaching degree. I mentioned that I found one close by, but admittance was not open until the next semester. The requirement was a CPR first aid course, but we could not afford it right now on Ata's salary. My stepdad had calmed down now that I was in Canada out of his reach. He gave me his credit card information so I could use it to sign-up for the course online. He reminded me to get rid of the paper I had written it on, as soon as I was done registering, to which I agreed. I signed up for the course, excited to go to a real school I was finally on my way to becoming a teacher. It was a dream for me to be like the teacher in the movie Matilda and shape minds through kindness and understanding.

When Ata got home that night, he asked how my day was. I told him about signing up for the course. "How did you pay for it?" he asked, "My stepdad gave me his credit card info." Ata glanced at the computer desk and saw the credit card info on a piece of paper. He said, "I'm going to use it to pay off my parking ticket," to which I replied, "No, it's not right, it was only to be used for my course." Ata looked at me and said, "This man beat you and raped you and you don't want to make him suffer?" I knew that if I took the right side, I would be condoning in Ata's mind what my stepdad had done. If I said, "Yes, I would be betraying the trust I had been given by my family." So, I stayed silent as he used the credit card number to pay his ticket and whatever else he could think of that was possible to pay for online back then. Which thankfully wasn't a lot.

The next day my stepdad called asking if I had used the card for anything else to which I replied "No." He asked me again. I lowered my head in typical fashion as I would have done if he was before me to show contrition and explained what had happened. He was outraged and said, "That should never happen again! You should not allow him to push you around that way." I nodded my head as he spoke over the phone and said, "Yes, Baba." Sadly, as long as my stepdad was married to my mom and as long as my mom and the kids remained in Saudi Arabia, he would be a part of my life. I just needed to accept it and play referee between him and my husband now. At least I was out of his house, and he would no longer be able to do as he pleased. Now maybe we could finally settle into some kind of more normal father daughter relationship.

It was hard to balance my husband's rebellious lifestyle and my duties to my mother-in-law and the community that loved her. Ata wanted me to dress more liberally, saying, "Your shirts don't need to reach your knees, they only need to cover your skin. Tight is not a problem. Look at what some of the other Syrian girls are wearing and ask them for some tips." So, I adjusted my wardrobe over time, modeling a lot of the covered girls we saw in the malls in Canada. One day, after a day at Ata's uncle's house, Ata received a phone call from his mom. She was livid. Yelling and asking how he could allow me to go out dressed so indecently. Apparently, word had reached her that I was wearing very tight-fitting clothing. After he hung up the phone, he said, "You need to start wearing your old clothes again, my mother said so." I huffed and said, "First of all, this was all your idea. Did you tell her that? Because it's not fair if she thinks it was me who wanted to dress this way in public. Secondly, you're my husband, why does she get to decide what I wear." He hung his head and said, "What can I do? If I don't listen to her, they won't send me money anymore. Just wear your long jacket when we go anywhere with the family."

It was an interesting dynamic to me since in my house and everyone I had ever known the man was always the boss but in Ata's house, his mom was the boss. The boys were raised to heed their mom.

It was Eid, our very first in Canada. In my family we would awake early for the morning prayer at sunrise and have breakfast with the family right after. Women don't normally go to the mosque in Saudi daily or even weekly like the men did. It was not technically frowned upon if a woman went but it was not encouraged. In the days of the Prophet Muhammad (ﷺ) the women actually went often and prayed in the same hall as the men just behind them but at some point, I guess it was decided that women were better off praying at home. We did however go for Eid Prayer since it was a special occasion. In Canada the Eid Prayer is offered in the mosque three times the first day of Eid to accommodate people who did not get the day off work so they could still make the prayer. Instead of breakfast we had lunch with the family.

It was great fun. I loved all of them already and since we lived far away, they never needed to know or bother with the other side of our life.

There was to be a big ladies' Eid party that weekend. I was so excited to be invited. Knowing I had nothing formal to wear, I decided I could try and catch a bus to the mall. Ata said he would be doing inventory which meant that he wouldn't be home until after 11:00 p.m. I thought I could go see him, buy a dress, help him with his inventory as I had done in the past and then we could come home together. I had never traveled that far alone before, but I was confident I could do it. I had my cell phone so what was the worry? I could surprise him. I was sure Ata would be so happy to know that I took the bus all the way to the mall by myself. I opened up the computer and looked up the map, wrote down the buses I needed to take to get to the mall and headed out.

I got on the first bus. It was the first bus I had ever been on alone, so I saved the ticket like a trophy of my newfound freedom. I got off on a street, walked to the next street and took the second bus. Then I could not find the next street to take the next bus I needed to get to the mall. I stood on the corner, my heart started to race. The icy rain started to come down. My mind started to scream you're lost but I wasn't going to cry. I calmed my mind, looked around and noticed a bus stop with an old man waiting for the bus. I was not accustomed to talking to strange men and especially not on the street. My mind filled with thoughts what if he knows I'm lost and tries to rape, kidnap, or kill me. No, Elise, my mind replied, he's just an old man you could outrun him if he's dangerous. I took a deep breath and said, "Excuse me sir. Do you know where I catch the number 9 bus?" "Yes" he replied, "Just down there on the left." I thanked him and ran to catch the bus. Finally, the mall came into sight, I felt proud I did it all by myself. I made it! I beamed with joy as I entered the mall.

I ran to Ata's store. When he saw me, he came over and said, "How did you get here?" Smiling from ear to ear I said, "I took the bus!" He said, "I won't be able to take you home until after we finish inventory. You're not going back on the bus at night." "I know. Not to worry I can help with the inventory," he smiled and said, "Okay."

I went off to buy a dress. It was to be my very first all-women's party where my parents would have no say in what I wore. Since it was all women, I could wear whatever I wanted. I tried on dress after dress and finally settled on my very first sleeveless sweetheart black silk top with a lace belt that fell like a tail and a mermaid full length maroon skirt. It was beautiful, classy, and feminine. I had never worn anything like it to a party before. I made my way back to Ata's store just as they were closing. Alex ordered a pizza, and we started the count. Everyone was assigned a side to count and then we all switched sides to recount the inventory and log things in. Unfortunately, the inventory came up short meaning either people forgot to log sales, or someone was stealing phones. We finished around 11:00 p.m. as anticipated.

We made our way to the cars and all of a sudden Ata said, "Hey, honey, go sit in the car, I just need to talk to Omar for a minute in his car." I said, "Okay." It was dark so I couldn't see them in the car, and my mind started to wonder. What was it they needed to talk about that could not be said around me? As far as I knew Ata told me everything. I settled on the idea that it was probably Omar who had a secret he didn't want to share in front of me. I waited for Ata to return knowing for sure he would fill me in later. They finished and Ata jumped in the car. Ata said, "Hey, sorry, we just needed to discuss some work stuff." I sat there silently thinking I had just finished doing inventory with them. There wasn't anything related to that store that I didn't know, what could they possibly have to discuss related to the business that could not be said in front of me? My mind raced. What could it be? I asked him, "What was it you needed to discuss?" Ata stayed silent the whole way home.

When we got into the house, I had nothing to say. I was appalled by secrets. Ata asked me to sit down and taking a deep breath he said, "We were smoking weed." I squinted and slightly tilted my head. "What is weed?" He laughed a little and said, "It's a drug, you smoke it." I asked, "And how long have you been smoking it?" "Since I quit smoking cigarettes last year." I said, "Why do you smoke it?" To which he replied, "It's either weed or cigarettes and you made it clear you don't want me to smoke cigarettes. Now I just smoke weed every once in a while with my friends." I stared at the floor and said, "When were you planning to tell me?" "Well, now," he said. "If I hadn't showed up at the mall unexpectedly, would you still have told me?" He stayed silent so I got up and went to bed.

He slept on the couch that night, thinking there might be a fight if he should try to go to the bedroom. I sat up most of the night thinking how close I wanted us to be and wondered why he would keep such a secret from me. I didn't want him to smoke cigarettes. Smoking this weed every once in a while started to seem like no big deal but why keep it a secret? Maybe he thought I wouldn't understand. I came out of the room and sat next to him, he started saying he was sorry about smoking weed and I looked at him and said, "Honey, I'm not mad you smoked weed, I'm hurt that you felt you needed to lie about it. I don't want secrets between us. I want us to be close." He bowed his head in shame. We made a deal that night. That we would never keep secrets again. He cried and said he was afraid I would leave him if I knew. I told him I would never leave him as long as he always told me the truth. I told him, "I can't promise not to get mad but being honest will never be a reason to leave you." We made up that night and I was glad in a way that it happened because it only brought us closer. We had the marriage everyone wished for. So in love, so close, so happy, and so devoted to each other. You can always tell the truly happy couples from the fake. It shows on their faces in the way they interact in public and when they think they are alone.

The day the party arrived I spent the greater part of three hours doing and redoing my hair. I finally got it right. It was a work of art, something I had never been able to do before. I was so proud of how beautiful I looked that night. Ata came home from work to take me to the party. He did his usual reaction of bending his knees and saying wow, you look amazing, so hot! I giggled in my usual way. I put on my head cover and jacket carefully so as to not mess up my hair and we were off. He dropped me off saying, "I'm going to go hang out with my friends at Tim Hortons. Take your time and call me when you are done." I was nervous. I had never been to a party like this without my mom. It was also my first party as a married woman, other than my wedding. I entered the hall and checked my coat and head cover.

As I walked in, I was surprised to be surrounded by everyone in the room. I was so unique, an American Muslim woman who spoke Arabic - everyone had heard of me. Not just because my mother-in-law was so well known, but because many of the mothers had hoped to marry their daughter to the son of the most respected woman in the community. Everyone had questions about my background as well as how I liked Canada and how my mother-in-law was doing. I found them all so nice and welcoming. Then the dancing started, and I headed to the floor before anyone else. In Saudi the girls all want to get on the floor as soon as possible to be seen. Here they all were shy and wanted to wait until more girls were on the floor, all except one.

She was a fuller girl; voluptuous you could say but a little bit past the standard voluptuous mark. Her name was Fozia. She knew my mother-in-law well and said she grew up with Ata. I was happy to meet her on the dance floor as she was a great dancer. After the first dance she introduced me to her sister and their childhood friend Alaa who was wearing a skirt just like mine and a black lace top. We laughed saying we looked like twins. She was a beautiful girl, short, skinny and with long brown hair like me. I looked at her and knew that we were destined to be friends but as outgoing as she seemed in the party, I saw a deep inner sadness that she tried to hide. Fozia was a happy talkative girl who stayed with me the whole party. She made me laugh and I enjoyed the company since it had been so long since I had any friends of my own. Noor was so far away, and it was hard to talk to her on the messenger with the time difference. We danced most of the night until it was time to go. I called Ata and said, "I was ready to go." He came and picked me up.

As I entered the car he said, "How was it?" I said "Oh, I had such a good time! I met a really nice girl. She said she grew up with you." "What was her name?" he asked as I strained to remember. "Oh, her name was Fozia." "Fozia," he said. "Yes," I replied. He issued, "You can't be friends with her." I said, "Why not? Why can't I be friends with her? You can't tell me who I can be friends with." He said, "You can't be friends with her and that's it." "Give me a good reason why," I retorted. He said, "She has a bad reputation and I made out with her once. Everyone knows her as a loose girl. You can't be friends with her." I folded my arms and said nothing more.

We got home and I went into the bedroom thinking since I looked so pretty Ata would have followed to make love to me, but he did not come. After an hour I went out to the living room to get him. It was dark, the lights were out but there was light coming from the computer screen. As I looked out into the living room there was Ata masturbating to the screen. I gasped. He saw me. I ran back into the bedroom and closed the door.

The next day I told him I was not mad that he was masturbating as much as why he didn't want to make love to me. Did I not look beautiful enough? Was he tired of me? What had happened? I felt hurt and I didn't understand. No one told me that men masturbated even after marriage. He said sometimes he just liked to watch porn and it had nothing to do with me or how he felt about me. I did not know what porn was for until then. I said okay and asked to see some so he showed it to me. We watched some together and all was well again. He left for work that morning leaving me with access to his collection with instructions to learn something by watching some videos. I watched a few and paid special attention to the blow job parts since it was something I was not accustomed to, and it was obviously something he was interested in. I was determined to be a better wife by becoming a better lover. I had no prior experience and so I'm sure for a worldly man, I might have been a little bit boring.

I worried about being the perfect wife. If I didn't get it right, would he grow tired of me, take a second wife, or go out and not come home to see me anymore? Would he leave me in this big world, alone? What would I do for money, would I turn out like my mother, depressed and unhappy? I thought of my family and remembered what my aunt used to say about how family is a woman's only protection even if they were good or bad, they were her family. I thought about why I was not yet pregnant. All those years of being told sex gets you pregnant immediately. Yet after all the sex we had had still my periods came like clockwork. Was there something wrong with me? Who could I tell? Definitely not Ata or my mother-in-law, they might replace me for being inadequate. I spoke to Noor who asked her mom who said, "These things take time." It wasn't enough to soothe my mind.

I walked to the grocery store that day and bought a pre-paid phone card and called home. My mom answered and I asked her a lot of pointed questions. "How do you know if you're pregnant? How can you tell if someone is high?" My questions were enough to make any mother worry. I'm sure I sounded sad that day and she kept asking me, "Are you okay? Why are you asking these questions? Do you think you're pregnant? Is Ata doing drugs?" To which I answered, "I was fine and there was nothing to worry about. I was just asking for a friend of mine." My mom said, "Well, I hope that friend of yours is married and I hope you told her no, you don't want any drugs." I sighed and placed my hand over my face as I realized what a bad idea it was to call her. I decided to change the subject and so I asked her to tell me about the news from home, but she said there was nothing new. The card gave it's two-minute warning. I said goodbye and sat still in my cold and quiet apartment for a little while.

It was getting close to the time when Ata would be home, so I dusted myself off, prepared dinner, and carried on. I feel like the years you spend alone in your head in Saudi Arabia can go one of three ways. You either learn to psychoanalyze yourself or you slowly break down, conform, become a shell, or go insane. I feel like I became the first. Learning to talk myself through my problems by talking through one question at a time: should I be worried about being pregnant? "Why, you two are supposed to be studying. Your parents did give you a box of condoms for your wedding and tell you no babies until after college. If anyone asks, just say you're waiting." and so on. One by one my concerns seemed to subside. In Saudi Arabia there was no going to a counselor. That was considered only suitable for crazy people. Talking to someone outside the family about the family's problems with documentation, oh no, that was not happening. Unless you have someone close, and I mean really close, who wouldn't judge or tell anyone what you're concerned about, you have got to work through it yourself. Even within the family we never know who to trust and where loyalties truly were. The best rule was to trust no one. Which is why I was so grateful that I found Noor.

Eid al Adha, the second Eid, arrived and there was to be a bazaar at the mosque. Selling headscarves, spices, toys, dishes and all sorts of items brought to Canada from the Middle East it reminded me of the market in Saudi. We went and I ran into Fozia again. This time we exchanged phone numbers. She said sometimes she and the girls go out for tea, I was excited. I broached the subject with Ata again. This time through his mom saying, I felt very lonely, and Fozia seemed like a kind girl. His mother, never liking to involve herself in gossip said, "I'm sure she is." We left it at that. There were not many girls of our age in our Muslim community. Therefore, it was hard to say I could not be friends with them since the alternative would be for me to make friends outside the community which would be worse due to possible non-Muslim influence. So, ultimately, I decided to go to tea with them.

Fozia and her sister picked me up in their car and we went to pick up the others. Alaa and a girl named Sarah, whom I had never met before. She was an extreme liberal Lebanese girl who did not cover. She was very beautifully molded in the sense that everything on her had been pushed, plumped, and dyed until the young girl looked like a woman ready to take on the world. She smoked, drank, and was free to come and go as she pleased. I wished I had grown up like her, so free and confident. We all piled in the car, and we went to a place I had never been, an Arabic *shisha*, café. It felt like we stepped out of Canada and back into the Middle East. It was crawling with Arabic boys who were all smoking and drinking coffee. Fozia asked me, "Have you ever smoked *shisha* before?" to which I responded, "No, is it nice?" She said, "Let's have some fun."

They ordered one and her sister glanced at the boys at the opposite table. Then taking a puff of smoke into her mouth, she leaned over and kissed Alaa to release the smoke into her mouth, and Alaa then blew it out in such a sexy way. I had never seen a girl kiss another girl and my mind was blown, were they lesbians, I thought? Fozia, seeing my face, laughed, and said, "It's harmless. We just do it because it makes the boys crazy, and we enjoy their reactions." She handed me the pipe. I took a puff. It was indeed really nice and relaxing. We drank tea and teased the boys at the other table until one of them passed us a note that we left on the table. This was where the girls would hangout. A place where they knew no one of their community would see them.

In Saudi if my stepdad had known what they were doing I would have never been allowed to hang out with them. In the grand scheme of things, they were virgins, just having a little fun. They weren't drinking, they didn't really have boyfriends, they didn't do drugs or go out late at night. For an American or a Canadian, they were just young girls and would have made good friends to anyone, really. In the Muslim community if a word of that day ever got out, none of them would be able to marry a good match. For me it was of no concern in my mind at this point, since I was already married and anything I did in this community would never reach my family, so my siblings were safe from scandal. It was such a freeing feeling, and they were fun, so I decided to keep them as friends. If only to be able to observe a different lifestyle than what I had seen my whole life. I had, however, forgotten to consider how my actions could affect my mother-in-law and Ata's family. They dropped me at home in time to start dinner preparations. I remember feeling great now that I had some friends to spend my time with.

We often got together at their homes. Sometimes they even came over to mine. When we went to Fozia's house, we went for the food. Her mom was always so happy to see me since she hoped I would be a good influence on her daughter because I was the daughter-in-law of such a great Muslim lady. We went to Alaa's house to play with her expensive wardrobe. She was the only girl in her family. She was in college and had a part-time job. She had no responsibility beyond that. Therefore, she spent all her money on shopping. My house was always the place they would gather when they had real trouble in mind. There was the time Fozia wanted to pierce her nose but was afraid someone would see her going to the tattooing and piercing place. She came over with Alaa and her sister. They used a needle, an apple, and an ice cube to pierce her nose in my living room. Needless to say, it was painful to watch. As far as I was concerned it was her body.

We became very close over time and over that year. I especially became close to Alaa. She was the only one in the group whose soul in a way spoke to mine. I saw a deep secret sadness in her eyes that reminded me of me, and I really wanted to help. She finally confided in me that her dad was very strict, and she was not allowed to go out very often unless it was to the mosque for Quran study, or to school. This is where we all came in, always pretending we were going to Quran lessons together. If her dad caught her in a lie or she wasn't where she was meant to be, he would beat her and keep her in the house for days, so she took extra care to make sure everything was set up correctly. Fozia seemed the most attached to me. She saw me as the wise, married girl who always had a good idea how to get out of trouble. After so many years of navigating my stepdad, her parents were a piece of cake to me. She came over often since Alaa was rarely able to get out and her sister was often busy with her upcoming engagement.

Ata's friend was getting married, so naturally there was to be a Bachelor Party. He told me he would be out until late and not to wait for him, so I invited Fozia over to spend the evening. I pulled out all my old photos and told her all about my life in Saudi Arabia. She shared all about her life in Canada. She finally asked me to show her my jewels and since we were very close in my mind, I trusted her enough, so I obliged. Every piece had a story since the ones that were given to me by people I didn't like or were just ugly I had sold. You see, unlike the other girls in my age group who loved the latest fashion jewelry from places like Swarovski, I took a note from my aunt's book. I only wore gold and what money I got from selling gold went back into gold. This way I was always building my own little nest egg that could be sold at any time in case of an emergency. Ata's mom did likewise. Every year on her birthday or their anniversary Ata's dad would always give her a gram of gold which she saved for a rainy day. Saving rainy day money is good but there will always be the temptation to spend it. With the jewels we wore it would be hard to part with them unless there was a dire need and so our little nest eggs were safe from our human weaknesses.

Fozia left around 10:00 p.m. and Ata arrived around 2:00 a.m. I was full of questions, "What was the Bachelor Party like? What did you do?"

"Well, we went to a club first and then to a strip club," he said. I said, "WOW! Can you take me to a club? I want to go dancing and see what it's like?" "No" he said sternly, "A club is no place for a good Arabic girl." I said, "Come on! I will be with you. Just once! I'll never ask again. I won't even dance, I just want to see." He said "No," and we went to bed. The next day I made his favorite dinner and asked again, "Please, baby, can't we go see! Please, please!" begging and pleading. "No, it's not a good idea. You have no idea what you're asking, it's not as glamorous as the movies." "Please!" and he finally gave in. "Fine, but you stick next to me, and do exactly as I say." I clapped my hands; I was so excited. "I promise. This is going to be so much fun!" "You will have to go without your head cover. Just saying," he said thinking it would detour me. I replied "Okay, it will be like I'm undercover, ha-ha."

The weekend came. It was finally the night we planned to go to a nightclub in real life. I got dressed up in a long sleeve sweater and a long skirt. My sweater showed a small amount of cleavage. I knew it was wrong, but I figured Allah wants me to follow my husband and since Ata said I could go I could pray for forgiveness later. Afterall, going without my head cover for a night can't be as bad in the sin department as drinking or smoking pot.

Ata was already in a bad mood when we got in the car. I begged him to cheer up, he was spoiling it for me. We drove to a club that was called Money. We walked in and ordered nothing. Ata watched as every single man checked me out. His blood began to boil as I took no note of anyone looking at me. I was too busy taking in the whole vibe. I looked out at the people. It was like nothing I had ever seen before. Girls dancing with boys, people drinking and laughing. I was in a daze when Ata said. "Let's go." I said, "Why? We just got here." "Everyone is looking at you, let's go!" Ata, like most Arab men, got very jealous when it came to other men looking at his wife. I suppose my typical head cover dulled me down just enough to make him less jealous when anyone looked at me. There was so much flesh walking around in Canada, exposed legs, cleavage, booty shorts, and more. With me being covered I was a lot less interesting than all that "*Lahmah*" as we called it, roughly translated as, "Meat, Flesh." Bottom line, Ata felt secure when I was covered, thinking

I would be the last thing a man wanted to hit on with so many easier targets. Tonight, without my head cover, even in the most conservative outfit in the club, I stood out.

We got in the car, and I was very upset. What kind of trip was this? He promised to take me and now we leave after 10 minutes. "Why are we leaving?" "All the men were staring at you, and I don't like it." "Ata, it's not fair, I feel like I am being punished and forbidden to go to all the parties you go to in clubs or otherwise just because you don't like the way men looked at me. It's like I'm being punished for being beautiful and that's not fair." He said nothing and I stayed silent the rest of the drive home.

On Monday I called Fozia and told her all about what had happened. Then she had a great idea. She said, "I can drive, all we need to do is tell your husband the girls are coming over. He will have to be out most of the night to give the girls their privacy. So, he'll go out with his friends and then we can get all dressed up, go to a club, and then be back before he gets home." It was the perfect plan.

Wednesday, I told Ata the girls would be coming over. He had no objection since I would be safe in the house. Fozia came over and we got all dressed up in the most vulgar clothes we could find in our wardrobes. We even put on fake tattoos to make ourselves blend in better with all the other skanky girls that would be in the club. Then we put on our jackets and headed out in the rain to the club Fozia had found online, called The Government. Since we only planned on going once in our lives, we figured this was a good one. It had four floors, and each floor had a different kind of music. If we didn't like one floor, we could move on to the next one. We stood in the line and handed the doorman our ID's. He let us in.

We checked our coats and were on our way. We had two rules: no drinking, and no talking to guys. We went to the first room. Pop music was playing, and I danced with Fozia. A couple songs later we moved to the next room where R&B was playing, the sound of my late 90's teenage years. I started to dance but the room was empty, so Fozia was not happy. "One song," I said, "Pleaseeeee"! Fozia said, "Oh, alright." We started to dance when a tall handsome Black man entered the room.

He looked at me intently, he was so intense. We stopped dancing. Fozia grabbed my hand just as the man grabbed my other hand. I looked at his eyes. I was married and yet I found myself extremely attracted to this utter stranger who just touched my hand. I admired his boldness and feared him in equal measure. If he was in Saudi, he would have not even been admitted to a list of suitors for one reason. He was Black, but in that moment, the second those eyes and that hand touched mine, it changed everything I was raised to think about Black suitors. I could not make out what he was saying. Fozia gave me a tug and we ran away to the next room.

This was the oddest room of all. It was a kind of music I had never heard before. Almost like electric pulses. We looked around at the laser lights flying around the walls. Then we noticed there were a lot of people, but no one was dancing. I asked Fozia, "Why are they just standing there staring at nothing and rocking back and forth?" She said she didn't know so we went to the fourth floor's room. It was very crowded with hardly any place left on the dance floor. We looked at each other and decided it was time to go home.

We ran to the car, getting drenched in the process, and drove home laughing. When we got back to my apartment building, we realized there was one very important part of the plan we overlooked. The door fob. The main door of the apartment building had two ways to access the building. A fob, which Ata kept with him, since he was always the one who might come home late. The second was the dial box that called ... Ata's cell phone. We stood in front of the door trying to think what to do. It was so late at night and waiting for someone to come by might not happen in time. If we called his cell, he would know for sure that we were outside when we were meant to be inside the whole night.

"I've got it!" I said and I dialed Ata. He answered and said, "Yes?" I said, "Hey, baby, so sorry! We ordered a pizza and came down to get it but got locked out." He laughed and buzzed us in. We both sighed a sigh of relief and went upstairs to change. Fozia went on her way, and I called Ata to tell him he could come home now. I was satisfied and thought I don't really like nightclubs, but I was glad I got to go.

Initially, I wished Ata had known me well enough to know that if he took me willingly, I would have realized on my own that I didn't like nightclubs. I grew up dancing at all women's parties, celebrations, and weddings, and they seemed like way more fun to me than the nightclub scene. His fear I think, was what if I liked them, I might change and start partying. What he forgot was that despite all my inexperience and being kept at home most of my life, I had grown up many years ago. I found the stories of people's crazy escapades more entertaining than actually being in one of my own.

My mother called on Sunday afternoon when Ata was home. Typically, my stepdad would try and let her call when he knew Ata would be at work to avoid the proper niceties of saying hello to him, since they both knew neither one wanted to speak to the other. Today, however, my stepdad was away in Dammam on a business trip. She decided since she felt so lonely, she would call and check up on me. Which really meant she was calling to gather gossip or share the gossip she already had. Being of the dramatic sort, she was never able to settle into a calm sort of happiness. Maybe it was her life with my stepdad, maybe it was just who she was. Whatever the case, happiness for happiness's sake was never in her DNA.

I picked up the phone laughing, and my mom asked why I was laughing. I said, "Hey mom, Ata was just being funny." She talked about the weather for a few minutes and the kids. Making it a point to tell me that everyone was doing better than ever. The kids were doing better in school, and everyone was happier, now that I was gone. My face changed and I felt I had been sliced by the very person whose role I had filled in for so many years. I answered her comment that was meant to get some crazy response from me with, "Well, I'm glad everyone is doing so great." Then she started prying, "How is marriage, does he beat you? You can tell me, sweetie." I rolled my eyes and looked over at Ata as I said, "No, Mom, he doesn't beat me." "You can tell me, Sweetie. Baba said he is very controlling of you, and you don't get to do anything on your own." I rolled my eyes again and said, "No, Mom, he's not very controlling. and I'm very happy." It was obvious that my stepdad was out of town, and she was looking for some drama to keep her occupied, which I refused to give her.

Seeing my face, Ata leaned over and tickled me to lighten the subject. As I giggled my Mom said, "Maha, this is no laughing matter. I'm very concerned about you." She pried and pried until Ata finally had enough and took the phone away to speak with her himself. I sat there, knowing full well this would not go well. He didn't know my Mom. They were both Pisces and therefore emotional by nature. He would surely set her off. He said, "Hello, Auntie, how are you?" My mom turned her questioning to him and when he didn't give her what she wanted, she turned to telling him how sorry he will be if he makes her daughter unhappy. I leaned my head back thinking oh, no, here we go. Ata took a deep breath and said, "Listen, Auntie, if anyone made your daughter unhappy it was you and your husband. I take care of her. I love her and our marriage is none of your business. Have a good day." He handed the phone back to me as my Mom started shouting, "How dare you!" and everything else in her playbook of dramatic sentences she had collected over the years from her American soap operas, no doubt. I told her I needed to go. I hung up the phone and didn't think much about it.

The next day, my phone started ringing early in the morning. It was my stepdad. I knew he was mad about the phone call with my Mom, but I didn't want to answer. I was tired of being yelled at. More than 6,400 miles away and he could still get to me! My heart raced with fear as the phone continued to ring. Then it stopped and rang again. He must have called more than 30 times that day, but I never picked up. I dared not tell Ata how many times my stepdad called out of fear that Ata might decide to answer or call him back. When I woke up the next morning there was an email in my inbox. It read as follows (errors retained):

> **Subject: Is your brain still alive**
>
> *I've got a call from your mother while I was on a business trip in Damam, she was crying from hurt and was very troubled. I'm not sure what took place, but she said things that really upset me. I never trusted that piece of garbage you call husband so I was not surprised from his low behavior; I was very disappointed from your reactions. As much as I was sad for you to allow him to*

walk all over you, demolish your personality, I was forcing myself to stay out of your business because it is your life and I trusted you will do whatever to live it happily. But to allow him to walk all over your mother in that way........that is way low.

I tried to call you from there but as usual, I get the answering machine. When I came back yesterday, I tried to call you more than 35 times, still no answer. I'm not even sure if this mail will get to you or it will be a public note viewed by that parasite. If he is then let him know that only a scum with inferiority complex like himself bite the hand that gave him generously, a real man he can never be as he have no clue what the word means. Maha, if your brain is still alive, not dead like his, I beg you to rearrange your life and retain back your responsible personality that somewhere, somehow you lost in your quest to please someone who will never be pleased because he does not have the brain capacity to see things clearly.

I read the email and sat back in my chair. Then I sat up and read it again. He had sent me many emails over the time that I had been in Canada. I had blocked him, as soon as I arrived, from my messenger and answered his calls as infrequently as possible. The manner of our parting made me wish never to see him again. I was done with the drama. Sadly, the drama and my stepdad were not done with me. I ignored the email as I had all the others that came through. To them my lack of availability meant my husband was keeping me captive, but the truth was I just started my life over to find some peace.

The summer was getting closer, and Ata wanted to go home to visit family, but we could not afford the tickets. We called Ata's parents, but their answer was, "Why doesn't her family pay for her ticket, and we will pay for yours?" I sighed, knowing the answer to that one. My stepdad would undoubtedly say, "No, if he can't afford to bring you to visit his parents, we won't pay for it." My stepdad and Ata were at constant odds with each other. Each one trying to find any reason to poke the other. It was exhausting. I wanted to see my siblings since I had only received one letter from Noura in the last year. My mom never told me enough details about them or put them on the phone so I could visit with them.

It was hard on me to have been like a mother to all four of them. As happy as I was to have my own life, I was missing them terribly. Every time my mom called, they were busy playing outside or at school. I knew the only way my stepdad would pay for my ticket home was if I was getting a divorce. That was what he wanted.

As we sat and discussed how we could go to visit his family for the summer, I recalled my stepdad's outrageous email where he called Ata a parasite. An idea came to mind. I told Ata, "What if I told my parents I'm considering divorce and need some time away from you. Then I could fly there to visit with my family for a month to see my siblings and Noor. Then we could magically make up. Then you come pick me up and take me to your parents' house." "I don't know how I feel about you being there with your stepdad for a month, it's not safe, and I would be worried. You remember what happened the night we left." "Yes, but I'm married. Yes, I know I was married then, too, but I'll call you every day and if I don't, you'll know something is wrong. Plus, I can always run away to Noor's house until you arrive if I sense any danger." Ata reluctantly agreed since it would be the only way we could both go home for the summer. Now all that was needed was to convince my stepdad. After so long of not emailing I decided to start by emailing him a short work of poetry I had been working on in the back of my textbook. He replied by asking if I wrote it and reminding me that I was a talented writer. Then I finally sat down and wrote him a more serious email. It read as follows (errors retained):

> **Subject: hi daddy**
>
> *hi daddy*
>
> *i was thinking about what we talked about and i dont want to get devoriced its too soon to be thinking about that i am in a marriage after all iwant to try and make it work as best i can only when i have tried everything can before i concider devorice...i was thinking about spending sometime apart i think it owuld be good for both of us but where to go thats my problem and would ata agree well i dont know i havent tlaked to him about it yet u tell me*

what u think daddy..

POTA (Princess of them all)

I waited for a reply and when it came this is what he said:

Subject: Re: hi daddy

Divorce is not easy, and so is getting married, and it will be twice as difficult for a divorcee, and 10 times worse for a divorcee with kids, at the end of the day, it's the loses and gain equation that makes us chose the one path from the other. Too soon or not is not the determining factor to stay together, does he want you, do you want him are the things that you need to look at. Trying to make a marriage works with some one who feel forced to live with you because of all the social and financial obligations that divorce may bring, is like filling up a cup with a hole, you hope to be able to fill it up by increasing the poured water (efforts) but even when you succeed it wont last, and your life turn to a continuous race with your own sanity to keep that cup full. A couple do not necessary have to have the same goals and interests in life, they do not even have to connect and carry a meaning full conversation all the times, but they must at least want each others and welling to cross the extra mile to see happiness and smiles on their partner's face. I don't know much about the way your life with him is going, but from the little I've seen and heard, you are the one who been crossing all the miles, he refused to even when he had the chance to do it he preferred not to. I could be wrong in my conclusions, but Princess, you are the only one who can judge that. As far as trying everything to work it out, is that even possible?

Yamama, it takes two to tango, while one is pouring the water the other need to put a finger on the hole to fill up the cup of life, then enjoy drinking it together. You need to confront him with your concerns your feelings and be able to say your opinion because it's yours not because it makes him happy. To me separation will not help solving any problems, it only allow more room for the men to lie about their feelings and what are they spending their time on, and keeps the women in dream land created by the few words from the man over the phone. Facing problems and finding solu-

tions together is what marriage is all about. Beside, as a man, if I have to be separated from my woman, I would not like to see her living any where except at her parents or mine (if I cared about her that is). In your case, living with his parents in 2 bed rooms flat with his 2 brothers with no chance to complete your studies is not really an option, is it?

The moral of this lecture is as follows:

* *Divorce should be the very last solution for marriage problems.*

* *Working out marriage problems requires both partners to recognizes these problems and face them up, separation is an escape way to avoid confrontation.*

* *A short period break from each other is OK, as long as both partners are comfortable with it.*

* *Do not let social and financial obligations be the reasons for eternal living hell. We live our day looking toward the future not the past.*

* *Test him by dropping on him divorce as a solution, if the first or the only thing he can think of is the money he spent or going to spend, then that is the only thing that is keeping him with you and that is sad. If he got shocked and seemed confused then he does not know what he wants and he is been moved by traditions, his family, and his parents, in this case, god help you girl you got your self a nonstop rollercoaster ride that will last you a life time. If he really doesn't want a divorce (by him or by you) and he want you in his life, then you got your self a starting point for confrontation and solving problems together, USE IT IMMEDIATELY, find out what he wants tell him what you want and get your life in the right track with all my blessing and wishes for an everlasting happiness.*

I know the above is a lot to read, but I can't help it I miss lecturing you, and as always, if you understand any of it please try to explain it to me because I don't.

A phone call and a couple weeks later, all was settled for me to return home to my parents. I got on the messenger and told Noor the great news that I was coming down, to which she replied, "Honey, you should not go back, it is too dangerous." She reminded me of the day I left and my stepdad's threat to keep me despite me having a husband. "Think, honey, think before you come back." I was scared but the plan was in place. The urge to see my siblings was a huge pull. I just wanted to see how they were, pick them up and remind them how loved they are. "I'm coming, honey, so we need to make an escape plan and we need your mom on board." "Okay, let me think." "Okay, what if we keep it simple. I'll call you every day just like Ata. If I can't, I'll text but remember to watch my language since it could be my stepdad. I'll start every message with your name as code for it's me writing the note. I'll delete them once sent so he won't know the pattern. Here, take down Ata's number and add him on the messenger, in case I need you to get a message to him." "Okay, honey, see you soon and good luck." Ata told me one last time, "if I don't talk to you every day to let me know you're okay I will be on the first plane to take you away from there. Worst case scenario, you're American. The embassy will surely help you get out." I put my fear out of my mind and looked toward the happy reunion and seeing my siblings again.

Ata took me to the airport and stayed with me until I passed through the security checkpoint. It was scary traveling alone. I was constantly worried someone would grab me, put something in my bag when I wasn't looking, or steal my purse with my passport, leaving me stranded in a strange place. Amsterdam airport alone was scary trying to follow the signs and make sure I got to my gate on time. I spoke to no one. My plane landed in Saudi late in the evening. It was the first time I had landed in Saudi alone. I put on my abaya and my black head cover on the plane just before landing. As I exited the plane, I covered my face completely as I had always done. I stood up straight and walked slowly. It was almost like all the changes I had gone through that year faded away and I turned back into my Saudi self. Proud and waiting patiently for someone to even try and speak to me out of line, so I could puff out my chest and say, "Do you know who my father is?"

I waited in the line where I was told that all foreign women needed to wait inside until an escort arrived to pick them up. I moved to the front and said in Arabic, "My father is Saudi, and he is waiting outside. The officer held out his full hand flat in the direction of the door as if to say, "off you go." I went to gather my bag and, like I had seen my stepdad do many times, I turned my veiled face toward one of the Indian men standing with the luggage carts. I insinuated with my hand that he should come grab my bag from the conveyor belt. He did so and took it to customs to go through the scanner. He lifted it up and put it on the scanning machine. Removed it from the other side and we headed out the door. When you exit the door, you find a metal fence where all the men picking people up are required to stand until the people exiting on the other side of the fence see the person there to pick them up. I saw my stepdad immediately. He smiled and came out to get my bag, tipping the nice Indian man who had helped me.

My stepdad opened the car door for me. I got into the front seat of the car and my stepdad told me everyone was waiting to see me and that everything would be all right. I remember looking out the window watching the city skyline go by. The place that had been my home for so many years now seemed dustier than I remembered. I asked my stepdad, "Were all the buildings always this dusty or is it just me?" To which he replied, "When you live here you get used to it. The dust storms, as you know, come and no one would be able to clean the buildings that often. It's only when you go away and see how other countries keep their buildings that you notice the thick layer of dust on the buildings here." I noticed the trash on the streets. The brand-new purple Mercedes left smashed on the side of the road for days at a time. The checkpoints at every highway exit. There were no people walking in the streets like in Canada. All I saw were workers, drivers, and men walking to the mosques. All the women dressed in black, and all the men wore their white thobes and yet, it felt and smelled like home. I was happy to be back despite having to cover again in my black abaya and having no right to go anywhere. I was happy to be home. There was a kind of comfort in the predictable and a peace in the slow pace of Riyadh that night. This world felt as if it moved slower than Canada with all its hustle and bustle. Riyadh, even though it was a city, moved slowly like a woman gliding around a ballroom one step at a time, pausing to be admired.

We finally arrived home and I was so happy. I took off my abaya and came into the living room. My stepdad apparently lied when he said everyone was waiting for me. It appeared that he had forgotten to tell anyone I was coming. He wanted it to be a surprise, he said. My mom cried as she approached me, holding on to me and soaking my shirt with tears as if I had returned from a war when she thought I was dead. I noticed that she was pregnant again, I asked, "Why after talking to me on the phone so many times, did you not bother to let me know you were pregnant?" She said, "Well, I thought it would make you unhappy." I leaned in and said, "What? Why?" She reminded me that the last time she was pregnant with Lina, when she was throwing up in the bathroom, I got upset and asked if she had heard of protection and why in the world, she kept having so many children.

She failed to understand that I was not mad she was pregnant as much as I was already exhausted taking care of her current bunch while she spent her days watching TV. I looked at her and said, "I'm happy for you, that's great!" Since in my mind now it would no longer fall to me to care for the new baby since I lived in Canada. If she wanted to add to her workload, more power to her. Then I saw Lina. I walked across the living room to the dining room and swept her up in my arms and twirled her around. I had missed her so but in doing so I didn't think that my shirt would rise up just enough to reveal my belly button ring. I had gotten it done a few weeks earlier. I did not notice my stepdad taking note of my belly button ring since I was too busy with my siblings.

That night once everyone was off to bed and I was all unpacked, my stepdad summoned me into the living room for what was often referred to as family meetings where we discussed matters that should not be overheard by the children. I sat down in my usual place on the floor facing the two of them on the couch. My mind flashed back to the time my mom walked in and Noor was comforting me by brushing my hair and I was called into this very room for a family meeting so they could ask me if me and Noor were lesbians. All I could think was, what now…

As I sat in the living room that night on the floor facing the two of them my stepdad started by saying how disappointed he was with me. "How could you pierce your body like a common street walker?"

I chuckled and said, "A lot of girls have them and my husband likes it." The sentence my stepdad hated most in the world. I enjoyed seeing his face when I said it. He said, "While you're in this house, you will not wear such things." I stood up and protested "Come on no one can see it, it's under my shirt. It's not like I'm parading it around!" "If I saw it then your brother and sisters saw it. So, you will take it out now." I protested some more, "But if I take it out, it will close up and I'll have to get it re-pierced." "Well, that's not my concern, you shouldn't have gotten it done in the first place." I stormed off to my room where I debated not taking it out at all and keeping a close watch on my shirts. I decided it was better to just take it out rather than risk the wrath of my stepdad, should he notice the slight hint of a belly button ring poking out from under my shirt.

I went to sleep in my old bed and slept well since I had been traveling for so long. Noura was so happy. She asked if we could stay up and play *Barbies* and I promised her we would another night telling her I was going to be there for at least a month. Yasmin was getting so tall and beautiful. I woke up at night a little and watched the two of them sleep. The next day I walked around the house, remembering what my mom had said about everyone being better now that I was gone. All I saw was that everything was worse. They had hired a maid, who didn't speak much English, to help with the housework. Mom still sat in her room all day. The kids' grades were suffering because there was no one to help them with their homework. My stepdad finally had to employ a tutor to help them get their grades up. A part of me wished they were doing better with me gone. At least then saying what she said to me would have been justified despite how it made me feel. I only ever wanted to see them all happy, safe, and taken care of.

I wondered why she would say something like that to me since it wasn't true. She must have meant that she didn't want me to come back, and the thought cut me very deeply. After all I had done. All those years, instead of hanging out on my computer, playing with my make-up, and talking on the phone to Noor, I took care of the family. All the times she had breakdowns and I picked up the pieces left by the dramatic scenes she pulled before hiding in some obscure place in the house until my stepdad found her. All the nights, I fixed dinner for the children, making sure they went to bed on time, tucking them in as their mother laid in her bed watching TV or reading the latest Steven King novel. A part of my heart felt like it died. I wiped the little tears that started to run down my cheeks and pulled myself together. I stood up straight and reminded myself I never did it for her. I did it for them. Then I rolled up my sleeves and began to make lunch for the kids. They were so excited as Noura and Mohammed told me tales of all the strange food mom had made in the last year since I was gone. We laughed like we always did as we cooked together.

If I could not be here, I thought, I might as well teach whoever can learn how to cook for the others. I spoke to Noura about being the oldest girl in the house now and the responsibilities that came with that. "You're the big sister now and I count on you to look after the others. Help them with their homework if you can, cook when you can." Noura and I stayed up that night with Yasmin and played *Barbies* together. When we finally went to bed, we heard a creak in the door and all of our hearts pounded. Theirs for fear of a spanking and mine for fear of everything else in the world that they could not fathom. As the door opened slowly in came little Lina who for the past year always slept in mom's bedroom. She crept in and climbed into my bed. I cuddled her, kissed her head, and sang her a little song as I had done when she was a baby until she went to sleep. A couple of hours later my mom arrived, hovered over my bed for a moment and then woke me to say, "I'll take Lina back to bed. Sorry for the bother." I whispered, "No bother, you go to sleep let's not wake her." She said "Okay," and returned to her room.

It was at that moment I realized why she had said what she did to me. I was the mother to them she never was, and it hurt her deeply. She forgot along the way that children need parenting and because she was always absent, only showing up for a hug, a play session, or a spanking, they looked to me. I never realized that even though she never put in the effort to act like their mother, she watched as I called them to attention. How I always knew where each one of them was and what they were doing without ever needing to leave what I was doing. The kids were always dressed properly, and dinner was always on time no matter how busy I was. I asked myself how a mother could be jealous of her own daughter? I sighed and realized that she and I were like the fat girl at school who hated the skinny girl. She wanted to be me. She watched me every day just like the fat girl in school who idolized and despised the skinny girl. Instead of going on a diet and going after that dream of being like the skinny girl, she ate more instead. Despite everything she had, my life was the dream she wanted. All her children looking up to her. Taking her advice. Thinking she was cool. Respecting her authority, not out of fear, but out of love. Being asked to play *Barbies* at night. Keeping their secrets and receiving praise for a house well taken care of and a delicious dinner prepared and served with warmth and love.

Why didn't she just get up from her cloud, leave her TV or book one day, come down and take her place as the mother they all wanted her to be? I felt pity for her in that moment. Even though she would never know what I had been through to protect her family and to care for her children. Even though she would never understand or appreciate all that I had given up for her. She was my mother and I still loved her. Forgiveness, when it comes from the heart, is the most beautiful and freeing feeling. How could I not forgive my mom, my blood, when I had found a way to forgive my stepdad time after time, even though he always took my forgiveness for granted. Holding on to anger, hurt, pain, and sadness would have never put food in the children's bellies. I knew from her example that if I had fallen apart the house would have fallen into ruin. I forgave and tried to move on. All I ever wanted in life was to make her proud of me and so I forgave her that night for hurting my feelings and went to sleep peacefully.

The next day the kids were playing in the afternoon, and I took a phone call from Ata. While I was talking and smiling, I told him how much I missed him. Just when my stepdad walked in the room. He waved his hand in front of my face and said, "Who are you speaking to?" I waved him off and continued talking. When I hung up, he again asked, "Who were you talking to?" and I said, "My husband." His face turned red with anger and then he said, "Why?" I said, "Because he's my husband," and my stepdad shot back, "You should not be talking to him! If I catch you again, I'll take your phone." I nodded and went upstairs. Once in my room, I called Noor and told her what had happened. We discussed what to do and we decided it was too risky to stay. If my stepdad took my phone, I would not be able to take Ata's calls, and Ata would be sure to show up. If he showed up, it would be a mess. If Ata was asked to call at random hours when my stepdad wasn't home, he would worry and also be sure to show up. I didn't want to leave, but the thought of having Ata arrive suddenly, the damage might be irreparable not just to me, but to my ability to see my siblings and my mom. How would I explain to them why my husband was acting like a lunatic and why their dad was fighting with him. We weighed the options and decided that the safest way for me and everyone was if I left and stayed with Noor while I waited for Ata to arrive.

My stepdad seemed to have plans that involved keeping me in Saudi under his control and I was not willing to put anything past him. He was Saudi, and my husband, despite being Canadian, was Syrian in the eyes of the Saudi authorities. I would not risk a conflict where my stepdad's influence would land Ata in jail or worse. The next day Noor said she could get there with the driver by eleven. I packed my bag. When she called saying she was at the backdoor with the driver, I pulled the children aside and told them they needed to keep mommy busy. They took up the challenge and talked to her until she fell asleep for her nap. I went to the back door and handed the driver my bag. Noor issued the order to the driver, "Run Ahmed, run straight to the car!" We ran behind him. Once inside the car we laughed and hugged each other. I was so happy to see her and relieved to be out of that house.

A couple hours later my mom went looking for me. Then she interrogated the kids who finally spilled the beans and told her that I left. My mom called and when I picked up, I said, "I'm fine." "Where are you?" she asked. "I'm safe and I'm fine." I replied. She asked again and I said, "I'm fine, goodbye." Noor's mom asked me if I was okay, to which I replied thank you so much for having me, Auntie. We went upstairs to the roof and looked out over the city, set up the shisha and smoked all day. We laughed and filled each other in on the last year that we had missed being in each other's lives. She told me about how the boy she had a crush on disappeared, so one day she called his phone but his wife answered, so it was over. I told her about Ata and how happy we were. We laid on a blanket on the roof, looking at the stars, and dreaming about her wedding one day and my future children .

We laughed about all our old adventures in school. We smoked until 5:00 a.m., we were high on life. As we stumbled down the stairs arm in arm, we sang one of our favorite Mariah Carey songs until we hit the bed and fell asleep. We slept better than we had in years. It was the first time I had ever slept over at her house. I didn't have to worry about my mom calling saying I needed to go home, or time was up. She was done with school and free to spend time with me. The next few days were some of the happiest days I had ever passed. We did nothing and everything. We never ran out of topics to discuss.

One day Noor said she wanted to go to the beauty parlor, where she and her sister had been working. I went with her and met her new friends. They were an interesting group of girls who seemed very friendly. She told me about all the things they did. The secret mixed parties with alcohol and the boyfriends they had. I held myself back from telling her how bad her friends were. My good friend was transformed into what my inner Bedouin described as scandalous. How would she marry? I thought, I must protect her from them, but how? Having a secret telephone relationship in Saudi is one thing, but the parties and the boys, this was dangerous territory. All it would take was one raid. One person accidentally telling the wrong person and there would be no going back, just straight to wherever the religious police decided she should go. After that, to accept whatever sentence was deemed appropriate.

One night her new friends invited us to a party they had planned to celebrate Noor's birthday. Every bone in my body screamed, "DANGER" when I heard that there would be prostitutes there, the son of the Ambassador to Bahrain was bringing the liquor, and there was a boy she had a crush on. I listened to the details with great reserve, trying to foresee an escape plan should the party get raided. It was her birthday. How could I ruin it by saying I wasn't going and if something should go wrong how could I forgive myself if I had not been there to help her escape? "Are you sure you want to go?" I asked, "It sounds dangerous." "Nonsense," she said, "I have been to many of these parties they are fun." I asked her, "Who knows where we are going just in case." She replied, "The driver will take us and if mom asks where we are, the driver will know." I thought for a bit, took a deep breath, and slowly let it out in a deep sigh, "OOOkay."

We got dressed up and started down to the car. At the last minute, her mom got in the car and said, "When he drops you off, I need him to take me somewhere." Noor was concerned that her mom would figure out what we were up to doing. A part of me hoped she would figure it out and stop us. I told her mom, "Auntie, I'm so happy you're joining us for the ride." Noor squeezed my hand which meant be quiet. I knew in my bones that her mom's sudden arrival was not by accident but to make sure she knew where we were as she turned a blind eye to the fun her girls were having. I was grateful and relieved.

We arrived at the *Istiraha*, which is a villa often with a pool that is kept or rented on the outskirts of the city. They serve as a kind of summer house, where whole families would go. Each family takes a room, and everyone gets together to barbecue, sit by the fire in the desert, or watch the children swim in the pool. As soon as the car stopped Noor grabbed my hand and we jumped from the car. Trying to get inside before some boy exited and gave the party away. My heart was in my throat, and I was on high alert. My eyes swept over everything as we entered the party. I saw the drink cart and the boys who were probably already drunk.

My mind started to map out the exit strategies as well as the number of boys versus girls and anything that could be used to defend ourselves, should it come to it. Noor seemed to have no care in the world laughing as she introduced me, and we greeted everyone. I sat down and stared at the sight I was seeing. I sipped some tea I had gathered from the kitchen, making sure none of the boys had had a chance to touch it. I looked out for Noor as she laughed and danced with a new boy she liked. The Ambassador's son sat down next to me, offered me a drink, and made small talk, as I told him, "Thank you, but I don't drink, and I'm happily married." It was important to be very clear that I was here for Noor's birthday and not a part of the menu for this evening. I dropped hint after hint that my father was a Saudi, to make sure he felt that there would be consequences since he had no idea how high up in the chain my father was. As he spoke to me, I pretended to listen and watched Noor constantly like a hawk.

Suddenly I noticed the girl Noor had pointed out to me as a prostitute leave the room and head to the back room. One by one, the men left and a little while later returned. I shuddered to think what was happening as we sat in the grand living room. The smoke was so foggy you could cut it with a knife, the music blaring in our ears. I finally needed to go help cut and serve Noor's cake in the kitchen. As I passed through the hallways to get there, I saw the prostitute lying face down on a couch. I kept my cool, but my mind kept thinking once these men are drunk enough who is to say we won't be next. My mind spun with scenarios of mass rape. Who could we call if something happened? There would be no one to tell afterwards. I helped arrange the cake, hoping all the while that my proud demeanor and the fact that my stepdad was a Saudi was enough to keep us safe until Noor's driver arrived to take us home.

We brought out the cake and everyone sang happy birthday as she danced with her new crush. I danced a little with her and then took my seat again. Finally, the driver arrived, and we left. Noor had a wonderful night, but I was on edge more than I had been in years. She talked the whole way home about the lovely time we had, never even considering the danger we were in. My blood started to boil. I listened and I listened until finally hours later at home, it came out. "How could you associate with such people! They are all sluts and pimps! Do you want to be seen as one of them? "They are my friends!" she said. "Some friends! You think they care about you or what happens to you?!... They don't!" I said. Our voices raised in Noor's bedroom, causing her little sister, now sixteen, to become concerned. She knocked and said, "Is everything alright in there?" and then tried to open the door. I went straight to the door, pushed it shut and locked the door from the inside, determined not to be disturbed until we were done.

Our anger built until finally we jumped into a knock down drag out fight. Her sister all the while banging on the door trying to see if we were okay. Finally, we stopped fighting and laid down on the floor as we had always done, side by side, but this time not speaking. I got up and unlocked the door as her sister entered to see what was wrong. We both stayed silent. "You two are crazy!" she said. I took the pack of cigarettes on the dresser and headed up to the roof with Noor in tow. For the next seven minutes we sat on opposite sides of the roof looking at the floor. We didn't really smoke cigarettes but with the lack of the *shisha* being ready it seemed like a good idea. Her sister snapped what is today probably the most important picture we have of us together. It was raw, real, and honest. When we finished smoking, we looked over at each other and laughed out loud, as we replayed our very first fight and how silly we were. Noor discussed how even though she knew her new friends were not the best in the world, she was lonely, and I was gone for so long. I took a deep breath and understood. Since I had a group of friends in Canada who weren't the best but were at least something for me to fill the time. I was wrong to judge. "Even my friends are not the best, *Hiyate*, but in Canada, it's different. If we go to a club there and get caught, we won't be lashed or worse, stoned as prostitutes. Remember where you are, I know you like to have fun, but how much fun is worth your life?"

Saudi Arabia, despite being filled with people, despite being a communal culture where everyone knows everyone, is a lonely place. Please don't misunderstand; I loved that country and miss it sometimes, but when you grow up portraying your proper side every minute of every day that you are in front of people, you tend to push your own thoughts, desires, dreams, wishes, hopes, and fears deep down inside until you find yourself sitting in a room sipping tea like everyone else but feeling utterly alone. I knew how she felt but she would need to find safer outlets.

My stepdad called and called but I never answered, for fear of hearing him yell at me for leaving and then issuing a threat of some sort. After his hundredth call I answered the phone and said, "What do you want?" He said, "Your mother fell and she's in the hospital, do you want to go see her?" It sounded like a really good ploy to make me come out from wherever I was hiding. Since Noor had moved since I left it would be impossible for him to find me. I have to say if you want to go missing, Saudi Arabia is one of the best places to do it. You don't go out without covering your face and as long as you stay away from the gatherings where someone might know someone who knows you, well, you can fall off the map forever if need be. I said, "No I can't." He called me selfish and unkind. I asked if she was going to be okay, and he said he wasn't sure. Noor was standing in front of me saying, "It's a trick, honey." After all, being in the medical profession, his not being sure if she was going to be okay sounded a little too vague, even for him. He asked me where I was and if I was coming back. I told him I would not tell him where I was but that I was safe and when Ata arrived I would be going back to Canada. he said, "So you never planned to spend time with your siblings and your mom?" I replied to him, "Of course I did! It was your choice to act the way you did and make me leave. He was furious and said, "You're not going anywhere. I'm going to call the police and report you missing. When you get to the airport, they will just bring you home," and hung up the phone.

I looked at Noor and said, "Can he really do that or is he just bluffing?" She said she didn't know, and we ran downstairs to talk to her mom, who confirmed that if he does call, it will be very hard to leave and suggested that when Ata comes, we might try the American or Canadian Embassy. Yes, I thought the Embassy would help. They wouldn't let some Saudi individuals keep an American citizen against her will. We put it out of our minds and went on with continuing to plan Sara's birthday upcoming party. Those many weeks passed like one long sleepover. We went to the mall, ate out in restaurants, went to the theme park on ladies day, and in the evening, we would sit out under the stars on the roof, drink tea, listen to music, and talk.

As it got closer to Ata's arrival, Noor broached the subject of telling my mom about my stepdad and everything he had done. I told her she would never believe me and her not believing me would hurt worse. Noor used her mom as an example and said, "There is no way a mother could not believe her own daughter in matters such as these. After all, your stepdad is not your real dad, there is no way she would not believe you, Sweetheart." I took a sip of my tea as I silently thought about her words, and finally said, "I don't know, what's the point? I'm out now, so who cares? She's happy with him, so why not just leave her the way she is." Noor leaned in and looked me in the eyes and said, "Honey, what about the other girls? Soon they will get bigger and if you don't tell someone, who can keep an eye out … won't you regret it?" She was right. I would never forgive myself for leaving and I could never be happy knowing that I could have told my mom. Now that I was not there to protect them, maybe she would.

There were a lot of stories like mine when I was in school, but it would be many, many years before I would ever hear them. Mine is actually a lucky case. Before you clench your fists and say the word "lucky" aloud sarcastically, consider this. A girl I knew once had many sisters, the eldest was raped and deflowered by her real father. This made finding a match for her almost impossible. When her younger sister grew up, her dad raped her as well. The mother tried to stop it because she believed her daughters. She contacted the police, and he was taken before a judge. The judge ruled in the favor of the husband and the wife was sent back to him with her daughters. The wife was beaten so badly that the daughters had to fend for themselves. When the next sister down the line got bigger, the father cornered her in the dark sitting room and removed his pants. The older sister begged him to take her instead. I know in truth none of us were truly "lucky," but by comparison, maybe I was.

I knew my mother was weak and had always been unable to talk back to him, but she was now the only one in the house to watch over the children. The children I had raised since they were born. None of them were old enough to understand the meaning of rape, let alone what signs to look for.

The next day we called Ata and told him that we planned to call my mom and tell her. He said he thought I should have told her years ago but issued a word of caution that once told, it cannot be untold. He didn't want to see me hurt. He spoke briefly to Noor and asked her to please take care of me. She told him not to worry. I sat on Noor's bed and dialed my mom as Noor held my hand. She answered, apparently miraculously out of the hospital. "Where are you?" she asked. I said, "I'm good, I'm safe." She asked, "Are you in Jeddah with Ata's family?

I said, "No Mom. Just listen, I need to tell you something." She said, "What is it?" I told her she should maybe sit down, and she told me she did. Then I told her, "Mom, he's not who you think he is." She said, "What do you mean?" I said, "When I was little in England, he raped me." She cried, took a deep breath, and said, "Did you sleep with him?" I said, "Mom, what? I just told you he raped me, not that way but from behind." She said, "So, you slept with him, then." I said, "Mom, no, I was a virgin when I got married. Did you hear what I said?" She said, "I heard you, but I need to go, you just like to make trouble." I cried and hung up the phone. Noor held me as I cried and cried. The only thing worse than being raped is having your own mother not believe you. After you finally find the courage to tell her. I at least took comfort in the fact that I had my own life now and if I had told her when I was little it would have been much worse. In a way I always knew she wouldn't believe me; she didn't believe my brother, and he was her favorite.

It would take me many, many years to contemplate her reaction. Why she reacted the way she did. Some people say only the selfish survive. Maybe she knew she could never leave him and hating me was easier than taking in the truth. After all, in Saudi, in case of divorce, everything would go to him except what she owned individually, which was nothing. All children under the age of seven would be allowed to live with her. At seven years old the girls would be returned to their father for protection and sole custody. While the boys were given the right to choose where they want to live. Yes, perhaps the selfish do survive longer but I think it's not the selfish that survive the longest, it's the learners and my mother was never a learner. When my stepdad hit me, he showed he had the great capacity to do more harm than he had done in my youth. Like many we knew. I believe it was because I studied him carefully that I survived. My mother, like her mother before her, had many words for strong, free, smart, beautiful women. Such as the flight attendant I wanted to be when I was four and her favorite word for that was "hooker." It would be another twenty years before I would discover that my mother's mother called her a "hooker" once because she lost her virginity before she got married, and the guilt she carried had to come out on someone I suppose. I guess she decided it was me and if so, that was okay.

Ata finally arrived, and Noor's driver took Noor and I to the hotel where he was staying that night. I was so happy to see him. It was a relief to know he would take care of everything now. I went to say goodbye to Noor before she left the hotel. I sat on the couch next to her and rested my head on her lap as she stroked my hair and told me everything would be okay. Ata snapped a picture that will forever remain one of my favorite photos of us. At that moment she felt more like a mother to me then my mother had been in many, many, years. Noor departed and Ata and I spent the night catching up and loving on each other. It was the first time we had been apart since we got married and as is often the case with young love, we missed each other terribly.

The next day we headed to the airport to get on a plane to go see Ata's family in Jeddah. I was scared that someone would stop us, but no one did. Upon arrival in Jeddah, we were greeted by his parents who were so tickled that their son and his new bride would be staying with them. His mom spoiled me, and I loved it. For the next two weeks, every morning I woke up and all the neighboring women were in the kitchen helping prepare lunch just like we had done in my grandma's house in Mecca. After lunch we took a nap. Then shopping and dinner. It was peaceful and I felt like I had never known how it is to be in a house that wasn't plagued by a constant cloud of misery, secrets, deception, and suspicion. It was serene.

When the time came for us to leave, Ata sent someone to ask whether I would have trouble leaving the country if my stepdad had put out an alert that I had run away. The news that came back was, yes. As you recall, my stepdad had outsmarted me when he suggested that it would be easier for me to visit my family if my custody remained under his name as a Saudi. It would guarantee me entry whenever I wanted. Ata, on the other hand, was considered a student and his parents were expatriates. There would be no guarantee they could stay. So, after we married, instead of transferring my male guardianship to my husband as is normally the custom, they all agreed to leave it under my stepdad.

Maybe he really did it for the reason he said, but in this case, now it was a problem.

Ata said we should go to the American Embassy and ask them to intervene on my behalf to get me out but upon arrival the embassy said they already had at least ten American women with Saudi children hidden in hotels around the city, because they were in danger, and they still have not been able to get them out of the country. They said at least I didn't have children but because I could not prove I was in danger they could not help. Ata steamed, paced, and thought as I called and told Noor what had happened. "Show them the video," she said. Ata's eyes lit up, "Yes, the video that will convince them." We went home and burned a video disc with the video of my stepdad grabbing me for them to see. When we arrived back and told the embassy what we had in hand they took us back into a dark room with black glass. After they watched the video, they decided they had a case but assured me that it would take many months, if not years, to take this matter to the courts. They also warned me that if it did go to court, I might not be allowed back in the country ever again. I nodded and said, "I understand, I just want to leave." They kept the copy of the video, and we headed to Ata's parents' house.

The days turned into weeks and still nothing, I called every day but every day we got the same answer, "We're working on it but we still encourage you to try and fix it with your stepdad yourself." "Fix it with that asshole?" Ata said. "No way, he doesn't get to decide." Time was running out and Ata's job was in danger of being lost if we delayed his return to Canada any longer. If he went back without me, that would place me under the full guardianship of my stepdad, and therefore there was no other option. Fearful that he might have to leave if this dragged on further, he sat his parents down and told them what was happening. His mother gasped in shock but said, "It all makes sense, he was always making trouble when we were debating the *maher* (dowry) and the wedding plans."

In an effort to fix things herself, she decided she would go ahead and throw the Jeddah wedding they had planned when we returned after college. She would invite my mom so she could talk to her directly about my stepdad. Invitations went out and the hotel was reserved. My wedding dress was taken to the dry cleaners, and she asked me to call and invite my mom. I did as I was told and called her, but she simply said there was no way she could come, and she hoped I would have a good time. She had decided not to pursue anything I had told her and continue as she had been before I came back. She was happy, I was gone, and that was that.

The wedding was to be a ladies-only event for all of my mother-in-law's friends. My hair was done, and my veil was hooked in a more modern style. I danced as much as I liked but at the last minute when they called for Ata to come down, but he refused, hating the show and that he would have to be the only man in a room full of his mother's friends. When the buffet was open, I did something no Saudi bride had ever done. I removed my shoes and stood at the buffet door with my mother-in-law welcoming and greeting every single guest as they entered the hall. Normally the bride never comes down to the dinner and she certainly doesn't greet people, people greet her, food is brought to her. She is the princess of the night, but I had already had my night. I wanted to let everyone know that I was a part of this family now. Everyone remarked on how down to earth and humble Ata's mom's daughter-in-law was. My mother-in-law was proud.

I received many gifts, all of them gold. Some I later sold, because they were gaudy or not my style. I used the money to purchase something else I liked better. Among the guests was a lady my mother-in-law insisted I meet. I greeted her and then my mother-in-law mentioned that her brother was Osama Bin Laden. I said, "Oh, okay." Sadly, I hadn't seen the news at all since I considered it boring and whatever I needed to know would undoubtedly be told to me by my husband if it was noteworthy. I had no idea who she was as she handed me a beautiful sapphire necklace as a wedding gift, saying, "*Alf Mabrouk*" which means "1000 congratulations." When the night was over, I asked Ata who Osama Bin Laden was, and he told me. I asked, "Why is your mom friends with her?" He replied, "He might be a bad person but that's not his sister's fault." I nodded and thought for a moment. I asked my mother-in-law to come shopping with me the next day where I sold the beautiful sapphire necklace, not wanting to have anything in my possession that would link me to that family. My mother-in-law might categorize people by their virtues, which is often right, but I was raised to categorize them by their reputation and the reputation of their family, so I did what I needed to do.

Time ticked on and still nothing had come from the embassy. Noor suggested that her sister's new husband, a Saudi named Abu Sultan might be able to help us. I never knew his real name but it's normal for men and women to not be referred to by their name once they have their first son. Rather, he was known as *Abu* (meaning father of) and their first son's first name. My mother, for example, was referred to as *Um* (meaning mother of) Christopher but once Mohammed was born, he was considered the first-born son, since he was Saudi. She was from then on referred to as *Um Mohammed*. Noor's sister had done some office work for Abu Sultan when he noticed her. Despite being much older and already having a wife, he decided to take a second wife and married her in secret. Why in secret? Sometimes it was done to avoid a jealous first wife and still have sex with a younger model without it being a sin. I also would assume that there was a large dowry involved that was negotiated by her father and mother, which allowed them to agree to keep the marriage secret.

He was a wealthy businessman who had some influence, so Noor's sister pleaded with him on our behalf. He agreed to meet with us, so we flew back to Riyadh and stayed with Noor. He met with us and upon hearing the story, leaned back in his chair, and said, "The situation is easy, give me your passport and his phone number. I will make him give you his permission to leave." He called my stepdad and spoke with him for a few minutes then invited him to visit his office. He hung up the phone and said, "He is on his way. You should go into the next room." We went into the adjacent room and abided there as he welcomed my stepdad in his office and proceed to threaten him if he did not return the next day with the passport and an exit visa. We listened at the door intently. It surprised me how calm and humble my stepdad was, agreeing without question to everything Abu Sultan said. Once my stepdad had gone, we came out and said, "How did it go?" Abu Sultan leaned back in his chair again, laughed and said, "He was trembling like a baby. All will be well you'll see." Ata thanked him, and I sighed a sigh of relief. Then we went to Noor's house for dinner. We spent the night waiting for the next day when my stepdad was to return with the passport. The next day we waited and nothing. Finally, Abu Sultan called to threaten my stepdad, but he took his stand and said, "If she wants to leave, she can ask me herself," hanging up on Abu Sultan and calling his bluff.

I felt like all was lost now, not only was I without an exit visa I had no passport anymore. The next day we went to the embassy in Riyadh and explained what had happened because we realized now my stepdad had my passport, things were even more tricky. Despite our efforts we had been unable to secure an exit, so the embassy officials finally agreed to expedite things through the court system.

When I look back now, it was obvious that once I no longer had my passport and I also had a damaging video, it had become a larger news story and the longer they kept me waiting, the more likely I was to tell it and that made them move. We had been trapped in Saudi for three months. Ata was at risk of losing his job, our home, everything. We stayed in Riyadh with Noor's family to try and save some money. When finally, the call came that we would meet with my stepdad and the judge the next day. I did not sleep that night from fear of not wanting to see him again. Afraid the judge would rule with a fellow male Saudi. Noor stayed up with me all night trying to distract me from my worries as we waited for the sun to rise.

The next morning, we headed to the courthouse where two representatives from the embassy were waiting. The elderly counsel woman came up to me saying, "There is no need to see the judge, after all, your stepdad has kindly agreed to give you back your passport and let you go. All he wants is to talk to you, why don't you just talk to him." I looked at him across the room and all the years of pain, fear, all the suffering everything rushed through me "NO." I said, "I won't talk to him, I want to see the judge." The embassy representative again using her diplomatic skills said, "Oh, come on, I'm here you'll be okay." I turned my head away and said, "I want to see the judge. It's enough. I have had enough."

The call came to see the judge, and we all entered the room. The judge addressed my stepdad and asked him, "Dr. Turkistani, why are you keeping her against her will, when she has a husband?" my stepdad said, "I was looking out for my daughter and until now I had no idea it was her wish to leave for all I knew she was being coerced into leaving against her will." My blood rose up with anger at his manipulation of everyone in that room, even the embassy officials. I turned my head away to avoid looking at his face. "Lies," I thought to myself, "Since he had spoken to me on the phone." I looked up and said the first thing that came to mind, "*Hiywan, Himar*! (You animal, you donkey)!" Two in a long list of the worst insults in the Arab language. The judge asked that we all calm down and then ordered that my passport be given back to me, and I be allowed to leave. The embassy representative continued to graciously thank my stepdad with all kinds of bowing and scraping as if he had done them a great favor. As we left, she said, "He still wants to speak with you." I said, "Fine." He said, "Take care of yourself, kid." to which I replied, "Go to hell."

Let this be a lesson to all. All the stories we're told and all the movie scenes we've been fed about how our embassy is there to help when you're in trouble do not apply on Saudi soil. If they can get away with not helping, they will. Their relationship with Saudi Arabia is so very important, you will be considered collateral damage. Unless you possess something that could cause an incident that was media worthy. I realize now that if I had not come back to the embassy with the video, they would have just turned me away again, just like they did the first time. I think back to the ten women they had put up in hotel rooms who had Saudi children. Who probably never left because they had nothing to prove that there was any kind of abuse and no way to reach an external media source. This is more than likely, based on the way the American council bowed and scraped to my stepdad, and how many times she urged me to resolve things with him myself. My guess would be that they put those women up in hotel rooms and had them wait until they were tired of being stuck in a small hotel room and decided to go back to their husbands. While the council negotiated with the husbands behind the scenes asking them to mend the fence.

We had a video and there was nothing stopping Ata from returning to Canada and telling the story of his wife, an American citizen who was molested by her Saudi stepdad at the age of eleven. Who was being held against her will in the country by the same man. Even though she was married, the American authorities did not intervene. Not only was it a bad story for the Saudis since one of their own had been bad but it was bad for their reputation of upholding Islamic law since I was no longer under his guardianship Islamically the day I married. After three months they all could agree that the best solution was to let me go as soon as possible. Since it was obvious, I was young and didn't know what power I possessed, and everyone wanted to keep it that way. Even today it is not like the movies, if you're running from someone and you don't have your passport, you're not going to even get past the external guard of the American embassy. I know because I had a meeting once, years later, when I forgot my passport and the guard, seeing my name on the list, still refused to call anyone, or let me in. You can call out, "But I'm an American citizen, this is my embassy, you have to let me in" but ... good luck with that. There is so much I love about the people and where I grew up but when it comes to being a woman, even an American one in Saudi Arabia, all I can say is Buyer Beware...

The next day we were on a plane returning to Canada and our life. I finally felt truly free of my stepdad, and I was eager to get back to my life.

Ata's parents came to visit us that summer. Upon their arrival, they stayed with Ata's father's cousin since he was the oldest relative, and his house had a guest room. They took us to dinner and came by our house for tea afterwards. His mother scanned the area, the apartment's conditions, and the noises coming from the neighboring apartments. While asking Ata, "How could you have your wife living in such an unsafe place?" Ata hung his head and said, "This is what I can afford." His mom looked around and her eyes rested on me as she said, "She is now our responsibility." Her husband silent. Nodding as he always did in agreement with his wife. I felt blessed to have them worry about me as if I was their daughter. It was touching.

As we drove them home, we stopped at a gas station. Ata and his dad got out to pump gas and get a few things from the convenience store. It was the first time my mother-in-law and I ever conversed alone. "You know we think of you as our daughter and if there is ever anything you need or that I can do for you, please feel that you can tell me anything. Men are not always good," she said. She added, "and if there is anything wrong or you need to tell me something, please feel safe to do so." The minutes passed in that car so slowly. As I looked at her face, my mind raced. Should I tell her about Ata's weed habit, his drinking, his partying? What did she know and even though I knew she could help and traditionally I would talk to her to knock her son into line, I didn't want to be like all the other wives. Exposing their husband's secrets. I knew it would just make him keep secrets from me and I didn't want that. Instead of smoking his weed and drinking with his friends in my living room he would stay out all night. I felt it's more dangerous for him to be smoking and drinking on the street. I felt like I was drowning. No one had prepared me for this. I needed her advice.

I longed for a confidant but to do so would be to betray my husband's confidence and do as all the women in the family did and lead a life of quite unhappiness. He would lead his life outside the house, and I would lead mine inside the house. He would never confide in me again; we would have children and he would act as he should, and our days would go on as if everyone was happy. I had watched my stepdad and my mom live separate lives for too long. I watched my uncles do it with their wives and I didn't want that for Ata and me. So, as the seconds ticked on in that car, I smiled and said, "Thank you, I will remember that if something comes up." I touched her hand and the men returned to the car. A part of me always wishes I had confided in her, but it just wasn't possible. If she had known everything he was doing, she would have had a heart attack. It really wasn't my place to tell her, it was his.

The next day we visited a real estate agency and discussed what it would take for us to buy an apartment instead of rent. I listened as more money was mentioned than I had ever seen in my life. I had no idea how much buying a house costs since it was a male topic that I had been taught not to worry about as a woman. I listened as my Mother-in-law took control of the situation like a commander in the army. It was so interesting to see such a confident and powerful woman. I looked up to her and hoped one day I might be more like her.

We visited a few apartments and found one across from a very popular mall called Square One. It was a two bedroom with ceiling to floor windows in the living room, brand new and gorgeous to behold. The front door entered into the living room. To the right was the kitchen that had a bar that opened to the living room. Past the kitchen on the left was a small room that could be a guest room or a study, followed by the master and a bathroom to the left. The washer and dryer were stacked on top of each other in a closet. I remember looking at them and wondering what is this magic? Who would have ever believed that you could stack a washer and a dryer let alone fit them in a closet. Back home they would have been on the roof in a hot laundry room so that the noise would not disturb the rest of the house. We all fell in love with the apartment at once and when my mother in-law said, "Yes, this is the one," I leaped into her arms for joy. She chuckled and patted me on the back. She had never had a daughter and she was used to having boys and men around the house. I was determined to be the perfect first daughter.

The next day we returned to the realtor's office and started on the paperwork. Ata's parents had decided they would give us the down payment provided Ata could get approved for the loan. We waited a few days for the phone to ring. When it finally did the news was too much to handle. He was approved. We all celebrated by going out to dinner and Ata's mom called everyone in her address book to let them know that her son was now going to be a homeowner.

It felt like our life was really starting the way it was meant to. We were happy but now we had a mortgage and with that came extra responsibility to make sure we made our payments on time. I think perhaps the pressure of marriage and a mortgage was a lot for us to handle, Ata, a man of only 24, and I at age 21. I had no idea how much that responsibility might have weighed heavy on a man.

I did my best to keep the house and make everything perfect for him every day. My walks now were to the mall instead of the grocery store. I listened to my iPod and danced in the snow pretending to be Mariah Carey, Christina Aguilera, or Britney Spears. As I sang along to the songs, something started to feel missing. I wanted a purpose, I wanted more and at the same time I felt guilty for feeling that way. It was funny how marriage was this big adventurous escape I was looking forward to my entire life and now I just felt selfish for wanting more. If I had told anyone they would have just said it's time for a baby, but we didn't have the money for a baby.

One day we stopped at the Arabic store to pick up some supplies. Ata waited in the car as I picked up what I needed. While checking out I overheard the owner interviewing a girl for a job in the store working as a cashier. My ears perked up when he said I would pay you cash because I don't want to pay taxes. She turned down the offer and left. I could not work yet in Canada since my residency was pending along with my Canadian social security number. I asked the owner, "Excuse me, how much does the job pay?" "It pays $5.50 an hour." I looked at his nails and the rotten meat underneath them wondering why his wife never made him scrub the dead meat from his nails that had seemed to be rotting there for the last few years by the look of it. I thought to myself how exciting it would be to have my own spending money, to not have to ask someone every time I wanted to buy a dress or a new pair of shoes. He took one look at me and leaned his head back in a chuckle saying, "The job is yours if your husband agrees." I said, "Thank you so much!" and ran to the car.

I got in and told Ata about the job. He immediately said, "No. What would people say if my wife was working in a supermarket? It's not a job for a lady." I begged and said, "Please let me do it. I can bring in some extra money and I would still be home in time to cook dinner every night. It might be fun, please, please!" "Fine," he said. I kissed his cheek and ran inside saying, "I can start tomorrow." The owner smiled and said, "Be here at 8:00 a.m. and we will show you the ropes." The large Egyptian butcher behind the counter nodded at me with his large knife in hand and said, "Welcome to the family."

The next day I woke up with so much zeal, excited about my very first job. I got Ata ready for work, tied his tie, and he dropped me off on his way to the mall. I bounced into the shop like a little girl going to Disneyland, as the owner came from behind the desk happy to have me join the team. The shop was small and like so many Middle Eastern stores, it was run down. A penny pincher serving a community of bargain hunters doesn't really keep the floor in good repair. The shop had a shotgun layout. The cashier on the right when you enter, and the butcher counter on the left, with a small sink in a tiny room in the front. It smelled like rust from all the blood mixed with the smell a freezer gets when it's had meat coming and going for years without ever being defrosted and cleaned out. I remember wondering as I walked around how they ever passed their inspection year after year but there it was on the wall: health inspection passed.

He showed me to the cash register. I wondered why his gloves were ripped but he didn't put on new ones. Then he showed me how the cash register worked. I thought it was so fun to use and pushing the button that made the cash register drawer fly open was so exciting. The responsibility of counting the change and making sure I got it right felt like an honor. Then he took me on a tour of the shelves and told me all about how things work. "If something expires and doesn't sell it is returned to the seller for credit or exchanged for other items that do sell, you understand? Now you're in charge of making sure nothing expired stays on the shelves, and also for checking the rice bags for bugs. Here let me show you how to check them." I had never thought it was possible for rice to get bugs in it, even in Saudi. I never saw such things on a supermarket shelf. Perhaps the supermarkets had people who checked their rice for bugs and as a consumer I just never knew. The idea of bugs grossed me out as he pulled one of the rice bags down and pointed out the tiny holes in the bag saying, "You see they bite through and lay their eggs inside." I made a face as he laughed but I thought at least they are inside the rice bags unlike the potatoes Ata left in the cupboard while we were stuck in Saudi which became a breeding colony for cockroaches. That was a night of gloves and bug spray and chasing the little roaches all over the kitchen. I will never forget that experience as long as I live. "*Umo* (uncle) I just have one request." "Sure, what is it?" "I don't want to work with the meat if that's alright? I don't like blood." "Of course, there is no need for you to work with the meat, but once in a while I will need you to help wash some dishes and the parsley for my *Kofta* (meat dish of seasoned ground meat)." "That sounds fine."

It all felt so exciting as if I was in a leading role playing a shopkeeper girl in a movie. As I climbed the ladder to wipe the shelves I felt a sense of honor, responsibility, and ownership. I worked hard to make the shelves tidy and checked out the customers as they arrived. The owner had one cassette tape by an Arabic singer from Lebanon named Fairuz who even today every Arabic person knows. She was a legend in her time. They say she had a beautiful voice and that she was a beauty but the more times he turned over that cassette tape and played the same songs again and again she started to sound like torture to my ears. They always asked if I was the owner's daughter since we were both white and had colored eyes and my Arabic was just as good as theirs to which he replied, "Yes, that's my daughter," and the three of us laughed at the inside joke.

At the end of the first day, he handed me my very first pay, $45 dollars. I was so happy I threw out my arms and hugged him like any girl would a father who had just given her a present. I skipped out to the car feeling like I was contributing to society one customer at a time. Ata was waiting to take me home and I talked the whole way home about how happy I was to have a job. He listened and smiled. My happiness seemed to be his happiness and there was so much joy in my heart that night as I spent the evening telling him about all the new things I had learned. Things like how to wash parsley that had just come from a farm covered in dirt and still crawling with grasshoppers that would jump out at you once you turned the water faucet on, "You should have seen how they jumped all over the place, it was crazy! And I got to organize the shelves and don't get me started on the cash register. It was so much fun."

Looking back now, I wonder about the nature of happiness. This is never to say that seeing the world as a child would and taking every new experience and making it a grand adventure is a bad thing, but not everyone can see the world that way. Too often, even if their job is the better one, your exuberance can cause them to question their happiness in their own job. Unfortunately for Ata I felt this excited about every new thing I did, even the simple walk to the grocery store. Happiness is something people crave. Just like the stranger who walks past a mansion and sighs, saying, "I'll never be able to buy a home like that one," people will look at people and say I'll never be that happy. I'm here to tell you this … happiness is a choice just like deciding you won't be poor anymore; anything is possible, you just need to decide.

Ata got a promotion to be the manager of a small store in the subway station. His promotion depended on him bringing up sales with the people he had. He was struggling and wanted to move up so desperately. One weekend when they had a sale going on I went with him for moral support. I noticed how his staff were shying away from customers and because of the store location people were leaving the station before ever visiting the store. I immediately took a stack of flyers in my hands and went to the middle of the station and began to shout, "Free cellphones, come down." People began to grab flyers and run down to the store. At the end of the day, we sold more than any store in the district.

That night after he closed the store and celebrated with his colleagues, he looked at me and said, "You can't do that." "Do what?" "You can't help with the store, and you can't hand out flyers in the terminal. You could get me in trouble." "I don't work for the store so there is no liability, you can say you never knew a customer would take flyers and hand them out in a subway." "Maha, everyone knows I'm your husband. I know you did a great thing and you're always a big help, but I need to do things on my own." I had nothing to say and just looked forward to getting home.

I did not understand then, as I do now, how sometimes it's important for men, but especially young men, to prove they can do things on their own. While I had helped him a great deal, I had also started a string of jokes among his friends about how his hot wife was a better saleswoman even in a head scarf. Ata was eventually promoted to manager of a store of his own in a mall called Van Mills. I was so proud of him and to celebrate, he invited his colleagues over to drink, smoke, and box in the living room as usual.

The next morning, I came out after he left for work to clean up the mess as I had always done without complaint. It was my most important duty to look after my husband. Beer cans on the floor, wine spilled on the white carpet, pizza boxes everywhere, and weed buds in the ash trays, I grabbed a trash bag and started cleaning. As I was cleaning the bathroom, I noticed my Mariah Carey album behind the backroom sink. I thought, "How did that get there?" As I pulled it out, I noticed a strange white powder on the album cover. I wiped my finger across it and tried to see if it smelled like salt or sugar, but it didn't smell like anything I knew, and my mind went all kinds of places. What is it, I thought.... flour?... what? Why was it in the bathroom?

I called Ata and said, "Hey, honey, I found my Mariah Carey CD behind the sink in the bathroom with some white powder on it. What is that and how did it get there?" His first words were, "Shit! I told them to put it back after using it and not leave it there." I said, "What is on it?" He said, calm as drying paint, "It's cocaine." I said "WHAT! How could you allow that in our home?" He said, "I never used any of it." I said, "But in our home! Weed is one thing but cocaine! Possession of it is manslaughter! Do you not think?" I hung up the phone and went to wash my CD immediately for fear of it being discovered as I swore his friends would never again be allowed to party in our home. When Ata returned home, I continued to lay into him about his responsibility and how careless it was to allow such things to go on in our home. We fought as we always did which usually ended in me throwing something or other, hoping to wound him.

The days rolled on. It was the year I learned to drink coffee to wake up in the morning before work. I especially loved to fill it with heavy whipping cream to drown out the flavor of the coffee, which I thought was grotesque. I finally bought my first hookah from the Arabic store/butcher shop I worked at so I could have a good smoke in the evening as I wound down after work alone. Ata's new promotion kept him very busy and after work he liked to unwind with his friends in the parking lot of a Tim Horton's.

Even though it was hard to go to work every day and still find time to pick up after Ata, I managed to do it all. He was the kind of man who left tea bags in the sink, his shoes in the hallway, his dishes wherever he was using them, his razor and hair clippings in the sink and he had never made a bed in his life. I had already been prepared for that. Men made a mess, and it was his wife's job to clean up after them. Even Ata's mom, the strong woman, still found the time to always have dinner on the table, keep the house in good shape and sit with her husband. After cleaning up every day after four children in Saudi, Ata seemed like a breeze although I made the typical mistake of asking him to come into the kitchen so I could nag in silence as I pulled the tea bag from the sink and placed it in the trash can that was right under the sink while giving him a look.

ILLUSIONS

We seemed to settle into our routines and despite our arguments and my silent nagging, we still shared everything with each other since we had established that rule in the very beginning. We laughed together about everything. Despite our hot-headed fights that often blew out of proportion, he was still my best friend that I could tell anything to. Growing up, fighting back, or disagreeing with my stepdad was not an option. As a result, when I fought with Ata I'm sad to say looking back that I brought with me 20 years of repressed anger and took it out on him.

One day Ata told me about his day and how a little Tunisian girl who was nineteen years old came to his store and kept giving him googly eyes. I laughed and said, "Aww, poor thing, she has a crush on you." She took his business card and since the store paid for his cell phone, she was able to text him a few days later. Ata showed me the text messages as he was leaving for work. She sent him messages about how much she liked him, and we both laughed about how silly she was.

Christmas Day, the Arabic shop was open. The owner didn't celebrate Christmas and neither did we. By being the only open shop in the area all those urgent Christmas last minute buyers came to his door. After making love that morning I started to get dressed when Ata said, "Where are you going?" "I told the owner I could work today." "But, my store is closed. What will I do all day? My friends are all busy with their families." I said, "Relax, I'll be back in the afternoon." "Alright, I might go get started on the inventory, let me drive you and I'll pick you up around 4 o'clock." I kissed him goodbye and started my workday.

That day the owner decided that the olives in the big bowls where people could buy them by the pound were looking a little moldy, so he had me sift out the olives, wash them, wash the container, and then return the olives to the container with new olive oil so that none would be the wiser. I felt so dirty afterwards, not just from the olives, but from the idea of selling moldy olives to our customers. It felt so wrong, but what should I expect from a man who obviously had not washed his hands in a year and who every night when we closed unplugged the fridge and freezer to save on the electricity bill.

It was a busy day, probably our busiest of the year and I had not checked my phone as a result, 4 o'clock rolled around, and Ata wasn't there. I worried a little since he had never been late to pick me up before. I assumed he was just stuck in traffic and waited. The kind butcher asked, "Where is that husband of yours?" "I don't know, he's never late." "Don't you worry, I'm sure he's fine, let me know if you need a ride home." I texted Ata again but no answer. Even on his busiest day he always found time to reply to my messages even when it wasn't urgent. At this point I was pacing the store and calling his cell but there was no answer. I wondered if he had been in an accident driving back from the mall and thought seriously about taking the bus home before the last one left. Two hours later he pulled up.

Relieved, I jumped into the car, and we began the drive home. "Are you okay? What happened?" I asked. Ata said nothing as we drove. Ata looked very nervous like I had never seen him before. I asked again if he was alright and he said, "I need to tell you something." "Oh," I laughed, "What is it?" He said, "I have to tell you because when we get home you will know, and I need to tell you now." I laughed again wondering if it was some surprise present he could not keep to himself. He continued, "When we get home you will see the beer cans and you will know, so I need to tell you." I said, "Alright," and he said, "Well, you remember that girl, the one who was texting me? Well, she showed up at the store and I don't know what happened but all of a sudden, she was in the car, and I didn't know where to drive so I took her to the house. We had a beer and hung out, but I took her home after, nothing happened I swear." I laughed it off. It was all too hard to believe. I felt sure he was playing a practical joke on me. When we stopped for gas, I texted my friend Alaa and told her about the crazy joke Ata was playing on me.

When we arrived home, I walked in and noticed two beer cans on the counter in the kitchen. I asked nothing and recalled what Ata had said in the car. I picked up the can slowly and looked at it as if I had never seen a beer can before and put it down again moving slowly as I scanned the house, feeling like my world was in a fog. I could think of nothing specifically. I heard the cat playing with something, so I looked down and he was playing with a small silver bracelet. I took it away and the first words that came to my mind to say were, "What is this?" He said, "It's her bracelet she was playing with the cat with it." "You let her play with my cat?!" My tone that should have been angry was so broken and low. I didn't know how to react; I knew how to handle a second wife but not an affair. No one had talked to me about what I should do if this happened. I walked to the bedroom to change, saying nothing. My response scared Ata since normally we would both go at each other over much smaller things but there was no anger, just utter confusion, shock, and disbelief.

I noticed that the bed was made, recalling that we had made love that morning and I had not made it before I left. My mind flashed as I stared at it. Ata never made the bed for me in his life, I looked at him and said, "The bed is made." He said, "Oh, I made it for you." I shook my head in disbelief, three years and he had never even picked up a sock. I turned to the dresser and saw his wedding band. I slowly picked it up to look at it and thought how I had never seen him take it off, not for bed, not for a shower, nothing. I had it engraved with the words, Two Bodies One Soul. I asked, "Why is your ring here?" He fumbled for words and said, "I took it off to wash my hands." I took a deep breath in disbelief as I looked at my bed and asked myself in my mind if he had sex with her there, but I dared not ask. I stared at his ring in my hand as he kept saying, "I didn't sleep with her. She kissed me and I took her home, nothing happened, I swear." I had nothing to say, no anger to display as I tried to figure out what I should do. At that moment the relationship I thought we had, felt like it had been a lie and everything around me felt like it was crumbling down.

As he followed me around begging for forgiveness, I changed into my pjs as he kept apologizing. I opened the sock drawer and pulled out his stash of weed and put it in my hookah. I sat on the couch in the dark, smoking and hoping to forget everything that had happened as my mind swam around the words, "What I should do?" I finally went to bed and started to cry. "Baby, let me hold you." "No, I'm fine, please just let me cry."

The next morning after he left, I called in to the shop saying I had some family trouble, and I wouldn't be in. I sat around for hours until I finally pulled myself up, got dressed, and remembered I needed to buy some things for the house, so I went to the mall.

Omta called me to check in and even though we were not close I broke down and told her what had happened while standing in the checkout line at a store called The Bay. I asked her, "What do you think I should do? I don't know what to do!" She said, "You should definitely lock him out of the house and teach him a lesson. He can't just do that." "I can't lock him out of his own house, that sounds crazy. He did tell me after all." "I can't tell you what to do but if Alex did that to me I would do way worse."

When I got home, I lit up my hookah and stared at the door, shaking my foot. Is that what you do? I thought. How would that make things better, if he slept in the car or at a friend's house? With all the questions in my head the most important question every wife or girlfriend should ask herself eluded me. Did I still want to make it work?

Knowing Ata would be home soon I finally got up and walked calmly to the door and twisted the deadbolt. When the knock came, and the doorbell started ringing I only turned my head slightly to hear him say, "Please let me in," but I didn't open the door. My insides wanted to let him in so badly, but I didn't know what to do. Omta was older and more experienced in these things. She must have been right but then why did it feel so wrong? An hour later I unlocked the door and texted him that he could come home. When he came in, I told him simply and calmly, "Get rid of her and we will move past this." He went to bed.

The next day I went to work as usual but when I came in the owner greeted me and asked if everything was okay. No one knows how much that question affects a person until they ask the right person at a moment like mine. I leaned into him to cry on his shoulder, thinking of him as a father figure. Telling him everything that happened and how my family was no longer in the picture, and I didn't know what to do or who to ask. The kind butcher behind the counter said, "I would never do that to my wife. She is *Taj Rasi* (The crown on my head) and I carry her as such." I nodded and the owner said, "Everything will be okay." I wiped my eyes and said, "Everything is going to be fine," and I went to sort the cans in the back.

Ata picked me up from work and we went home without saying a word the whole way. Once he went to bed, I did something I had never done before. I had always had all his passwords, his phone password, his email, his Messenger but I never used them. Trust ... it's such a big word even if it has only a few letters, it's impactful and mighty. I trusted him and never felt the need to check up on him. My aunt called it one of the worst things a wife could do. We should never distrust and check up on our husbands. We should be happy in our ignorance by not asking questions we didn't want to know the answer to. But once he was asleep, I picked up his phone and checked the messages.

My aunt was right, I should have never looked for answers to questions I didn't want to know. Sadly, I found recent messages from her saying, "Are you okay?" and "If she locked you out just come here." Once I had finished reading the correspondence I put the phone down, went to the living room, and lit my hookah. I asked myself why he would cheat when we had been so happy, when we had just made love that morning? She was 19 and I was 19 when he married me, so maybe I was too old now. Was it my fault? How could I fix my marriage? I fell into despair and slept on the couch that night. The next day Ata asked, "Do you need a ride to work?" I half smiled and said, "I'm good, I can take the bus." "Okay, see you later, *habibti* (My love (Female))." He kissed me on the cheek and left.

As I sat on the couch sipping my coffee that morning something came over me. I called work to say I would be out again. I got dressed in the sexiest thing I owned, put on my makeup, perked up my boobs, fixed my head cover so it showed half my hair and ran to catch the subway train to go see Ata at his work. When I arrived, I didn't see him in his store. I asked his colleagues, "Hey, have you all seen Ata?" They all looked nervous for some odd reason but told me he was at lunch in the food court. My heart beat fast like it had never beaten before, wondering as I walked if I would see them together having lunch, and what would I do?

My aunt assumed I would never need a lesson on what to do about a mistress, this was because she thought I would marry a man in Saudi where discretion would have been almost guaranteed. Therefore, she focused on what to do in case of a second wife. Saudi men, you see, to avoid trouble and scandal, don't typically bring their mistresses to their wives' homes. What if the neighbors saw? What if the maid said something? It was just too risky. Instead, they would have their affairs on business trips in places where no one knew they were married or cared. Thailand and Malaysia were popular spots for their little dalliances, so was Dubai. Some, to keep it Islamic-ly correct, would fly to Syria and find a small village where a family had a beautiful young daughter. They would then make an offer of marriage including a large dowry, more than that family had ever seen, They would then marry the farmer's daughter that day, sleep with her and then divorce her in the morning and fly home. In all these scenarios I would have never known anything and if it was a second wife, she would have never been in my house and as my aunt would say, I would not have to see her at all.

Here I was feeling hopeless. I was taught that a man only takes a second wife when his wife is lacking something, but what was I lacking? It would be many, many years before I realized that that is not the case at all. I wished I had spoken about mistresses with my Aunt Iptihag since she was the only person I knew who experienced it so brutally. It was a big cover up within the family that would have never been possible for her to talk about. She would have been insulted and shocked if she knew that I knew what she went through in the beginning of her marriage.

The story goes that my stepdad's younger brother, Latif, got a job at the King Faisal Hospital and met a beautiful Filipino woman. He was living with my Uncle Shakoor on his third floor. He would sneak her in to be with her. My little cousin was only seven when she saw her dad shouting and beating his younger brother while she watched a half-naked woman sneak out of the back gate. I was 16 when the maids relayed the story in complete to me. He fell in love with her but when my Uncle Shakoor told the family, measures were taken. He was to be married at once to a good Bukhari girl, my Aunt Iptihag in Mecca, and thereby removed from Riyadh and his relationship with this woman. It was an easy fix. Give him a new beautiful young virgin to play with and he would forget. They were wrong. He continued to see her. One night as Iptihag was returning from visiting her mother she caught the woman standing outside her house waiting for him or leaving after just seeing him. Unfortunately for her, Iptihag did not know who the woman was, since everyone agreed not to tell her, so she ignored it. There are rumors that she was caught in the house by my Aunt Iptihag, but I'll never know for sure. Until today he still sneaks away to see her. At some point he convinced his wife to move back to Riyadh to be closer to his mistress without her knowing that was the reason. Maybe she did know but she was happy in her ignorance, I guess.

It's in these moments that we all experience a rip in time as if the moment took centuries. As I passed the corner, I feared what I would do, what I would say, and how I would navigate a wave that was sure to take my marriage out to sea. There he was with one of his staff, who immediately excused himself when he saw me. I sat down and said nothing, putting on a firm exterior. He looked at me and said, "You just missed the Postman." "Postman?" I asked. He said, "Yes, she was here, but I told her to leave because I had called you and your phone was off, so I thought maybe you were in the subway." I looked at him and stayed silent. It was another situation I didn't know how to react to. We sat until he was finished eating then he headed back to his store. I stood there for a few minutes and decided to remove the yellow diamond wedding ring on my hand. I slapped it on the counter and said, "Call her or text her and tell her to come back." "No, I won't, she won't come. I told her not to be here since I knew you might come." "Are you an idiot? She will come if you ask her and if you won't, I will come take your phone and text her myself as you and she will come. Ask her to come or take this ring."

He texted her and we waited. I paced around the fountain. I recall looking at the water falling until suddenly she was standing before me. I had never seen her before or heard of how she looked. She was tall, skinny, dark skinned, black curly short hair, and boyish in her features. All my mind could think was, "Shit, there is nothing I can do to alter myself to be like her." If she was blonde, I could change my hair for him, If she was tall, I could wear higher heels, but she was everything I could never be. I stared at her for what seemed like an eternity as Ata arrived and said, "We should take this outside." Afraid and anticipating a cat fight, I lifted my hand and held up my palm pointing it towards the doors, meaning, "Lead the way" inviting them to start going outside and I followed behind.

We exited the back door of the mall. As soon as we were outside, she opened her mouth and said, "I am so sorry. I never intended to break up a marriage." I raised my hand indicating stop and said, "No, no, you don't get to talk." Then I turned to Ata and glanced back at her. I said, "When do you two intend to marry, because if not, I'm filing for divorce today." Neither of them had anything to say so I said, "Well, then, have each other." With that, I started to walk away, not knowing where I was going. Home and then what? I didn't know. I had no plan, no map, despite all the things my aunt taught me. I was lost. Suddenly Ata called out to me, "Maha! Maha!" he ran after me as she cried and ran inside the mall in the opposite direction. He picked me up in his arms and said, "You're the only one I ever wanted. I love you, you're my everything."

When we got home, we talked and I told him, "The only reason I'm still here is because you told me and I didn't find out on my own, that would have hurt a lot. You get rid of her, and we won't talk about it again. I'm not going to ask how you're going to end it and I honestly don't want to know. She's your problem." "She's gone, it's over, I promise." I nodded and went to make him some dinner. As I cooked, I told myself I would never again dig around for the answers to questions I didn't want to know the answers to. If this was going to last, I had to find a way to trust him again

Life seemed to go back to normal, but Ata started to fall into a deep depression I could not understand. He said it was normal for him to have periods of depression. I tried to help by picking up the pieces, he smoked weed more than usual and missed work often. Trying a new tactic, instead of scolding him as I had always done and reminding him of his responsibilities, I enlisted Alaa's boyfriend at the time, Sammy, to take me to the bad side of town to buy Ata some weed as a gift. I was going to give it to him and say, "Hey, get high, take some time off and then maybe you will feel better." Sammy, a recovering addict, if given the money would have surely just smoked whatever he bought for me. I had to guarantee delivery.

I recall the bus ride, watching the buildings and the people become more and more run down every second we moved. We exited the bus and Sammy said, "Stay very close, it's very unsafe." As we walked, I recall thinking all the while how dangerous everything looked. Sammy warned me that undercover cops were everywhere, and I needed to follow his instructions exactly so that we didn't get caught buying drugs. I nodded and followed everything he said. I was determined to buy some weed to make my husband happy. We arrived at an old apartment building. Sammy said, "You should wait downstairs in case there is a raid and to keep you safe. I don't know what these guys are on, and I don't want them to see you." I nodded as he went up to buy the weed. I waited for what seemed like an eternity looking left and right for danger until finally he came down and said, "Let's go," I said, "Did you?" He said, "Shh, let's go now." We left, and he dropped me off at home, handing me a small package of weed. I skipped upstairs and dressed up the weed as a gift, knowing for sure Ata would adore the gift and it would cheer him up.

When he arrived home from work, I handed him the gift. He smiled and said, "Aww, how sweet of you," opened it and immediately said, "Where did you get this?!" I started to relay the story and he jumped up from the couch in a rage, "How could you go to a place like that! Do you know how dangerous that was?" I stared at him blankly as he continued, "Ugh! You don't know how dangerous it was…." I tried to explain that I just wanted him to be happy, but it was no use. He was mad and stormed to the bedroom to go to sleep.

The next day I went to work and asked for more hours. The owner asked me again if I was alright, but this time I decided to act as I was taught and keep my personal problems away from those who were not close. I did my best to smile and bury the sadness. Anyone who knew me would have noticed that the happy, bubbly, bouncy girl, who marveled and smiled at the simplest things was gone, taken over by a solemn girl who kept to herself.

One day Abu Muhammed the butcher called in sick. As I was climbing the ladder to restock the cans the owner came up behind me and grabbed my ass. As I turned to look at him, he walked away laughing and winking at me. My face was blank, and my mind was turning. What just happened? Did that really happen? What should I do? If I tell him off, I will lose my job. My husband is depressed. He barely goes to work. How would I pay my bills? I said nothing and continued with the day.

I took the bus home that evening and sat in silence on my couch, thinking and thinking. In the end I decided it wasn't as bad as all that if he does it again, I will just ask him politely not to do it again and remind him that I am happily married. "Yup, that's what I will do." The next day Abu Muhammed was out again, still sick with the flu. The whole day as I completed my tasks I was highly on guard, purposefully moving out of his way as he passed me. If I could go back in time, I would tell myself that the one thing we don't know in that moment. Men like this, when you don't say anything, make up a story in their minds that you liked it, that perhaps you were too shy to express your feelings, and they won't stop. The fear you feel never crosses their minds.

In America they call people like me a hugger. I am very affectionate with everyone I care for and, like most huggers, I'm known for hugging strangers, or helping interns through the hardest times in their lives by sitting on a bathroom floor with them and listening. For grabbing a colleague by the arm and taking her into the bathroom to stitch up a hole in her skirt so that she would not be embarrassed, even if she had never been kind to me. At that moment I recalled my first day of work, when I hugged the owner for giving me my very first pay, when I cried on him and told him my husband was cheating … and then I asked for extra hours. I worried that I had given him the wrong impression.

I went home and found Ata asleep already. He had skipped work again. As I prepared my hookah, he woke up and something made him ask me, "What's wrong?" I sat him down and told him about the shop owner. His rage came out and he said, "I'll kill him." I let out a deep breath and said, "Sit down. Let me point out how much we need my income. I will very likely not find another job that pays cash so close to home for some time until my Canadian Social Security number comes in. There is no need to kill anyone since nothing really has happened and I am being vigilant. If something more happens then we will revisit the issue but until then there is nothing more to do." We left it there as I contemplated what to do if he tried it again.

Even though I needed the job, he was bigger than me, a beast of a man with large arms that were longer than his legs. He was bald, grotesque with an ungroomed red mustache and prone to getting very angry at customers when provoked. I wished I had hit him for touching my ass or shouted at him, but I feared he would retaliate and give me more things to remember him by, not just the loss of a job. One might say you can call the police and report him but in addition to working illegally with the risk of being deported I grew up in a country where that was not an option.

Ata's depression grew worse, so I invited his friends over to have another night of drinking, gambling, and rough housing. I thought his friends were strange, unruly, irresponsible, and a bad influence on him but I bore them because my husband loved them and seeing him happy made me happy. I know a lot of people say that, but it was true and if I sent his friends away, I could only imagine how depressed he would get then.

Ata got worse and worse. I took on a lot of the household bills making sure everything was paid on time and begging Ata to go into work, knowing full well that if this continued much longer, we would not be able to keep the apartment. I went into work and was asked to wash the parsley to make the *Kofta*. The owner started giving me more and more responsibility, like washing the bloody plastic bins after the meat had been in them, something I had told him early on I would not like to do. It was as if he knew I really needed my job now.

Abu Muhammed left early one night and as we closed up, the owner said I could have a bottle of the cherry soda I liked so much. He said he would put it in a glass for me as I finished tidying up. When I finally went to take a sip, I noticed that it tasted a little funny like something I had never tasted or smelled before. I looked up to see him staring as I drank with a smile. I looked at my watch and said, "Oh, I need to go." He said, "Finish your drink, don't waste it." I said, "My husband is waiting, I really must go." As I tried to walk out, he stood in front of the door and as I tried to pass him, he grabbed me with both hands with a grip like a vice and kissed me. I kept my mouth closed and made a face of such disgust because of how revolting I thought he was. He let me go, smiled, and said, "See you tomorrow." He let me pass and I ran to the bus stop. I cried the whole way home. What was I to do? If I told Ata he would end up in prison and if I fought back, I would lose my job and he might spread rumors about me far and wide out of spite for not getting what he wanted. If I stayed it might only get worse. I needed a plan, but nothing came to mind.

The weekend came and I was at home. While Ata ran some errands, I went to use the computer, but the room was a bit messy, so I started picking up this and that. I heard the messenger ding, so I checked to see if it was someone from home, his mom or anyone. As I looked at the screen, I saw her name. I lowered myself slowly into the chair as she typed the words, I miss you; I didn't think I would see you online and I love you..." My mind was spinning. "Alright, Maha, you got this. She's just trying to get him back; it doesn't mean anything," I said to myself. I wanted to reply and call her something like a home wrecking prostitute, but I had no words as I saw that he had been talking to her as recently as yesterday. A part of me loved him so much that if this is the person he wanted, why was I wasting my time trying to cheer him up? Maybe he needs her, and his happiness was all I wanted. I closed the computer down and sat on the couch to think about everything as I was taught to do.

I thought about our life, my inability to go to school, working in a grocery store. Would I be there forever if he kept depending on me? He would never go to school as long as he felt he needed to support me and then it hit me. He would never learn to stand on his own as long as someone was there to pick up the pieces and I would probably spend my life fighting off the inevitable until I was old, had children, and was stuck going nowhere. I recalled the words of my stepdad as much as I hated him, when he wrote about how divorce is never easy but it's even harder with children. My mind spun around and around.

When Ata arrived home, he said, "Hello," and I said softly, "You're still talking to her? I asked you for one thing, Ata." He replied, " I don't know how to break it off with her, I feel bad to hurt her." I pursed my lips together as I looked down, thinking how was it okay to hurt me, but not her? I raised my head back up and said, "I think you should sleep in the study from now on until I decide what I want to do." I felt as if I had cried enough and went to bed. I was tired of fighting a battle I felt I could not win anymore. A lot of women, when they get married, they let themselves go, they gain weight, couples stop taking care of each other, giving gifts for no reason, going on dates, eventually leading to "I love you" becoming just a meaningless phrase. They start making love on a schedule or not at all. In America we call this getting comfortable, but my aunt would have called it just plain lazy.

I spent weeks going over everything I had done and asking myself what I had missed. I followed the road map so clearly laid out for me and then I decided it was because I allowed him to stray so far from the right path that is, after all, what his mom would have said. All the things I let him do when I should have insisted on religion in our home then maybe God would have kept us together. I began to pray like I had never done before in my life, hoping God would guide me and forgive me for failing to do the one thing I was raised my whole life for, to get married and care for my husband and his children. Now what? Would I move out and work forever in that horrible store? The days seemed like I was frozen in time, stuck, and lost.

I kept going to work and eventually just stopped caring if he rubbed up against my ass or tried to kiss me. I needed time to figure out my life and not having a job wouldn't help. I decided he didn't seem so dangerous, after all I could leave anytime, not like with my stepdad and as long as Abu Muhammed was around, he stayed in check. One day as I entered the store I noticed two tall men, a skinny man with long hair, half his face was scarred, wearing a fur hat, and a very chiseled man with short hair who seemed very American. They both came up to me and the owner jumped out from behind the counter and said, "Maha, this is Ziyad and Eyad. Ziyad is the co-owner here and Eyad is his brother." I was delighted to make their acquaintance and happy to have people in the shop when Abu Muhammed was away.

Eyad was very typical in his mannerism of talking all the time but so pleasant, funny. and a little angry at the world. Ziyad took a particular interest in the shop and wanted me to show him all the things I knew about stacking, packing, and cleaning. He was gentlemanly, very polite but much older than me. I was barely 22 and he was 41 but his mind, his gentle and respective nature. stood out. I enjoyed his company. I looked at him and wished he had been the owner of the shop. Perhaps then the choice to stay would have been an easy one despite my marriage falling apart. He came many days at a time, and it was always a pleasure to see him. One day they came in the morning and said, "We won't be staying today because we want to see Niagara Falls before we leave." "That's fun!" I said as I stood on my tip toes for a nano second. Looking at my excitement Eyad said, "Hey, would you like to come with us?" "Well, when will you be back?" and they said, "By 5." I looked at the owner and said, "Can you manage? Do you mind if I go? Please!" Since I had not had a day off in a while he said, "Go." I jumped in the air excited about spending the day with two of the friendliest and kindest men I had met in a while, caution to the wind. If my stepdad had seen me, he would have told me I was crazy to go with two men to a place far from home, but I had seen a lot in the last three years and had changed.

We got on the bus and rode all the way to the Falls. They were fun and funny. We ate lunch at a fancy restaurant. "Order whatever you want, it's my treat" Eyad said. I recall feeling free of my constant thinking as I spent the whole day getting to know them. They asked me where I came from and all kinds of things about Saudi Arabia. I had my girlfriends but in recent years they had all fallen away. Alaa was more and more often confined to the house because her father found out about her Egyptian boyfriend, Sammy. Fozia, after I confided in her about my stepdad, told someone who told someone and my mother in-law had to stop the spread, and Sarah and I were hardly close since in my mind, she was so loose morally.

Eyad talked about his life in California, his place in Huntington Beach, and Ziyad talked about how he got the scar on his face by picking up shells after they came down in Palestine to sell for the metal. He also talked about his work at the bank in Abu Dhabi, an Emirate in the United Arab Emirates. He told me how beautiful and free it was there. As I listened, I dreamed of home and being back in the Middle East. Being in Canada so often felt as though my religion and my head cover made me an outsider everywhere I went. I recall even the day Saddam Hussain died how the butcher swung his knife and said, "And they call us barbarians, the man was the leader of a country, and they killed him like a dog." I agreed but in the West such opinions are hard to explain to people who live with so much freedom and never really know a world where even death should be honorable. Saddam may have been a dictator, but some countries need one. During his rule Iraq had stability and now with his death it fell into chaos.

During the trip, somewhere by the Falls when Eyad wasn't looking, Ziyad accidentally touched my hand. I moved my hand back and blushed, not expecting to feel anything. It was a simple polite romance, an experience I had never had. There was no family involvement, no traditions to follow, no negotiation that needed to happen. Just two people getting to know each other. He would leave soon so I decided to enjoy his company. Despite my traditional moral compass, I thought, my husband has someone else and he doesn't look like he is going to give her up anytime soon, so I should try to move on as well. Not to get back at him but to move on. The expression "nothing gets you over the last one like the next one" is true in this case and in many cases. His presence helped me separate my emotions from my marriage and see it only for what it was: a broken relationship that very likely would not survive.

A DIFFICULT DECISION

Those we love when we're young often turn out to be not as we expected. Some couples can stick it out and find a way to merge the dreams of both the wife and the husband but in this case, I dreamed of bigger things and staying where I was, caring for a depressed husband with a mistress, was not one of them. Ata was like a child, and I knew after trying so long to keep him from seeing the hole we were digging to keep him from getting more depressed wasn't working. It was obvious that he would only do better if the weight and stress fell on his head alone.

The best thing I could do for the man I loved was finally clear. It was time to leave him so he could give up the drugs, go to work, and think about furthering his life. If he wouldn't listen to me, it was time for a reality check. Knowing someone means often knowing what is best for them, even if they don't know what is best for themselves. If he didn't have to support and care for me and vice versa, we both would thrive. I owed him a new life after he had given up his to save me from my stepdad. You can call it justification but only time would tell. You can lead a horse to water but that doesn't mean they will drink; you must make them thirsty.

Eventually Ziyad had to return to his job in a bank in Abu Dhabi. We kept in touch by email and sometimes he would call. When he did, I would leave the apartment to spare Ata any unnecessary pain. He may have hurt me, but I refused to hurt him in return. We talked about daily life, the shop, his work, and about my marriage. The time finally came a few months later when I finally made the decision to divorce Ata. The night I decided to tell him, I suddenly recalled again the words of my stepdad saying, "Throw out divorce; if the first thing that comes out of his mouth is, 'what about my family, a scandal, money, or reputation,' then run for the hills. But if he says 'because he loves me' then we have a starting point to make it work. I waited for Ata to get home. I sat him down and said the two words no one in a relationship wants to hear, "Let's talk."

He timidly sat down as I continued, "It's time and I think we should divorce." He put his head down and the first thing that came out of his mouth was, "What will I tell my parents?" Disappointed, I said, "Tell them whatever you would like. I will not tell them about your affair, or whatever else you are doing, that's up to you and you can say it was my fault if that makes it easier." The second comment only made his case worse, "But what about your *Mutakhar* (Divorce money/remainder of my dowry)?" I said, "You don't have it and honestly, it's fine. I will be okay." He said, "Where will you go?" I said, "I don't know yet, I have family in California, maybe I will go there." All the wrong questions and all the wrong expressions for someone who was losing the love of his life. He said, "Okay," then walked to the hallway and punched the wall, leaving a whole in the drywall. That was how he tried to express that he loved me but it's hard to see when the expression of losing something you love comes out through violence.

The next morning, I set out to see how we could be divorced as soon as possible. In Saudi it's as simple as the man simply uttering the word divorce and the woman acknowledging that he said it and even without her permission he can go anytime and divorce her. Some say divorce is more simple than marriage. The only trouble is the Islamic waiting period for after a man divorces a woman. She must wait through three menstrual periods before remarrying. Unlike in some countries, where the law stops them from being divorced for six months or so, it's the society that keeps the couple together, not by law but to save their marriage. Many marriages in Saudi are made for important alliances that must be kept at all costs. Other reasons could be that the family sees that they are young and hot headed and need time to calm down. Or maybe they help because they fear the gossip mill will engulf the family in scandal. My aunt used to say it was just because everyone cares. I knew if we didn't get a divorce soon, word would get out and my in-laws would fly down to help us fix it. At that point they would find out about all the things Ata was doing, pack us up, and take us to Saudi, talk to us about family, responsibility, and all the things I knew would make me buckle and try again to stick it out. When I saw clearly that it was broken.

It's very expected and especially in my family that when a first divorce takes place ... well, let me explain what I mean by "first" divorce. If your husband says, "I divorce you," once, he can take you back and if he says it a second time, he can still take you back but if he says it a third time, there is no going back unless you marry another man and get divorced. It was very normal for the family to step in after a first divorce happens and the husband would be forced by the family to take time off work. His company would be very understanding of this necessity. The couple then would be confined to their home until they worked out their issues. The family would drop off groceries and food, but no one would see them for at least a month. In most cases it worked. I knew it would work on me, but it wasn't what was best for us. We both needed to fly but together we were weighed down.

I went down to court and filed a petition for divorce. Someone told me that we had to sign saying that we were separated for a year at least before we could go to court, but we were not required to provide any proof of separation, so I said "Fine." I asked Ata that night if he would sign the document stating that we had been separated for a year and that our marriage had broken down. He said, "No, that is lying." I said, "So?" He said, "No, someone will read it, what will my mom say when she sees that paper and asks how we were separated for a year and never asked for help." "Ugh!" I said. I went to my room to go to bed and see if he would change his mind in the morning.

Ziyad called and asked if I had enough money to get to my family in California. I confessed I had 100 dollars to my name and even if I went to my family, they were all Mormons, and I didn't want to live with people who didn't share my beliefs. I asked if I could come visit him, but he said it was too soon and he wanted to make everything ready for me. He said he would ask his brother if I could stay with him and his girlfriend, this way, I would be close to family but separate for a while. After that phone call I went to Ata and said, "It's time." "Time for what?" he said. "Time to say it, you need to say the word." "No, I can't." I said, "I need to go and since I won't be back to Canada or Saudi Arabia it will not matter if the courts granted us a divorce. All I really need, in my mind, is my Islamic divorce as was my right." The strain on his face was clear: the word *Talaq* (divorce) is the hardest word he had ever uttered in his life. In that moment as he did, I felt for him, for us, and for everything we had wished we would be but now it was over. The word *Talaq* in Islam is never used even as a joke, for if said, even if the husband was just joking, his wife and he will be divorced.

I packed two suitcases, leaving anything that was not of sentimental value. Taking only the clothes I really needed to start over, not wanting to be too heavy. The call finally came that a ticket to Los Angeles would be waiting for me at the airport. My cousin, Cecily, said she would pick me up and take me to have dinner with them at her mom's house and then she could take me to my friends' place. Obviously, I had no intention of telling them that my friend was the brother of a man I was interested in while by their standards I was still married.

The last night in the apartment was hard on the both of us. I went into the study where Ata slept, unable to sleep myself. I cuddled up next to him, he held me tight and then attempted to have sex one last time, but I got up realizing I wasn't doing him any favors by flirting and giving him hope. For me one last time would have been just that, but for him it would have meant he could have me back. I measured twice and cut once. There was no going back. Five a.m. rolled around. "Time to go," I said. Ata took me to the bank so I could take out the $100 I had. Crying he said, "I wish I had more to give you." I said, "No matter, you take care of you now. Don't worry, I'll manage." He drove me to the airport, helped me load my bags, and we hugged goodbye.

Seeing him disappear as I passed airport security would stay with me the rest of my life. I thought hard on the plane and realized that ours was a perfect friendship but due to our society, suggesting that men and women shouldn't be friends, it was marriage or nothing, so we married. Had we remained friends only, we would have had the best relationship, but our personalities created too many clashes and that was how it was.

In Saudi we didn't date, we married. See a girl you like? Hear about a girl from your mother, sister, aunt? If she sounded good you married her, period. Dating was never allowed. I wonder how much would have been different if we had been given more options.

I walked to the gate solemnly, looking out for anyone walking too close to me. I feared being kidnapped since I had only traveled by myself once before. The whole time I was recalling all the stories I was told about smugglers putting something in your bag when you're not looking, people who make conversation and then slip something in your drink when you're not looking, and worse dangers.

LOS ANGELES

When we landed in Los Angeles, I went through to baggage claim, got my bags, handed them my little card which I had no idea how to fill out and the TSA agent said, "Okay, off you go." I said, "Thank you," and struggled to push my two giant bags on the cart. I was wearing a gray full-length raincoat, my gray head cover, and flat, plain black shoes. Since I am only 5'2" I struggled to get my bags through the exit, the weight making the cart always want to go the wrong direction with me struggling to redirect it.

Suddenly a big TSA agent passed in front of me. Thinking he wanted to pass I tried to go around him, but he blocked me. I looked at him from behind my bags, and he said, "Do you live here?" very casually, I said, "No, I just got divorced so I don't live anywhere yet." He gestured with his hand to the other side of the hall and said, "Come with me." I said "Okay?" I was wondering what I had done and what he wanted. They took me to a bag check counter where they proceeded to remove every item from my bags, asking me, "Why did you come to LA?" I said, "My grandpa and aunts live here so I'm coming here to regroup, is there a problem?" I asked, "No, no, not at all this is just standard procedure." Looking around at all the other people who had been pulled aside for random checks I couldn't help but notice all the Indians, Pakistanis, Arabs, and covered women. I knew there was nothing standard about what I was going through.

They pulled out my laptop and asked me to unlock it as they went through every folder, until they found my Quran audio files. They were in Real Player format and since my laptop didn't have Real Player installed at the time, they asked, "Why don't these files open?" "What are they?" I said, "These are Quran files. Just recordings of someone reading the Quran so I can memorize Surahs. They aren't important. I can always get new ones, delete them if you want." "No, no," said the TSA agent, "that's fine." "Okay," I said.

They pulled out my wedding photos, my personal photos, and went through every single one. I wasn't covered in any of them, and I felt violated but there was nothing to be done. I thought it's not their fault that they were not educated on how to respect people's beliefs about how important it was for a Muslim woman not to be seen by strange men without her cover, even in a photo. After the photos, they pulled out my books. I had 6 or 7 books on Islam that I was finally planning to read. The TSA agent said, "Why do you have so many books on Islam." I looked at him for a second, thinking it was a very under-educated question. I said, "I assume you're Christian, is that correct? "Yes," he said. I said, "Well, don't you ever wonder why it is that you pray the way you do, why you go to church?" He said, "Yes," I said, "Well, then, that's why I have them so I can understand why I pray, how to wash for prayer properly, and why it's important to cover." The TSA agent took a breath and said, "Wow, that's a great answer." Three hours had now lapsed, and they sifted through my underwear and everything else. My legs started to get tired so I tried to sit on the table "No, umm, ma'am you can't sit there, sorry it's taking so long." I said, "No, no, you said it's standard procedure, so take your time. Can I sit on that chair?" "Yes, of course," they said. When they were finally done, they thanked me for my patience. I said, "It's no problem, you're protecting the country after all, have a good day." I'm not sure how long I was there when they finally finished but it was close to six hours when I was finally able to exit the airport, exhausted.

I saw my cousin Cecily waving. I smiled, so excited to see her. We headed for the car and started the long drive to San Diego to see my brother, grandfather, and Aunt Angela. Arriving at my aunt's house I asked to be excused while I washed and completed my last prayer of the day. I looked around the house and wondered how anyone can live with so much cat and dog hair everywhere. The bathroom had hair and dust bunnies in every corner. I wondered if this was a typical American house, feeling not that it was the wrong way to be, but it was not the way I intended to spend my life. The carpets were old, stained, and had clearly never been cleaned. As I bent down to pray, they smelled as if they had not been cleaned in many years.

I was excited to see my Grandpa, but he looked so run down, his nails too long for words curving around as if they had not been cut in many, many months. His beard was all ratty. I wondered why his daughter had not helped him take care of himself, he was in her house after all. When I was young, I would consider it an honor to care for my grandma on my stepdad's side. Help her out of bed, get her breakfast, cut her nails, whatever she needed. It was a different culture. We felt it was an honor to care for those who spent their whole lives caring for their children and now needed help. The sight of my grandpa so run down made me feel bad that I could not stay longer and care for him. I did my best to respect their way of life after all, if they were happy that way it was not my place to judge or try to change anything.

I knew my Mormon aunt hated the use of the saying, *"Oh, my God,"* so I struck it from my vocabulary while I was there and expressed curiosity about their religion. My mother was always prone to shooting my aunt down if she talked about the Mormon church, always accusing her of trying to convert her and her children, which I always felt was ridiculous. It was the first time I had ever spoken to my aunt without my mother there to argue and monopolize the conversation. It was the first time someone was able to have a conversation with me about my biological father.

My aunt pulled out the information she had, like his birthday, their wedding day, and what she knew about how they met. I asked if he was ever in the army, since my mom had mentioned that he was. My aunt said, "No, he was never in the army, that was a previous boyfriend she had prior to your dad." "I'm confused, my mom swears my dad was her first everything. She said that my grandma had forced her to marry him." My aunt said, "On the contrary, she arrived at the wedding on the back of his motorcycle and apparently sang him a song during the reception." I felt like I was trying to put a puzzle together, but I was missing the middle pieces that would reveal the full picture. My stepdad had given me a picture of my biological father and my mother on their wedding day standing outside the Mormon Temple in Utah. He also gave me her wedding band which he managed to save from the bonfire my mom had had in the front yard burning wedding photo after photo as she cursed my biological father's very existence. My stepdad said I should look him up but to no end. I found nothing and when I contacted the church they refused to confirm or deny they had any information about him. After searching for so long in Canada when I had time, I had settled that perhaps he was dead. I took comfort at least in the discovery of the letter which my grandmother hid from my mother in a book to stop my mother from burning it in the fireplace. At least that letter disbanded one lie, he did love us.

My grandpa took me to his room and showed me some things that belonged to my grandma, handing me a gold necklace that had eight gold 1-gram bars, each one 9.999 percent pure. He said, "You should have this, I'm sure you remember when she had it made." I smiled and said, "I did." The supermarket was doing a special where for every X amount of Riyals you spent they would give you a gram of gold and every time we went grocery shopping if the total was below the needed amount my grandma would turn to grandpa and just say his name "Charles," to which he would always respond, "Yes, dear," immediately picking up a stick of gum or a box of something to make the total allow her to get that gram of gold. She collected as many as she could and then took them to a jeweler who turned them into a necklace which she loved until the day she died. He said there was also a monogram "E" necklace, a simple silver charm. He said, "I thought it was for your Aunt Elizabeth," but I picked it up and started to cry and said, "It was mine. When I was four, I was in the front seat of a taxi. I had a habit of running the charm across the chain back and forth until the day the chain broke. Grandma took it away, saying that she was not going to give it back until I learned to take care of my things. I never saw it again and as children do, I forgot about it." Seeing it there I realized she had kept it for me all these years. I dried my eyes not wanting to set off my grandpa. I knew her death was a great loss to him. He showed me all the things he found that she had hidden in books and so on, producing the original letter from my biological father. I touched it as if it was a piece of him, the ink was faded but its worth had not. Grandpa said he would keep it safe since there was only one letter and two of us, it was best not to give it to either of us at this time. I agreed.

Cecily drove me down to Huntington Beach where I would be staying with my friend, Eyad, and his girlfriend. Cecily helped me up with my bags, said hello to them and headed back home. I got settled into Eyad's office. Unlike my Aunt's house, his home was very clean, his girlfriend had a cat but there was no hair anywhere to be found and I felt more at ease.

I went to sleep and the next day after Eyad's girlfriend went to work, he handed me an envelope saying it was from Ziyad. I said, "Thank you." Looking inside it was more money than I had ever held in my life, $1000 dollars. Eyad then took me to the grocery store to get the food I liked. I remember marveling at the grocery store that seemed like being in Europe and nothing like America at all. When we got back, I helped him put everything away and we ate lunch. He handed me a new prepaid phone sim for my cell phone then said he had to go to work.

I sat down and sent an email to Ziyad to thank him for the money, saying it was too much. I asked him what we were doing and what were his plans for me here. He said, "For now, just rest and recover." I said, "Okay." I spent my days reading, praying, and meditating. I spent the evenings with Eyad and his girlfriend, and sometimes the neighbors, smoking his hookah and watching the television show, Rome. I sent my new cell number to Ata through email saying, "If you need me to sign anything with regards to the apartment or the divorce papers you can reach me here."

Unfortunately, my cell phone number ended up in the hands of my mother-in law who had heard of my departure to the States. She called more than five times a day, leaving messages asking me to please tell her what happened. Ata apparently was not talking. She sent me numerous emails asking how she could help. I felt for her, but I could not tell her anything because that was the deal I made with Ata. I finally replied and said, "I can't tell you anything, but if you want my advice, you should get on the first plane, not tell Ata you're coming, and just go to the apartment." She asked me what I meant. I replied that I couldn't say anymore but this is what I suggest. I know she thought I was cold, unfeeling, and perhaps even a coward for running away so she told me a story about the early days of her marriage. Her husband used to go and sit with his friends every night chatting, playing cards, and drinking tea, leaving her alone at home for long periods and once she got her mother-in-law involved and put her foot down all was well, and he didn't do that anymore. I knew she could not understand, her problem was so simple compared to what I went through with Ata.

I still kept in touch with Omta, Alaa, and some others. One morning the phone rang. Eyad answered and handed it to me. It was Ziyad. It was so nice to hear from him. He asked me how I was, and I asked how he was. He said he was just getting things ready so that one day he could bring me there, and then he said very seriously, "Maha, can you do something for me?" "What?" I said. He said, "Don't smoke." I said, "Of course," realizing that smoking was a sin and I had disappointed him and probably God, so I no longer enjoyed the hookah in the evening with Eyad and the neighbors. That night, however, when everyone was sleeping all I seemed to think about was smoking and since Eyad smoked cigarettes I thought there must be one lying around somewhere. I reasoned I could smoke without anyone knowing or anyone telling Ziyad but as I crept out of the room in the dark of night and looked around the apartment, I started to realize how ridiculous I looked and headed back to my room and went to bed.

Ziyad and I corresponded almost every day. He talked a lot about me being sure I wanted to come there and whether I was sure I wanted to be with an old man like him. I told him that Islam did not consider age a big factor in a good marriage. We went back and forth for a while.

I understood his concerns. I was very young, and I had just gotten out of a marriage. He told me about his first wife. She was Turkish. "I still love her," he said, "but she and I have been estranged for a long while, living in one house as strangers." I asked what happened and he said it was simple. When they first married their idea of religion aligned but as he learned more and more and changed, she remained the same and could not understand his deep need to pursue Islam fully.

She didn't cover her hair even though he wished she would, she drank when she was in Turkey with her family and friends on special occasions even though it bothered him, and over time they grew apart. As is the case in many marriages they lived in the same house but had very different lives. She was in Turkey now with the children, he said. He talked about his two children, a boy who was extremely smart for his age and his daughter who was his joy.

I thought about the idea of being a second wife a lot. I had uncles who had second wives and even though I had never planned to be one out of pride, throughout all our correspondence I felt like he was the right one for the path I was on. I decided I need to pursue Islam now since it was the only thing my previous marriage lacked. I remembered Ata and realized that even if I had stayed, we might have grown apart as I started praying and dressing more conservatively. He would have resented being married to someone who didn't fit his rebel liberal lifestyle. I felt as though Ziyad's wife had abandoned him, and I told him he should accept her as she is and try to fix things if only for the children. He thanked me for my concern. There was a strange feeling that now I was the other woman, but I rested my mind on the fact that many men had two, three, and even four wives on our side of the world and there was no shame in it.

A month had passed, and an email came one day from my mother-in-law letting me know that she had flown to Canada after the neighbor had discovered Ata on the floor of the apartment unconscious. She said he was paralyzed from the waist down and all he kept asking for was for me to come back, blaming himself for what happened. A part of me seriously considered going back. I prayed about it and thought long and hard but even if I had gone back and nursed him back to health then what? They would fly us home to Saudi and force us to work on it until we finally reached an understanding to live together but separately like so many couples. Overtime we would resent each other, and I still loved him enough to want a better life for him and myself.

I emailed her and thanked her for letting me know. I expressed my regret for whatever he had done to himself and while I did feel for him, he was once my husband after all, I did not feel responsible for what he had done to himself in my absence. In my mind he had many chances to make things right while I was still there, even when divorce was brought up it was clear that our marriage was not something he truly wanted and the dramatic display he caused after my departure would not convince me to come back. It felt too much like a child who didn't want a scolding from mom, so he had to be sick. I had made my decision and I would not go back so I asked her to please help him move on.

ABU DHABI

Finally, the email came with an airline ticket to Abu Dhabi, and a few days later I was on a plane and on my way. I had used the money Ziyad sent to buy whatever I needed and had even given some to Eyad to cover any inconvenience or extra cost he had incurred during my stay with him, keeping only 100 dollars or so. I boarded a plane to a country I had never been to be with a man I barely knew. There were so many risks involved but sometimes you must jump.

Abu Dhabi is an emirate of the United Arab Emirates. In contrast to Saudi Arabia, it is one country, but it is also not one country. If you had three gold necklaces and you wanted to make them one you could melt them down and turn them into one necklace to be worn by one person but if you had three diamonds, you could only bring them together by creating a setting of a ring or what have you. They would be together, strong, and united but they would never be one. Each would always hold its own beauty, its own glimmer, and its own being. Saudi Arabia was turned into one necklace by King Abdul Aziz, while the Emirates was united by agreement to unite but never really surrender power. Each Emirate still has its own ruling family, and each emirate still acts and feels like its own country. Abu Dhabi is conservative but not as much as Sharjah, and Dubai is liberal and modern. Saudi Arabia has one ruling family, the Al-Sauds, while the Emirates has six. Al Nahyan ruling Abu Dhabi, Al Maktoum ruling Dubai, Al Qassini ruling Sharjah, and Ras Al Khaimah and Al Mualla ruling Umm Al Quwain. While they are indeed one country, if you ever get a chance to see all seven emirates you will see how different each one feels.

Abu Dhabi was more open than Saudi Arabia. While both had people from all walks of life, people in Abu Dhabi are allowed to pursue their way of life within the bounds of respect for the culture of the Emirate where they are residing. During Ramadan, for example, almost all restaurants are closed, and eating and drinking in the street is not allowed but a foreigner can eat in a hotel restaurant with all the window curtains drawn. The reason for this is that while the people understand that some people do not fast, it can be hard on those who do fast to have people eat in front of them. As an Islamic country, they do have a duty to help their flock follow the right path, and unlike the Wahabis of Saudi Arabia, they feel no duty to impose Islam on a person of another faith, so in this way they appease everyone.

Women are free not to cover if they so desire, as long as their clothing is not overly provocative or skimpy. If you want my advice, save the miniskirts for Dubai, but in Abu Dhabi, wear an Abaya even if it is only ornamental and left unclosed. Unlike Dubai, the people of Abu Dhabi still judge, stare, and treat people differently if they feel you are boldly opposing their traditions. Respect in the Middle East is as high as honor is in Japan, and reputation in all of the Gulf Countries is one notch higher than that. A woman who wears a pair of tight jeans can be thought of as a poor child who was not raised properly and just didn't know any better, but a woman who is, as my aunt would say, half naked strutting around like a peacock, if attacked or even raped, can be seen as having asked for it. The men who are not overly religious will gawk at you, but the women will secretly wish you harm. Respect the culture and you will not find a more loving people than you have ever met. Disrespect the culture and as we say in Arabic, *"Allah Maak,"* God be with you, or depending on how it is employed, it can also mean, "On your way."

I deplaned and made my way into the airport terminal, and, hearing Arabic being spoken left and right, I felt a great sense of home being back in the Middle East again. So many Indian drivers and women in head covers that I seemed to blend in perfectly, never realizing how much I had missed being like everyone else. I exited the terminal and there he was smiling at me. He put his arm around me and said, "Welcome." We walked to his car, a black Mercedes. I sat in the front with him, and he pointed to the back seat where a bouquet of twenty-four white roses was waiting for me. He said, "My cousin is waiting for us at home. If you're going to be here, we need to make it official." There in the car he asked me officially to marry him. I accepted, agreeing that it would not be right for us to stay under the same roof unless we were husband and wife. The Islamic saying goes, *never does a man and a woman sit alone together without the third being the devil.*

When we got to the apartment, I greeted his cousin, who extended his hand to me but by my placing my hand on my chest and bowing ever so slightly, I signaled that while I received his hand extension with great happiness, I did not touch the hands of men who were not my husband or a relative, something every Arab man understands immediately, and so he placed his hand on his chest and bowed ever so slightly as well. His cousin was a good-looking young man who seemed very kind. He stayed with Ziyad for a while when he was getting settled after he came to Abu Dhabi a few years earlier, and now he was engaged to be married and well on his way to finishing his medical training.

We sat on the couch in the dim light with a beautiful cake on the coffee table. I was so caught up in the romance of the moment as Ziyad explained that the minimum requirements for an Islamic marriage were that we both consent verbally and in writing, that a witness be present and that a dowry is received. I had no knowledge of the Islamic requirements, so I leaned on his knowledge. He said since I was not a girl anymore, there is no need for my *Mahram* (usually a girl's father) to be present to negotiate on my behalf. I nodded that I understood.

Then Ziyad showed me the marriage contract he had drawn up on a simple piece of paper and pointed to the amount for the dowry, which was blank. He asked how much my last *Maher* (dowry) was? I told him it was 100,000.00 Riyals, split 50,000.00 upfront and 50,000.00 in case of divorce. He said okay and wrote 200,000.00 Dirhams (100 halala make up one Saudi Riyal. The difference in the currencies is just about 2 halala. Basically, they are worth the same) on the paper in front of me. I was shocked and said, "It's too much," to which he replied, "You're worth much more." We continued with the ceremony and his cousin read to us a piece of Quran and then asked us if we both consented. We each responded yes, and then we signed the paper, followed by him. Ziyad then pulled out a very simple gold band. I blushed as he placed it on my hand. It was too big, so it was placed on my middle finger.

We were now husband and wife, we celebrated by eating some cake and having some tea, then his cousin left. Ziyad took me on a tour of the house, the living room being the entrance with a balcony on the left that overlooked the ocean, then on the right the small kitchen, then the master bedroom, the little maid's room, the little boys room, and the girls room. Ziyad told me he knew I understood that we both could not sleep in the master out of respect for his first wife. I completely agreed thinking that would be very strange. His daughter's room had an extra bed. He pointed out that it would only be temporary, because after all this was her home and it's only right that I should have my own as soon as he found an apartment for us, and I smiled. His respect for his first wife made me respect him more. We consummated the marriage and slept in the tiny single bed that night.

The next day he had to go to work but before he left, he introduced me to their live-in maid. She was an Eritrean who spoke great English and Arabic. She had been with the family for years and was considered one of its members. Ziyad asked that she look after me, she nodded as she looked at me from top to bottom. She was Catholic and her complete loyalty lay with her mistress, Ziyad's wife, but Ziyad paid her salary, so she tried to keep her opinion to herself. After he left, I had my coffee on the balcony overlooking the ocean. It was higher up than I had ever been in my life, but so peaceful. The maid brought me the best fruit salad I had ever eaten in my life as I spent my day reading. Ziyad came back for lunch and to take me to the grocery store to get whatever I needed. There was an interesting way in his mannerism. Instead of insisting on anything or suggesting an alternative to something I wanted to buy, he would always start the conversation with, "What do you think, maybe fruit is better for you than potato chips?" I understood right away that it was not a question but a strong suggestion, so I said, "Of course you're right, fruit is better."

It was a peaceful few days. As we drove back from the grocery store one day, I saw a church and said, "Ziyad, is that a church?" "Yes" he replied. "In a Gulf country!" I said, shocked. "Yes, actually many Islamic countries allow for their people to worship openly as they like." I was floored. I had never thought there could be a church in a country like the Emirates since they were in the Gulf like Saudi, but there it was. It was a whole new Arab country and entirely different from anything I had seen before. When I was young, we only went to Mecca, Jeddah, and Bahrain, in the Middle East, and now I felt like I knew why.

As is always the case in Arab marriages, the family got involved. It came to my attention that although Ziyad and his wife may have been living separately under the same roof, the family, as is often the case, saw them as a happy couple. When he returned from Canada, he suggested that he might bring this girl he met to Abu Dhabi to help give her a new start. His wife knew full well that I was not another one of his charity cases from the look in his eyes ... a wife always knows. She said, "No, you won't!" Time went on and eventually he insisted. So, she took the children and went to her parents' house in Turkey, saying she wanted a divorce. As often happens, it was suggested to her that if she left him alone without the children he would come to his senses and come get her or send for her to return, but he didn't. The family got wind of my arrival from his cousin and immediately informed her. In response to this news, she said she was done and never coming back, but like I said before, when the family gets involved, decisions change. Someone suggested to her that she was weak saying, "How could you just abandon your home to that prostitute? Go back and get rid of her." Being the strong woman that she was, this touched her pride and so when Ziyad got home that day after work he pointed out that she was arriving on the evening flight from Turkey. He chuckled and said, "Apparently to get rid of you, ha-ha." He laughed but I was afraid. He touched my hand and said, "Not to worry, she is kind, and I will be here, nothing will happen to you, but say nothing to her until I explain things to her slowly. She is not like us, and second wives are not something they do a lot in Turkey." I nodded.

He went to the airport to pick them up and asked his cousin to sit with me while he brought them home. We sat on the couch in almost utter silence. It was a situation I never thought to be in, but I was determined to give her all the respect she deserved as the mother of his children and first wife. When they arrived, Ziyad allowed her to enter first, it was the longest stare I had ever received from a woman. You could feel her blood boiling. I slowly lowered my gaze as Ziyad tried to make everything light, introducing me to his family. His children greeted me with a friendly resolve They did not understand what was happening yet but wondered why I was the reason their mother had shed so many tears. Ziyad got them settled and she went to the master bedroom and slammed the door. I also retired to bed.

The little girl was so excited to have another girl in her room, she asked me about makeup and anything else "grown up" that she was fascinated with. The next morning Ziyad went to work, and we both spent our time on opposite sides of the house. I kept to the girl's room at all times, except when I was going to the bathroom, until he returned. When he got back, he told his wife that he had to go to Dubai for a few days on business and he would be taking me with him. She said, "Why?" he said, "I have set up a few job interviews for her." She said something in Turkish and went to her room. I was excited to go, since I had never seen Dubai. I packed a few things in my small carry-on bag, leaving the rest of my things behind, and we departed early the next morning.

It was my first time in Dubai, a shining city of wonder, the buildings seemed as though they would fall on you because in order to look up to see where they end, you need to lean pretty far back. The hotel was luxurious and perfect. The food was amazing and the next three days flew by like a honeymoon with pure joy and without any problems. It felt like we were in the Middle East but not all at the same time. Unlike Abu Dhabi, the women wore less, and parties could be heard on every drive back to the hotel. When we arrived back at the house, Ziyad went to the kitchen to speak to his first wife about something she said was pressing and I went to the girl's room. I have always been a person of great detail. When I was a teenager and came back from school I knew if someone was in my room because something had moved an inch. My brothers and sisters learned early on that nothing got past my eye for detail. When I entered the girl's room and looked at my suitcase that day, I noticed it was upside down under the bed instead of right side up as I had left it. I thought maybe the maid was cleaning and moved it, maybe his wife went through it, but it was of no consequence. I had nothing to hide so I forgot about it and went to bed.

The next morning when I came out, his first wife was standing in the living room with his cousin, the same one who was a witness at our marriage signing. I looked at them and she said, "Sit down." I sat slowly, wondering what was going on. "Where is Ziyad?" I asked. She said, "He's gone, and you'll never see him again," I stood up and said, "What?" She said, "I have contacted your mother and told her what you're doing to my family, she said you did it before to her family." My mind pondered how she found my mother, but then I remembered Facebook. I wondered how my mother could say such a thing but realized that my mom has always been a follower, if someone she was talking to hated someone, she hated them, too. In Arabic, we call this *Maahoom maahoom aalaihoom aalaihoom* (with them, with them, against them, against them) and that is how she was.

His first wife continued, "You're either going back to Canada to your husband or to your mother in America, but you're not staying here." I moved towards the door, but his cousin blocked me. I tried to push past but it was no use. I was not strong enough. She said, "You're going nowhere except on a plane." I tried to push past again but to no avail. My mind raced. How could I convince him to leave his post as gatekeeper? Then I saw the balcony. It was a risk but what option did I have, I thought. I ran to the balcony and climbed up on the ledge, he left his post as she screamed, "She's crazy, you see!" He grabbed me and brought me down at which point I bolted for the door as fast as I could. I ran to Ziyad's office which was not too far from where we were.

When I arrived, I went up to his floor and asked for him to be called out. He came out. He looked at me and lowered his head. Tears welled up in my eyes as I asked him, "What happened, what did I do? Why did you leave me there with her?" He reached out his arm and we took a walk, he said, "She hacked your laptop and showed me pictures of things that just didn't seem like you, photos of you in a very indecent outfit." (Photos from the night Fozia and I snuck out to the night club. My stepdad's words rang in my ears. *It's not what it is but what it looks like to someone else*). I said, "So I took a picture in a skimpy outfit in my home, it made me feel pretty. Was I in the street in the photo?" He said, "Well, then she showed me the picture of you and Noor sleeping next to each other." I said, "So her sister took it, and it is a good memory. You can't tell me your first wife never slept in the same bed with her sister?" He put his head down and said, "Well I'm just confused, she made me feel like I didn't know you, like you're pretending." I said, "You know me, I am what you see right now and I'm your wife, too. It's not fair to bring me here and then just leave me with her without even talking to me." I cried, and he held me and said, "Let's go get this worked out, you're right, it was not right to judge you before talking to you, after all, we have all done things we're not proud of, but it doesn't make us bad people."

We went back to the apartment, where she proceeded to tell him that I tried to jump off the balcony. I explained why I went to the balcony in the first place. He asked her to lay off and I returned to the girl's room as they argued. Things went on as normal for a few days, I avoided her, and she avoided me. I went out all day spending my time in parks, reading, and in the library, until I knew Ziyad was home, vowing never to be alone with her again. She started shopping and shopping, spending money left and right on the kids, on herself, and on the house, as a way to cope and get back at him. She and Ziyad would argue about it every night and as a result it delayed him being able to find me an apartment which meant I would be stuck with her for a little while longer yet.

One day Ziyad had some time off work, and we went to lunch in the mall. It was a great day. He took my hand in public, proud to have me on his arm. As we were leaving, someone saw us, a friend of his first wife, and that person called her to tell her. When we got home, she was waiting only speaking in Turkish to him so I could not understand. He had learned Turkish for her years earlier but sadly she never bothered to learn Arabic for him. They started arguing again so I left them to go pray. As I went down for the first bow, I heard a crash, but not wanting to interrupt my prayer, I continued. The little girl screamed, "Baba, NO!" as I saw him holding her arm near the bedroom door, she was hitting him over and over as he tried to hold her hands back. I had never seen two people fight as they did that day. Finally, everything stopped for a moment, and then in the silence, I looked up to see the half-closed bedroom door fly completely open, and she entered the room with a coat hanger in her hand. She came at me with the sharp hook. As I moved back, Ziyad came in and pulled her out. "Get your things and meet me at the car," he said. I grabbed my suitcases and ran out the door to the elevator.

When I reached the car, I looked up at the balcony where I saw any clothes I had left behind, along with his clothes, flying off into the air as she threw them in clumps over the balcony. Ziyad finally appeared, helping me get my bags into the car. I asked him what happened, and he relayed the story that someone had seen us, and it was too much for her. He said, "We need to call your mother and you need to go back to America until I sort this out." I said, "I didn't care if we had a fancy apartment, anything would do. I want to stay here with you." He said, "No, you need to go where you are safe, and I'll find something nice for us. Please do this for me." He called my mother who said she would call her sister, Kathy, in California, who could take me until she arrived in a few months. He thanked her and drove to the airport. He bought me a return ticket, knowing I would have never gotten on the plane if I thought it was forever. He gave me some cash and then pulled out our marriage contract. Whereby he proceeded to write on the back in Arabic, *we divorce until god decides what is best,* and then he asked me to sign it after him. "No, I won't," I said. He said, "It's just in case you meet someone or change your mind." His eyes welled up with tears and I sobbed as he held me while I signed. Then I left and got on the plane to San Diego.

It was a long flight and I played back everything that had happened, recalling my aunt saying that divorced women never marry again since no one wants a spoiled flower. I worried if this was my last chance to have a home, be a wife, have children, and fulfill everything I was raised to do. Should I have fought harder? Was it all over? Was a life in America living like my mother's family my destiny now? Was everything I had ever known lost to me?

Arriving in San Diego, my cousin, Britney, picked me up in her car and we talked about small things until we reached the house. My aunt ran out to greet me. She looked so much older and sicker than I remembered her. She was injured in a car crash and now the head trauma had left her debilitated most of the time.

I spent my days praying and studying my books. I never was a reader, but I needed to know, why did we pray the way we did? Why did we cover our hair? Who the Prophet Muhammad (ﷺ) was? Who were his wives? Occasionally, Ziyad would call to ask me what I was learning and how I was doing. I would ask when I could come back but with every call and email came another reason why it was too soon. The calls became fewer and the emails more spread out. I started to run out of books. I felt as though I was waiting on the edge of a cliff for water, for hope, and for my life to start again so I could get it right this time.

I went for a walk the next day. I enjoyed contemplating and listening to my iPod as I imagined the world was some kind of music video. When I came back, I went to my room which had also been my aunt's study. As I walked in, I noticed the computer screen was on, so I moved closer to turn it off and noticed an email was open. I reached out my finger to the button not wanting to pry, and I saw my mother's name. I started to read and ended up sitting down to read it slowly. I was shocked as I read my mother saying to my aunt things like *she is crazy, keep her there I'm coming soon, she needs help and she's not stable*. After reading it several times I turned the screen off, went to the bed, and cried. I felt like the person who was meant to support and love me the most, the person I had tried to help and protect every day of my youth, taking everything onto my young shoulders, thought I was a lunatic. I contemplated calling my mother and screaming at her but realized that if she was saying this to my aunt, she was saying it to everyone. As a result, any move in the extreme would only add to her story and prove I needed to be kept until she arrived.

Looking back now, knowing what I know, this has a common ring to it in the stories of many women imprisoned for "acting out." Be it in their homes or otherwise, the answer to the question, "Where are they?" is always, "They are hysterical, crazy, and need to calm down so we are letting them rest." while they put us away, so we don't influence others. The illusion of freedom can be very appeasing to most but when a girl starts seeking actual freedom, well, that is dangerous.

The next day I decided even though there were still three months left before my return flight, I called the airline and decided I was getting out of here. I requested the soonest I could get out of San Diego, but they said there wasn't anything soon unless I was willing to fly out of Los Angeles instead. I said, "Yes, sure." They said, "Okay the flight change will be $150, what card would you like to put it on?" I said, "Oh, I don't have a card." I could hear the woman on the other line pondering in her mind who doesn't have a credit card. I asked if I could pay with cash at the airport, but she said that was not possible. I told her thank you and told her I would figure something out and call her back.

I couldn't go to my aunt since she was probably on my mother's side. When my cousin, Britney, got home from work, I explained to her that I needed to change my ticket, but I didn't have a credit card and asked if I could give her cash in exchange for her using her credit card. She said, "Sure, of course." We called the airline together; I gave her the cash and she paid the change fare on her credit card. It came up at dinner. My aunt said, "Oh, you're leaving so soon? I thought for sure you would wait for your mother." I said, "Well, I need to get back to my husband, so it's time." The next day miraculously my mother called, she talked to my aunt for an hour. My aunt had her on speaker in the bedroom and I heard my mom say that Britney should check her credit card or the cash. It might be a scam. I sighed and felt confused. First, she is better off without me, now I'm crazy, and she really wants me back. The scent of my stepdad was all over it, after all, I was divorced as far as they knew. My aunt said to my mom that she would not keep me against my will. My mother said she would call Grandpa to pass final judgement. He was the only person in the world my mom could never be mad at, and she trusted his opinion.

I cried as I prayed that night trying very hard to forgive my mother. I knew maybe in her mind she was protecting me from making a mistake and this was the only way she knew how. Drama and depression had always been her closest companions. I knew that and so I forgave her that night and knew for sure that I needed to be calm and ready for Grandpa tomorrow.

The next morning, two days before my flight out of Los Angeles, at breakfast my aunt said, "How are you planning to get to LA?" I said, "I assume it's not far, I'll just schedule a cab," but when I called the taxi service, they said trips that long needed to be scheduled a lot sooner. I hung up the phone and looked at the GPS. I could walk it, I thought. If I could get an early enough start, as soon as I got halfway I could maybe find a hotel that had taxis and one of them could take me the rest of the way. Grandpa arrived that afternoon. He sat down at the table in front of me next to my aunt. He started the conversation by laying out on the table everything my mother was saying about how she was worried and how she had asked them to take care of me until she arrived. I took a deep breath, looked into my grandfather's eyes, and said, "I do understand that she is worried, as any mother would be, but respectfully, it is my life and yes, this man has a first wife, but I need to go back and sort things out for better or for worse. I can't leave things as they are. It is my life and I need to find my own way. I can't go backwards; I must go forward." "What if something happens to you?" They asked. "Then it was meant to be that way, but I have to go back." My grandfather looked at me for a moment, then he said, "Well then, how are you getting to the airport?" I explained that I could not get a taxi, so I was thinking of walking to somewhere to get a taxi. My grandfather touched his long leprechaun-like beard and said, "Day after tomorrow there will be a car waiting for you in the morning to take you to LA." I asked him, "How much will it cost?" and he made a face, I knew it meant I had upset him. I lowered my eyes and said, "Thank you, Grandpa." I hugged him and my aunt and he left.

The day of my trip, I got my things together. I went to my aunt's room to say goodbye, but she was asleep after taking some pain meds that morning. I tucked her in, kissed her forehead and left. Outside there was a black Mercedes waiting for me with a driver wearing a black hat. It felt like something you see in the movies; I sat down inside, and we took off for LAX.

GAMBLING WITH YOUR LIFE

I had decided once I changed the ticket not to tell Ziyad until I was already on the way since there was a chance he would find a reason to delay me. My life laid in the hope that he would not abandon me once I was in his neighborhood. Once I landed in Amsterdam, I found one of those Internet computers, signed into my email, and sent him an email saying that I was in Amsterdam and what time I would arrive in Abu Dhabi. I pushed send and got on my flight. It was a gamble that he would even see it before I landed, but it was a safer bet then telling him in advance as he might have tried to talk me out of it or worse, cancel my ticket somehow. Arriving in Abu Dhabi, I went out to look for him all the while trying to calculate how much money I had left and where I would go if he wasn't there. There he was. I was so happy to see him, but he greeted me with the anger a father gives to a child who has disobeyed. "How could you just get on a plane and not tell me, what if I had not seen it, what then?" I said, "I missed you and I guess I would have figured something out." We got in the car, and he said, "My cousin, luckily, is in Syria and his home is empty. I'll take you there until we figure out what we need to do." I knew from the tone he already wanted to send me back.

We got to the house, and he put down my things. I made him a cup of tea and kissed him, but he turned away, saying he was very confused, and he needed more time. I calmly said, "You married me, why didn't you take more time before you did that?" He didn't have an answer. He finished his tea, gave me some money, and left, saying he would check in. I went to sleep that night on a mat in the living room behind the couch. Their home was very small. They lived as the Prophet (ﷺ) did, simply, only a kitchen and a living room for guests, otherwise, they too slept on mats on the floor with their newborn son.

The next day I went out for a walk to see what was around and found there was a small market, but not much else. I took a taxi to the city center to buy a few things I needed and returned home to wait for Ziyad. A phone call came from Ziyad saying he was otherwise detained tonight. I said, "Of course I understand." I prayed and prayed that everything would be as it was before his wife arrived. Then one day he called saying, "It is the Prophet (ﷺ)'s birthday and everyone is gathering to pray for him. Would you like to go?" and I replied, "Of course." "Okay then," he said. "I'll pick you up at 6." I was ready to go when he arrived, and we went to the gathering. I entered through the women's door, and he went in through the men's. We would not see each other the rest of the night as women and men in very religious circles don't often mix just as it was when I was growing up. One day you're 10 and a half, playing soccer with your boy cousins, the next day you're 11 and no longer allowed to see them anymore, but that's just how it was.

It was a simple home with not much furniture, all the women spread out throughout the house sitting on the floor rocking back and forth listening to the public address message from the Sheikh on the other side who was issuing out sayings of the Prophet (ﷺ) and everyone was praying for him. I sat down and tried to do the same but wondered if the Prophet (ﷺ) would have approved of us celebrating his birthday? It was not something they celebrated back when he was alive, and the Prophet (ﷺ) never wanted to be worshiped in any way, shape, or form. But just as Buddha had requested that they make no graven images of him and now it's the most mass produced graven image, here they were doing almost the same thing. I felt it was not my place to judge as I knew very little, I thought. Although it seemed cultish in some way, but I went along. The women were gracious and so kind. They asked about my husband and offered me tea. It was a great night, one of the few where I was proud to be his wife and free to say I was. When we left, Ziyad was beaming and so happy he got to share the experience with someone, and I was so happy he was happy again.

Soon the Islamic women's community started to invite me more and more and Ziyad was more than happy to give me a ride to the ladies' gatherings. They were similar to the Sunday school gatherings or visits the Mormon side of my mom's family had. Everyone would get together, talk about their children, drink tea, and then one of the ladies, more advanced in their learning of Islam, would speak. I felt for once that I was a part of a family again, loved for no reason except that I deserved to be loved, and accepted for who I was today, not rejected for something I had done before.

I met Doctor Zayina, we called her *Doctoria*, which is the female for doctor in Arabic. She was a short and very wise pediatrician who had a practice and spent her free time serving the Islamic community. She always wore the same navy-blue rain jacket and a navy-blue scarf. She was always so light, smiling, and happy. I asked her how she stayed so happy, and she replied, "When you really put your faith in *Allah* (God) and know everything that happens to you is his will, you relax knowing everything will be okay." I realized I had a long way to go if I was to reach her height of enlightenment. I bought a book on *Fiqu*, which are the rules and ways of doing everything in Islam, how to wash, how to sleep, how to pray, what you need to do if you're late for prayer. I even fasted every Monday and Thursday just as the Prophet (ﷺ) did. Every meeting I would talk to her about doctrine and ask questions about the interpretation. After a while she discovered that I had read so many books so many times that I had a lot of interesting insight. When the ladies spoke about something I quoted the Prophet (ﷺ) in a story I read, and it was not long until I was well known as the American girl who spoke Arabic and loved Islam.

I knew that Ziyad's cousin would be back soon, the day of the conversation was finally upon us. Ziyad arrived and told me that I needed to go back, that he loved me, but he needed more time. I said I would not go back again. He sighed and said, "Well, then, you need to sort out somewhere to stay because I can't afford to get you an apartment right now." I took a deep breath and headed for the kitchen.

I called Doctora Zayina and told her of my situation. She pointed out that in Islam he is responsible. I told her he said he could not afford an apartment and living with his first wife was not an option since she did not accept me as a second wife. She said, "Wouldn't it be better to return to your family in America?" I sighed and said, "I was there; I saw how they live, and I can't live that way, they worship things, and because I cover, I am seen as an outcast. I want to stay here with you." She took a deep breath and said she understood, she would call around and see what she could find. Two days later and she had not called back. Ziyad said his cousin would be arriving soon and I should be ready to go to the airport the next day.

The next morning, I gathered my things and grabbed a taxi to a mosque near Ziyad's work. It was in a great park and always open. I put both my bags down in the women's section. I knew this mosque well, since from the time I had lived in Ziyad's house, I had taken my walks near there and had always stopped to pray. It was in a good neighborhood and barely ever saw much traffic since it had no service on Friday. It was there just for someone walking to stop to pray. Ziyad called and asked me where I was. I said, "I'm in a mosque, I'm fine don't worry about it." He was furious, but I calmly told him I would not leave again, and I could figure this out with some time. The mosque had facilities, I had my books and my prayers to pass the time. I had enough cash to buy a sandwich every now and then to survive. There was no air conditioning, only a fan, but it was enough. Since it was winter the weather was really beautiful. At night I laid on top of my suitcases, clutching my purse in my arms as it held the essentials: my gold, my money, my passport, and my cell phone, in case someone should try to rob me as I slept. I stacked a bunch of prayer rugs as a pillow. There I stayed for a few days, Ziyad hoping that I would soon give in and go back to America.

I got a prepaid card for $25 Dirhams and called Noor who immediately scolded me for leaving Ata and not calling her sooner. I said, "Look, honey, it's not going to work. I know you like him, but it's just not." She said, "And this other guy, who has a wife? That doesn't look like it's going to work out either." I said, "He wants to send me back to America and my mom keeps saying she will buy me a car and send me to college, all the things they could have done when I finished high school at sixteen." She said, "I never thought I would say this, honey, but you're crazy living in a mosque. Maybe you should go home, at least you will be in America, and if you're stepdad tries anything, you can call the police or go back to Ata, he still loves you and he's worried about you." I said, "I knew he would contact you, what have you told him? What does he know?" "Nothing, he is just worried about you, and he asked me to ask you to come home." "No, listen to me, if you want to talk to him, that's fine with me, but I don't want him to have any information about my life anymore. We're divorced and the only way he will let me go and get on with his life is if he has no hope and no contact," I said. The phone card gave it's one minute warning as I said, "I have to go, I love you, honey, I will call you when I can."

I tried to go to the library to use the Internet but having two bags and pretending you just got off a plane really only works once before you start to look suspicious. I found a local newspaper and tried to scour the want ads for anything I could do. I thought about hiding my bags somewhere and getting online at the library, but I dared not leave them unattended. I was too proud to ask Doctora Zayina for help again, so I continued to pray that God would send something my way. Noor gave my mobile number to my mother because she was worried about me all alone and sleeping in a mosque. When my mother called, she said, "Where are you?" "I'm fine." "I heard you were sleeping in a mosque and why did you go back there, why didn't you wait for me at your aunt's house? I was going to come and put you in college and buy you a car." All I heard was: I will put you in college maybe if you do as I say and I will buy you a car if you do as I say. Then when I want to go out on my own, travel, and get married to the man I choose it will be: well, I'm taking back the car. If I get in an argument with my stepdad over something it will be: Well, you're not going to college anymore because we're not paying for it. Everything was a tool to keep me obedient. Even in the US this can be accomplished. All they needed to do is find something I wanted and use it to move me like a pawn … and I was done playing their game. "I don't want anything from you. I would rather sleep on the street then come back to live with you and that man," and with that, I hung up the phone.

One morning while I was sleeping, a group of ladies came in to pray and gather. They caught me sleeping and woke me softly asking if I was okay. At first, I said I was fine and tried to gather my things then one of the ladies asked, "Sweet girl, do your parents know you're here?" I cried and told them my story. I mentioned that I was looking for work but not many companies are willing to pay the hefty amount of money to complete my residency and the ones that do like to keep your passport for safe keeping. I mentioned Doctora Zayina, and one of the ladies knew her. She picked up her phone and called her right away to tell her they had found me in a mosque sleeping. She immediately said she had a place for me with a member of her flock, but I needed a ride to get there. I said maybe Ziyad can drive me. I called Ziyad and said, "I have a place to stay, can you take me there?" "Yes, let me know where you are, and I will be there right away." He arrived as happy as a man who won the lottery. He had two cherry flavored cigars that we smoked in the car, the only kind of smoking he didn't hate and his feeble attempt to say he was sorry. We arrived at a girl's PreK School that was owned by a woman and her husband. I was ashamed when I entered, and they asked why I smelled of cigar smoke. "My husband" I said, "he smokes sometimes." She nodded and showed me to an empty classroom. "You can rest your bags here and then come down for dinner," she said. I put my things down and set up the mat I was to sleep on and headed down to eat.

Despite owning an entire school, they lived in a little house in the back, only big enough to have one small entry room no bigger than your average American bathroom, a tiny kitchen only big enough for a sink, a two top stove, and another room where the whole family slept. As she served the food which was a broth that included every part of the lamb imaginable, eyes, stomach, brains, and kidneys, she said, "Forgive my humble home but we have chosen to live as the Prophet (ﷺ) lived, simply, and without excess. Even though the food frightened me into not being hungry anymore I ate some, thanked her, and a part of me admired her for how she chose to live her life simply and without care of judgement from others. There is always something to be said about living without the desire to collect things, simply, and soulfully. I finally retired to my room where, as I laid down to sleep, I caught the distant smell of human pee. I covered my nose and said a prayer. There was something eerie about sleeping in a school among all the small desks and chairs, but I was grateful for a roof over my head and a safe place to sleep.

I didn't have a TV for the first time in my life and since I needed to be out of the school when it was in session, I spent my days in the library. I found reading difficult at times. Every time I went to the library to excite myself, I made up a game. I would say to myself, today I'm going to learn all about the Prophet's first wife. As I read, a new character would emerge and the next day, I read all about that person. My days were spent in that library learning and job hunting. Eventually one evening, on a Thursday, I decided I would break my fast in a restaurant in the mall instead of with the school owners. I had seen the restaurant weeks earlier. It was an Arabic café on the top floor of the mall. No one was there on a weekday, so I ran little risk of being spotted by my new religious community. I took the table facing a wall and the chair that faced the wall as well so that if someone did come in no one would be able to see who I was. I feared being seen by one of Doctora Zayina's flock and being thrown out.

I ordered a hookah, the first one I had had in a while. I ate some soup and smoked and smoked and smoked. I thought about Ziyad, I asked myself if I had lost him? Would I ever marry again, remembering my upbringing how no one wants a flower that has already been plucked? Was this my last chance? Would I be alone forever? The thought scared me.

When I left as I was heading down the escalator my heart rate increased more and more as I watched the world around me turn dark slowly as if I was in the end of an old film where the black circle filled more and more of the screen. Finally, it happened, and all was dark. I passed out and fell off the escalator to the mall floor. I recall now that I was prone to similar attacks as a teenager but since I was always at home when they happened, I would just lay down and be fine.

Three men who were passing by came and tried to wake me, asking if I was okay. I tried to get up out of embarrassment, but it was too late, the ambulance had already arrived. They put me on a gurney and took me out to the ambulance. I kept saying I was fine, just tired maybe. They asked if I ate today. I told them I had been fasting. They asked me if I knew what day it was. I answered them. They asked me if I had any family. I cried and said, "My husband, Ziyad, his number is in my phone." They called him and when we got to the hospital, they placed me in a bed for an IV and then he arrived.

I cried as I reached out to hold him. He held me and leaned back to say, "Have you been smoking?" "Yes, I'm sorry." His face filled with disappointment for what I had done. He checked me out of the hospital and in silence took me back to the school I was staying at. I could feel it – it was over. It was my very first big anxiety attack in my life. I had no idea how thoughts could affect your physiology, but they did.

A few days later, the ladies found me a room in an apartment. The rent was 500 dirhams a month, living with a Jordanian family, a daughter, and her dad. The mother had died years earlier. I told Ziyad and he agreed to pay my first month's rent while I looked for work. He drove me there and introduced himself as my uncle who was looking out for me. The despair I felt, knowing he was not willing to introduce himself as my husband, saddened me. It was a plain room with nothing but a bed in the right corner and a small window in the middle, but it was mine. I sat up that night and said a special prayer in Islam that is called *Istikhara* when you ask God for something knowing he will only grant it if he thinks it's good for you, or when you need help with a choice. I prayed to become so busy that I would not have time to think about Ziyad anymore and be able to start my life anew. It was then I realized that I had decided to come back, not because I knew he was the one, but because I knew Abu Dhabi was where I wanted to be.

The next day I went to one of my Islamic women's meetings. I walked around as I overheard a woman saying, "Poor Um Salem, her son was convinced to join the Taliban." "How?" I asked. "Ah, it happens; some of these mosques have leaders here whose only purpose is to recruit young men." "Can't they just tell him no?" I asked. "He is already on a flight, it's too late. Oh, his poor mother." "Isn't there someone we can tell?" I asked. She sighed and said, "The only thing we can do is pray for his mother now." I nodded and continued to drink my tea. As I finished taking a sip, I noticed a large, white pigeon-like woman coming towards me through the crowd. She was plump with a small head, pale as snow, and had dark circles under her eyes. She kept saying, "Excuse me" as she passed woman after woman. She looked at me and I greeted her properly. She said her name was May. I called her Ablah May. "*Ablah*" being the old proper way to greet a woman older than you who was not of relation. You could also use *Khala* which means aunt for a non-relation, but I enjoyed using the word Ablah as I was taught.

She was impressed and said, "I heard you were American." "Yes," I replied. "And that you speak Arabic very well." "Yes," I said. "Good." she said. "Then I need you to help me with something." She explained that she worked for an organization that helps refugees from the Iraqi war find new homes, the United Nations High Commissioner for Refugees, UNHCR. Her English, however, was not as good as expected, and so she had been looking for someone to help translate the interviews from Arabic to English. I said of course, I'm happy to help. She grabbed my arm and said, "It is hard work and I need to tell you, my dear, that most days I excuse myself to the bathroom to cry." I nodded and said I could be there tomorrow if she needed, since I was still looking for work. She lit up with delight, gave me the address, and left.

The next day I was happy to wake up with a purpose. I went to her office where she told me about how transcribing means not removing anything from the story at this time and to record everything the lady said. The woman came in and spoke about her life in Iraq, how it was calm and sweet but then when the war came, her daughter who was only four years old, got shot. They didn't have time to see a doctor and fled Iraq as soon as possible. Her daughter was dying, they could not get work, so they ate out of trash cans behind supermarkets. My heart ached; I had no idea there were people who ate out of trash cans. I realized in that moment how sheltered I was. I remembered the Gulf War, but I had never heard of anyone dying. This was because when the Gulf War happened, the Saudi Royal family and the Wahhabis still controlled the media. We only had two TV channels, one in Arabic and one in English, so they got to decide what their people saw and heard.

Because we were expats and my grandpa worked in the TV department in the hospital, he was better informed. He had a bomb shelter built in the backyard. I was too young to understand and thought it was just a really cool playhouse. We had gas masks, but again, what do children think anything is except a toy? I recall the night the Scud missiles were flying over the house. My mother woke me up in a fright but since she was prone to being dramatic as far back as I can remember, I went with her to the living room and promptly fell asleep in front of the television set which was supplying few accurate updates on the events of the Gulf War. I was known in my family after that as the girl who slept through the Gulf War. Ablah May predicted rightly; when I finished the interview, I went to the bathroom and cried for them.

I came back once a week to transcribe interviews and eventually Ablah May, through her contacts, found me a job at a school as a Kindergarten teacher. It was like a dream come true. I went to help Ablah May every morning I could and after school, every afternoon I could. I enjoyed the work I did with her as much as teaching. It was fulfilling to know I was helping someone in need. Eventually I started volunteering at an Emirate charity to teach children English and Quran on the weekends. Just like that my life was busy, so busy I barely had time for anything.

MAHA BECOMES ELISE

Since it was a new start, I decided I wanted to be known by my legal first name Elise. I had always loved my name but had been told I needed to use my Muslim name, Maha, my entire childhood from the age of 8. I was told that now I was Muslim so keeping a Christian name was sinful. My mother and stepdad had found a way to change my last name on my passport from Evans to Al-Turkistani but my first name remained unaltered. All around me I saw girls with all kinds of names I never saw growing up and none of them were considered less Muslim for having them. I confided in Doctora Zayina that I wanted to be known by my name but I was not sure if it was a sin. She said "There is no sin in a name, it is your name. of course, if your name meant something bad like demon or devil then of course you should change it. I have many converts who keep their names." I felt relieved and began to introduce myself as Elise.

Time passed quickly; before I knew it, three months had passed. One day after school Ablah May was talking about the weekend volunteer work when I said, "You know, Ablah May, I said *Istikhara* to ask that I would be so busy I would forget him, and it happened. I'm grateful to God for answering my prayer." Her nickname for me was *Habiba* which means "my darling" or, "my love." "*Habiba*," she said, "Tell me about him." "My husband?" I said. "Yes," she said, "Does he provide for you?" "No," I said as I lowered my gaze. "Do you see him?" she asked. "No," I said. "Well far be it for me to get involved but I think it's time we sent him back to his wife." I nodded in agreement as she picked up the phone and dialed Doctoria Zaynia. You see, Doctora Zaynia's husband was a member of the same mosque as Ziyad. She said she would make arrangements to have this put to rest as soon as possible.

Since the mysterious marriage contract was still in Ziyad's possession, if I should ever think of marrying again, he could come back and say I still belonged to him even though we signed the back saying we will divorce until God decided it was best. Islamically, he still needed to say the word out loud. These two remarkable women had come into my life and taken over my heart instantly. It was the first time in my life I didn't feel a need to doubt a person, question their motives, ask myself what they wanted from me, or if they really were all they portrayed themselves to be. I just loved and trusted them fully like a daughter does a mother. They made me feel precious, loved, smart, and unique, and I rested my every decision with their insight.

Every evening after work I would head to the library and read. When I was done and ready to go, I would put my headphones in and since there was hardly ever anyone around I would walk that way down the gallery to the door with a little dance or sway, depending on the song I was listening to. On one of these evenings a girl from Yemen about my age had been doing some college studies in the library as well. In normal cases because of the dialect and my white skin people at first glance thought I was Syrian or Lebanese but when she saw me, she knew I was not an Arab. Later she would tell me although I looked like an Arab girl, the way I was dancing around like no one could see me would tell her that I was something else. She introduced herself as Samira. I greeted her and smiled, introducing myself with my Islamic name, Maha. She mentioned that she was meeting a few friends for dinner in the mall and asked if I wanted to join. I smiled and said, "Sure." It was the start of a great friendship. I had been alone without girls my own age for some time, and I was grateful for the invitation.

At dinner I met the crew: Wala, a beautiful Syrian girl from Damascus. She had a very cute, squeaky voice and was always ready for fun. Sameria's older sister, who had beautiful piercing brown eyes. An Emirati girl who was very critical of everyone and constantly pissed at life, and Reem, another beautiful Syrian girl from Halab who had the kindest heart and the softest voice I had ever heard. This was where they hung out, in the food court of the Marina Mall in Abu Dhabi. They followed the rules that they were raised with for the most part and all of them were covered but they had discovered a loophole in the guidelines. It would not have been acceptable to take boy's numbers and text them but turning on your Bluetooth and receiving random drops from strange boys around the food court was fine. We all laughed at what we received and shared around the table, love messages, photos, emojis, everything. To them it felt like a safe way to get male attention without ever having to worry if the boy knew who they were since everyone in the food court was on their phone. The girl receiving the message with her pin name could have been anyone. They dropped me home and I smiled all night long, I pulled out my secret stash of cherry flavored cigars, opened my window, placed a wet towel under the bedroom door and climbed out onto the ledge. It was only big enough for my butt, so I held on to the window frame dangling my feet outside three floors off the ground. With one hand I lit my little cigar, I would take about two puffs, and then I would retire to bed, throwing the evidence into the street below and spraying the room with perfume so no one would know it was me. It was not illegal for a woman to smoke, and it wasn't mentioned on my lease, but it was not socially acceptable for a covered woman to smoke and so if I had been caught the father might turn me out for being a bad influence on his impressionable daughter.

The next few weeks were packed with activities. I loved my Kindergarten class and made sure I took the time to invest a few moments during lessons to focus on every single child. As any teacher knows, each one would struggle here and there in their own way, and I loved watching them light up with excitement when they finally drew their first letter "A." There was one little girl in my class who refused to work. Her maid brought her every day and held her all through class as she cried. I tried excusing the maid from class, but this sent her into a state of panic and disruption. I tried everything I could think of, but it was no use. I went to visit the principal after school. "What's the problem? Just let her sit there, her mother has paid, and she is the daughter of a Sheikh of Abu Dhabi. To turn her away would be the end of the school," she said. I said, "If she doesn't do her work and continues to disrupt the other students she cannot stay in my class. I have to think about the rest of them as well. Please put her in another class." The principal agreed and moved her.

It was only later when I relayed the story to Ablah May that I realized that what I had done would have normally gotten a teacher fired. "Really, is she that volatile?" I said. She replied "Yes, worse than that, she doesn't even care what the parents think but you see, *Habiba*, you're special, with an American teacher on staff she can charge more and because you speak Arabic, you can speak to the parents, which makes you very important and that is why she speaks to you on her level." Ablah May began to tell me the stories. Once there was a little girl who would come to school with a clip to hold her bangs back. Her mom had been trying to grow them out. On her normal rounds of the school the principal saw the little girl and asked why her bangs were in her face? The teacher said, "She pulls the clip out, what to do?" The principal issued a warning to the mother saying if she saw her daughter's bangs in her face again, she would take matters into her own hands. The mother tried braiding the bangs and then putting them in a clip, but no matter what she tried, the little girl freed her bangs every day. On the next round the principal took a pair of scissors and cut the little girl's bangs as short as they would go. "Didn't the mother say something?" I asked. "She did," said Ablah May. "But that principal is so scary even the parents don't want to talk to her. Unless you are from an Emirate family like that little princess, or of some note like a Saudi with the power to do something, it's best for them to keep their heads down. She could make it difficult for them to get the children into another private school." I said, "What else?" She told me the story of a little boy who was "cutting" class, so the principal locked him in a closet. The principal forgot he was in there and they only found him when the bus failed to drop him off and the mother called the school asking about him. I was shocked to hear story after story and the rumors were worse.

I received a letter the next day from the school office saying my file was incomplete. My Teacher Aide Diploma needed to be translated and attested by the UAE Embassy in Washington. It had not returned yet. The letter mentioned that if I did not provide it within thirty days I would be let go. I went to the principal to ask for more time, but she said they were due for an inspection, and she could not give me an extension to the deadline. I went to Ablah May and asked her what I should do if it didn't arrive in time. She said not to worry too much. *Allah* has already decided my destiny and I should trust in his path.

A month later the certificate didn't arrive, and the school gave me notice. I took the letter to Ablah May and asked her what I should do. She said, "I'll handle this, *Habiba*." She picked up the phone and talked to the principal, somehow buying me some more time. I relaxed for a moment. I did the work she needed my help with and went home. I prayed for guidance and the ability to be strong. The next day when I arrived at Ablah May's office after work she said she had a surprise for me. "What?" I asked, "I have need of a translation assistant with this crisis we are facing in Iraq, would you be interested?" She showed me the contract and the pay was double what I was currently making at the school. I covered my mouth and said, "Yes, of course, I would love to help you." "Okay, then," she said, "Sign that and tomorrow go to the school and collect your things."

She invited me to dinner at her home to celebrate my new position, and that is where I met her husband. A frail, tall, skinny man who worked for the Japanese embassy. She shared with me about the struggles she went through before finally deciding to cover her hair. "As you can see from the photos, my daughter is not covered," she said. I gazed at her photos and Ablah May relayed her story of choosing to cover her hair when she got older. My mind went into a small state of shock as it screamed, "Wait, there was a choice? I was never given a choice, it was what I was to do, and I was told not to question." A part of me in that moment wondered if, had I been given the choice, would I have taken it so early in life or waited like Ablah May until I was older. As I looked at her daughter's pictures, I wondered what it was like to go to college, wear pretty things outside, swim in the ocean, and get a drink at a bar with girlfriends. Her life seemed like a Hollywood movie to me as I stared in wonderment at all the wondrous adventures she had, all without ever covering her hair.

She continued telling me about where they came from. "We are *Sharakus*, which is a tribe in Jordan and Syria. We're all over the place, originally Russian but we fled many, many, years ago. We're Muslim, but it's not uncommon to find a bottle of wine on the table at breakfast in Ramadan." A strange sentiment I never thought possible with any Muslim, especially one as pious as Ablah May. She talked about the small rituals that made them unique. For example, in Saudi, the men made all the marriage arrangements and then the young woman, covered, would serve the juice in order to get a glance of the boy, which should tell her everything she needed to know. The *Sharakus*, on the other hand, would throw a party with a lot of boys and girls of the same age. If the girl didn't like the boy, she put salt in his coffee before she serves it. This way, she said, he is the only one who knows when he tastes it that she is not interested and so there is no insult taken and the two may part ways without hurting anyone's ego. I thought how wonderful it would be to be born into such a wonderful tribe.

Her daughter arrived, took one look at me, and went to her room without dinner. I would learn later that her mother had been talking to her about covering for some time and I was seen as the covered daughter Ablah May always wanted. Someone who went to her meetings with her and lovingly discussed doctrine, while her actual daughter showed no interest in doing any of those things with her mother. Being an only child often means no one else can be allowed to occupy a place in your mother's heart, even if they share something special with your mom that you, the only child, don't value.

That night, I pondered over and over that single sentence Ablah May mentioned about how hard it was to choose to cover. The fact that there was once a choice saddened me, because I knew that if I had a choice once, had I not grown-up Saudi, I knew removing my head cover now would be next to impossible to pull off. Here is why: In Abu Dhabi, this was a community that respects a woman who feels unready to cover when she converts. They respected other ways of life and religions that don't cover even though there is always an underlying amount of pity for them for not being on the right path. It was a community that would not interfere if a Muslim girl of age from a family that previously didn't cover didn't feel ready to cover, like Ablah May's daughter. But for a woman to cover and then uncover was impossible and would cause a great backlash. The only way I was ever going to be without a head cover was if I moved to another country and left everyone behind.

I played out the scenario in my head and saw it clear as day. While Ablah May might understand, she would side with Doctora Zaynia and the others that I was making a mistake. I would no longer be welcome at the women's gatherings to study Islam, since I would be a bad influence on young girls, like Doctora Zaynia's daughter, who were soon to cover. Eventually, if I continued, Ablah May would no longer want me by her side, at work or otherwise. My roommates would see it as one step to a slippery slope and not want the reputation of their house tarnished by allowing me to stay, and just like that, my world would fall apart.

You see, in the Middle East everything is not about you, the individual, but the community. Without your community or connections, it can be very hard to go anywhere or do anything. I loved all of them and so I made the decision that the idea of being without a head cover should be put out of my mind. The freedom to try a life without a head cover, even if it was only for a short while, was not worth more than the people around me who helped me when I needed help the most. I reminded myself of all the great freedom I already had. I worked, I went out whenever I wanted without needing to let anyone know where I was going or when I was coming back, and no one ever wondered if I was doing something I wasn't supposed to be doing. I was blessed, I had more freedom than I ever thought I would and wearing or not wearing a head cover seemed like a frivolous idea in comparison.

One weekend, Samira called and said, "You know I have been wanting to bring this up for some time, my mother is struggling to pay the rent while my dad is still stuck in Yemen, and I was wondering if you would like to come live with us? The rent would be lower, and you would have your privacy. Also, my mom cooks at night so you will always have a meal waiting for you." I immediately said yes, gathered my things, gave my notice, and moved within days.

The room was larger than my last room and painted purple, a color her sister loved. Her sister moved into Samira's room with her. It was a wonderful time, I loved living with them experiencing what it was like to be with a family from Yemen. We ate with our fingers as the Prophet (ﷺ) did. We all prayed together, shopped together, and went everywhere together. They showed me the city as I had never seen it and we all watched TV together at night. One of our favorites was a Turkish TV Drama called *Noor* (named after the main female character) that was dubbed into Arabic. It was out of sync and badly dubbed, but we all had a crush on the leading male character. He was handsome and so chivalrous. He was our Jamie from the TV show *Outlander*, so to speak, and we all swooned over him. Another show we all enjoyed which came out only during Ramadan each year was called *Bab Al-Hara* (meaning the neighborhood's gate/door). It is possibly the most famous TV show in the Arab world to date. It was about life in the old city of Damascus in the 1930s and 1940s.

The city was easy to get around by taxi and, for the places that weren't, the Syrian girl in our group, Wala, had a small, green car she lovingly named, "*Zatunia*" meaning olive. In Abu Dhabi there was little to no chance a cop would stop us for packing so many girls in one car or not wearing seat belts, as they had bigger things to worry about. We went camping in the desert, rented a small house for the weekend where we cooked outside and danced until morning. We visited each other's houses, and I even got the chance to see the inside of a girl's college that they all attended together.

Despite the glorious display of wealth to the average visitor, I was surprised to find that the college was much more primitive than I expected. The computers were old and male teachers would give lessons via recorded lessons on big TV's that were wheeled into the classrooms on carts. Just like Saudi Arabia, a shining modern city in so many ways because of the wealth, and yet the education system for women still lacked so much.

The girls and I were all aligned until eventually, I started to show signs of change. My smoking started to get more reckless, trying to find a moment to sneak out of a party and find a dark alleyway where no one would see me, only to be caught many times by Samira, who said nothing and just gave me a shameful motherly stare. The more I learned about Islam the more I assimilated it and that was a problem because everything started to feel so stressful, wondering if the sound of my heels on the pavement was considered a sin, I bought flat shoes. I decided plucking my eyebrows was a sin since it used to be associated with street walkers, so I stopped doing that. Jumping out of bed because I realized I might have overslept and missed a prayer time. With the opportunity to learn also came a curious need to question. Were the rules of the past really meant to be carried on into the modern world? But I kept these thoughts to myself.

Another few months went by and on a calm day in the office, we were doing the normal paperwork. Ablah May had mentioned that a delegation would be arriving that day from Riyadh. She often spoke of her boss, Yacoub, with so much grace and admiration. I looked forward to meeting him. The door opened and a man walked in. Tall, white skinned, green eyes, curly, black hair and as clean as a shiny penny, so perfectly put together. I looked at him and melted. In an effort to not show how handsome I thought he was I looked down at my papers and began to file them vigorously, asking random questions of Salem and pretending to work. Behind him came Yacoub, a short Sudanese man who was sweet-tongued (*Lisano Heloo*, meaning he would say all kinds of nice things all the time) as we would call it in Saudi, truly a great man. I smiled, looked down, welcomed them, and then subsequently went back to pretending to look busy while they worked.

I worked on my refugee interview while listening in and taking glances at the stranger. It was the first time in my life that I had ever felt this way. I always went for the personality or the character but in my mind all I could think was I had never seen someone with such a beautiful smile. I secretly texted Samira and said I have just seen the *Amar*, which means moon in Arabic. She laughed and texted back and said she couldn't wait to hear about it. The men mentioned they were tired and wanted to head to the hotel so Salem offered to take them and Ablah May, being smarter than was good for her, suggested I go along and then Salem could take me home. She didn't think she could drive me today, she said. Yacoub got out first, and then the man moved to the front with Salem. He spoke so eloquently I could not help but be beguiled. We reached my apartment; I got out and he got out to politely say goodbye as I did in my traditional way and I politely walked calmly to the doorway where once out of sight, I bolted for the elevator. Jumping out of the elevator, I ran into the apartment and shouted, "To the balcony, to the balcony!" All the girls followed me. As we reached the balcony and leaned over to see him talking on his phone outside the car, each one added her commentary as is normal for girlfriends. "He's cute," "He's tall," "Oh, he's well dressed," and then he looked up and we all fell backwards onto the floor, like something out of a romantic comedy, laughing because we had almost been caught looking at him. When I come to think about it now, how could he have seen or known who was looking at him from such a height but nonetheless, we fell back. We talked about him all night and I gushed about how perfect he was.

The next day the two men finished their work and left back to Riyadh. Many months passed. I was busy and hardly found time to think of him until one day Ablah May said, "I need the number for a person I can't find. Can you call that boy - he will have it." I said, "Who?" She said, "Oh, what was his name … oh yes, Firas, call him." I turned red and said, "Me call him?"… she looked over at me in the way a mother would when her child would act weird and said, "Oh, do you like him?" I said, "No, me? No, not at all." She said, "Don't lie, it's okay, he's a good boy. I like him, now call him." I picked up the phone and called. As it rang, I wished he wouldn't pick up, but he did. I said, "Hello, it's Elise from the Abu Dhabi office and Ablah May wants a number from you for so and so, what is it?" He answered, I said thank you and hung up the phone, trying so hard to hide my trembling from Ablah May. She tilted her head back, laughed out loud, and we went back to work.

DIVORCE THE UNTRADITIONAL WAY

Late in the afternoon in Ramadan I was to have my *break-fast* with Ablah May, so I left home right before sunset to walk to her apartment. It has always been my favorite thing to see, how in many predominately Muslim countries, come Ramadan, right before break-fast the entire country looks like a zombie movie, not a single soul to be seen in the streets. You could walk down the middle of a busy street without looking behind you and never see a single car until after break-fast time. All the shops are closed, and everyone is at home about to eat. I loved the stillness that happened to a city that would normally be bustling at this time of day. Even the Christians and those practicing other religions were either at home eating or had been invited to a Muslim's home to break-fast. Ramadan is a great time for racking up as many good deeds as possible because they were worth more during that month. Likewise, a bad deed is multiplied during Ramadan as well. It is said that every single evil devil is chained by *Allah* during that month to free us all from temptation.

Following break-fast, Ablah May, her husband, Doctora Zaynia, and I headed down to the mosque to meet Ziyad's Sheikh. We entered the mosque, and they spoke on my behalf, explaining that Ziyad had brought me here and abandoned me. "The girl says he divorced her, but we need to be sure," Doctora Zaynia's husband said. The Sheikh only glanced at me briefly, not wanting to commit a sin by staring at a woman who was not his wife, as he said, "To be honest, I have been visited by the man's wife and family, they painted her as a monster. A girl with loose morals but what I see before me is but a child and a pious woman."

He picked up the phone and called Ziyad. "*Salamun Alaykum,*" Ziyad said, as the Sheikh pushed the speaker button, returning his greeting, "*Waalaikum issalam*" and said, "I have some people here and I need to ask you about a marriage contract you have." "What contract?" Ziyad said. "The one you made with this girl you brought here," the Sheikh said. "I have no contract," Ziyad replied. "Well, that's not what they tell me," the Sheikh said. Silence filled the room as the Sheikh said, "Did you divorce her like they said?" "Yes, yes, I did," Ziyad said. The Sheikh said, "So, you divorced her then?" "Yes, I did," Ziyad reiterated. "Well then, there is nothing more to discuss today. Goodbye. Hanging up the phone, he turned to us and said, "If it was not done right before, you are all witnesses that it is done now. She is divorced." I felt a wave of relief, we all did, but I feared the text message that might come from Ziyad knowing full well no one could have gone there without me and now his Sheikh had seen me and understood the truth of the situation. The next few months were hard. All my friends urged me to forget about him, but it was hard.

My contract ended with UNHCR (United Nations High Commissioner for Refugees) but there was a vacancy in the UNDP (United Nations Development Programme) that was located upstairs in the same building, so I moved up there and assumed the role of an assistant to an Italian woman named Gulia. We worked on women's empowerment and helping those who had been sexually abused, a field that today I am proud to have worked in but at the time, I didn't want anyone to suspect that I was all too familiar with it. To make up for the fact that the salary was a bit lower than what I was bringing in before Ablah May found me a position as an after-school English tutor with an Emirati family. For the tutoring position, three times a week after work a driver would pull up in a Maserati lined with fur to take me to their small palace to tutor their two children. In the early afternoon the head housekeeper would call on behalf of the cook to ask what I would like for lunch when I arrived to which I would always reply, "Anything will be fine," or, "I'm not really hungry." After napping on the 40-minute drive in the back of the car I would awaken at the small palace and a find a beautiful gold dining table laid for me with at least five main courses along with all kinds of pastries, dates, nuts, pickles, olives, fruit, and sweets. I would like to say I was in awe, but my mind normally just thought I said I wasn't hungry and now that they have gone to the trouble of making the food, I had to eat something or fear offending them. Not to eat when food is already laid in your honor can be interpreted as you think it's poison or you're a bad cook, either way, it's an insult.

I always ate alone and when I was done, I would head upstairs to the nursery where the children were finishing their homework. After my lesson we would spend a few minutes talking about their day in Arabic and I became especially close to the little girl, who was turning eleven and about to start covering her hair even in front of her cousins. I felt what she was going through. For many it was a choice but for us it was not really a choice. She talked about how she felt how she didn't want to stop playing outside with her boy cousins. I stayed as neutral as I could knowing full well it was not my place to interfere and anything I say could be misinterpreted. I tried to do a lot of nodding and offered suggestions about making her head cover more fun with jeweled pins perhaps or another color when it was appropriate. The little boy had a crush on me and only turned red when I spoke to him, but he was not my main student, the girl was. Since he was so young, he was there only to observe and absorb.

I only met the mother on two occasions. The first day I went when she said hello and introduced me to the children, and the last time I was there. The last day I was there I arrived at the usual time and the food was on the table but there was shouting coming from upstairs. I heard words like, "How could you do this?" "Are you without a mind?" I walked slowly closer to the stairs and saw the housekeeper standing by the kitchen doorway. A slight head tilt on my part towards the upstairs was all that was required to ask what is going on up there for her to gesture that I should come into the kitchen. She closed the door slowly and related the story of how the little girl had picked up a boy's phone number while she was out one day, and she had been calling him regularly. I bit down on my lips because I understood completely what was going on and in this the Emiratis are no different than the Saudis. She had put her reputation and the reputation of her family in danger. I put my hand on the housekeeper's shoulder and whispered, "I won't say you said anything, but thank you." It was the look in the housekeeper's eyes that told me how much she loved that little girl, probably having been the one who raised her from infancy along with a nanny. She could not interfere with the mother yelling at the girl but perhaps I could help. I nodded my head out of respect, walked to the staircase, took a deep breath, and headed up the bright pink carpeted stairs.

I followed the sound of the mother's voice down a hallway to the little girl's room. The door was closed, and the mother was standing outside telling her, "Open this door right now," and then shouting at the house staff to find the extra key. The mother heard my footsteps whereby she turned and looked at me, mortified at what I might have heard. She was concerned about how much I knew about the scandal her daughter had brought on the family and wondering who in the community I might tell. "Is everything alright?" I uttered, hoping to put her at ease that I knew nothing, saw nothing, and suspected nothing. Her reserve turned to humiliation as she said, "It's time for her lesson of course, I completely forgot." I placed my four fingers on my chest and then held my hand out to the door as a way to say, "May I try?" The mother nodded and left.

I leaned on the door and said, "Hello, it's me, Ablah Maha, can I come in?" The sound of the key turned in the lock and there she was in tears. I entered the room and sat down with her on the floor. She leaned in and cried on me for a little while and then I said, "What's wrong? What happened?" "There was this boy I saw when I was with my friends at the mall. He dropped his phone number for me and one night I called him." I exhaled as she continued, "I love him! But my mother and father found out and now they took away my phone. I'm not allowed to go out, see my friends, go to school, and my mother said my father will be home soon and I know he will beat me." I felt trapped in this tight spot. If I offered her advice and she revealed it to her family, it could be dangerous for me. I did not know if they were royal, but for sure they were close to it. A royal is a royal, and sometimes when up against a powerful person, you need to just exit like you would when you tiptoe around a baby's crib once they have fallen asleep. I looked down and told her something my stepdad had once said to me when I was young. "I know you're young and you have feelings. You will see many boys that you will like as you grow, but you can't talk to boys, not like that. The risk is too high. There will always be someone who knows someone who knows your family. You don't have the luxury of being invisible or having a relationship this way like those other girls. All it will do is put you in danger." She nodded her head in defeat and looked down as the tears came running down her cheeks. I reached out my hand and lifted up her face to look at me saying, "One day you will be married and have a life of your own, but you won't be able to do that if this goes too far." I paused as I recalled my Aunt Zakia and my mind made out a list of all the things that could come to pass if she continued in her open defiance.

I asked, "How angry does your Baba get?" "Very angry, he beats me with his belt." "Did they say what else was going to happen?" thinking there was a chance they would marry her off as soon as possible but in this day and age, the relationship would have had to be more public and gone a little further for that to happen. "They just said I would not go anywhere until they said so." "Okay, then. Here is what I need you to hear and it's just between you and me, okay?" "Okay." "Listen, you may be too young to hear this, but you need to say you are sorry to your dad and your mom and tell them it was a big mistake, and you won't do it again." "But I love him! I won't say sorry, my dad beats me with a belt, and my mom is shouting at me all the time." The boy was Emirati and supposedly well off like her so I said, "Listen to me, you can only get what you want by giving them what they want and being careful. Very careful. This was your first time doing something like this and more than likely, they will keep you here a short while and then you can do all the things you used to do, even contact this boy as long as he promises not to tell anyone either. Don't call him from your cell, get a prepaid one at the mall and only talk to him when no one is in the house. If he is worthy, one day maybe he can come and ask for your hand from your father but until then you need to protect yourself. You need to be the most important person to you. Do you understand?" "I think so," she said as she dried her eyes. I gave her a hug and told her to go say sorry to her mother before her mother got angrier and I left for the car that was ready to take me home.

The next day Ablah May let me know that the family had decided to send the girl to an English school somewhere and would no longer need me to tutor her. "Here, Habiba, they sent over your money." It was more money than what was agreed upon and I didn't know if it was a tip to never mention what I had witnessed that day or a thank-you for asking her to apologize to her parents. I wished I had more to offer her that day but even I knew that running away was not the answer, if she was even considering it. There was nowhere for her to go.

I heard recently about a princess who ran away from her family in Dubai but in the end, they brought her back and put her on house arrest, followed by prison and torture. The Emiratis have come a long way from how Saudi Arabia is today, but the inside is still the same. The only way to change the furniture in a room is to enter the room and move it out. No change will come for these women from the outside. It is the women who need to find a way to move the lines drawn for them, slowly, from within. Through careful planning and tact. Only then will change be real and long lasting for the next generation who will move the line a little further and soon enough change will come. Running away and refusing to play the game is not the answer, in my opinion. I feel for the princess but believe in the expression, *With Great Power Comes Great Responsibility.* If I was a Saudi woman, I would be there beside them, planning, holding tea gatherings, discussing ideas, and sharing my thoughts with my fellow women. But I was born American and so I was called to write this book and stand on the sidelines of social change and history. I do not judge the princess' decisions. Everyone's threshold for suffering is different. Often just because you were born with great power does not mean that you were born with the shoulders to carry that great responsibility. If you must run, run, but if you can stay and affect change, do so.

I was always an observant, careful, and strong child. My older brother paved the way for me to learn, unbeknownst to him. His constant habit of breaking the rules and defying laws taught me caution and tact, patience, and planning. We're not all strong enough to stand tall in the face of the unknown and to plan for outcomes impossible to fathom in advance. We're not all mountains that never bow when the wind howls. Some of us are palm trees that sway and bend with the wind. We all get to decide what role we need to play, if we want to see a different tomorrow.

My mother finally reached out through the MSN messenger asking if I was okay. I ignored her for days. After what she had done, telling everyone I was crazy, I never wanted to speak with her again. When my friends found out they encouraged me to speak to her since in Islam, Heaven is found at the feet of your mother. They said my salvation would be in danger if I disappointed her. "Ugh," I uttered as I typed, "Hi." She responded, "Sweetie, how are you, are you okay?" "I'm fine, what do you want?" "Well, your dad will be in Dubai on business in a few days. You two should meet and talk. Let's put the past behind us." "He's not my dad." I replied. "Meet him and forget the past," she said. I reluctantly said, "Fine," since I was on my own two feet now and he was coming to my playground this time. I arranged to meet him for dinner in a very public place for fear of retaliation. When the taxi pulled up, I got out and there he was standing in all his Saudi glory in his white thobe, head held high as if he ruled the world. I stared at him for a moment. He looked at me and I looked at him and just like that a wave of forgiveness came over me. I missed having a family no matter what they were. I missed having a dad even if he was evil. My hate and love for him always seemed equally powerful. Unfortunately for me there was never anything he could do that I could not forgive him for, and he knew that.

I walked up to him, hugged him, and said, "Daddy." I said to myself it will be different this time, I taught him a lesson and I don't live with him anymore. We had a great dinner. He told me about my mom and how the kids were doing. My mom has a habit of just making everything seem like it's rosy, like her life is perfect, the kids are perfect and not to worry. The reality is always grimmer. Lying is just something she does without even thinking. There is a certain kind of person who makes up a story in their head, however small. Lies like her child is a straight-A student and she would tell so many people over and over until one day she convinced herself and now it was a God-given fact. In essence, she even believed her own lies. I enjoyed hearing how the kids were struggling in school with the Arabic since there was no one to help with homework anymore, and I was not there to offer my advice as I had always done. He asked me how I was doing at work and romantically. He asked if I had met anyone, and I told him about Firas, how there was nothing yet but who knows. I told him about my friends, how happy I was, and that one of them was getting married but I didn't have a dress. He suggested since he would be in town a few days we should go dress shopping. The inner little girl in me said great, sounds good, and we made plans for the next day. I slept that night with a real sense of happiness that my dad had finally taken up his role as a father and I was grateful to have him.

The next day we went dress shopping and had lunch. He bought me a beautiful turquoise dress of the like I have never seen again. He dropped me back at my apartment and I was so happy to tell him goodbye. Had I fixed everything, I thought? Might we now be one family that played Monopoly and laughed at the old days? I didn't know but the idea was soothing as I sat at my desk at work the next day. Things had changed. I had my own little tribe here making it difficult I suppose for him to have control again. I also think that he had tried his original plan to just assert his authority and failed miserably.

My American passport meant now that I was older and more versed with the world, if he tried to kidnap me and take me back, he would face the possibility of my going to the media. It was set and match, but he wasn't going to give up that easily. If he wanted to have a chance at influencing my life, he would now need to tread carefully and be patient like the spider he was. I was asked recently why I kept putting up with him. The answer is too complex even for me. He was the man who abused me, and he was also the man who raised me. He no longer had a say in where I went, who I saw, what I did, how I dressed, and what I was allowed to think. But he did have control over some of the most valuable people to me. My siblings, and in a way my mother, despite everything, she was my mother. I knew that until my siblings were out from under his control my only hope of looking out for them would rely on me having the stomach to accept he would have to be in my life for a while to come.

A year or so passed and Ablah May said, "We needed to talk about finding you a husband." I said, "I didn't think anyone would want to marry me now that I was divorced twice." "Nonsense, you're a beautiful, smart, pious, Muslim girl. You weren't running around everywhere with God knows who. You got married and that is good. Leave it to me, Habiba, I will find you someone nice." I nodded my head silently and we continued working. A few days later Ablah May asked me to go have passport size photos taken. "Why?" I asked to which she replied, "Because I need one. Go today." I got her the picture, and she placed it in her wallet. Then she revealed that she was going on assignment to Riyadh, and she was going to see Firas there. I said, "Ablah May, I don't think he likes me at all, he barely noticed me last time he was here." "Nonsense," she said, "I'll talk to him." I said, "Okay." I thought he was handsome, but I really didn't want to be with someone who didn't like me.

Syrians and Sharakis courted very differently then what I was used to. Normally if my family was around, I would be getting to know Firas's mom, for example, or his aunt would be appraising me, but for Ablah May's tribe it was the two people who might be married who appraised who they wanted to spend their lives with. The parents would have some opinions, of course, but with Firas being as old as he was, the old ways would not work for him. As I came to learn, Firas was an expert at finding flaws in every girl he asked to court.

She asked me to help Salem while she was gone, in case he needed anything. Salem was Ablah May's administrative assistant, a short, bald, very intense Indian man. They had worked together for more than 10 years. Ablah May would tell me later that he was an amazing assistant. He was never late; everything was done quickly and properly. He was knowledgeable and fun, but his only downside was that he never had a new idea of his own. If she asked him to put these files in red folders moving forward 'till the end of time, he would buy red folders. He never tried to improve anything, never had a new idea, which was his only downside.

Three days later Ablah May returned and said nothing about Firas until the moment when Salem left for the day. Then she looked up and said, "Okay, here is what happened. I didn't have a lot of time with him, but we talked about how a good boy like him shouldn't be single. He is getting close to 40 and needs to start a family." He said, "Yes, I know, but I still haven't found the right one." "What was wrong with the girl I sent you out with last time you were in Abu Dhabi?" "She was great but not for me." Ablah May had been setting him up for years. Firas however was a skilled politician and as such he never voiced why he didn't like the girl so as to not offend anyone.

Frias was a pureblood Syrian from Damascus (often in Syria you find the class distinction of Syrians who actually could trace their blood lines back in Syria and the ones who arrived as Palestine refugees and married a Syrian. Firas took this class distinction very seriously). He was above all, very vain. In Syria he was seen as the successful boy who found a way to get an American scholarship, get straight A's, prove himself worthy, and now worked for one of the most important international organizations in the world. Any one of these items was enough to make him very popular with mothers. So as is often the case when you have a lot of options, you get more picky, you make up a checklist in your mind, and stay single longer.

Ablah May had made a personal project to see him get married. She said, "Well, not everyone is a good match, but I have the right one for you." She pulled out my picture and handed it to him. He looked at it and said, "*Muhijiba* (covered girl). May, I don't want a covered wife." May responded back, "Shame on you, what kind of wife do you want, wasn't your mom covered?" "Yes," he replied. "I'm not saying to marry her right away but if you let this one get away it would be a great loss, just consider her." "Okay, May, I will think about it."

Firas' mother had passed away when he was young and Ablah May was a mother figure to all who knew her. She gave unsolicited advice and told almost everyone what the right thing to do was, but she was so beloved no one would tell her "No" or that she was wrong. "Come on, Ablah May, there you see he's not interested, what about your daughter? She seems like his type," I said. "That may be, and I love Firas so much

I would give him my daughter in marriage, but her father and I want her to marry from our tribe to make things easier on her," she said. We left it at that.

On his next trip to Abu Dhabi, Ablah May pressured him into taking me to dinner. He said yes and asked me if I was free the next day. I said, "Yes." I picked a place, and we took a taxi from the office to the Marina Mall.

There was a nice restaurant that I liked on the water, one of my favorite spots to go at night. I knew Firas smoked so I figured he might appreciate the thought that the restaurant allowed smoking. We arrived and sat across from each other. He leaned back in his chair, one leg across the other and began to interrogate me. "Did you go to school? How old are you? How is your Arabic?" Picture with every question his head doing a slight jerk upwards. As I answered him, he constantly mentioned all the reasons why he was such a hot commodity. "I'm a Fulbright Scholar, I have risen higher than anyone expected. My brother lives in America and so I don't need a nationality." I was nervous because I had liked him once, but I had never really been on a date with a man before, which made the whole thing weirder. His lack of sensitive consideration made him less appealing by the minute. All the comebacks I could think of now were, "You don't need a nationality, well guess what, I'm not offering one. You got a full ride to a college in America, so what? I was raised in Saudi. You can take your arrogance and shove it, I lived arrogance." Instead, I did what I was taught to do. I sat and listened, nodding as I ate, wondering when the date would be over. Firas, being who he is, didn't notice or care, all he cared about in that moment was crossing me off a list so he could fulfill his promise to Ablah May to consider me and he was determined to accomplish his purpose.

We departed the restaurant and he said he had to run off to do something, which was always code for another date. Even though I had not been on a date it didn't mean I had not heard thousands of stories. He was only in town a short while and it was his right, as it was mine, to shop around. I decided to go home. All my friends wanted to know how it went and what he was like. I told them he was "*Shaaif Haalu* (vain or full of himself), arrogant, and he doesn't like me. I'm glad I found out early." I was certain he was a bad match until I went to work the next day. I told Ablah May about the date, but she insisted that he liked me. I told her there was no way, but she protested and since I felt sure I had bad judgement when it came to men I ignored my own senses and agreed with her.

Time stretched on and Doctora Zaynia brought her suitor to the table, her brother. She was Syrian, of a very conservative nature, so even though she thought it was acceptable for a couple to get to know each other she didn't think it was right for them to be alone, even in a restaurant. Just like Firas, he was vain and never married but at least she was kind enough to warn me of her brother's arrogance when she brought him up and suggested a lunch with her brother, herself, and her daughter, which I agreed to attend. After all, to meet him would do no harm.

When the day came, I arrived early and sat in the living room where he was sitting while his sister set the table. He sat in the chair and leaned back as Firas did. He asked questions and held himself so high and mighty. I answered his questions but when lunch was served and we sat down at the table he told off his niece for eating ketchup, to which I snapped back at him, "Let her eat her ketchup, it's none of your business." Until today I cannot explain why I would ever tell off a stranger and perhaps not having the courage to talk back to Firas factored into that, but his face was almost pale with shock as I issued a gesture to her that she could have her ketchup, completely overriding him. If my Aunt Zakia had seen me in action, she would have grabbed me by the arm, taken me to the kitchen and given me a stern lecture on how women should behave in the presence of a man and especially a wealthy, well-established, good-looking suitor.

We finished lunch and talked a little. I had no interest in him and so I had no problem putting him in his place for his arrogance every time it sprung up. "My sister says you have been married before?" "I have, but why haven't you been married at your age?" pointing out that if he thought there was something wrong with me there could certainly be something wrong with him. Often a good negotiation tactic is to point out the flaws, this way you can bring the price down. Afterall a white, pious, well-respected Muslim girl, who was also beautiful, young, and American wouldn't come cheap, but he needed to know there was going to be no negation should I decide to marry him.

The next day Doctora Zaynia called to say he had left on his next business trip but was very taken with me. I was shocked, since I had done nothing to draw his affection. How could he like me at all? But she insisted she had never seen him so smitten with anyone as he seemed to be with me. There it was, he, like Firas, was wealthy in his own right, had everything and had no need to marry so he took his time and every girl that came along got swept up in everything he had to offer as if it was a fairy tale and they wanted to play the leading lady. I was the first woman to put him in his place in a long time and that excited him. Like all great hunters, if the prey comes too easily it's not as exciting. She asked for my feelings to which I replied, "I will pray on it, but I feel like he is not for me." Unlike Ablah May who would not take no as an answer, she said, "I understand," and we left it at that.

The days moved on, and soon I found myself slipping away from my religious path. Everything in my mind was so clear at one point but now I started to question everything. My friend Wala said everything bad that had happened to me in my life was because I smoked but since I had never seen any doctrine to say it was forbidden, I could not understand why God would be angry. I continued to read, take my Quran lessons, offer counsel to those who wanted to convert, and help them decide if the call to Islam was for them. Unlike Ablah May or Doctora Zaynia, although I was an advocate for Islam, I was of a different nature. I believed in the idea that each of us has the right to choose if the path is right for us while many of the ladies used influence to convince others to convert. "Think about your children, think about Paradise, think about how much God will smile on you if you take the oath and become a true Muslim," they would argue. When I converted at the age of nine, I felt the pressure of my parents to do so or be left out of the family and I would not impose such pressure on anyone, no matter their age.

Once there was an American woman who was married to a very pious member of the community. She was studying Islam and considering converting but the biggest obstacle she faced was whether or not she wanted to cover her hair. The ladies said, "You're American, you cover, you should talk to her and tell what a blessing it is to be covered and how God smiles on such things, how her beauty was for her husband alone, you're the best one to do it." I took a deep breath and said, "I'll talk to her happily, but that is a decision I don't want to have any influence on. Wearing the *hijab* (head cover) is not an easy decision and she should take all the time she needs. If she covers too soon, she will take it off later and that could cause problems for her in society and with her husband. But if she covers when she is really ready. even if it takes years, there is nothing wrong with that. We all need to come to things in our own time." They all leaned back and said "Oh, we had not thought about that, you're right, yes, talk to her."

My work contract with UNDP was up for renewal but it was made clear that the head of office wanted to save money, so my contract would not to be renewed. When Gulia heard, she said, "I will talk to him," and strolled down the stairs to plead that she could not do without me but to no avail, my contract was to end. The same day I went home to find Samria sitting down on the steps mentioning that our building was assigned for destruction by the government to make way for a new, bigger, brighter, high rise and so we needed to move. In the face of all of this I tried to get another job, but nothing came about and even if it did, where would I live? With the inflation in Abu Dhabi going up every day due to the mass influx of rich Iraqis fleeing with bags of money and willing to pay any sum, renting an apartment would be impossible to do alone. Samira offered for me to move with them to Sharjah where the rents were cheaper, but Sharjah seemed so quiet compared to Abu Dhabi and way more conservative. I had traveled there with Gulia to meet Sheikha Fatima, the wife of the ruler of Sharjah who was a big supporter in our work with women, but it just didn't seem like where I wanted to go next. If you ask me what it was like to sit in the presence of royalty, it was like watching a graceful swan softly move across a lake. You could tell her mind was like the swan's legs moving at great speeds but her every move was like a smooth dance. She was beautiful, grateful, calculated, and most of all, unapproachable. We sat when she sat, we rose when she rose, and we drank when she drank.

Ablah May found me an internship at the United Nations Department of Safety and Security, but the only problem was it was in Riyadh, a place I had sworn never to return. My mother had by this time moved to Iowa with the children, and since this was an unpaid internship that might lead to a job, I would have no means to secure lodging, I would have to live with my stepdad again. This time, alone.

I called my stepdad and mentioned that I might have an internship in Riyadh, and he mentioned that he traveled a lot to the US to see the kids so he would not be around much, but I was welcome to my old room or any of the other rooms. I made my calculations. I had contacts now, I had worked for the UN and Firas was there, even if he didn't like me as a potential wife. His honor and respect for Ablah May would call him to look out for me. In the past when I was in Saudi under my stepdad's guardianship, he had all the power. No one would interfere but now if I felt in danger all it would take is getting in touch with Firas. If my stepdad tried to take my phone away Ablah May would notice and call Firas. Then all Firas would need to do is put me in his car that had diplomatic plates and I would be untouchable. I was no longer afraid to run away if I had to, as I had been as an adolescent. I decided the job was important, so I packed my two suitcases and left for Riyadh.

My stepdad picked me up at the airport in the afternoon and drove me to our family home. We sat and ate. When we were done, we spoke for the first time about what had happened when I was little. He expressed his grief if he had caused me any pain, a part of me wanted to throw something at him and say, "How could you!?" A part of me wanted to cry on behalf of a once very confused and scared little girl and for my mother who didn't believe me, but instead all the years seem to have made me hard, so I told him, "It's okay, don't worry about it, we're starting over." I asked what mom thought of me being here to which he replied, "Don't you worry about your mom, I will handle her." My mind flashed back to the times when he felt I would break as a child and say something to my mom or my brother. He would walk me to the corner store in England and talk about his plans to poison my mother. "How could you? The police will find out," I would say, and he would reply, "I am a biochemist. I would do it slowly in her daily Coca-Cola, in fact I have already started, so if you want her to live you will keep our secret to yourself." I'd like to say things were different now, but I dared not let myself believe that he was done manipulating me or anyone, it was simply who he was. I nodded and went to bed. I chose to sleep in my old room at first with a lock on the door but eventually moved to my brother's old room because it had a desk I needed for my laptop, plus that room had so many memories, wonderful and horrible, and with my sisters no longer in the bunk beds, it felt too big for me.

In Saudi, if you don't have a driver, as a woman you will have to rely on taxis but if you had ever seen a taxi on the street in Riyadh, trust me as a woman alone, you would have second thoughts about getting into any taxi. If you were lucky, you got a new one but most of them were old and breaking down. Some had no AC, and the poor Indian driver would sweat all day as he drove around the city. Let's just say if you don't have a strong stomach, you would vomit and you would be grateful for your veil that could be used to reduce the smell. Then there was another problem: many women like me were never taught to navigate the streets since we relied on our fathers and trusted drivers to get us safely where we needed to go. To be honest you could have dropped me in the middle of the city, and I would only know how to navigate to a road named Takksussi, which is where the King's hospital was. The houses have no addresses and so you would need to be able to give directions based on the large street names and landmarks around. That would be easy enough but what if the driver took a liking to the color of your hands or the sound of your voice. We knew a girl who got in a taxi alone from the mall. The driver took a new turn saying he knew a shorter way and a few turns later they were in a remote area. When they finally did find her … Well, let's just say she was lucky, or maybe unlucky, she was still alive. The taxis do have license plates if you thought to text it to someone before getting in, and ID cards that must be displayed but they could have been sick and had a friend drive for them that day. Like I said before, it is very easy to disappear in Saudi Arabia.

My stepdad had no car since he walked to the hospital for work. The hospital offered a car service for their employees, mostly to keep the single nurses safe, and since my stepdad was a doctor, this service was also available to us. I called the service, and they sent a car with a very respectable man from Africa. As is customary, they don't speak to you as a woman for fear that they will get in big trouble but when we pulled up to the diplomatic quarter and he dropped me at the UN, he said as I was stepping down, "You work here?" I found his inability to stick to protocol rather refreshing, whereas in the past I would have found him highly inappropriate. I smiled and said, "Yes, Mubarrak, I work here." "That is so cool!" I smiled again and said, "Can you come back and get me at 3:30 p.m.?" "Yes, Madam, I will be here."

My first day at the UNDSS was interesting, to say the least. On my first cigarette break I met a boy whose name was Haisum. We sat together as we smoked, and he said, "So what's your name?" "Elise," deciding that it was more professional to start using my legal name to avoid the confusion of using Maha, which was not the name on all my paperwork. "That's cool, so where are you from?" He asked a question I always struggled to answer. "Well, I'm originally from California, but my stepdad is Saudi." "Wow, dude, that's super cool!" It was the first time someone had called me dude. "Where are you from?" I asked. "I'm from California too." he said. He was popular among the staff and if it wasn't for the fact that he was doing an internship for his college back in California. I would have worried he would get the job. He was smart, funny, and exceedingly kind. I had never had a male friend before. Someone who I was not afraid was just interested in sleeping with me or marrying me, but rather there to really listen and provide advice. Until this day he blames me for his addiction to cigarettes, but those days we spent together were some of the best in our lives. I affectionately named him Guy since he was my first guy friend.

I attended meetings about security and took notes which I was never allowed to take home to edit. I did research on this and that and I was always being told not to do any of it at home. Then we were assigned the task of presenting a presentation on bomb safety since Riyadh was considered a dangerous place for expats. Even I could recall an occasion when a bomber had driven his car into a compound filled with expats before detonating it. I recall the after blast once cracking our windows. Even though it wasn't as common now, it was still a real possibility. I took this assignment very seriously, even going as far as to count every bomb attack in Riyadh versus every other city in Saudi Arabia, proving that this was no laughing matter. We were all in great danger if we were not prepared. Haisum and I worked on the project every day, planning out what we needed to say and what kind of drills we would have them all do.

On my second day, Firas asked if he could take me to dinner in the diplomatic quarter, one of the only places in the city where the religious police could not enter. There was a little Italian restaurant that we met at. We sat in the corner so no one would see us and gossip about us dating. He talked about his life, his family in Syria, his great education, and found every opportunity to remind me that there were a thousand girls lined up to marry him. He drove me home in the diplomatic car, which by law can't be stopped by religious police, so I was safe.

My stepdad made plans to travel to the States to see my mom. I was left alone in the house. Life, when I returned to Saudi as an adult, was much more free for me. My stepdad didn't question where I was, why I was late, and who I was with, and while he knew about me seeing Frias once in a while he only ever offered advice when it was asked for.

While looking for some of my papers while my stepdad was away, I came across a document I had never seen or thought I would have any interest in seeing. My mother's divorce decree. I opened it and read through it. I noticed that my biological father had joint custody. My mother had told us he took everything from her and wanted nothing to do with us. My mind wandered as I searched for my first passport, only to find a visit visa to Saudi. I felt as if the puzzle pieces were finally coming together. She would have never been able to take us out of the country without his permission, so she told him we were going to visit grandma and grandpa in Saudi Arabia and upon her arrival she got a job, changed our visit visa to a residency, married my stepdad, and changed our names so he would never find us. My heart broke to know that my father, who really loved me, had no choice in this matter. How could my mother do such a thing? All these years telling us he never loved us, that he was cruel and unkind, and now I knew the truth.

My heart felt angry as if I had been betrayed in the worst way, knowing now that my father might be dead, I might never know him because my mother insisted he was a bad husband. In my mind, even if he was a bad husband that did not make him a bad father. I closed the envelope and made my peace, deciding that there was no point in confronting her since she would just make up another story to cover her tracks. I knew now that I had to find him, no matter how long it took, even if I only found his grave.

THE PERFECT MAN

Firas and I went out many nights after work to the same restaurant. He talked and I listened every night. I would come back home and walk straight to the balcony to smoke and sit in silence, so I could get some rest from being talked at. He would talk about how I wasn't good enough; I was undereducated, too skinny, and too religious. I would sit and contemplate his words, asking myself why I would ever want to see him again. But in a lonely city like Riyadh, even bad company was better than no company at all. There was a part of him that showed up sometimes when he was reminiscing about his homeland or talking about his family that I liked, but for the most part, even though I knew he was a good person and perfect as Ablah May said he was on paper, it felt like a bad match.

As the days went on, I realized that I was the only covered woman in the whole building. I felt out of place and one night Frias mentioned, "I like meeting with you, but I will need to see you without your head cover to make sure I am attracted to you." It seemed like an honest request, so I went into the bathroom, took off my head cover, fixed my hair and came out. The waiter was shocked into silence as I emerged, having seen me so many times as a covered girl. Firas said, "You look okay but there is room for improvement." My brain flashed. No man had ever said that to me. He preyed on my insecurity about being divorced and every other button he could push.

The next day I received a call from my stepdad, and I took the opportunity to ask him what he thought about me going without my cover when I was at work. Afterall I worked in the diplomatic quarter and there was no chance of the religious police picking me up for indecency there. He said, "If that is what you want to do go ahead." Unable to believe my ears I said, "Really?!" "Yes, you're all grown up but just be careful." "I will, daddy, thank you, daddy!"

I woke up and blow-dried my hair, put on my makeup, and covered myself to get from the compound to the car. Once the car passed into the diplomatic quarter, I lowered my head cover. Mubbark turned his head slightly and said, "Elise, what are you doing?" "It's okay, Mubbark, my dad said I could, but only in the diplomatic quarter." "Okay, Elise, but be careful." "Thank you, Mubarak." I went to work the next day glowing like a beam of light in the darkness. I recall standing on the steps of the building entrance as a slight breeze blew past my neck and caught my hair. It felt so different and strange, and yet so exhilarating, not that I had never been outside without my cover. It's very hard to describe but it was a defining moment. A moment when a great perception in me changed.

Upon entering the building, the shock of everyone was real since it was unheard of that a religious covered girl should one day decide to uncover, but there I was. The women started a whisper campaign to try and figure out why I would decide not to cover, while the men enjoyed the new view. Firas was out of town on business that day and since he worked in a different building it would be sometime before he saw that I was without my head cover. Haisum said when he saw me, "Dude, going all rebel on me, ya! Good for you."

Mubbark called and said he would be running late so my supervisor offered to drive me home. I was grateful. On the drive home he opened a conversation about how he had been ill. "Oh, I hope you are feeling better," I said. He said, "Well it was an operation on my dick." I froze in my seat, my mind raced and as he continued, "but it's still good. I'm like a horse despite my age." I nodded and wondered if I could jump from the car if it slowed down enough. He already knew my father was away, but he didn't know if my neighbors were close to me I thought, so I sat still as he continued. Once he stopped at my house, I jumped out saying my neighbor was waiting for me and thank you for the ride. I went inside, watched TV, and went to bed.

When I awoke for work the next day, I laid in bed thinking about what had happened. I thought about how I needed this internship. If I reported him, it would only mean that no other agency would hire me, and he would be reassigned. My mind raced as the hours ticked on and I realized I could not go to work today. As I lay there, a call came from Alaa, my supervisor. It rang but I decided not to answer. He called again and again and finally I decided the best option was to stay home for one day to let him sweat and then to return to work as if nothing happened. He called again and I answered. His voice was in a state of panic. "Are you okay?" "I'm ill today." "Oh, I thought maybe something I said yesterday might have upset you." I said, "I'm just ill but I will be in tomorrow." My tone was stern, and I didn't even try to sound sick. I hung up the phone feeling stressed, there was a thin line. On the one hand I had everything to lose by telling someone but if he felt it was okay, he might get worse. The next day I returned to work as if nothing had happened. When he brought the conversation up, I changed the conversation to his wife who was in Egypt, asking if it was hard to be so far from her all the time, and eventually he dropped the idea completely, hopefully for good.

Haisum and I were in an area we called "the shithole." It was the smoking area. There were no chairs, so we sat on the side of the planters and threw our cigarette butts in them. Hassium eventually asked if I was seeing someone and I asked him if he saw that tall visitor from the neighboring office to which he replied, "Evans, him? No way." I said "Yes, but it's not for sure yet, so you can't tell anyone, we're just talking at this point." He agreed to keep the secret and poked a little fun at the fact that he was known around the office as Mr. Squeaky Clean. I smiled and said, "I can see that." With that, we headed back to work.

The time came for our presentation. We were to present in front of all the agencies and it was scary. Haisum said at the last minute, "You should do most of the speaking, Evans." I shrugged my shoulders forward and back indicating I'm not good at public speaking to which he replied, "Too bad, Evans, you got this." The people arrived and filled the hall as Haisum did our intro. Then I began discussing the statistics. By the time I got to the safety procedures, half of them were rolling their eyes like this was never going to happen and the other half were wondering why a little girl was talking to them like they were in the army. So many of them had never been in Riyadh during the compound bombings that took place, since the staff rotated every two or four years. For me it was a scary thought, but if it happened before, it could definitely happen again. I wanted to stress how critical this was to their safety but to no avail. Our supervisor stood at the end and advised everyone there would be a random drill very soon and they should all read up on what they needed to do.

The next few days were spent putting together a plan. How could we scare them enough that they would take the drill seriously? We took our plan to our supervisor for approval to which he said, "Sounds good." First: We made a phone call telling someone in the building that there was a bomb on the premises. That person would need to know who they needed to call next down the chain to help evacuate the building as soon as possible. Not a second could be spared when there is a risk of a bomb. The next step was to set off the fire alarm, which didn't go off, so we had to climb up on a desk with a lighter to get it to go off. Then we got to take the megaphone and run up and down the hallways saying, "Leave now! A bomb threat was received!" One of the staff actually jumped out of her chair and ran outside screaming. When she realized it was a drill, let's just say she was not a happy camper. The anonymous drill was a success, and our supervisor was pleased.

I talked to Ablah May almost daily to give her reports on Firas, as I am sure she did the same with him. Every time I felt like it was a bad match, she would insist that I was wrong and ask me to be patient with him. I would always lower my head and say, "Yes, Ablah May." My stepdad finally returned and noticed an unsettling pattern of how every time I met with Firas after work, I would come back stewing, angry, and unsettled. Not wanting to interfere, he kept his thoughts to himself. Firas decided my Syrian Arabic needed correcting so that it would be perfectly matched with his. So, he only spoke to me in Arabic and the conversation restarted over and over every two minutes as he had me repeat the word I had fumbled up over and over until I got it right. These lessons would go on even as he drove me home. Reaching a point when I didn't even want to speak anymore for fear of being corrected. He promised much and delivered little.

"When I make my decision, I will make my wife the happiest in the world with flowers, dinners, and presents. I will lavish her and take her places, so just wait for my decision and you will see," he said. The patience he required took a lot out of me, but I stuck it out for Ablah May and because despite being many things, he was a good man. I had married twice for love. This time I wanted someone stable, honorable, and kind. Like my aunt always said, "I'm sure love will grow with time."

The time came for my internship at UNDSS to end and on our last day, Hassium gave me this letter (errors included):

Elise Marie Evans

24 today, eh? 24 is just before 25...Where your life really starts. So what you do this next year really sets you up, I guess. But then again, nothing in life really sets you up for anything.

So, I have a lot to say to you. I didn't know how to say it in any other way. I usually DO end up doing something which has major amounts of expression for people that are close to me - my mom got a FAT email, my best friend in Davis got a video b-day card, and well my ex-girlfriend got a few months worth of journals about how much I thought about her, lol. Oh well.

Here's what's up. I can pick people out pretty easily. I can read into them, figure them out, understand how they would react under certain situations and in a nutshell, judge them. I could never do that with you. In all honesty, you had me baffled. You are literally one of the most complicated people I've ever met. At the same time, you appear as one of the most straight up women in the world. You don't create drama, do your own thing, let it be known that you care and make your goals obvious, transparent, and understood.

The balance you maintain between a semi-troubled past, a quest for truth about your father, a distrubed first experience of a relationship and a continuous run-in with independence really sets you apart. You are such a deep person. There are so many things you are capable of doing, but until you get to know YOURSELF first, you won't get anywhere.

You keep getting crushed under other people. You keep letting their opinions take a toll on you.

Don't.

Why do you do that? Look into the mirror, bud. You are a strong, charismatic, and extremely sentimental person that is capable of changing the world. Why would other, weak, not-so-amazing people have any sort of effect on you? You know I'm not saying [sic]"oh fuck the world, do whatever you want and fuck the rest". All I'm trying to say is figure yourself out.

Understand yourself and appreciate yourself. Not for your beauty, not for your charm, not for your "womanly powers" (these are all external things that you show to OTHER people and that THEY see about you), but for who you are inside that only YOU know about.

I don't know why I'm telling you all this. I just feel that you need to hear it. I felt it, and when I usually feel something so strongly about someone I let them hear it. You know what it is that makes me feel so strongly? Just like you said...the little things.

Remember how you walked in that second day, and I was having a shithole time and was kinda balling on the phone and you said "are you ok? You looked like you were crying"... well that meant a lot. Just you caring and giving a shit meant a lot. And then when you asked about my ex-girlfriend, that meant a lot. You were a stranger, outta the blue [sic], and you wanted to hear me out. You didn't know that I'd been CRAVING to vent to someone about how much I missed her. How much I missed her arms and missed holding her tight. How much it hurt that someone else had that liberty now. But you still asked, and listened and that's what mattered.

Sometimes you don't listen, and I can tell. We'll be sitting there, talking, and you'll just be checking yourself out in the big window, lol. I notice that. And then I'd notice how things I said would just kinda fly over you… But when it mattered, you'd listen…

There was the time when Salwa's kid was over, on my second last day at work. We were all smoking, you were smoking, and the kid was there. You didn't even know the kid but you put out the cigarette (It was half done...I was cringing from the wastage) and you took her away and picked out flowers. Elise, little things like that change the world. Not for me and not for you, but for the big fucking world itself.

Little things like that show what a person truly is made of, and it's little things like that that have made me feel so strongly for you. You are such an amazing, complex, and intricate person. Everybody around you is just so simple. They've tried to dump their simple lifestyle onto you and it's because of all these reasons that I feel I need to talk, you know? When something is bugging you in your stomach, and you just HAVE to let it out...you tell the person exactly how you feel.

That's how I feel.

You have potential, oodles of it. And you know it. It's not just your beauty. And you should know that beauty will only take you SO far...so don't dwell on it. Don't rely on it, use it as a sidenote but don't base your life on it. It's your brains and heart that take you places at the end of the day. Let them work, and let them do all the talking.

Be yourself, Elise. I know I'm a kid who's stupid at times and doesn't know much but I've seen a good chunk of the world and have been through a few situations that have made me not only articulate and really ponderous, but also someone who appreciates life for what it is, tries to bring a smile to everybody's face and for people that are closeto him, tries to bring a smile to everybodys heart.

I hope I brought a smile to yours. Because honestly, you've made mine laugh. I have had one of the best summers of my life and you are the main reason. I loved coming to work because I looked forward to fighting with you about whether we were going to the lounge or the shithole, I looked forward to seeing that childish gleam in your eyes when you talked about making bombs, lol. In short, you WERE my summer. Thanks for that. Thanks for all the good talks, positive words, and for saving my ass on so many occasions.

I know you're trying to quit, but I have a snagging feeling you won't anytime soon. Which is why I got you this little thing - I hope it comes in handy once in a while.

Take good care of yourself and stay in touch. You remember that time I was asking you how many 'good guy friends' you had? Well, I hope I can be included in that honorable list - because you are ;)

I always got your back, bud. Through thick and thin.

Have a great birthday,

Guy.

A letter, the first I had ever received where someone saw me, really saw me. It would take many years for the words of this young 19-year-old boy to be heeded. The first time I read this letter I thought he was crazy. How could I as a woman impact anything? But now I draw strength from this letter and that boy who told me I could change the world.

A position opened in one of the other departments, but they picked one of the other interns. Another position opened in the UNHCR which was located in another building. It was where Firas worked so I asked if he knew if they had settled on anyone. He said he thought they settled on someone, but he would ask. Ablah May good as promised me the job and started calling her entire Rolodex but to no avail. Apparently, the head of finance was to supervise that position and wanted someone he knew, a relative of his. Firas thought it over and realized there were only two female candidates for this job. The rest were male and the one they were advocating for was male. Then he looked around the office and noticed how of the entire staff there were only two women. He realized what could convince them to hire me wasn't to sing my praises but rather to sing to Geneva about the lack of diversity in the office.

When they called the managers meeting, Firas took the opportunity to point out the diversity issue he had noticed and said, "If we don't hire a woman for the HR position, I will write to someone." The head of office agreed that they needed to hire a female and so I and one other female were thrown into the mix. Upon further interviews I came out on top since I had previous UNHCR experience, and I got the job.

I admired him at that moment. How smart he was. He seemed like a knight in shining armor in that moment and that was the moment I started to love him. That night we went to dinner as we normally did and sadly with Firas' track record, he managed to turn my dreamy sparkling eyes into the eyes of someone who was just slapped for no reason. He pulled out a piece of paper and drew a pie chart of his ultimate woman that he had been looking for. He explained to me where I was lacking on that chart. My eyes got bigger as I sat there and asked myself if this was for real. When he was done explaining how I fit most of the criteria, but I just needed a few tweaks here and there, I looked up and told him, "Maybe you should go buy a car since they come custom made, if you want to add a cool stereo or something they can do that, all you need to do is pay more." His face looked like mine had three minutes earlier. He was in shock, and I wondered if any girl had bothered to tell him off instead of just deciding not to marry him and sending a messenger to say they were a bad match very politely.

He was engaged once to a Syrian girl but when he relayed his plans to have her give birth in Canada so they could get another nationality she refused. He broke off the engagement immediately. My mind was so puzzled when he told me as I immediately took the side of his ex-fiancé saying, "I would not want to give birth in Canada without my mother either, I mean a strange country and having a baby for the first time can you blame her for not wanting to?" He immediately got defensive about his decision and since I knew he was great at arguing until he was declared the winner, I dropped the subject.

Despite his long lectures about how a thousand girls are lined up in Syria waiting for him, how he had unlimited options since he knew he was a good catch, I learned over time with his stories that he was greatly unaware of how many women had actually rejected him. He told me once there was a beautiful Syrian girl that he really liked and fit all the criteria but for some reason she met with him once and relayed a message through her family members that she was not interested in a second meeting, his ego took it pretty hard.

I started my new job with the eagerness of a rabbit to eat a carrot. The MENA (Middle East and North Africa) region had never had an HR representative and because it had grown so much, they needed someone to look after personnel issues. My new supervisor, Khaled, a short Indian man who was often afraid of his own shadow, told me that in addition to my HR duties I would be in charge of security, and handed me a manual for safety procedures for the office. I was happy to oblige since I felt that safety was important especially after everything I had learned at the UNDSS. Then he took me to see the files I would be using. Opening a long closet behind the kitchen he revealed stacks and stacks of papers. None of them were in files and all of them were covered in dust. I looked at him, nodded my head, rolled up my sleeves, and went to work. Carrying one stack at a time to my office where I made new stacks for each staff member and their region. I then ordered binders in different colors so I could color code the staff making their files easy to find. When they called with a question, the manual became my life and in about a month I had pretty much memorized many of the procedures and benefits entitled to staff.

As I filed, I read the papers, making notes of mistakes that needed to be corrected. Hour after hour as I filed away in my office the door alarm would go off. The office door was a large metal bunker door with an alarm that would give you a headache. I would run out and say close the door, it's not safe to leave it open. The cleric, Mustafa, whose desk sat near the door would look at me and say, "Relax, nothing is going to happen, and it will go off in a minute." I would reply, "Relax! Mustafa, it says in the manual that the door needs to stay closed unless someone is entering or exiting. It is for your safety." "Safety from what? We're so safe here we don't need that door," he said. Annoyed, I said, "Mustafa, please close it. I was put in charge of security, and I say it needs to stay closed."

He closed the door and as I turned around, I heard him chuckle and say, "The little girl is telling me what to do. She thinks she is going to keep us safe when we are the men here, ha-ha." I kept walking back to my office.

I made a trip to visit our security guards in the garage beneath the office the next morning, to introduce myself as the new head of security for the office. They were two men from Pakistan and extremely polite. I asked, "Tell me what you do every day." Ahmed said, "We check the cars for bombs, Madam, and make sure people do not enter the garage unless they have an appointment." Their location was very important because should a car with a bomb somehow make it past the main diplomatic quarter gate and get parked in our garage, the explosion would take out the office and everyone in it. I knew this well from the research we did for our bomb training in UNDSS. I bowed a little and said, "Thank you, Ahmed. Just keep doing what you're doing and remember that no one enters unless their car has been checked and if you ever can't get a hold of someone to confirm if that person has an appointment, you can call me directly on my cell phone. No one should pass without confirmation, okay?" He bowed and smiled, I returned his bow, and told them both how important they are to everyone's safety at the complex.

We had a driver, a poor soul from Yemen. I had spoken to him many times about his children but realized after reviewing his paperwork that he had never been told that he was entitled to extra pay monthly for each child he had on his paycheck and the back pay was ten years' worth. He had seven children. When I called him into my office, he looked a fright, like he was going to be let go, but after I explained that I would be letting Geneva know the mistake and he should expect a check soon, he wept. It was life-changing for him. The staff were my refugees now, my calling and their rights were my duty. I took phone calls and replied promptly to email even if I didn't have the answer, I would assure them I would try to find a solution if there was one available and get back to them as soon as I could. I enjoyed the work so much and there was little to do at home in the evening, so I tended to work long nights especially when Firas was traveling. When the head of office would leave every day he would say, "Oh, you're still here? Go home, it's late." "I will, I'm just finishing something," I would say. Sadly, I did not realize that this was a request not out of concern that I was working too much but to tell me to go home and not use the Internet to chat with boys as the rumors around the office suggested, after all who works that hard? Especially a woman....

Firas and I would smoke together on the office balcony with another staff member, Mahmoud, a newly married man who was very funny and laid back. We would talk about the world and this and that. Mahmoud always found a way to lighten an otherwise stressful topic like Palestine, events in Syria, Egypt, and everywhere that seemed to make Firas would go on at length about how the Jews were evil, that the regime in Syria needs to be taken down, how the Egyptian president is corrupt, and on and on. Mahmoud would laugh and say, "It's a beautiful day in Saudi Arabia, at least we're not there anymore, so relax." Firas forbade me to come to his office unless absolutely necessary, less people in the office begin to gossip. Day after day the door would sound the alarm and I would run to close it promptly. Mustafa would chuckle and say, "Look guys, the little girl is going to save us if someone gets through the door!" I would roll my eyes and return to my office. Despite their teasing, I always jumped to my feet and closed the door and ignored their laughter and comments. I was a natural protector as I had been for my siblings and it was hard for me to not fulfil my role once it was given to me, even if those I was asked to protect did not care for my protection.

When Firas and I went to dinner, I would leave first, and he would follow later to avoid people knowing we were courting. Everything seemed to be going well. I excelled, learned, and worked hard, but it turned out that wasn't a good thing. You see most people in the office left early, came in late and Noha, the employee who had offered her niece as a candidate for my job, spent her days sending forward emails to everyone about the "lady boys" in Vietnam to explain how depraved their gay lifestyle was, and leaving by two o'clock. The truth was that I didn't realize as one of the youngest people in the office, I was making everyone else look bad and that wasn't a good thing. Especially Noha, with every compliment I received, she hated me more. She possessed what is known as an indefinite contract, which meant firing her was almost impossible. I, on the other hand, had a contract that was renewed every six months. I felt for her as she had lost a child in a bus crash many years earlier. I assumed that was why she was always mad, why she hated me so, maybe she needed someone to be mad at, but my work had little to do with hers, so I decided I need not see her too often.

As is often the case with woman-on-woman combat, the prettier you are the more enemies you have in the world. At no fault of your own except that genetics made you fit a stereotype that people think is pretty when in fact even Noha was pretty. All the insecurities in the female domain can be rooted back to self-confidence. If you're confident and know you're worth, truly, you will have no need to be jealous, suspicious, spiteful, or malicious. I was brought up Saudi and even had I not been beautiful, confidence was something every Saudi possesses in spades, unfortunately Noha had none.

They put me on a committee to decide on things around the office. Noha was also on the committee, and I was afraid of getting it wrong and giving her ammunition, so I recorded the meetings so I could better type up the notes accurately, and then deleted the recordings. After the meeting Ablah May got wind that I was not covering in Riyadh, obviously from Noha, and was very disappointed. "Habiba, why are you not wearing your head cover? "I don't know it's something I want to try; I never had a choice like you." "It's frivolous, put it back on and go make friends with Noha." "I know Ablah May, but she hates me. It won't matter what I do." "Good girl, Habiba, she's nice just try talking to her." I got up the courage and went into her office and asked, "Noha, I get the feeling that you don't like me, and I would like us to be friends," she insisted she didn't. I cried. She said, "You know it's not you, I just don't think you are very good for that job." I told her, "Thank you for the input," and left her office. I continued to avoid her, hoping it would help us learn to coexist.

While my stepdad knew I was seeing Firas after work for dinner most days which was sanctioned and since I came home most nights disturbed, my stepdad didn't feel the need, I guess, to ask how it was going. Perhaps he assumed it would fizzle out on its own. One night out of the blue Firas called while I was cooking dinner and my stepdad was in the kitchen. Firas said, "Habiti, I have made a decision." My heart raced. Was this THE decision? Then he said, "Well, I have decided that even if we don't end up married, I have decided to pay for your college tuition." I sighed in disappointment and said, "That is very generous, but I can handle that myself." He said ,"Well, think about it, I want to do this." I thanked him and before I hung up, I said the word *Habebe* which means "my love" (Masculine).

My stepdad's head whipped round as he asked, "What did you just call him?" I said, "Habebe, why?" He said, "I didn't think you two were so far along." I said, "It's just a word and we have been dating for almost a year." He said, "No more!" and went straight to sit in the empty guest room in the dark. He sat in a chair staring at the wall, his cheek muscles flexing as if being stimulated by electric shock, which was always a sign that he was really mad about something. All my attempts to get him to talk failed so I had to leave him be until he decided to come talk himself.

The next day after work he said, "It is time that Firas came to talk to me and formally ask for your hand." I said, "Of course, I totally agree. I will put it to him." When I told Firas his response was, "While I completely understand your dad's position, I really can't make a decision like that until you meet my family. Since my stepmom's heart is so weak and she can't travel, you will need to come to Syria with me to meet them. Also, I would like to have you checked to make sure that you can have children by a doctor since you're not on birth control and you have been married twice." Spoken like a true politician and lawyer but knowing my stepdad as I did, I dared not think of what would happen if Firas said those things to him. I told my stepdad Firas would be very busy with a project the next week or two, but he said he would come talk to him. My stepdad agreed to wait two weeks.

Back in the office, everything went wrong when it turned out my keeping of perfect notes for the meetings backfired since most of what Noha said in the meetings she did not want to put into the minutes. She came into my office like a rolling boulder down a short hill. Shouting and saying, "You made up whatever I said in the minutes?" I didn't dare tell her that that could not be the case since I had the recording on my phone. Instead, I calmly said, "Please do not shout at me," but that only made her louder. I then calmly asked, "If you're going to shout at me could you kindly leave my office," to which her elevated voice replied, "It's not your office, it belongs to the organization." Then I said, "Okay, if you won't leave and insist on yelling then I will leave." I went straight outside for a smoke knowing she would not follow for the displeasure of the smell of smoke.

My hands were shaking, and I wanted to cry but I dared not, since very soon someone would be on the balcony to ask what happened. Mahmoud came out. While not a smoker he liked hanging out and occasionally he bummed a cigarette from someone to feel included. He asked what happened and informed me that she was in the head of office's office right now wailing about how I disrespected her and that I said the office I am in belonged to me. My mind felt dizzy so I went down to my boss and said I would be leaving for the day. He said that might be best. In a small office like ours everyone knows about everything. My only ponder to this day was with walls so paper thin, why didn't anyone come to help me when she barreled into my office? Was everyone that afraid of her?

Things eventually moved on and settled. Firas was invited to many embassy events where he could have taken a plus one, but he made a point of mentioning to me that he could not take me because we weren't official. I went home early those nights. One day a contact of mine at the US Embassy invited me to the ambassador's house for an election watch party. I have to admit I was a little pleased to tell Firas. His eyes glowed for an invite to the one embassy he had had a hard time getting into. I said, "I'm sorry I can't take you; it is a ticket for one and due to the time constraint I can't get another, sorry." It was my first embassy event, and it was the first time I went to an election party. Living abroad I had never had the opportunity to vote so it was exciting to see the patriotism all around me, including the handsome soldiers, the army, the diplomats, and everyone enjoying the night chatting.

When I arrived, I noticed how the house was built on a high hill with fall offs on all sides. It was a great safe house for the ambassador and his family. I had the privilege of bumping into the ambassador at the buffet table. I asked, "Are you excited about the election"? He said,

"Yes, of course, but if Obama wins it means I will be relocated." I didn't know much then about how things worked so I asked, "Why?" It would normally be at about this point that Firas would chuckle and start apologizing to the ambassador for my ignorance. He would give his excuses that I had not been around the diplomatic community very long and I, feeling embarrassed, would swallow my saliva and shut up for the rest of the visit. But Firas wasn't here and the Ambassador, being such a gentle soul, was more than happy to explain it to me saying, "Well, depending on what party is in office, they normally assign someone from their own party to serve in important countries such as Saudi Arabia." I thought it was all so fascinating! He seemed a little sad, so I asked him how his family was, to which he mentioned they were back in the States. I felt like he was lonely so I told him, "Well, maybe Obama will win and then you can go see them soon." He smiled and said, "Thank you."

THE IRISHMAN AND THE DAMASCENE

I excused myself and walked around the room, all the happy people, everyone watching the screens and hoping for the candidate of their choice. We were all there from 11:00 p.m. to 7:00 a.m. the next day waiting on the results. During this time, I met the head of Embassy Security, an elderly gentleman who mentioned the Marine Ball to me. I heard the word "Ball" and my brain rang with romance Cinderella and glass slippers! "How do I get tickets?" I asked. He said they were sold out, "NO! Please John, how do I find a ticket? There must be at least one somewhere!" He pointed to a tall Colonel named Russ and said, "He might have an extra one." Russ was a towering handsome Black man. I stood up straight and pranced over to him saying, "Hi, I'm Elise, and I heard you have an extra ticket for the Ball?" He smiled and said he was sorry, but he didn't have any more. I lowered my head and said, "Oh, well," and continued in conversation. He was a great man with kind eyes and his blue uniform was so striking. We talked about life in Saudi and the election.

A phone call came from one of the other guards in rotation in the garage under the UNHCR office. His voice was hard to understand though his tears, "They took him! They took Ahmed," I said. "Slow down, who took Ahmed? What happened?" He sniffled and said, "A Saudi man came and refused to have his car checked. Ahmed told him he could not enter without being checked. The Saudi man said, "You're Pakistani, you don't get to tell me what to do." Ahmed said, "No, my supervisor said no one goes through without being checked," and he blocked the man's car from entering the garage. The Saudi man got out of this car and beat him, he beat him, Madam! Then the Saudi man called the police and them that Ahmed insulted him, and they took him, Madam, they took him." I covered my mouth with my hand for a moment and said, "Take it easy, nothing is going to happen, I'll take care of it. For now, since no one is in the office anyway, best you don't stop anymore Saudis, so nothing happens to you." He said "Okay," and we hung up the phone. I stood for a second and tried to figure out what to do. I called Firas but his answer was, "It's probably nothing, they will just keep him overnight and let him go. As long as he didn't strike the Saudi back he will be okay." "How is this okay, he was doing his job?" I asked. "Calm down, Habiti. This happens all the time, he will be fine."

I hung up the phone and called my old UNDSS supervisor, Alaa. I relayed to him what happened, and he said, "That poor man, let me make a few phone calls and find out what happened." "Thank you, Alaa." I returned to the gathering, but part of my heart was with poor Ahmed who was in a Saudi jail because of what I had asked him to do.

Suddenly John showed up and said he had good news; he had found a ticket for me. I was so overjoyed and excited I threw out my arms and hugged him and then turned to Russ and hugged him too. John said, "I don't have it here but if you just show up Friday night at six at the Embassy and ask for me at the guard station, I'll come out and get you in. I thanked him over and over and then he had to return to his duties. Smiling from ear to ear and buzzed on too much coffee, at 2:00 a.m., I headed outside to the tables near the pool and under a stunning moon. It was a beautiful desert night and the moonlight on the pool was breathtaking. When I went outside it was empty, but once the second round of food arrived, it started to fill up, until every chair was taken except the one next to me. Suddenly I looked up to see a tall man with red hair standing near the chair near me asking, "Is this seat taken?" "No, it's not," I said. He then replied, "Do you mind if I sit here?" "Yes, of course, please sit down."

He made a joke about something that I don't remember to this day. I had noticed him earlier and I knew that he waited until all the chairs were full except the one next to me before he sat down, he had been waiting for his moment. I admired the tactic instead of all the normal really awkward pick-up lines I had heard in my life. His subtle way and polite manner were intriguing to me. He didn't ask for my number or if I was seeing anyone, we just talked like two expats in Saudi Arabia. His way surprised me since all I had ever experienced was Arab men and their abrupt direct often off-putting way of approaching me. He just seemed like he wanted to get to know me, not measure if I was a good match, what family I was from, if his parents would like me and everything else I was accustomed to. It was just easy.

His name was Robert and he worked for the Irish Embassy. I had never really met an Irishman before, so I had lots of questions about his country. He was informative, smart, and extremely funny. It had been a long time since someone had made me laugh so much. We talked for more than five hours but hardly felt the time. Finally, it was time for the election results, and we all cheered as the results revealed that we would have our very first Black President. A moment in history not many people can forget, no matter what party they were from. It was a great move forward for our country.

At the end of the night, which was now morning, we all headed out. Robert handed me his colleague's card saying he had just arrived, so he didn't have his cards yet. He took out a fountain pen, crossed out his friends name and wrote his own then asking if I had a card. I said of course, handing him my card which only had my work line and my email address. He asked if I was going home to which I replied, "No, I have to go to work." He said he was going to work as well and finished with, "I'll see you around."

My driver picked me up and dropped me near the office. I walked the rest of the way so I could grab a sandwich for breakfast. Despite being awake all night, I didn't feel sleepy. My head was in a daze. My heart was light as a feather, something I had never felt before. I was smiling from ear to ear. The desert stones and palm trees seemed to sparkle with gold, not dust as they usually did. I got to the office, closed my door, and opened my email to find an email from Robert saying how he was planning to lock his door and take a nap, I laughed to myself and said that sounded like a good idea.

As I giggled, my office door opened, I reacted by minimizing my computer screen and what I was looking at. It was Firas. He said, "Good morning, how was the Embassy?" I cleared my throat and said, "It was great, I'm just tired. Were you up all night?" He asked, "What's so funny?" I said, "Nothing, just something funny." He smiled and said, "Okay," and left to start his day. I reclosed my door and continued emailing Robert. We went back and forth until he went to take his nap and I put my head down on my desk and took a nap, too. After work Firas wanted to meet for dinner but for the first time, I said I could not because I had to go get some sleep. I added that maybe tomorrow before I went to the Ball we could meet for dinner. "Ball?" he asked. "Yeah, someone had an extra ticket, I tried to get one for you, too, but they were sold out." I could see the disappointment in his eyes. The American Embassy parties were something that had eluded him since he had arrived in Riyadh. The fact that someone as uneducated and low on the chain of command career-wise was suddenly invited to Embassy events bothered him to no end. He asked if I could try with my contact again to get him a ticket. I said I would try and left to go home.

When I got home my stepdad asked, "How was the Embassy?" I told him all about all the wonderful people I met. When I mentioned Robert, my eyes sparkled and my stepdad's head tilted slightly to the left stopping me saying, "You like him." I said, "I don't know, he's funny but I'm seeing Firas." My stepdad said, "He has not proposed yet so as far as I am concerned you are free to consider other options." I said, "I'll see what happens." He said, "I think the Irish man sounds really nice." I smiled and said, "I need to get some sleep," heading to my room, and falling back on my bed thinking about the great night I had had, my iPod playing an old Mariah Carry song called *Underneath the Stars.* I felt so euphoric, like I was floating outside of my body. For the first time I felt like I was in a romantic movie of some kind wishing the night had never ended. I looked forward to our next encounter and fell asleep.

Ahmed was released from prison the next day, but his courage was greatly depleted. I told him, "I'm sorry for what happened to you, Ahmed. If you ever have trouble again don't even speak to the man, just call me, and ask them to talk to me. It was very brave of you to stop him like that. I'm proud of you but in future don't put yourself at risk." He nodded and thanked me for the call I made to Alaa that resulted in his release so quickly. He was a lucky soul who worked for someone who cared and knew someone who could do something. Many others are not as lucky and find themselves deported or worse for doing nothing except what they were told. I decided that morning when I saw Ahmed that I would stop caring about security and return them to the lax state they were in before I arrived since it turned out security and safety were not what they wanted, rather, only the illusion of it just so they could tick a box for Geneva. Politics, Protocol, and Phantasm. That would have to be enough to keep them all safe.

The next day was Friday. After the Friday prayer was over my stepdad took me to buy a dress. I had no Ball gowns to speak of and it was a Black-Tie event. We looked everywhere until we came across a black dress, it was off the shoulder. I looked at my stepdad, surprised that he was even suggesting I buy it. I said, "Baba, it is indecent, and the Ball will be mixed company." To which he replied, "You can get a sweater, you're grown up now, you should wear something that helps you blend in." I wondered who is this person and what has he done to my stepdad? I bought the dress and went home to get ready for my very first Ball. There was no time to go to the hairdresser, so I did my hair myself. I was so nervous that I over did the hair spray and was running late. I got to the restaurant in the *DQ* (Diplomatic Quarter) for a quick bite with Firas. He told me I looked pretty and asked if I had had any luck getting him a ticket to which I replied "Sorry." He said, "They didn't have any extra?" He was kind today, less critical than usual but even if he had not been I don't think I would have noticed because I was too busy wondering if I would see Robert again. Firas dropped me at the Embassy and asked if I would need a ride home to which I replied, "No, that's okay, my driver is coming for me later."

I stepped down from the diplomatic truck and as my heels hit the ground, I took a deep breath and walked towards the Embassy. When I arrived at the gate I said, "Hi, I'm here for the Ball, I don't have a ticket, but John said you should call him, he will know who I am." They called for John, and I waited. When he arrived, the first thing I noticed was the machine gun hanging across his chest. It was the first time I had ever seen such a thing up close. He motioned for me to come through and he gave me a side hug. He started to walk me to the Ball, saying, "So, I managed to find you a ticket. Please meet…," pointing to a tall blond diplomat whose name I cannot recall until this day. I was not accustomed to the idea of dating and blind-date setups, which are a very common thing in the States. I thanked the man for having me. He offered me a drink, which I declined, my eyes scanning the room for Robert but to no avail. The man started making conversation about the room and the history of the Marine Ball. I tried to be polite, but my mind was elsewhere as we entered the buffet line. He seemed like a nice man. He was good looking, well built, blonde and polite but for me, he just wasn't my type. If I had a type, blonde skinny, White boys did not fall into this category.

As we exited the buffet, the music started, the dance floor opened and there he was, in the center of the dance floor jumping around like a very tall leprechaun. My face that gave away how out of place I felt suddenly changed to the face of someone who just wanted to dance. I asked the man to excuse me and walked to the dance floor. Robert saw me and smiled as we started dancing. He taught me some of my first Western dances. All I really knew how to do was Arabic dance, Saudi Dance, Iraqi Dance, Belly Dance, and many other tribal dances but none of those applied to this music. I leaned in and told him, "I didn't know how to dance." He leaned his head back and laughed when an MC Hammer song came on and then he started showing me a dance he called the *big box little box.* We laughed and laughed. His colleague was ripping up the dance floor, flinging his jacket around left to right before resting it on his shoulder like John Travolta in *Saturday Night Fever* and sweating as if he was in a hot yoga class. For a moment it seemed like the world slipped away and all that was left was the dance floor and us.

Finally, 11:00 p.m. rolled around and for fear of over abusing my stepdad's newfound willingness to let me go out to a mixed party by myself, I told them I had to go. Robert and his friend cried out, "No!" but I insisted that I had to work the next day. Robert asked if he could walk me to the gate and once again, not being aware of the customs of the West, I thought I didn't want to disrupt the dancing, so I said, "No, thank you, I will be fine," and waved goodbye.

As I strolled through the American Embassy parking lot, gazing at the stars, and thinking about one of the best nights of dancing I had had in a very, very, long time, the desert night air filled my lungs with an intoxicating coolness. Suddenly my day dreaming was interrupted by a Saudi man stumbling towards the gate carrying a large water bottle but the liquid inside wasn't water, it was almost yellow. My mind went to the things I thought it could be. Was he carrying his piss? I thought? Why? Suddenly from the shadows came John with his machine gun still strapped across his body only this time, he put his finger on the trigger. He gestured for me to get behind him, so I moved slowly aside as he raised his voice to the Saudi man, "Hey! What's in the bottle?" "It's none of your business," said the man as he started to move closer to the exit. John signaled for his guards and asked again, "What's in the bottle?" to which the man replied, "It's just some beer, now let me go." "Sir, you can leave, but the bottle stays here." The Saudi man protested and pleaded for them to let him take it out of the Embassy, but they held him down, took the bottle, and escorted him out of the Embassy.

John then turned to me and asked how I enjoyed the Ball, to which I replied, "It was so much fun, thank you so much, John, for getting me in." John looked at me for a moment and asked, "What do you do for the organization? "I'm in HR," I replied. "Do you have a college degree?" he asked. "I'm working on it," I said. "Well, then, when you get it let me know, with your language skills you would be perfect for the Agency, and I can help you with that." Handing me his card he said, "Call me when you're ready," I nodded and headed for the door. When I heard him call my name, "Elise," I turned as he said, "Is your car outside?" "Yes," I said. He said, "Okay I'll walk you, that man just left so I would feel better putting you in the car." He walked me, machine gun and all, to my driver's SUV, helped me step in, and closed the door. John, if that was even his real name, would tell me later that he was leaving for an assignment in Yemen and reminded me to call the number on his card when I'd completed my degree. After he was gone, no one at the Embassy would remember seeing him, who he was, or have any information about how he was doing. I realized later I was being recruited by the CIA. People often ask me why I didn't join the CIA since I was an obvious candidate. I knew the language but better than that, I would pass for an Arab easily and I knew the customs. My answer to the question why not join the CIA is, "because I don't want to die."

My driver, Mubarak, was so excited to hear what adventures I had had. A very jolly fellow, always asking about my day as if he was living vicariously through me. I told him all about the Marines doing their march at the beginning of the ball and about the Saudi Man I saw trying to leave carrying beer. We laughed the whole way home. When I got home my stepdad was waiting up, so we got some tea and went to the balcony to have a smoke. My stepdad had safety-pinned an old sheet over the balcony ledge so that I could go out and smoke on the balcony without being seen by our Bedouin neighbors. It was not becoming for a young girl, technically a daughter of a Saudi household, to sit out smoking for everyone to see. It would bring scandal and since my sisters might marry from here one day like always, I needed to be on my best behavior. In the Diplomatic Quarter where I worked it was a different world; the rules were different. Saudis did not go there very often and not without good reason, so there I was free to be myself.

As we sat that night sipping our tea and smoking, I told my stepdad about the Ball. We talked about Robert some more and my stepdad seemed to be pushing me towards him and away from Firas. I told my stepdad although I was really enjoying the magic of just letting things develop on their own and even though I really liked Robert, Firas was discussing marriage even if he was dragging his feet. He was a good man, well educated, good looking, and came from a good family. It would be foolish for me to give up Firas for someone who has yet to make his intentions known. Besides, I didn't even know if he liked me that way at all. My stepdad nodded and said, "See where it goes, don't feel guilty you're not married, you're not engaged, and he has yet to even announce he is courting you or visit me to ask for your hand as he said he would. You're allowed to see other options just as he is." Holding my cigarette in my mouth I looked down at the ground, took a deep puff and said, "You're right." He got up and went to get ready for bed. I sat for a while and then headed to bed myself.

The next day Firas asked me how the Ball was, and I told him it was alright. He asked if we could grab dinner. "Sure," I said. We met after work in the usual place. He talked about himself a lot and I spent a lot of my time off in my own head wondering why he continued seeing me if I was not what he wanted. Finally, he said "I have decided to turn you into my dream girl." I looked at him, puzzled, and he kissed me on the cheek as he continued, "Isn't this great news, Habiti?" "Sure," I said. Then he broke out his diagram of his perfect wife and started listing all the things I needed to fix. First, he said, "Is your Arabic, we need to work harder on making you speak with a better Syrian accent." I remained silent and then asked simply, "Why?" He said, "Well, because I want to make sure my children speak proper Syrian and when I travel, I want to always come home and speak my native tongue." His dear friend had married an American and like so many other families, he had seen the Arabic language seem to get lost and never learned by the children. I understood his logic in a way but wondered why his dialect was the more important one? I loved my Arabic and had every intention of teaching it to my children. In the end, my old upbringing kicked in and I convinced myself that a good wife would honor her husband, and in this case, future husband's requests.

The list went on, I was too skinny and needed to gain weight to which my reply was, "I eat everything. I have always been the same weight, it's not possible!" To which he dropped the line, "We can try and if it works, I'll buy you an entire new wardrobe!" My brain went, new wardrobe heck ya! "Sounds good," I said. The list went on and I started to feel hurt and unpretty. He said I dressed too conservatively but in my mind I dressed classy. He didn't like the way I did my makeup. He wanted it to look more Syrian. I sat politely and listened.

When I got home my stepdad asked how it went and I relayed to him the diagram of the perfect woman story. I was about to continue and mention all the faults I apparently had when my stepdad stood up and said, "Who does he think he is?" I said, "You're right" and went outside to smoke in peace and try to let go of how ugly and hurt I felt. It was a learning moment. I had never felt ugly or inadequate before since I had my first suitors at fifteen.

The next day I went into the office and said good morning to everyone and went outside to smoke. Firas followed, came out, smiled, and said, "Good morning." I half grinned and looked down, holding my cigarette. He asked me what was wrong to which I replied politely and calmly, "I really think you need to go buy a car, like I said before, they can be customized however you want. I don't think I am what you're looking for and you should try and find her." He counter argued and said, "No, no, we can just work on these few things together." His eyes and his face and the fact that I loved him convinced me to continue so I nodded quietly, and we agreed to meet after work for dinner.

It's hard to explain the influences the people around you have on decisions even as big as marriage in the Middle East. Firas was the one Ablah May wanted and I respected her wisdom. Many of my friends and I, myself, had married men less than worthy of them, who beat them and refused to give them a divorce, took their children away, abused their children, and more. Despite all his faults Firas was an honorable man. He wouldn't lie, trick, or deceive and had shown no signs of violence. He was well educated and successful in his career and had plans to go much further. On paper what more could a good Arabic girl ask for in a husband? I thought to myself, am I being too picky? Everyone I knew loved him except my stepdad who was on the fence, but I couldn't use him as a baseline for obvious reasons.

The next day as we were taking a smoke break outside, Firas asked me if he could see my divorce papers sometime for me and Ata to make sure all was legally sound. "I don't have them, and I don't think they are important since you want to get married in Syria and not here. This is the only place where there is a record of my marriage to him." "So according to the Saudi Government, you are still married?" "I guess so." "Elise I travel all over and need to not fly into a country and apply to get you a visa only for them to say sorry she is married to someone else. You need to get this settled now." "I never thought I would come back here or go to Canada so I figured it wouldn't matter. Islamically we are divorced." "Of course, it matters!" "Ok, let me make a call." Luckily, I still had Ata's cell number and had kept good ties with him after enough time had passed, we kept in touch. I called and he answered. "Hi, I need a favor. I might remarry and I need you to come to Riyadh and legally divorce me if you could." "I'll be on the plane tonight and we can go to the court tomorrow." "Thank you so much," I said, and I went to Firas and told him, "Ata is flying in, and he will go with me to the court tomorrow."

Firas went and made the appointment with the judge and the next morning I met Ata at the courthouse. When I arrived, Ata opened my car door for me and helped me from the car. He smiled and was so happy to see me. We talked a little then headed in to wait in our separate waiting rooms until we were called for our turn. It was time and we both entered the chamber together. The judge asked if I had finished my iddah? An iddah is about 3 monthly periods. The purpose of this requirement being that if I was to remarry there needed to be no doubt of the paternity of a child. An old tradition since in the old days there were no paternity tests or pregnancy tests, but it is still observed today. He then asked if Ata had paid me my Mutakhar, which is the part of the dowry set aside in case of divorce. Since he had flown all the way down in an instant for me, I looked at the judge and said, "Yes," thereby releasing him from that financial burden. The judge asked if we were sure we wanted to get divorced. He said, "You look like a good couple." Ata bent slightly and made a gesture like it's not up to me, then pointed in my direction. My immediate reaction was to take a step back and shake my head no at which point Ata addressed the judge again saying, "As you can see, we are sure we want to divorce." The judge sighed, signed, and stamped the paper saying, "The original will go to the woman, since it's very important for her to have it if she remarries and since you can have four wives you will have a certified copy. Allah be with you both." We went down and got the copy then as we were leaving Ata asked if we could grab dinner and talk. I agreed and invited him to grab dinner at a hotel that is known to turn a blind eye to non-married people having dinner, especially two foreigners. Even though we had just gotten divorced we still had the old marriage booklet that would help appease the religious police if they should ask us.

I messaged Firas and thanked him for setting up the meeting with the Judge. I told him all went well, and I was divorced and that I would be having dinner at home tonight so I would see him in the morning to which he replied, "Sounds good, Habiti." Ata and I sat together for the very first time since we got divorced four years earlier. He told me he was sorry for all that happened and although he knew I had moved on he wanted to keep in touch, and I agreed. Even though I felt we were no good as a couple he was still one of my best friends. We hugged tightly after dinner, and it seemed as if he was about to cry. He held on as long as he could, and it seemed as though he was trying to record everything in his mind in case he did not see me or hold me again.

My heart broke for him and a part of me, although unwilling to consider remarrying him, still loved him deeply and always will. He was so close and dear to me during one phase in my life and despite everything he was there when I needed him and still there even when I asked him to come divorce me. If you were to ask me if love ever dies, I will have to say it cannot. Once you have loved someone, no matter what occurred they have affected your life and will be the love of that given time frame. You can say you hate them now, but all of the people of our past influenced who we are today and for that they deserve at least a small degree of respect. Ata and Ziyad were not the men I was meant to finish my life with, but they nevertheless changed my life forever.

I told him about Robert, Firas, life and of course how things were going with my stepdad now that I was back in Saudi under his roof. Ata was the only husband I ever talked to about my stepdad since I knew I would need my stepdad's approval to stay in touch with my siblings and I didn't feel like dealing with the constant battle I went through between Ata and my stepdad at the beginning of our marriage. Firas also would have never accepted to be married to someone who was sexually abused by her stepdad. He had a hard enough time accepting that I was married before. If I ever told him, he would suddenly treat me as a pity case. He would still help me and stand for me, but he would not want to marry me for the thought of scandal should anyone find out. I would be disgusting to him, that was plain as day. I was made unworthy in his eyes by getting married twice, I can't imagine what I would have been in his eyes if he knew I was raped.

Ata said if there was ever any trouble with my stepdad, he was only a 45-minute plane ride away. It was a comfort. He would tell me about the girls he met, lovers, friends, his family, and I would happily listen and offer advice. There was no one more able to listen and understand me as he did and vice versa. We knew everything about each other despite our years apart. It was like speaking to someone who has always been with you. Our marriage didn't work but our bond was very real. We both wanted happiness for the other beyond ourselves, something even Noor could never fathom possible for a couple, especially an Arabic couple, let alone a divorced couple. So, we kept our calls to ourselves to avoid too much commentary from everyone around us.

Noor's relationship with a Jordanian named Eymad she had met at a mixed party started progressing. He worked in a tape shop in Riyadh and was about her age. She talked often about how romantic he was, how unlike the Egyptian she had fallen in love with at school.

The Jordanian came into her life like a phoenix giving her rebirth from a broken heart and the feeling that she would never find true love. He called her and texted her all the time, wrote her poetry and left her presents outside the outer gates of her parent's house in Riyadh. On a few occasions she convinced me to help her meet him. "You're crazy! What if you get caught by the *Mutawa*?" "We won't get caught, honey, I asked some friends of mine, and they said that the Hilton on the edge of the city is full of foreigners and rarely checked by the *Mutawa* we should meet him there." I said, "What's your plan, woman?" "Um, well, we will pretend we're having dinner in the restaurant and then when he arrives, I'll meet him in his car and then I'll come back in to sit with you." "I don't know, honey, it sounds so risky and how well do you know him anyway? What if he does something to you, I won't be able to do anything if he just drives off with you in his car. Are you sure you trust him, honey?" "I'll be fine, you're always worrying too much." I let out a sigh and said, "Alright, let me know when you want to go."

The day came and we rode with my driver to the Hilton, since her driver would wait and be very likely to tell her mom where we had gone and what he had seen. My driver was safer because he would drop us off and come back and didn't know my stepdad at all. We pulled up and went into the hotel restaurant and got a table. I ordered tea as she texted Eymad to let him know we had arrived. Once he was in the parking lot, he texted her and she sprung up from the table, giggled, and headed out. The parking lot was poorly lit and had no attendants so the risk of being seen rested only with the people visiting the hotel. Since most of the visitors were people from out of town and foreigners, it was likely they would not suspect anything when they saw a woman leave a hotel and get in a man's car.

Thirty minutes passed and I texted her, "Woman! That's enough we should go." Forty-five minutes later she came back inside the restaurant. I said, "What took you so long? I was worried something happened to you!" She placed both her hands over her mouth and said in a hushed voice, "We were kissing, and he touched my boobs, Honey." I just about got up from my chair to slap her when I remembered that people were around us. "What are you thinking! What is wrong with you?" I reached my hand up and grasped the arch of my nose as I said, "Yella, let's go home. Mubbark is here to take us."

When we got to her house I came up to her room and began scolding her. "How could you! What do you think he thinks of you now? These men take what they want and then don't marry you because they think you are easy like a slut. If this was America or Canada or anywhere it would be different, but not here." Noor sat on the bed, broken. "I know, honey, but I'm alone and I just want someone to love me." I sat beside her and placed my arm across her shoulders and said, "I know ... I know ... Just be more careful, okay?" She nodded as I hugged her and said, "So, was he a good kisser?" Her mood changed and after hearing about how dreamy he was I headed home.

Time passed and Robert invited me to celebrate Saint Patrick's Day at the Irish Embassy. I was excited to see the inside of the Irish Embassy, so I accepted the invite and when Firas asked if I was free for dinner that night, I just said I already had other plans. When I arrived, it was a fun mix of people, everyone drinking, laughing, and celebrating the day. Robert took me on a tour and told me all about Ireland. He was drinking a beer and offered me some to which I replied, "I don't like beer I had some once." "What kind?" he asked. I replied, "Budweiser," his face crinkled up and then he said, "I can understand, try this one. He passed over his bottle of Corona. I took a taste and went, "Oh, wow, that's not so bad after all." He got me a new bottle and I enjoyed my very first beer, starting a lifelong love for light beer.

Robert and his coworker were remarking on a story about a French diplomat who had done something naughty. When thrown in prison his Embassy argued with the judge that he had diplomatic immunity so therefore he could not be held or tried. The judge looked at the man and said something to the effect of, "You come to our country and do as you please, but this time I will make an example of you and then maybe you will remember to obey the laws of this country, diplomatic immunity or not." The judge ordered that the man's hand be chopped off which is the punishment for a first offence of stealing. His Embassy argued and pleaded but the judge would not resend, his decision was final. Robert began to laugh, and I said, "What! What happened next?" "Well, you see they kept begging the judge to change his mind, but he would not. Finally, the compromise was reached that they would chop off the man's hand, but they would allow for a jet to be standing by with medics to reattach it." "That's crazy," I said. But even I could understand the masterful diplomatic skills of the judge. The judge needed to appease his Wahabi religious clerics and use the man as an example. At the same time, he did not want to damage their relationship with a European country, so he chopped the man's hand off and allowed for him to leave and have it reattached if possible out of sight and out of the country, never to return again.

When the evening ended, and I went home. I walked in as I did every time I saw Robert, like I was light as a feather and walking on air. I would sit up in my room at night listening to Mariah Carey love songs and replaying every word that was spoken. It was something I had never felt before. There was no pressure for decisions, marriage negotiations, it was just a really great time with good conversation. My stepdad finally had enough of Firas dragging on with no decision since we had met a year ago. He asked for a meeting with him, this time with no negotiation of time. "I have given him enough time," he said. I told Firas he needed to call my stepdad and set something up, so he did. It was set for Thursday night.

On a cold night on the first day of the new year and after a year of getting to know Firas, he was finally coming to ask my stepdad for my hand in marriage. How nervous I was! Since 9:00 a.m. I had kept busy by cleaning, cooking, taking deep breaths and hoping all would go well. My stepdad talked all day about family, reputation, honor, and then half an hour before Firas's arrival, making himself a drink from the wine he had smuggled in a few months earlier. It was easy enough since the wine was in a box and the airport security normally only looked for glass bottles.

The buzzer rang and my stepdad went to the door. I sat in the kitchen waiting to be called once they had agreed, worried, wondering what was being said between the two. Hearing only the sound of voices going up and down. Staring at the door trying to make out the conversation. Hearing only a few words here and there, "Trust" and wondering why that issue was raised and hoping my stepdad would behave himself.

I received phone calls from friends, including Ablah May and Noor, who wanted an update. At that point my stepdad and Firas had been in there for an hour and a half. I had to know what was happening, so I slowly opened the dining room door and stood quietly to listen. I listened; they were discussing plans for the future. Firas would throw out an idea and my stepdad would reject it. Being completely unreasonable as usual. I kept thinking about interrupting and placing myself in the middle and then backing up. Hearing the tone of Firas's voice I had a feeling he was going to leave. The conversation went on for more than four hours until I was called to serve the juice. I was then informed from my stepdad in a text message before entering that no agreement had been reached and that there would be no engagement tonight. Saddened to hear this I soldiered on and entered the room carrying the juice. My stepdad sitting in all his glory, full of himself, and Firas, broken and trying so hard to smile. My heart reached for him as I served the juice and offered to heat up the food that had gotten cold for the last four hours or more. Then I removed myself, showing my objection to the way the night went.

They sat at the table. While placing the food down for them I kept asking myself if I should ask why or just stay silent, the silence won out. My stepdad had acted like a child, and it was clear Firas had lost his appetite and was hurt from the expression on his face. Firas excused himself since it was after midnight and I expressed my disappointment by smoking in the kitchen, something forbidden in the house while asking my stepdad for details, but he wanted to speak upstairs so the neighbors would not hear the conversation through the kitchen window, a thing not uncommon in our compound.

I was patient. We put away the food and headed upstairs where my stepdad explained every single word. According to my stepdad, Firas was unable to say the words he was waiting for, "I love your daughter and I want to marry her." Knowing Firas's indecisive nature, it did not come as a shock to me. He continued, saying that Firas told him he couldn't do any engagement until his dad met me, but his stepmother was very ill and unable to travel, so he asked if my stepdad and I could fly to Syria with him to meet his parents, but my stepdad, being the proud Saudi that he is, refused, stipulating that Firas's parents by tradition should always come to the bride's house not the other way round, no exceptions. I started wondering why I brought my stepdad into the picture in the first place. It's in moments like these that any child wishes they had no parents.

Listening to him finish his side of the story I started wondering if I should run away before I hated him again. My stepdad continued, mentioning that Firas had also asked if I could have some fertility testing done to make sure I was capable of having children since I was married before and had none, to which my stepdad replied to him, "Would you also like to take her upstairs, spread her legs, and see if you like her in bed? You're not buying a cow, you either love her and want her despite having children or not." I realized then what set the tone for the next four hours they spent in that room, so I decided to hold on and try and patch things back together since both were at fault. It was the clash of the titans between two arrogant, stubborn, men with massive egos.

The next day I spent the whole day in bed, snapping at my stepdad at every possible moment and then apologizing. At noon I spoke to Firas and asked to see him so I could hear his side of the story but of course my stepdad, hearing that I had the intention of seeing Firas so soon after the meeting, refused to let me go. At that point I decided I was not going to tell him anything anymore and went to cry myself into a long nap. Upon waking up I decided to go out alone. Before going I made a few phone calls to Noor first, who said my stepdad was in the right and Doctora Zaynia, who suggested I talk to my stepdad and ask him not to complicate things for me since I was not a virgin bride. Things don't need to be so by the book. It is no less honorable to go to their house than if they came to yours. Honestly, I liked her opinion although this is something I had been telling my stepdad for the last year without much luck on the issue, but I promised her I would try again.

Saturday came around and I decided to call in sick since I was dealing with my own drama and didn't think I was up for handling other people's drama calmly that day. Before my stepdad left for work, I pointed at him and said, "Play nice, the man will be your son in law." He turned and left to work without saying anything. I took the day and found my inner peace again reminding myself that *Allah* had a plan, and everything was for the best even if it doesn't feel that way at the time. I may have taken off my head scarf, but my faith was still intact.

When I went to work on Sunday, I got a chance to speak with Firas and although he didn't want to talk any more without my parents or his parents approval out of honor, which I greatly admired, I convinced him that in the end it was my decision, so we made plans for me to travel to Syria with him. He asked how I would explain it to my stepdad, afraid secretly that he would be accused of kidnapping a Saudi man's stepdaughter to which I replied, "I'll handle it."

Tickets were bought and plans were made, my exit reentry visa was still valid (Which is a stamp you get on your passport that says your *Mahram*/Guardian has given permission for you to leave the country) so we were good to go. Robert texted me out of the blue and told me he had just purchased a Wii and wondered if I wanted to come over and play it the following week. I mentioned that I had a trip to Syria coming up, but I would come by this week if he had time. He told me a good day and time and I went after work to go play video games and hang out. He gave me a tour of his compound and his home, and we played video games all night. Bowling was my favorite, and we had a great time running towards the screen, laughing, and pushing each other to make the other one fail and then right before the last game was over he pushed me, I laughed and pushed him back, and suddenly we were kissing.

The phone rang and interrupted us. It was my driver, "I have to go, but I'll see you when I get back," I said. He asked to walk me out to the car and make sure I was safe. My driver took me home. I twirled around my room like I had never been kissed before. The magic of the natural flow of things instead of the world of procedures and processes I was raised with was exhilarating.

I packed Tuesday night and hid my bag in the guest bathroom downstairs knowing that my stepdad does not use that bathroom late at night. I was scared because of my past experience defying him and if he should find out I was heading to the airport against his wishes I was well aware how easy it would be for him to report me as missing. No American passport could have helped me leave the country. By law I was under the guardianship of my stepdad and he and he alone got to decide where I go. I hardly slept all night, planning out what I would say about why I was going to work a little late and making sure I was calm enough not to be suspected of keeping something from him. Above all people, my stepdad was always hard to lie to. He is a master at detecting inconsistency in tone, behavior, and body language.

The morning came and I dressed as slowly as possible to waste time until my stepdad went off to work. I was ironing my Abaya, as he came out to leave. He looked at the floor as he spoke. We had not been on good speaking terms since he met with Firas and often his way of showing his displeasure of the choices, I made was to ignore me until I broke. In those episodes he would not even look at me while talking to me. "You're late for work," he said. My reply was a calm, "No, I'm good," and he continued on his way. I crept out the balcony door to watch him leave the compound and then called Firas to tell him I was ready to go. He came round the corner, and I jumped in the car. We were on our way to Syria.

DAMASCUS, SYRIA

You learn a lot about people when you travel with them. Firstly, I learned that Firas hated flying. He was absolutely terrified, making it an uncomfortable journey for the both of us. I spent most of my time trying to calm him down. Secondly, I knew he could go on and on about himself when we went to dinner, but I had no idea he was capable of doing so for an entire flight. I wondered why he never asked me how I was doing. If I was scared? If I was nervous about flying to a foreign country? Had I ever been to meet a family formally against my stepdad's good wishes? When you grow up in a culture that is very family oriented, defying them is one of the hardest things you can do. It often feels like betrayal even when you know you're doing what's right for you, it still stings deep inside like a knife that was plunged in and was never removed. No matter what kind of family you have in Saudi Arabia it's still not something that was done.

When we landed in Syria, Firas asked me not to look around too much or make eye contact with the various secret police wandering the airport. I thought it was silly, but I listened just the same and spoke only when I was spoken to. When we exited the airport there was Firas's father and stepmother waving and excited to welcome us. I greeted them in the traditional way, took their hands, and kissed them on their cheeks. It was customary that until Firas and I were married I would refer to his father respectfully as *Umo*, which meant uncle, and his stepmother as *Khala*, which mean aunt. Since we have many respectful options it's even common to ask what they would like to be called but of course if they say, "Just call me by my name," it is also proper to refuse and tag on a respectful salutation such as *Umo* and *Khala*.The other word for aunt (Uma) was reserved only for my stepdad's sister, Ablah (Big Sister). While they say they don't mind and maybe they don't, they are a people of old traditions and respect for one's elders is high on that list.

As we drove, they welcomed me to Syria and his father started to tell me all about their heritage and the sights. Then I saw a beautiful building, so I pointed and said, "What's that?" Firas pounced on me and said, "Don't point at anything! That is a government building." I didn't understand why it would be wrong to point at a government building since I was remarking on its beauty, but I started to notice there was a cover of fear that layered the city. No one dared speak the president's name without whispering even when saying good things so that it would not land them in prison or worse. Later I would hear the stories about the secret police that would show up unexpectedly at people's homes, even those of foreigners, knock them unconscious and just like that they would disappear for days. People said when they returned, they would pack up and leave the country as soon as possible. The secret police would interrogate and torture them until they were satisfied they were not a threat to the political stability of the country. The reason that landed them in that situation would have been a friend who made an anonymous call or a person at the table next to them in a coffee shop that heard them utter the president's name, "Bahar Al-Assad." Just like Saudi Arabia, knowing who to trust and how much to say was paramount to survival, not just for you, but for your entire family.

I have heard stories about how one person in a family spoke out against Bashar's father Hafez al-Assad and following his arrest, the president ordered the arrest of everyone with the same last name. Hafez Al-Assad feared the Muslim brotherhood a group that opposed his government. In 1982 the Massacre of Hamma was called one of the deadliest acts by any Arab government against its own people in the modern Middle East. Forty thousand people died according to the Syrian Human Rights Committee. Although if you ask a local, they will say that it was much more than that. Some say the president shot civilians from his helicopter as they fled but most of the carnage was scrubbed from the history books. Bashar Al-Assad became president a month after his father died. Firas told me that he was too young at the time so laws were altered to make sure he would be able to be president.

Syria was a place where if the regime wants someone in power, they walk house to house and ask people who they are going to vote for, and no one wants to be the one under suspicion for saying they were voting for the wrong person. As a result, even after everything Bashar's father had done and how terrible he was, Bashar ran uncontested and received 97% support. Need I say more … in Saudi, we have a Layanrchy that has ultimate power but here you get to vote for the president, giving the outside world the impression that the government is elected by the people. To be honest I don't know which is worse.

Someone asked me recently if I wished for one thing to change in Saudi and I could only have one wish, what would that be? My answer was freedom of speech. The right to openly and peacefully discuss everything. The ability to question our leaders, their decisions, and laws, openly without fear of the consequences that seem to befall anyone who appears to be creating a disruption. Political dissent, public speaking, and gatherings for the purpose of open discussions that question the king, or the royal family, are criminalized. We are raised to memorize, take orders, submit to the decisions of our betters, and then after they have raised a bunch of sheep, they wonder how the country can turn those same sheep into soaring eagles? If you want your country to fly to its highest possible height you must start by allowing people to use their wings.

I was to stay in a hotel during this visit so that no shame could be attached to my name by the neighbors and friends who would undoubtedly see me enter Firas' family home and have lots of questions. Firas, now forty, had become one of the more sought-after bachelors for all the line items I mentioned before, but in Syria, his bloodline made him even more desirable. It was a strange hierarchy but just as the Bedouins of Riyadh, we're proud to be the original inhabitants of the area. So too, Firas' family was proud to say they were pure blooded Damascenes, as they are called. If Firas strutted like a proud rooster normally, here he was a golden rooster.

The stories of the girls he turned down were endless. Normally it is more often the woman who says no, especially if they are beautiful, but in Firas' case, it was the opposite. While many had turned him down, he had turned down even more. His former finance, for example. Like so many things about Firas, his needs and desires were all he cared about. I don't think he did it on purpose but when he thought he was right that was the end of the conversation.

We went to the hotel first. I went to freshen up after the long flight while Firas and his family headed home to prepare lunch. The hotel was beautiful and much more modern than I had expected based on the way the media portrays Syria. Firas arrived about an hour later to pick me up and take me to see his family home where he had grown up and where they currently lived. When we arrived, I climbed the steps to the apartment which was one level consisting of a kitchen, a living room, a formal room for entertaining, two bedrooms and a large balcony. His father came out, walking with his arms open so excited to see me again and his stepmother was happy as well. I could not remember the last time I felt so welcome and loved by strangers.

I smiled and sat down as Firas's dad called him into the kitchen. We both heard a loud smacking sound as his dad slapped him over the head saying, "This is what you can't make a decision about? Have you seen her?!" Khala Nawal and I giggled under our breath and then stopped before they exited the kitchen. We ate and his father asked me all about myself, my plans, told me all about the city and served me as if I was a very great guest. He was everything a father-in-law should be and more.

In the morning when I would arrive for breakfast, he would bring my coffee out to the balcony along with a fresh cup of warm milk and would say, "Here is some milk, it is good for your bones when you get older." Then he would excuse himself to let me smoke. He appalled smoking, but being an ex-smoker himself, he totally understood and made no comment and pushed no agenda that others should quit. Instead, he would just leave the area and come back later. He had a beautiful canary that he would put out every morning and her song filled the area with peaceful tranquility.

Firas' father constantly recited poetry to me and offered up an endless list of compliments. In Saudi we used to say if your daughter needs to be complimented a great deal, marry her to a Syrian. They were known as the Arabs whose tongues were always filled with honey and his dad was the embodiment of that.

An example would be: A Saudi man asking his wife for tea. He would say, "*Ya Hirma* (Woman) bring me tea." When the tea arrived, he would just grunt and say, "*Shukran* (Thanks)" and the wife would either sit or leave, depending on the situation. A Syrian husband would say, "*Ya Omri* (My lifespan) or *Ya Ahla Bint fil Dunya* (Oh most beautiful girl in this temporal world) or *Ya bint Al-Halal* (bint halal, means daughter born in a pure (acceptable way) which is basically marriage, this is used for people who are generally associated with good traits) would you mind bringing me tea?" As the wife is arriving, he would say, "*Ya-Salem Idaike* (meaning basically thank you to your hands)." Every action or request comes accompanied by a compliment which is normally hard wired into the request.

I wondered why Firas was not the same. Was it his dad's first wife's death that sparked a great appreciation for women, I wondered. I later found out he was always a romantic and it was why the three sons were named after three Syrian poets.

He always wanted a daughter, but his first wife died from breast cancer before they could have one so for him, his daughter-in-laws were like his daughters. I had never been in a house where the rule was women sit and men serve. I tried so hard to get into the kitchen as in a traditional Saudi household. Even if they refuse help it is expected that you go in and at least offer. If you just sit even if they told you to when you left, you can bet someone is talking about you after you leave. In Firas' family home it was not the case. After attempting many times to get into the kitchen I realized his dad was serious, which baffled me, but I enjoyed watching Firas work in the kitchen with his dad. I fell in love with his family instantly.

We went out to see the market area and the surrounding sights, none of which I have heard still exists anymore. The atrocities in Syria have completely destroyed what was once a beautiful and vibrant city. The bustling marketplace near the mosque was a wonderful sight to behold, one I shall never forget. All the spices and the colored cloth put up to shade the stalls from the sun. The Prayer call (Adan meaning also *to listen*) blared over the loudspeaker in the mosque.

Firas' aunt and stepmother, Khala Nawal, said we should pray. As we got close to the mosque the attendant said, "She can't enter. She is uncovered." Pointing at me and the fact that I was not wearing a head cover. Something struck me. I was refused the right to pray. While my mind understood why it was disrespectful to enter a mosque without my head cover, my conscience ate away at me. Tears swelled up in my eyes and I told Firas and Khala Nawal to please go pray, I would pray at home later. They refused and bought me a simple head scarf from the market. As the tears rolled down my face Firas chuckled and said, "There is nothing to cry about Habiti, it's not a big deal." I nodded and entered through the woman's door to pray with Khala Nawal. He could not understand the journey I was on, the hard choices that I battled with internally every day. Cover or not cover. Salvation in the hereafter or hell. Be an outcast or stand different and alone. He did not understand what I would lose if I decided not to cover at all and I could talk to hardly anyone about it. The internal and external conflict we as the women of Arabia face is bigger than covering or not covering.

At night we would go to eat with Firas' friends at beautiful restaurants with amazing service. I enjoyed getting to know everyone we met. Everyone was so friendly and happy to meet me. I was also aware that as soon as I left the table for the ladies room, Firas was asking everyone what they thought of me, but I took no mind. It was his way, and I was confident enough in my own skin to not worry what they thought.

The next day Firas and his dad returned from the market with fresh *Molokhia*, a green leafy vegetable. I have not seen fresh Molokhia outside of Syria. They brought in bags and bags of it since it was in season. Khala Nawal washed and laid out every single leaf on the balcony to dry. When she was done Firas came out to smoke and I had the conversation many women wish to have but find it hard to have the right temperament for. "Firas, tell me about your friend from school Sarah, the one on my left at dinner last night." "What is it you want to know? She was in love with me, but I never made a move." "Why not?" I asked. "Yes, she's beautiful, from a good Syrian family, adores you, has a law degree. She possesses the body type you like, why didn't you ever consider making a move?" Firas stood stunned for a moment like all men, perhaps thinking it was a trap for an argument, but it was an honest question. "Firas, if it's your perfect girl you're looking for, she looks like it to me, I think you really should consider her. I love you but I will understand if that's what you really want. Just think about it, your happiness after all is the most important thing. If you're happy, I'll be happy for you." "She's not the one." "Why not?" "I don't know why, but she's not. Now come, let's go in for dinner."

Time began to run out and so on the last day Firas' father asked him to make a decision, remarking that leading a girl on for so long without a decision was not right. They agreed it was a go. Firas drove down to my hotel and knocked on my door. When I opened the door, he told me how excited he was. "Habiti, we're going to get married." I backed him up and said, "Are you sure?" He replied, "Yes, I have never been more sure of anything, I feel so good about this," and then he kissed me. It was the kiss I was waiting for but somehow it just felt like someone was just pushing their face against mine and squishing me on the bed. He got up and said, "Let's go see Baba," which was what he called his dad. We drove down to the house for a final meal. Everyone was excited and then we were off to the airport.

INDECISION

The plane ride back began in much the same fashion as the flight there, with one major exception. Between his panics and in the middle of him speaking his mind, I heard it. He was talking himself out of the decision he had just felt so good about one hour ago. I said, "What do you mean you want some more time to think about it? You just said you felt really good about it, you said you were excited." He said, "I know, but I just need a little more time to think things over." I felt exhausted by the back and forth, the indecision, the time wasted. I had defied my stepdad and for nothing. It felt as though no matter how much I loved him he was set on chipping that love away one tiny piece at a time. I told him, "Look, take tonight and let's meet tomorrow for lunch. Then you can give me your decision." He agreed that should be enough time. I went home.

My stepdad saw me arrive and said nothing as I made a face of utter frustration and went straight to my room. I washed and prayed a special prayer called *Istikhara*. It's a prayer done when you are uncertain or trying to make a decision about something. It is done right before going to bed and the idea being that in the morning you should know what you need to do. I went to sleep and woke up late the next morning and called Noor to give her all the updates. "Good for you, honey, he really needs to make a decision. You don't need to be wasting your time. You're not young after all, you're twenty-seven."

11:00 a.m. rolled around and I headed to the restaurant and waited. We had agreed on 11:30 a.m. but 12:30 p.m. came and he had still not arrived. I was very close to leaving when he came barreling in saying, "So sorry, I overslept." I sat back, crossed my legs, and said, "Okay" as my eyes uttered, please continue I'm here for only one reason. He pulled out a notebook he had been scribbling in all night long by the looks of it. And of course, there it was, the diagram of his dream girl. He took me through his entire thought process all night about how he had convinced himself he could do without certain aspects of his dream girl because he had not factored love into the equation, and he has decided he did love me. "I also forgot to factor in your American passport, which gives you extra points," he said. I felt like a small wire in my brain snapped. I'm not looking for a romantic carriage ride to tell me you love me or to propose, but come on! I thought. I might have let all of this slide before seeing that he did have a good role model for how to treat and talk to girls in his father. "Continue," I said. He continued, "So, Habiti, I have decided we should get married since you almost fit all the criteria and we have both invested so much time already. I just have a few conditions and then we can get married right away."

I stared at him for a moment, then I looked down and raised my hand to hold my mouth and took a deep breath. It was as if the prayer I did the night before was working. I had no tears. I felt my heart go cold for a moment and only these words came out very calmly. I said, "So, conditions, that's your proposal? First of all, you were very late, then you tell me basically I'm not what you really want but I grew on you, so you guess you'll take me since we have already invested so much time in the relationship … I don't think I want to be someone's "almost perfect" and then when their dream comes along, they ditch me. Actually, you know what, I don't want to get married." With that I rose to my feet and said, "I need to go home." He said, "Come on, Habiti, let's talk." I said, "No, I can't, it's enough. I'm tired." He drove me home and talked a little, but I could not hear anything, I was so exhausted and felt so sure of my decision.

When I got home, I called Noor to tell her what happened. She said, "Oh my God, are you sure?" I said, "I feel very sure. I'm tired. It is not hard to just show up on time and just say I love you; I want to spend my life with you, will you marry me but like always it was all about him. He's the catch and I'm supposedly leftovers that should kiss his feet for him agreeing to marry me. I'm worth more, I'm a catch too!" Noor said, "Well, if you're sure *Hiyate* (My life)" and we hung up the phone.

The weekend arrived and I didn't reach out to Firas at all to give things time to calm down. On Friday I started receiving phone calls from Syria saying how hurt and broken Firas was over the whole thing. The callers pleaded with me asking if I could give him a second chance and saying how he loved me. But all I could do is explain that I'm not sure. "I'm not sure it will be any different if I take him back," I said and to that they left me to think it over. On Saturday the call I had been dreading came in, it was Ablah May. I answered and she started with, "Hi Elisooosa, I heard that you broke up with Firas. Good for you ... to teach him a lesson for dragging his feet but now I think he learned, and you can forgive him." I took a deep breath and replied, "Ablah May, I was not teaching him a lesson. I think it really won't work. He doesn't like me; he thinks I'm ugly. I don't match what he is looking for and that's okay. I wish him all the best, I really do but..." "Now Habiba, you listen to me, of course he thinks you're beautiful or else he would not have even considered you and maybe he's not good at sharing his feelings the right way. Go on, give him another chance." I said I would pray on it, and she let me go after that.

She called back the next day and thc next. It seemed as though Firas was also calling her which was understandable since he was like a son to her just as I was like a daughter to her. She always had a profound influence on me and through her antidotes, short stories, and way of talking she was very good at convincing me to do as she thought was best. Firas went on a quick vacation to Syria to recover which helped us avoid any awkwardness in the office, but it also increased the frequency of calls from his friends and family and even though I thought of just not answering I took the calls for the love I bore him still. They told me how much pain he was in, and I told them what he had done. They advocated that I forgive him, but I didn't feel ready to do so. I told them thank you for calling, please take care of him, no one deserves to be in pain, and I said I would pray on the matter.

Noor's Eyad started to get clingy, jealous, and possessive. Noor, unlike Saudi girls, had a mother who understood young love since she herself had been denied the ability to marry her cousin since Noor's father was considered a better match. She allowed her daughters their secret romances and would have helped them pursue marriage if and when the time arrived, and the man was ready to step up. Unfortunately, Eyad would never be ready; he could not afford to get a house, a proper car or pay the marriage dowry on what he made at the tape shop. Despite all this he got more and more possessive, and it scared Noor as he threatened to tell her family and everyone else what they had done if she ever left him. She called me crying and said that he would park outside her family's house all the time and if she didn't answer his calls, he would send her messages like, "I'm here and I know you're home, answer me." She would go along until he went to sleep but didn't know how to get herself out of the volcano she had invited into her life. I called for Mubarak and went straight to her house so we could talk in person. We strategized on this and that and decided that the best course of action would be to tell him she loved him, but her family had found someone who was a good match, and she could not refuse her father's wishes.

This happens all the time in Saudi, so it was not unbelievable. I sat with her and coached her not to reveal that she was happy about it at all, that he was the love of her life and that it was just her duty as a good daughter to obey her father. Thankfully he backed down and then he said they could still talk even if she was getting married. "Um no I can't, my mom said I should change my phone number since my new husband wants to get me a new one as a gift, beside it will be safer that way for you. I will miss talking to you. I'm sure he will be awful but what can I do?" He said, "I wish I had the money to marry you...." When they got off the phone, I seriously resisted the urge to say I told you so, instead I pulled out the non-alcoholic Holsten beer and said, "Well *Al-Hamdullah* (thank God) that is over."

I ran into Robert again at another embassy party. We danced until it was time for me to go home. I got home a little later than usual. My stepdad and I had not spoken since my return from Syria. I had sent him a text message on the plane just as we were taking off, asking him not to worry. He came out of his room as he heard me climb the stairs. He looked at me and said, "If you come back as late as this again, don't come back, you can't just run around with Firas all night long without a decision." I looked at him and said, "I was with Robert. Firas and I actually broke up when we got back from Syria because he could not make a decision." My stepdad changed his face and said he was sorry about that, and we said no more about it.

The next week Robert asked me over for dinner and a movie, which he had rented. I said "Great," expecting we would order takeout or a pizza. When I arrived, he was in the kitchen on the phone with his mother speaking in Gaelic. I said, "What's for dinner?" to which he replied, "My mother gave me her recipe for stuffed chicken breast." "You cook?" I said as I attempted to close my jaw. I was floored. I had never heard of a man who cooks, except in movies and I had never been cooked for nor had I ever expected to be, period. Firas' dad cooked but this was way different. I smiled ear to ear as I said, "You were on the phone with your mom getting the recipe, how nice." He smiled and acted as if it was no big deal as he set the table for me and opened the wine. Everything looked and tasted like it came out of a five-star restaurant. We talked a little as we ate. He asked about me some more and I asked about what it was like to grow up in Ireland. It was a beautiful two-way conversation where neither of us was intellectually superior to the other even though he, like Firas, had a master's degree and I had only just started my bachelor's coursework.

We started the movie and halfway in as we sat side by side on the couch he yawned, stretched out his arms and his arm reached around my shoulders. I giggled on the inside at how obvious it was. I would come to discover later; this was the classic guy move in America. Evidently this was also the case in Ireland. A few minutes later he leaned in, and we kissed. Suddenly I was on his lap facing him and we were making out as his hand reached to rub my breasts on the outside of my shirt. Naturally my hand reached down to feel over his jeans, my hand moved down and then moved to the other side then back again and back again. My mind was racing? Why could I not find his hard on? Then suddenly while kissing me he picked me up and carried me up the stairs. I was over the moon feeling like I was in a romantic movie or a novel. We got upstairs and he placed me down on his bed as he started undressing me. In the midst of kissing my brain checked in and I said, "Do you have a condom?" His face looked surprised. At the time I didn't understand why but now I see that it was because most girls would have been on birth control, but I was not since technically I was not supposed to be having sex unless I was married. I was surprised that I didn't feel as guilty as I thought I would. It just felt natural and right. As he placed the condom on my eyes glanced down to see his member as I tried not to make a face at the very small size. In the end it didn't matter that night. He cared so much about my pleasure and when it was over, I recall feeling light as a feather as I laid next to him on the bed.

I looked over and asked about the flag he had hanging on his wall. He said, "You don't recognize the Irish flag?" Feeling inferior and ashamed I backpedaled, "Oh, yes, of course, sorry." I glanced at the clock and saw that it was 11:00 p.m. Not wanting to be late home and arouse my stepdad's temper, I started to get up from the bed. Robert pulled me back and said, "Sleepover" to which I replied, "I can't, my stepdad will be worried." His face showed that he didn't understand. I knew it was an odd culture to him. That a grown woman would be so concerned about what her stepdad thought but in the Muslim culture it was not okay for a single woman to be out late, especially not in the company of a man. I dressed and texted my driver to come get me. He arrived ten minutes later. I kissed Robert goodbye and headed out to the car trying all the while not to display on my face the happiness I was feeling until after I got home and entered my room lest someone should figure out where I had been by the dreamy look I wore.

Luckily my stepdad was asleep, so I went straight to my room. As I closed my bedroom door, I leaned against the back of it and sighed, replaying the night in its entirety as I put on my headphones and played the Mariah Carey song that seemed the most appropriate. The words went, "Touch me baby it feels so amazing," a song I had not previously really enjoyed since most songs relating to sex seemed inappropriate to me. But this night it seemed the perfect match for the cloud I was on as I fell asleep.

I awoke the next day to find Firas had returned from Syria. He seemed fine in front of everyone, but I knew better from his eyes that he had been suffering from late night tears. I felt for him and asked if he wanted to meet for dinner after work to talk. He nodded and after work we followed the same routine. I left first and he followed later. When he arrived at the restaurant, he began with how I had hurt him, how I had led him on and broken up with him, how he had introduced me to his family and then I broke their hearts, how he didn't mean to be so unaffectionate but in Syria it was normal not to show too much affection or else the woman might think she is the boss and take the upper hand. He said he had seen this happen with too many of his friends and he didn't want that to happen here. I sat and listened. Then he drove me home where once again I entered the house mad at everything, I could not bring myself to say so I decided to sit down and write him a letter, and this is what it said (errors preserved):

> *I don't know where to start that's why I'm writing it down. I will start with the word "3arshra"(a life together), the other day when we were in the car, you were expressing what your dad had said about how love doesn't matter it comes and goes, that's true and I believe I said it to you during our first few dates but you won't remember, it's ok. You don't know how you stab me when every time we have any meaningful conversation you insist on saying there are 1000 girls lined up waiting for you in Syria and all over the place. Glad to hear that you will marry in a heartbeat, it's nice to be reminded that you don't need me. I'm sorry but I don't recall ever doubting your worth, if I had hinted that you were below caliber, I apologize but I don't think I ever have. I know that I have given you all of me plain as it is and tried to show you love as best I can.*
>
> *"3arshra" is when you would want someone regardless of whether or not they have a 1000 girls running after them or not, it would not change whether you do or don't care and want to spend the rest of your life with them.*
>
> *"3arshra" its when you think you are comfortable with that person enough that even when they grow old and become slightly less attractive, you feel you would still like to spend your days with them and feel relaxed knowing that they would hold you as you slept. Let me make this point clear, I see in you an "3arshra"*

someone I can see myself spending my days with and taking advice from. Someone I would feel happy to go any distance to place a real smile on their face. That does not mean that I do not have 10,000 men waiting on me, men would line up in the street for me and when I walk in a room it lights up. God has gifted me with a beauty that is inside and out.

"3arshra" it has to be a two-way street both willing to go the distance no matter how far to get the other one, its[sic] something you just know. To love you did not make me a silly girl its exactly the opposite you forget my dear I am different from other girls. I love you because I see this "3arshra" in you if I did not I would not be here.

"3arshra" 1000 girls waiting for you! Why? Did you ever ask yourself that question, lets see… Is it because they think you are good looking, your family name, roots, the way you talk, your powerful job, that they think you might be very rich? You say you're looking for an "3arshra" and are searching for a wife but all that I have mentioned above are very superficical and unfortunitly they don't last, a woman who would marry for any of the above mentioned reasons… Well lets just say there is a reason why most of your friends are unhappy.

"3arshra" is when you marry someone knowing them and accepting all, to stand beside them through thick and thin, hard times and good. I would have traveled to any place and brought you happiness through any hard times to come, would have taken care of you and placed you on my head (Ala Rasi, meaning like carry you on my head to protect and love you), money or no money, job or no job, been there to hold you when you needed comfort and be your support system to help you get where you need to go. Is that not an "3arshra"? Syria or no Syria these are just details, you see I would do it for you but would you do it for me? When you have 1000 girls waiting for you why would you want to run after a girl who is "divorced" "uneducated" "not chubby enough" and "not Syrian"? Perhaps it was because you saw in her an "3arshra" someone you could see yourself coming home to everyday?

Marriage is not something you do because you think you're getting old, if you just do that you will end up unhappy it's very hard to find a lifetime partner and when you find someone who is not perfect but you see in them a partnership, then you just you just go for it because if not you lose them. No father would ever hand his daughter over to a sea of uncertainty just as you would not hand over something that you think of as very precious without some kind of commitment, you would probably want a contract or a word of honor before someone took a piece of you to another country. Its commitment that was asked for by my father something you could not give and honestly he didn't ask for anything much, you know the other day he said, "I just want to know he will take care of daughter that he really wants her, if he would just say that he is wants to marry her regardless of all the formalities he keeps laying out then I would not ask him to do anything I would feel he was committed and go and buy him the airline tickets for Syria." You were never willing to commit to this relationship, you always wanted me to go on in extreme uncertainty and now after more than 1 year you can't even say that you really want me so that we can take the next step.

I am afraid that you will never be ready and it's a big fear but like they say when you really want someone you go the distance. Because you never want to be without them, but it seems like losing me is as easy as, you will just go choose from your harem of women. Then I am not the one for you and I wish you all the best. I hope you don't end up married to someone for the wrong reasons to a girl who won't travel with you and when things get bad, and you can't provide for her as her family used to leaves you to return to her family. I hope for the best. "3arshra" is someone who would happily stand by you through everything and still find a way to put you at peace when you are stressed. It's a lifetime decision <u>no one can promise forever, but we commit to do our best because we found someone who is worth doing our best to have</u>. I will miss you very much, but I guess we were not meant for each other.

Warm regards,

The next day a reply came, and I read it, but I felt so confused, knowing that he had read my letter, but it seemed as if it went in one ear and out another. Here is what it said.

Baby I heard a sentence in a movie couple of days ago and I think it applies to us amazingly. Three things that are true in life. You are born, you die, then things change and don't remain the same. Everyone has his or her own soul mate somewhere in this world waiting to be found. When you find that person, stick to him with all the powers you have, simply because no one else in this world will ever come close to that person. This is what I have been trying to do in the last two months, and I thought you are trying to do the same. Now I realize that it is not the case.

Baby, I loved you, but I feel so hurt because it was your choice to come into my life and now you are leaving it with your choice. Really, I was only responding to what was happening around me and what hurts me the most is that when I did exactly what you wanted me to do, asking you to marry me, which is loving you so much you withdrew. Maybe it was a mistake to give away my heart, but this is what happened. I will be fine baby, do not worry. I will manage and survive but the scars of this love will be around a long time. Now I realize it was not probably right to give away the most precious things I had, my heart. It is something I never fully gave to anyone. And when I did, it was damaged. Until today, I was so weak because of your love. But now I am strong again. Actually, I have never been stronger.

I'm sure I will move on, and you will move on. It is a blessing from God that wounds heal and recover with time. But when I look back at the last year now, I see that I was a complete idiot. Why did you give me the impression that you loved me so much if you did not want to continue loving me? Why did you make me experience how nice you are if you want to leave me? Why did you go to Syria with me and made me experience how much it is beautiful to have you as my wife if you do not want to marry me? Why baby why? It is just not fair. Maybe you are not seeing it now, but the decision you are doing now are not yours, it is someone's else.

I am sure I have done mistakes, sorry, it is my first real experience. But I am afraid you are doing again the same mistakes. If you look at the things objectively, there is really no reason for breaking up, there was no reasons for the fights we had in the last two months and there was no reason for letting this love go. On the contrary, I see all the reasons that we should continue and get married today before tomorrow. Because if the movie sentence that I wrote up in the first para is correct, i.e., we are soul mates, no one else in the world that you will meet in all your life will probably come close to me. Likewise, no one else in the world that I meet in the future will ever come close to you.

I will love someone else in the future, I am sure. But now I know that I should only love my wife, not anyone else. I will share with her everything I have, even my life. I will give her all the love she deserves. I just need to start searching for her again. Until today, I thought that this wife is you. Now I realize that it is not the case.

Baby, there are so many things that I want to say, but they do not matter anymore so I will not say them. I just want to tell you that I loved you from the bottom of my heart and it is so difficult to see you leave now. With all the hurt in my heart now, walahe (I swear to God) I still hope that you marry the best person in earth, be the most successful person in this life, and live the happiest life ever. I tried my best to keep you, but I ran out of options. It hurts so much to let you go, but I guess I will have to do it. This is the last time I will tell you the word "habibti" and I will say it.

If we cannot say farewell in person at least let it be on paper.

Goodbye, habibti, and good luck, I will miss you so much

Firas

I felt sad for his pain but mad that he could not see what he had put me through this last year. How he had caused my self-esteem to suffer as he downgraded me every day. For me once I pulled away, I felt like a wave of stress was finally lifted from my heavy heart not being ready to consider reconciling. At this point I folded up his letter, put it away and pretended all was well. Justifying that in his case it eases his pain to blame me since after all anger is a more useful emotion then sorrow if you need to keep going.

At work we were courteous and during smoke breaks in the beginning we went separately. Mahmoud expressed his sadness one day and I confided in him that I was sad, too, but maybe we just need some time apart for now.

I decided to take a trip to the U.S. to visit my mother and siblings in Iowa. This would be the first time I had seen them since I ran away from the house all those years ago, when I was married to Ata. I took ten days off work and before leaving I asked my stepdad if I should cover while I was there or could I just go without. He said, "I would wear it when she picks you up to lessen the shock but then once you get to the house and go out again just forget it, she will adjust." It was surprising to me that my stepdad had agreed for me to go without it as long as the family never found out, but my mother would be the one to make a fuss now.

There is no way to explain my mother when it comes to religion. She didn't pray really; she didn't read Quran or know any of the other things that were required of her as a Muslim woman. Yet she had selected this one thing, the hijab, and made it her Islamic torch. My sisters were also of covering age now, Noura, fifteen, and Yasmin, thirteen. I landed and after exiting and before calling my mother to let her know I had arrived I placed my head scarf lightly on my head leaving some of my hair exposed. I will never forget arriving in the Des Moines airport looking out and thinking where am I? It was so run down, small, and all the people were in sweats, while I was dressed to the nines. It's interesting how when we travel, we were always taught that you should be dressed your best since you never know who you will meet, and people tend to treat people differently depending on how they are dressed. Many Americans dress down when they travel presumably because in their mind, they are on vacation.

My mom walked up to me crying as if she had missed me terribly. It was always so confusing to me. We drove home through the heavy snow and when we arrived, we walked through a garage that was piled high with things. I wondered how in just a couple years in the States she had already amassed so much junk. We entered through the laundry room, which was dark, because the light bulb had not been changed and we stepped on the dirty laundry to get to the kitchen which looked as if it had been stepped on for months without anyone thinking to do it. The dishes were piled high as they had not been done in months. I had always thought it was Saudi that made her that way. I thought maybe it was the lack of freedom to drive or go and come as she chose but nope, here she was in America, and everything was in exactly the same condition.

All the children were in the living room, along with my brother Chris, who had fallen on hard times, and moved into my mother's basement. Delighted to see them, especially Osama, whom I had never met before, I pulled out the five red envelopes I had brought with me for each of them, each containing a fresh $100 bill. Osama danced around as they all did, except Noura who turned, left the envelope, and went to her room without saying a word. My mother said, "She's angry at you." I said nothing to my mother since more often than not she didn't understand the situation at all. I turned to Yasmin and said, "Take her envelope to her, I'll be up in a minute." Yasmin nodded and headed up the stairs. My mother quickly changed the subject and said, "Where did you get all that money? Are you doing something bad?" "Mom! I have a great job and I have my own money. I haven't seen them in a long time, and I wanted to make it special." She backed down and I headed upstairs to see what was going on with Noura.

Noura didn't seem to want to talk, and I noticed why, as we both heard my mother creep up the stairs to listen in, so I decided to wait until everyone was asleep to talk to her. Knowing Noura, she would be up late playing in her room. My mother shouted, "Who wants to go to Blockbuster to rent a movie?" a trip they all enjoyed. I conveniently forgot my head scarf and jumped in the car with them. Yasmin sat still in the back seat as my mother turned around laughing and saying, "Elise, you forgot your scarf." "No, I haven't worn it in almost a year, I'm good." My mother said nothing, she only turned around and started driving.

That night I crept into Noura's room, took her by the hand and we went into the only room in the house that might be soundproof, the bathroom. "Honey, what's wrong?" I said. She started to cry, "You left me." "No, honey, I got married and grew up, but I never left you. I would have come anytime you asked me to, you know that." She hugged me, and I comforted her as I reminded her of all the fun things we used to do together, then suddenly, the bathroom door swung open. "What are you two whispering about?" my mother asked, concerned. This was a common theme for her. She couldn't stand to feel left out of anything. She was always sure people were talking about her. I looked at her like she was crazy. "Umm, Barbies, old days, don't believe me, ask Noura." Noura nodded. "But why the bathroom and why the whispering and why is she crying? "Well, she hasn't seen her sister in I don't know how many years and we didn't want to wake anyone. Good night, mom." I walked Noura to her bed and tucked her in and told her, "In the morning we will talk some more."

I understand now that my mom was very concerned that I would share with Noura, now that she was old enough, all that I had told her about my stepdad years ago but in my mind if I saw no signs of abuse, I didn't feel I had the right to ruin their relationship with their real father. I wasn't his real daughter and hopefully it stopped at me. We never talked more indepth about why she felt abandoned. I wonder now if I should have asked more questions and if what happened to me had also happened to her, but I guess I'll never know.

My stepdad arrived a few days later and now that he was there, I started asking, "Why are they covering in the States? In Saudi I understand it keeps you safe but technically in the United States after 9/11, it doesn't keep you safe, it makes you stand out and makes you a target for people to snub you and throw you in a stereotype. The kids will get bullied, and my mother fights with everyone she meets about it. What are you doing here? I went to middle school in England, and I was bullied daily. Is that what you want for them?" "But what about hell?" my mom said. "God is not that petty; he won't send you to hell for not covering." I replied. The next day I bought a hair dryer, a curling iron, makeup, and perfume that I purposefully used in front of my sisters to teach them how to do their hair. When I left, I left it all behind as if it was mine and I would be back, but they knew it was all for them. I had lit a match and now I would wait for the embers to catch fire. The next time I would come visit none of them would be covered.

When I returned, I called Noor to tell her all about what happened when I was away. She said "Honey! I met someone." "Okay, who?" "Well, I met him at a party, and he is tall, handsome, and a Virgo like you." "Honey, Virgo men are not like women. That does not mean just because you're a Pisces and I'm a Virgo that you two are perfect for each other. Besides, honey, you met him at one of those parties which you know I hate. You have no idea what kind of man he is." "He's so sweet and nothing like Eyad, his name is Muhammad, and he really wants to marry me." "Well, *Mabrouk* (Congratulations) but be careful, honey, okay? Don't rush into anything." "I won't, I promise." "What about Firas, honey, anything new?" "Not really. He's being ridiculous as usual and honestly, I'm just tired." "He's a good man, Honey, try to work it out." "Let's just see how it goes, what is meant to be will be. Okay, I need to head to bed now I have work tomorrow." "Love you, honey." "Love you." I didn't tell her about Robert right away since I knew it would send her into one of her long lectures about how as a Muslim women I cannot marry a non-Muslim man. After all, none of them are circumcised, they eat pork, and worship idols they call Jesus. For me Robert was something worth exploring even if it was not worth keeping. He made me happy when I was around him and that was all that mattered. In Saudi we often frame relationships in one straight forward way. Would I marry him and will he marry me. These questions are asked mentally by everyone of us whether we realize it or not the first time we speak, meet, or look, at the opposite sex. While I had asked myself this question about Robert, a part of me for the first time in my life didn't feel like it mattered. All the rules, traditions, stipulations, and customs seemed ridiculous after everything I went through with Firas and my stepdad. So, for the time being at least I decided that Robert was my secret to enjoy without any religious mood poisoning.

There was a party at the American Embassy which Firas and I already had tickets to so we agreed we could still go as friends. That evening

Robert texted me asking if I was going and if I thought he should wear a vest, a bow tie or both. "Both," I said, excited to see him there. I entered the ball room with Firas all excited to see Robert but as we entered the bar area and Robert turned around there was a distinct awkwardness in the air. I tried to break the silence with a quick, "Hey, so good to see you again." Firas looked him up and down, then stretched out his hand saying, "I'm Firas." Robert, looking understandably confused, held up his drinks and signaled as though he better get them where they needed to go and promptly left the room. No matter how many times I try to disprove it in my mind the saying always tends to ring true. "It doesn't matter what is but what it looks like." To Robert, that night it looked and felt like from Firas's tone that he was touching another man's property. Even Robert knew better than to go head-to-head with an Arab man about what he considers his property. I tried to find a chance to talk to him all night, but Firas didn't want to dance and broken up or not, it would be rude to ditch the person I came with to go dance with another. I did not wish to hurt his pride anymore. We sat most of the night watching the people get drunk since the liquor could not leave the embassy in any other form except inside a human and with it being unavailable outside, the embassy party guests tended to drink more than their fair share.

I was invited to another Embassy party; I can't recall which one. It was a grand night, an outdoor party in a large garden. They were doing a raffle with prizes. It felt all so very exciting and since I had come alone, I found myself with no lack of constant attention. There was a young British man named Mike who was very sweet. He was good looking, and I loved his accent of course but there was a lack of boldness that I craved in a man. Robert was there so I went over and talked to him. He finally asked me about Firas and in my hopes not to make it too long a story I said, "He was just a suitor, but it didn't work out." Robert nodded, we danced, laughed, walked around, and then the raffles started. I sat on the wall and cheered for the winners with one man on either side of me, Mike sweetly handed over his raffle ticket saying, "You can have mine." "Thank you," I said, taking the ticket, thinking in my mind since in Saudi culture it would be rude to take something without at least refusing one time I assumed Western culture was the opposite and not accepting, I feared, might come off as rude. As the raffle was finishing up, they brought out the last prize, a box of fine Cuban Cigars. They called the number and as we all read over our tickets the speaker said, "I hope it's not a lady." I jumped in the air, hands up high yelling, "It's me, I won!" I ran to the stage, grabbed the box of cigars, hugged them, and jumped up and down. Everyone cheered. I had no idea what I would do with them, but they were mine.

Robert drove me home that night, we talked a little in the car and somehow, we got on the topic of engagement. He was curious how things worked in Saudi, and I was curious about Ireland. When he mentioned that he would be saving three full paychecks in order to buy his future wife's engagement ring my brain could not compute it. "Three full paychecks? For one ring?" "Yes" he said. "Well, that seems a little silly. Wouldn't the money be better off spent elsewhere like on the honeymoon or buying a home?" His face twitched a little and I felt that it was a tradition he was attached to, so I changed the subject and somehow the topic arrived at sleeping with prostitutes and how many diplomats tend to indulge. I asked him, "Hey, have you ever slept with a prostitute?" His face twitched as if I had insulted him, and I know now that I had done so unknowingly. It would not be uncommon for young men in Saudi culture to go out and sow their wild oats, as they say, before they got married. Since the laws on dating and sex in Saudi were very serious a lot of times the boys and men would drive across the border or fly to neighboring countries to seek pleasure wherever they could find it. It was not always necessarily a prostitute, but you get the idea. Robert and I were so different.

The following week something happened in the office and Noha decided to come after me again. This time I knew without Firas as my champion she would get me for sure. The formal meetings happened again and again but just as the head of office was ready to appease Noha and write me up, Firas called the head of office in Abu Dhabi saying, "I know you are in need of someone to fill in until your accounting person arrives. Would you consider taking Elise?" He said, "Yes." It struck me, how I had not asked for help, and I was no longer dating him that he jumped in and saved me asking nothing in return. It felt as though my heart spoke to me and said, "He has his faults, but he is there when you need him and that counts for a lot." Not yet ready to consider getting back together I thanked him for his help and started making plans to move to Abu Dhabi.

The next day on my way to work I texted Noor to get an update on her new man but the message I got back was, "Don't text me or call." My mind raced as I pondered how my Noor could ever send me such a message. I held the phone for a moment in utter disbelief and then thought maybe there was something going on. Maybe her new guy heard I was divorced and wanted her to distance herself from me. This was not uncommon since divorced women in Saudi are often seen as dangerous because they are no longer virgins and therefore could get up to all kinds of trouble and because more often than not the gossip mills always blame the women in a divorce. Then I thought maybe she was trying to tell me something like, *I'm sending you this because he asked me to, but I'll reach out to you later,* so I decided to respect her wishes. In our world one can often be left in the dark especially if the other person is not at your side one can never know the circumstances they are dealing with. She could for all I knew be in the middle of a big fight with her father, future husband, or both. To avoid a beating, she would need to stand down and at least appear to have acquiesced to their request. I knew she would call me when it was safe to do so. Therefore, I sent nothing back for fear of putting her in danger.

My stepdad returned from the States the day before and when I came home from work he was making soup. I had purchased a few things for me to cook with when I had my friends over. Among them were some fresh herbs and vegetables so my stepdad, looking to add some extra flavor to his soup, threw in a bunch of garlic cloves, some cilantro, and so on. Ten minutes after eating his soup in the kitchen he started to turn red. "Dad, I think you need to go to the hospital, are you okay?" "No, I'm fine, I'll just take a shower and I'll be fine," he said. I waited for him to come out of his room following his shower. Knocking on the door to make sure he was alright he opened the door, and his entire face was breaking out in hives. "Nope, you're going to the hospital, no arguments!" I said as I grabbed the keys and called for a car which was five minutes away, knowing full well that the ambulance would never arrive in time. I put his arm over my shoulder and walked him out to the street where we could meet the car when he suddenly collapsed on the sidewalk.

It's a funny moment in a life when you look upon the person who has caused you so much pain and in that second you consider doing nothing. In these seconds there are many thoughts that run through a victim's head … Should I let him die? Would I carry that guilt and regret the rest of my life if I did or if I didn't? Suddenly the world came back into focus, and I screamed louder than I have ever screamed in my life, "DADDY!" I tried to wake him, but he would not wake. I was crying but thought he's breathing. "I'll just let him rest until the car arrives" I thought. A neighbor who was a doctor came out of his house running and asking what had happened. I told him, "He looks like he's having an allergic reaction, I'm trying to get him to the hospital." The doctor said, "We must turn him over." "I thought maybe to let him rest until the car arrives." "No," he said, "He will choke on his own vomit if we don't turn him on his side." He turned him over and sure enough my stepdad threw up. I thanked him and he then ran to get his car in case the car did not arrive in time but just as his car was pulling out of the driveway, the driver arrived, and my stepdad managed to stumble into the car. The driver drove as fast as he could. We arrived at the emergency room. Once inside I informed them of the situation. They asked us to have a seat and just as he sat down, he collapsed again I screamed, "Someone help!" They immediately took him into the ER, put him in a bed, and gave him a cocktail of antihistamine.

As I waited in the emergency room, I thought about my mother knowing she would never forgive me if he died, and she didn't know. At the same time, I did not want to scare her unnecessarily since she was so far away, so I waited. I wished I could call Noor but she was gone.

As I sat there in the waiting room waiting for news, I called Firas and told him what had happened. He jumped in his car and came down to the hospital. He asked how he could help, and I said, "Once I know he is okay I would like to go home and change. I have some vomit on my

Abaya. Would you mind driving me home?" "Of course," he said and then he waited with me. Finally, I was allowed in to see him. He was asleep in the bed. The doctor explained that he would be fine, but they wanted to keep him for observation just in case. The doctor then looked at me and said, "You did the right thing by ordering a car and bringing him here. If you had been five minutes later he would have died." I could not hold back the tears swelling up in my eyes for no matter his faults, he was after all, the dad that raised me and to see him in that hospital bed saddened me greatly.

Firas drove me home. I changed and came back. I hugged him and thanked him for coming. It meant the world to me. I sat by my stepdad's side until it was very late and then returned home to get some sleep. The next day they released him, and I brought him home, got him into bed and made him some food. I called in sick to work explaining what had happened and that I needed to look after my stepdad. They were very understanding and so I spent the next few days yelling at my stepdad for overdoing it. "Get back into bed all that can wait." He would laugh, knowing that my appearance of anger was really so much love and concern. He knew it was just my way.

Once my stepdad was fully recovered, he got back on a plane to the States to see my mom and the kids again. He asked if I had everything, I needed for my move back to Abu Dhabi. I checked my exit re-entry visa to make sure it was still valid, and it seemed to be, so I said, "Yes, I'm all set." In Saudi Arabia women are required to have an exit visa which could only be obtained from their male Guardian. There are a great deal of stories of women who are old and have no brothers, fathers, or sons to apply on their behalf, so they spend years in the courts fighting for the right to be their own *Guardian*.

Firas took up the task of driving me home after work while my father was away. One night we saw a young girl walking out of the Embassy alone at night. We both knew it was very dangerous for a young woman to be out at night alone so far from the city, so we asked if she needed a ride, she was grateful. "I was trying to find a taxi, but there were none," she said. We introduced ourselves and told her a little bit about where we were from. She was Lebanese and so sweet. When we dropped her off at her home, we gave her Firas' card, and I wrote my number on it in case she should like to keep in touch. The same night my phone rang, and it was a number I didn't recognize.

I answered and said, "Aloo." It was Noor; she was crying. "*Hiyate*! I have missed you! My friend!" she began telling me the story about how a nice Syrian man and an American woman picked her up and drove her home, and an American that spoke Arabic perfectly?... "What was her name?" I asked. When she told me I started to cry. "*Hiyate*, my fiancé took my phone and messaged you like it was me and then my phone was lost, I lost all my numbers, my emails, everything. I had no way to reach you. I'm so sorry, *Hiyate*!" I told her how I thought it was strange but wanted to respect her wishes. I was so overjoyed to hear her voice and we both felt like it was God or the universe bringing us back together again.

The day arrived for me to leave for Abu Dhabi. Firas offered to drive me to the airport and see me off. I checked in and handed over my bags to be placed on the plane. Then I proceeded to passport control where I handed over my exit re-entry visa to the officer. Upon review the officer said in Arabic, "This is expired." I said, "No, it's not." "Yes, you see the date it's expired." Since the Saudi calendar, which is called the Hijra calendar, is so different I had mixed up the dates.

I looked at the officer and said, "Okay, I understand, but I'm American and this is not my country so you can just let me go. I need to go for work and my dad is in America right now." The man leaned back in his chair and chuckled for a bit and then said, "*Ya bint al halal* (meaning proper and upright girl) I'm sorry, but you are not leaving until he gets you another exit visa no matter what nationality you are."

I left and went straight to ask to have my bags removed from the plane before it took off and Firas drove me home. I was upset and felt like a piece of property, but I knew full well here the law is the law even when sometimes it doesn't make sense. There is nothing to do but work with it or around it. I called my stepdad, crying, explaining how I was going to miss my job and I didn't know what to do. He said, "There is a solution. Go to my office in the top drawer there is a stamp of my signature. Take that to my secretary and she will give it to a messenger who can go on my behalf to the ministry and renew your exit reentry visa." "Thank you, daddy, I'll go right now."

Two days later I was on my way to Abu Dhabi, unsure of how I would navigate not being covered now and Ablah May. Ablah May found me a room with a good Muslim family since she feared for my safety if I stayed somewhere alone. It's not that there was any real danger of me staying alone, girls did it all the time in Abu Dhabi. But as a mother she worried since she did not have space for me to stay with her. She wanted to feel that I was out of any potential danger, and it was better for my reputation if I stayed with a family.

For example, if I was having dinner with a potential suitor no one could come to any conclusions since they knew I lived with a respectable family. I covered my hair when I arrived at the apartment since the family were highly religious and Ablah May had most definitely sung my very religious praises since that is who I was when I left her last. The wife was very sweet and kind. I was given my room key and a key to the front door. I never met the husband since he observed the religious practice of not laying eyes upon any woman who wasn't his wife, sister, daughter, aunt, niece, or mother, and so on to avoid sinful thoughts. If I arrived home and he was in the living room, I would lower my gaze and only say Salam softly as I went straight to my room. He never turned his head, as far as I knew.

The next day I went into the office, wrapping my scarf lightly around my head showing some of my hair unlike I used to do. Ablah May said nothing at first and showed me to my office saying, "Well, Habiba, it's good to have you back." She nodded in her way and returned to her office. At around 3:30 p.m. I entered her office to ask her a question and she asked if I would like to grab some coffee with her after work so we could catch up. "Of course, I would love that." She smiled and said, "Okay, Habeba." I exited her office, looked down and sighed. I felt it coming. The intellectual mother scolding me for abandoning my head cover. I loved her dearly and never wanted to disappoint her, but I wished she would love and respect my choices more often.

We got to the coffee shop and sat down. Ablah May, started right into the subject at hand. "So, Habeba, tell me about you not wearing your head cover." I said, "It is something I wanted to try since I had been covered since a very young age." She responded with a "Well, now you have tried it. Now you can go back to covering. There is really nothing exciting about it anyway." There was nothing to say except, "Yes, Ablah May." After that she was happy again.

A temporary staff member arrived at the office a few days later, an Egyptian man named Belal. I had met him briefly while we were on an office retreat in Bahrain. He was tall and his body was very disproportionate. I recall thinking to myself he must have swallowed a tire and forgotten. He was a very respectful and kind man. I enjoyed his company and, unlike Firas who scolded me whenever I was silly and carefree, whenever I would show the slightest silliness Belal would laugh, saying how wonderful I was. He loved the fact that I was covered again. With Firas on a short leave in Syria to think about whether he wanted to get married to me for the 100th time, the office felt lighter since I was free to be myself.

After working together a few days Belal called me out of nowhere one evening and asked if he could possibly have my permission to speak to my father. I was in utter shock, frozen into silence. He continued saying that he had feelings for me and would like to take the next proper steps in order to get to know me better. I knew he liked me, but I had no idea it had gone this far. I asked if he had spoken with Ablah May, perhaps that would be the best place to start. He mentioned that he had, and she was delighted. I was stunned again since I knew she knew about Firas and favored him, plus she never said anything to me about Bilal wanting to marry me. I told him I was honored that he would think of me and knowing how religious he was I simply said that I would need to pray about it. Bilal responded, "Oh, you're so wonderful and pious, I am sure you will be perfect for me!" The expression on my face could only be rendered by imagining a cartoon character's eyeballs slowly exiting their sockets.

The next morning, I went straight to Ablah May's office and closed the door. "Ablah May!" "Ah, Habeba, so he called you." "What about Firas, does he know about Firas?" "Firas has not really made a concrete decision yet and so you're still on the market." I tilted my head slightly since that's the same thing my stepdad said when I was considering going on a date with Robert. "Alright, I guess we can see, but he can't talk to my father yet, I don't even know if I like him that way. He's very kind, don't get me wrong, but…." I held out my hands to allude to his physical appearance. "Looks are not everything, Habeba. You could marry a very good-looking man and regret it. No, no, Habeba, a good husband that adores you and is religious would make a fine match. Plus, he is just as educated and well off as Firas." "Okay, Ablah May, you're right." "Good! I'll tell him he can take you to dinner tonight." "Okay, should I tell Firas?" "No need, he will find out soon enough and he hasn't made a decision yet so it's his loss not yours."

The workday came to a close and Belal entered my office and asked if I would like to go to grab some dinner to which I replied with a smile and a nod. Picking up my handbag I walked beside him to the office car where Salem the driver was waiting for us. He sat in the front and I in the back which was very proper, and Salem dropped us off at this little European restaurant which was always crowded. We sat and he talked ever so eloquently. It was obvious that he was educated and worldly. He was older than Firas as well but that didn't matter. It made me giggle to myself how Firas had always used his age as a reason for us not to be possibly compatible when here was a man sitting before me, complimenting me every five minutes, who had no concern that I was much younger than him. As the night went on, I started to see what Ablah May meant about Bilal. He made me feel adored, beautiful, and respected. He begged me to talk and tell him stories about my life and my travels. I was shocked to find out that Ablah May had already told him how many times I had been married before and it didn't even phase him. It was a very refreshing change to be able to laugh at a joke without being told that I was acting like a child in public.

The next day I arrived at work smiling and skipping around to which Ablah May took it to mean that dinner went very well. "So Habiba how was it?" She asked. "He is very sweet, and it was nice talking to him," I said. "So, should you give him your father's phone number? Or if you like I can talk to your father first?" "Too soon Ablah May, I'm not sure." "Well, you will need to be sure soon. He is very sure; in fact, I think if he spoke to your father he would ask to marry you tomorrow, ha-ha," her head flying back in an open mouth chuckle. I said, "Let me pray on it and talk to Doctora Zaynia as well." Ablah May agreed to give it more time.

Let me pray on it. This is a sure way to make any religious person slow down, especially in the Arab world. We also use words like *Inshallah* (God willing) and *Han Shouf* (We'll see). Buying time when it comes to a good marriage proposal is tricky, since long drawn-out courtships are frowned upon. There was only so much time that would be given for me to pray on the matter, so I had to get some help.

I called Ata that night to talk through the fact that Belal was in love with my religious side, while I didn't feel very religious anymore. "Once upon a time when I first arrived in Abu Dhabi, I would have been perfect for Bilal but now I don't even want to cover, and I don't pray nearly as much as I used to." Ata told me that he sounds like a great match on paper but if I was going to marry him, I would have to tell him that I don't want to cover my hair or I need to decide to cover my hair and go back to being the very religious woman I was before. Ata had said the same thing I was telling myself all day, but I knew if Ablah May knew that I had told Belal such a thing she would be angry enough to stone me herself. I agreed with Ata that it had to be done otherwise it just would not be fair to Belal to continue giving him hope and keep him waiting. I myself was currently experiencing the torture of waiting for Firas to make up his mind and did not wish that on anyone.

We went on our second dinner. It was as delightful as the first. This time as the dinner was coming to an end he unexpectedly reached over and touched my hand. I turned red and looked down. "Forgive me, if I startle you but I would love the honor of speaking to your father and making you my wife," he said. I trembled a little in silence as I gathered my thoughts. "Belal, there is something I need to tell you before we consider anything, but you have to promise not to say anything to Ablah May," I said. He looked frightened as I am sure a million bad things rolled around in his head … I took a sip of my tea and proceeded as best I could to explain where I was on the covering issue ending with, "You see, I am not sure if I will really cover again but I am also not sure that I won't. I was told to cover my whole life and now I am at a point where I am just not sure I am ready to cover my hair again. But Ablah May insisted I should put it behind me and cover, so I do. I think you might feel better marrying someone who is at the same point you are."

A part of me felt so relieved and thought that was that. A religious man like him would want someone to share his location on his religious journey which was as it should be. He let go of my hand and brushed his hand across his red beard laughing a little. He said, "You had me scared for a moment there. Let me ask you, Maha, do you think any of my sisters cover"? I lifted up my shoulders slightly suggesting that I had no idea and he continued. "None of them do and if you aren't ready to cover that is just fine with me, you'll get there. I don't think it's right to rush anyone when it comes to religion," I was floored. My mind pondered what I had done to this man to make him so eager to marry me? Perhaps this is what they called bewitching in the old days when they hung women as witches. I nodded and took a deep breath as he said, "Not to worry, I would never tell anyone anything you ask me not to, ever." I nodded and said, "I need time to think." He smiled and said, "I understand."

That night I called Ata again in a panic. "I told him, and he said he didn't care." Ata laughed and laughed saying, "Well, you're in a right old mess now, he is definitely in love with you." "I know, and Ablah May won't let me turn him down without a good reason there is nothing wrong with him besides the fact that I don't find him attractive. She will say I am just stalling for Firas and push it forward. While maybe I am hoping Firas will suddenly come to his senses at the same time, I know any girl would feel honored to receive such a proposal." "Well, she can't make you marry him so just see how it goes for now. You know my opinion on love. I think it should always be two-sided but according to custom it's very common to marry someone you don't know or love at first. Your aunt, my parents, none of them married for love, so just see if you change your mind about his looks."

Belal got called on assignment for a few days which would give me time to think. Before leaving he asked, "Maha, could I call you while

I am away? If it would not get in the way of your thinking, that is." I smiled and said, "I would enjoy that."

A normal day of work consisted of the secretary and I laughing over this and that, the refugee letters pouring in on the fax machine and the phone ringing endlessly. Nine out of every 10 calls started with, "What countries can you send me to?" to which my mental reply was this is not a travel agency, but the correct response was always the same. "We don't choose, actually it would be the country that would choose to offer you a new home." "Wait, so if I start the refugee process I won't get to choose where I end up?" "You can choose not to go once a country makes an offer, but yes, it will all depend on the country's criteria, how many people they are taking and many other factors." "How long does the process take?" "For some people it takes a matter of months but for most it is years before they are approved." "YEARS?!!!" "That is correct." "Is there someone I can pay to make my application go faster?" "I am sorry, but no." Finally, I would direct them to the fax number or the email and ask them to write their story. How many people were in their family and so on and send it in so the process could start with the opening of a file. They would say thank you and then call every day following sending in their story to see if there was any update in their status. My heart went out to them living in a country with no legal status, unable to return home for fear of being killed or worse, children eating out of garbage cans with no access to medical care. There were thousands of refugees but most of them we knew by name and voice. There was no happier day then when the final round of questioning takes place, and a family is told they will soon be on their way to their new life. The joy will forever be indescribable. The next day brought with it a storm the size of which none of us expected…

HURRY UP AND WAIT

Firas decided to cut his trip short and come back. When I arrived in the morning, I found him fully pressed and put together as normal in Ablah May's office sitting down with one leg crossed over the other. I found an excuse to bring her a letter as I stood as close to the cracked door as possible to hear what was being said. "Tell me about Belal and Maha; is it true he is trying to marry her?" "Yes, he is most eager, and I think he is a very good man." Hot air blew out of Firas's nostrils as he smirked and said, "He's no match for her, have you seen him and he won't climb up the chain very soon, be serious Mrs. May." "I am serious, he is just what she needs, and he loves her in her hijab. I think he will spoil her, and they will make a fine couple. He's already asked for her father's number." "He will get nowhere. I have tried speaking to her father." "Well, I know her father so I'm happy to help put in a good word if that is what Maha decides." Firas drew silent, so I knocked on the door to bring her the letter. "Maha," Ablah May said, "Look who's back early." I smiled and said, "Welcome back, Firas." His well put together grin which revealed nothing to anyone else revealed volumes of jealousy to me.

I turned and went back to work and as usual before lunch I headed out back to smoke. Firas, hearing the door, followed me. After lighting up and taking a long drag on his cigarette he looked over at me as I asked, "How are your parents? How was Syria?" "Great, everyone is great. What about you? I heard Belal is interested." I gathered my thoughts as I took a drag of my own cigarette and said, "Yes, it took us all by surprise." "So, are you considering or not?" "I should consider every marriage proposal, should I not?" "You'll be miserable with him, he's Egyptian, he's only interested in your passport and besides he has no future, he's just a Protection Officer." I smiled a little, trying to hold back a giggle at his obvious jealousy as he continued. "Listen, if it's him you want, you best let me know so I don't waste my energy." "Is there a decision after your trip"? "Not yet, I had to come back early and didn't have enough time." "I see …Well, I don't know; I am still thinking." "Well. think fast, I have a lot of offers to consider as well." Tossing his cigarette to the ground, he left. My eyes rolled at the ridiculousness of the situation. I should make up my mind as soon as possible. While he needed a trip every few months to make up his mind with no results. I was to not entertain other suitors because he had me on hold? The entire situation sent me into an outrage from which I could only find release in writing in one of my notebooks (errors preserved):

Can he ever focus on anything good!!!!!! In allah maa as'sabireen (For God is with the patient) that's all I can keep saying to myself… All I have heard in the last few years is how many things are wrong with me, how we don't have anything to carry a marriage. I should not have to sit and defend us getting married to the other person in the relationship. We should both of us believe and know that we want to get married. All I keep hearing is how he is so much older than me so "were not compatible," how he is so much smarter than me so "were not compatible," how he is much more experienced than me so " were not compatible," how he is Syrian so "were not compatible." Then at the same time when someone else comes along who finds me perfect and accepts me as I am suddenly I need to make up my mind right away, hurry up and wait for Firas his royal highness to declare his decision… Fuck that shit.

Firas and I barely spoke over the next few days as he steamed around the office. Once Belal came back the sight of him looking at me sent Firas barreling upstairs to his temporary office. A national holiday arrived which meant we would have a long weekend. Ata texted me saying he would be in Dubai over the weekend for business and asked if I wanted to grab dinner. I texted him back, "Yes of course." Ablah May asked me the next day what my plans were for the long weekend. My brain stopped cold then I said, "Well, it's not for sure but I might head up to Sharjah to see my old roommates and spend some time with them."

The day before Ata arrived in Dubai, I started to map out in my mind the plan. If I went to Dubai and had dinner it might be too late for me to get back. Renting a hotel room would be too expensive and after all, I did want to spend as much time with Ata as I could. I felt it was time to give him and myself more closure. I texted him and told him that if he didn't mind, I would stay with him in the room. Although completely unorthodox and if I was discovered it would be a big scandal but luckily no one knew me in Dubai at that time. While everyone in Abu Dhabi knew me since I was associated with two of the heads of Arabic female society there. Ablah May the social side and Doctoria Zaynia the religious side. There was hardly anything I did that was not witnessed by someone who knew them in one form or another. Plus, since I know he would never think of raping me I figured why not go have a nice weekend getaway with my old friend and ex-husband.

I packed my bag and caught a taxi to the Dubai hotel he was staying at, placed my bag in his room and we went straight to dinner. It was an outdoor place with live music and *shisha*. I was happy to see him and we laughed and shared old stories. He filled me in on how he had been, his recovery from what happened in Canada, something we had hardly spoken about before, and his family. I filled him in on Firas, my struggles, Ablah May, and my journey since I left Canada. I felt for the first time now that I was not his wife, he spoke to me differently. He listened better and offered his male advice as neutrally as he could. I told him about Robert which was something I had not shared really with anyone except Haisum. "Wow, Maha, three guys at once shame on you." I smiled and slapped his arm. "Robert just happened, and I know it's not serious, but I'm enjoying it. Firas won't make up his mind and Belal just came along and started proposing. Technically if there is no decision, I'm free to do as I like besides I'm not a virgin anymore." "Ha-ha I'm not judging you, calm down and tell me more." I asked him if there was anyone special in his life and he said he had been on a few dates but there was nothing serious yet.

At the end of dinner not wanting the night to end Ata asked if I wanted to maybe go to a nightclub, to which my shock compelled me to say, "You want to take me to a nightclub? Where all the men will be staring at me?" He laughed and said he had changed so much these last few years and that it might be fun to go dance and have a drink since there was nothing like that in Saudi. I said "Sure," and he asked me where I thought we should go since I lived in the Emirates. I said "I don't know actually; I only just became uncovered a little over a year ago. I have never been to any night clubs in Dubai or Abu Dhabi." He asked if there was anyone I could ask so I texted Robert who loved dancing and he suggested a place. I was very excited to have a wish fulfilled that I had asked for all those years ago when we were married to let me try new things with him, not without him.

We got to the club and the music was rolling. I went to the bartender and said the line I had wanted to say since I first saw the movie, *How To Lose A Guy in 10 Days,* "Can I get a Dirty Martini, please?!" wearing the biggest smile, bigger even then when a child meets their favorite Disney character in Disneyland. The bartender nodded, mixed the drink, and handed it to me. It was perfectly like in the movie. I felt so classy and excited to drink my very first martini. Holding it and walking around like it was made of gold. I placed the glass to my lips, took a sip and immediately spit it back into the glass. I felt like I was drinking rubbing alcohol with the flavor of olives, and I hated olives. I walked over to the bartender in shame looking down saying. "Would you mind swapping this for something more sweet maybe?" He laughed and said, "You have never had a martini before, I guess?" I shook my head no and he mixed me up a sweet pink drink. Ata and I danced like we had never danced before. He wasn't jealous anymore like he used to be, he just enjoyed my company and I his.

The next day we woke up and went to breakfast still finding so much to laugh about and catch up on. He was kind, gentlemanly, and careful not to overstep any lines since we were no longer married. Afraid to frighten me I suppose unless he saw a signal, which I appreciated, and which also took any pressure off expectations. We spent the rest of the day going to shops and seeing the sights. That night we went out to dinner and danced again. He seemed different that night since he was to leave the next day almost like he had something to say but could not find the words to say it. When we returned to the room that evening, he finally found the courage to say, "Maha, I'm sure you know by now that I had no business that brought me here." I nodded and he continued his hands trembling as he said, "I spoke with my parents and at first they were opposed to us remarrying since they blamed you for leaving me but once I opened up and explained all that had happened they agreed. If you are open for us to remarry, then you can come live with us in my family's house until I get on my feet more."

The words *"live with me in my family's house"* rang in my ears. I was supporting myself now and free in a way I had never been. I had a good job here, friends and although I loved him still, Firas was still present in my mind. I lowered my eyes and told him that I loved him and wanted to always have him in my life, but I could not marry him and that I was sorry. His sad eyes will remain in my memory always as a part of me wanted to say yes but my mind would not allow me to forget how incompatible we proved to be as a couple. However much he had changed over the years my biggest fear was as soon as I said yes and became his property again things would go back to the way they were. We agreed to speak no more about the subject and enjoy the night. We ended up making love. I thought he deserved one last great night. The next day when I awoke, I said my goodbyes and asked him to always keep in touch because I would love to know his next wife when she appeared and that I was always here for him.

I returned to work running around trying my best to clean things up before the new accounting person arrived who would take over the accounting side I was covering and then I would move back into HR again. I had minimal accounting experience but did my best to clean up things and follow procedures as best I could. Two pieces of news arrived that day. One that Firas was going to be relocating to Abu Dhabi instead of flying back and forth for meetings. I also heard Robert would be relocating as well. Firas was to go a few months to Syria to see his family and contemplate again if he should marry me and Robert said he would be in town that week. I was excited to have Firas in Abu Dhabi on a more permanent basis and I was excited to see Robert soon as well.

The weekend came and I asked Robert if he wanted to grab a drink which he seemed hesitant to do for some reason or other. We agreed on a place and a time and since the family I was living with were away I did not see any impediment to leaving the apartment without my head cover provided I did not run into any neighbors or the door man. I normally wore my black Abaya and head cover when I left the apartment. I was afraid it might freak Robert out a little if I wore them since he was not used to me being so covered except in Saudi when he drove me home once. Plus, I was pretty sure an Abaya and a head cover would not be allowed in a bar. Along with the fact that it would make me more recognizable to everyone who knew Ablah May in Abu Dhabi. I put on my Puma sports jacket. I straightened my hair in a way not normal for me, lifted up the jacket collar to cover half my face and headed out the door making sure not to make eye contact with the security guard who would surely gossip to my landlords if he recognized me.

When I arrived at the bar, I felt shamed by the door man checking ID's since my ID showed me covered and clearly at this moment I was not. Once I entered the bar me and Robert sat down, and he asked me how I had been. Sadly, after all the steps I had to take to get to the bar uncovered and all the worry I was going through if anyone who knew Ablah May or Doctora Zaynia had seen or recognized me, the stress levels were too high so I attempted to explain the situation I was in. His face like so many times before showed how much he failed to grasp why an American woman who supports herself should care what anyone thinks about her choices to cover or not.

After appetizers and drinks, we took a walk by the beach. He told me that he was sorry, but he was not looking for anything permanent right now. I sat down beside him and kissed him for old times' sake and caught a taxi to go home. I wished him all the best and hoped we would stay friends. So often I think men expect a scene of tears but that wasn't me. I just wanted to kiss him one last time. After all, he was a good kisser. I knew it wasn't permanent, but I was so happy for the memories and the experience of what it was like to date someone from another world.

Two nights later I was sitting up in bed, thinking about Firas. I knew in my heart that Belal would always want me to cover one day, and I could never commit to that for certain. I started wishing Firas and I could just run away and get married like in the movies, away from everyone's opinions, thoughts, and traditions. I texted him and told him that I loved him and wished we would just run off and get married and he texted back that he loved me as well and we would talk when he got back to Abu Dhabi.

I went the next day to Ablah May and asked if she could let Belal know that it would not work. I wanted to let him down easy, and I knew she would know the right words to do it. Since he came to her first it was more than proper for her to be the last person to discuss the proposal with him. Ablah May, not wanting to hurt his pride, decided to tell him that Firas had stepped up to the plate and I just liked him a little better, nothing to do with him, just chemistry. She said, "You know, Belal, our receptionist Fatima is very lovely as well. What about her?" Belal leaned out to peek out of Ablah May's doorway to get another look at Fatima, then he shook his head and said, "Thank you Ablah May but I had something else in mind." "Well, not to worry, Belal, I'll keep my eye out for someone perfect for you. Don't you worry," Ablah May said. Belal put in for a transfer after that, took his vacation time, and I never saw him again. In the end it would have been very hard to sell an Egyptian to my stepdad since according to my stepdad Egyptians were very low on the totem pole if not scraping the bottom. All I knew growing up was that it was because they were considered loud, quick tempered, and dirty in their habits.

I wonder now, why? But when you look back through history, Egypt's relationship with Saudi Arabia has been more than bumpy. In 1938 Egypt put Faisal ibn Turki Ibn Abdullah Al-Saud in prison. During King Saud's and Egypt's President Gamal Abdel Nasser's reign Egypt sent five Palestinians to try and blow up the king's palace. In 1962, Egyptian soldiers entered Yemen as Nasser announced on the radio that socialism would flourish in Yemen and bring down the Saudi Royal family. After the Camp David Accords Saudi Arabia, along with other countries, broke relations with Egypt and started boycotting their products. The list could go on forever. In short Egypt and Saudi Arabia have been poking each other for years.

In Abu Dhabi it felt like there were a million eyes upon me each one having their own expectations of me. The family I was staying with watched me for any sign of scandal, evaluating if I would or would not be a bad influence. Luckily, they were so conservative they did not go to the places I went, so bumping into them when I was with my friends was not likely.

Then there was Doctora Zaynia who often brought me in as an example to Westerners looking to convert. The guilt of what Doctora Zaynia would say if she knew I was not really covering anymore was REAL. Ablah May continuously poked and said how I need to give up any thought of going without my Hijab anymore and made sure I knew every day that God's wrath would surely come upon me if I did not. In order to change the subject one day before Firas got back, I told her that Firas and I might reconcile. We were going to talk when he got back from Syria. She was overjoyed for a moment and then sure enough she came back around to how if I don't start wearing my Hijab again God would make sure I don't marry him and of course he will never respect me if I persisted.

To get a change from the constant guilt trips I texted my old roommate, Samera, looking forward to talking to her. I knew she would not approve of me being without my Hijab as well, so I wore it and put on my less conservative clothing that I had been wearing for over a year now. In the past if I went without my Abaya, I would wear full length skirts that were not too tight and long sleeve shirts. Now I wore skirts that came just past my knees and my short sleeves came just past my elbows. As soon as she saw me her face changed from happy to see me in the back of that taxi to a scolding stare as she expressed how disappointed she was with me as well.

When I returned to my room that night, I felt utterly alone in a city that had once been full of friends and happiness for me. I laid in my bed that night staring at the ceiling asking myself if I should just go back to covering to make everyone stop so that I could be just loved again and not lectured every five minutes. Then I would shake my head in silence.

If I do that, I'll never be able to enjoy not wearing it as I had been and there might never be any going back. I knew it was not a game to put it on and take it off.

Asma, the accounting girl, arrived the following week almost the same day as Firas from Syria. The head of office was pleased with my performance and asked me to start the handover of all the accounting work. I started to show her my systems and the handbook. She spent a great deal of time in Firas' office talking to him about Syria and killing time, a place I was forbidden by Firas to go since he was afraid of scandal. Even though I was not his direct report he still asked me not to spend too much time up there. I felt like she didn't like me right from the start. I could not put my finger on why and looking back now at how young I was, I think I was jealous. Not of her but of the connection they shared being from the same country and the fact that I was always ordered to stay away from him when we were in the office together while she could sit for hours with him and there was no talk about them.

Fatima, our receptionist, was also from Syria, just a different city than Firas. She was from Halab like Ata was. A young and bubbly girl, we connected right away and spent a great deal of time giggling throughout the day. She told me how the new driver, Harriri, had a crush on me and how she had a crush on Firas. A lot of the staff thought Firas was kind and proper. At times they talked about him, and I listened but never planned to tell him all his nicknames: Mr. Squeaky clean, the tin soldier, the charmer, the one who is always late, and so on. A lot of the staff found him unreliable. Harriri told me a story once about how he was late to do his other work because he agreed with Firas to pick him up at 9:00 a.m. but ended up waiting half an hour because Firas had kept him waiting. I felt for Harriri since I above all others knew how it felt to wait for Firas.

Firas and I had dinner and agreed to give it a try. My eyes rolled secretly every time he mentioned how he needed time since I hurt him so badly with the whole Bilal issue. I decided instead of bringing up the past like he was I would just leave it in the past and give it another try. I felt beat down with no allies except sweet Fatima who had not known me as I was before and loved me as I was today.

Firas would come down from his office upstairs often to order me to do some assistant work for him. I had my own work but since he was giving me a second chance, he felt he was entitled to me helping him with his. I helped him a few times but then one day he came down and asked me to scan something for him. I looked up at him. Puzzled. since I knew he had a scanner …. My brain snapped a little since I wasn't allowed to come to his office to even say good morning, but he was allowed to come down and ask me to scan something? I said, "Firas, you have a scanner and I have work. I don't work for you; I work for the agency. Maybe you need to get an assistant?" He was furious as he stormed out of my office. I went out to smoke feeling like working together in the same office didn't seem like it was going to work out. Over time it became more and more apparent as every dinner we had turned into a fight about who was right and who was wrong when we talked about any office gossip. I had a side, and he had a side, and there was no convincing Firas he was wrong about anything.

I had a great relationship with Chris, the head of office in Dubai and so I contacted her to see if there were any openings I could take. When Firas heard he was furious, wondering how I could apply without asking his permission. My response was simple. "We're not married, you haven't even decided if we're going to get married, why would I need to ask your permission?" This of course angered him, though he kept it to himself. I could see it, but I knew he knew I was right even if he didn't like it.

When the job offer arrived, I spoke to the head of office thanking him for allowing me to work in his office but since Asma was now in place there really wasn't a place for me any longer and of course I would continue to help with their HR from Dubai since I would still cover MENA. He gave me a glowing recommendation. I packed my bags and Firas offered to take me to Dubai. I was grateful for the ride. Upon arrival and because I still did not have my residency, I could not rent an apartment, so I planned to stay in a hotel.

When we arrived, we informed them I would be staying at least a month, so they offered me an extended stay rate which helped. Before I could pull out my card Firas pulled out his and said he would take care of it. I was grateful and wished not to wound his pride anymore that week, so I said, "Okay." I got to my room, put my bag inside, sat on the bed alone and cried. I felt alone in a city I really didn't know facing a new job with people I had talked to on the phone but never really met. I had escaped from so many prying eyes and criticism but now I was in a place where there was no community safety net for me like in Abu Dhabi. Although it was not the first time I had to learn to rely on myself alone, it had been a while and the lonely hotel room scared me a little. Even though I didn't like living with strangers there was a kind of safety in living with someone.

The first day started well. I grabbed a taxi to the office and introduced myself to my new head of office, Chris. Chris was an amazing, strong woman role model who was delighted to have me on her team. It was so fun to be away from the pressures of wearing my head scarf that so often came up in Abu Dhabi. It felt like a great weight had been lifted from my body. I was trusted to do more and sent on many special meetings to translate for staff sent from Geneva to negotiate with the Emirate Government. The team was undivided, something I had never seen in an office before. Everyone helped everyone and no one spoke ill of the others behind closed doors. Every day at 5:00 p.m. when I got off work, I would pass through the Dubai Mall, pick up dinner, and head back to my hotel. The hotel had a common area on each floor and on smoking floors it was permitted to smoke there so I spent most of my awake night study time there until I felt sleepy, when I would wander off to my room to sleep.

Working a full-time job and taking classes online full-time was difficult but I was determined to have my B.A. sooner rather than later so I could grow with the agency. Firas would call every day after work and sometimes at lunch and come down to visit me on the weekend for dinner or lunch, depending on his schedule.

We argued less now that we were not working in the same office. We had our separate lives and our dating life, and for a time, our relationship seemed simple and happy. I felt independent, free, appreciated, alive, happy again and I loved him in those moments. Ablah May would call almost every other day to see how I was doing and ask about the progress with Firas and if he had made his decision about whether he would marry me. "Not yet," I would say with a sigh. The answer was always no, not yet.

Weeks turned to months, and it came time for our office to do an inventory of the warehouse. I had never been inside it before as I volunteered to help do the inventory with everyone. As I walked in the door, I remember thinking how marvelous and vast and endless it was. It seemed as though there were enough supplies in there to help an entire country recover from any natural or unnatural disaster. Beds, tents, jerry cans, and anything else one might think necessary in a crisis were stored right there. It was a hot day in the summer, but we all had a great time running around the warehouse just getting things done. I felt as if I was a part of something more than a team, almost like a family, but without all the dysfunctionality families often have.

When we had finished, we spread out the plastic on the ground which in Saudi we called *Sufra*. As I grew older, I discovered *Sufra* was actually the name of the first company to brand the plastic we sat and ate on, so everyone called this plastic table, regardless of the brand, *Sufra*. This was common when it came to all manner of things in Saudi. For example, since Pepsi was one of the very first soft drinks to enter

Saudi Arabia way before Coca-Cola, it was the name adopted to refer to Soda Pop. Until today, if you want to ask if a store sells soda, you would say "Do you sell Pepsi?" and then ask for the type of "Pepsi" you wanted which could be Fanta, Sprite, and even Coca Cola. To squeeze everyone in we all sat shoulder to shoulder on the ground and shared all the food, laughing and talking.

One day I got a call from Firas saying he would not be able to make it down to see me on the weekend because he needed some time to think. "Some time to think?" I asked. "Well, you see I have been talking to Mrs. May and I just need to think about a few things," he said. My mind rolled around as I went back and forth trying to extract the true nature of his conversation with Ablah May and then it became clear. Ablah May had heard that I was not wearing my head cover in Dubai and had put it to Firas that if someone was able to abandon so easily something as sacred as covering their hair, what might that say about her? Knowing Ablah May as I did, I saw the plan clearly before me. It meant so much to her that I cover and while it was not her intention to break us up, it was however, her intention to get Firas to request that his wife wear the cover thereby accomplishing both her goals. Putting me back on the righteous path and helping him want his wife to cover as his mother had done when she was alive.

The guilt hit Firas hard since he could not argue that he believed in his religion wholeheartedly and adored his mother who had covered all the days of her adult life. Firas was unable to contradict or argue with any mother figure. Ablah May, being a strong mother figure to all who knew her, sent him into doubt about everything again. After Firas revealed this information to me, he then added his own concern that I seemed to be doing well in my current position and since he would eventually need to travel again due to the nature of his job being on rotation every two to four years, he did not know how my working in the agency would work if we were to marry. I took a deep breath and calmly told Firas that if he needed time I understood. I hung up the phone and looked at the sky that summer's day. I lit a cigarette and started to pace on the walkway outside the office. Back and forth, my mind, my heart and my soul arguing back and forth. Then it came to me, and I knew what I had to do.

Despite all of Firas' faults I loved the calm side of him; the man I had witnessed with his family in Syria, the man that would come to visit me in Dubai. My logical mind kept yelling that I had invested too much time in the relationship for polite Arab society. Everyone had attached my name with his already despite what Firas thought. If we didn't marry it would surely harm my prospects while his would remain intact since he was a man and has the right to choose, unlike me who was a mere divorcée and should be grateful for what I was offered.

Feeling defeated, I threw away my cigarette, ran up to the office, sat down at my computer and read through my contract. Then when I had found the clause that I was looking for, with a heavy heart I typed up my resignation letter, took a deep breath and pushed the send button. It went straight to my counterpart in Budapest. Then I jumped up and quickly headed out of the office to grab a taxi straight to Abu Dhabi. Leaving early was easy to do since we didn't have set work hours just as long as we did eight hours or made up the missing hours the next day. I had the taxi driver drop me off at the mall where I walked into the first store that sold headcovers, grabbed one, paid for it and jumped back into another taxi straight to Ablah May and Firas' office.

I arrived with my headcover on and walked straight into Ablah May's office to the shock of everyone there. She looked up from her desk as I closed the door. I stood before her and said, "I'm done, I'm covered, I'm sorry." She nodded and came around and held me as she said, "*Habiba* I'm proud of you, now let's call Firas in here." I knew what was coming and I hated it but there was nothing to do. It was the only way.

Firas came down and walked in in his normal manner, well put together, smiling, seeming happy to see me but his eyes, his eyes always gave him away to me. His shock was real as he sat down slowly. Ablah May shared with him that I was now covered and that he should not influence me in any way but be proud of me as his future wife for choosing the right path, for that meant the marriage would be blessed. Firas, unable to say anything to the contrary, said, "That's great, well, congratulations." Then Ablah May excused herself saying she had a prior engagement and Firas asked if I wanted to go get dinner then he could drive me back to Dubai. I nodded and we left silently.

We talked in circles over dinner for a bit and when he asked why I decided to cover again I kept to the simple explanation. "It was time." I didn't know how to tell him I had also resigned from my job knowing full well come the morning, everyone would know. He already thought I was impulsive and reckless, so I remained silent. He drove me home and I went up to my room. I walked into my dark, cold, hotel room, took my head cover off, and laid down on my bed to cry. Freedom and the right to have anything for myself seemed like it would never be in reach. I felt as though I needed to give up dreaming about being successful as anything but as a wife or a mother down the road. That was what I was brought up to do, after all. I felt my spirit slip into a deep silence as I decided to lower my head and go along as I was told by Ablah May and Firas. I realize now, how many Arabic women with spirit come to this resolution and resign themselves to a place of irrelevance and subjugation. If you are an Arab man, you have the world by the tail and can do whatever your heart desires. If you are an Arab woman, well, there is marriage and having kids, and that is about it.

The next day Chris called me over to her desk after finding out I had resigned and asked if it was something she had done wrong. "Why did you resign?" she asked me. Unable to hold back my tears she stood up and took me for a walk. I told her about Firas, Ablah May, and the pressures I was under from what seemed like everywhere. She asked me not to resign and instead that I finish out my contract and then decide. She said, "I won't say much but it sounds like if this man really loved you, he would not keep you waiting this long for an answer and be pressured so easily by others but only you can know that." I listened to what she had to say but it would not soak through. As you get older you learn that there is a very big difference between listening and hearing. You can listen to a song without ever knowing any of the words or you can really pay attention to the song and decipher the lyrics, it's true meaning and it's deep feeling.

A phone call came from Firas once the news was out that I had tried to resign. "Why would you try and resign?" "I figured it was for the best since you are going to be moving every two to four years. It's probably best if I don't have a career and look for something more temporary like you said." "How will you pay for anything until we're married? I can't afford to take care of you yet, I'm not ready." I took a deep breath wondering when he would run out of reasons why he wasn't ready, why he needed to think it over, why he needed more time alone to think, and then I said, "I have taken care of myself this long, I think I can manage. Don't worry about that I can always go home and stay with my stepdad in Saudi." It seemed as though the answer was too easy for him, but we ended the conversation, and I went back to work.

There is a certain amount of thought and reflection that comes when one ends, enters, or chooses to stay in a relationship. To err is human but to seek out perfection is also human. It's hard to explain but I wanted to try. I had married for love the first time. I had chosen alone and sought out no one's opinion but my own and in this case, there were so many close to me that kept saying, "Firas is perfect, he's a catch, wait for him, don't marry for love, marry for stability, marry for care, marry for good family and a proper upbringing." Were they right? Could I be making the biggest mistake of my life if I walked away after so much time had passed? In normal Arab society we would have been married by now. If I had been a virgin there would be no way anyone would agree that we continue as we did but because I was "flawed," it was thought okay for me to wait for him. My gut tugged me one way and my mind tugged another, and my heart only felt sadness most of the time, but as with every time I reflected, I decided I would do what I was taught to do this time instead of listening to my headstrong mind.

The agency was pleased with my work and offered me a renewal of my contract. I was so flattered and saddened as I stared at the contract knowing that if I was to marry Firas another six months with the agency would not have been possible at all. I don't envy anyone who feels they need to give up one dream to pursue another when both are always possible. As I sat at my desk Ahmed, who sat across from me, said, "I just wanted to tell you that working with you has been a great joy. I will always remember you." I looked up and wondered how he knew I was thinking of turning down the renewal and then he mentioned that he was not asked to renew his contract due to budget cuts. I knew he had three small children to support, and his wife did not work. I said, "That can't be right," as I typed away an email to my counterpart in Budapest inquiring secretly as to the real reason behind his non-renewal. I knew that we had just received a large donation and budget could not have been the reason. The reply came that there were no performance issues; they just thought the job could be more effective if they moved it to one of the European offices. I took that as code for: someone wants the job who has better connections and since creating a new job was always harder than moving a job from another office, I assumed that's what they were doing. Since he did not have the right nationality that would have allowed him to enter Europe easily, he was out of luck.

I looked up from my computer at his sad face. The concern of how he would feed his family poured out through his eyes as he worked. I sat down and started an email to my boss and my counterpart in Budapest letting them know that I have decided not to renew and since Ahmed's post was being cut due to budgetary reasons I asked if they could use that money to keep him on instead for six more months since this would give him more time to find another job and take care of his family. My phone rang soon afterwards from Budapest and my supervisor came by. They were both so sad that I was not going to renew but they could find no reason why that plan could not work so a new contract was sent for Ahmed to sign. The tears rolled down his face when I handed him the contract. With that I felt as though I had done what I was sent there to do, and I was ready now to move on to my next adventure, marriage.

I moved out of the hotel and back in with the family I had lived with before in Abu Dhabi, having saved enough money to remain in Abu Dhabi at least for a little while. Firas and I did some apartment hunting for him. He had been staying with a friend of his but now was ready to get his own place, now that his position looked like it would continue there for at least two years. "This does not mean I made a decision but having a woman's eye always helps." I sighed as he once again made sure to suck any hope and any joy out of the process.

The apartment market in Abu Dhabi at the time was hot. Buyers took the old, large apartments and turned them into two or three apartments so they could make even more money, not to mention renters then secretly subletting since rent was typically locked in for 1 year, paid fully in advance. You might ask how anyone could afford this but more often than not, the companies would offer to pay the rent in full for their employees and then deduct the amount from their paychecks every month without interest.

His budget was tight, so he did not have as wide a selection available to him. As we looked at every apartment, Firas always found something wrong with it. To me it was not important to have it perfect, it just needed to be in a safe area. But apartment after apartment to Firas was too small, too big, or had a funky layout, none of which were really big deals in my mind. Although when you spend time locked in a room, sleeping at a mosque, or renting a tiny room from a family with no TV, I suppose you become less picky. Only the thought that it might be called my home one day seemed important to me.

Firas finally found an apartment he considered acceptable. I thought it was beautiful, he negotiated the yearly rent and then right on time, there it was, the mood poisoning time. "Habiti, now, I see you getting excited. You need to remember that just because I get an apartment that doesn't mean I have made my decision." I stopped smiling and sat in silence as he continued his usual speech. I wondered how hard it would have been to just leave me in my cloud for a moment. Let me enjoy the joy of finding an apartment that we might live in as husband and wife. I know in his mind perhaps he was trying to protect me from having a broken heart but all he really did with each time he brought me back down was teach me not to get excited about anything, which was hard since it was so contrary to my nature. I loved to express my joy, I loved to jump, dance, skip, sing and smile. I loved to celebrate the little things as well as the big every time I could. Firas seemed intent on sucking all of that right out of me.

He dropped me home and I began calculating the cost to stay, how long I could pay for rent and essentials before I would need to head back to Riyadh. I decided not to discuss my finances with Firas and went to seek council from Ablah May instead. I told her that I would not be able to stay much longer after giving up my job. She waved her hands in the air saying, "And I know you gave it up for him because he didn't want to have his wife working at the agency. When will this boy make a decision? It's like we fix one thing and something else is wrong. This has gone on long enough; I could have had you married with a kid by now. This just won't do! Leave it with me Habiba, I will talk to him." Ablah May had a conversation with him alone. I never knew what it was they discussed but this was the custom of marriage negotiations. Even if it had been my stepdad doing the negotiations I would not have been allowed in the room.

Firas came back saying he needed to go to Syria to see his family and take some time to think without any outside influence. In the meantime, he suggested that I stay in his apartment to avoid paying too much rent, making it easier for me to stay in Abu Dhabi a little longer. I arrived at the apartment just after he finished his coffee. He handed me the keys and said his farewells noting that he would be out of touch until he had a decision. I agreed not to call or text him. After he left, I noticed his coffee cup on the table. I was about to be a good future wife and straighten up a bit. But then I decided the coffee mug needed to stay just as it was because every time, I saw it I felt like he was around still knowing I might not hear from him for a few weeks at least.

A few days passed and I spent most of my time in the apartment heading out daily at night for a short walk and dinner in a small café alone with a book. On the fourth day as I was having my coffee my phone rang. It was from Syria. I answered and it was Firas's dad and stepmom on the other line asking how I was and saying how much they missed me, how Firas should have brought me along and not to worry, they told him he should marry me. There was such great joy in hearing their voices and it also greatly helped with the anxiety I felt as I waited for Firas to make a decision. I didn't understand what was so scary about at least getting engaged and then deciding the big things later. It would have been much better for my reputation if we broke off an engagement rather than waiting as we were doing but there was nothing to do now except wait. The journal entries from that time period are full of worry and despair, of doubt of self-worth, of fear for time wasted as I was not considered a very young woman anymore.

A few days passed which seemed like years until the phone rang again. It was Firas letting me know he would be coming back the following day on the 3:00 p.m. flight. I asked how his thinking was going and he said, "We will talk when I get back." His dad was in the background saying, "My son, don't keep her waiting, just tell her," I smiled, and Firas reiterated, "We will talk when I get back," adding a small laugh at his father's comment. A nervous tick of Firas's was that he would always laugh to throw everyone off what he was thinking at the time.

I greeted him with much anticipation as he sat me down and said he has decided he wanted to move forward but we will need to get married in Syria in a place of his choosing. I had no disagreements. After all, this would be my third wedding and spending a lot of money for a wedding was overrated to me. I suggested we get married in his family's home to make it special for him. He said he would think about it.

I called Ablah May and gave her the good news to which she replied, "I told you I would handle it Habiba, now go and be happy." I then planned a trip to go back to Saudi to attend Noor's wedding and talk to my stepdad one last time to see if he would agree to the match. I was concerned about Noor's groom since the last time we spoke she told me about an incident that happened when they had an argument. "He got so mad, Honey, that he raised his hand up like he was going to hit me." "What!?" "But, don't worry, Honey, he won't do it, he was just mad." "Honey, listen to me, a man who raises his hand like he was going to hit you while you are still in your family's house and you're still not his wife yet will very likely hit you once you're in his house and you're his property." "I don't think so, Honey, I just made him really mad." "Alright, Honey, but I would think about that."

When I landed in Saudi my stepdad picked me up and we went for lunch at one of our favorite Italian. We talked about Firas, the wedding in Syria, and he sighed and said "I will not stand in your way if you think he is the one for you, but I cannot agree on principle since it would make me seem weak. Like I have no pride. I still think his family should come to you since you're worth that much at least but if you want to run off to Syria and marry him then go. I am sorry to miss your wedding, but I cannot show that I agree." I was grateful for his honesty, and his willingness to accept me as the headstrong adult I was, and for allowing me to make my own decisions. Although to many it seems like not something to be grateful for but for my stepdad to set me free this way was a very big step for him, and I appreciated that. I knew full well that many girls in Saudi would never have been given the luxury of being free to choose on their own and would never dream of disobeying family and tribe for anything.

I went to see Noor and stayed a few days to help her prepare for her wedding. Upon arrival I was cornered by her mother who looked at me and said, "We don't like the groom; can you talk to her? There is still time." "I can't, *Khala* (Auntie), I have told her what I think but she still wants to marry him, and I won't be the one to talk her out of marrying him even if I could. She needs to make that decision herself. Otherwise, she might hate me for interfering. Trust me, I see what you see but there is nothing we can do about it." Her mother nodded and left me to return to Noor.

Through good and bad nothing could have separated us. Not men, not customs, not distance, not time, and not family. There are so many pictures of that night and videos as well which are cherished memories. We laughed so much our sides burst and we looked like we were drunk or high, even though all we had were cigarettes and tea.

She made me her famous eggs with tomatoes in the morning and as we ate, she mapped out the plan for the day to go see her finished wedding dress. When we arrived at the woman's only dress shop Noor pointed at her dress. I struggled not to giggle as I said, "Wow, honey, it looks like a cupcake." She said, "I know it's not your taste, but this style is the height of fashion right now." I had forgotten over the years that Noor was raised to keep up with the current styles through magazines and music videos while I was always one to wear what suited me best or what I liked or what was proper. If I ever wanted to buy her a gift like the one I gave her for her wedding, all I needed to do to find the perfect one would be to pick out the flashiest, ugliest thing to me and she would love it. She was my polar opposite in taste. I smiled and screamed at her, "YOU'RE GETTING MARRIED!"

The night before the wedding I went home so I could go to my hairdresser in the morning which was close to my house and to get my dress for the wedding. The wedding was set to begin at 9:00 p.m. so I planned to arrive for her dressing, hair, and make-up and of course to help with any anxiety that would surely arise. It is interesting to point out that the Arabic word for bride is *Arousa*. Coincidentally it is also the word for a female doll, a Barbie, or a baby doll.

When I arrived at 4:00 p.m. Noor was already in the chair having her hair done. Her nerves showed through her eyes. She looked up at me. "Honey, how does my hair look, is it okay?" I said, "You look so perfect, honey, don't you worry. she is doing a great job." She settled in as I sat beside her and talked of old times when we would dream about our weddings. Then we moved over to makeup, nails, and any last-minute waxing.

It was almost time. She was ready now for pictures of her alone and some with the groom. This would take at least two hours

Because Noor's contract signing had been done, if she did cover normally, it would be totally fine for him to see her without her cover now, even before the wedding. The tradition that the bride should not see the groom before the wedding was rarely done since getting those wedding pictures while the bride's makeup was fresh was way more important. Once the photos were done the groom retired to the men's section to hang out with the men. In more liberal families like Noor's it would not be uncommon for the men's section to have a band, a male singer, cigars, and of course, *shisha*. The men sometimes danced. Some Saudi tribes did this as well, but in my tribe, the men's section was a place of men sitting eating seeds, nuts, biscuits, drinking tea, and discussing the world.

Noor was brought out to her spot where she would take her first steps to being a wife. We all embraced her and then left to take our seats. As the *Zafa* (wedding march) started all the women began to do the wedding call. It's like a thousand birds calling up to heaven. The sound was in perfect pitch to the music. We continued until she reached the top of the stage. Then someone calls out a blessing, usually the mother, grandmother, or aunt. A common one might be, *"Alf Salat Wa Salam*

Aalaik ya Habeb Allah Muhammed" (A thousand prayers and greetings on you the beloved of God Muhammed). Really it can be whatever was decided. It was important because some families fear the evil eye might set upon one so beautiful and something bad could happen. The women in the crowd called it out again as loud as we could as the bride stands in all her shyness with all eyes upon her on the stage.

A dance song chosen by the bride plays and the bride traditionally will dance first with her mother, sisters, and the women of her new family. Arabic dancing is not like couple dancing. It is done in groups and often all dances are seen by outsiders as just belly dancing but in fact there are many different kinds. Saudi dancing for example involves less shaking. You walk towards the girl you're dancing near with your hands in a rested wrist position almost like how hula dancing uses their hands to tell the story. As you walk towards another girl they walk back and so on. Palestinians, Syrians, and all Arab countries have their own versions. Another example is Iraqi dancing, which involves more twirling of the hair in a circular fashion, a skill I never mastered without it making me dizzy. The dance they did was modest since a bride often finds it difficult to move too much in her dress and tripping is not an option.

Once the family has danced then the bride will more often dance with her friends and then take a seat to rest for a bit. Then all the single girls and some young married women take to the stage to show off their skills as the mothers look on from the tables. Dancing in the Arab world is such a big part of expressing joy and happiness for any occasion and throughout the next couple of hours the bride will rise to dance many times and even be asked to dance with any girl who wishes to celebrate her.

Women will also during this time take turns approaching the bride on the stage and offering their congratulations on the marriage, wishing her many children but in particular, sons. There is an Arabic saying that is similar to the Western saying, "You're still newlyweds until you have kids." The Arabic version is "*Lissatik Arousa E-lan Mat Gibi A-Sabi*" (You're still a bride until you have a son).

After enjoying some dancing with her friends, the women are given a 10-minute warning so that anyone who wishes to cover in this case should do so as the male family members are about to enter with the groom. Noor exited to the hall and met her groom for a few seconds and then they began their first walk as husband and wife. Everyone cheered and the wedding call was employed once again. As I watched her ascend to the stage with her new husband, a sadness came over me like none I have ever known. She belonged to him now, as if I was a mother losing a daughter to marriage. Things felt as though they would never be the same again. No more sleepovers, mall trips, long nights sipping tea or staying up all night smoking *shisha*. Noor's youngest sister saw me, and we hugged as we both cried for the sister we felt we were losing to marriage. Now she was a wife she would be busy setting up her home, cooking, and pleasing her new in-laws.

It is the custom that when a woman marries, she becomes the daughter of her new family and should do her best to heed their traditions and ways of doing things. For example, while in the past Noor would have asked her father or her mother for permission to go out, she would now rely on her husband and in-laws for direction. For example, her family celebrated birthdays (some tribes see birthdays as a Western and improper custom), if her new in-laws did not, she would need to give up that tradition. She was now the member of a new family and there would be a lot to learn if she wanted a happy marriage.

After all the traditions were observed, Noor donned a beautiful white head dress designed to cover her hair without messing it up along with a small jacket so that all the men could enter to congratulate the couple. Noor's husband decided soon after their engagement that he would like her to be covered like his mother and sisters did. He was a jealous man and since she was now a member of his family, she donned the head cover officially for the first time in her life. I recall when she told me about his request, and I asked her how she felt about it. She said she was happy to do so for her beauty was for him and no one else. I listened but knew deep down she would miss the summers she spent in Egypt swimming in the sea in her bathing suit, going out to cafes with her sisters, and doing her hair. We had made a pact once as girls that one day we would go to Egypt and dance in a night club, but this dream would now not be realized.

The men arrived at the hall with drums playing and the traditional Dabke dancers performing a Levantine folk dance. The line formed from right to left and the leader of the Dabke headed the line, alternating between facing the audience and the other dancers. They were all dressed in very traditional attire, all donning the Palestinian black and white checkered *Ghutra* (Male headdress) wrapped around their heads or placed on their shoulders. The different colors of headdresses for men was a regional thing. The Emiratis, for example, prefer the white Ghutra rather than the thick red and white checked version the Saudis wore. In winter, however, they could be seen in a thicker white cloth. The reason they preferred white is probably because the UAE was hotter and more humid than other places on the peninsula, and the loose white material of the Ghutra was more comfortable in heat and humidity. There are also some tribes throughout the Arab peninsula who wore different colors and patterns of the Ghutra so they can distinguish each other at first sight. The best example would be to compare it to the Scottish Tartan, which Scots wore as kilts. Each Tartan had its own pattern which helped them distinguish which clan you were from right away. The fishnet pattern made famous by Yasser Arafat appears to be quite popular among Yemenis and some Jordanians (perhaps due to the Palestinian connection for the latter), and Saudis descended from those nationalities will tend to wear that pattern.

Most of the men were their cousins, chanting, jumping, twirling, and dancing to celebrate the bride and groom. It was not uncommon to hire a professional dance company for this but with their families having so many able young men, it was not necessary.

After the dance, I watched as they cut the cake and then they called for the buffet to be opened. Men and women would each eat in different halls for the comfort of the women who were covered so they could relax, uncover, and eat without fear of being seen. I did not attend the dinner and instead once everyone had exited the hall, I went to Noor to bid her goodnight. Knowing that since her husband did not like me, I knew it was not likely I should be involved in the family walk as the young couple were escorted to their suite. To save Noor from feeling bad I simply made the excuse that it was very late for me. "We'll talk tomorrow, good luck, Sweety!" She held my hand tightly for a moment that seemed like all the years we had known each other as she said, "Okay, *Hiyate*." I kissed her cheek, turned to her new husband beside her, bowed slightly, lowered my gaze as a sign of respect and said, "Dear-*Balic Aalaiha*," meaning take care of her or look out for her. He nodded in the affirmative and I took my leave of the hall.

Noor loved him so much in those early days. His jealous nature, however, could not stand for a rival to his affections, and he saw that rival in me. I would like to say if he knew that I was the reason her mother was unable to talk her out of the wedding he would love me for refusing to use influence where I felt I had no right to do so. But alas, he was possessive and wanted everyone to keep their distance. She was his property now and that is why he felt he had to get rid of me. He knew that if he wanted complete control, he must isolate her as so many men commonly did. I was an uncontrollable force that he could see she admired and listened to, making me very dangerous to him indeed.

Fear the people who fear the people, who ask you to ask
the right questions of yourself for they are weak-minded and
afraid that their true nature will be revealed.
- Elise Martin

The next few days Noor would be busy, so I took the time to call on an old friend from school, Wajdaan. It was my reaction in choosing Noor over Wajdaan that day at school which gave her much to contemplate. We had kept in touch through text messages over the years and she never insulted Noor in my presence again. I often wondered why I was so important to her, but I suppose talking to me was like looking at a life and a world she would never have. She had married her dreamboat, the cousin she had loved since the moment she set eyes on him. From experience I knew that although unknown to her, her marriage was all planned by the family from their infancy kind of like my betrothal to Fahad but in their case, it was done on the downlow.

I entered her home for the first time. She was always very religious; she never wore an Abaya that displayed her figure. Unlike mine, which started from my shoulders, hers started at the top of her head creating this penguin-like shape so no one could tell what her body shape looked like. When she was in the street, she wore black gloves, closed-toed shoes so no one could admire her feet or see if she was wearing nail polish. She never wore heels outside of an all-women's gathering, wedding or tea, so that the men on the street could not be attracted to the sound of the heels hitting the floor. She never plucked her eyebrows because it was considered that doing so was considered a sin. I recalled how she scolded me for plucking mine in school.

Although they had money she lived simply. They ate on the floor, slept on the floor, and prayed and fasted regularly. As I looked around, I knew I was right to refuse my cousin's marriage proposal all those years ago. This could have been my life. She spoke of the joys of motherhood; how happy she was that she had a boy and a girl. She talked about school and asked about Noor. She raved about how much she loved her husband and towards the end of tea I asked her the one question I had always wanted to ask her. "Are you really happy here? You have no freedom to go anywhere alone. Do you ever dream of going away and walking on a beach as your hair flows in the wind like in the movies?" She smiled and reached for my hand and said, "I am more than happy, I love my home, my children, my culture, my religion, and my husband. I have no dreams of doing or being anything else. Sure, I could have married someone more liberal and done different things but this and he are what I wanted." I realized in that moment something that had never crossed my mind before.

In her mind she chose to follow tradition and have an arranged marriage, she chose to cover, she chose to give up her higher education to be a mother and a dutiful wife to her husband. However, in her case, she had no choice not to cover, not to get married, not to have children, and not to live as she did. The optimal word here is "Choose." If the women of Saudi Arabia wanted to do things differently, they needed to start with choices and those choices need to be their own. Some like Wajdaan will choose to stick to the old ways of the tribes while others may not. But the point is that they need to have the right to choose where their journey will take them.

Perfection is not found in being like everyone or doing what everyone says is right all the time. It is found in finding one's own idea of perfection and working on oneself until one is satisfied. Cut, then polish, then buff, and you will find out what kind of jewel you are. I left her home that day awakened to the idea that maybe there was nothing wrong with me. I was just seeking my own perfection, even if it did not line up with everyone else's idea of perfection. It was mine alone. The problem would be, ever being able to help anyone understand my journey and love me still.

After a few days Noor finally was able to meet me at her parent's house where I would be trying on dresses for my wedding to Firas. I tried on a few colors but knew that Firas would insist I wear white to be as people expected. I understood it was very important to him that he keep a certain reputation and I would now be an extension of that. It was bad enough in his mind the shock everyone he knew was having over the fact that Firas, the man who could have had any virgin in Syria or elsewhere, who waited until 40 to marry because there was always something wrong, would choose to marry a divorced woman. Something he made sure to always remind me of.

I told Noor I was so nervous to go to Syria and get married with no one from my side in attendance, something that was almost unheard of in Arab society. "People will talk and say I disobeyed my family by marrying without consent, and if I disobeyed my family, what does that say about how I will treat my new husband and his family?" She said her mom was meant to be in Jordan around that time so maybe she could convince her husband to let her go along and then convince her mom to visit her aunt who lives in Syria, so that she could be at the wedding. I hugged her tightly saying, "*Inshallah* (God Willing) I hope you can come, Honey, I need you with me."

I returned to Abu Dhabi. Firas had already headed to Syria to prepare for the wedding. Ablah May, at the request of Firas, took me shopping for my wedding and engagement clothes. A whole new wardrobe was in order to turn me into the perfect Syrian bride. Her selections were strange to me. Designs and colors I had never worn before. Since I was covered now all my dresses needed to be at least knee length even if just barely to show modesty. Then we found a rabbit fur wrap that would be perfect to cover the top of my wedding dress since the wedding would be a mixed wedding and I would have to be covered the whole time.

There was one more piece of business that needed to be taken care of before I left for Syria. Although I was Muslim, Firas said it would help us to get married in the Islamic court if I officially take the Shahada. It was a morning like nothing I could possibly describe except perhaps like the day a nun takes her vows. I entered the court in Abu Dhabi and was greeted by a woman. She was fully covered in her black abaya as was I out of respect. She giggled joyfully at the sight of an American converting to Islam officially. She read the Shahada which is like a pledge that there is one God, Allah, and the Prophet Muhammed (ﷺ) is his messenger. Tears swelled up in my eyes. It was a pledge I took seriously committing to embrace the religion I was raised in. She handed me a certificate and I hugged her. Islamically there was no need to have a Shahada made official in this way since you can convert as easily as saying the words out loud, but Firas liked everything nice and tidy. The next day I boarded the plane to Syria and was ready for my next big adventure to start.

Upon landing, Firas was there with the family to greet me. His father carried flowers for me, smiling and boasting about how excited he was to have a daughter. His enthusiastic nature always made me smile inside and outside. We dropped the bags at home and set off to find a ring in the gold market. Stall after stall, store after store Firas kept saying how expensive everything seemed. I told him. "I didn't want a diamond. I find them very common." But for the sake of appearances, he said, "What will people say, if I don't get you a diamond? They will say I'm cheap." So, I suggested, "If that is the case let's get a white gold setting with a cubic zirconia. After all, they imitate diamonds so well these days. Who would know the difference and then later on when we have more money you can just replace the stone." His father was so overjoyed at my care and Firas quietly agreed as we found the perfect ring and band.

We then went on to look for my *Shabka* or my dowry, normally a set of gold jewelry. As we looked for a set of my liking, we came upon a necklace. It was some of the most beautiful craftsmanship I had ever seen. It was tear shaped the size of my hand with diamonds that spelled the word *Allah* in Arabic. As I held it, I knew it was what I was looking for, it spoke to me. Firas commented, "It is meant to be a set. If I just get you a necklace what will people say and if I get you this necklace, I will not be able to afford the rest of the set." I replied "That's fine, I am going to be covered anyway so no one will notice if you didn't get me a set, plus this is big enough so it will show up. I don't think anyone will have anything to say except how rich and generous you must be." My sister in-law then interceded knowing full well help was needed saying, "Oh, yes, it's beautiful, look, it has a clip so you can wear it on pearls as well." Firas smiled in his way and asked the store owner to get it ready to go, I smiled and held back a girlish twirl, knowing Firas would not be happy if I acted like a happy child as he would put it.

I had hoped for a small wedding at home but as is often the case you can't invite one family without inviting another and you can't invite one cousin without inviting all the cousins. People would feel insulted if not invited even if they were going to be out of town. As the guest list grew it was clear that we needed to find a larger venue for the wedding. Firas had his mind set on getting married in the place where so many prominent families in Damascus had married, the Cham Palace Hotel. This hotel was highly sought after due to its very traditional Syrian décor.

Upon our arrival it was discovered that they were booked up for a while due to the season. Firas's face sunk in despair until the salesman offered that we buy-out the restaurant and host the wedding there. Firas's face lit up as he appraised the restaurant asking if there would be a band, handing out instructions as to how the setup should be done and what kind of food was appropriate. I followed along feeling like a waste of space with no say in anything. Suddenly the salesman looked at me and said, "Now the cake; would the bride like chocolate or vanilla?" I was shocked someone was asking my thoughts on something. I said, "Vanilla." Firas jumped in saying, "It must be white on the outside but let's do chocolate, more people will like it." I sunk back and hoped we would finish soon so I could go smoke on the balcony and hide.

That night I had a hard time sleeping since tomorrow we would be off to the courthouse to sign the marriage contract. Firas' family had decided that instead of me staying at a hotel this time since we would soon be married, and his parents were there to chaperon us they didn't fear much gossip. I took over Firas' room while he slept on a mat in the formal sitting room. I woke up early to get ready, putting on my engagement dress Ablah May had picked out for me. Khala Nawal, Firas' stepmother, was kind enough to take a few pictures of me in my dress before we left for the courthouse.

We drove down to the city, found a parking space, and walked the rest of the way. Firas' Dad held my arm, charging along as happy as could be. Firas walked far behind us as if he was trying to slow down his doom. I wondered why he was unhappy, why he was not excited like everyone else? Marriage papers signed, his father and stepmother leaped out of the courthouse with so much joy. Firas was quiet and for some reason his silence made me feel like I had no right to be happy. I placed my hands together and quietly followed my celebrating in-laws as we all went to lunch. Firas' silence continued for most of the day.

After a nap we went out in the evening to coffee shops to meet Firas' friends. This coffee shop in particular was called 1st Cup and in addition to serving coffee, they served dinner and drinks as well. For Firas and his Syrian friends this was their hangout place almost like a bar in the U.S. but with a five-star food menu. Some of his friends drank and some did not. Some came out to talk and some would come to play cards. Either way we would go out every night in order to squeeze in as many of Firas' friends and old classmates as we could when we were in Syria. Even though this trip was so similar to my last, Firas was different. I spent most nights reflecting on words, actions, and cross-comparing them to our last trip here, was it wedding jitters, I wondered.

The next day I decided I would not stand for this cloud of gloom he kept walking around in. While we were having our coffee in the morning and once we were alone, I very calmly popped the question, "Are you okay, you seem sad or unhappy, is it the wedding? Do you want to push it back or cancel?" He sighed and looked down at his feet and said, "Of course I'm happy to be getting married, it's just not as I thought it would be. At my wedding I wanted to show the world my bride as the most beautiful girl in the world and instead, my wife is covered. I'm not saying you're not beautiful in your Hijab, but I just saw it differently." I nodded to express my understanding while at the same time giving him enough space in my silence to freely say whatever else he had on his mind. When he was finished, I added, "If you want me to go without my cover I will but it would be kind of difficult now that everyone has seen me in it. The story that Firas' new wife flip flops between being a true Muslim and not would be a way more juicy a story then Firas' new wife being covered." "The wedding will go forward; everything is already paid for and luckily they all got to see you on the last trip uncovered so hopefully they will remember how beautiful you are." I sat for a bit wondering if there would ever be a moment where pure joy would just wash over him? Would there ever be a moment when I was just the most perfect creature he had the opportunity to behold, or would I always have something wrong with me? Something that needed adjusting to make me perfect, and then something else to make me more perfect.

The wedding day arrived and the men by tradition went to the Turkish bathhouse in the morning, leaving the house for the women to get ready. In the bathhouse they would be scrubbed, shaved, get their hair cut, have a massage, and sit in the steam room congratulating each other on their accomplishments. I took the opportunity to prepare myself for our first night as husband and wife. With the exception of the hair on my head no single hair on my body could remain. I asked *Khala* Nawal if she knew of a place nearby that provided hair removal, but her answer was that she did not since it was not something she had done in years. "When I was young a lady would come to the house to prepare the bride before the wedding," she said. I took on the project myself, starting with the most difficult parts and moving on to everywhere else. Three hours later it was time for a shower and then off to get my hair and makeup done. Noor had arrived a few days before, but the schedule was so packed I had not had the opportunity to see her yet. I asked her to meet me at the hairdresser, but she had to get her hair done as well so we planned to meet at the venue right before the wedding.

My hair was perfect, just as I had wanted it, and my dress hung ever so beautifully against my body. *Khala* Nawal and the hairdressers kept saying how beautiful I was and how happy Firas will be when he sees me. My girlish joy arrived as I giggled with them happily in that moment thinking how happy he will be when he sees me. Once ready I went to his brother's wife's parents home for pictures with Firas. Their home was chosen because it was thought to be more photogenic and larger than Firas' family home. I waited in the formal sitting room until I heard the groom arriving.

In Syria it is very normal for the men to make a big fuss as they escort the groom to the bride's house to pick her up and also when they are both on their way to the hall. This duty would fall to his friends, brothers, cousins, and any other male family members. You can always tell a wedding is going past when you hear a great deal of honking, shouting, cheering, and whistling in the street in Syria. The people in the city cheer for them from the balconies and despite the late hour everyone is happy to see a wedding go by. In the past it was even traditional to fire shots into the air, but it happened too often that a stray bullet would end up somewhere or in someone, so the tradition was abandoned in the city.

Firas was dropped off with all the noise the group could muster. As I heard them, I arose from my chair and stood in a position so as to be seen by him when he opened the door. He walked in laughing from all the attention that had been lavished on him by his friends. Then he closed the door and stood silently. I smiled bashfully and looked down a little as he said, "You look great, *Habiti*." Then turning to the camera woman, he said, "We don't have much time so let's get started." We shot picture after picture. My eyes would be the only place you could see my self-recognition that I wished I had not built up the idea of him being overjoyed to see me. I was happy to be getting married and excited about our future together. I realized I just needed to try and accept him as he was. When we were done with the pictures, I removed my wedding veil and placed on my head cover and rabbit wrap, and we headed out to the cheering mass that would be honking and escorting us to the hall.

The best way to describe this type of *Zaffa* would be like a prince and a princess traveling in a carriage to somewhere while the crowds cheered, and strangers waved. Everyone wanted to see the bride and groom. I even saw a mother lift up her little girl and point at us saying, "There, there is the *Arosa* (Bride)." When we arrived, the cheering continued as we were escorted from the car and into the hall. Then we went to the upper section to take photos once more, this time with family and friends. Firas huffed and puffed that my rabbit fur wrap was covering his new suit in hair, making it a very uncomfortable photoshoot as he tried his best to smile for the photo and then pull away to pick the hairs off his jacket. I tried to help but it was of no use. I had no way of knowing the rabbit fur would shed since I had not worn it before today. I understood how distressing it must be for him to feel like everyone in the world that he knew was going to see him. But somewhere in his distress he forgot that there was a woman beside him who was without her family, had only one friend in a hall filled with strangers and a husband who barely noticed her.

I shook it off and looked forward to seeing Noor. She was the last to take a picture as I embraced her. I whispered in her ear, "I need a cigarette." She smiled and said, "I'm sure you do." Before Firas' and my big entrance to the party, Noor and I snuck off up the stairs and found an empty room where we could smoke. In Syria back then it was permissible to smoke indoors in most places and if it was not allowed you could bribe any worker to pretend they saw nothing. They would have understood the need for discretion, especially for a bride. Since it would be distasteful for a bride to be seen smoking anything except *Shisha* at her wedding table.

"He doesn't like me, Honey, I feel like he still doesn't like me. Why is he marrying me?" "He must like you, Honey, he's marrying you and you said he could have had any girl, but he chose you, so don't worry about it. I bet he's just nervous." I nodded and then changed the subject to a more fun conversation. We talked about a girl in the crowd Firas had been in love with from a far since his school days. I discreetly pointed her out to Noor from the upstairs room that looked over the restaurant. Noor chuckled saying, "Oh my God, Honey, she looks like a man." I tilted my head ever so slightly and gave her a second look. "I never thought about it, honey, but you're right, the big shoulders, her build, and her square strong chin." We had another good giggle and then I was off to make my entrance with Firas.

In a mixed wedding it can be normal for either the bride and groom to enter together or for the bride to enter alone, depending on preference. In this case since the restaurant had no official walkway or throne for the bride and groom we entered together to the drums and the cheering of the crowd, the wedding call being pronounced as often as possible until we reached the middle of the room. Firas held up my hand and everyone cheered. I smiled bashfully looking down and then we were seated. The *meza* (appetizers) started to come out of the kitchen, normally hummus, olives, sour yogurt, all of which are served cold and in the winter months it was more common to serve hot appetizers like green beans in a tomato sauce, spinach pastries, and so on. In Syria it was more common that the meal is served during the wedding unlike in Saudi where the meal is served after the groom arrives since most of the weddings are segregated there and here many of them were mixed.

As I started to remove my white satin gloves, I heard a song I knew so I jumped from my chair to go dance, causing the crowd to cheer for Firas to join. He got up smiling and waving to the crowd as he made his way to the dance floor. Then after dancing a few steps, he whispered to me, "You should sit down, you will get overheated." "I'm fine." "No, you're face. It's getting red. Come sit down, we can dance later." I bowed my head, shrugged my shoulders, and took his arm as we smiled our way back to the table. We had conversation after conversation with so many people about everything. Where we would live, where we were going on our honeymoon, if I was going to work, all of which decisions had been made without me as I sat in silence trying not to embarrass Firas any further.

After a little while the cake arrived with sparklers. We sliced it with a traditional sword, and everyone was happy. We danced a few dances and made the rounds to say hello to everyone and then I discreetly stole Noor away for another cigarette. We talked about her marriage. Still a newlywed herself, she felt as though he was overly jealous, suspicious, and controlling but then as she said this, she also corrected herself saying, "But it's because he loves me so much, Honey." I nodded as I always did and told her, "If you ever feel afraid or need anything you let me know, Honey. If you're happy, I'm happy, and that is all that matters." She gripped my hand and said, "Don't worry about Firas, he will come around, he's a good man you're lucky, you'll see." I looked down, knowing that she was right. He was a match any mother would have wanted for her daughter. Accomplished, successful, good looking, and there would be a lot of travel, what could I possibly have to be sad about?

I returned to the wedding, we finished dinner, and then headed for home. I went into the room and changed into my wedding night gown. Then, putting on my robe, so that I could join the family on the balcony for some late-night tea. His father and stepmother finished their glasses and promptly excused themselves to leave us alone, giggling as they left. I stared at him all starry-eyed as we smoked and recapped the wedding. Then he got up, so I arose to follow him. As we entered the house he walked me to his room, cleared his throat, kissed me on the cheek and said, "Goodnight, *Habiti*." Puzzled, I said, "Aren't you sleeping in here?" "I'm so tired I think I will just sleep in the other room." I nodded and shut the door. I sat up most of the night wondering what was wrong with me. Was I so ugly he didn't even want to be in the same bedroom as me? The next day his father made eggs for breakfast and funnily poked newlywed jokes as I tried not to show that anything was wrong so as not to upset anyone.

A few days passed and invitations came from all over inviting us to lunch and dinner. It is considered a great honor not to mention good luck to host a bride and groom soon after their wedding. Every evening when it was time for bed Firas would wait for everyone to go to sleep and then head to his bed in the other room. We were set to leave for a few days in Lebanon for our honeymoon. One morning over coffee as I sat smoking on the balcony *Khala* Nawal came out pretending she wanted to talk about neighborhood gossip and then slyly sending Firas to get her a glass of water. As soon as he was out of sight, she whipped her head around saying, "Why is he sleeping in the other room? Are you on your period? Is he mad? What's wrong?" I shrugged my shoulders saying, "I don't know. He said he wants to sleep in the other room." She half squinted her eyes and said, "Let me see about this." I nodded, and she was gone.

That evening, Firas' dad having been informed of what was going on by *Khala* Nawal, waited for Firas until he said he was tired and then asked him why he was not sleeping in the same room as his wife. I exited the room since such conversation would normally not take place in front of women. I listened at the door crack with Khala Nawal as excuse after excuse arrived. "It's more comfortable in the other room, it's cooler at night, I get hot," he said. His father then pointed out that he slept in that room his whole childhood and every single time he came to visit but this time he would not? Firas agreed to sleep in the room with me and marched to the door. As he entered and closed the door, he took the opposite bed saying, "Goodnight, Habiti." I looked over and asked, "What is wrong?" to which he replied, "Nothing. I just don't want to have sex in the same bed I slept in as a child and not with my parents next door." I nodded and wished him sweet dreams.

The next day we were off to Lebanon. He took me around to see all the sights and eat in a famous restaurant on the beach but all the while he seemed far away, distant, and unhappy. I asked again, "What's wrong?" "It's just when I am on this side of the world, I like to spend all my time in Syria with my family and friends. I don't see them very often and I feel like I'm losing time with them." "Then let's go back," I said. "No, we can't, it's expected that we honeymoon. I don't want people saying I didn't take you on a honeymoon, it will be fine." I sighed and let it go, trying to enjoy Lebanon despite Firas being so unhappy. I tried to convince him to take me to one of the famous night life places for some dancing, but he was tired, so we just went to bed. It was a slow honeymoon, and we went to all the sights so we could get the traditional collection of pictures proving our happiness.

He was finally convinced to consummate the marriage but in the time it took to convince him, it felt like an uneventful occurrence. An obligation and a burden more than love. Once we decided to head back to Syria it was a relief to see him smiling again. His family welcomed us back and now that it was the one-week anniversary of our wedding his brother hosted a dinner at his home in our honor. As a surprise they got me a little veil and had me enter the room to dance. Firas for some reason did not like me to dance, it was almost like it embarrassed him. His family cheered me on. I felt so underfoot as if every time I smiled it made him uncomfortable and fighting my happy nature was bringing me down.

My wife training took over and I smiled and tried to be as pleasing and conformed as possible. Never having a thought of my own, I smiled, nodded, agreed, and went along with whatever my husband thought was best. Always displaying a happy honest display so that no one would have reason to think that we were anything but the most happy of couples. Only his dad seemed to enjoy my giggly, girly ways. Always making me coffee while sitting with me when I went out to the balcony, telling me Firas' childhood stories, reciting poetry, and smiling as I laughed out loud, something I tried not to do too often around Firas since he liked me composed at all times.

I sipped my tea and thought the truth was when I looked around, I was happy in a way. I reminded myself that I was lucky, my husband had a good job, I was not expected to work, we would travel, my in-laws were amazing unlike Noor's mother in-law who reorganized Noor's entire kitchen to make her a more efficient cook. This was very common and like so many girls it's never a good idea to say anything but thank you to your mother-in-law. After all, she could make your life a living hell, bending and dealing was always safer.

If you wonder why, I will re-mention the fact that in Arab society and Islam, Heaven is found at your mother's feet. If she was upset with her daughter-in-law, she would tell your husband she was displeased and then he would make you listen to her. Sometimes by force, sometimes by a conversation, but in the end, she will win every time. You might think the man weak but when we look at it from a new pair of eyes, we don't blame a Catholic for fearing the fires of Hell, and this is just that. If heaven sits at the feet of the mother, then if she is displeased, she might ask God to deny you entry into Heaven and no one wanted that.

I thought of all my friends, their marriages, the ones who never got more than one marriage proposal because they weren't from a prestigious family, weren't as pretty, and didn't have as many opportunities as I did. I got to travel alone, I got to go out and really see life, parties, I got to fall in love, I got to dance before I married Firas. A million girls would have killed for my life. My husband didn't beat me, left me alone most of the time, allowed me to continue my bachelor's coursework and therefore I decided I had no right to be sad but rather just to be happy where I was. My life was just as it should be, and I would do my best to be the wife he wanted. A small smile came over me as I put my tea glass down as I nodded pretending, I had heard everything they discussed in the last ten minutes.

We returned to Abu Dhabi where I collected all my things from the room I'd rented at the family's house and moved into Firas' house. Everything I had with me fit into two suitcases as it had when I left Canada, so moving was simple for me. When I arrived, I took some time to unpack and made a cup of coffee while Firas went straight to work. When I was done unpacking, I went for my very first grocery shopping trip as Firas' wife. Taking my time on every aisle, loving the way my ring sparkled as the lights shown down on it. I was excited, tonight I would cook our first dinner since we got married. I knew he liked fish and despite never having cooked fish well before, I was determined to do it this time.

As I picked up the fish my aunt's voice rang in my head. As I looked at the fish, I heard her say, "When serving your husband, never test out a recipe you have not tested before. Always serve him something you know." I nodded to my own memory and put the fish down and headed to the beef section. I decided it had been a long day. I would just make him a simple chili; I was good at chili. In Saudi we always served it with rice, well to be honest in Saudi we served mostly everything with rice.

I got home, put everything away and got straight to work cooking dinner. I put it on a low heat to stay warm, leaving enough time to shower, wash the food smell out of my hair, get dressed. and apply my makeup. Two aprons are normally kept on hand, one you cook in and one you wear when your husband gets home. or your guests arrive, and you serve. This way everything is perfect, always. It is the illusion that you cooked the entire meal and never spilled a drop. The table was set, the candles were lit, the food was ready, everything was timed to perfection. I sat down on the sofa to have a cigarette as I watched from the window for the car, excited to show him my awesome wife skills.

Sitting in front of the TV happy and smiling. Six o'clock turned to seven and seven turned to eight. I didn't want to call and bother him if he was busy. Finally. a ring came on my phone. "*Alo*? (Hello in Arabic)" "So sorry, Habiti, but we have some stuff that needs to be finished here. Please don't wait for me, I'll just have the driver pick me up a sandwich and see you when I get home." My heart sank but I responded as I should. After all it was my duty to support his career and there would be other nights. "Of course, Habebe, I'll see you when you get home." I went to the bathroom, washed my face, changed out of my sexy lingerie and not feeling hungry, I sat for a little bit watching TV and went off to bed. When he got home, he showered, changed, and climbed into bed. He put his arms around me and said, "Hello, Habiti," as he kissed me all over my face with the exception of my lips. Just like that, all was forgotten.

The next day I woke up at 5:00 a.m. for the morning prayer and prepared his coffee before he left for work. He kissed me on my cheek as he left for work, and I returned to bed. At around 10:00 a.m. Ablah May called to say she and Doctora Zaynia wanted to swing by for tea to congratulate me on my marriage. I was delighted to have them as my first guests. They were so happy to see me and I them. They asked how I was doing and if I was settled. All the normal questions on that side of the world. I would expect many such visits just like in Christianity when you visit the sick, you also pay calls on the newlyweds.

Ablah May asked me if I had everything I needed for the kitchen to which I replied that I needed to buy a few things but other than that I thought I was fine. Ablah May, in all her motherly nature replied, "You must have a proper dish set for entertaining and nice pots and pans for cooking. Make sure he knows he must spend money on the good kind. It will make all the difference." I took a deep breath and said, "Ablah May, I don't think Firas has the money for that and I can get by on what I have," not wanting to mention my ring, knowing it would conjure fire from her eyes if she knew I gave in. "I don't need anything fancy, Ablah

May." "No, Habiba, you're starting off all wrong. You must fight for what is due to you and not settle for less. If you let him be cheap now, he will continue this way for the rest of your marriage." I nodded, thinking what she didn't know would not hurt her. After the whole wedding ring back and forth in Syria, I didn't feel like serving dishes or pans were as important and after all I wanted to make my husband happy and avoiding the subject of money was a big part of that. I took what he gave me for shopping and personal items. Beyond that I stayed away from the topic of money since it was not considered a woman's place and on top of that, Firas was very touchy about the subject, since he was raised with a mentality that women always waste money. Ablah May mentioned, "Our group wants to throw you a small wedding party since they missed the wedding, in a week's time." I was delighted and excited to dance in my dress without my head cover since it would be an all-ladies party.

When Firas came home, I served him the dinner I had made the night before. He ate it quietly and when I mentioned the party he simply replied, "Whatever you want, Habiti." "I pressed my hands together under the table to contain my excitement as I smiled, then came the boom, "What is this we're eating?" "Chili. Do you not like chili?" "No, I like chili, but I would prefer some Syrian food, ask Ablah may to get you a book, or call *Khala* Nawal and Baba. They can teach you a few simple recipes until you learn." I nodded and gazed at my plate. I felt like a failure then I shook my head and said to myself, "No, I'll prove I can cook Syrian food yet, he will see."

The next day I remembered that our neighbor in the compound growing up was Syrian and she taught me how to make a dish called *Bamia* (okra in a tomato sauce served over a bed of rice). I made a trip to the grocery store to get the ingredients. I cooked it just as I was taught while adding my own flare to it, it tasted great. Firas got home a little late, but I still served him dinner. I was hanging on the edge of my seat as he took bite after bite, I leaned in smiling, "How is it?" he chewed and said, "Better, but I still think you should call my dad or ask Ablah May for help. This is not done the way we do it in Damascus. They can give you some tips. Did you change it somehow?" I shuddered. Should

I tell him the slight changes I made, was that wrong, I thought? "Well, I added some more bouillon. I thought it gave it more flavor." "That's okay, you'll learn soon." He was always so calm, calculated, and collected, making him hard to read at times. Was he disappointed or just indifferent? It was so important to him that his house be Syrian and every inch of me that was ever American was to be done away with like stomping out a virus that has infected its host. Anything that made me less Syrian had to go.

The days went on as such. I kept up the house and waited patiently for him to get home. The weekend came. When we woke up, I asked if he would like to go out, maybe get lunch in a restaurant or dinner. His answer was always that if he moved the car, it would be hard to find a parking space. I sighed and sat on the couch next to him. "Well maybe we could watch a movie?" The news was on. He pointed at the screen and asked if I knew who was the president of South Africa? I answered "No." He started explaining what was going on in South Africa, who the president was, and why it was important for me to know. I listened and nodded knowing he meant that if we had an event, I would be expected to know such things.

In Saudi growing up, women only associated with other women. They sipped tea and talked about marriages, children, cooking, personal grooming, the latest fashions, and the latest gossip but in his world, it was more open. The endless balls, embassy events, dinners with royalty and all sorts of networking would soon be all the outings we would go to together unless we were in Syria where all his family and friends were. Thus was his life: to build his career. Watching the news all weekend was part of that. The weekends turned into my least favorite time of the week. At first, I was so excited to see him but soon I just felt like the house was more peaceful when he wasn't there. We only had one TV and so when he was home, I just tried to concentrate on my schoolwork and sit with him so he could teach me things I needed to know. I told myself that when he called me over to watch the news with him so he could explain something. It was his way of saying he missed me. But mostly I just felt like an ornament most of the time. There to get him more tea and clean up when he was finished with something.

When he wanted to have sex, he would just stand up from the couch and say, "Let's have sex." and then proceed to the bedroom. Like a drill sergeant giving an order for me to march. I knew that meant to follow him. It felt so impersonal like it was just something we did when he was in the mood. I couldn't for the life of me figure out what on the news turned him on, but I knew for sure it wasn't me. Every attempt I made to dress up, wait for him or put on something I thought would be sexy was ignored. He was too tired, or my dress wasn't to his liking, but I kept trying. I would figure it out eventually, I thought.

The day of the party arrived; I got my hair done. I was so excited to dance and laugh. I donned my wedding dress and said, "I'm ready" He said, "I'll drive you," as he arose from his seat, I pointed out that he might want to dress up since they are planning to bring him in so they can celebrate the both of us. He shook his head and said, "No, I don't want to be there, it's a woman's party." I didn't know what to say. "But, Doctora Zaynia's husband will keep you company." "No, just call me when you're done, and I'll come get you." I nodded and went to the party. When I arrived Ablah May asked, "Where is the groom?" I replied with a "He had some work to do so he is going back home." Ablah May, not wanting to make a sad bride sadder at her own party, just smiled and said, "Well we will have a great time without him, then."

It was a great party; no music was employed since music among conservatives is considered the devil's work (actually pretty much all Muslims agree music is the devil's work but not everyone goes as far as refusing to listen) since it is thought to lull you into a kind of trance. Just like the story of the Pied Piper; how he led the mice and later the children with his song. Certain instruments are approved though, like the handheld drum called a *darbuka*, often used at weddings, and songs could be sung. The voice as an instrument is allowed. You can find many beautiful plainchant Islamic songs that despite the lack of music are exquisite in their own right.

One might ask how they could live without music, but you just do. Just as some live without TV, movie theaters, Western food, shelter, and all sorts of modern conveniences, and yet they are happier than most people you see in the United States chasing fancy cars, the next season of Game of Thrones, that new house that is going to make them perfectly happy for a day, a week, a month, and then they move on to the next thing that might make them happy. For the Arabs I have found that it is the people that make their own lives so joyful. The community that comforts, consoles, offers help, shares the meal they made just today for no reason other than to just be together.

In Syria if you go out alone it's not uncommon to meet a stranger at a coffee shop and sit down for coffee, be invited to their home for dinner and suddenly become lifelong friends. If you go out on a boat, it is customary to wave to the people in the other boats as you pass. This is done even though you don't know them and might never know them but tribal traditions like being on a boat in a large body of water means that one day you might need a friend to save you if your boat tips over. Likewise, your neighbor might save your life one day. It is built into us, and I have to admit there is a kind of peace in knowing that a community is there for you. The same kind of security people find in going to church and being a part of that community. The same thing you feel when you know your mother or father is a phone call away. This was my community and even though I still listened to music, missed some of my prayers at times and smoked secretly, I respected their choices and loved them all so immensely. The sad part is the day you choose to no longer conform, you will lose it all in the blink of an eye and I was mentally halfway down this path, but I dared not show it.

It was at this party that the realization came to me that despite all my girlish notions about having a partner who would really love me and share a life with me, a best friend, a confidante, and lover, that was not what I had with Firas. My aunt was right all those years ago. I would need to resign myself to having two lives. One where I would see my lady friends where I got to be myself (at least part of myself) and another life where I was a proper diplomat's wife. Cooking the food he liked when he was home and eating the foods I liked when he traveled.

It may sound sad to someone who only lived in a world where true love prevailed above tradition. A world where passion and connection are tested before marriage. But here in the world I grew up in it was all too common for marriage to be this way. Surprisingly most girls were perfectly happy with the status quo. Firas would not involve himself in women matters and in turn I would never ask about the business of men. I enjoyed the party. Firas drove me home with a smile, asking if I had a good time. I nodded and smiled. When we reached home, I went straight to change and to bed.

The next morning, I awoke as normal to make sure Firas got his coffee. Once I saw him off to work with a smile, I closed the door. I silently walked slowly to the bedroom, where my wedding dress had been hanging in the closet. I looked at it. I felt a sense of leaving my fantasies behind. It was time to embrace the role of a good Arab wife as it had been done for centuries. I gently picked up the wedding dress, walked outside the apartment door and pushed it politely into the garbage shoot. Returning to the apartment, I poured myself a cup of coffee and lit a cigarette. It felt like the scene of a movie when the woman is just done and sets the whole house on fire while she sat outside smoking and watching it burn.

The months passed. My cooking was well on the way to better I hoped. I knew I had been out of practice since I left Ata, but I did my best to make sure I did things right. I spent my days working on my college courses and deciding what I should prepare for dinner, then going shopping for the ingredients. I found grocery shopping alone peaceful, a kind of meditation. I would visit each aisle even if I didn't need anything from it. Just slowly strolling from aisle to aisle like a Stepford wife, saying hello to women as they passed. In the Middle East when we stepped out of our homes, we were taught to always look our best. You never know who you might run into and with Firas' status I would never want to risk any gossip placed on me for looking frumpy even if it was only a grocery store trip.

My group of roommates fell off like flies who had tasted bug spray, because even though I covered again, I still wore tight clothing and mid-length skirts. To them, cutting me off from their friendship was a way of asking me to think my choices through and eventually when I returned to dressing properly, they would welcome me back with open arms. That day would never come. In all my time between the wedding and my new life as Firas' wife, I forgot someone. Fatima, the receptionist at the office in Abu Dhabi. Visiting the office was different now that I was the wife of a high ranking official. I tried not to go too often since Firas did not want me in the office where he worked. How would it look, he would say, if my wife is visiting me all the time at work? I passed by that day to see everyone, to say hi to everyone. I was lonely and wanted a glimpse of what my life was and could have been. I had enjoyed the hustle and bustle of the office. Reading the refugee letters and helping answer the questions asked by those refugees who came by the office. When I arrived, Salem came out of his office and said, "Oh, Miss Elise, it is good to see you." I smiled and asked if Ablah May was busy. "No, no, she is just in her office, go in." I went in and she was on the telephone, I sat and waited for her to finish. "Allooo Aroosa! How is married life, Habiba?" "It's good, how are you? Is there anything I can help with?" "Not at all, you just take care of your house and your husband." I nodded as she said, "Did you hear the good news?" I tilted my head back slightly signaling, "Tell me." She said, "Our Fatima is getting married! Didn't Firas tell you?" "I half smiled and said, "Where is she? I must congratulate her."

Ablah May called Fatima to come in her office. She came in timidly clasping her hands together in front of her. When she saw me, I got up from the chair and took her hands in mine. "*Alf Mabrouk* (A thousand congratulations) my dear! When did this happen?" She said, "Just last week." I took her hand to see her engagement ring and said, "How wonderful! You must tell me all about him!" "He's Syrian, from Halab, and he has a Canadian passport." For a moment I wondered if it was Ata. I smiled and said, "And how did he hear about you?" "Oh, his father and my father are friends. I'm so nervous, I don't know him. The wedding is in a month and then we're moving to Canada right away! Didn't you marry a Canadian once? Could you tell me about it?" "Of course." Putting my arm around her shoulders I walked with her into the courtyard so we could talk out of ear shot of everyone, especially if Firas should come downstairs. He would have hated I was there but if he knew I was talking about my ex-husband I would be in big trouble.

"Tell me what you're nervous about Fatima, really?" "I don't know anything and I'm going to move far away from my family, I'm scared."

"It's not easy. I moved to Canada when I was younger than you and it's a big adjustment but I'm sure if your father chose him, he's a good man." "He is very handsome," she said as she giggled and showed me his photo. "I want to ask you because I can't ask anyone else." "What is it?" "Will it hurt?" "I, unlike the generation that raised us, will tell you, yes, it does hurt, but only for a little while, then it can be really nice. Just ask him to go slow and everything will be okay." She looked down at the ground and nodded her head. "Will you come to my wedding; I don't think I can do this without you." I held her hand. "Of course, I'll be there, don't you worry and if you need anything before that you just ask." I hugged her and headed back to Ablah May's office. "*Yella* (can mean hurry up, let's go, I'm in a hurry and so many other things depending on its employment and the context) I am going home." Ablah May stood up and said, "Don't you want to see Firas?" I looked at her, leaned in and whispered, "He doesn't like it when I come here." "Nonsense! I know he loves you." "I'm sure, Ablah May, but I shouldn't bother him, I'll see him at home."

That night over dinner Firas asked me what I was studying so I talked about my latest Psychology course that I was really excited about until he interrupted and said, "You should be studying Communications, not Psychology." I paused and mentioned that my stepdad had said the same, my stepdad having mentioned once that I would have been well suited to be a TV news anchor, but I loved psychology. He pressed the issue until I agreed I would look into it. The next day I looked at the courses that were required for a communications degree. A few sounded boring but it would not stop me from taking the psychology courses I wanted so I wrote to the school to change my major from Psychology to Communications. When I told Firas that night he was overjoyed. I liked seeing him happy.

The next morning as I went to work on my schoolwork, I felt drained. Almost like I felt there was no point in getting the degree anymore. I caught my reflection in the mirror and asked myself again if I really wanted to go into communications? I felt a strain on my soul, the kind that makes you want to cry. I had left high school not thinking I would want to go to college, and it was the love of psychology that I found from watching videos of a psychology professor at MIT that made me feel passionate enough to go back to school and get my degree. I liked studying when what I was actually studying was what I loved. I called Noor and used her as a sounding board for my thoughts. She agreed with Firas and my stepdad that maybe communications was a better route since it might offer a better job prospect in the future. "After all, *Hiyate*, in America they might have psychologists but here we don't go to them unless you're really crazy," she said. I knew she had a point. You see in the West it's normal to have a therapist but here in the Middle East that role is played by a person's family, friends, neighbors, religious leaders, and so on. In essence the community is the therapist since so much is considered improper to discuss outside the family, especially to a stranger. Marriage problems, sex problems, addiction, feelings, everything. It was also considered embarrassing to see a therapist, almost like admitting you had major problems, and no one wanted that kind of gossip attached to them or their family. For example, you go to see a therapist because of grief, simple enough, but word flies on the wind that someone saw you and the gossip mill starts that you might be insane. If you're insane suddenly your entire bloodline is called into question. A man, for example, planning to marry your cousin who heard you were seeing a therapist might wonder if she will go insane or if his children will be insane and eventually he would call off the wedding in search of a more pure bloodline.... Everything is hushed up because when you have a population of women with nothing to do they fill their days living vicariously through the rumors, stories, gossip, and suspicion. Good news cannot sustain a bored mind; they must dig for bones.

I hung up the phone and sat down on my kitchen floor for a moment. Then I sprung up, pulled out my laptop and emailed my school again asking them to change my major back to Psychology. No matter what anyone said I wanted to get my BA in Psychology. I would worry about a job later. I decided if you're not enjoying what you're doing right now then why are you doing it? I would not spend four years getting a B.A. in a field I was not passionate about.

When Firas got home, I told him I switched it back saying, "Communications really wasn't for me." He shook his head and said,

"Well, you will see, I tried to tell you but if you want to get a degree in Psychology you go ahead." For me it felt like a big victory to be able to choose what I studied. So many girls I knew had their degrees chosen for them by their parents or husbands. It was common to hear mothers talk at tea about how their son or daughter is going to be a doctor, a lawyer, or engineer. These were degrees to be proud of, not someone studying Psychology. I knew how very blessed I was to be able to decide even if everyone thought I was wasting my time studying something that fit nowhere to them.

The night of Fatima's wedding arrived. Firas dropped me off and said he would be back to pick me up when I was done. The groom's family decided that it was not necessary to rent a hall for the men since they didn't know many people in Abu Dhabi, so the wedding was for ladies only. They could not afford a DJ so one of her relatives brought a CD player from their house so they could play some music. The hall was bare, and the guests were few. There were no flowers, no sweets on the tables, no tea being served, and everyone was dressed as if they were going to a ladies' gathering not a Middle Eastern wedding. Tea dresses instead of formal gowns. As I walked around waiting for Fatima to arrive, every mother I met asked if I had a sister, a question that meant I like you, but you're married so is there another one I can get for my son? My favorite answer was no, to end the conversation but Ablah May would surely call me out since she was there so I said, "Yes, but their father will want them to marry Saudis and they are in America now." With that, the women moved on to other potential prospects.

Fatima walked to her *Kosha*, solemn and sad. She didn't look like a bride on the verge of wedded bliss but rather like someone who was attending her execution. Fatima's dress was red, one of her favorite colors. As I mentioned before it is still not uncommon for women to marry in any color dress they fancy although the trend has turned towards white in recent years. Fatima actually wanted to be married in white, she said, but the red dress was cheaper. The music played as she sat and yet no one was dancing. I waited until everyone had finished greeting her and headed up to see if she was alright.

"Are you okay? Can I get you some water?" "Oh, you're a guest, you shouldn't do that!" "Nonsense, I'll be right back." I brought her a glass of water and sat beside her on the stage for a moment. The music was loud enough so no one could hear us as I said, "What's wrong?" "I don't want to get married; I don't want to go to Canada and leave my family." "What happened? Is he mean?" "He's very cold and jealous; Hariri from the office called me when he was visiting me and my family. It was about a refugee file he could not find. I didn't pick up but when he saw his name he was upset and told me I should never take calls from other men. I'm afraid it's all been a mistake, but my family thinks it's a great match."

I wanted to tell her come and let's ditch this wedding, but I dared not. There was no getting out of it now, she was married. Her family would not permit her to change her mind before the wedding so surely, they would not permit her to get out of it now. She was being married to him not just for her own good but for the good of the family. She would become Canadian and so her children would have a better life in Canada. I wanted to tell her that great matches on paper do not always make good matches in real life, I wanted to tell her about me and Firas, but it was already too late. I said, "Don't you worry, I'm sure it will be fine. Just know that you can call me from Canada, day, or night, and I'll answer. Listen to me, I'm not just saying that I mean it." Her eyes met mine and I felt as though I could see her aching, scared heart through them. Standing up I held out my hand and said, "This is your wedding, we can't have you sad on your wedding day. Let's show these old ladies how to dance!" With that we opened up the dance floor and she started to smile. The groom arrived and I hugged her as I was leaving. I whispered in her ear, "Call me, if you need me." She smiled and I turned to her husband and said to him while bowing my head and not making eye contact, "Congratulations" He only nodded, and I left to go home.

I got into the car and Firas said, "How was the wedding?" "It was sad, she's scared to go to a new country with a man she doesn't know." "She's a silly girl and should be grateful that she made such a good match. He has a foreign passport and now she will be Canadian. She is lucky she should be happy." I nodded and said nothing else. I knew he could never understand. He was an Arab man who didn't know what it was like to be an Arab woman. What it was like to marry and have sex with a man who was a complete stranger to you, to leave everything you know behind for only the hope that it would all work out. I did.

Summer came around and we took another trip to Syria to visit Firas' family. Every vacation was always to Syria, that is the way it would be, but I enjoyed seeing them.

The next day I woke up with the strangest rash I had ever seen covering my whole body. I showed it to Firas and told him, "It must be allergies, I have so many allergies to dust, pollen, fur, and my brother is allergic to cat antigens. Maybe I should see a doctor." Firas rushed me with his father and stepmother to the best hospital in Syria where we were shown to the doctor's office. The doctor was tall, skinny, and his glasses were thick enough to be used as a microscope. He asked me some questions and I told him what I was allergic to. He then placed his hands in his pockets and took two turns around the room before saying, "Yes, the answer is simple. It's allergies." He handed me a paper filled with things I should stop eating. "This will fix it," he said and then administered an injection of antihistamine, it made me almost faint. They took me home and I slept for a while until I awoke to find the rash was worse. I panicked wondering what it could be. I wasn't sick very often but just like the time I cut my leg by accident in the bathroom as a child and could not stop the bleeding of a cut no bigger than a pinhead I was sure it was my end.

Firas' dad suggested he take me to the local doctor down the way. It was late at night by then. As we walked down the streets, I saw the tall new buildings of the city drop away to reveal a poorer side of Syria. The houses were old, and many were in grave disrepair including missing roofs. There was a great lack of sanitation, and the dogs and cats took over every garbage bin in sight. We walked up to a small villa that had no door. The floor was dirty and the smell of urine on the street was apparent. The doctor was a short, elderly man who looked at my rash and within a few minutes said, "Yes, I've seen this before." Firas said, "Doctor, what is it?" "Well, you say your wife is American, well this is an American disease." I cringed as he continued, "Her blood is too sweet.

The mosquitos seem to have taken a liking to her." He laughed and said, "Just close the window when she sleeps at night, they will go away." I felt so relieved as Firas thanked him, paid him and we left. I recall marveling at how in my mind the doctor in a big fancy hospital must be the best since he is employed there but in fact the best doctor in the area spent his days treating people who could barely pay, who traded for treatment. The doctor in the big hospital seemed snobbish and superior in a way and the doctor in the villa seemed joyful and human. He was everything a doctor really should be; he cared more about healing than making money.

Two days before we were set to leave Syria, Noor sent me a text with two pictures of her harshly bruised leg and neck, telling me to not reply without the password. A system we had put in place years ago. I looked over the pictures and felt enraged! I pulled up flight schedules to fly to Riyadh to teach him a lesson. Firas entered the room and said, "What are you looking at?" "I'm looking at flights to Riyadh, Noor's husband beat her! Look, he broke a table on her." Issuing my usual Saudi expression, "*Ha Gatta Rasoo* (I'll cut his head off)" Firas laughed and said, "You will do no such thing and go on no such trip. You're my wife and she needs to deal with her own marriage, and we have no right to interfere." I scowled at him as he issued the line "Who knows, maybe she deserved it."

He left the room as my phone rang; it was Noor. I said, "Honey, are you okay?" "Yes, I'm fine. Just keep the pictures I had to delete them from my phone in case he finds them." "I'm checking flights I'll come and beat him; no one has the right to hurt you." "No, Honey, that would be dangerous; just stay with your husband. I'll go to my family's house for a while and maybe that will teach him a lesson." "No, Honey, it won't, it will change nothing. Tell me more about your life, is he even working?" "No, Honey, I swear it's so hard to call you because he sits on the couch all day and any money I make from doing makeup for brides, he takes. To call you I had to wait until he went out with his friends. I don't know what to do." "Honey, okay, listen to me. If you don't make enough money, he will have to go back to work. Here is what you do. Next time you go on a makeup job you take half and hide it and give him half, this way he is not suspicious but still he does not have enough to sit around. Then you buy yourself another emergency phone with a prepaid SIM card and hide it somewhere with the money. This way you have enough money to get out if you need it one day and an extra phone if he takes yours for fear you will call someone like your brother or family to come help you. *Gaadah*, my friend, wished she had done this during her first marriage but alas she had no way of anticipating how badly her new husband would treat her." "Okay, Honey, I'll do that."

We hung up the phone and I knew she would never follow through with the plan I had laid out for her safety. She would need to first overcome something a lot harder to overcome and that was years and years of being told to submit to the man of the household. It is like a house arrest ankle bracelet that was attached to your conscience. Every time you move an inch from its specified perimeter, you would feel the beep and feel compelled to return. Noor, like many, would suffer from battered woman syndrome and fall into an endless cycle of beatings followed by elaborate apologies that make them unconsciously place less thought on the past beatings instead of seeing the pattern they take the apology and try again and again and again until one day, we find that there is nothing left of the once vibrant, willful girl who had inhabited her body. My only wish for Noor now was the hope that she would not have children and eventually leave him and ask for a divorce.

We finally returned to Abu Dhabi. I tried to be the most perfect wife my aunt could have ever imagined. The nights of getting all dolled up and waiting on the sofa grew tiring so I tried to find other ways to fill my time. Volunteer work with Ablah May was a great distraction and every time she would ask how marriage was going, I would reply, "He doesn't seem to like me." She would laugh and say, "He was single for a long time, if he didn't like you, he wouldn't have married you." I would nod silently and continue whatever it was I was doing. He cared about me that much, I always saw. Like a knight, he was always there when I needed him. If I was sick, he would drop everything to make sure I was alright, but when it came to matters of the heart and sexual compatibility, that we did not have. It was not so much the sex I wanted but for him to look at me with desire once in a while, notice a new dress, lie, and say my cooking was great even if it wasn't Syrian, cuddle with me now and then. But like many wives not all things come right away so I would be patient.

Our lease was almost up in Abu Dhabi and with the shortage of apartments and the crowding the prices kept going up. We discussed moving to Dubai. It was only about two hours away, so not too bad a drive and even with the gas calculation we would still save money, plus we would have a much nicer place, so we went apartment hunting in Dubai. After the recession many apartment buildings were abandoned. Expats who lost their jobs even left their cars at the airport knowing there would be no way for the car companies to come after them to pay the remainder of the debt on the car if they were in another country.

We saw many apartments and I knew my role as a good bargainer. I was not to look excited if I liked a place but rather, I would provide a slight look to let Firas know I really liked a place. We finally looked at a place that looked over the Marina and I knew it was the one. I could barely hold back my excitement. It wasn't big but it was a good size one bedroom with a bathtub that was big enough for a queen, marble floors, a good size kitchen and twenty-four-hour security along with a panic button inside the apartment if I should ever feel in danger.

Firas negotiated the deal, and it was settled. We would move in a month. I was excited to move to Dubai, the restaurants, the malls, the Marina, the beaches but most of all it would be nice to live somewhere where less people knew me, I was so well known in Abu Dhabi I could barely go anywhere without being recognized as the protégé of Doctora Zaynia and Ablah May. I loved them but freedom was at hand, and I could not wait. We moved to Dubai and Firas would leave every morning for work. I enjoyed taking walks on the Marina, visiting the Mall, shopping, and cooking for Firas upon his return home from work.

I was alone a lot more, but it was really nice and peaceful. No stress, no rushing, everything I did flowed like a slow piano piece easily, planned, and timed to perfection. For Firas everything was last minute, he was always in a state of panic which put me on edge. I had all the washing and dry cleaning picked up and delivered including the sheets which were always pressed by the two maids that arrived twice a week.

One would clean and iron while the other would help me chop and prepare all the vegetables for freezing so all the cooking went faster without the prep work. I stopped waiting and wondering when Firas would be home and instead settled in, enjoying the calmness I found in Dubai.

Firas said he needed to go on a trip for work for a week and so I asked if I could fly down to Saudi to see Noor, to which he agreed. I packed and he took me to the airport. I was excited to see my friend again. We never talked as well as we did when we were together. The reason being that in Saudi all communications are monitored greatly so many topics are off the table unless you're in person. And if the government wasn't listening there was a big chance someone else like her husband was. Even today, the *Whatsapp* app call feature is blocked in Saudi Arabia, so every voice message I sent her had to be recorded.

When I passed through the airport in Dubai, I saw a set of liquor chocolates and thought why not? We could try it together. Bringing alcohol into Saudi is dangerous. It is one of the worst crimes to commit but since the chocolates were not shaped like liquor bottles, they might make it through the scanners. I called my stepdad to see what he thought, and he said, "If they catch you, just swear you didn't know they had liquor in them. They should let you go, and I'll be there to pick you up."

It wasn't the first time I had been privy to a smuggling job. I had seen my mother do it on many occasions. Once when we went to Greece when I was a child, my mother bought a small hand-sized statue of a Madonna or a Greek goddess. All I remember is that she was naked. My stepdad insisted that it could not enter the country. My mother had a plan. My brother was a bedwetter and was sure to wet himself on the long plane ride back to Saudi. When he did, my mother did what all mothers would do. She changed him into a fresh set of clothes and placed the peed-on clothes in a plastic bag. After that she placed the small statue into the middle of the wet clothes in the bag. When the bag of wet clothes went through the scanner the security guard asked what was in the bag. My mother grabbed the bag pointed at my brother and said, "My son, he peed, see?" placing the bag directly under the security guards nose and opening it for him to see. The man covered his nose and waved his hand saying, "Go, Go." There are many stories like this since everyone had something or other that they felt they could not live without in a country that asks you to live without a lot of things.

I was nervous the entire flight of being caught but I remembered what I was taught: keep your head up, you are a Saudi. I landed and the women as usual were being moved to one side until their male escorts arrived. I moved to the top of the expat line saying my father is Saudi and he is waiting for me outside. They examined my visa and then let me pass.

We talked as he drove to our favorite restaurant. When we sat down to dinner, I caught him up on all my news, he tilted his head as he did when I was a child and asked, "What's wrong?" I looked down and discussed my time in Abu Dhabi, the pressure I felt to cover when I really didn't want to.

After listening to me go back and forth for a while he said simply, "Just take it off now that you're in Dubai they can't see you." "But, Firas will not like it, he will be concerned with what his family will say." To which he replied, "To be honest I don't think it's any of his business." I was floored that my stepdad had said such a thing. The man who would not let me cut my hair until I was married so my husband could decide what he liked. Time had clearly altered a lot, I stared at him with the stare that said that sounds like a battle. He added, "Look, if he wants you to get a tattoo on your face, should you do that too?" I responded with, "We'll see," which he always knew meant I need to think about it. It was a common Arabic expression pronounced *"Han Shouf."*

He gave me much to ponder that night as I laid in bed. I decided I should seek Noor's council the next day when I would be spending a few days sleeping at her new place. Her husband was out of town, so the timing was perfect. I was excited to see her and spend some time just hanging out. I packed up the chocolates and had her on the phone as I had the driver pass by the grocery store on the way to pick up all our favorite snacks, alcohol-free pink champagne, indomie (Indonesian ramen noodles), chocolates, and anything else she needed for the house. When I arrived, I grabbed the bags and hurried up the stairs. Seeing her always made my heart sing with joy. I hugged her and we sat down for tea and a cigarette to talk about life.

So often I have found that none of the people I grew up with liked to share much on the phone. There was always a risk that someone would overhear the conversation only hearing part of it and then misunderstand and spread the information. So many things can be interpreted by the Saudi Government as intent to cause unrest and the risk is always high. Now that we were alone, and her husband was out of town, she told me all about his temper and how many times he beat her. I held her as she cried and pretended to be strong as I offered to hurt him if I ever saw him again. Noor was known to talk back but when spoken to the right way she was the kindest softest soul I had ever known. She didn't deserve to be beaten by someone she loved. None of us deserve to be beaten at all.

She covered all the time now. It was the first era in our lives where we both really covered. She, because her husband wished it. I asked her about my issue with covering and told her the story. She leaned her head back and took a long puff of her cigarette and said, "Honey, your husband is good to you, you have everything, you get to travel, he leaves you alone to do as you please, you get to go shopping, you live in Dubai ... honey, just leave it, it's a small thing and nothing worth losing a good husband over." I nodded and took her advice under consideration.

Part of me knew she was right, but my mind wandered off on how often people dispensed advice dragged from their own experiences. How often we pass out advice based on where we are instead of where they are. So often our inner self guides us, but we don't know how to listen to it or something, a tradition, a person, a learned habit, or programming affects our decision making. If there was ever one thing I'll always keep from Islam, it would be the stories of the Prophet Muhammed's (ﷺ) constant ability to sit alone with himself in silence, no music, no distractions and reflect, on his day. Who he wronged, what he could have done better, on his year, on the questions he wondered about, on doctrine, on everything. I often found myself in a great silence, pondering reasons for steps taken, choices made, people I might have wronged along the way and everything else almost like a trance staring at nothing out the window and everything all at once.

The weekend was beautiful. Filled with coffee mornings filled with stories, movie, after movie, after movie, which I managed to download to my laptop using a program called *Bittorrent* while I was in Dubai so she could watch them. There were also trips to the mall. Finally, I pulled out the chocolate and we spent a long while biting off the tops of the tiny chocolates and pouring the inner liquid into a wine glass. Each of us ending up with maybe half a shot mixed with our non-alcoholic champagne. Needless to say, it had no effect and Noor said, "I don't know what all the fuss is about?"

We practiced our dance moves as we used to do as girls before we were married. Back in the days of weddings and suitors we were a force to behold. When we got up to dance at a wedding the girls backed away to clap and enjoy learning as we danced so perfectly in time with the music. All girls learn a little dancing if their families are not too conservative when it comes to music. Not everyone however has an ear for the beat, can predict the next beat and is able to dance perfectly to a song they had never heard before. People often think the hardest part to dance to in an Arabic song would be the fast parts, but Noor always used to say the hardest part is being able to slow down when the beat suddenly drops. A famous song that is always played at least once in every Arabic wedding or party is called *Shik Shak Shouk*. It has been redone by many artists and has many versions, but it demonstrates so fully the sudden fall in the music from a rigorous beat that goes very fast to a sudden slowdown that requires you to slow your breathing at a moment's notice until it picks up again. The song in total can last up to six minutes which is quite the workout. Belly dancing for the entirety of this song was something that would not go un-admired among women. When we were young, we always made sure to include it in our practice.

The visit ended and it came time to return to Dubai. There were a couple of days at home until Firas got back. I came back early to make sure the house was in order since the maid service would not come when I was away. If Firas was alone even one day in the house, I could be sure the house needed tidying up. He had a habit of leaving everything where he opened it, where he finished with it and where he took it off. This was not untypical of Arab men with the exception of my stepdad who, being the psycho that he was, was very meticulous in putting everything in its proper place as soon as he finished with it as I was taught to do. It was normal that the man brings home the money to support the wife and we make sure they never need to worry about where the trash can is.

The maid service was booked up, so I did all the clean-up myself, which I found very therapeutic. Once everything was in its place I sat down on the sofa and lit up a cigarette along with a cold 7up. As I smoked, I decided I would discuss the idea of me going without a headcover with Firas. Surely, he could not object since it would make me happy and especially now that we were away from Ablah May and married.

Firas arrived in the afternoon, and I had dinner ready to go. We never really ate at the table since Firas preferred to eat in front of the TV to watch the news. I offered him a blowjob since I knew he enjoyed that more than sex. Sex for us was always so disconnected. He didn't like me to look at him and I was often bent over waiting for it to be over. He said he had lovers in the past who had raved about how amazing he was but knowing a lot about his past lovers I know that they all wanted very much for him to marry them. I was very petite, and they were not. The largeness of his appendage made it very painful for me, something I tried to explain to him, but the answer was always the same. "Every girl wants a big one, everyone knows that." I always disagreed saying, "It's all about puzzle pieces, some girls have more space than others." Since I had never really had lovers, I was a tighter fit than most, but it was no use.

CHOICES ARE CALLED CHOICES BECAUSE WE NEED TO MAKE THEM

After he was all settled in, I broached the subject, asking what he thought about me not wearing my headcover anymore. He immediately sprung up from the couch and said, "You can't be serious! What will my family say? What will everyone in Syria say? Wearing the Hijab is not a game. If you did not want to wear it, you should not have put it back on." I lowered my head in silence for a moment. I remembered a proverb from the Disney Movie, *Mulan*, where the Emperor said, "No matter how the wind howls, the Mountain cannot bow to it." But I was never raised to be a mountain, I was raised like a palm tree trained to be pliable to the wind. When peer pressure came, I bent to it all but once the wind went away, the palm tree returned to its natural position, This is what was happening to me.

He paced as he lit a new cigarette then he said the comment that changed my mind from a palm tree to a mountain. "What would your father say about this, you know he wouldn't like it." I tilted my head, feeling like it was a low blow to try and use my stepdad to make a point, but my stubbornness kicked in, it was too late. I responded, "Actually, he said it was none of your business if I decided to wear it or not, it was my decision." Firas was furious as he lashed out saying, "Well, that's just because he doesn't like me." I sighed and said, "I'm going to bed." I cried knowing that taking this decision could have great repercussions, but I wasn't happy being covered anymore. I knew the decision was made in my mind; I only needed the courage to do it.

I broached the subject multiple times, but I always got the same answer "No." The weekend came, and I said I needed to go to the mall for a few things. As I walked around, I saw an army green dress, knee length, a pencil skirt with short sleeves and it was so elegant. I walked into the store covered, bought the dress, changed into it, and walked about uncovered. It was done.

I went straight from there to find a hairdresser to blow dry my hair since the head scarf had flattened it out. I walked into a salon in the mall. In the Middle East, unlike the West, often a salon is a one-stop shop. Waxing, hair cutting, massage, everything in one place. Many are segregated for the comfort of women who cover, and all the attendants are women, but this one was not. I walked in and asked for a wash and a blow dry. The woman directed me to a seat, then a man arrived. I was still uncomfortable with men who were not a relation touching me. I didn't know how I felt about him as he touched my hair and said, "You asked for a blow dry." I sat up straight to display my confidence and said, "Yes." He said, "I can blow dry it but if you were my client I would not let you leave this salon with a haircut like that." I said, "What's wrong with it?" He held up a piece of my hair that was obviously cut wrong by mistake, shorter than the rest but hidden from my eyes in the back. I said, "So, fix it." He bowed and said, "With pleasure." He mixed up color, cut, did my blow dry, and I was on my way. A sense of guilt swept over me since I knew Firas would have been in an outrage if he knew I let another man, even a hairdresser, touch me, but then I recalled his own bad habits and all the contradictions I lived with every day.

Firas liked to get massages from women when he traveled and I had never made a fuss, how was this any different I thought? Firas had many habits that his family would have disapproved of: going to strip clubs, bars to watch Russian hookers arrive, getting innocent massages by women, or so he said. To be honest I didn't mind anything he did even if society would have. I trusted him and that was that. In the interest of keeping him happy I turned a blind eye and never told anyone. We lived and grew up in a world of contradictions and to be honest I was starting to get sick of it.

That day as this strange man washed my hair and blow dried it, I finally got the male attention I had craved from Firas. However platonic it was, he will never know how much it helped me remain in our marriage. I never washed my own hair again as long as I lived in Dubai. I would shower and head to Robert, my handsome new hairdresser. He would wash and blow dry my hair every two days. What Firas was unable to give me in terms of non-sexual attention I found in Robert just washing my hair and flirting with me from time to time.

When I arrived home Firas had employed the deadbolt, so I had to ring the bell. He opened the door and saw me in my new dress, scarfless. He was silent. I smiled and entered the house. Firas began his rant about what people will say. Nothing meant more to him than what people might say about him, and I now was an extension of him. I listened quietly as I moved around the apartment putting my things away and preparing lunch saying nothing at all since, I knew it was useless to argue. He needed to say what he needed to say. I knew by now how important it was for him to speak and feel in charge, in control, and powerful. It was already done in any case, so I absorbed him gracefully as I was taught to do. For unless he intended to beat me into wearing it, he knew deep down there was no going back once my mind was made up on this note we knew each other well.

The next morning, he informed me that we had an Embassy event a visiting Qatari Prince was hosting. He asked me to be ready to go when he got home. I nodded and wondered in my mind why I had not been to any events since I had decided to cover my hair and suddenly, I was to accompany him to an Embassy event again like we did when I was uncovered when we were dating in Saudi. The appointed time arrived, and I was dressed in my black skirt suit, hair done, and ready for the evening. Firas escorted me to the car and off we went to the event. There was something charming about him when he knew people were watching. It was very important to him that everyone knew how kind he was to his wife, what a good provider he was, and how much his wife loved him.

We entered the event and unlike I had done in the past when the Prince reached out his hand I shook it, bowing my eyes as a sign of great respect. Firas spoke to me at length on the way over about staying close to him and saying as little as possible so as not to reveal how ignorant I was about world politics. I nodded as I always did and secretly wondered why he was bringing me along if not to be a softener for some political plan. A pretty face can always go a long way in negotiations. It's why some of the best salespeople are smoking hot. It's not discrimination. It's gifts put to good use. And now that I was not covered, he could show me off at his leisure. We went to many events, banquets, receptions, and dinners like this all of which were beautiful, elegant, and impressive. I felt as though I was surrounded by people and yet, completely alone. I enjoyed Firas most when he was out. He was more attentive in front of people. The man I loved would come out and I enjoyed watching him articulate things so elegantly, always knowing how much negotiation was appropriate at dinner and how much was not. A skill not many people possessed as well as he did. He was a true politician.

The days stretched on and there was a silent compromise between us. Since we were not planning to go to Syria right away and because Ablah May and Doctora Zaynia were in Abu Dhabi, there was little risk anyone would find out that I was not covering for the time being. Since the people at the events we went to in Dubai did not know me when I was covered, and even if they did mention me to Ablah May when they saw her, they would not think to mention if I was covered or not. Only that I was elegant and beautiful to which Ablah May of course would respond, "She is like a daughter to me and Firas a son, a great match I arranged." He would tell no one yet for fear of what people would think and I would not offer up the information for fear of Ablah May's wrath and disappointment.

The Arab spring arrived starting with Tunisia. Firas called one afternoon to ask me to pack for him since he would be heading there right away as a spokesperson. He was very good at redirecting questions when placed live on news networks like CNN, Aljazeera, Al-Arabiya and many more. Along with being very charismatic and handsome he was perfect for the job. When he arrived home, I had his bag laid out on the bed ready for him to pack whatever else he felt he needed. I asked him how long he would be gone to which he replied, "I don't know; it will depend on how long this lasts."

It all started with a street vendor in Tunisia named Tarek el-Tayeb Mohamed Bouazizi who set himself on fire. While there are many reasons to remember him one of mine was that it annoyed Firas when he would say Sheikh so and so said the man will go to Heaven and I would gladly quote the Quran and the Hadith saying, "No, he won't." "How can you say that the man is a hero?" "Ya, but in Islam if you kill yourself you go to Hell, so hero or not he is going to Hell."

It wasn't that I really thought he was going to Hell but there were few things I could win in the battle of intelligence with Firas. The subject of Islam was one of them and I enjoyed every minute of it. At the time none of us could have predicted the spill over of the Arab Spring from Tunisia all across the Arab world or that this was the beginning of many events that would take place all throughout Arabia. Changing it forever.

He left that night and following that I continued my normal routine. It was peaceful and Firas would call once in a while to tell me he loved me, missed me and if I would make sure to record his interview on TV when it came on. Since he would not be coming home for dinner anymore, I would cook once every three days. Because I was so used to cooking for my large family. I tended to overcook, but I didn't mind eating the same thing for lunch and dinner every day. In the afternoon every other day I would go shopping to fill my time and the BeBe store always expected me as I walked in and said, "Has the new collection arrived? Great, please bring one of everything in my size to the dressing room." I then left loaded with everything I wanted. Firas was a rising star in the organization and money was more available to us. He was a penny-pincher most of the time but when it came to me looking and dressing like his wife, he had no comments or questions. After all, these are the places where a wife is meant to spend money, shopping for groceries, clothes, and household items.

In the evenings after I had my dinner I would head down to the Marina on the water where there was a café that always had live music. I would sit in the ocean breeze, order a *shisha* smoke, and read my book with a glass of tea. The servers came to predict my arrival. They loved me for my calm, undemanding nature and so it was every night for a month. If there was ever a day when the café was full a table would be brought out from inside along with a chair so I could sit. I recall this period of my life as one of the most peaceful and calm. I read a lot, pondered a lot, and explored my inner self. Reading and pondering in Saudi Arabia was not a past time often taken up by women since with so much censorship it was hard to get as many books as one would want, especially the types of books you would want. Even magazines have all the women blacked out with a permanent marker. I think a great slogan for Sharpie would be, "This will permanently get rid of it, the Saudis use it all the time." Many women spend their days like my mother off in space watching approved outdated TV dramas and wasting time.

One night I walked home from the Marina café at around 2 a.m., as I was entering my well-lit apartment building, I noticed from the corner of my eye a group of boys standing on the street. I entered knowing full well the security guard would not allow anyone to enter who did not live there. As I entered the elevator, they all appeared and tried to get on with me but I stepped out as the doors closed. I pressed the elevator button and took the next one. When the elevator doors opened on my floor there they were. Despite my insides trembling, I recalled what my stepdad had said, "Stand up straight, show no fear." I looked at them, realizing that I must have hit my floor button when I had gotten in the other elevator. The hallways had no cameras, but I knew if I could manage to make it through my door the panic button was right there to call up the guard. I reminded myself that for all they knew I had a father inside or a husband ready to beat them. I walked tall and calm to my door, placed the key inside then as I twisted it, I turned my head and boldly asked them in Arabic if they plan to leave or should I send for the police? They turned and headed for the elevator. I rushed inside and pushed the panic button. The guard came right away and said he would review the tapes and find out who they were. I double locked the door that night and did not leave the house for a few days. It was discovered that they were young men staying with a family member on another floor for a few days. That was the end of my nighttime outings.

Soon enough, Firas returned home. I was happy to see him, I jumped up to hug him as I always tried to do but the reaction was always, "Calm down, it's nice to see you, too," as he held back both of my arms as if the sight of me was insane.

Entertaining was a frequent occurrence. When a foreign dignitary was visiting or a staff member from another duty station would visit, I would work all day on dinner making sure nothing was left to the last minute. The food was served more often in buffet style to create more room for people to sit.

A tradition developed in our home before guests arrived. Moments before they got there, Firas would collect every item on the bookshelf that suggested I was American. A book, a teddy bear, a bookend, a picture, a tiny flag, or snow globe and as I was setting up the table, I would notice they were missing from the bookshelf. I would then wait for him to be distracted on a phone call or in the bathroom getting ready and simply put them back without a word. Then I would continue what I was doing. As he moved around, he would remove them again and I would put them back again. Silently we continued this until one of us succeeded having them either on or off the shelf when the doorbell rang, knowing full well that if we talked about it, he would meet opposition and arguing from me which wasn't really something we liked to do.

I would always greet the guests, smile, serve, and have no opinion where possible. All the while I wondered why something like a snow globe was so annoying or embarrassing to him on the shelf, while none of the artifacts from Syria were ever moved out of sight when guests arrived. I was not entirely very American on the inside, but I was not ashamed to say I was.

Once in a grocery store a woman came up to me and asked if I was married. Firas interceded saying, "Yes." Her next question was what house I was from to which he replied with his house and then proceeded to say I had no sisters. The proud Saudi in me came out and I corrected him as I should not have done since it is very wrong for a wife to correct her husband in front of anyone. I said I was half Saudi and American and my family name was Al-Turkistani. Firas ran circles around himself to explain the misunderstanding since he made it sound like I was Syrian. While he was not wrong, I was married to him and as I mentioned before the wife does become a part of the husband's household after marriage instead of her families but at the same time women in the Middle East do not normally change their last names. This is so that they still keep a piece of where they originated from proudly. But, for Firas, me not being Syrian always felt like such a shame to him.

As time went on, I waited day after day for him to become the man he had bragged to me about when we dated. The one who would spoil his wife with love, flowers, romance, but that man never seemed to appear. People tell stories of knights in shining armor like Lancelot and King Arthur. The reality is sometimes the Knight is just an honorable man who doesn't know the first thing about love or how women work and in Firas's case, he showed no interest in learning. He was perfect in every way in his mind and that was that.

It was the year I had four wisdom teeth pulled in one day. Firas was at home watching the news and I asked was he going with me. He said he would be along shortly. I headed to my appointment. It was an outpatient procedure and so in his mind it seemed as if nothing important was happening. After they pulled my teeth there was so much blood, I could barely keep myself conscious let alone stand. I called him but no answer, so I paid and proceeded to walk home alone. When I got home, there he was in his undershirt on the couch. I found it hard to speak so I didn't. He said, "How was it?" My weepy eyes looked at him and I then wrote on a piece of paper, "Where were you?" To which he replied, "Well, I was going to come but I feel so tired so I figured since it was so close you would be fine." I sighed as I realized he had no idea. I showed him the doctor's instructions about food, how everything for the next few days would need to be chopped very small to stop me from opening up my mouth too wide. Hard foods were forbidden, and cold foods were preferred. I laid down on the couch to nap and when I woke up, I was hungry so I wrote a note asking if he could get me a banana. He got the banana and placed it in front of me still whole. I felt like a starving person who was given a jar of yummy food but no way to eat the food.

I felt alone in my head every single day, but I was grateful for my TV shows, books, schoolwork, and the environment in which I lived that allowed me to be without his constant scrutiny and correction. He never held my hand in public since he said it was improper despite the many couples, wife covered or otherwise, who did so in Dubai. When he was away, I got to be myself. I would smile more and skip down the street without being told not to act like a child. I ordered what I liked off the menu and enjoyed it with my quiet mind. I understood him well, his reputation and what people thought of him was important, more important than anything, even me. He never saw that perhaps when we were alone it would be okay for me to be myself, a deal I tried to broker once but to no avail. Those conversations normally ended with "My wife will be …." In his mind if I laughed and jumped around at home, I would be more apt to do so in public, so I was like a horse that needed to be broken and put back together as his wife and nothing else.

Although it sounds very harsh, I bore him no ill will since in reality this was the way it was, and I knew I needed to find a way to accept my new role and forget who I used to be. There were days and sometimes weeks where I felt as though there was a piece of my soul being slowly buried. I tried to fill the void with shopping for new clothes to help me to see the wife he wanted when I looked in the mirror, but it seemed now instead of getting dressed up, smiling, and twirling in the mirror, I would just sigh and finish getting ready.

I was a rare Arabic girl because of my upbringing. Every time my mom would fly off the handle about a woman who stared too long at my stepdad, my stepdad would ask me to take a hard look at what jealousy looks like and how it ruins marriages. He would go on to talk about the impact on the feelings of the innocent party who is being mistreated because of something a stranger did, then he went on to remind me that I should never lose my self-esteem. “It is better to be full of yourself than to feel ugly and worry constantly whether you are enough for your spouse. For this will breed insecurity and ultimately lead you to become like your mother.” This was one of the most profound lectures he ever gave me, and my mom was a frequent case study for jealousy.

The older and fatter she got the more insecure she became. Khala Jan, who lived across from us when I was a teenager and often taught me to cook new recipes, was the exact opposite. She took care of her body, ate well, and carried herself with an air of a middle-aged woman who knew she was still beautiful and desirable. She was calm, collected, intelligent, and unafraid to age. I knew that was the kind of woman I wanted to grow up to be.

Firas liked to go down to the hotels in the red-light district in Dubai. He would order soda water with lime so he would not look out of place without drinking and watch the girls arrive he said, to which I always replied, “Of course, go have fun.” In my mind it could not be much different than heading to a strip club and if there was anything I knew it was if Firas wanted to do something, he was going to do it. I had a choice, as many wives, girlfriends and lovers do, to take him as he was or not at all. Looking did no harm. After all I thought, I could choose to know where he was or I could choose for him to go and just not tell me, which is a very common place in the Arab world and elsewhere, I imagine.

The two biggest pluses was it got him out of the house on the weekend so I could have a peaceful evening free of the next big lecture on whatever country was featured on the news that night. When he returned, he was so grateful that I let him go and was not jealous at all. I never asked why he was late, I only ever smiled and asked how it was. In truth I always wished I could go and see all the girls arriving at the bar, but it was a side of town where respectable girls opted never to be seen. When he would get home, he would hug me and kiss me all over my face with the exception of my mouth, with the affection so lacking in our marriage. I was happy to let him go to see him happy when he returned. It seemed like these were the moments when I finally did something right in his eyes.

One evening as I was getting dinner ready for Firas, he called on his way home. He was excited beyond measure saying, "Habiti, you won't believe it!" "What is it?" "They have decided instead of making me head of the office here there is a position for me in Geneva, Switzerland." I got quiet. "Is it decided for sure?" "No, they said if I wanted to stay here, I could apply for the head of office here and if I wanted I could apply for the position in Geneva and they said I am sure to get it, I'll be working in headquarters." "Okay, but why not apply for the position here, I like it here." "But this is an amazing opportunity, I can't pass it up." "We can talk when you get home, Habebe." When he arrived, I pleaded with him to just apply to stay here. "I know I agreed that one day we would have to move as is the nature of your job, but we just got here, why not apply to stay and then in two years apply for Geneva, this is all happening so fast we would need to leave in a few months." It was no use though, as was always the case, there would be no compromise or discussion. A wife must follow her husband.

The next day Ablah May called to try and ease me through this first of many transitions. She too, being a diplomat's wife, knew that it can be hard to move every two years. I contented myself with the fact that there was no point in crying over spilt milk. It was done and it was time to go.

Firas took care of all the needed paperwork for our upcoming move since almost everything had to be pushed through the office, while I planned and packed.

One day I went to the mall. It felt like any day but upon my return I found all my furniture gone and Firas standing in the living room. "Where is everything? My dishes? Our couch? The bed?" "I gave it to a newly married Syrian couple I met." he replied. I stood there in the empty room with no words, it wasn't anger I felt, but despair for not even being consulted before my home was carried away. They may have been things but maybe I wanted to mentally say goodbye. "That was kind of you, but you could have just consulted me, Habebe, so I don't come home and just find everything gone like this, I knew we weren't going to take it with us but…." No apologies were made, after all it was his decision to make, and I went to gather the suitcases so we could go stay in a hotel. Moving to a new country without sadness is completely possible. In fact, it can be very exciting but for me there was always a ritual to it, a last walk in my favorite places, a last night in my bathtub, a final meal at my table, and a last look at the city. Most of which was ripped from me which made closure and leaving the simple peaceful life I had made in that apartment in Dubai that much harder.

GENEVA

Arriving in Geneva was like stepping into a Beauty and the Beast novel. The cobblestone streets, the winding narrow roads, and the short, old buildings were everywhere. It was the polar opposite of the shiny new city of Dubai with all its tall buildings and modern conveniences. Firas had rented a small sublet in an apartment building in an area called Petit-Saconnex, which was within walking distance from the Palace of Nations, close to his work location. It was to be our temporary apartment until we found a more permanent solution for the long term. The apartment was already furnished with some dishes, a couch, and a bed. It had a tiny balcony which except for in winter, would prove to be its greatest aspect with the view of all the trees and a mountain off in the distance.

I headed over to the supermarket. I recognized none of the brand names and everything was in French or German, so I did my best to get the essentials.

When Firas got back from work, he asked how my first day was. As always, in my very excited tone I started to relay all the wondrous things I had seen, but as was always the case I was stopped halfway with, "Well, that's nice Habiti, and then he proceeded to talk about bank accounts, apartment hunting, and his plans for the next couple of days. We headed to dinner but with Halal food being so hard to come by and the fact that neither one of us could understand menus very well, we finally settled on eating in a small bistro on the corner. We ordered half a chicken; it came with no sides and two Cokes. The bill came to 50 francs. My brain thought about how expensive everything was down here and how

I didn't want to eat half of half a chicken every night so I decided that tomorrow if I wanted to really eat, I would need to start cooking.

The next day I did a map search and found out that there was an Ikea not too far from me. I put on my walking shoes and headed to the train station. The thing about having no car meant you needed to remember that whatever you buy you will have to carry. At Ikea I purchased a small cart which I strategically loaded with only what I absolutely needed to cook very simple meals. I decided I could make as many trips as I needed but if it didn't fit in the cart it had to wait. On the way home pushing my cart up the hill from the bus stop I saw a familiar sight, a McDonalds. When McDonalds came to Saudi Arabia, the Arabs pronounced it how they read it - *Mack-dough-nal-ees*. Since it was getting close to dinner time, I stopped to order something for dinner. I got two Big Mac meals but when the bill came, it was around 14 Francs. I was shocked trying so hard to wrap my brain around junk food costing so much, but I paid the bill and headed home.

The next day I cooked our first meal. Since there was no Arabic store near enough to go to without a car, Firas had no cause to complain for the moment that it was not Syrian food. I spoke to him at dinner about the money we'd save by eating at home after I'd stocked the kitchen with Ikea finds, but there was no praise to be had. Only a comment about my taking the train by myself and how I should have asked him first.

I often ponder if, in my life, I have always reached for one particular goal, to make others proud. Perhaps it was bred into me by my Aunt, my stepdad, my mom, Ablah May, Doctora Zaynia and now Firas, but it always felt like no matter how much I tried, I was always lacking. It was like a never-ending mountain I climbed named Proud. It's funny how important those words can be to anyone, "I'm proud of you," and if they never come how hard you push yourself to hear them from others. I started to get the hang of the bus system and the different cafes where I could take my books to study. It was a lonely place where people kept mostly to themselves. As usual we went to many diplomatic dinners in fancy restaurants where I sat and did my best to be pleasing. In Geneva I felt isolated. In Dubai, even though I had no friends, I knew the language and carrying on a short conversation with the waiter in a café, my hairdresser, or at my nail salon, was enough to help soothe the loneliness I felt at times. I was good at being alone but now I could not even have a conversation with the check-out girl at the grocery or bargain with vendors for goods in the market.

One day I decided to take a bus to go see the Montblanc store I had heard so much about. I loved to write, and pens were of special interest to me. When I got on the bus, I showed the map to the bus driver and spoke in what broken French I had, in an attempt to ask if this was the right bus to go to the area that had the Montblanc store. The bus driver could not understand. Then a man in the middle of the bus stood up and said, "I speak English." The relief on my face was so joyful and thankful as I moved towards the man saying, "Thank you so much, I'm just trying to go…" but before I could finish, he said, "But I'm not going to help you." Bewildered, I looked at him for a minute as he continued, "You know why? Because when I go to your country, I have to speak your language, so when you come to my country you need to speak my language." Then he promptly sat down again. I slowly exited the bus and began my walk home. The tears began to roll down my cheeks. My mind knew he was right that if he went to America, they would expect him to speak English, but this was not my home and if he went to an Arab country, I knew that everyone would do their best to help him even if he never spoke the language. I went home and took a nap. A habit of mine to calm my mind when sadness would take me over. Everything was always a little better after a nap.

When I woke up it was time to fix dinner. As dinner cooked, I looked for a French language class for expats in the area. Unfortunately, it was not close by and would take at least 4 busses to get there. If I was to live here and be happy, I knew learning the language was very important. When Firas got home, I told him that I found a place where I could learn French to which his reply was, "I'm not going to drive you." My mind always twitched a little when he would make a comment like that since there was no mention of him driving me. You often see the case with Arab marriages and in much of Western culture men are subconsciously trained to assume that when your wife or girlfriend shows you a picture of a car they think is cute, or an item in a store, what they are actually saying is "Will you buy it for me" or "Will you drive me there."

I always wondered why, despite the years we had already spent together and my constant display of extreme capability to get things done on my own, I was still put into a checkbox as a female who needed a man in order to do anything. I'm either asking for money or something else, when in this case, I was only seeking to share my plans, and maybe make him proud that I was attempting to integrate into my new environment. An expression often used is 'Happy Wife, Happy Life.' The truth is I needed no one to make me happy. I was perfectly capable of making myself happy. Unfortunately for us, what he thought should make me happy such as: not working, staying at home, not needing to worry about things like money and being married to the most perfect Arab man on paper the world had ever seen … in his mind was not enough for me. Despite my efforts to explain this to him, it just fell on deaf ears.

I took the four busses to the French class which was held in the teacher's home. It was so nice to meet other expats. The class was intense, and I did my best to try and catch up to everyone. I met a woman who worked for a woman's expat organization that was looking for volunteers to help with an election party they would be putting on in a few months. I eagerly volunteered to help, excited to have a purpose outside of Firas, his work, and the housework.

When I mentioned it to Firas, I was met with great disapproval that his wife should be working on an election party. He expressed his concern that, "Being around too many Americans will make you more American and that was not what I want in a wife." I felt like I heard crickets as I replied, "But your wife is American." I argued that I was only going to help with decorations, and I could not see how this affected anything. He expressed his disapproval again saying, "Your studies and the house will suffer. What if I have a dinner that we need to attend pop up suddenly?" I said, "You're my first priority but this is something I am going to do whether you like it or not." "Aha!" he said, "There it is! No Arab wife would say that to her husband. You see! This is what I am talking about. It's already started." I rolled my eyes and headed to bed.

Most of the volunteer work took place in the daytime and as I suspected, Firas barely noticed how much time I spent with them. It was a great joy to work alongside people who spoke my language again and the Marines who helped us were always the most polite and kind group of service men I had ever met. The night of the election party came, and I told Firas he should come with me. I said, "It will be fun, we can grab dinner beforehand and you can meet all my new friends." He agreed to dinner since me being out at night without him seemed absolutely out of the question. We ate dinner in the hotel where the event was. When we finished dinner Firas said, "You go say hello and then we need to go home; it's late and I have work tomorrow." My mood changed from so excited to introduce him to everyone I had told how wonderful he was to a solemn mood of disappointment. I did not speak the whole way home and asked myself over and over why it was okay for us to sit with his friends and coworkers until the early hours of the morning but making one round in a ballroom for me was too difficult? I never went back to the volunteer group again, feeling embarrassed that I had talked him up only to look like a fool to do so. Slowly the disapproval for my French classes came up over and over again until finally fatigue on my part for the topic created so much discouragement that there was no point in going.

I walked one day to the Place of Nations to study and noticed a job board for a position in the office where Firas worked, for which I was qualified. I was so excited; this perhaps is the middle ground I thought. If I was working alongside his coworkers and friends maybe, then we would both have what we wanted. After collecting all the needed paperwork, I got home, filled everything out and made dinner. When Firas arrived, I jumped up telling him about this great position I wanted to apply for. He took a drag of his cigarette, looked down and said "I can't have my wife working in the same office as me. That would be embarrassing. People would say we need the money and what if you make a mistake, they will include me in the blame which would hurt my reputation in the office." I argued, "We met while we both worked for the same organization and eventually, we worked in the same office. If I make a mistake that would be my problem, not yours. Besides I won't even be in the same department as you, we probably won't even see each other." He stood up. "Out of the question and that's the end of it." I nodded silently and headed to bed early.

Once we were married and Ramadan came around, I continued the daily routine as I always did, getting up and kissing him as he left for work but as I leaned in he put out his hand to hold me back saying, "What are you doing? It's Ramadan and I'm fasting. You will break my fast." "But we're married," I replied, with a very confused look as he left for work. It was a battle line he had drawn. I avoided kissing him after he was washed for prayer even though he was wrong and there was no wrong in it. I thought but for God's sake a whole month every year without any human contact - that was beyond ridiculous. I could not lose my temper while I was fasting since that could make my fast invalid, so I waited until he came home and our break-fast was done.

"Now explain why you can't kiss your wife during Ramadan?" "It will invalidate my fast. We can't have any sexual contact, you know this." "Sexual contact…? It's a kiss, not a blow job and unless me kissing you causes you to come in your pants, of course it is allowed." "No, that's not correct, we should avoid all contact." I pulled out the Hadith and began to read him a passage. A story about the Prophet Muhammad (ﷺ) kissing his wife Aisha during Ramadan and said, "See here." "Well, the prophet was different, not like the rest of us." "Alright, how about the story of the man who went to the prophet in shame saying he had made a mistake and kissed his wife and invalidated his fast. Did not the prophet then ask him if he took water into his mouth to wash for prayer? To which the man replied yes, and the prophet asked if that invalidated his fast?" "No, you're misinterpreting it, we can have no contact during the daytime in Ramadan." "I can go on forever, Firas, but there is no misinterpretation, it's black and white." Round and round we went. It was a normal routine when I would not back down from the fight which I did out of sheer headache more often than not.

Then Firas issued the line I always loathed, "Well, listen all your books are written by Saudis, Indians, or foreigners, so it can't be correct unless the books are written by a Syrian. I'm just saying we know religion best." My head twitched a little as I contemplated the stupidity of his argument and wondered if continuing was even worth it. Then the idea came to me. "Okay, let's call a Syrian, a well-respected Syrian, who is well respected by you and me and ask him for his judgment on the matter. Your DAD. He's in Syria, he was raised with your version of Islam that's so superior to all others. Let's ask him what he thinks." "This is silly, Habiti, to involve my dad." "No, no, we need a Syrian opinion you're right." I dialed the number. When his Dad picked up, Firas jumped for the phone asking his Dad the question, if it was allowed for a man to kiss his wife during Ramadan, to which his dad replied in the affirmative as long as there is no sexual desire attached to it. I folded my arms and leaned on the wall, gloating. I knew Firas would still avoid kissing me despite what his Dad said, but from a knowledge base standpoint, I had won and that was enough for me today. When you live with someone who constantly reminds you that they're more knowledgeable and superior, you can find yourself looking for opportunities to remind them that they don't know everything.

One evening Noor's husband decided to visit his friends. She texted me with the password and I replied with mine this way we were both sure who we were talking to since her husband was prone to taking her phone and texting people to make sure she wasn't up to anything. His jealous mind had made him paranoid. Noor, however, never gave him cause and over time, developed a strong voice of her own, at least inside the house. She started to fall into the routine of keeping her house in good order and working as a makeup artist for brides and paying calls to her in-laws regularly. We got on a call. "Hey, Honey, how are you, how is Geneva?" "It's fine, Honey, but I miss Dubai, I was so happy there and here the people are so strange." "Tell me all the news from home" "We are all great. Muhammad has finally realized that he can't push me around if he threatens to hit me. I warn him that I will beat him back. I beat him the other day after he pushed me, ha-ha." I cringed that she had normalized this behavior. I said, "I wish you never married him, Honey, *Wallahi* (Swear to God)." "It's fine, Honey, a lot of girls have worse husbands" I sighed as she took a deep breath and continued. "Honey, I need to tell you something, but you have to promise not to be mad." There was a long pause before I said, "What is it?" "Umm, well,

I'm pregnant." I let out a deep breath and said, "You're still having sex with that monster? Why aren't you on birth control? What were you thinking?" "Look, Honey, I tried to leave him, you remember. I went to my family's house, and it was awful, I was not allowed to go anywhere, and they would not allow me to get my own apartment. There was nothing to do all day long. My dad is retired now and always at home and asking me to sit with him. They were all on Muhammad's side and I just couldn't take it anymore. The only way I could have some sort of a life is to have a man. At least I have my home and I can do as I like most of the time. Then after I came back everyone kept pushing for a baby and I thought I'm bored, and it would be nice to have company. Also, who will take care of me when I'm old if I don't have a child?" "I wish I could take care of you and get you out of there." "I know, Honey, but it is what it is. I'm happy, really. I'm going to have a baby." "If you're happy, Honey, I'm happy for you, just try not to have more than one. If you ever decide to leave him one day, it will be hard enough with one. Mabrouk (Congratulations), Honey."

It was done. She was glued to him and there was nothing more to say. Getting angry would not help the situation and I wanted her to be happy in spite of whether or not I thought it was a big mistake. I still always believed that it was her life, and these were her mistakes to make. Unlike her mother, who was probably right to ask me to help stop her from marrying him in the first place, I wanted her to make her own decisions and cut her own path through stone. How else would she learn to navigate the dark waters of the world she lived in and would be living in for the rest of her life?

A delegation arrived the next week from Dubai and among them was our old friend from the Riyadh office, Mahmoud. I was so overjoyed to see him. I made a special dinner and we all sat and laughed about the news from the Riyadh office and how everyone was doing. After dinner Firas implied that he was going to take Mahmoud to see some of the sights ... they shouldn't be too late, he said. In Geneva mostly everything is closed by 7:00 p.m. with, of course, the exception of the red-light district, which is why I was not invited to come along. "I'm sure you're too tired after cooking to come with us," Firas said. I nodded and said my goodbyes to Mahmoud and started on the cleanup as they left.

Firas was late coming home but as usual he came in happy, hugged, and kissed me on my cheeks as he headed to bed. Sometimes we would go months without having sex and as you might imagine I didn't mind at all. The reason, according to Firas, was that anytime he got a massage or went to the red-light district and noticed afterwards that he had a small cut somewhere on his body he would panic assuming he might have contracted HIV. He would order home test kits which were sent off on a regular basis taking at least two months for the results to arrive. During this time any contact was out of the question to keep me safe, he said.

Once we were trying on shirts for him in a store and he accidentally pricked his finger on a pin. He cried out, "I pricked my finger, Habiti!! Ah!" He sounded like a wounded beast of some sort. "It's alright, it's just a little blood," I replied as I wrapped the finger in a tissue. He asked if I had made sure to throw away the top 10 tissues from the tissue box in case the person who put them in the box in the factory had HIV. I assured him I had done so but nonetheless the pin in the shirt might have pricked someone previously who had HIV, so to no avail. I attempted to educate him on the impossibility of contracting HIV in all the ways he imagined, even attempting to say things like, "What if the person who filled the tissue box put the tissues in upside down. Should we waste the bottom 10 as well?" Unfortunately, that backfired resulting in us removing both the top and bottom layer of tissues in a tissue box. The same rule applied to toilet paper rolls and all manner of items. At some point the insanity reached such a point that I would find ways to freak him out on purpose for my own amusement and when he asked me if I thought he had HIV from one incident or another, I started to reply to the affirmative, since logic was nowhere to be found and he would most definitely send off a test anyways. We kept at least three HIV tests at home at a time and when one came back negative, sometimes he would send off a second just to make sure there was no mix up at the lab.

It was the night of the United Arab Emirates Independence Day ball that a lot of things changed for us, at least on my side. In the Emirates, the day of their independence was always a large celebration throughout every city. People waving flags as they drove down the highway, women wearing head covers striped with the Emirati flag, fireworks, and vendors in the streets. Truly a joyous occasion. Naturally it was the ball I looked forward to for weeks, knowing way in advance exactly what I would wear. The night before Firas stressed how important it was for him to collect as many contacts as possible that night to which I replied that I bet I could collect twice as many as he could. He made a kind of "Ya, right" sound, and we headed to bed. The challenge was accepted.

The next day Firas and I were on our way. When we arrived and we checked our jackets, Firas's face turned white as he noticed the Emirate flag I had draped over the front of my gown to cover my cleavage. "Take it off, you can't wear that, you're not Emirate." "I can take it off, but it will show my cleavage," something I knew he didn't want. "Besides, they will love it, I am celebrating a country I love," I said. I could see his blood boiling as we entered the ball room to greet the Ambassador. All eyes were smiling upon me as the Ambassador said to me, "How wonderful, are you Emirate, my dear?" "No, but it is my favorite country in the world," he smiled from ear to ear as he replied, "I am so glad to hear that, welcome." I looked over at Firas and made my I told you so face. Once inside, Firas moved from one group to another, talking to people to make connections and collect business cards. While I stood proudly in the corner of the ball room knowing full well that I didn't need to jump from person to person, they would most assuredly come to me, as they did.

I met and spoke to so many people who complimented my patriotic ensemble. At the end of the night the Ambassador came over to introduce me to his wife who said that she wished more people were like me and loved their country so wholeheartedly as they did. I thanked her with all the Arab graces and terms I was taught to use for an Ambassador and his wife. Firas, seeing them both talking to me, headed over in my direction where he made excuses for my wearing the flag to which the Ambassador's wife made a face as she looked at me and said, "Why would you need to apologize? It's so lovely to see someone so passionate about our country!" Firas backtracked saying, "Yes, of course, and you will find that we both love the Emirates a very great deal." I rolled my eyes in my mind but smiled and bowed on the outside. Then Firas said that it was time we get going so we collected our coats and headed towards the car.

Once inside the car Firas blew up. "How could you embarrass me like that?" "How did I embarrass you? If I was in the Emirates on Independence Day, I would have been wearing the exact same outfit and the Emirati Embassy is Emirati soil." Yes, but you stood out." "I'm a beautiful woman, I'm always going to stand out." "Well, I didn't get to talk to some people because they talked to you instead of me." "I should think that's a good thing, I collected a ton of business cards and now you have a connection through me, we divided and conquered." "No, that's not how it works, I'm the man, the diplomat, and you're the wife. How does it look if my wife is talking to people without me"? The argument continued as we entered the house. I said, "I thought you would be glad, I thought I was helping you. Your friend's wife does it and she's a diplomat's wife just like me, and you're always praising her for helping him at events." "She's different," he said. "How so?" I asked. He replied, "Well, she has an advanced degree and more experience." I paused and said, "Oh, I see ..." and with that I went to bed.

Firas was always the golden boy at events, the Syrian who had nothing, who gained a Fulbright scholarship to America. Top of his class, he was offered a job to work as a lawyer in Washington but instead, joined the Agency and rose faster than anyone could have imagined. At events everyone wanted to talk to him and congratulate him. Having his wife shine brighter with all of these accomplishments in his mind brought him down a notch. I understood that night that I had bruised his ego somehow by trying only to do what he asked of me, be a diplomat's wife.

It's funny when you grow older how your memories become such a comfort. When one is young one finds comfort in food, friends, drinks, and even entertainment. All the while unknowingly creating something more important than all of those. When you grow up, the oldest and dearest friend who never fails to sit with you in hard times and good is one's own ageless memory. Please don't misunderstand my words when

I say ageless, I don't mean that memories don't gather dust in the mind, get jumbled up, or even suffer loss, but overall, they are our time machines whereby only sitting in a chair or lying on a bed or any place at all, one can be transported to a very comforting moment, time, place, and even be in the company of those lost to time and circumstances. Memory can, as we grow older, be all one has during a time when the world seems to be too much to handle, The comfort memories provide can often be better than anything else. I found myself so often alone with my own thoughts and memories, thinking of happy moments and friends lost to time as I went about my day in silence until Firas got home. I did this most of the time when he was home, sometimes even during a lecture he was giving me on some diplomatic affair on the news or other.

SIRED BY BUT NOT FATHERED BY

It was February the 15th 2012. I was sitting at my desk in Geneva completing my college assignment when the Facebook messenger popped up. It was my mother's sister, Angela. "Your father sent me a message." I giggled, thinking she was trying to say she was insulted that my stepdad sent her a message or something since he was the resident family barbarian. "Lol which one?" "Your biological father." "That's not possible, it must be a fake. He's dead. I looked everywhere." "It's him, he has your baby pictures." I went straight to the page and looked at the pictures. He was older, but it was him. I began to cry as I messaged him.

It was confirmed by my aunt that he was who he said he was. With the time difference, we made a plan to speak in two days over video chat. I wanted to talk to him, but I wanted to be dressed and do my hair for when he saw me for the first time. Firas got home from work and came in as I was crying my eyes out. He let out a chuckle. It was his way of diffusing tense situations. "What's wrong. Habiti?" "My dad. He found me. My dad is alive. I thought he was dead!" "Well, that's great news, Habiti, but there is no need to cry. Come calm down," and then promptly turned on the news. I retired to bed. It was a moment when suddenly, someone with all the remaining puzzle pieces had arrived, to answer all the questions I had.

Two days later we had our first video chat online. It was weird and happy all at the same time. Here was my father who was also not my father since I had been raised by my stepdad. I was all grown up now. He was remarried to a lovely woman his own age. Since he lost me and my brother, he never wanted to have any more children since he feared he could not bear the loss a second time. My dad filled in the blanks about how he had actually gone to Saudi and worked with my grandfather while my mother was back in the States giving birth to my brother and later, me. He would send as much money as he could back to us and visit as often as he could. Eventually my mother proved unable to manage the money. When he sent her money to get the car fixed, she bought shoes, which resulted in the brakes giving out and her getting into a horrific accident that almost killed my brother. He decided to come home since it would take him a while to rise high enough to be allowed to bring his family over.

You see, if you were a laborer, you could not apply to obtain a visa for your family without a royal exception. Once you moved into management, then having your family with you was a perk that came with the role. Laborers were often housed together as single men on the hospital's dime but if they were to bring their families, then the hospital would need to assign them their own residence, which was more costly along with an extra allowance for their family's maintenance. The higher you rose the better your housing assignment, in a nutshell. Doctors, surgeons, and such got to pick and choose which compound they wanted to live in. Managers with families were offered a couple options, single nurses were only allowed to live on the hospital grounds. Single men shared villas or were put up in apartment buildings. All of these properties and compounds belonged to the hospital and the Royal family. I don't know how many compounds they owned, but with more than thirteen thousand employees and their families, you do the math.

When my dad got back to Texas where my mother was living so she could be close to my dad's family, she asked to move back to California to be closer to her family. So, my dad went to California and looked for work and rented a small house for us. When he returned, we were gone. She took us to Missouri where she had spent a great deal of her childhood. Then she took us to California to my Aunt Angela's house, where my grandmother was vacationing from Saudi.

While my mother filed for divorce, my Dad would send letter after letter addressed to me and my brother at my Aunt Angela's house since he knew that my Grandma would keep them for us. He hoped someone would read them to us one day, but my mother burned them all without opening them. My Grandmother took pity on him and did her best to save the letters, but only one survived. One day we were just gone and there was no finding us after that.

The next day I asked Firas to go visit my family in the U.S., since they had just moved to Texas, and I was eager to see their new house and maybe fly down to Colorado to see my biological father for the first time. Firas agreed. Pulling up the bank accounts on the TV screen before I traveled was a common occurrence, and he went through what we actually had and what was in some investment or retirement fund or other. He liked round numbers, so he would say so my spending money from any of the accounts was dependent on keeping the accounts round so if 10,000.00 settles at 9,534.37 for example it would drive him nuts so my allowance should not disrupt his round number system. Normally I would just sit there until he worked it out, out loud based on what was coming in, what was going out that month, and where the amount would land. I really didn't need any spending money but to send me without it would look bad on him, giving my stepdad ammunition to say he was cheap and didn't care for his daughter properly, so I took whatever he thought was appropriate.

I never used to enjoy traveling alone but without Firas to panic about being late and then leave at the last minute to insure he could panic to his heart's content, traveling alone became a joy. Now I could stroll through the airport, calm as melting butter. Like so many people who didn't really drink, I would always order a glass of white wine making sure to pay in cash so as not to alert Firas to the fact that I had been drinking. I hated the taste, but the single glass was enough to put me to sleep. I always slept with one leg connected to my handbag and my legs covered by a blanket. This way I would not alert anyone that I was worried about having my passport stolen or worse, someone trying to put something in my bag.

Trust no one outside the tribe. This is the Saudi way I was brought up with. I was ever vigilant about strangers and their intentions. Adding of course the fact that a beautiful woman traveling alone can often face interesting characters along the journey.

My stepdad would always pick me up at the airport, forgetting as usual to tell anyone I was coming, making me a surprise for the family. As a former smoker himself, it was a kindness given that I would want to smoke after such a long flight and once entering the house, finding a moment away from my five siblings would prove impossible. When we got home, he would always walk in the door and tell the family something like, "Honey, I was walking, and I found this woman and thought she might need a place to stay." Then I would enter. Osama, my youngest brother, the only one of my siblings that I had never changed his diapers, would run to the door saying, "MAHA" and hug my legs, holding on until I bent down to hug him. To him I wasn't his sister like the others, since they all lived with him. I was this beautiful, magical woman who would visit from time to time. As little boys do, he followed me around as much as he could.

The house was built to specification for them, making it the house my mom had been waiting for since she married my stepdad. Now, with his retirement check, he was finally able to make her very comfortable. She showed me her expensive new leather living room set that my sisters named the most uncomfortable couches in the world.

The house was mapped out to perfection with the girls having their own suite upstairs with a connecting bathroom which was used for any and all top-secret conversations we didn't want our parents to hear. My arrival was always an exciting one since I was appalled by things like the disorganization of the nail polishes sitting in a shoebox. I would quickly replace it while the girls were at school with a proper shelf. I would hear all the pleas for things like the idea that mom had forbidden the girls to have perfume, since in her mind, it would attract the wrong kind of attention. I would take Noura and Yasmin shopping and make sure they had everything young women should have. Being the rebel in the family already, they knew that if caught I was happy to take on the fight and the blame.

Noura was now in her first year of college at the Art Institute in Dallas while Yasmin was in her final year of high school. In the daytime, to avoid my mother talking to me all day while I tried to work, I would have my stepdad drop me off at a local coffee shop or library nearby.

There I would spend my day studying and taking smoke breaks without the fear of my brothers and sisters seeing me. My stepdad was very clear on this one rule. We both agreed that if they smoked one day, neither of us wanted to be the influence that brought them to it.

I found an evening when the children were asleep to discuss my biological father with my parents since my mom would undoubtedly find a way to make a dramatic scene at his reappearance. "Does he know where I live?" She asked. "No, he doesn't know where you live, calm down, but I need to go meet him," I said. "No, you can't go alone, he's dangerous." I looked at my stepdad in disbelief since she had lied enough about him for years. At the same time there was always a concern about "a grain of salt" once the statement was spoken. My stepdad said, "I'll go with you to meet him." It was agreed. I messaged my biological father and told him we would be coming to see him, and he sent me his address.

We landed in Colorado and as I exited the hotel to meet him for the first time, I had the first panic attack I had had in years. I was very prone to them, and they were often triggered by uncertainty. My stepdad caught me and sat me down on a bench saying, "Breathe, we don't need to meet him if you're not ready." I said, "No, I just need a minute. What if Mama is right, what if he is a monster? Do I really need to know?" He said, "Listen, honestly there have been many a time where I had to hold myself back from hitting your mother. I don't blame a young man who could not keep his temper with her, she is a handful." I took my time and finally got up and headed for the car.

When we arrived, we both walked up to the door, but I was unable to knock. I was frozen in the driveway. My stepdad rang the bell, and my biological father came to the door saying, "Yes?" "Are you David Evans?" my stepdad asked. "Yes." "Then this is your daughter," my stepdad said, holding out his hand as if to say, "Here she is." My biological father leaped from the doorway and held me, my arms to either side of my body as I tried to figure out what to do. It was my dad. I wanted to cry and at the same time he was a stranger hugging me. I finally returned his embrace and then we went inside. His wife refused to greet or recognize my presence. The tension was real. My "Bio" (which is what I have taken to referring to him by ever since) took us to eat at one of his and his wife's favorite restaurants. I recall wondering why the cleaning staff had not picked up all the peanut shells and why anyone would throw them on the floor to begin with!

He looked so much like my brother, Chris, and had so many questions about my life and who I had become. Surprisingly, he had no questions about my mother. Whereas I knew as soon as I got home my mother would interrogate me for information about him. It's an interesting thing about hatred. I always used to say that if my mom had really gotten over her feelings for my "Bio," she would have just become indifferent. Yet, she was always so angry about him. I think it was a way to cover the fact that she was still in love with him and that is what made her angry.

When we returned from dinner, my "Bio" walked me around his house, showing me this and that. He stopped at the basement door saying, "I'll show you that next time." My heart pounded at all the crazy stories my mom had told me about all sorts of things. I thought, what could be down there? Torture equipment? Guns? But in the end I found out it was his guitar and his record collection. We would prove, years later, to have the same genes but very different lifestyles.

His new wife's extended family all welcomed me so warmly and told me how much joy my return meant to my dad. It turned into a beautiful visit. I love him and until this day, enjoy his company, but we will never have much in common since I grew up so differently. And, trusting another father figure will always be hard for me.

When I arrived back home, my mom started her line of questioning. "Is he remarried? What does she look like? How old is she? Where does he live? Does he have other children?" To which my simple reply was this: "Mama, do you want me to tell him all about your life?" "No!" "Then don't ask me to tell you about his life. If I tell you about him, I will have to tell him about you, it would only be fair." She backed down and never asked me about him again.

The library in Frisco, Texas, became my day home where I would spend more than eight hours a day studying. At times Ata would call and we would talk about life. One day when he called, he mentioned that he had met a girl that he really liked. "Tell me about her." "Well, actually

I think you know her." "How?" "Do you remember Najla?" I paused and laughed. "The cousin of Hiyfa and Zulfa? Wow, what a small world!" "Yes, I started to tell her about my ex-wife, and she stopped me and said, "Is her name Maha?" I laughed and said, "Ha-ha, Yes, I remember her, how is she?" he continued. "She's great, not extremely beautiful as you know, but she responds well to me, so I am seeing how it goes." "Well, that's fantastic," I replied.

He would go on to talk about their meetings, the trip they found a way to plan to Dubai without her family knowing she was meeting him there and how far she was willing to go without losing her virginity. I always enjoyed listening to men talk to me like they would talk to men. It was fascinating to hear the difference in mindset, judgement, emotions, and roadmaps. For Najla, you see, I could tell that it was all set in her mind. When the time was right, he would come and ask for her hand which is why she was willing to go as far as she did like so many girls I knew growing up in Saudi. For Ata, however, at this stage, it was nothing of the sort. More of an exploration to see if he enjoyed having her around. He was dating her, but she was courting him. I advised restraint on his part in going too far and breaking her heart, along with her reputation. "If you must date her, be cautious," I told him, and he agreed.

Arriving home from the library I would be met at the door by my siblings all holding their hands out for the coins they knew must be in my pocket after a long day out. Noura, Yasmin, and Osma would always say something like, "College fund!" as I would empty my pockets and hand them the coins. Then I would head upstairs and enter Noura's room, since that was where I slept. She would tell me about her day and after a while, I would ask where Yasmin was to which Noura would often reply, "Ms. Scrooge is probably on her bed counting her coins." We would head through the bathroom, open Yasmin's door without knocking to avoid disturbing the counting.

Noura and Yasmin, when it came to money, were so amazingly different. Noura liked to buy anything and everything that took her fancy like our mother, leaving her always broke. Yasmin saved every penny she could find until she had enough to buy exactly what she wanted. Noura's room was filled with clutter, Beanie babies, and trinkets. Yasmin's was organized and minimal. It was as if my personality had split into two girls. The side of me that would spend money on junk to don my shelves as a girl and the minimalistic woman I had become.

Our adventures were small infractions of the rules of which there were far too many. Every time I visited, I tried to push the bar further and further but slowly so as to not cause too much of a stir. We would steal the car in the morning to go get donuts. Noura would carry a change of clothes to school. Change and then change back before my stepdad picked her up. He kept only two cars even though Noura was in college. This was said to be a money issue but one look at our mom's fancy couches, and I knew that it was a control issue. If Noura had no car she would need to be driven and picked up. Thereby, my stepdad felt he could keep her in check. I could see the opposite happening. The tighter he closed his fist the more the girls pushed the boundaries. It's a common mistake with parents of older or adolescent children. Instead of being inside their bubble they place themselves above it. I, on the other hand, placed myself inside the bubble listening, understanding, and keeping them safe without the need to place hard rules, judgments, or restrictions on their shoulders. Mistakes needed to be made so that they could grow, and I was there so they could make those mistakes safely.

I would tell them the truth. If Noura would ask if I ever had sex with someone I wasn't married to, I told the romantic story of the Irish man I met in Riyadh. If they said they wanted to watch a movie on our parents' forbidden list, we waited until the parents went to sleep, and I would rent the forbidden film on my iTunes account so we could all watch it together. This way I could answer any questions they had about all the things they were shielded from. Sex, boys, drugs, drinking, and so much more. I felt that to have the right information on purpose was always a better idea than to end up with inaccurate information accidentally. In Saudi I was taught simply that this and that was forbidden, alcohol was forbidden, talking to men was forbidden, eating pork was forbidden, and so on. Problems so often arose when you suddenly find yourself placed in a situation. What if you're at college and a boy begins to talk to you? What if you were like me, told the wine needed a little vodka, but you didn't know which was which or the difference? Without knowledge, when placed suddenly in a situation or in proximity to the forbidden, the outcome can be ... well, you get the idea. Think of the line in Disney's *Beauty and The Beast* animated movie:

> ***Gaston***: *"Belle, it's about time you got your head out of those books (tossing book into the mud) and paid attention to more important things . . . like me! The whole town's talking about it. It's not right for a woman to read–soon she starts getting ideas . . . and thinking."*
>
> **Belle**: *"Gaston, you are positively primeval."*

My stepdad was out of Saudi Arabia, but he was still primeval. I, however, was not primeval and was intent on helping my sisters avoid being thrown into a new world without the proper information they needed to navigate it.

A month went by, and it was time for me to head back to Geneva. I called Firas to make sure he had my flight details so he could meet me at the airport. I had two very heavy bags and would need his help getting them home from the airport. He said he had missed me, which made me happy to be heading back. Deep down I loved him dearly and missed the small infrequent moments when he showed how much he loved me, too.

Upon arrival I went to collect my bags, which were heavy now that I had filled them with items not available in Switzerland. I waited by the conveyer belt for Firas, but he was nowhere to be found. After waiting a while and calling him, I propped one leg onto the edge and struggled to lift my suitcases. Once they were off the conveyor I looked around again for Firas, but he wasn't there. I called his cell phone to see if he got stuck in traffic but there was no answer. I waited by the curb and smoked a cigarette. I called him again but still no answer. There must have been an emergency meeting that was called at work or maybe he overslept, I thought. I grabbed a taxi home. Upon arrival I struggled to get my bags inside to the elevator, and I called him again. With no answer I decided I just needed to do it myself. Loading the suitcases into the tiny elevator was difficult, but I made it up to our floor where I lugged the heavy bags to the front of our door and retrieved my keys from my purse.

The door was bolted from the inside, so I rang the doorbell and Firas opened it. I looked at him for a second as he said, "Habiti, welcome home." Joyful and cheery, he kissed me on the cheek as if he had never intended to come and get me at the airport. I said nothing as I struggled to bring my suitcases inside. He continued talking, "Hey, aren't you going to say hello?" "Where were you? Why didn't you answer your phone? If you weren't planning on coming to get me, why say you would? I waited!" "So sorry, Habiti, there was something so interesting on the news and I'm just so tired from work that I figured you would be fine." I had no response to the fact that the news took priority over helping his wife return from the airport. That he was always tired by working at a desk all day while I had been traveling for almost thirteen hours. I felt as though I had brought it on myself by hoping he might wake up and be so excited to see me that he would pick me up from the airport, but it was not to be. In my mind I'd made him something he was not, and that was nobody's fault but my own. We can really only disappoint ourselves by setting up inaccurate thoughts that don't reflect reality.

As I looked around the apartment, I sighed. The place had not been cleaned in a month. Dishes had not been washed, takeout boxes were piled in the corner, the toilet was growing an army of bacteria and my favorite note of all, every cup we owned had been turned into an ashtray so that he didn't have to empty the one ashtray we had. Firas quickly retired back to his couch saying, "I'll let you get some rest, Habiti." While my mind asked myself how could I possibly rest in a house this dirty, I rolled up my sleeves and got to work immediately. Once the house was clean, I went to the supermarket and picked up a few things to make dinner. We ate in front of the news and after dinner I went to bed, all the while asking myself why I had bothered to come back.

Here I was in Geneva, a place that when I told people, "I lived there," they'd respond emphatically, "Wow!" but for me it was a very hard time. In Dubai it didn't matter much if Firas was messy. I had a cleaning service. Now everything was up to me. I was up for the job but just wished he would show a little more consideration. Empty an ashtray, take out the trash, help me carry the groceries once in a while, or just pick me up at the airport.

The routine went back to normal, his work and my days alone. I started to find new parts of the city to explore and new cafés to study in. I watched people, birds, and life. I thought about all the conversations I had had with Firas about my needs. I thought I was simple. Kiss me once in a while not on my cheek, tell me I'm beautiful instead of finding something wrong with my outfit, buy me flowers when I'm coming home or for any reason at all, but his response was always a lecture on how such things are silly and as his wife I should need none of them to know that he loves me. My response was always a nod in order to make him stop talking. I had no ammunition since using a past relationship as an example was out of the question.

He said my past marriages were a disgrace and I was lucky to have made a good match in him. I was to forget I was ever married before him because none of them were his equal. Shamed into silence, I would think about Ata twirling me around when he got me from the airport. How even a week apart was torture for us. I thought about Ziyad bringing me fruit salad and making it a habit to speak to me in the softest of tones at the beginning of our relationship. Sometimes an argument would escalate to the point of me deciding not to back down. Then Firas would call his dad and his dad would suggest he buy me a present and for an hour or a day he was attentive and sweet but when that hour or that day was over, he would slip right back into who he was. It makes me wonder how someone outside the house who was so liberal, kind, courteous, and open minded would switch on "full Arab" once we were in the house.

Firas had a business trip for a few days. I took the opportunity to talk to Ata as often as I could now that the time difference was not important since Firas was not home at night. Ata said he was taking Najlah on a trip (They had married earlier that year) and asked me not to send anything in case she should see it. She was what he called, "jealous of her own shadow." While Ata and I understood that we were never getting back together, she would have never agreed for us to be speaking. The next day my email account was hacked, and the hacker emailed everyone in my contact list with one line, "Where are you?" I know because my other email address was in my contact list too. As soon as the emails went out, sure enough, there it was: an email from Najlah. It was in Arabic and very long. She used a lot of language calling me a prostitute and making sure to write the word "bitch" as often as possible. The gist of the email was, "Don't contact my husband ever again. I have all your pictures from Ata's hard drive, and I'll put them all over the Internet."

I recall feeling sick as I read the email to Noor on the phone. We understood her anger and Noor made sure to scold me for letting him keep the secret of our talking from his wife, knowing full well she would have never agreed. I had changed so much and felt it was his place to tell her or not. The truth was I needed him to talk to and I was selfish. I didn't care if she released my pictures since she had no idea that I was no longer covered as she still was. The threat would have been very scary to a covered woman in Saudi like her, but for me, it was just air. She threatened to release the video of my stepdad grabbing me that Ata had saved. The only concern with that threat was Firas. I could see the cycle of pain coming back around again. My stepdad and Firas already did not get along and if Firas knew what he had done I would have never been allowed to visit my family again. I finally decided, come what may, she can do as she likes with my pictures and the video, but I don't want Ata to suffer. I also knew Ata better than anyone and I knew he would have never agreed to let her send me that email. Above all we loved and respected each other. I sat down and drafted a short email to her.

It read something like:

> *Dearest Najlah, I'm so sorry. My email was hacked. Of course, it is your right to ask me not to speak to him. I will no longer contact him and if he contacts me, I will always send him back to you.*

I copied Ata's email address so that he could be aware of what had transpired. The reply came from her again just saying, "bitch you bitch you bitch." I blocked her and quietly mourned the loss of a dear friend. We both knew the day would come, but now at last it was real.

Relationships between men and women once they married others was not often done. Firas would have never agreed and likewise neither would she. I swore I would never do that to someone I loved.

Firas had made me give up Haisum a year earlier, even though he was like a little brother to me. Now I had lost Ata, my only real confidant who had lived outside of the Saudi world I grew up in. Noor would always offer advise based on what she knew but Ata could advise based on all the different interactions, worldly experiences, and relationships he had had. I needed them both, I needed them all, but perhaps it was time.

Firas called, saying he had to extend his trip because they have asked him to go to Austria for a couple days. I said, "Austria, can I come?" "Why would you want to come to Austria? You would be bored. I won't have time to see you at all." My mental response was I'm bored here, and you don't have time to see me here … instead I replied, "I could see the sights, I love Austria. My favorite historical princess from childhood is from there and there is the Freud museum. I'm a Psychology major, Habebe." "Alright, but when you get here don't be asking me to come with you anywhere, I'll be busy, and you'll be on your own." My mental response was "why would I want you with me making commentary about everything?"

Austria was everything I imagined it would be. I walked around the square, found the most breathtaking cathedral, and attended my very first Catholic mass. Something Firas would have found very unacceptable. While I found other people's cultures, traditions, and customs fascinating, Firas's commentary was always how they were wrong, and we were right. A typical lawyer, he picked his side and would argue until he had won the argument. At the end of the first day Firas returned from his business early. I was getting ready to go to a Mozart concert I had bought a ticket for earlier in the day. Firas looked at me puzzled and said, "Why didn't you get me a ticket?" "You said you would be busy, and I assumed you would be tired when you came back and not want to go, but I'm sure there is probably an extra ticket at the door if we go early." He got dressed and we headed to the theater. The champagne was included but of course we didn't drink, so we gave our bottle to the table next to us. I secretly wished he had worked late so I could have tried the champagne, spoken to people, and cheered for the amazing performance at its end instead of clapping properly like a diplomat's wife.

The next day I visited the Freud museum with so much excitement to see his fainting couch and have a glimpse into someone I had been studying with fascination for the past two years. When I returned, I laughed and told Firas how I got lost walking back but then found my way. His response was, "You shouldn't want to go see his museum. That man was disgusting, and everyone knows he slept with his own mother." "If you feel like bashing what you don't understand please keep it to yourself, I had a lovely time." "You know I'm right." "No, I don't. Tell me, then, what do you know about psychoanalysis? ... Anything...." A pause happened for a bit, I knew full well he had no idea what that word even meant or anything about Freud. Like so many Arabs, for Firas, Freud was persona-non-grata for one easy reason, he was born to Jewish parents.

The issue of Israel vs. Palestine when it appeared on the news was an easy way to upset Firas as he called the Israelis every curse word he had at his disposal. I would state an obvious fact or make a peaceful suggestion such as, "Why don't the Israelis just give all the Palestinians nationality and live together in peace?" to which he would respond, "They took Palestine away from its people who were there first, they should give it back." This would provoke a history lesson from Firas about everything the Israelis had done. I would bide my time as he spoke and then insert, "Fascinating, Firas, tell me how long Israel has occupied Palestine?" "More than 45 years." "Okay, so what country in history got their country back after 45 years of occupation? Can you name one, and if there is one, isn't it still better to just let Israel have the country and nationalize the Palestinian's so people like my best friend can have a passport and see the world, instead of wondering from country to country with nothing but a travel document? My best friend will never see Europe, America, Asia, or most of Africa because she will never have a passport unless she marries for one. Wouldn't that be better than the endless killing, backstabbing and back and forth? Just end it already." "Palestine will never surrender to Israel, it's a matter of principle. The Israelis are evil and need to be stopped." At this stage he would return to ranting at the TV while I withdrew to our balcony, sick of the entire issue.

After Austria, I tried to fill my days when I was not studying with projects; I sewed curtains for my pantry, painting, and finding a way to get Netflix in Switzerland through a proxy. Noor could rarely talk unless her husband was out, Haisum was gone, Ata was gone, and I felt as though the world was a dark and lonely place. I used to leave the TV on in the background all day playing movie after movie that I had seen before as a kind of way to bring voices into the house so that I would not feel so alone. Since I was a full-time home student I took on average four courses each term and when possible, six. The end of a term was a stressful time with exams looming, which meant I was awake sometimes late into the night.

One particular night Noura Facetimed me. We normally just messaged each other, so I knew something must be up. We talked for a bit about random things until she spilled that she had met a boy. She was as giddy as a girl can be with her first potential boyfriend. I enjoyed listening to her happy, dreamy, girly talk about how wonderful he was. While at the same time mentally logging potential problem clues, she would naturally overlook the clouds where she currently resided. She talked and talked until something stuck out, "Well, his mom is a prostitute, and his brother deals drugs but that has nothing to do with him." I controlled my face as I asked her to tell me more about that. She told me everything she knew, and I said, "Cool (which really meant *Oh, Shit*). Do you have a picture? I want to see."

She texted me the picture, a good-looking Black man, charming even, but something was very off with the way their relationship was going. Noura felt pressured to have sex and my question for that was, "Do you want to have sex?" Her reply was, "No." I advised her to just avoid going to his place and stick to the courtyard at school. "You should be fine." We said our good nights after two hours on the phone and I immediately started looking for a flight to Dallas.

When Firas woke up, he asked me why I was packing to which I replied, "I need to go see my sister, she's involved with a boy, and I just want to make sure she is okay." His response was, "Serves your dad right for raising his daughters in America." I rolled my eyes and finished packing, all the while replaying everything Noura had said about the boy. I thought about what Baba might know, which was very important. My stepdad being Saudi disowned me for marrying a Syrian, twice. A nationality he said was, "unfit to even clean his car." Egyptians would have been worse and a Black man .... Well, if he found out she would be a dead woman. While I would have no problem with her dating or even eventually marrying a Black man or even a Jew, I knew that until she was sure it was going to stick, she did not want to have Baba find out. She would most definitely find herself on a one-way trip back to Saudi and married to someone of his choosing soon after or dead.

Let me touch for a moment on what seems like a ladder system. The Gulf countries population, even though many of them will not speak of such things outside their own circle, see each nationality as having a rung on a tall ladder. The top rung is the Gulf countries. Saudi Arabia, Kuwait, Qatar, the United Arab Emirates, Bahrain, Oman, and Iraq. Saudis think they are the top on the ladder, the Emirates think they are, and so on. After the Gulf countries according to my stepdad, are Jordan, Lebanon, Syria, and Egypt (Egyptians being very low since my step-grandmother used to say they were not Arabs because they are technically Africans. Which was actually an insult meaning they had dark skin. (Therefore, only considered working class. Until today in fact there is still a great struggle happening to convince Saudis to work in certain jobs that require manual labor. They feel very strongly that such work is beneath them.). Followed by Sudan, Nigeria, Somalia, Algeria, Yemen, Djibouti, Africa, India, Pakistan, and so on. All at the bottom of the ladder. All the other countries in the West were not really thrown into the mix very often since they were just infidels and didn't know any better. Foreigners were often treated with respect but if you were born in India, for example, you would find that you are spoken to and treated like a 4th class citizen. As my stepdad would say, "Not good enough to clean my shoes."

Sadly, where you were from had a direct impact on your life in the Middle East and still does to a great extent today. I volunteered once at the King's Hospital in my mid-twenties in the Administration department where I stumbled across a pay structure listing nationalities and alongside them how much they got paid per hour based on their country. India, the Philippines, Sudan, Nigeria, Somalia, Algeria, Yemen, Djibouti, and Africa were all at the bottom of the pay scale. I'd like to say I felt appalled at the time, but I grew up in this system and when I asked the very nice Filipino lady in the admin office why this was, she said that it was based on an average salary in their country of origin. "I know that means that they can send money home and it will be a great deal over there, but how do they survive here?" She asked me not to talk that way for it would get them all in trouble. I dropped the issue. It was the way things were.

In truth even the United Nations still uses a system similar to this one. Firas, for example, got paid less than his friend who was Jordanian, because his friend was hired after he got his American passport while Firas was Syrian. I traveled and made friends from all nationalities; I encouraged my sisters to do the same even when it came to love. My stepdad, however, will never change the way he was brought up. In a world where he was put down because their family, while Saudi now, were once somewhere lower on the list. Once the family had a few generations on the ground they took great pride in their position on the ladder. It still surprises me that my stepdad's best friend was from Sudan. He loved him and confided in him, which was a rare thing for my stepdad. At the same time, he would still refuse to even consider a marriage for one of his daughters from his best friend's sons so our families never had dinner or even tea together.

My mind raced the entire plane ride to Dallas. Noura had no idea the possible danger she was in. Not from her potential boyfriend but rather her father. While they knew how clever their father was, none knew how cunning he was like I did. If he didn't know already, he would very, very soon. I could not decide what to do, having only Noura's info to go on knowing full well she was not deliberate and careful like Yasmin was. When I arrived, my stepdad picked me up at the airport as usual but asked about the sudden decision for the trip. Normally they knew weeks, sometimes months in advance. "I'm happy to see you, Princess, but is everything okay at home?" he said. Here it was, the moment I had been dreading the entire plane ride, the man could sniff out lies like you or I would smell burning popcorn in the next room. Rule number one of any interrogation is always to stick to as much of the truth as you can without giving away everything. I lit my cigarette, inhaled looked at him and said, "It's something with Noura, she said she needed me, so I came." Which wasn't the truth, she had no idea that I was coming for her. "What is it?" he asked. "I won't tell you now, I can't. I have it in hand, just trust me, if it's something you need to know you will, otherwise just let me take care of it." My stepdad said, "Alright." It was the first time I didn't have to lie too much or tell him the truth. The years seemed to have proved to him that I always had my siblings best interests at heart.

At home, Noura spent the greater part of the night talking about her new boyfriend. Likes, dislikes, how they met, and everything else her brain could remember. She said she was scared Baba was getting close. I said to myself I bet he already has the boyfriend's phone number but hasn't made the call yet. Before I offered any of my how-to-get-away-with-having-a-boyfriend advice, I wanted to make sure this was a real thing. Thus far all the signs seem to be pointing to college sex, considering her sudden fascination with the topic with Noura being the sacrificial lamb in the scenario. I dug deeper to see if he was asking her to have sex with him and how often. Once, twice, or does it come up every time they meet? My questions went on and on until the night ended, and the sun came up. I gave Noura some advice about not seeing him anywhere near where Baba could drive by and accidently get a glimpse. Second, I said, "Don't ever be late to get to the car. If Baba is on his way you should have already said goodbye, so he is nowhere near you when Baba arrives." "Baba won't recognize him, he has never seen him," she said "No, my dear, Baba would look at him if he glanced at you for just five seconds and then he will look at your facial expression and you will give it away and it will be game over, trust me. Not my first camel race." Noura nodded.

The next day I began running interference because Baba had started giving Noura less and less warning that he was almost to her school. When he would leave, I would text her and eventually I discovered that he had ordered a full record of every phone call she made in a given month. He had already isolated her best friend's number and everyone else in our family. Since Noura only had one friend at the time it was easy to figure out that there might be a boy and as I suspected he already had his number. Noura and I would meet in the bathroom while Yasmin was at school to talk about him. Noura did not want Yasmin to know anything either. Yasmin, however, another person Noura underestimated, had noticed a boy kept liking all of Noura's Instagram posts and she had grown suspicious all on her own. One night when we were watching a movie, *Burlesque*, about strippers since they were curious about the topic, Noura started to talk about her friend in class, a boy. I felt like taping her mouth shut. By the smirk on Yasmin's face, I knew she was sure now.

Yasmin made a suggestion that they message him from one of our phones and pretend to be a stripper just for fun. I volunteered my phone since it was the only one my stepdad didn't have access to the phone bill. Plus, I was more able to handle things if anything went wrong. Noura, in her effort to prove to her sister that she didn't like the boy, agreed with a laugh saying, "He has a girlfriend, he won't be interested in a stripper texting him." I shuddered at the young girl before me. I knew better than anyone that even the happiest of married men would still be curious about a stripper texting them. It was male nature.

In Saudi and in Islam, looking at another woman with lust is a sin and wives start arguments over their husband's just glancing in another woman's direction. Some of the more ridiculous arguments start that way. When the truth is they can't help it, anyone would look at boobs if they were placed before them. I knew she would not take it well if things went like I knew they would. We gathered around my phone in the dark as we googled stripper names to find a picture and agreed on our stripper's identity, we settled on the necessary information and Noura put in the number and sent the first text:

Noura: *Hey*
Greg: *Who is this?*
Noura: *It's Misty*

Greg: Do I know you?

I turned to Noura. "Is there a bar he likes to hang out at. somewhere he might go drinking?" "Bar Louis, it's near campus." "Okay, got it, was there a day you know he was there recently, hurry, Noura, he's going to get suspicious." "Umm, Yes, he was there on Wednesday."

***Noura**: Ya, we met at Bar Louis, remember, I work as a stripper if that helps you remember ha-ha.*

***Greg**: Cool, so what's your stripper name?*

***Noura**: Misty-Dream.*

After that, like clockwork he asked guy question after guy question leading up to him asking for our picture. Once sent, the flirting began, and the giggles started to turn to a deep silence from Noura as I suspected would happen. She passed the phone back to me slowly signaling that it was time to end the conversation and we texted him that we had a show and had to go. I blocked him as Noura talked about how lame he is since he has a girlfriend. My eyes caught hers as I tried to convey with no words how silly the whole exercise was.

A few days later Noura said Greg had told her he was moving back to California and didn't know when he would see her again. I started my usual round of thought-provoking questions. "Was this something he has been talking about for a while, or was it all of a sudden?" "He never mentioned it before." "Odd, and when you were at his place did it look like things were getting packed, or maybe a plane ticket?" "Nothing," she replied. She looked at the bathroom floor, I could see the wheels in her head slowly starting to turn so I continued, "So, after he told you he was moving away and he might not see you again for a while, did he ask you to have sex again?" A slow and quiet, "Ya" came out of her mouth as she looked up at me. I asked one last question, "So, do you think maybe he is saying he's moving away to get you to have sex with him?" "Do you really think that's what he is doing?" she asked. "I can't know, Noura, only you can answer that, you know him, and I don't. Give it a few days and see for yourself."

The next few days proved that he had never intended to move anywhere and at 11:00 p.m. on a Monday night, after a month and a half in my parent's house, he broke up with her. She was heartbroken but not too severely since she had contemplated breaking up with him after the stripper joke, and after the California incident. My work was done, she was safe, and it was now time for me to head back to Geneva. In the car ride to the airport my stepdad asked me if everything was all good, to which I replied, "As I am sure you already knew there was a boy, but he's gone now and that's all there is to it, no need to worry about it." He nodded, and we didn't speak of it again.

In a normal American environment, there is nothing wrong with exploring your body, having sex, and having all kinds of different relationships, but for my family, even though they lived in America, the house was like Saudi soil and the rules were the same. Shame the family and there will be consequences, disobey the rules and there will be even bigger consequences. They had grown up partly in Saudi and while they were aware, the extent of their awareness was nowhere near mine. The safest course for them in my mind was to keep the freedoms that I had rallied for them to have and to play the game until they moved out with my stepdad's blessing. Then freedom would start, and this would give me time to educate them on the new world they were about to officially enter.

I would spend most of the next two years flying back and forth from Geneva to the U.S. only being able to bear Firas for short periods of time. The summer came and Firas' brother and his wife were both doing their residencies at a hospital in Shreveport, which was only a two-and-a-half-hour drive from my parent's house. I suggested I fly down early and then he could meet my parents and then we could head down to see his brother together. He agreed. Upon arrival back in the U.S., I relayed the plan to my stepdad and suggested we could have lunch with Firas at the house so he could meet mom and the kids. My stepdad grinded his teeth and said, "He's not coming here," walking away. I followed him asking, "Why not, come on be reasonable." He turned around and said, "It was your decision to marry him, but he still married you without my permission, which is disrespectful. You can have him in your life, but he will not be a part of ours." "It's just lunch, I'm not asking for him to stay." "Fine, have him over for lunch, we will be out." "Now you're being even more ridiculous." I stormed out to go smoke by a large willow tree on the other side of a pond in the back of the house, a place I called my thinking spot, where I contemplated everything.

As things stood everything was fine. I came to visit my family and Firas was more than willing to send me but if my stepdad insulted Firas by turning him away, well let's just say I knew better than anyone that slight would not be forgotten, and I would hear about it every time I mentioned my family. I begged and begged my stepdad day after day for a compromise, citing that he would cause problems in my marriage and undoubtedly it would affect how often I could visit. He finally relented to him coming by for coffee. "No sweets, no snacks, just coffee." It was to send a clear message that he was only there because I begged, since in a Saudi home, you never just served coffee. Not to offer something more to an Arab guest was an insult but it was better than the alternative: no visit at all.

Firas flew down and rented a motel room. My mother was kind enough to drive me out to meet him. Upon arrival my mother asked if I was sure I was going to be alright as we looked out the car window at the dark, creepy motel. I replied, "I'll be fine." As I headed up the stairs to find the door to Firas' room, I noted the people in the parking lot, the trash on the floor, and peeling green paint on the doors. I knocked and Firas said, "Habebti, so good to see you." I tried to smile as I clutched my bag and looked around the floor. He said, "It was the only place I could find that allowed smoking and was close to the strip clubs." "Well, that's not surprising," I said as I cringed, noticing all the black cockroaches wandering around the floor. Firas said, "Oh, ya, I already called. They are going to send someone to get rid of them. The place looked really nice in the pictures."

I sat on the corner of the bed and noted the state of the room as I uttered, "I think I will call my mom to come get me. I can stay there tonight, it's really dirty, Firas." Firas went into Arab pride panic mode and said, "Wait, we can move somewhere else, no need to go home." I just wanted to sleep without things crawling around, but I forgot the ongoing chest beating game my stepdad and he were playing. If I had gone back after my mom dropped me off and told them what the motel looked like, my stepdad would have used it to prove his point that he was a low Syrian and not worthy of his daughter. Firas looked at his phone for a few moments and finally settled on the Intercontinental in downtown Dallas. As he drove me there, he relayed his plans for the evening and asked if he could get me some food from the drive-through Taco Bell on the way. I nodded.

After we checked in, Firas looked at me and said, "Is that okay, Habibti, I have not been in America in so long and I really want to go see the American strip clubs." I nodded, smiled, and said, "Yeah, of course." "Thank you, Habibti, I'll be back soon," kissing me on the cheek and leaving. I sat on the bed with no appetite for eating anymore. He had not seen me in a month and his first thought was always the news or strip clubs. A sinking reality hit my stomach and I changed clothes and went to bed, feeling hurt and alone.

The morning came and we packed up early to make a stop on the way. We needed to buy gifts for my family which is customary when you meet your future in-laws for the first time. In Firas' case, he did not get to meet them before the wedding so he would need to treat this meeting as such. Everything had to be perfect because my stepdad would be waiting to pounce on anything he could call a slight. My stomach was in knots the whole way there.

When we arrived, I found my mom had put on her gaudiest gold embroidered woman's thobe, a traditional dress worn by Bedouins. I looked at my sisters with a look that said, "Really?" They shared in my embarrassment. The show had begun. On a day-to-day basis, we were really normal and casual in our dress. Today, however, my stepdad was putting on his "I'm better than you" show as he was purposefully late leaving his room to show he was disconcerted about a guest who was much lower than he was. Dawning his full Saudi thobe complete with his red Saudi Ghutra and holding himself like a King Cobra ready to strike. He walked over to Firas and held for a second so Firas could extend his hand first. The time before Firas extended his hand was painful. Finally, he did, saying how good it was to see him again, to which my stepdad just nodded.

My brothers and sisters piled in and sat all over the room watching as if it was the climax of a really great horror movie. Something was going to go down and none of them wanted to miss a moment. I introduced my brothers and sisters to Firas. He smiled and greeted them one by one. As I poured him some coffee, it happened … My mom was oblivious of course to customs, signals, or slights. My sisters however cringed like the movie just got gory. You know the part where you need to close your eyes because blood just splattered across the screen? Ya, it was that bad.

My stepdad sat down in this chair and put his feet up in Firas' direction. I closed my eyes for a moment hoping I had imagined it out of panic, but it was so. Firas drank his coffee and made conversation with my mother for a moment and then promptly said, "Well, we really should start driving, we have a long way to go before we get there." My stepdad sat up and said, God be with you, and promptly went back into his King Cobra cave (his bedroom). God be with you or in Arabic "Allah Ma-aak," can also be used as an insult. When said with a tone that actually sounds like "Fuck off" or more politely, "Get going."

You see, Arabs normally walk their guests to the door and spend a great deal of time telling their guests how good it was to see them, how much they hope to see them again soon, and wishing them a safe journey. My stepdad just retired to his room. This would be the part in the movie where the fight was over, and my siblings could now collect on their bets on who would insult who first.

The drive was unbearable. Firas started his rant as soon as we were out of sight. "How dare he insult me!" I attempted to diffuse the situation by saying, "He sits with his feet up all the time. Maybe he didn't mean anything, he was just resting his feet." "Oh no! He knew what he was doing, and he did it on purpose. I'm just as good as he is, better. Of course, you could not possibly understand, you're not Arabic," he said. Here we go, I thought, now I'm just a dumb American. I decided to stay silent, knowing there was nothing I could say and no side I could take that would help the situation. What was done was done. Halfway down the road I donned my head cover again. A compromise we agreed on to not disturb the image his family had of me. In their minds I was still covered, since they had not seen me after I decided not to cover in Dubai. I felt like a fraud, but it was his family and what he said had to go.

We arrived at his brother's house and were put up in the guest bedroom. I wanted to stay there the rest of the trip since in order to come out I needed to cover my hair. I felt as though I had gone backwards. I sat with them at the table as we ate dinner, and their daughter watched her cartoons. His brother explained that we were not to speak to their daughter in English. Since they wanted her to learn Arabic, everything in the house needed to be in Arabic. Phone calls were taken outside, all of her cartoons, toys, and books, were in Arabic. A great idea to help her learn the language from an early age, I thought. If the two-year-old girl asked her father for water in English, she was to be ignored until she said it in Arabic. After an hour of crying, she finally produced the word. I felt like that was going too far but of course it was not my place to say.

I spent most of the visit in silence, day in and day out. We stayed there for about five days. His brother was much more religious than Firas was, prayer was not an option, his wife lowered her eyes when we went out and of course we walked behind the men. Firas' brother constantly lectured Firas on smoking, praying, and making sure he ate only in *Halal* (Halal being that the meat was sacrificed in the proper way and in the name of the one true god) restaurants. The best lecture of all was about the importance of having children. Firas said that we weren't settled enough for children, and he wanted to wait but his brother cast out the "God will provide" quote and when Firas nodded, I knew what was coming next.

That night Firas told me that he had decided that it was time for us to have a child. "You decided? Shouldn't we decide things like that together?" I asked. "I'm the man and I've decided it's time," he said. I took a deep breath knowing a fight in front of his brother would not be appropriate and after almost three years of marriage, it was the logical next step, at least the HIV random testing will be put on hold … hopefully.

On the drive back to Dallas we managed to argue for two hours about what I should do if my car ever stopped on the side of the road. Firas said, "Listen to me, if your car stops on the side of the road you need to call the police." "The Police!? My car stopped, I call triple A or a tow truck. Not the police." "No, you have to listen to what I say, so you need to agree that you will call the police." I knew how this cycle went, if I agreed he would puff up and end the argument. Winning was everything to him but over the years I started to take more pleasure in not agreeing and so we would go back and forth like this for hours until one of us conceded which was usually me because I was getting tired.

Back in Geneva, baby making attempts would surely commence. It was during the final semester of my BA. As we sat one evening in front of the TV watching the Tudors, the first show Firas agreed to watch with me as long as I agreed to exclude the homosexual scenes. If I forgot he would scream, "YAK! Go forward, it's disgusting." I, of course, would insist on leaving it on, saying it was important to the plot. Unfortunately, it was always impossible to hear what they were saying as he covered his eyes and ranted about how disgusting it was to watch. While I like that Firas grew up in a world where homosexuality was not accepted and, in most cases, punishable by death, his overreaction to every scene of this nature made me wonder. Was he really that disgusted or was he trying to avoid me noticing something? A look or a tick? Often in olden times when a person was accused of a crime, such as homosexuality or witchcraft, the crowd would throw rotten food at them as they were escorted to their place of execution. The people knew that not to do so would show sympathy and they might then be accused of being homosexual or a witch as well. Was he overreacting so as not to reveal something, I wondered?

As the semester moved on, my stress levels rose and rose as I found myself without sleep trying to read all the material and turn in my work on time. I asked Firas if I could go get caught up on my schoolwork at my family's home in Dallas. "What if you're pregnant, you should be here," he said. "I'll be fine, and it would be better for me if I was pregnant to be there with nothing to concentrate on but my schoolwork," I said. He said, "We'll wait to make sure you're not then you can go."

After getting off the phone with his father that evening he told me that he wanted to remind me that when we did have children, I was never to tell them anything about my past ever. I looked confused as I said, "They will know eventually, the whole world will." "No, they won't." I took a deep breath, "Firas, I'm going to write my book about my life, of course they will read it one day." "No, you will not, I forbid it." "Yes, I will." "No, you won't, I forbid you to write a book, it would bring only scandal." I knew there was no winning the argument, so I left the room to go to bed and to try and get some sleep.

That night I got up again with deadlines swirling around my head but more than anything the fact that being forbidden to write my book felt like one more piece of my life was being ripped away from my soul. I had been working on my book on and off since as far back as I could remember. A journal here and a piece of paper there. I even minored in literature just to help me put it all together later. I stood on the balcony looking out into the night sky. Listening to a song by Owl City called *Silhouette* with the lyrics:

> *I'm a silhouette, asking every now and then is it over yet will I ever smile again.*

As I replayed the song over and over, I felt as though I was nothing but a shell of myself. Everything I wanted was wrong, stupid, forbidden, disgraceful, or silly. My past had to be deleted since it would only bring scandal and so too my memories were forbidden to be recalled or shared with anyone at all.

I glanced down off the balcony to see how far down it was to the ground. I found myself pondering if I jumped would it be high enough to kill me? Or, would it just immobilize me for life? I stared at it for some time before deciding the latter was worse than the former. It was not high enough. Instead, I called my stepdad and told him I needed to come home for a while. The stress of my final semester was getting to me, I said, deciding not to reveal to him my real concern. I woke up in the morning and told Firas I needed to go see my family to finish my semester. He agreed and then started to talk about HIV, politics, and other things.

As he spoke, something snapped in my head. "Enough!" I shouted, throwing my fine China coffee cup into the sink so hard it smashed. It was the first time I had ever displayed such outright anger to Firas. "You broke the cup, we need to talk about this, that kind of behavior is not acceptable to your husband." I looked down and took a deep breath as I replied calmly, "Be grateful it didn't end up in your head." Firas was stunned into silence as I passed by him to pack my suitcase.

Once I was back at my parents' house in Dallas, Firas said I could stay a few more weeks but while I was there, I needed to get all the fertility testing done that he had requested I do. This request possibly came because his parents said if we have not been using any contraception for almost three years, then something must be wrong. The doctor suggested Firas get tested first to save on the cost of tests. I explained to her that Firas would not agree to get tested, he said he didn't have time. Her face looked like she wondered why anyone would want to have a child with a husband who didn't have time for such a simple test. Test after test and the doctors could find nothing wrong so I headed back to Geneva.

On the same evening I arrived, Firas decided it was time to get started trying again so we went into the bedroom, removed our clothes and I leaned in to kiss him but he leaned back saying, "No, I want to make sure *Allah* will bless this creation," and proceeded to say a *Duaa* (Which is a kind of prayer that does not involve bowing, it's more like supplication). I laid there cold and naked until he finished. I thought to myself how turned off I was. Then as usual I was not to look at him as I gave him a blow job, followed by me turning over while he jerked off until right before he was about to come and then sticking it in and finishing. Afterwards he told me I had to sit with my legs in the air for at least twenty minutes as his father had suggested. I thought maybe he would sit with me, maybe bring me my phone, but he quickly left the room to turn the news back on.

The next day as I was washing some glasses in the sink, I started pondering what it would be like if we had a boy? A mini-Firas. I could barely handle the one I already had. If we had a mini-me well that would be fine, I guess, unless he insists that our daughter live in an Arabic time warp at home like his brother's daughter. I started to get sad about the fact that I knew if I had a child, that child would be kept away from any ideas, thoughts, mannerisms, way of dressing that reflected the American side of me. They would be his children and they would be Syrian.

I reflected more and more until I suddenly broke the glass I was washing and sliced the flesh between my index finger and thumb almost right down to the bone. There was too much blood for me to handle so I called Firas. "I sliced my hand; I need help to get to the hospital, it's really bad." He said he was on his way and hung up. He helped me into the car and took me straight to a walk-in clinic. They did an ultrasound to make sure there was no glass inside my hand before stitching me up. It was these moments that kept me with him, he had dropped everything he was doing and come to help me. He sat beside me the whole time telling me everything was going to be alright. That was all it took for me to forget about everything he had done or not done in the last three years since we got married. I realized that I loved him because I felt like no one really protected me my whole life. I had to look after myself. No matter what, Firas would be there when I needed him and perhaps that was more important than anything else.

Returning again to the States, I spent my days in the library as I normally did, finishing up one paper after the next. I would take my smoke breaks between finishing papers as a sort of reward. It was in these moments in the silent library that I thought about my past. Not so much in a longing to go back. I regretted none of my decisions. All of them were right at the time. You see, great love stays with you always. Deep inside, hidden from your mind, and resurfacing like the way a violin reaches into a classical music piece. In that moment all the world turns silent as you recall their face. Almost like a ghost that haunts you in these moments. You look over at the empty seat next to you and imagine them sitting down and as a result your heart beats a little bit faster. Then time starts again, and they're gone, like a coin that fell from your pocket and disappeared out of sight. It was something Firas could never understand having never been in love, as he said, before me.

I don't know if we really ever move on. After all, the lives we touch along the way and the lives that touch us are with us always and a part of who we are today. We all bounce through life making choices and getting bruised but, in the end, everything adds up and then we emerge. I pondered much during those hours at the library. I felt Firas' place on the shelf begin to shift. A Psychology professor of mine once said that you don't just hit someone over the head and now, they are insane. It takes more than that, nothing happens overnight.

YOU CAN GRADUATE MENTALLY AS WELL AS ACADEMICALLY.

After being in the States for two months, I thought there wasn't any point in going back to Geneva until I was done with school. The day came when my final results were finalized: I passed! I ran around the house shouting as if my whole universe had suddenly changed. All the kids danced and jumped around with me. To celebrate I decided I would go out for a smoke. As I slipped away from the house, I traveled across the street to my secret place. I climbed down the grassy hill and sat next to the water. I looked up at the beautiful sunset and then out across the water. As I smoked, I thought about my life. Sadness came over me as I realized that I worked so hard and yet I was celebrating a Bachelor of Arts degree I would never be allowed to use. A minor in literature I would never be allowed to put towards writing a book. My life would always consist of me standing in the shadows, an empty shell of a person. Victor Hugo wrote, *"diamonds are found in the depths of the earth and so truth is only found in the depths of reflection."* It was at that moment, the day I got my degree, that in the depths of my reflection I made my decision.

I called Noor from my special place to tell her the good news of my graduation and ask how her delivery went. When she told me she had a boy I was relieved; in case of divorce, she might be able to keep her son since male children at the age of nine get to choose where they want to live, unlike girls who always belong to their fathers. "Oh, honey, Alf Mabouk! Your little prince!" "Thank you, Honey, I never thought I could love anyone more than I love this baby!" "What was it like? The delivery?" "It was awful! I never want to go through that again! They forgot to give me the anesthesia when they were stitching me back up and I could feel every single stitch!" I cringed at the thought and said, "Too bad you're not in the States, we sue doctors for doing stuff like that!" "Well, it's over now, Al-Hamdullah! You should have one with Firas, Honey." I got quiet and said, "Honey, I can barely handle him let alone if there was a mini-him running around. Honey, I have decided I want a divorce. He's just not right for me and he doesn't like me." "Honey, I can't agree. He's a good man, he lets you travel, he gives you money, he doesn't beat you. You have everything, Honey." I sighed, thinking that this was my world's definition of a happy marriage. That you are fed, clothed, and not beaten. Where everything you want to aspire to must be agreed upon by your husband. To me it felt more like the relationship between an inmate and a prison warden, and I wanted out of the psychological jail I had been in for too many years. "It's over, Honey, I'm sorry, I know you like him and maybe for you he would have been a great match, but for me he is not." "Pray on it, Honey." "Okay. Talk soon!"

I went back into the house straight to my stepdad's study and told him I was going back to ask Firas for a divorce. "Whoa! What brought this on all of a sudden?" he said. "It's not all of a sudden, I'm not happy and I finally made my decision." "Okay, but why? I thought you were happy." "I am married to an Arab. All Arab marriages are happy on the outside." I proceeded to list out everything I had never shared with anyone over the years about my marriage to Firas. His responses when I took a breath were, "What!?" "Wow," and "Get out of there!" as I continued to spill my story. He noted my sudden change in spirit, as if a spring in my bouncy feet had been returned to me. I called the airlines and changed my flight to the next day. I was not set to go back for another two weeks. I also decided to take nothing with me and not tell Firas I was coming, as a sudden flight change would only freak him out. I wanted to do this in person calmly, which was only right out of respect for the relationship we had.

Upon arrival in Geneva, I took a taxi to the house. Firas would be at work which would give me time to start packing up my things to ship to my parents' house. I walked inside to find the place twice as dirty as normal but instead of cleaning up as I normally did, I headed down to the market to purchase some boxes and bubble wrap. When I made the purchase by credit card, the credit card transaction sent a text alert to Firas, something he had set so he could ask me about everything I bought. I had been so used to it, after a while I forgot he was notified for every purchase. He never asked if I bought anything at the grocery store but everything else was questioned.

He immediately texted my phone, "Are you back?" to which I replied, "Yes." This meant that he would be on his way home at any minute. I opened the fridge to get something to drink as I waited for him only to find a bottle of Whiskey and a bottle of Vodka. I was surprised that someone so adamant about not drinking, suddenly had two bottles in the fridge. I recalled the night I begged him to try having a drink in Geneva and how I said, "We don't have to be drinkers but if you've never had it, you should try it." He agreed and bought a small bottle of Whiskey and as I poured myself a glass with him, he said, "No! You're my wife, you can't drink. I won't have that sin on my head." I sat and watched him drink and then throw the rest of the bottle down the trash chute saying, "It's not for me." I felt defeated that night, since I had hoped it would loosen him up and we could have a great night, but it did not go as I'd hoped.

When he arrived, I was standing on the balcony, smoking. Taking in the view in my mind for one last time. When he came in, I turned around and greeted him. Everything had changed with my decision. I now had no expectation of anything beyond doing what I came to do. I no longer cared if he would kiss me or if the house was clean. When he came in, he started talking right away as if he had been caught with the liquor. "I'm so happy you're back, Habibti, but what brought you back without telling me? I would have come to pick you up from the airport." I took a deep breath and looked to one side since I knew even if I had called, he would not have picked me up. He always said he would, but he never did.

He continued talking since my silence was obviously putting him on edge. "What time did you get in?" I understood with that question he was wondering if I had seen what was in the fridge yet. I replied,

"Firas, why don't you sit down and let's talk." "Is everything alright? If it's about the bottles it was just something I wanted to try again and I figured the best time would be when you were away." "Firas, I don't care about the bottles. I wished at one point that we could have tried things like that together, but it really doesn't matter to me if you drink or don't. Even I tend to have a glass of wine on an airplane now and then. I don't understand why no matter how many times I pushed, you refused to try things with me. Why you refused to let me have one glass of champagne in Austria, but you have two bottles in the fridge? It's just silly."

He looked down for a moment as he gathered his thoughts for his argument. I took the opportunity to continue, "Firas, forget about the bottles. I came back because I think that we should get a divorce." He looked surprised, naturally. "What! Why?!" "Because we don't work, Firas. I want to have a career, friends, and to write my book, and you refuse to let me. Once I got my B.A., I realized that I would never use it. You just wanted me to have it so you wouldn't be ashamed when people ask where your wife went to school. Every time I try to make you proud it's never enough. You don't find me attractive, and you put me down at every opportunity. I don't know why you keep me around. You could get a cleaning lady who cooks and that might be just as if I was here. We hardly ever have sex and when we do, you can't stand it if I look at you. Ah, none of that matters now. I just came to tell you in person that I have decided." He replied, "I have given you a grand life. Any girl would fall on her knees, thanking God for a husband like me."

I exhaled through my nose and pressed my lips together. I said, "I'm glad any girl would be honored to be your wife. I was honored, but that is not the point. Firas, try to understand. Once when I was in a supermarket in Dallas, the checkout girl smiled and asked me about my day. Then she listened and wished me a great day. I left the store thinking about how genuinely happy she looked, and I wished I was her. I would rather give up all of this. The balls, the diplomatic dinners, the travel, the money, the shopping, everything, and work at a supermarket if that means I get to be just genuinely happy every day." "That's a low blow saying you would rather work in a supermarket then be married to me," he replied. "Firas, look, you don't have to understand. I have decided and I'm just here to pack up my things and head home again."

Just like that, the magic words arrived. He said, "What will people say?" I did my best not to roll my eyes as he stood up from the couch and said he needed to take a walk. Which meant he wanted to call his dad out of earshot from me. I stayed out to the balcony to smoke as I watched him pace back and forth on the phone in the parking lot with his dad and his brother. He was gone for over an hour.

He walked back in the house standing tall and he asked me to sit. He said, "I have spoken to my dad and my brother. My brother agrees that, you owe me at least to give me the American nationality." I was bewildered at such a request as he continued, "Yes, so we need to stay married for at least five more years, then you can have a divorce," he said proudly as he nodded his head. I blinked twice and said, "No." "What do you mean no, it's the least you owe me," he replied. "Owe you, why do I owe you? Besides five years being way too long, giving my nationality is not something I owe to anyone." "Well, I'm not giving you a divorce until you give me the nationality." "Okay, Firas … let's get one thing straight. You can choose not to give me a divorce, but you will never get my nationality from me. If you persist in this, I'll make sure that when we do go for an immigration interview at the embassy, I will tell them how much you hate America, Americans, and how you tried every day of our marriage to make the American side of me disappear. When I'm done, you'll have a pretty hard time getting the nationality from anyone." His brother, Anas, had married an American before his now-Syrian wife for the nationality and now it was clear that was the only thing that mattered. Looking back at it now, my responses were coincidentally very humorous since that day was the 4th of July, America's Independence Day.

He turned around and went straight to the bathroom. I followed him saying, "Firas, there is no need for us to part badly, come sit down." He locked the bathroom door. I stood by the door for a moment but when I heard him crying, I went to clean up to give him his privacy. He emerged only to depart again. I cleaned and packed as much as I could until I felt tired, and then made dinner in case Firas was hungry. Before he got back, I called my stepdad to let him know I was okay, since I knew he must be worried. When he heard what Firas had said about the nationality he said, "Well, it looks like you made the right decision after all, Princess."

When Firas got home, he threw down an envelope on the bed, telling me it was the rest of my bride money, $5000.00. I looked it over and felt insulted at his action throwing the money onto the bed instead of just handing it to me like an adult. "Firas, let's talk. There's no need for it to be like this." "No, I'm going to bed and since you asked for a divorce you can sleep on the couch." As he closed the door, I wondered what made him think I was planning to sleep in the bed in the first place, but no matter.

I couldn't get to sleep so I watched TV happily, since in the past, when he went to sleep I had to sleep too, he would not accept it any other way. The door suddenly swung open, and he told me to come sleep in the bed. Since the couch wasn't really comfortable and we really needed to talk, I got up and went to bed. He laid down next to me and held me tightly as he had never done before and began to sob almost uncontrollably. Every time I tried to turn around to talk or comfort him, he asked me not to look at him. I laid there wondering when the night would be over so I could get out of the bed and finally dozed off.

In the morning I found him sitting as calm as paint drinking his coffee at the kitchen table. I got myself a cup of coffee and sat next to him. He said, "So, how are we going to do this and how much longer are you staying?" "I'm just staying until I'm packed, and don't you have work today?" "I can't go to work today; I need to get all the details sorted out because I don't see us getting a divorce soon. I don't have time to go to Syria and we're not getting divorced in America." "I agree, if we get divorced in the States we would have to go to court, and then communal property comes into play. I don't want any of your money. I would not do that to you. I know how fond you are of it. I thought if you just give your brother in Syria power of attorney, he can divorce me there on your behalf." "So, you've thought it all through then. Well okay, just hurry up and get packed. I need to go call my brother."

I recalled when I left Canada it was a similar feeling, only this time I would be going home. I left so many things behind when I left Ata and the visual of all my things left in the apartment had sent him into a deep depression. Despite all of Firas' short comings, in his own way, he had loved me. I did not want to see him go through the same thing as Ata. I went through the house drawer by drawer, cupboard by cupboard, making sure to throw away anything of mine that I was not taking or shipping. Even the smallest things, like a bar of my soap in the shower, could make him very sad once I was gone.

The time came to buy my ticket. My books were all packed along with the quilt my mother had made us. Firas said he would make sure they got shipped to my parents' house. That night I stayed on the couch unable to sleep. I never pondered if I was doing the right thing, I just wanted to know if he would be okay. He had worn me down over the years, making me almost numb, but there remained in my memory a place which contained how much I loved him.

After getting back to America, the next few weeks were full of a superb feeling of freedom. I felt exactly like Rapunzel running around shouting, "I'm free, I'm free!" I was free to read whatever I wanted without judgment or criticism from Firas. I was free to get a job anywhere I wanted, pursue a master's degree, and at last, even to write my book. The only thing that would bring me down was Firas' messages. I did my best to answer his calls, since technically until everything was done in Syria we were still married, but every call brought with it a comment like, "Your books cost me $800 dollars to ship to you and I had to repack them." "Okay, do you want me to send you the money, Firas?" "No, I don't need money and this jewelry box that was in there didn't go because it won't scan." "It's made of lead and doesn't go through scanners well, it was my grandmother's, but you can throw it away. I don't need it." "It was your grandmother's, and you don't want it? You're so cold," to which my reply would be silence. He then added how he saw the blanket that was in the box and broke down crying as he wrapped himself in it. I told him I was sorry he was sad but like clockwork he bounced back, realizing he was showing weakness saying, "I also put into the box all the photos I have of us and things, I don't need any reminders of you so feel free to do with them what you like." "Thank you, I'm sure I'll see when the boxes get here, was there anything else?" I said. He replied, "No, goodbye." "Goodbye, Firas."

I continued to spend my days out of the house at the Starbucks or the library. I no longer wore my wedding ring (in the Arab world, in cases of divorce it would be very unrespectable to take back a wedding ring since it was part of my bride price, it was mine to sell or keep). I was free game for men who got up the courage to approach me. One day while at the library the man sitting across from me noticed my necklace. It was the Saudi emblem, something I had stopped wearing because Firas thought I should wear more Syrian-styled jewelry. The man got up and walked over. Standing in front of me, blocking my only means of escape, then placing his arm down in front of me on the table way within bubble space. He said, "I saw your necklace, have you been to Saudi?" I looked up from my book and replied in Arabic, recognizing right away that he was Palestinian saying, "My father is Saudi." He then let out an "Ohhh" sound as his brain began to turn its gears. I could hear his thoughts, "American passport, speaks Arabic, Muslim, and maybe rich," all of which was ascertained by one simple statement, "My father is Saudi." The next thing that came out of his mouth was completely unexpected. "You know, I do Karate," he said as he flexed his arm muscles. I contemplated how I would escape as I said, "How nice for you," and I started packing up my things. He began to panic and started to tell me all about how he was studying to be a doctor and how his mother would surely love to meet me. I smiled and said, "I need to go but it was nice to meet you." Taking my leave, I called my stepdad to come and pick me up and take me to Starbucks instead, since my library suitor was not likely to give up very easily and I really wasn't in the market for another marriage.

Time passed and the relaxation that came with being husbandless felt like I had had high blood pressure for years and now had been cured. Time passed for Firas as well but for him, time seemed to be moving much slower. I decided to have no contact this time with Ablah May as well, even though I knew I would always miss her. I knew she was the only one who could convince me to fall on my sword and go back. Firas therefore had no update on me and the silence that was so often between us now appeared too loud for him to handle.

On July 18, 2013, the longest email I have ever received in my life arrived along with a text message announcing its arrival [errors retained].

Elise, ya habibti,

I wanted to write this message to you a week ago. But I eventually decided to delay it in order to give you some time to think and reflect before you hear from me again. I am writing these pages to you, reflecting the flow of thoughts that are coming immediately to my mind, putting them down in the email immediately, without editing, proof reading, or even reviewing, without worrying about putting them in proper English or not. Simply, I am writing them as they are coming out of my mind.

Since you left on 06 of July, nothing has been on my mind except you, your face, and what happened to us. I know you said that your decision is final, but I am sorry, I will not go with that. I want to ask you to think again, to reconsider, I urge you to take a step back and think deeply about the decision you are making and about its effects on both of us. No matter how you justify it to yourself right now, on the merits of it our problems are no different from the problems experienced by millions of other married couples. I urge you to reconsider and I urge you to change your mind.

As I said in my messages today, I am still surprised by how you suddenly came back and asked for divorce. That easy!!? Divorce? Have you forgotten habibti? Have you forgotten our days together, our time together, the process and the pain we both, not you only, went through to reach where we are? Our marriage is collapsing in front of our eyes, and it is of a rushed decision that you made. Have you forgotten habibiti that my love to you did not come suddenly, and it will not go suddenly. Have you forgotten that i grew over time, over all these days we spent together, over all these places, cities and countries we have been to together, over all these situations of both joy and pain that we went through together. It grew stronger and stronger with the days passing. It grew stronger and stronger from the time we spent together Fal compound, the dinners on on the swimming pool smoking shisha, the time we had in scalini restaurant, the trips we made together to Damascus, the one lovely day when we rented a room at Cham hotel, the time we spent in that one bed room apartment in tourist club in Abu Dhabi, the Mag 218 days in Dubai, to the trips to Cairo, Vienna, Paris, Beirut, Denver Shreveport, and more and more and more. Have you forgotten all of that suddenly? while only remembering a problem or a quarrel here and there? You threw all of this and came in one day to ask for a divorce?

In no way am I saying the last years were perfect, of course they were not. But even with all the problems that we had, they were still lovely years. I understand and recognize that there were issues in our marriage, many of them. I understand and recognize that I may have not showed you how strong my love was to you, how much I appreciated you, how much I love having you around and I loved the fact that you were my wife. I understand all of that habibiti, clearly.

Maybe I expressed my love to you over the last years in ways different than what you wanted or expected. Some men ya omri show their love with words. Others with actions, gifts, or financial ways. I guess I was more of the second group than of the first. At the end of the day, you are the only woman I loved truly, with all my feelings. You are the only woman I shared everything I have or I know with. You are simply the wife that I made a commitment with, before Allah, to love, care, and cherish when I am poor or rich, when she is healthy or sick, when she is young or old, with or without children. And by far you are the only women that understood me the most.

I do not know if it is a coincidence or not that the last three months in particular made me realize how much I value you and how much I love you. I decided and determined to make it up for you in the near and far future, when we go to the UAE and beyond. I was looking forward for the days we go back to Dubai, get you the apartment you want, ask you to choose the furniture you like, have you enjoy Dubai like you did when we were there and even more. I wanted to show you all of this with words but also with actions.

If you think that I was happy everyday with you then you are wrong habibti. I was not every day. If you think the divorce did not cross my mind then you are wrong. It did. But the difference between you and me is that I turned out to be a lot more patient that you. I did not take a rushed decision that is just based on change of circumstances. Unfortunately you did. I always said to myself, I married this woman for better and for worse. If I, as her husband that loves her, don't take it in and endure, then who will. I was patient. And I always told myself that Elise with all the problems she is having is the wife I want for the rest of my life.

It is true that she could be a pain in the ass sometimes, but for most of the times she is the loveliest wife ever. It is true that she could be harsh and even rude with me, but for most of the times she is the nicest and sweetest person on earth. She is my simply my wife that I love and her name is Elise.

Equally, you loved me, took care of me and cared for me when I was down, upset or in a bad mood, your treated me well, and you gave me the position of being your husband. These are not only emotions, these are facts. These are basis for a marriage that should last for long, not one that ends very suddenly and quickly. We can learn from our mistakes. I know I did and continue to do.

Even with all our problems, I cannot remember that I said no to something you asked for or requested. This is due to many reasons, one of them was because making you happy was a goal deep inside of me, whether I stated it or not. Another reason of course was that you understood me and knew exactly how to get what you want from me. I liked that a lot from you. and I would agree to what you want immediately.

I really hope that no one in the future inflicts pain on you as much as you inflicted on me since 04 July. You have no idea what I have gone through in the last two weeks. I have been on constant pain killers prescribed by the doctors. I developed what could be an ulser in my stomach, if not treated immediately, from the severe stress I suffered from. I am now on more than ten different kinds of medication that I take every. I am just saying this so you know the effects of your decisions on others the next time you make one like the one you did with me. It hurts so much habibti, so much. It is so deep, enormous and mountain-breaking pain that you made me feel. Any you know why? because you were not just a girl that I knew, just a girlfriend that I hang out with for a month or two and never see for the rest of my life, just a casual friendship that I just pumped into here and there. You were my WIFE, if this word means anything to you. You were the woman that I devoted my life to, you were the woman that I was making plans to spend the rest of my life with, share everything I have with, build my future with and grow old with.

Now we come to what you said when you came on that miserable Thursday when you asked for divorce. You said you drink, you do not fast Ramadan, you were praying just for me, and you have no problem marrying your daughter to a Christian guy. If this is true, then you should not blame me for my mistakes, you should blame yourself first and foremost for a much bigger mistakes than the ones I did. You presented yourself to me as a person who while liberal, is still a true Muslim. Like me exactly. While not so conservative, but at the end of the day prays, fasts Ramadan and tries always to do istifgfar (Ask for forgivness from god). On this BASIS habibiti we got married. You should never forget that. So do you think coming to me after three years and a half and saying walaa I do not fast, I pray for you and I would marry me to Christian guy, you think this is fair? If this is true then you have a lot to blame yourself for than to blame me. It is not fair to Firas that you marry him on a basis that is not there. If this was not the case, and you have changed later, then you are also to be blamed because you have broken the terms of marriage on which we committed to each other.

However, habibiti, thinking about it deeply, I honestly and truly think that you are not what you said you are, even if you think now otherwise. I hope you were only saying this just to make me say the divorce word, just to make me hate you, just to make it easier for me to let you go. I do not believe it is you, because it is not you. I know you, as much as you think I do not, I know you. When I met you, you used to fast every Thursday and Monday. You taught me things about Islam that I did not even know. You informed me about riyad al saleheen (Hadeeth of the Prophet) that I did not even read. This is why I can never believe that you really meant what you said. It could just be sins that you do here and there. All of us sin here and there, starting with myself. But the basis is there. The true belief in Allah and in Islam is there inside you, inside your heart, and it will always come back, no matter how much you sin.

Habibti, in case you have not noticed I was under immense pressure during since the last year or two from all angles. I have a very busy and hectic job, am trying to build a career that will benefit me, my wife and kids. That will bring them good life, will secure a life time pension after I retire and a life time pension for my wife and kids if I die god forbid. Furthermore, my country is screwed. My savings and the house that I bought in Damascus could be lost at any time. My parents are living under the shelling and bombing. Anything wrong could happen la samaha allah. My wife is away from me most of the time. This made me restart my thinking of the future that I want to build for you and me.

Finally, Elise, please think again. Nothing wrong in reconsidering a decision you made and nothing wrong in even changing your mind. You are cleaver habibiti, so please do not let stubbornness cloud your good judgment. Don't let the devil win over the angles. It is no mistake to change your opinion and give this marriage a chance. No mistake to listen to someone who loves you and who is willing to put your happiness a priority over his own. I am ready to give this marriage a chance on the same basis we got married four years ago. And those are that we both love Allah and follow his commands, even if we sin here and there, we always do istigraf and we know our mistakes before Allah, that we both love each other, and that we both will care and respect for each other. I do not promise that our life will be problem free, but what I do promise with all my heart and feelings that my ultimate goal will be your happiness, your interest, and the interest of the kids that we will have together. I promise to respect your family as much as you respected mine, but I also expect that they treat me with respect. I promise that I will do what I can to make it up for you, ease your pressure when you are stressed and be there next to you when you are sick. I also expect the same from you. I promise that I will live for you and for your kids, not for myself, and I expect the same from you. I promise to support you all the way, in work, education and life, as much as I did already and even more. And I also expect you to do the same, support me all the way as much as you did and even more. I promise to endure you when you are angry, upset, sick and old. You need to promise me also the same. In addition, you need to promise me that you will love me and do not flip on me the moment circumstances change. I promise to be your good caring and loving husband, and I want to you to promise me to be the same. Lastly, I promise to cherish you, spoil you, give you the hanan (compassion and kindness) that I did not give, and to put your needs before mine. And on this one habibti you do not need to promise me to do the same, because I know you will do these things and even more. You already proved to be very cherishing, kind, caring and much more. This is why I love you so much and I want to you come back.

I am not being emotional ya habibti, am being very reasonable. If you decide to come back, you will find me the happiest man on earth with all open arms. You will find a husband that will considers you the best and most beautiful woman in the world, that will consider you his own half. If you decide not to, I will be very sad that Iost you, but time would then be my hope as a great healer.

I still stand on what I said, we still have a wonderful life ahead of us, waiting for us in Dubai as close as next September, and much more beyond.

Habibti, take your time in reading this email. You do not have to reply immediately. Reading it once or twice, consider it, before you make your final decision, or before your change your mind.

With all my love.

Firas

I recall feeling angry when I read this email before heading to bed. The next morning, I read it again and this was my reply (errors retained):

Dear Firas,

What to say, you think that this is just me being stubborn and that just shows yet again that you don't know me. I know when I am being stubborn, but this is not the case, you think I told you all the things I did to make you hate me and that's not true either. I told the truth as plain as it is, I don't lie, for that never helps anyone learn from mistakes. I would marry my sisters to even a Jew if he was a good man. Today is the 11th day of Ramadan and I have not fasted one day thus far, and I feel no guilt. I will never cover again. I discovered that hated it, I tried to be religious for a long time and there was a time when it was everything, but I realized over the last five years that I was never happy that way. You say I taught you a lot more about religion then you knew but you forget that every time I tell you something you say, "Well let me ask my dad," "Well that book was not written by a Syrian," and of course, "Well I know better." Out of my kindness I let you have your way as much as I could to keep the peace in hopes that one day my word might be enough but that day never came. You never saw me or treated me as your equal as you say but rather as your subordinate. You might disagree but these are the facts, they were the same before we got married. Since my journey to discovering what made me happy started long before I met you and continued all the time you delayed deciding if I was the one for you, people change all the time.

You're thinking now, of course, if this was the case why did you marry me? So let me explain after you showed up with your list of conditions and said, "so I decided we should get married," I went home and I realized that this was not gonna work, and when I told you the next day you broke down, you changed and you became sweet. I saw a side of you I never saw, I saw someone who loved me as I was, whereas before, I only saw the man who was full of himself, put himself up as better than me. I suddenly saw a kind person and I could not help but be moved then because I loved you. I remember the letter you wrote and left on my desk and everything else and so I agreed to marry you against my father's wishes and went to Syria without even saying goodbye to him. We went to Abu Dhabi and what happened... You changed back into the person I broke up with, but I was patient, praying and hoping one day to see that other person again but he did not return. You bring up the days in fal compound with good memories now but when we were married, every time I brought up these memories I was forbidden to even mention them as us being alone was a sin, a sum of regrets for you that you would rather not remember and so I did as you wished and tried to make new memories but it did not work. We lived in Dubai, and you always picked on me, I was never good enough, never dressed the way you liked, you don't remember all the times we talked and all the times I cried, begged you, to just love me for me as I am, as I had loved you the way you were, but you never listened. You went away for 5 months and when you came back for 5 days, I tried to make those days good for you even though you thought you had HIV at the time and wouldn't come near me, you talked non-stop about politics which you know I hate, I bore it all with a smile so that you could rest and sent you back again - that was love. I accepted you as you were.

I don't want to hurt you, but I don't know what you expect me to say except the truth, your love came with time perhaps but just as it took you time to love me, in that time you slowly poisoned my love for you, and it died. Every time you shot me down, put me down and insisted you were always right without any care to listen, I disliked you more and more.

It's funny how strong a human being is as one can often grow numb to all kinds of things. I learned not to listen when you talk and just nod since nothing I said seemed to matter. I tried to just make the best of whatever, you forget when I cried and begged you to kiss me and when you did, you did it with a two seconds and then asked, "is that enough?" It was a real turn off, I said to myself, well I don't need sex, hugs, kisses, affection, partnership, or friendship. We have always slept on opposite sides of the bed, and when I tried to move over you would say, "it's too hot," or "I can't sleep like that." Your only concern was always yourself despite your protest that your only concern was for my happiness, you spent almost five years showing me the opposite.

Unfortunately, I have experienced love in my life and that was not us, I know how it feels to be adored and listened too and that was not you. I have been unhappy for so long Firas, but you never bothered to listen or notice and if you did, it was always a here, take this piece of gold or vacation or this or that and go be happy. Money, Firas, can make someone happy for an hour, a day and then you realize how empty it really is, you saw it as affection and that is how you are, I understand. You don't know how many times I wished I could die rather than continue our relationship, you say you were lonely when I was away, I was lonely everyday living with someone who could not see me.

But none of this matters now, Firas, you are who you are and a good person, but I hate how your mind works, all your calculations and your obsession with money makes me crazy, I don't care about your politics, I got tired of freaking out with you every time you thought you had HIV. You think if I work you're entitled to all my money and I think we either share it or I keep all my money. You dream of having a million dollars and I don't mind being poor struggling but happy, I hate moving and I hate change and you love change. I thought in time you and I might have adapted to each other, but we did not.

Even when I knew it was not working, I tried to make friends in Geneva; you shot me down with your negative comments, you never wanted me to associate with Americans all the while forgetting that I am American. You did not want me to apply for the job in the US embassy, you don't want me to write my book about my life which we agreed on while we were dating, as long as I don't include you and then you changed your mind. I wanted to go to a party and just have a good time, you could not even do that for me, if it wasn't your friends, you event, it was not worth going, only adding to my feelings that this was not working. This is the truth I tried so hard… and now it is just done for me, burned, and closed. I cannot even shed one tear anymore, I cried a river over you long ago and now it is just over, I am happiest when we are apart and that's just the truth, no stubbornness involved even if all that you say is true, you will just change back and after so long I hate to say it, but I don't love you anymore. I don't want to sound harsh but it's like you keep asking me to tell you things you just don't want to hear.

I wish you all the best and hope you find someone you can connect with, who makes you happy and you her, our time came and passed.

Elise Evans

I knew it was a blow, he never liked hearing the truth like so many Arab men I had come to know, he was the center of the universe, and a wife should be content to revolve around their undying light. I sent a text message letting him know the email was in his inbox (errors retained).

***Firas**: I'm reading it now*

***Elise**: I think if you reflect well you will see that I'm right. You are who you are, and I am who I am, we won't change. I am kind but only to the point where I feel walked on and then in all calmness of mind, I realized that there was no need to continue it will only be more damaging if kids got involved and we ended up buying a home, now at least we both have a chance to start over. We tried and that it.*

***Firas**: I wish I can forget about you that easily, but I cannot. I wish I can stop loving you but my heart aches when I try. Despite everything that happened you are the only woman that I truly loved in my whole life. You are only woman that became my wife. I surrounded with people at work, yet I never felt so lonely like I do now. I see tens of girls every day in the streets, but they all appear faceless to me. I cannot stop seeing one face and one smile* *that is engraved in my mind. It is your face and your smile. If you think that time is helping me get over you, it has not so far. The last 20 days have been nothing but painful.*

It would be a few more days before I would hear from him again. I tried not to reply in too many sentences since his words started to wear me down. In truth I wished that I believed the poetry that had suddenly started spewing out of him, but I knew that if I went back, he would be so sweet for a day, a week, a month maybe even a year, and I would forget about the past and he would return to normal as he had always done. A part of me was glad he took to writing and didn't get on a plane and yet a part of me wished he had come and showed me this other Firas that only shows up in letters, emails, and text messages. It was for the best because if he had showed up, I know I would have gone back. He started doing things like sending me texts that were meant to go to his boss about a hospital procedure he had, how dizzy he was, that the nurses had to put him into the taxi and so he won't be able to make it to work today. Tugging heart strings in this manner only made me more certain of my decision.

Text messages:

***Firas**: I wish you know how much I love you; I wish you know how much I miss you, I wish you know how much I value you now. I am sorry if I didn't express it all before, I am sorry if I did not show you how strong my feelings are for you. I am deeply sorry. That was so stupid of me I realize it now. I know how much you meant to me. Simply put you are life for me. Without you the world is so dry, without you, life has no meaning. This is what I'm feeling now this is the suffering I am going through now. I know you might say to yourself this is not the real Firas, this is not the Firas I know, this is not the Firas I am used to. But this is him, Habibti, this is him. I wish I had a chance to express to you and how much I love you now. I'm sorry for all my mistakes I regret them all deeply, God knows I do. This is the real Firas speaking, your beloved husband. Not a stranger. This is the person who is willing to do whatever is necessary in life to make you happy. You are rejecting this person while he is at your fingertips. Think* *it again, Habibti, think it again. I promise to change, in fact I changed already but you are not here to witness it happening unfortunately.*

It took me an hour to reply, reading it over and over again. Time is a funny thing. Sometimes when a moment passes it passes. There was a moment when these words, if said in person, would have softened the heart of a woman who was so much in love with one man that she bore everything that was put before her for seven years (dating and married). But it was the lines about how he wished he had a chance to show me, and I have changed but you are not here to witness it that glowed in the dark. I wasn't on the moon… A man who could have jumped on a plane at any moment, his job would have given him leave at a moment's notice, the money was available. Instead, he chose to make himself sick and sit at home. His pride, as always, would not allow him to bend and come make it all up. In his mind, I was the party in the wrong. I left him so I should come back and so on. Proving once again that nothing had changed.

I learned from life that to continue to communicate with him would only give him hope as it did with Ata all those years ago. Time was what he needed more than anything, perhaps then we could be friends one day like Ata and I were. I lied and let him know I would be changing my number, that I wished him all the best and that if he ever needed me, I was here for him. He could always reach me by email. It sent him into a flurry asking if I hated him to that degree and how could I be so mean. But what one interprets as mean when they are hurt can often be a kindness and a cure. I knew what he was going through. I had seen it before, he had not. The only way to get over an addiction is often to slowly phase it out. I would still be available to him but not as easily or frequently, which would help him stand alone.

A month later an email came [errors retained]:

Hi Elise,

Please read this email until the end. I am sorry it is a bit long, but I need to say what I have written to you below. Email is unfortunately the only way left to communicate with you.

It's been over a month now since you left, and what a month. The words I am writing to you below are the outcome of all the reflection and thinking that I have gone through in the last month, being alone.

I start by saying I apologize for all my mistakes. I apologize from all my heart for everything bad I did. I apologize for not being nice with you every day and every minute. I was wrong not to pamper you the way you deserve. I apologize for all the problems we had, and for not solving them quickly. I am not perfect, and I did mistakes in this marriage, I confess. I am sorry if I caused you any pain at any time in our relationship. It was never my intention. I was inexperienced, so please do not hold it against me, it was the first time in my life that I get married. But you need to remember Elise that I was never a bad person with you, that I was a good man who loved you, who was generous with you, who did not say no to whatever you asked, who shared with you everything he has or owned, and who adored you when you were with him and when you were away. I was wrong in not showing you how much I loved you, and not saying it to you every morning and every night. But it was in my heart all the time. I was wrong in trying to show you my love only materially, and not emotionally as well. I was wrong in taking for granted that you know how much I love you and how much emotions I have for you. Even if did not show it all, loving you was always there in my heart and it kept getting stronger and stronger with time, whether I said it or not. In the last four months particularly, I was here alone missing you dearly every day, missing my wife that I realized how much I love. I was figuring out a lot of my mistakes on my own, and waiting for the day you come back to hug you and show you the love I have for you.

I know now that I should be very caring and loving to Elise, that I should respect her, pamper her and trust her judgment. I now understand my wife Elise a lot more than I did last year, and surely a lot more than the time we got married. I now know that I should do my best to make Elise happy all the time, bring her flowers every day, hug her when we are watching a movie in the evening together, and please her the way she likes while making love. I now know that I should not be shy of confessing to the cleaver Elise that in many things she knows a lot better than me, that I should hold her hand every time we walk together, that I should keep hugging her at night, kiss her lips and neck and every part of her body, and tell her all night how much I am lucky to be her husband. I now know that I should be very proud of her as my wife, that I should introduce her to the whole world as my partner, my equal, my other half and as the love of my life. I am saying these words with all truth and honesty Elise. They are coming out of my heart, soul and mind, all together. I knew nothing about these things when we got married. It is you Elise who taught me all of this, and it is you who deserve to benefit from it more than anyone else in the world.

You may say to yourself, he had his chance, it is too late. I will say that it is never too late, and never have I understood how much you mean to me more than I do now. I am talking to that soft spot in your heart, to tell you that I genuinely have all the love, respect and honor for you Elise. I know that re-gaining you love will take time. But I promise to be there all the way while at the same time showing you how a good, loving, and caring man I am. I promise to be there for you when you are healthy or sick, when you are young or old, when you are rich or poor, when you are in a good mood or in a bad mood. I promise to be guided with what is best for you, and to love you like no one else in the world. I promise to make you happy and to respect your decisions whatever they are. If you don't want to fast or pray, then don't. I will respect your decision. If you want to drink, then I will bring you the bottle myself and drink with you. I promise to love and respect your family like mine. All of them, you dad, mom sisters and brothers. I realize now that the most important thing is not my job at UNHCR, not my career with the UN, it is my wife Elise. You Elise, you are the most important thing in my life and the best thing that happened to me. I realize now that home is not Syria, Geneva or the Dubai. Home is not even where my parents are. Home is where you are, home is with you and around you. Home is wherever I am with you. What I am trying to say that after these years we spent together, and the time we had together, good and bad, you have simply become the center and core of my life, and the love of my life.

Please give this marriage a chance and give our children a chance to be born. I will live for you and for them. I will tell them one day that they came to this life because their lovely and beautiful mom gave me another chance.

I know I am now a better Firas, the same good and generous Firas but a lot more considerate and caring. I know your value now Elise, and surely I know what you mean to me. This is the same Firas talking, the Firas you met for the first time on the noon of Sunday 07 October 2007 in Abu Dhabi, the Firas you looked at when you sat next to him that day on the couch with such beautiful eyes, the Firas that realized straight away the electrical charge and the chemistry between you and him and who deep inside of him wanted to make love to you immediately, the Firas you loved and you later married on 07 of January 2009. It is you who taught me how to love, and I am very sorry it took this long. But loosing you made me realize that my life has no meaning without you, made me wake up, and made the image very clear ahead of me. Again, I am saying these things with a calmness of mind and I mean every word so dearly.

You can choose to work or to not, it will be your decision, and I will be very supportive either way. You can choose to continue your master and PhD, and I will pay your fees. You can go anytime to visit your family. If you are bored of the UAE or if you do not want to go there anymore, or if you want to live in the states instead, then I will work on getting a job with the UN in the states with all my powers. All I want is to be with you and to be able to show you how much I love you. All I want is to regain your love and care. We have come a long way, we suffered already. Now is the time we benefit from our suffering.

You have the power to make a decision now, to continue for a divorce or to give this marriage a chance. Use this power wisely habibiti, use it wisely. The decision you make will change the course of time and the course of the events in our future years. How I wish you change your mind, and how I wish you give me and this marriage another chance. If you do, our children will come to life because of this decision you make.

Baba and Khaleh Nawal are coming to Geneva tomorrow and I will take them to the states in ten days. I wish from all my heart that you talk to me or see me when I come. I wanted to say these things to you in person to show you how honest and genuine I am. But I have only the email now as a means of communication with you.

I am trying my best to show you how much I sincerely wish that you change your mind, I am trying to prove to you how much I genuinely love you, and how much I will be good to you. Unfortunately I can only prove this if you do come back. I ask you to trust me for I know now the meaning of true love, I ask you to trust me for I know now your value to me. You are my wife that I loved, married and that I will continue to love and cherish until the last day of my life.

Come back ya omri (My lifetime, Love/Darling. It can mean all of these), come back to me, and you will find nothing but the loving husband you wanted me to be. The Firas who will love you, appreciate you, pamper you like you deserve, and who is ready to go to the end of the world to make you happy. I love you now more than ever Elise, and I will be grateful to you forever if you decide to give me and this marriage another chance.

I am attaching one photo that will hopefully remind you that the person who wrote this email to you is not a stranger, he is the Firas you once loved and you married.

Best

Firas

There it was, finally, the email that should have come first. The words that he had three days with me in Geneva as I packed when he could have shown and said all of this, but he did not. I do not blame him since I suppose sometimes shock can generate pride and even anger. But I do blame him for the fact that he knew for seven years after all how to make me happy, but he didn't because he didn't want me to know the power I held over his heart for fear that I would take advantage as he said so many of his friends' wives did. He forgot that I was not those girls. I understand that it's hard to give someone the power to hurt you by opening your soul, but true love cannot come without trust that they won't abuse the great power given, the power to hurt you.

It was no use. The bridge was burned and there was no going backwards, only forwards for his sake and mine. He was hurting but I had hurt for seven years. He had a month to come and show me but the best he could do was an email. He didn't want to risk coming if he thought I would reject him again. What he didn't realize was that in doing so he gave away the chance that I would say yes. My decision was final so I decided the only help I could give him now was to make him angry. I knew anger was a more useful emotion for moving on than despair. Sometimes loving someone means pushing them out of the nest and out into the world if they can't do it themselves. I sent my reply two days later:

Dear Firas,

You're like a broken record, repeating and repeating over again the same stuff. Since that is the only system you seem to understand, let me REPEAT myself again, I don't care to receive such emails from you. I don't love you, if I never see your face again that will make me happy, I am happy without you and I will never come back. I don't care to hear about your feelings and your regrets, they are your own.

Have a great life,

Elise

He called me cold, but I had to be. It was over. In Arabic we have a saying about marriage that it is like a piece of hair held on two sides by each person. When one pulls the other must follow because if both sides pull at the same time it will break. I was glad to hear that my time with him had taught him so much, but I was tired. I had been the follower for all the pulling he did over the years and the one that absorbed his every wave, fear, concern, thought and manner but it was now time to cut the hair and to follow the path to who I wanted to become and be happy once again.

Over the next few months, I spent a great deal of time trying to sort one thing out after the next. I had never lived in the U.S. prior to 2013, and there was a lot to learn. Even an American who grew up abroad can feel like an immigrant when they move to a country that had never been their home. My stepdad turned his study into a bedroom for me. It was a tiny little room barely big enough for a bed, but I was happy. I went down to the Department of Motor Vehicles to get an American driver's license so I could stop carrying my passport and my international driver's license around every time I wanted to buy cigarettes or drive the car. Everything was strange and scary but I was happy to be living in the land of the free.

THE EGYPTIAN AND THE JORDANIAN

One morning as I sat at Starbucks drinking my morning coffee and smoking, my ears picked up a conversation at the table in front of me. Without removing my headphones, I paused my music to listen in. It was clearly Arabic and since I looked nothing like an Arabic girl, I tucked my Saudi necklace into my dress and listened in happily. There was a kind of feeling of home in hearing people speak in Arabic but what was especially interesting was the fact that these two men thought no one could understand them. They stayed for a while and then left and came back in the afternoon, all the while I listened in.

I would share with my sisters all the things they talked about. Me, the girls that came and went, politics and judgements about the barista inside. We would have a good giggle about the two men who assumed no one could understand anything they said. One afternoon as I smoked outside, I noticed a lot more teenagers coming and going from the Starbucks than usual in the daytime. I assumed it was a field trip that stopped to get coffee and thought nothing of it.

When I got home that evening I entered through Yasmin's room since I was sharing her closet. "Hey," I said. "A friend of mine said she saw you at the Starbucks … SMOKING!" she said with the gleeful tone of someone who had discovered a secret. I was already facing the closet hanging up my jacket so the shock on my face had time to be mended before facing her. As I hung my jacket I said calmly, "Your friend, you said, which one?" "Sarah, she saw you," she said as she wobbled her legs in her chair grinning. I continued changing, "Does she know me?" "Ya, she saw you at my concert." I calmly replied, "Hmm, well, I don't know maybe she was mistaken."

I watched as her eyes looked down wondering if she was wrong and she dropped the subject. Knowing my sister, she would text her friend and say, "Hey, maybe it wasn't her?" and her friend would insist it was me and offer to go get photo proof the next day. With this in mind I went to a different Starbucks that day and any day that my sisters had a school holiday. They were old enough to understand but there was a chance that my stepdad might insist I quit instead of ever letting them find out. I lived under his rules now and I wasn't ready to quit.

After listening to the two men day after day, I managed to figure out where they were from based on their accents. The tall skinny one was Egyptian, and I could hear a slight hint of Palestinian, meaning one or both of his parents could in fact be Palestinian, and they migrated to Egypt before coming here. The big one was clearly Jordanian. Since I didn't know their names when I shared their funny stories with my sisters in the evening, we referred to them by their nationalities. This went on for a month or so until one day after I thought they had both left, I took a phone call with Noor. Talking away in Arabic and making the exact same mistake they had. I didn't notice that the Egyptian had come and sat down at the table right behind me.

When I hung up the phone, I heard a voice say, "Where are you from?" busted, I thought to myself. I told him I was American. "American? But how come you speak Arabic like a Syrian?" he said. There was no choice but to replay my story in as simple a way as possible. We talked while all the while he kept to his table and I to mine. He stayed at his table out of respect. It would not be appropriate for him to ask to join me at my table and he especially didn't want to be sitting at my table if my stepdad drove by. He told me about his family, how he got to the US and finally about his fiancé, which put me at ease. I would hate to lose another smoking hideout like I had the library due to another hunter.

The next day it was raining. One of my favorite types of weather and I enjoyed sitting outside in the rain more than anything. As I got my coffee and sat down, I noticed the Jordanian was sitting outside on his own, waiting for his friend I assumed. As I sat down, he asked me in Arabic where I was from. It had come as no surprise that his friend had told him. "Ah, I am discovered," I replied in Arabic. He laughed and said, "So it is true, wow, so how do you speak Arabic so well?" He had no idea how flattered I was for him to say so. Firas had always found my Arabic never quite good enough for him. We talked about the world, families, traditions, the Arabic community in Dallas, the food we liked, and all manner of topics. The conversation lasted for almost three hours and one hour after my coffee had finished, I didn't want to leave the conversation, so I pretended to continue to drink it the whole time.

It had been a while since I had a chance to speak Arabic with someone other than Noor without fear of being corrected like Firas used to do or being proposed to as often was the case. My stepdad could not stand hearing me speak in Syrian and I didn't enjoy speaking in Saudi, so we only ever spoke in English. Jordanian, just like his Egyptian friend, stuck to his table until he had to go, and I wished him a good day. Moving forward we turned into a little Arab group. We talked about women and they both came to find me very easy to talk to and take advice from. All the while sitting at separate tables. We didn't exchange phone numbers or make plans; we just saw each other when we all ended up at Starbucks at the same time.

I enjoyed their company; it was easy to laugh and just shoot the breeze so to speak without any expectations or plans. One day, I talked to them about work since I was growing bored of being without schoolwork or a home to care for. My days seemed to be long, and I longed for purpose. When I asked if they knew of anyone who was looking for an admin or an HR worker, the Egyptian said he would pass my number along to a friend of his who owns a company. I gave him my phone number but felt that it was rude not to also give it to the Jordanian as well, so I did. The Jordanian never texted me and the Egyptian didn't as well, and things went on as they always did.

One day neither of them arrived and then the next. It was strange not to have my coffee buddies, so I texted them. I asked if they planned to come to Starbucks today? The Egyptian whose name was Ahmed replied in the negative since he was getting prepared to go home to get married soon. The Jordanian whose name was Jacob said he would be there in about thirty minutes.

Jacob confided in me that day that he never finished high school only returning later to get his GED. He had a great aptitude for electrical work and worked with his friend Ahmed who was an electrician. He told me that one day he was planning to sit for the electrician's exam and then have his own company. I commended him often for following his dreams. He had one brother and one sister who were both in Jordan. His family owned a large grocery store, and his mother and sister took over its management after his father passed away a year earlier. He came to America as the oldest son to make a better life for himself since Jordan had little to offer him. He lived with his aunt while he figured out his next steps.

There was something commendable about Jacob. He was manly but always soft spoken with me. He loved jokes and made me laugh every day. He was also a gentleman, a sign of someone raised well, never overstepping his known boundaries which I greatly appreciated. He asked about Firas and how I was holding up. Then he quickly retreated from the question by saying, "Of course if you don't want to talk about it, I completely understand." I smiled and said, "It's no problem at all." In fact, I was happy to find someone to talk to other than my stepdad. Day after day we talked and laughed. There was never any discussion about anything more than friendship which put me at ease to be myself and just enjoy our time.

One day my stepdad came by to pick me up and Jacob was sitting at his table near mine. My stepdad noticed us talking and rolled down his window to glare at the man who dared speak to his daughter. When I got into the car, he asked me, "Who is the ugly brute talking to you?" I took a deep breath wanting so badly to defend my friend, but I knew to do so would not end well. I just said, "I don't know he's here every day, and he just decided to say hi. There is a big group of us that is here every day working on this and that, men, and women." My stepdad left it there and we went home. I knew moving forward that I would need to make sure Jacob was not visibly talking to me when my stepdad arrived. I knew I wasn't allowed to have male friends according to my stepdad's rules, but I felt as though I did not leave Firas to have another man like my stepdad no matter who he was telling me who I can or cannot be friends with.

The next day it was windy and as Jacob talked, I had a hard time hearing him. I lifted my hand and signaled that he should come sit at my table. He looked like I could have knocked him down with a feather as he asked if I was sure. I chuckled and said, "Yes, just come sit I can't hear you and it's silly for you to be at another table." He asked about my stepdad and if he had gotten me into trouble to which I relayed to him the intricacies of my stepdad and his way of being. "He won't harm you, I don't think, and I told him nothing about you. He would only ask me to go get coffee somewhere else and to be honest I am 29 and he doesn't get to tell me what to do, I just don't want the headache of setting him off."

As I was driving around one day, I noticed a hiring sign at the daycare center behind the Starbucks. I went home and told my stepdad I planned to go down and apply, to which he replied, "It's too soon to be thinking about working. Take some more time." I told him I could not sit around anymore. I needed something to do.

The next day I donned my best suit which was probably worth more than a month's salary at any daycare and headed over to apply for the job. I was excited that I had the power to just go get a job. There was a great joy for me in teaching children, their eyes so bright and filled with wonder at the smallest things. There was too much adulting in my past life and sometimes I wished we all had a switch on our eyes to make us see things differently like how a child looks at the snow. At times we remember that feeling, when our eyes open wide, and we feel so peaceful just watching it fall and in that second, we see the snow as a child. All the stress melts away, the world, everything. In that moment you are a child again. Yes, I wish we had a switch so whenever the world is too much, we could just click it and take it easy.

I walked in and met with the owner of the daycare, when she looked at me and my resume, she asked why a girl like me with a B.A. and so much experience would want to work here? I told her the truth, "I'm figuring things out after my divorce, my parents live nearby, and I have always loved children. If I like it I'll stay and if I don't I'll help you train a replacement." She asked me when I could start to which I replied, "Tomorrow, if you'd like." "Very well then, we're excited to have you, my assistant will help you fill out the paperwork." I walked out of the door and jumped in the air. I blared my favorite song of the day Mariah Carey's *Beautiful* as I drove home slowly to take in the moment.

My first day was so much fun, singing and getting to know all the children in my class. There is an ease about children. If you talk to them like little people, they respond well to being acknowledged and understood. My kids were between ages 3 – 4, one of my favorite age groups since they were potty trained and happy to sing, dance, play, and give hugs. I enjoyed singing and dancing with them and my enthusiasm was noted by everyone since I was happy and peppy all the time while most of the teachers, including mine, had grown tired of children, hated their jobs, and many felt there was nothing else they could do with their lives.

After a few weeks, I started to notice that all the new assistants were sent to hangout in my class before being placed. Anytime we were doing tours my class was always shown first.

Jacob and I started seeing each other at Starbucks on my lunch break and sometimes after class if I had time. After a month he got up the courage to ask if I wanted to go to dinner. I said, "Sure, why not? We can go on Friday." He was so excited like a little kid who had been told he just won all the candy in the world. He was not my normal type, he wasn't financially secure, had no advanced education and no plans to pursue any. He wasn't handsome, he didn't have a home, an apartment, or a stable job. In fact, from an Arab marriage arrangement standpoint, he had nothing to offer. Any Arab mother would have told him to go make himself ready by acquiring at least some of the basics on the list before considering him for their daughter. Firas was, by comparison of the check list, a better catch. Yet Jacob made me smile, laugh, feel safe, listened to, and respected. He was everything Firas was not. When he looked at me and he saw me, he never offered his opinion on my life, he just listened, and he talked about how one day he wanted to get married to someone he could build a life with.

I decided to see how it went but first I would need to find a way to go out at night for dinner without my stepdad knowing with whom. I knew better than any he would never approve, especially so soon after getting a divorce.

I went home and made my plan. With a personality like my stepdad's, one can't go head-to-head like a bull would. That would only end in disaster. I knew I had the right to do whatever I wanted but I was staying in his house, which gave him the right to say what went on with those who lived there. Since dating was out of the question for my sisters, it was certainly out of the question for me.

I waited until after dinner when he was having his tea and said, "The group of Starbucks people and I are thinking of grabbing dinner on Friday. If you don't need the car, I won't be late." In this way I was asking out of respect while informing him at the same time. I didn't need the car, but it was necessary since my stepdad would not drive my mom's big van and this way, I could prevent him showing up to check if I was really with a group. "Oh, where were you all thinking of going?" he asked, and I answered, "Not sure yet; something near here for sure but I think we're planning to decide Friday when we meet at Starbucks." I said, "Alright," and calmly retired to my room to text Jacob and let him know it was a go.

I always made sure to leave my phone in my room since my stepdad knew the only person who would really text me was Noor and never as often as Jacob would blow up my phone. Which was a welcome change from Firas, who once in a while would text or call but it would alert my stepdad every time it lit up that there must be a boy and if I even tried to reply to one message my face muscles would betray me for sure, so great care had to be taken.

After work I came home and changed for my dinner date. I chose one of my favorite dresses. A tightly fitted army green colored dress, knee length, short sleeves and showing no cleavage. I had chosen it because it was attractive but not too much so to imply anything improper. While entering the kitchen to grab the car keys my stepdad walked in asking me what I was wearing. "It's a dress," I replied, wondering what his problem was with it. "It's too tight and you need to change," he said.

“I wore this all the time even in Dubai, Baba,” I said. “It’s too short and you need to change, or you can’t have the car.” he said. I thought about fighting back but with the late hour I didn’t want to keep Jacob waiting. My stepdad was obviously already suspicious by the sound of his tone, and I dared not offer up more confrontational clues as ammunition for him. I changed into some jeans and a nice shirt. I came out for his final approval before grabbing the car keys and heading out.

I met Jacob at the Starbucks where I parked just next to his car. He opened my car door, something I had rarely ever had done for me except by a driver. Stretching out his hand to help me out of the car, we walked inside to get some coffee. We sat at Starbucks talking and laughing until we realized we had forgotten dinner. Looking over our shoulders we decided to walk over to the Subway which was in the same plaza and pick up something to eat. We ate at Starbucks and continued our endless conversations. It was almost like we could never run out of things to talk about. I never felt belittled by him or less than him nor he of me, like I had when I was with Firas. When it was time for me to head home, he walked me to my car which was parked by his. He asked me to wait as he got into his car and played a Mariah Carey song so loud, he could have woken up the whole neighborhood. And then he asked me to dance. I had never danced in the street with a man before and the fact that he picked my favorite singer for the first dance showed that he really was listening. He melted my heart as he kissed me.

When I got home, I sat in the car in the garage as long as I could in case my stepdad was awake. I needed to shake the sappy smile off my face. I entered the house and went straight to my room. As I lay there still dressed, I thought about how magical it all was, to be romanced by someone I had only just met and how wonderful it felt to be looked at like a treasure again. Headphones on, I replayed the song over and over until I fell asleep.

The next day was Saturday and I got up to head to Starbucks for my morning coffee. My stepdad again scowled at my dress, saying I would need to change. I looked at him for a moment and said, “I have worn this dress before when I came to visit. What is different now?” “You’re under my roof and now you’re not married,” he said. I rolled my eyes and went to change. When I came out I found my stepdad in the car saying, "I'll drop you off. I need the car." "Sure," I said as I panicked internally thinking there was no way to text Jacob now and tell him to avoid being seen by my stepdad. Which was exactly why my stepdad wanted to drive me on a Saturday when he didn't need the car for anything.

We pulled up at the Starbucks and my stepdad took note of Jacob sitting in the corner alone as he said, "I think I'll come in and get some coffee too see what all the fuss is about Starbucks." This way he could get a good look at whether or not there really was something going on based on Jacob's reaction and mine to being in the same proximity. It was the same scenario I had warned Noura about, so I thought on my toes and said, "While you're here why don't you sit with me for a little bit while I smoke." "Sounds good, there has been something I need to talk to someone about," he said. I was unable to concentrate on anything except the possible explosion if Jacob should feel so inclined to be manly and approach my stepdad. The only word I could utter was, "Hmmm" as my stepdad spoke. He continued by telling me that he came to the States with his retirement package, which consisted of a million dollars and a lifetime salary of $6,700 dollars a month. With that money he bought my mom the house she always wanted and all the expensive furniture she dreamed of. He'd invested the rest in the stock market but something went wrong in the market, and he lost the rest. "Your mom continues to overspend, and Noura is unwilling to accept a scholarship from the Saudi Government because they did not recognize Art as a degree. So, I have that on my plate as well." In my mind it was as simple as putting a harness on my mom and telling Noura she needed to pay for her own college or take the scholarship and study something else. As I thought Jacob moved from his table, my mind got stuck in tar for a moment and all I could muster was, "Hmm."

Luckily Jacob was smart enough not to approach me with my stepdad in tow. My stepdad and I talked about ideas to give my mom something to do, such as a job or maybe a business, so that she would not sit all day on her phone idle playing video games and wasting money on frivolous purchases. After an hour or so he went home. Jacob by this time was nowhere to be seen but once my stepdad's car was out of sight he came out from inside. I smiled and said, "I'm so sorry but he wanted to come, and I couldn't have said no." "Why don't we just tell him we want to get married?" My face about turned white, one kiss and we're getting married! I thought. "Jacob, we have not known each other that long, I just got divorced and it's not as easy as all that," I said. "Why not, I love you?" he said. I shyly looked down and said, "You're very sweet and in a way, I care for you, too, but it's not as easy as all that because of many things. My stepdad for one and the bigger obstacle is that you're Christian and I am Muslim. Even if by some miracle I got him to agree, I don't think he would agree to me marrying a Christian." His face went sad a little because he knew this was the case.

In Islam, a Muslim man can marry a Christian woman as my stepdad had done with my mother, but not vice versa. When I asked my aunt why once she said, "Well, because the man is the head of the house, and his religion will undoubtedly be what is passed down to the children." I didn't care about such things, in fact I thought being an orthodox Christian must be so exciting, with their pastors that stand and preach in the movies, and all the candles and incense used in their services. I loved my religion but saw no reason why I could not marry a Christian and teach my children both religions, allowing them to choose. Stopping my train of thought, I realized I was actually considering marrying him. I told myself I was crazy and put it out of my mind. I wondered if Jacob was a virgin and maybe that was why he was in such a hurry after just one kiss. He was not, and was even engaged before.

Despite everything he had really become my best friend in this strange new world. I didn't want to lose him by turning him down, but I wasn't ready to move on anything yet. I thought about doing some digging. Normally in the Middle East this would be done by asking people who knew his family and even his family about his character. Both the man and the woman would often do this as a way of making sure the other person had represented themselves properly. In Saudi the women would ask the women and the men would ask the men. In such a communal culture as Saudi and the Middle East, the size of the population didn't matter. Families always knew someone who knew something about another family. Gossip always spread like wildfire but in the Middle East it spreads without evidence like an asymptomatic cold leaving no trace until someone asks the right questions. Unfortunately, in America the individualistic nature of the culture prevented this.

I decided to ask his friend Ahmed, since he was the only person I knew who had known him for a long time. I asked him about Jacob's past and if there was anything worth noting. He looked at me for a moment and grinned with his cigarette between his teeth as he said, "Wait a minute. You and Jacob, ha-ha, how wonderful." "Well, I don't know it's too soon for that, I just wanted to ask about him. Is he really as kind as I see? Is there anything about his family or in his past that I should think about?" "No, I have known him since Jordan and he is the kindest soul, but he's not very driven and will need a great deal of pushing before he makes something of himself." "I see. I also wanted to ask why he is in such a hurry. We have only just met, and he is talking about marriage." "My girl, have you seen yourself and seen him? If I was him I would be afraid you would get away, too." I blushed at the compliment and ended the conversation there.

My stepdad was always judge and jury but never liked to pass sentence until he had collected enough evidence to put you away forever. As we exited the car for the Starbucks I asked him if he wanted to sit down for a bit again. I tried to keep the conversation very hypothetical. I asked him how he felt about my sisters marrying Christians or other religions? "What brought that up?" he asked. "Oh, it was an argument Firas and I had once and I was just wondering your thoughts on the issue, after all, they are growing up in a country where they are more likely to marry from another faith." "I'm fine if they marry a Christian, even a Jew, but," he said as he leaned in to continue, "No more Arabs!" "What's wrong with Arabs, you're an Arab?" "I'm different." "You can't be serious, what about me? Only an Arab could understand that side of me?" to which his reply was to repeat himself, "No more Arabs." I finished my coffee and told him the Starbucks was cute but they had no desk for my laptop so I would like to go back to my regular Starbucks.

As we drove I found myself forgetting my own good advice and probing the subject a little more. "Why no Arabs, could you just explain?" "I'll tell you why," he said as the car speed started to increase which was never a good sign as he went on. "Because the Arabs that come here are more often the rejects from their own countries, making them garbage. Do you understand?" "Not really, it makes no sense at all. Everyone here is an immigrant." He swerved the car suddenly as he looked at me and said, "I know you think you like that Jordanian at the Starbucks, but he's trash and not for you." "I wouldn't call him trash, he's not like Firas, but he's not trash and what's the problem I just like him as a friend." "I SAID NO MORE ARABS!" he shouted at me. I knew at that point I needed to back down, so I looked down at my hands folded in my lap and said, "Yes, Baba." "Good," he said.

As he dropped me off at my Starbucks he leaned out the window as I was walking out and said, "I'm glad we understand each other." As I walked in, shaking on the inside, I knew that this had been a warning not to take this relationship any further. After that my stepdad started with his common tactic. The silent treatment. Something we all hated. For the next few days, he would pretend I was invisible unless he had a reprimand to hand out. Even eye contact would be avoided making the house extremely uncomfortable in the evening.

I relayed to Jacob what had happened but instead of understanding my tactic that we should slow everything down until my stepdad had time to adjust and we could see where it goes, he was overjoyed. He started saying that he can come and talk to my stepdad, ask for my hand properly, and move things forward. I shuddered at the thought of him and my stepdad having a conversation, knowing very well that there was no way it would go well. "Don't you want to get married? We could rent an apartment, I have some money put away, I love you," he said. He was endearingly sweet, but I could not help this underlying feeling that my stepdad was right in a way. It was too soon after my divorce, he was Christian which could create all sorts of problems down the road. Plus, the fact that I just found some kind of freedom for myself even if it was under my stepdad's roof. I asked him to let me think about it for a few days and ended the conversation.

I didn't go to see him after work for a few days and when I took my lunch break at the Starbucks I didn't call him to see if he wanted to meet me. I pondered all the trouble that could come by letting this go any further and at the same time, I enjoyed being in love with someone who loved me. My head and my heart seemed to be at odds with one another. Jacob had left many messages and missed calls on my phone while I was at work despite my asking him for time to think. I knew I needed to call him back, so I picked up my phone and took a deep breath as it rang. He answered, "Koko (his nickname for me), I miss you, I love you, how are you?" "I'm good Jacob, yes of course, I miss you too, but we need to just slow down for a little while. This is a lot to ask so quickly." A change in his voice happened as he said, "I don't think so, I'm happy to give you as much time to think as you want as long as when you're done you promise you will be mine." Silence overtook me. "I need to go, I have to get back, we will talk later." I could hear the panic in his tone as he said, "Okay, I love you. Call me when you get off work."

Deep down I saw the signs but I, like so many, forgot to follow my own good advice. I didn't call him after work that night and tried my best to avoid my phone as I sat with my sisters painting our nails. It was sweet, I thought how simple he made everything sound that we could just run away together, build a home and be happy. But he had never been disowned. I had. He had never been prevented from contacting his siblings, I had. He had no great ambitions besides his simple happiness and although I didn't know what my ambitions were yet, I had them. He was naive to think that my stepdad would even meet him. Jacob was proud as most men are and thought if he was a good man there would be no reason for him to be turned away, but the past was proof enough for me. If someone like Firas was only offered coffee and insulted while he was in the house Jacob would definitely not even be admitted to the street where my parent's house was, let alone be allowed to address my stepdad in any way.

When Saturday came, I decided to put it all aside when we met at Starbucks. My stepdad yet again broke his silence to tell me to change before going out, something that annoyed me immensely. I wished he would just grow up and talk to me as the adult I was, as we did when we talked about anyone else except me. I told Jacob that I didn't want to talk about marriage anymore right now while I tried to come up with a plan. I didn't have the heart to tell him that while I was falling in love with him, marriage was not on my mind. I wanted to be able to enjoy his company as Americans did and see how things went. But in typical Arab fashion that was not how things were done. My stepdad would forever be harping, and Jacob would keep insisting we get married. That night I felt a kind of sadness thinking how it was unfair that I could not just date him. After being so long in a relationship that offered no romance, here was a man who was all about romance, after being so long in a marriage that had no passion, here was a man who felt more passionately about me than anything in the world and on top of it all I didn't want to miss out on spending time with my sisters.

As I sat on my bed pondering all this, my stepdad flung open my bedroom door. Holding the handle, he stood tall and looked at the floor as he said, "You are to take all your short skirts and put them in a suitcase and hand them over to me." I looked at him, thinking how ridiculous he looked and asked, "What short skirts? I don't have any short skirts; they are all knee length." His response was typical, he repeated, "You are to take all your short skirts and put them in a suitcase and hand them over to me first thing tomorrow," and he shut the door. My blood boiled at the thought of being told what to do, being treated like I did something wrong when I did nothing wrong and being treated like a child when I was no longer a child. Sick of being ignored until I made the decision he wanted I jumped up from the bed and did something I had never done before.

I marched across the hall to my parent's bedroom. I knocked on the door. My mother answered. "Where is he!" I said in an angry tone. She started saying he had already gone to bed, so I pushed the door open only to see him standing behind her giving her instructions. Still unwilling to look at me. I said, "Do you want me to leave, is that it? Because if not, you best tell me now or I'll make arrangements tomorrow to find another place to live." He looked down, clenching his teeth, still unwilling to talk to me, so I made a decision. "Very well then," I said. "I'll make arrangements to move out tomorrow," and returned back to my room to search for an apartment nearby.

This was the stubborn determination both my stepdad and I had all too much of. Our inner Saudi's would never admit a wrong decision and once we started down a road it would take a miracle for either of us to do anything else except keep going until one of us broke.

It would be years later while writing this book, in fact that I would finally see all the strands of an elaborate web that my stepdad had been weaving around me over the last seven years. Brainwashing ... to control you must isolate and control the resources. I just never saw it at the time. He had to get rid of Firas, because with him, I was untouchable. So, he pushed for Robert, a man he knew who was only looking for some company while in Saudi Arabia, where the pickings were slim. A man who also would have probably, in the interest of his career, not have wanted to be involved in a conflict between a Saudi and his property (AKA me). And Firas would have relished the idea of taking down a Saudi who thought he was better than him. I didn't follow my stepdad's web, I married Firas anyway. The next person he needed to get rid of was Ablah May and my band of religious friends like Doctora Zayina and to do that was as simple as encouraging me to not wear my head cover anymore. He knew that I would lose them as a result and I did, along with any friends who were associated with that time period in my life. When I decided on my own to divorce Firas, he was beyond happy to once again have me in his clutches with no one at my side and perhaps he had been biding his time for this throughout my marriage to Firas. All my stepdad's advice sounded like he had shed his skin and changed. But as George Clooney once said, "Never re-friend a person that has tried to destroy your character ... a snake only sheds its skin to become a bigger snake." When Jacob arrived on the scene all his plans were spoiled. Once again. He had taken the direct conflict approach years earlier and failed, this time he played the waiting game, and he did it well.

The next day I set out to look for an apartment. I left the car and walked the two miles to my Starbucks to imply that I needed nothing from him. Something my stepdad hated since his claim to power with all of us often rested on our needing him. Be it for money, a place to stay, a car, contact with the family and so on, which is why we all worked around him instead of fighting his rules. Jacob had said the night before that he would meet me, but he didn't show up or answer his phone. I decided to continue to look for an apartment without him since I was not moving out for him. I was moving out to show my stepdad once and for all that I would not be bullied. Just as I was having my coffee and making plans to walk another four miles to an apartment complex nearby, Ahmed arrived and offered me a ride to go see the apartment.

Upon arrival I looked over the floor plans and rented an apartment that would be ready two days later, sight unseen. As we headed back to Starbucks to celebrate over a cup of coffee, I stopped at the bank to remove all of my money from the joint account my stepdad had me open when I first arrived. His reasoning at the time was that it would be best for building my credit if I added someone who already had credit to the account. I set up a private account since I knew he would see the apartment charge and might feel the urge to move my money to keep control of the situation. It was an intricate game of chess where I needed to always be two steps ahead if I was to win.

Jacob arrived, apologizing that he was working late and overslept. We sat for a little bit and then I told them I needed to get home to pack, to get ready for the move. Instead of talking to me, my stepdad decided to communicate through email (errors retained):

It's 4am and I can't go back to sleep thinking of you, how did you end up doing the one thing I thought I'll never see you doing, your mother does it all the time, she assumes or finish's what I say to fit what she wants to hear out of it and then bases her actions on that assumption. You did not wait for me to finish my sentence when I said (put you short dresses in a suitcase till the day.....) you jumped ran down to my room and said (till what the day I leave. Fine I'll leave) and you stormed away and apparently your basing you actions based on what you heard yourself saying. All what I can tell is that's not what I was about to say, but I guess that does not matter now .If anything came out of it, you managed to put a joyous grin on your mothers face when you told her you are looking for an apartment, and that same freaky grin comes out every time she sees us talking (or not talking more correctly).

Look kid I don't have much left in my life to spend it on useless arguments or petty you said, I said fights. All what I was trying to do is provide you with a better life and I guess I failed and for that I apologize. I just wanna live in peace till the day I die, and if you decided to continue not talking to me till then, there is nothing I can do about that except wishing the happiest of life.

Farewell Princess

Dear daddy,

You send me messages and emails and as always you make the same mistakes, you assume that I assume and we could go on forever assuming whatever but at the end of the day I am as tired as you of the fighting, If I don't talk to you it's because I am tired of arguing with my dad who should at least at this point in my life look at me and see the smart and accomplished woman I have become. Although as a parent I can understand that I will always be your little girl but there comes a point where every parent needs to let go and pray they already provided them with all the tools they need while always knowing that if they need something they can always lean back on family these are the values I know we agree on along with others.

But anyway Daddy every time I try to stand up for what I want and it's something you don't agree with instead of respecting my right as an adult to choose you do this and when I fight back suddenly there is a filter or I am acting like my mom. Why can't you just say to yourself she is acting like her, she always knows what she wants and she dose it so why do I fight her and why do I push her away. You and I both know that the whole short dress issue was not about the dresses but what disturbed me the most was your approach, you know me well and had you come and made a "request" I would never say no but it was not a request it was your way of trying to talk to me by finding a reason I guess, but you did it wrong.

A request normally includes things like please and this is why. Perhaps I seemed to over react but the truth is I have been wanting to move out for some time and I thank you for giving me this time to get on my feet, not much will change I guess I will just have more privacy which is what is best for everyone, especially me, I like my privacy and my independence allot and moving out will just help me gain that, if you ever need me I am always here for you, I am never going to be very far but sometimes there just comes a time when people need to make their own way and my time is now. I am sorry for causing you not to sleep, that was not my intention.

Sweet dreams.

Your Princess

His reply:

I'm sorry for getting emotional about the whole thing but honey as much as I'm proud of what you accomplished and how mature you have became, as much as seeing you jumping into this with full thrust, daily meetings, weekly outings, dressed for the kill, makes me think it is my duty to slow you down to protect you from regrets. You know me well, I don't want to be in your way, I want you to find your own way I always did, and this time is no different, when I said no arab's all what I repeatedly asked of you is to slow down, give yourself the time and space to absorb this new situation and be in the right state of mind to make the right choices. Instead, the minute I asked you to slow down, you push even faster, I know 3 years was an exaggeration from my side, but I'm old 3 years in my life is like 3 months in yours, but seriously 6 to 12 months is not that long of a time to set clear plans for the next 30 to 50 years of your future life, is it?. Stop this hopping as if you are trying to impress someone or in a race and you must meet a deadline before a certain age, it puts a huge pressure on any women, I understand, but a little time won't hurt. I'm very happy to see you feeling strong and ready to move out and be on your own, but as a person who has a little more experience in life, I'm asking you again to please slow down, give yourself the time to gain more knowledge about your surroundings, your professional and social circle, increase your negotiation strength (in the US that is money), oh and get yourself a car. Staying with us a little longer and dealing with our weird requests is not that hard for you I know that, specially if I stopped talking about your bad choices of men (oh yeah I still think it is a bad choice, at least at this time).

Oh this communication through texting and email is killing me, it took me 90 min just to text on my phone yesterday, I would like to talk to you face to face, but I did not want to disturb your day before work beside I don't like the way you swash your claws on my face when I criticize your choice of men, however I'm free Saturday if you are.

(Serious note: Just because I criticize your choice of men does not mean I see you as any less accomplished, smart, or mature. Choices are affected by the circumstances we are in at the time we make those choices).

So says an old man

Hi daddy,

I am on my lunch break, I love your email and although I understand where your coming from and I know we need to talk face to face, we will daddy not to worry. I know you want to save me from regrets, I know you always have good intentions but until now I don't have any regrets not from the past or the present, I take my decisions and never regret anything that's why I am always happy, always on the bright side no matter what tomorrow is another day. I am guessing from your email though that mama did not tell you which I figured knowing her she would have but that's ok, I rented an apartment yesterday and I move in Saturday, I am planning to tell everyone at parlay over dinner today, I want you and need you to be happy for me I am excited about getting started, my work is going great and I know this is the best thing, I don't feel pushed out its not because of anything, it's just time. Don't worry I will still be around eating out of your fridge and coming over to tuck Osama in bed.

I love you Daddy

His Reply:

That is just great you all mighty. Thank you for illustrating to your siblings how to deal with instructions from the old man when they don't agree with it or don't like it, just run away with the first stranger you meet at the coffee shop and have him rent you a flat or whatever. Just great just great.

At the moment I'm so upset I don't even want to look at your face. What are you thinking. Spontaneous decision for what? Don't lie to yourself and say this is not because of anything, we could've planned this before wasting all that time fixing you a room, we could have better used the resources setting you up in your own place and used the time to have everyone share your excitement and knowing you moved to your own place because you are a mature adult not because you ran away from home. If this was planned in your mind long before then thank you for lieing and making me believe you're coming home to stay for a while.

I don't know or have anything to say. After all it doesn't matter what I say to you all mighty will do whatever you want to do regardless. Thank you.

What was done was done. There was no going back now, he could assume and assume, and I was tired of arguing. The day of the move arrived; Jacob offered to drive me home from the Starbucks to help me collect my belongings. I knew that would blow my stepdad's brain and I didn't want him to think I was moving out for Jacob when the reason was so much bigger than whether he approved of who I loved, dated, or married. I called a girl I had met recently at work and asked her if she was up for a little adventure. I relayed all that had happened, and she drove me home to help me collect my things.

The house seemed empty since everyone was at school except Noura. When Noura came down I quickly sent her away telling her not to put herself at risk. I grabbed a bunch of trash bags from the kitchen, and we began to quickly throw everything into the bags. I urged her not to fold anything but instead to hurry. The air in the house felt like the night I underestimated his anger before I married Ata, and I didn't intend on being there long enough to find out what he would do.

As I was bagging up the last of my things I heard my friend in the hallway saying, "Hi, I'm Saline, it's nice to meet you, Dr. Turkistani." As she extended her hand he stared at her like a rabbit that had entered his carrot garden. I came out and asked her to help me with the last of the bags. Noura, upon hearing the introduction not returned, bravely stood on the edge of the stairs in his sight to make sure everything was okay. I picked up the last bag, looked at him and said, "Goodbye, I'll be living close by if you need anything," and on that final note, I placed my house keys on the side table next to him and left.

I felt exhilarated to have my own apartment at last. Jacob and I swung by Walmart and bought me a blowup bed and a bottle of wine. After we finished bringing all my things up we opened the wine, laughed, talked, and then made love. He held me all night long, he brought me water at night if he got up and made me feel more loved then I had in the last seven years of my life. Like clockwork the next day an email arrived from my stepdad (errors retained):

> *Bringing into the house a complete stranger this morning without at least informing us, that is very considerate of you, but then I should have expected that much from someone who never looked at this house as hers, it was just another bridge to you and we were the bricks to step on.*
>
> *This house does not appreciate strangers running around its rooms, and that applies on those who consider them self strangers, they are just not welcomed around the house or members of this house.*

The email was the announcement that my friend was a stranger and now I was as well. No longer welcome for dinner, to tuck in my little brother or to spend time with my sisters. It was my excommunication email and I had expected as much. I replied:

> *I love you and you are my daddy whether you consider me a stranger or not for me you will always be my daddy and that's forever. You know me better than anyone and you can say that I never considered your house as mine but that's just not true but your entitled to your opinion. You also know that I don't stay*

where I don't feel welcome and I seemed to have worn out my welcome with you and mama more than two weeks ago. Everything upsets you and causes you not talk to me, I did my best to ease and help you to talk to me the first time you went silent but to what end daddy. As for the complete stranger, if you really ever considered me as a part of that house then my friend would have been welcome and if anyone of your other children had made a mistake and had forgotten to take permission to bring a friend into the house you would have just reminded them that guests need to be announced but with me I get an email that says that I am no longer welcome, wow. There are just so many things for example Mohammed comes and goes as he pleases and no one even thinks twice where he is or what he is doing but me I get put under the microscope and isolated into silence, how do you expect anyone to talk to you when you do that.

But that's ok there always seemed to be different standards for my siblings then there were for me, they are informed by you that when they turn 21 they can do whatever they want and me who dedicated so much of my life to doing whatever I could to help you bring up this family even after turning 29 still out of my kindness asks permission before stepping out of the house.

I am still here, still around I don't want us to end up back where we were 9 years ago but whatever makes you comfortable daddy. Still I will always say your my daddy and I love you if you ever want to talk you know how to get in touch with me and where to find me, life is short daddy and everyone looks to find happiness, I miss you but if your happier without me around then I will leave you be, god knows I never like to force myself on anyone.

Your old Princess

His reply:

Amazing how you try to convince yourself that you are the victim here, when you are the one who took the radical decision on your own to run away from home without any consideration to anyone's feelings but yours. To a father who tried hard to provide everything he can to his kids, when one jump up, split and run away it is a painful stab in the back of his fatherhood specially when it takes place at a time of anger or during stressful periods of his life, you did that 9 years ago, when I was stressed about my new assignment at work (Lab head), but back then as painful as it was, I've never blamed you for it at all, I convinced my self with all kind of excuses, she is young, trying to show off her powers, and most of all she believe's she is doing it to protect her marriage (and I was proud of you for that). Today, you've repeated the same thing and decided to stab me in the back just because you can, but this time around it is hurting 100 times more because I've allowed myself to trust you beyond and more than I ever trusted anyone in my lifetime, I was under the belief that I was doing everything possible to make you feel welcomed, you are more experienced, and you are not doing it for any reason but to show how powerful you are as if you are taking revenge for something. This time around the stress on me is 10 times more as I'm faced with a situation where I cannot feed my own kids because I ran out of money and what I've got is not enough and that started to show on me the past few weeks, a situation that you are aware of, and fool me tried to run through my options with you before anyone else because I thought I had a friend to bounce ideas with, and all I got was hmmmm....(you were too busy with yourself to notice anything else). Of course you translated that stress in my face as "you are not welcomed" because you wanted to see it that way, and instead of helping with the situation you kept adding more stress to it, giving yourself the needed excuse to split and run away, and whammm comes the stab.

I've never ever wanted to go back to where we were 9 years ago, and that's why I gathered my shattered self and pushed my other issues away to try and talk to you, tried to ask for your help to settle down for few months, in the hope that you be considerate and give me the time to get back on my feet before we go through another round of changes (that was from the first and only time, there was only one time where I got upset seeing you exchanging admiration looks and laughs with Jacob, and when I came down I told you what it is flat out. The next time we did not talk till you stabbed me, was because you got upset about me asking you to change your short dress before you go out on your date, sorry "friends gathering", and to continue on your silence treatment you took off Saturday all day to avoid talking, and even when you decided to talk you came late at night to my room and wanted to hash it in front of mama, then next morning sure enough you are out all day and night, and the silence continues, in spite of all my messages and emails). Was there anything so sever that I did to cause this, well in your eyes there was, and I learned from experience that no mater what I do I can not change that, hence I am accepting my suffering quietly, till such time comes and a miracle happens or I leave to hell in peace.

We can talk, talk is good, taking actions while angry is not what we do. What type of talk is left after the china has broken, You keep convincing yourself that you looked at this house as yours by repeating words like "you can say that I never considered your house as mine but that's just not true" However deep within your thoughts that is not it, your true feelings are reflected by words like "god knows I never like to force myself on anyone," family members are never forced on each other, a thought like that never crosses their minds, you however think that way. I wish I knew of a way to change the above and more than I already tried. Don't fool yourself by trying to make it a simple comparison with your siblings, hash out the nitty gritty details of the way I deal with my kids and start to point out average discrepancies as major reasons for your actions, as if you are a stranger and I must be careful not to offend your "not belonging" feelings. More than any of them you know the way we look at boys and girls when it comes to leaving the protection of home, even with that you need to correct your info, Mohamed never leaves the house without informing me except for work and classes. With all that said, Mohamed did not even thought of "not belonging" or "forced myself" when I asked him to hand out his PS3 (his life support) to me, he did not feel un-welcomed because of that, he knows things like this happens all the time within a family unit, it is not a cause to break up the unit, not in that way or any way. Have you thought of it like a family member, you would not have taken actions based on anger feeling and given yourself the time to seek advice or at least an opinion, but that's not you.

You try to compare a completely unusual situation with normal everyday ones, none of the kids ever brought unknown "friend" to the house to empty their rooms content, completely unannounced. On top of all that almost in all situation's you always had the upper hand as I talk to you openly to help me set examples for the others, and that's what created what seems to be a double standard but if it is there it was always in your favor as I considered you my trust-able adviser and my favorite one, I depended on you to lean on, but I was wrong, you showed me repeatedly that you can vanish at any given moment and leave me to fall and apparently you are proud of it too based on your words "I take my decisions and never regret anything." When a family member is ready to leave the nest, the entire family gets involved with all kind of comments, supportive or discouraging, opinions, suggestions, they are all part of a sweet experience that include a fight over the decision itself and then when agreed upon, comes the selection of the place, the furniture, the stupid little fixes that a dad shows off with, just so he can see the thank you smile on the kid's face as she embarks on her life journey. In my case, all that was taken away from me and the others, because of your "un-regrettable" selfish decision of running away from home, and sharing those moments with your "coffee shop friends"........ Thank you.

If you think this is making me happy then you are wrong, hurt is never fun for me. Everyone should look for happiness, I just never expected your happiness can only be achieved by stabbing me in the back the way you did. The last thing I need at this stage of my life is more stress, I can not handle seeing one of my kids isolating herself in this manner (yet convincing herself to be isolated by me), and even though it hurt like hell, I cannot stop in the way of your happiness the way you believe it to be. At this moment I cannot mentally or physically sustain another blow, but sadly yes, I am vulnerable at this time of my life, waiting for another stab from you or from one of the other kids as you managed to show them the way to do it, but there is nothing I can or want to do anything about it, as any action of retaliation among family will only hurt both ends.

A thought to reflect on:

Strength is not having the power to do what you want, rather it is having all the power in the world but restrain yourself to use it to hurt others. Thank you

oh great now grandpa has lung cancer, can this stress get any harder?

I wanted to reply and set him straight, but I knew we would just go on forever. He was right in his mind, and I was right in mine. After mentioning the fact that my Grandpa had cancer, I offered a parley, as we called it every night at the dinner table, which meant a chance to talk. But even with that we went back and forth over email and text (errors retained):

***Me**: Daddy lets talk, let me know when your free.*

***Stepdad**: I'm always free, that's what my price tag says, $00.00*

***Me**: Lol ok daddy well I am free after work normally and this Sunday cause Saturday we have to do class set up at work. Which day is better for you?*

***Stepdad**: How long and where, will determine my availability.*

***Me**: To see you for one minute daddy is good for me, wherever you want.*

***Stepdad**: I can accommodate one minute now, where at?*

***Me**: Wherever you want daddy, there is Kroger, Walmart, Starbucks, subway near my work, McDonald's.*

***Stepdad**: That was last night when I had a minute, now its Saturday or Sunday.*

Do you have a car?

***ME**: Sorry daddy I sleep early cause they changed my hours. I can do Sunday cause we have to volunteer on Saturday for class setup. I don't have a car by I can get someone to drop me off wherever you want on Sunday.*

Stepdad: Another hit on the same wound, hurt is all what I'm getting, why do I continue to do this? It is more natural for you to ask someone to give you a ride than to ask me to pick you up, I get the picture.

***Me**: Daddy I was just trying to make it easier for you, if you wanted to come and pick me up why did you ask if I had a car, of course you can always come and pick me up.*

I felt as though this would continue forever anytime a sentence sounded like I was talking about Jacob, there was a problem. We finally agreed to meet at the Kroger next to the house. My stepdad picked me up after work and drove me there. I tried to clarify a lot of things based on his emails but so much seemed so lost in translation. He told me about my grandpa's sudden illness and how bad it was and then he drove me back to my apartment complex. Before getting out of the car I asked if I could maybe come by for dinner one night to see the kids. He said, "No." I protested that he was being unreasonable to which he replied, "You chose to leave so go live your life." It would not have mattered what I said in the end, if I didn't break down and ask for forgiveness nothing within his power to control would be available to me and that included my siblings.

I spent a few nights alone in my apartment when Jacob had to work late and the silence of the empty apartment made me feel very lonely, so I had a key made and asked him if he wanted to move in with me since he was living with his aunt. He looked as though he was offered a winning lottery ticket. Standing up so happy he picked me up with his big arms and twirled me around. He had no way of knowing the happiness I felt and the immense joy I felt from being twirled around like a real princess.

Three months later I decided it was best that we get married. I wasn't on birth control and having a baby with someone I was living with was still too liberal a thought for me. Jacob was over the moon with joy and called his family to make arrangements for the wedding. My one private condition with him was that if he wanted to get married in a church that sounded fine, but I would not be baptized to do so. I was still a Muslim to which he agreed happily. So, he planned to tell his conservative orthodox family that I was baptized as a child when I was a Mormon to ease their minds. It was all set. We were planning to be married on December 31, 2013, so that we could start the new year as husband and wife. Jacob bought a small diamond ring for me which was more than he could afford at the time. His uncle owned a jewelry shop and gave him a good deal. That ring meant more to me than the ring Firas had promised to get me once. It was small and simple but full of love.

We decided to merge our finances to make paying the bills easier than me asking him to transfer half the rent every month. We went down to the bank, I added him on, and we closed his account. While we were there the bank reminded me that I had a small savings account that had something like a hundred dollars in it. When I realized my stepdad was still connected to it I asked to shut it down. They told me all I had to do was take all the money out of it and it should close on its own. When I emptied the savings account an email was sent to my stepdad alerting him of a very low balance in the account which prompted him to email me about my current financial situation (errors retained):

> "*Let me start by apologizing for the silent treatment that started all of this, I guess I can not control my self when I get upset for someone specially those I care most for. It's who I am, an old man who depend to much on his family for understanding and tolerance, and I depended on you a lot, after all you are my first daughter.*
>
> *Anyhow, I've got concerned about the recent dramatic changes in your finances, you probably in full control of that and I have and should not worry about it at all, but cannot help myself. The thought of how stubborn ass you can be sometimes, and all that self pride and ego shit make me in vision you pushing yourself into unpleasant situations instead of reaching for advise or maybe assistance. So here I'm again asking you to let me know if everything is okay with you.*
>
> *If you don't want to reply that's ok too but at least send me "OK" message so I know that you are OK.*"

I replied:

Hey daddy, ya I am ok so far so good sailing along lol. Thank you for being concerned I am sorry for the silent treatment too, it's good to know my daddy still cares and worries.

I love you daddy, I was actually thinking of just coming by the house on Sunday I figured the silence has gone on long enough, since I know everyone is normally home Sunday and now that I got my car I am able to drive over and get around more easily, let me know if that's ok.

Princess of them all.

His reply:

I just wanted to know if you're OK... I did not say anything about you coming over.

My reply:

Dear Daddy,

I guess you are probably not interested in hearing from me since it feels like we're never ever getting back together but I need to tell you my news if for no other reason except that your my dad. To get straight to the point Jacob proposed and were planning to get married soon, he asked to speak to you and take your blessing because as he said it is a matter of honor because your my dad. I know your mad and probably your bent on staying this way for a while but just like the last time I got married, I would love to have you there to dance with me on my wedding day and share in my happiness.

Good night daddy, will love you forever even if you think we should never see each other again.

His reply:

To my dear lost daughter

If you made up your mind and decided to choose yet another man over your own family, knowing how much hurt you're bringing me to see you go like that, then I guess I have nothing left but to wish you success with your choices.

This time around however, I cannot close my eyes and accept you forcing your ill choices on the family, or waste the effort to work out a compromise to please you only to find out that you didn't know what you wanted yet one more time.

Finally, I will be grateful if you don't communicate with your siblings from here on, it will be easier on them if they keep the good memories, and not be in the middle of a conflict that they don't understand.

Wish that one day you will find the happiness you are looking for. Good luck and goodbye.

Your f..........??

Whatever you consider me to be

It was the final cut of the string. There was nothing more to say except go and be happy. I had hoped my sisters would still reach out but with my stepdad watching all of their phone bills it was not possible. They knew I would have never advised them to put themselves at risk to keep in touch with me.

I focused mostly on my wedding and embraced Jacob's family as my own. They were kind and welcoming and it seemed wonderful to be introduced more internally to what it was like being Christian Arabs since almost all the Arabs I knew growing up were Muslim. The ease of how male and female cousins, wives, and husbands hung out together was a whole new side of the Arabic world than I had known. Almost like a merging of who I had been, a conservative Muslim, and who I had grown into, a liberal. Who although still loving her religion, felt no need to stress about every little religious matter. It was always funny to me how the family life I always looked for was only ever found in the family of a husband when my own could have done the same. It makes all the difference in a marriage when you feel your family welcome your partner as a new member, too, but my stepdad couldn't understand that or as I see it now; he just never wanted me to leave. I wonder at times if my family really welcomed any of my husbands, what a difference it might have made?

The wedding day was closely approaching, and everything was planned to perfection. Jacob's mother arrived with his sister and brother from Jordan. They gave him a cash gift to help pay for the wedding expenses but as soon as she did the meddling began. I didn't mind since it was Jacob's wedding, and I was happy. My sisters were able to sneak out of the house to help me choose my dress and it was so great to see them, even for a moment.

The cousins planned a Bachelorette party for me in a Mediterranean restaurant called Sanabel. At dinner they asked me to open the gifts, which was unusual to me since in Saudi I was taught that the gifts are normally not opened in front of the guests. Instead, we would wait until the guests were gone and then make a mental record of who gave what. Presents that were not really your taste or duplicate gifts were put aside to regift to someone else when an event arose.

Since they were Christian, and their traditions were different, I agreed. It was a Bachelorette party, my first and my only knowledge of such things was in the movies. As I opened up bag after bag, box after box of lingerie, I did my best to say, "Ooh la la." I giggled and then somehow expressed slightly that Jacob would love them. When the belly dancer arrived, she pulled me up to dance and I danced as much as I could. Unfortunately, I had forgotten that while they were Christian Arabs they were still Arabs. Jacob got an ear full of his mother and sister about his future wife dancing in front of everyone at the restaurant and pulling out lingerie with no sense of decency. I reminded myself that I needed to be on guard around them. No matter how much they welcomed me like family I would always be an American who didn't know how to behave. I knew better than most girls how important it is to keep your in-laws happy.

The night before the wedding day Jacob was out with his brother while I was attending to last minute wedding favor wrapping when an email arrived. My heart stopped beating as I read (errors retained):

> *Hi Elise, I want to let you know that I am currently in Shreveport on leave since five days now. I don't know why I am telling you this but I thought it won't hurt to inform you that I am here close by and that I am driving to Dallas alone today to spend one night*

there. I really hesitated before sending you this email because part of me still wants to see you, while another part prefers to continue moving on. But I decided to send it anyway to see what you think about meeting. Let me know. I am staying at the Le Meridien, 13402 Noel Rd, Dallas.

I leave back to Shreveport tomorrow afternoon, and I leave back to Geneva next Sunday.

Take care

Firas

I pondered my reply quickly not wanting to hurt him again by saying why I couldn't see him and knowing at the same time that if he had any hope of seeing me he might decide to drive down to my apartment since it was the address where I had asked him to mail the divorce papers. My reply (errors retained):

Dear Firas,

It's great to hear from you and I am glad your are getting a chance to spend sometime with family. I got a new job working in the public school system so it gave me two weeks off for the holidays so unfortunately I am in Colorado my dad who brought me down for Christmas and New Years so we won't be able to meet, but enjoy Dallas and happy new year.

Elise

His reply (errors retained):

Hi Elise,

I just arrived to the hotel in Dallas and read your email. I actually have a confession to make which is that I came to Dallas only to see you and say the things that I could not say during the transitional period after you left because you would refuse to speak to me then. No worries, maybe it is God's wish that we don't meet again. I will probably drive back to Shreveport now as I have no other business in Dallas being alone.

Since we may never be destined to meet again in this life, I would tell you now what I wanted to say, in a civilized way, in person today. That is how much I deeply, honestly, faithfully and genuinely loved you with everything that I am made of, but also how much I am deeply hurt, humiliated and disappointed from the way you treated me at the end, and the way you ended our marriage. Believe me I had no intention to open old books again, but rather just to bring this to its final closure, as that closure never came to me in the last six months. Now it should come as I move on with my life and you move on with yours.

I would like to wish you and all your family a happy and joyful holidays and a prosperous new year. My very warm regards, in particular, go to your father in Denver for whom I have a lot of respect. He was able to show me in two days how good a father in law can be with his son in law even if they had never met before.

A thousand congratulation for your new job, which you greatly deserve. I hope you continue to move from one success to another and receive all the satisfaction you seek. At this final word, I can not but to wish you all the best of what life can offer. And again, if you ever need anything do let me know for I will be nothing but a good man and a gentleman until the last minute with you, as I was before.

All the best Elise.

Goodbye.

Firas

He decided not to spend the night in Dallas and promptly drove back to Shreveport. I often ponder about how difficult it was for him and his pride to write that first email. I also wish, as was the case with most of his efforts, that he had just said what he was feeling more clearly in the first email, but we can never know the impact of a change in the past. Perhaps I would have seen him if he had said simply I want to see you, I want to have a chance to talk for closure, I have missed you and I'm driving all the way to Dallas to see you for closure. Even when the second email came he decided to add notes like *I came to Dallas only to see you and say the things that I could not say during the transitional period after you left because you would refuse to speak to me then. No worries.* His bruised ego always popped up along with his lack of memory that I kept in touch with him for quite some time after I left Geneva.

I'll never know how much might have been different if he had learned to bare his heart instead of constantly talking like a medieval knight using terms like I would like to inform you that I am here and I will be leaving the next day. Meaning "Don't take too long, because I wait for no woman," but for Firas this was the only language he knew. While I could translate him after so long together I still knew I didn't want to spend my whole life trying to interpret love while all the while doubting that the translation was accurate. I decided not to tell Jacob about the email since it would only make him uneasy. There was always a silent irrational fear he carried that someone would steal me or convince me to leave him and watching him voice his concern was never a fun conversation.

In the morning I found time to reply to Firas' email:

> *Thank you for your words, same to you Firas should you ever need anything let me know and I wish you and your family a happy new year. I wish all the best for you in everything in the future you deserve a lot, may God bless you with success is everything you do.*
>
> *All the best Firas,*
>
> *Elise*

I was glad we parted well this time and I truly wished him all the best.

It was the wedding day, and it would seem like Jacob's mother and sister knew how to panic at every single moment in typical Arab style. The term, "*What will people say,*" was employed at every turn but I let them enjoy their panicking while I enjoyed my daydream. I was excited that I would be getting married in a church like all those romantic comedy movies I had seen. My biological dad arrived from Colorado to attend the wedding and stay with us. I was overjoyed that he got the chance to walk me down the aisle, just as he had probably wished for all those years he was looking for me.

We had a church ceremony in a small chapel. We could not do the wedding in the Orthodox church because I would need to convert which would take time and the fees were too outrageous. This small chapel agreed to do it without question of what religion I was and cost next to nothing. I wanted us to write our own vows, but Jacob didn't feel like he was articulate enough to write something, so we went with the normal vows and repeated after the minister. I have to say there is a romance in getting married in a church. We left the church in the freezing cold. I recall feeling really warm since Saline had given me a shot of whiskey right before the ceremony to calm my nerves. Jacob's friend, who owned a car dealership, could not attend and so his gift to us was a limo to take us from the wedding to the reception and from the reception home.

The limo driver dropped us off. I asked him, "What time will you be back?" "I'll be waiting here with the limo until you're done." "No, you should come in and have some food, it will be fun." The reception was in the Bass Pro Shop Restaurant in Garland, Texas. An odd choice of venue but the restaurant, despite being decorated with dead stuffed animals, was really lovely. Shotgun style and large enough to pack in everyone, a big fireplace at the end and an empty area near the door for the dance floor. We had visited the Bass Pro Shop when we took our engagement photos since it was on the water. When we noticed there was a restaurant we inquired if they ever did weddings. The manager said they didn't do much in the winter and never did anything on New Year's Eve. He offered the venue for free and gave us a great deal on the liquor and food.

The wedding party was full of dancing, and I could hardly stay still. His cousins lifted me and Jacob up in chairs to parade us around the dance floor singing. Which was a custom I was not familiar with. I was so scared I might fall but I felt as though no moment in time could ever be greater. The cake was cut, and dinner was served.

The wedding brought in the New Year and then we retired back to the apartment. As we walked in I headed for the balcony to take in the cool air and promptly leaned over the balcony and threw up. I was not used to having so many people buy me shots. Jacob got me some water and took me to bed. I wanted to sleep feeling so tired, but Jacob kept nudging that he wanted to have sex. "When my dad leaves, honey, and I'm tired, let's just sleep." He huffed and said, "But, it's our wedding night!" "Alright," I said.

I started to look for another job, but following interview after interview, no one called me back. Jacob's friend owned a sandwich deli in downtown Dallas and one of his regular customers owned a temp agency. Her name was Dobbs. It was the perfect opportunity to try out different places, get paid, see where I wanted to settle and show the companies how good I was at what I did. I have always been bad at interviews. I wasn't ready to get a job that demanded as much of my time as the Agency in Dubai. So, I asked the temp agency to send me to places that needed an assistant or a receptionist. I just wanted a job that made me happy. Unfortunately for me, in interviews the answer to the question, "Where do you see yourself in five years?" wasn't going to be, "I'll be happy…" so temp work was the best way to showcase my skills while avoiding the grueling interview process.

I was sent to many different kinds of businesses. When it comes to temp agencies who call when you don't have another job, you go without question. I worked almost seven days a week and was sent all over Dallas. Jacob started to get annoyed, saying, "Why do you go every time they call. Surely you need time off?" "Jacob, this is how I'm going to get a good job. I must go to everything they give me to try them out. If I turn them down they might not call as often. Then how will we pay the bills? I'm sorry, I miss you too, but I need to work hard right now." He found reasons to call while I was at work, bringing up excuses like, the bird is sick so I should leave early. My reply was always, "I'm sure it will be fine, I can't leave early. I told them I would be here until five and I will be here until five. I'll see you when I get home."

Jacob wasn't good at being alone, I was a kind of security blanket that needed to be kept in his sight at all times. My being all over Dallas everyday made him nervous. Who would I meet? Would I change my mind? Did I miss him? I tried to sooth him by making sure I kept in as much contact as I could. I would text him when I arrived, when I took a break, and when I was on the way home. This is the nature of insecurity and lack of self-confidence. It tears you apart from the inside and then tears apart your outer world. We are our own worst enemies.

D MAGAZINE

One day I was sent to cover for a receptionist at D Magazine in downtown Dallas. I thought it was odd when Dobbs called all giddy, saying, "D Magazine, you know it right?" The truth was I had never heard of it and on top of that, I thought magazines were a waste of money not to mention paper. When I arrived, a lovely young woman, Chelsey, showed me to the front desk and loaded up a cheat sheet to help me understand the routine and my duties. I loved precise instructions, order and everything being done just so.

I did well but all the while I wondered if everyone in the whole office were on happy pills. They all seemed to glide and bounce about all day long. I was the only person I knew who did that without use of medication. When the day ended the young woman came back to let me know it was time to go. I said, "Thank you so much, it was fun, but I need a supervisor to sign off on my timecard" "Oh, I can do that," She said. I looked at her, puzzled for a moment as she smiled and stood silently. "No, you see I need a supervisor to sign off," I said "Yes, I can do it," as she took the form to sign off. I was mortified to realize that while younger than me she actually was my supervisor. I felt ashamed of my upbringing that had taught me only men and older ladies could be supervisors, managers, or heads of departments. At the same time, I was in complete awe of Chelsey's accomplishments at such a young age. For me she was the essence of the American dream.

After working through the weekend at a real estate office in an area far from where I lived and not being offered a lunch break or even a bathroom break all day, I was delighted when Dobbs called and said D Magazine would like to have me back again on Monday. The request caused Jacob to groan, saying, "We haven't had enough time together," to which I replied, "I know, baby, but I'm trying to find a permanent spot, so I need to go when I am called. Sometimes working all the time is necessary." Jacob was very attached to me, and I loved that he loved me so much but at times it felt like I was a drug more than anything else.

Monday morning came and right at nine o'clock everyone started gathering in the main lobby. This wasn't covered in my cheat sheet, so I stood by while I waited for further instruction. Chelsey arrived, jumping on to the computer as cool and as joyful as can be, loading up a slide show to the big screen from my computer. I watched attentively, determined to know what to do next time. I was in awe of how many people there were in the office since on Friday it had been pretty quiet. People sat on desks, kitchen counters and stood in a large circle as one person talked about what her department was up to. I continued to watch the people as one would watch wildlife in a zoo. It was such a different culture and environment than I had ever seen in any office before. This was the weekly huddle where everyone got updates and accolades were announced.

At the end of their weekly huddle an award was always given out. It was called the High Five and was given to the staff member who did something above and beyond. To add to my awe, it was Chelsey. The exact words of what she had done escape me now, but I watched as they all truly adored her and I saw how modestly she received her High Five award from the President of the company. I was struck as if in a time warp. At that moment I decided I wanted to be like her. The thought that women could be accomplished, not just have a job, was amazing and I decided that one day I would be one of them.

When I got home and shared my day with Jacob, his response was, "I doubt her husband likes that." As I took a sip of my beer I realized that I had forgotten again that I had married an Arab man. He grew up, as I did, in a world where a woman having a serious career, aspirations, or owning a business was more a novelty than anything, just like a monkey playing cymbals in a traveling band. Women worked to fill their time until children arrived, and the men were the providers. This concept always surprised me since I had studied the wives of the Prophet

Mohammad, whose first wife was a very successful businesswoman who he worked for, but that story would do no good in a conversation with Jacob because he was Christian. In the past such a comment would have started a great debate between me and Firas about how the Prophet's first wife had owned her own business and he was happy working for her. Jacob, however, not being a Muslim, meant such a debate would fall on deaf ears. He was simple in his way, and I loved him, so I smiled and leaned in to cuddle with him as we watched TV.

I had arrived near the end of the summer when the owner, Wick Allison, was still away fishing. Chelsey passed by my desk one morning to let me know that he would be arriving today. I thought it was odd at first that I would need to know in advance, since I could not fathom what the owner would have to do with me. As she left I gazed around the office, and I noticed a certain buzz happening as people started to put off the scent of panic. Almost like the scene in the movie The Devil Wears Prada with the assistant screaming, "No! No! No!" and Stanley Tucci walking around saying, "Alright, everyone, gird your loins." I watched as person after person buzzed about. Cleaning their desks, hiding things, pulling up what they were meant to be working on onto their screens and rushing to make sure they printed the final draft of an article he had requested. Spitting out their gum and sitting up as straight as possible. Suddenly, the elevator door dinged and slid silently open.

The manner in which the man strode into the office and turned the corner with such determination taking no notice of me immediately gave him away as the owner. I stood to attention with both my hands behind my back watching as he walked down the hall. Suddenly he came to a full stop for a second before pirouetting, suggesting great confidence in his mannerism, and briskly walking back to stand before my desk. I smiled at him as he looked at me for a moment and then he said, "Who are you?" I confidently reached out my hand making sure to look him in the eyes and said, "I'm your temp, Elise." He nodded, spun around, and headed down to his office. I exhaled loudly and receded back into my chair. Humans are so much like animals when a stampede happens. I knew none of the stories. I had never heard of him or even seen his picture, but the sight of everyone else's reactions to his imminent arrival made me panic.

On the weekends, Jacob and I would go and visit his aunt, whose daughter lived with her. Aunt Nawal was old and unable to work, and the daughter, Sohair, was always between jobs. Sohair mentioned how she would love to get a government job since the work would be easy and the benefits are great. Like so many in Jacob's family she was prone to being melancholy, short tempered, and instead of bettering herself through reading or taking a class so she could get a better job, she preferred to complain how life in America was hard and people were prejudiced against her. Jacob would always nod and commensurate with her. I just listened and sipped my rosé wine in silence.

I remained a temp at D Magazine for a good while until the night of a big storm. The wind and rain hit the building so hard that the windows leaked water onto the carpet. We didn't have towels, so Chelsey and I did our best to blot up the water with paper towels. I laughed at the sight of us on our hands and knees saying, "I think in a few years this will be one of our fondest memories, the time when we had to clean up a flood with paper towels, ha-ha." Chelsey smiled and said, "There is something I need to talk to you about." My heart almost stopped beating as my mind raced with questions like, "Did they fill the position? Was this it? Did I do something to upset Wick?" She walked with me into the conference room where she told me they would love it if I would stay, and she offered me the permanent position. "You don't need to say yes now. The salary is not high. Take a few days and think about it." My composure flew out the window as I reached out and hugged her, "Of course I want the job! Oh, thank you, Chelsey!" I danced all the way back to my desk.

The next day Chelsey passed by my desk and said, "He wants to meet you today, I'll let you know when" "Me? Why?" "Shhh, don't panic, he just likes to personally meet every new member of the staff." I panicked anyway. I felt like I was back in Saudi preparing to be presented to a prospective groom. I was so nervous. An hour before lunch she came and took over the desk saying, "It's time." I took a deep breath and slowly walked to his office. Upon entering he asked me to have a seat on the large couch in the middle of the office. I sat and looked at the whiteboard that had lots of interesting plans written on it. As he moved out from behind the desk I smiled and offered him my full attention. He sat on the chair and issued the question, "Who are you?" My brain was thrown for a loop as I pondered how to answer.

In Saudi the answer was as easy as *I'm the wife of so and so or the daughter of so and so or the mother of so and so.* But who was I? I answered, "I am who I am…" reluctantly thinking it was the wrong answer, whereby he started to elaborate, "Ah yes, what the burning bush said to Moses." My mind spaced off wondering what that line had to do with anything biblical. He asked me to tell him about myself to which I obliged as if I was in a job interview. I was two sentences in when he said, "Well you should be on your way now." I stood and then did a small curtsy followed by a head bow to offer respect which made him smile. Exactly as I would have done if I had just met royalty, because within that domain his power was that of a king and everyone worked hard to avoid his displeasure.

Jacob's pay was modest and less than I made but it was only a steppingstone until he passed his journeyman's electrical license exam, followed by his master electrician's exam, which would allow him to open his own business. I did my best to make sure he had the books required but like so many things, studying and reading seemed too difficult for him. At times I wondered if he had ADHD like my brother had, since just like my brother, the ability to concentrate on a book appeared stressful. I asked him one night why he didn't study to take the exam like he had said he wanted to. His excuses stacked a mile high, *"I'm tired after work," "I want to rest on the weekend," "I want more time with you," "It's harder than it looks."* I rendered my typical, "I would have passed it already and I know nothing about being an electrician, when you do." Of course, the reply was, "You're good at studying and school, I'm not." I sighed as I thought about how I was horrible at school. Until I taught myself how to learn, I hated reading, and I hated reading until I decided I wanted to read. I decided I would not push the subject since we made enough money as it was to support ourselves and since I couldn't possibly study and take the exam for him.

It would be less than a year before his shiny job at the YMCA would disappear. They decided he was no longer necessary. I recall him being mad at them. I wondered if it was his fault. With all the long dinner time stories about everyone he didn't get along with it was no wonder in my mind that they decided to let him go. Jacob moved from job to job, moving into construction work eventually, but the time for him between jobs put strain on our budget.

We decided to move somewhere cheaper. We found an apartment in Garland, closer to his aunt's house and closer to downtown. I drove myself to work now since he no longer worked across the street from me. His aunt was an elderly woman who reminded me so much of Khala Nawal Firas's aunt and my former stepmother. It was funny that they both had the same name. I adored her and enjoyed visiting her. Her daughter, however, was a burly woman who always seemed to be angry about her lot in life and enjoyed commiserating with Jacob on the issue. I often wondered if their constant declarations about how they were treated differently as Arabs in America only increased the likelihood that they would be. After all, Jacob could have studied his books and taken his exams, but he chose to continue as he was.

I was never one for sitting idly by while wanting something different. I had spent too long being told what I couldn't have by other people and was not likely to let anything stop me from getting to where I wanted to go. But that was me and they were different. We all get to decide when it's time to climb out of our own wells and no one can help us do it.

I started enjoying my early coffee mornings alone again since Jacob no longer worked close by me. After the last year and a half, I started to feel a little smothered with love. Now I could sit alone, listen to music, smoke, sip my coffee and ponder the world as I had done before I met Jacob. With him no longer with me to place the coffee order and give the evil eye to every man who looked my way, I was able to make friends with the Starbucks staff.

I understood that being married to an Arab would always involve a degree of hot-blooded jealousy when it came to the protection of their women, but for Jacob there was always an underlying self-confidence issue that was ever apparent. Men often assume a woman cannot tell but more often than not, we all know. It's like a scent men put off when they are scared every minute that one day you'll wake up and realize you could have done better. The truth however was that this thought had never crossed our minds.

I enjoyed the stroll from the Starbucks to the office with my headphones on, taking in the sky and skipping across the crosswalk, when the song demanded it. Happiness seemed to reside in everything I did. My stepdad would have said, "Never let yourself be so happy, you'll just be disappointed." But I felt no need not to be happy when the world seemed so beautiful.

Jacob's mother and sister decided to return to the U.S. from Jordan and upon laying eyes on our tiny apartment, decided on our behalf we should buy a house. The conversation made me stand up straight like a tin soldier. I knew where the conversation was going but knew to intervene at this point would be a bad idea. Jacob said, "I can't afford to buy a house, mama, and we're okay here. We need some more time to save." His very strong and opinionated sister, Majida, replied on his mother's behalf, "We can get a house all together, this way we all save money." I cringed on the inside as I looked over at Jacob as his sister turned to me asking, "What do you think?" to which I issued the safest Arabic reply I could think of: "*Han Shouf* (We'll see)."

Once they left for the evening Jacob and I agreed that we did not want to live with them. If for no other reason than it would be weird having sex with them in the house. Add to that he knew his sister was very opinionated and given that both of them are older than me, they would both out rank me, so we would actually be living with them, not the other way round. We waited until they signed a year-long lease with an apartment complex. Which seemed the best way to end the conversation without ever saying no to them living with us. Then we met with a realtor and started our search for a small house of our own.

Problems that had been covered up began to bubble to the surface when I discovered Jacob was in debt to the amount of almost two thousand dollars! The realtor pointed it out after doing a credit check to see if we were eligible for a mortgage. "Jacob, why didn't you tell me this before? We could have paid it off by now in installments, made cutbacks."

"I'm sorry, Koko, I just thought it would just go away." "Debt is bad, and it does not go away for a long time, you need to call the collection agency and get it sorted now." He lowered his head and said he would call them in the morning. He negotiated the amount down to about seven hundred dollars, since the seven years was going to be up soon. I cut costs and paid the debt off so we could start looking for a house again.

Christmas brought with it an unforeseen bonus from D magazine. As we got in the car he asked if I noticed the deposit in the account. "What deposit?" I asked as I pulled up the checking account on my phone. I saw a deposit for $500 dollars from D Magazine. There was an email from Wick & Christine Allison, the President, in my personal inbox thanking me for making D an even better place.

An air of jealousy murmured in Jacob's tone as he said, "I wish I worked at D Magazine." There it was again I thought, in his mind, I wasn't doing well because I worked hard, was nice to everyone and made sure I was always reliable and polite. It was because I was a white American pretty girl, a distinction I loathed.

A few months later we found a little house that had the most lovely pink brick exterior. The inside needed a lot of work since the previous owners seemed to be prone to never opening the windows and deep frying all their food. The layout was perfect for us. Two small bedrooms, one large master bedroom with a beautiful bathtub, a large open kitchen that looked over the living room and a backyard just the right size.

Unfortunately, our savings did not amount to enough for the down payment. I suggested we consider renting for a time in the city near my work. I had envied so many of the staff that simply walked home on their lunch breaks and after doing the calculations for gas and so on it seemed like a great idea. Jacob felt that a house would be best if we planned to start a family and if we had his family over for dinner. Despite all my pleading about the dangers of accepting money from his mother for the down payment and the requests that would follow, Jacob insisted that the money they would give us was still partly his money and everything would be fine.

We closed on the house two weeks before our apartment lease was up, giving us enough time to make the renovations. It was a bad time of year to ask for time off. It was one of our busiest times. We would drive up every night after I got off work to clean and make renovations. Since money was tight, we would have to do it all ourselves. I rather enjoyed watching YouTube videos before work in the morning and on my lunch break, figuring out how to stain concrete, lay tile, and degrease a kitchen that had not been cleaned in years. Every night we worked until around midnight when we returned home to shower and pass out from exhaustion. The normal nine hours of sleep turned into six, but happily so.

When it was time to move into our new house, money was so tight that we had to rent a truck and do it all ourselves. Jacob's brother, Qais, came by and lent us a hand which was helpful, and the move was successful. Qais was often between jobs, which didn't surprise me since I had seen the same from Jacob. Qais always seemed to be high or on something when we saw him. This didn't bother me except there always seemed to be something they were talking about that stopped as I entered the room. Secrets bothered me.

It had been three years since I had spoken to my stepdad or my siblings and one night I decided to text Noura after watching the Disney movie, Frozen, with the line, "Do you want to build a snowman?" She replied with, "Hi" which led to us having dinner. It was the first time I had decided to go out after work alone since Jacob and I had married, and the fact that I was meeting a member of my family made it all the more scary for him.

"Let me come, I want to meet your sister," he said. "Not this time baby, I haven't seen her in a long time, and we will have sister stuff to talk about. Why don't you go see your family?" He slumped over like a kid denied going to the movies with his friends. I met Noura after work at North Park Mall in Dallas. We got a table at PF Chang's and ordered. We had so much catching up to do that we lost track of the hour and closed down the restaurant. I asked her if she was okay going home so late to which she replied that she has stayed out many nights and Baba just turned a blind eye when she said she's staying with a friend. I looked down at my phone with more than twelve text messages and six missed calls as I sighed and said, "Hey, do you wanna stay at my place tonight because Jacob looks like he's going mad with worry about where I am. I bet he thinks I'm not with you at all. He is just very attached." She said sure, and we headed to my place.

Jacob started to become clingy more than usual, which was bothersome to me, but to be fair it had been he and I on our own for so long and now our lives were evolving. My sister was back, I had made a few new friends, which for him didn't always come easily. When we arrived at my house, Noura said hello, made herself a cocktail and sat on my couch as we picked out a movie to watch. I remember Noura's eyes looking at me like my friend, Noelle, when she was over wondering why he was sitting with us the entire time. Making it impossible to have any personal conversation from her end. As I sat I wondered why he would be so panicked that he needed to leave me so many missed calls and messages when he knew I had not seen or spoken to my sister in over a year. I wondered if his self-esteem was getting to him since us as a couple was always odd to people; it was bound to have an impact on his ego. I brushed it all off as he headed to bed.

In the morning as Noura was getting ready to leave my phone rang, it was Yasmin, my other sister. I glanced over at Noura, asking if Yasmin knew where she was, but as I answered Noura took her right hand, flattened it out and swung it under her chin signaling *I'm not here.* Yasmin was driving and in a state that I would describe as mad fear. She asked, "Did you tell Baba!?!?!" "What would I tell Baba and why would I? He disowned me, remember?" I replied. "Well, it's just… it's just…" She began to cry as she continued, "He has a picture of me with a boy in a car and you were the only person on my Instagram I could think of." I listened to her sob for a few seconds before laying on the questions, knowing for sure that if Baba had a picture and told her about it, we had no time to lose.

"Yasmin is your Instagram account public? Do you have any of the relatives on there from our Saudi side? Cousins and so on?" She sobbed and began to tell me how Baba had told her she could no longer work and needed to hand in her notice and concentrate on college. "Yasmin, never mind all that now. What are you sure he has on you and if you're driving home, pull over so we can talk about it." The car pulled over as

I attempted to think in my stepdad's mindset. I asked her to start at the beginning. "Who is the boy, what was really going on?" and so on. I evaluated the facts and being very familiar with the scare tactics which my stepdad often referred to as scratching.

You see, when he was on the verge of knowing the story but could not yet prove it with evidence, he would 'scratch' his opponent to see their reaction. Which would send whoever he was scratching into a state of panic, thereby accidently giving themselves away. Yasmin's reaction to him asking her about the picture and ordering her to quit her job was playing right into his hands. After she had cried for a good while, talking about her job, the boy, and everything else, I calmly asked her to dry her eyes and to listen to me very carefully.

"We need an alibi close enough to the truth so that he felt victorious in his discovery but not enough to cause more of a lock down." I asked her to send me the picture and upon seeing it, it didn't seem as bad as I thought, since they were far enough apart to be just friends. I broke it down for her. "Listen to everything I am about to tell you carefully. When you get home, the first thing he is going to do is call you to his room and sit you down. Don't panic. Tell him the boy was a friend from school. That's all. No matter how much he grills you, stick to your story. That you thought it was harmless to just grab a bite to eat nearby and he offered to drive you. He will look for gaps so just repeat yourself. Now, this is the most important part. When he says he doesn't believe you and starts in with the trust speech, which he assuredly will do, you need to cry. I mean ball your eyes out then you say this exactly, "Daddy, I love you, and I want to tell you about things like this but you're so unapproachable and always seem like you'll get angry. I want to talk to you, but I feel like I can't." If you say and do as I say he will calm down and everything will be fine. Trust me.

"Once it's done you have to be more careful about posting things on the Internet. It's not only him who watches everything, but also your grandma, AKA *Omi*, the cousins, the aunts, everyone. Our behavior is fun gossip but the whole reputation of the family is at stake since we're rebels living in America uncovered. They tell him everything and trust me they have nothing better to do with their time."

I repeated my speech for her twice along with the timing for tears to make sure she had it down. I wished her good luck and told her to call me afterwards when it was safe.

When I got off the phone I mentioned what was going on to Jacob, but his response came from the Bedouin inside of him. "Well, if she was my daughter and I found out she was running around with a boy, I would have questions, too." "She's old enough, Jacob, and you had girlfriends at her age and more." "Yes, but I'm respectful, I'm Arabic, white boys are not the same." I rolled my eyes and ended the conversation since it was clearly going to go nowhere.

The call didn't come until Monday when Yasmin got away to work, a place where he could not listen in on the conversation. Just as I had predicted, everything I said played out as I expected.

I took my first long vacation from D Magazine. It was ten days and I decided to use that time to finish setting up the house. Jacob again moaned about how nice it must be to work for D Magazine and how he wished he had time off, to which my brain would internally reply, "Well, you could have kept your job at the YMCA or the one after that or the one after that," but I said nothing aloud. I enjoyed every project I undertook to make my house more and more like home, including turning one of the smaller rooms into a giant closet and glass painting the back door.

Yasmin and her boyfriend came for lunch. Jacob was meant to have work that day and I told him he really didn't need to be there for the lunch, which he took as my not wanting him there, and he changed his hours to make it work. I introduced them to Jacob, "Jacob, this is my sister, Yasmin, and her boyfriend, Cole," and we sat down to a hearty lunch. I asked little to no questions of the boy. I rather preferred to watch his interactions with her and she with him, which set me at great ease.

Following lunch, I asked Yasmin if she would like to come and see my closet which was our way of breaking away from the boys. Jacob and Cole had nothing to talk about as Cole sat in the living room feeling abandoned. Yasmin and I talked about sex, since I knew if it hadn't happened yet, it would soon. She had so many questions and I obliged her with the answers. "Is it okay to have sex if you're not married?" I assured her that if she felt comfortable having sex then she should go right ahead as long as she remembered to take precautions. I stressed that I preferred birth control to condoms but for now with her medical insurance being provided by her scholarship from the Saudi Government and all the bills being sent to my stepdad it didn't seem very doable. I was surprised that day at how much I had changed over the years since twenty-year-old me would have thought sex out of wedlock was disgraceful. She was growing up in a different world than the one I grew up in Saudi Arabia and the traditions of the tribe would not go very far in these very different waters. I hugged her and we sat with the boys for a while then she headed out with Cole. She asked me not to mention the meeting to Noura because she was not ready for Noura to know yet.

My work was going well, and I was moving along, receiving an employee of the year award along with two pay increases the following year. My morning coffee was often interrupted by the odd traveler or jogger looking to pick someone up or make conversation in the hopes of picking someone up. I made sure to practice my "resting bitch" face. I always kept my earbuds in and only replied with short non-conversational words, "You, too!" "Thank you," or "Ah ha." I also decided it was best not to mention how many times I got hit on to Jacob since I knew the response would be that I should not go there anymoreI vaguely remember a guy who appeared homeless. I thought he must be homeless, after all, who wears sweats, a t-shirt, and a ball cap on a workday? He would arrive at Starbucks, get coffee, and sit down at a table outside. He looked sweaty, tired, and he was always there around 7 ish, which was way too early for most people. I was afraid of him. Since I didn't know who or what he wanted, I did my best to avoid eye contact. He tried talking to me on a few occasions. I blew him off like all the other men who always tried to talk to me at Starbucks. Little did I know, he would reappear in my life a year later.

Of all the emotions in the world, I would say irrational jealousy is the worst, especially when one of the partners has no need to be so. However, Jacob's jealousy was rooted in something far worse than just simply jealousy, since it came from his addiction to external affirmation which provided him with a short-term burst of self-esteem. He was very insecure, so he was jealous of my time if it was not fully dedicated to him, my attention if it was directed elsewhere, even if it was caring for our birds. However, it seemed manageable as long as I kept reassuring him.

One Saturday afternoon while we were watching TV, Jacob looked at my parrot Yoshi flying about the house playing and said, "You should hold him more, so he knows who is the boss." I casually looked over and smiled at Yoshi's obvious happiness with his toys. I said, "I hold him plenty, besides, if he wants to cuddle he knows where I am. He's his own little man." Lulu Jacobs parrot was being grasped in Jacobs hands as he scratched her head and I noticed that every time he loosened his grip she would fly into my lap. After he took her back a few times I said, "Why don't you just let her be where she wants?" "No, she's my bird, she has to like me." I assured him that animals just like humans, will not like you better if you force them. Lulu had a habit of sleeping on her back, a common trait among Sun Conures. I said, "Why not let her fall asleep and then I'll move her into your lap." He agreed reluctantly and sure enough, no sooner had I moved her that she was back in my lap again. Jacob was enraged, stood up and shouted, "Stupid bird! I want a different one!" and threw Lulu into the TV and stormed out. I cuddled Lulu knowing that I would need to rehome her as soon as possible to avoid a recurrence of the incident. No creature deserves to be abused or scared in any way, but now also a deep part of me worried about this side of him I had never seen before.

When I was invited to attend a dinner, or a Friends-giving, Jacob grumbled and said he wouldn't be going. Which was intended to mean I shouldn't go either. For me after Firas, I decided it was not up to him whether I went, it was only up to him to decide if he wanted to go, too. In the past my conscience would have bothered me for disobeying my husband's desires. It seemed like all the American in me that had been daily suppressed by Firas was now rearing up and being fully expressed to Jacob.

I wanted so much to include him in my world and introduce him to the colleagues I adored. At the same time, I understood that in his mind it was a world of educated, beautiful people with interesting things to discuss while he always felt like the odd man out, and I knew that feeling all too well. Jacob would pick me up, drop me off and text me continuously until I was back in his sight.

Jacob's brother made a habit of coming over a lot and one day while I was making the tea my ears picked up the word 'jail.' I slowed down making the tea as I strained to listen in on the rest of the conversation, but they got quieter as I entered the room. I served the tea and as usual the conversation changed. I sat down and waited for the evening to end. After he left I looked at Jacob and asked him to tell me what they were talking about. He rolled his head and let out a long exhale. "It's nothing for you to worry about besides, it's in the past." "What's in the past, Jacob?" He put his hands together and looked at the floor as he relayed the story.

"Qais was arrested once for beating up a girl," "What! Why would he beat up a girl?" "She was his girlfriend, but she was a bitch." My skin began to crawl as I said, "Jacob, what else?" "Look, it's no big deal. He beat her up, she went to the cops, he got probation and that's why he has been in Jordan all this time." "So, he skipped out of the country when he was on probation?" "Ya and now the lawyer is saying he might have to serve time because the judge is pissed." "Geez, Jacob, why didn't you tell me this before? You mean I have been serving tea in my house to a man who beat up a girl just because he considered her to be a bitch? How is that okay? What if he gets pissed at me one day?" "It's all okay, Qais would never hurt you, you're my wife."

I was less than convinced. What I did know for sure was that I would not be having him in the house when I was alone ever again. I felt deceived because Jacob hadn't shared this information with me sooner. I had the right to know what kind of family I was marrying into. As usual, his lack of self confidence in himself proved destructive once again. I hated secrets and most of all, coverups and lies. I spent days wondering what else might have been a lie. The supermarket their father left them? The money his mother loaned us for the house? The reason they decided to come back to the States and stay? I decided to take a more cautious approach to anything regarding his family. Meaning every request was carefully examined and talked through with Jacob. It felt like layers of a delicious lasagna but when the layers were peeled back, all you found was a gruesome scene of ground up flesh.

Jacob's mom and sister had a hard time getting a car loan because they had no credit, so Jacob decided it would be best if he just gave them his car. It was completely paid off, and we planned to replace it with a newer car on payments. I was reluctant since with the new house, the budget was already squeezed a little too close to the nozzle. After balancing a few things, I came up with a reasonable amount we could afford to pay as long as we stuck to the budget.

Saturday came and we went to his mother's apartment for lunch. After we finished eating Jacob and I went out to the balcony to smoke and as we smoked, I went over the budget again with Jacob. Since there was not enough room in the car for me to go with them, I would not be there to offer caution when the car salesman or his sister said something like, "Go ahead, you only live once" or "I'll loan you the rest." I said, "Jacob, remember that you can't get anything that costs more than $175 a month. We can't afford more than that and we don't need to be in more debt to your mother and sister. They already put the down payment on the house." Jacob nodded silently. When we finished smoking we came into the apartment to find his sister storming off to her bedroom and slamming the door.

I sat down slowly, looking at my mother-in-law, who let out a nervous smile saying, "It's nothing." Jacob went into the room after her, we sat in silence as the shouting reached an all-time high. I had seen his sister shout and get angry before, in fact, the whole family was a little hot under the collar most of the time, with the exception of Jacob. I had never seen anything between them at this level. The door swung open, and his sister came barreling towards me shouting, "That bitch telling you what to do every minute. Who does she think she is?! Ah? Who do you think you are?" I stood up slowly, knowing that a response would do me no good. If I retaliated, I would forever be the woman who disrespected her elder sister-in-law, no matter the circumstances.

Looking at Jacob standing in the corner asking her timidly to calm down as she continued her tirade, I headed to the door to leave but she put her hand on the door, blocking my exit. I asked her, "Please stop speaking to me in this way and move away from the door. I'm leaving." She said, "Stupid bitch! Cow! Tell me, is my family not good enough for you, are you so much better?" She pushed me again and again, trying to provoke me into a fight. I kept looking at Jacob, wondering why he was just standing by as his sister pushed me around. I contemplated jumping through the balcony since they were on the first level but knew I wouldn't make it out before she blocked me again.

Qais got involved saying, "Ya, bitch, are we not good enough for you?" She slapped me and I was finally able to get the door open. I ran outside and realized I didn't have the car keys. I pondered ordering a taxi but heard them coming behind me. I headed toward the car, realizing it was unlocked I sat inside, locked the doors, and picked up my phone, leaving a message for Noor on WhatsApp. "I don't understand, Hiyate, I just wanted to make sure we didn't go over budget and... and... and... Jacob just stood there. He could have said something to stop her, but he just stood there." I started crying. Noor would tell me later that it was one of the saddest messages she had ever received from me. She could feel my broken heart even though she was far away.

When I looked up, I saw Jacob unlocking the door so that his sister could get inside. She sat down and said, "Elise, look, let's talk about this." I turned around, looked at her and said, "You see my face? Remember it, because you will never see it again. No one treats me that way, no one!" With that I looked at Jacob and said, "Either we go, or I am calling a taxi."

The car ride was in total silence. Jacob knew there was nothing he could say to ease what had just happened, and I had much to think about. In all my efforts to look out for Jacob's mother, I had overlooked one big thing: Jacob's sister. She was the oldest sibling; with their mother's amiable personality, Jacob being in the States and Qais always in and out of trouble, his sister was acting head of the family. Everyone turned to her for advice, and I had rendered Jacob no longer in need of her advice. She was unmarried and unlikely to be. I was beautiful and adored by everyone, which only added jealousy to the bonfire.

She had been seething for months and I hadn't even see it coming. Jacob at the time felt trapped. He might be able to stop his sister but the wrath she would unleash on him later was unimaginable to him. Since blood is always thicker than water, we had ended up here.

For the next few days, I kept my distance, leaving for work without saying goodbye and answering as few of his messages as possible. One evening as I arrived home, there they were sitting on the couch. I was outraged on the inside that he would invite them into my home without my permission after what had happened. Jacob stood up to greet me at the door saying, "Welcome home, look my sister came to say she's sorry." For me there was no sorry that could excuse her, but I nodded and allowed his mother to talk through how sorry his sister was.

It's customary in these kinds of situations that the eldest takes this role but the American in me could not accept an apology that was not made by the party at fault. While the Saudi in me wanted to see her flogged forever thinking she had the right to lay a hand on me. I said nothing that night as they had tea and pretended all was well again. Jacob then drove them home while I made a phone call to Noor to ask for guidance.

"Honey, he let them come without asking me, when he knows how I feel about it." "Hiyate, you forget that in their minds, this is not your home and Jacobs home. It is their son/brother's house, and you are his wife. They will never ask for you to agree and he will never tell them they can't come, no matter what happens." I realized that she was right. I had forgotten once again that despite being Christian Arabs, they were still Arabs. I was to obey and respect my husband's family. I would always be younger than his sister and therefore always ranked lower on the family scale. Jacob would never stand up to his sister, therefore, right, or wrong, I would always lose the battle.

When Jacob arrived home I asked him how he could bring them here without telling me. "After what your sister did, and you just let her?" "She came and said sorry, that's the end of it, that's my family." A silence grew over me as I lit my cigarette and slipped back into the couch. For the next few days, I wracked my mind going back and forth. After all, many Arab girls and American girls hate their in-laws. I could avoid seeing them except on formal occasions, living my life nodding and agreeing as his sister bossed him around. But there was one thing that nagged me and that was the fact that she had been seething that long because Jacob was too scared to tell her he had decided on something with me. Instead, he would say "Elise said no," or "Elise didn't agree," and when he didn't stand up, a barrier of distrust formed between us. One I could not shake and in that fatal moment, my cuddly man was replaced in my eyes by a cowardly lion.

I tried to dust myself off and continue as usual, pretending that nothing had happened. One day his brother came over to see Jacob and as I walked past, he uttered under his drunken breath, "Bitch" while Jacob was out of the room. I pretended I didn't hear it and went to work the next day without saying goodbye. As I sat sipping my coffee I thought about all the good memories we had together before their arrival and then I realized. While I could put up with them, if we were to have a child there would be no way to keep my child away from his family. I started to imagine his sister's influence, his brother babysitting my future daughter or son. I didn't want my future children around them in any way, but I knew that to make such a request would only cause Jacob to do so behind my back. The thought made every hair on my body standup.

When I got home that night I told Jacob that he should sleep on the couch. I needed some more space to think about everything. His child-like mind could not accept one night out of the bedroom. To him it meant it was over while to me it meant space without him holding me all night saying he loved me and to let it go. I knew that if I was to think clearly I would need space and oftentimes taking your own good advice requires a closed mental session. As I laid in the bed I heard him begin to shout. His tone awoke a fight or flight sensation in me as I removed my phone from the charger near the bed and placed it inside the pillowcase for safe keeping. Then I tried to remain as still as possible. He kept yelling, "IS THIS WHAT YOU WANT?" followed by a large crash as he smashed bottle after bottle from the bar. I mentally talked myself through the night.

As he continued, I knew he wanted me to come out and fight with him but once the first bottle smashed I knew what kind of danger I might be in should I leave the bed. I also knew what kind of danger I was in while I was still in bed. I texted my sister telling her briefly that if I didn't text her in the morning to call the police and then quickly returned my phone to the inside of my pillowcase, placing my hand under the pillow to hold the phone like a security blanket. Unable to sleep even when the house got quiet, I laid in bed wondering how one night apart could send him into such a rage. I realized that if something that simple could send him into a rage what would happen if it was something more serious.

Four a.m. rolled around. I slowly slid out of the bed, putting on a pair of socks near the bed so I wouldn't make the slightest noise. I inched into the bathroom, where instead of taking a shower, I dampened a washcloth and used that to wash my face and underarms. Followed by the use of mouthwash instead of brushing. My heart was racing as I crept past him on the couch almost like trying to get past a sleeping grizzly bear that you found near your tent one morning. I grabbed my dress and put it on. Shoes in one hand and jewelry box in the other I glanced at Yoshi's food and water trying not to wake him up as well. He would sing his usual breakfast song which would be sure to wake up Jacob. I made it to the door but upon opening it, the door creaked. I moved swiftly to the car, not looking back. I jumped in and drove downtown.

As I hit the highway, I started to tear up but talked myself down saying, "It's okay, you're okay, everything will be okay." I walked up to the Starbucks. The door was locked. It was still dark outside, but I saw a light and waved to Eddie the barista from the window. "Eddie, Eddie can I come in?" He looked at me, puzzled. As he opened the door he said, "Girl, you up early? Come inside, it's not safe out there yet. There are homeless people sleeping all over the place." I plopped down on the couch staring at the floor, clutching my hands together. Eddie realized something was wrong as he tilted his head he said, "You okay?" "My husband just went crazy, he was smashing things, I couldn't sleep all night."

It was obvious he had something to say but he bit his tongue and said, "Well, you're here now so let me finish opening up and get you some coffee." I nodded and proceeded to text my sister, implementing the next safety procedure by telling her I was out of the house but if I didn't text her when I got to work at eight she should call the police. Her response came back in the affirmative. At 6:30 a.m. the Starbucks officially opened. While sipping my coffee outside at my table, I started to continue my thought process. I felt safe enough with Eddie inside and lots of people around me. At seven thirty I glanced at a shadow coming around the corner and my heart stopped still as I saw Jacob. His work would have already started and was way across town. He looked at me with a look I had never seen before.

We stared at each other for a second. As he approached the table, his face muscles became more docile. He sat down and said, "You left so early." "I couldn't sleep, you scared me all night long." "I'm sorry, I was just mad. I love you, Koko, come on let's talk." "Jacob …" I took a very deep breath as I looked away to gather my strength "Jacob… I don't think this is going to work." "No, why? Because of the stupid, small thing my sister did? You can't be serious. Do you think marriage is a game?" I looked at him with disdain for that underhanded comment alluding to my past marriages as I continued, "Jacob, it's bigger than that, you are who you are, and I am who I am. For you it was nothing, for me it was a breadcrumb to what I can expect from them. Last night was a breadcrumb of what I can expect from you every time you get upset. I love you and while I might be able to put up with all of that, if we ever had a child, I could never accept that my children associate with your family. Your mother would never accept not being a part of her grandchildren's lives. I would not want your brother to touch a single hair on my daughter's head, enter my home anymore or be anywhere near me." "Baby, Qais will say sorry, I'll make them all say sorry. Qais is just like that, I'll tell him to make it up and …" "Jacob, the time for sorry has passed and even if they really said sorry, they would just do it again. In the end I know it's going to be fight after fight. When we have a child you will take them behind my back to visit your family and I don't blame you for that. They are your family, but I would never accept it. I don't want to live that way with so much anger all the time, I'm tired."

With that I stood up saying, "I need to go to work, we can talk some more later." "I'll walk you," three words that normally would have sounded sweet but for some reason they sent chills down my spine as he walked with me to work he kept saying, "I'll see you when you get home okay, you're coming home after work right?" I nodded and nodded, thinking only of getting into my office building. He said goodbye, kissed me on the cheek and I walked calmly inside, holding it together as I opened the office.

When Chelsey arrived, she bounced in like always but stopped as she leaned forward for her eyes to meet mine. "What's wrong?" I shook my head as I tried to hold back the tears. She held out her arm as if she was going to hug me and we moved into the conference room out of ear shot of anyone. I relayed what happened and asked if she knew of some place I could go. "There's no way I can go home after last night." She directed me to a room rental website and as the day's end got closer and closer, I got more and more scared that I would have to go home. I called my sister, Yasmin, and told her the situation. "I can't find any place to go, I might have to call Baba and go home." "NO! Don't go home, he will never let you leave again and besides he will just use it as a way to show everyone he was right. Let me ask my boyfriend's mother if she has an extra bedroom. Maybe you can stay with her." "Ask but I don't know them, and I don't want to make things weird for you, Babes, this is my problem." Time ticked on, and it was finally clear that there was no answer. My choices seemed like I had to either go home or call my stepdad and be the mountain that bent to the wind's will.

I headed to the car, sitting down inside. I cried and cried. I reached for my phone as I called my stepdad and uttered the words I swore I never would, "I'm sorry, daddy, you were right, and I was wrong." Hearing my sobbing he decided to forgo his traditional, "I told you so" speech and said, "Elise, where are you?" "I'm in my car." "Can you drive, or do I need to come and get you?" "I can drive," I said, pulling back the snot pouring out of my nose. I put my parent's new house address in the GPS and started down the highway. It was pouring rain and since

I had never been to my parents new house I needed to watch the GPS carefully.

As soon as it hit five o'clock Jacob called, interrupting the map. I rejected the call but that only caused him to call back again and again. My battery was dying, and I had no idea where I was. I decided to answer since it was clear he would not stop until I did, or my phone died. "Hello?" "Baby, why are you hanging up on me?" "I need to see the GPS." "Why, where are you going?" "I'm going to my parent's house just for the night." "No, you need to come home so we can talk right now." "Listen, I'm going for the night, and we can talk tomorrow, okay? I have to go now." Hanging up, trying to memorize the directions before he called back again and again.

When I finally made it to my parent's house my stepdad came out and got in the driver's seat and we drove to get coffee. This way I could tell him what was going on without scaring my much younger siblings or my mother. I relayed the story to my stepdad and at the end he said, "Well, *Ya'Mama* (an Arabic term of endearment), what to say. I wish you hadn't married him in the first place. It was obvious he was not for you but at least he showed his stripes in time for you to see them before it's too late."

He brought me back home; I went up to the guest room and I passed out right way. There is a safety one feels when they go home to their parent's house wherever that may be' even when it's not the same house, it's a sense of extreme security and rest, a feeling that I am unable to do justice explaining.

The next morning, I woke up to find an email from the bank saying my account had a low balance of $43 dollars. My mind spun around at the fact that Jacob would move every cent we owned out of my reach because I slept one night at my parent's house without his permission. I paid a visit to the bank to close the account since if the account went into overdraft it would surely hurt my credit score. The whole way to the bank my stepdad avoided chiming in on my attempt to rationalize how he could just move all our money like that. I certainly never contemplated such a thing, when I knew we had bills.

He finally commented saying, "When you deal with people like this, *Ya'Mama,* this is what you get. He assumes everyone is out to get him, so he took the money before you took it. In his mind that's what people do, i.e., I stab you before you stab me and so on." I left the bank and sat down on the curb to smoke, while my stepdad waited in the car. Reality was in front of me, but my heart and my mind were having such a hard time realizing that the man I had loved with all my heart would suddenly just turn into a monster. If I didn't know any better I would say someone must have dropped something on his head at work.

So often we see everything right from the beginning, but we refuse to admit to ourselves what we know it until the page is written, the ink is dry, and it's time to close the book. Suddenly a text message flashed across my phone screen. It was Jacob. It said, "I didn't go home yesterday, I slept at my mother's apartment." I paused, dried my eyes, and called Chelsey, telling her I might need an extra day if that was okay. "Take as long as you need," she said. As she hung up the phone I looked at my stepdad and told him that Jacob was not at our home. Now is the time to go get my things, Yoshi, and give him back this car which is in his name." "Are you sure he's not home? What if we get there and he is home?" "If he's home we won't go in. He always parks his car on the street so if we see his car, we will just drive by." My stepdad agreed, and we drove down to the house. Not seeing his car, we parked, and I went up to the house and went inside. Sitting in the corner in the dark smoky living room was Jacob, his leg crossed over his other knee, staring at me as if I was a dead woman.

My stepdad came in behind me, which caused Jacob to stand up and change his facial expression to that of a little iamb, as he reached out to greet my stepdad. My stepdad knew that escalating the situation was in no one's best interest, so he shook his hand and had a seat. As I walked straight into my dressing room with trash bags to grab only what was important, leaving behind anything that was not essential, then moving on to the bedroom to grab all my essential papers and my passport. As I was finishing up Jacob came in the room and tried to put his arms around me saying ,"Hey, I'm sorry, come on let's make it work." I kept moving, knowing full well that if I looked at him or let him hold me I might forgive him, and I could not allow my heart to dictate to my head. The decision was made.

As we were about to leave Jacob called out, “Hey, leave the engagement ring. It’s mine.” This might not seem to be a strange statement since this is common among many cultures and people. Common enough even in the Arab world. If an engagement is called off returning the ring would be expected but after the marriage has taken place and the couple has consummated the marriage, to ask for the ring back showed how low he was willing to go to try and get someone to fight with him. I removed the ring, placed it on the counter along with my car keys. I took Yoshi in my hands and walked straight to the car with my stepdad without looking back as Jacob started yelling, “What about your car?” When we drove off he texted the same question, to which I replied ,“I don’t want the car, sell your car, and keep this one, since your car is dying. I don’t want to leave you without a working car.”

People say it’s hard to do the right thing when someone keeps doing the wrong things to you, but the truth is being kind and doing what’s right is always as easy as we want it to be. Anger, hatred, jealousy, and the entire range of emotions are very potent spices. A little will wake you up but a lot will dull the senses. I kept my head on tight as I tried to navigate the fact that I would be getting divorced one more time, that I would have to mend my broken heart and shattered dreams again.

I moved into the spare room in my parent’s house and borrowed my stepdad’s car to get to and from work. The no smoking rule still applied, so after work before coming home and after dinner with the family, I would take walks around the park nearby to smoke, clear my head, and reply to any texts from Jacob. I opened a personal checking account and had my paychecks transferred there so that Jacob could not repeat the incident of emptying the account again. Jacob started living with his family, leaving our house empty. At first everything seemed to be going very amicably, he would ask for help switching over the electricity, gas, phone bill, and ADT security to his name and I would oblige, but soon the ever-present influence of his family started to appear as the texts went back and forth (errors retained):

***Jacob**: I need you to sign a power of attorney too so I can sell the car.*

***Elise**: Just find a buyer and I will sign whatever forms are needed you don't need power of attorney. Why don't you sell your car and that car and get another car on lower payments from the money you make on selling your car wouldn't that be better?*

***Jacob**: I can't add any bills now because you left me hanging.*

***Jacob**: I have no money*

***Elise**: And I do. You could live in the house and go to work. I don't have any money either you emptied the entire house account.*

***Jacob**: You know all the house bills is over $2000. What about the house? There is no equity in the house if I want to sell it.*

***Elise**: Did you ever think about renting it out or living in it?*

***Jacob**: I cant rent it out.*

***Elise**: You could rent it out for $1200 or whatever you think is good it would help cover the bills.*

***Jacob**: Can you call me please I hate texting.*

***Jacob**: Can you yes or no*

I called and talked to him about the house finances. I understood that it all might be a little overwhelming since I was the one always taking care of things and now he found himself in over his head. In my mind, just because it wasn't working out didn't mean I wanted him to suffer.

***Elise**: Listen I don't want you to have a hard time so if you want I can stay living in the house in the guest room until we finish everything up.*

***Jacob**: No, one of us has to go.*

***Elise**: And so I am gone. So you need to call the realtor and figure it out. I will sign whatever you need to sell the place but that is all I can do. I don't want anything. Then call the lender tell him were getting a divorce and ask him what you need to do to sell.*

***Jacob**: You think its that easy I asked you to give me power of attorney so I can sell the house that is what I need.*

***Elise**: If that's what you need fine I can do that.*

Back and forth we went. Me guiding him on how to do everything from navigating getting himself approved for the house mortgage alone to how to add a new contact in his phone. I found a rental agency for him to rent out the house that would have covered all the bills, but he refused to do anything until the court date. He said, "I want to wait and see what the judge will decide." We met at the courthouse to file the paperwork for a divorce, which would take sixty days until we would see a judge. There was a form he could sign that would not require him to be at the judgment. Since it was hard for him to get away from work he signed it. This way I could handle it for him. The back and forth started to get tedious with the endless *This happened... What do I do?* messages. Then, a severe storm hit, blowing over the fence we shared with our neighbor. He sent the following message (errors retained):

***Jacob**: Hi Elise yesterday I went to the house I found the whole fence was tipped over I got some one to estimate $2500 it'll split between us and the neighbor and I don't have money to fix it what should I do and it have to be fixed before we sell it.*

***Elise**: $2500 to fix it cant they just put it back up*

Jacob: no its all broken from the posts I need help I'm in deep trouble. I don't deserve all these can you get me solution please.

***Elise**: I don't have a solution Jacob cant you fix it*

***Jacob**: No I cant. I need help with that. The house still under our name you should help me with that. You left everything on me that's not fair I never did you bad. Allah forgive you Elise. Just tell me what to do I need help please*

***Elise**: Jacob, stop talking to me like I don't know the bills and everything .There was 1000 dollars in the house account which I would have never taken but you did... That was for bills and the mortgage is not due, you sold the car what is left? I paid all the last bills the electric, the gas, the internet and I owe ADT a* *penalty of more than a thousand dollars because I canceled the contract. I paid off my phone so you would not have it on your credit. Do you just care about money ?!??? The hosue is full of furniture that you can sell and use the money to pay whatever. You have two extra rooms you can rent out if you don't want to rent out the whole house.*

Jacob: *You think it's that easy. I need to sell the house I cant refinance.*

Elise: *Jacob its your house sell it.*

Jacob: *ok Elise I don't know what happened between us but I think of you every second.*

Elise: *Ask about a quick sale, if you get nothing at least you owe nothing and that also means we lived rent free for 6 months. Post the furniture for sale for cheap on craigs list that will at least give you some money.*

Jacob: *Ok how is Yoshi I miss him. I miss him I'm sorry for what came out of me I didn't mean it*

Elise: *it doesn't matter now Jacob we just need to finish everything so things can get better for both of us.*

Back and forth we went as he refused to follow any of the ideas I put before him and simply asked for money. The court papers were filed, and I was advised by my lawyer to avoid too much back and forth with him, now that it was just a matter of waiting. The silence of course brought out his other side in the next message (errors retained):

December 2nd 2015

8:01 a.m. - Jacob: *You have to pay me half the mortgage by law your name is on the loan.*

8:09 a.m. - Jacob: *Aha no answer of course you always talk about Arab how bad are they you are the WOREST.*

8:28 a.m. – Jacob: *How's your new boyfriend by the way do you tell him lies about me.*

8:29 a.m. – Jacob: *What a wonderful life you have all lies.*

9:09 a.m. – Jacob: *So let me know by tomorrow if you going to pay half the mortgage or not if I didn't hear from you by tomorrow morning I'll hire a lawyer and I'm going to let him postponed the divorce waiver and it'll take sex months until we sell everything and pay off everything.*

9:56 a.m. – Jacob: *and something else no one can destroy my life like you're trying to do* فشرة عينيك وسخه *(A curse which is too nasty to even translate).*

5:39 p.m. – Jacob: *You know what that mean it is Khayna the best think that describes you*

5:41 p.m. – Jacob: *Khayna means a person who lies and cheat on them spouse*

5:43 p.m. – Jacob: *So what did you decide Khayna let me know ASAP*

December 3rd 2015

7:40 a.m. – Jacob: *KHAYNA what did you decide*

At around 4:00 p.m. with no response from me he went on Facebook and found an old post of mine, when Firas and I were in on the Nile in Egypt and sent a message with a screenshot of it writing (errors retained), *"you're new boyfriend sound rich good job,"* all the while not bothering to notice that the image was posted in 2010. Blocking him on Facebook did no good since he just resorted to attacking everyone that I knew in order to get a response out of me. Despite all his aggravating attacks, I remained silent. I asked my lawyer about a restraining order, but her response was that by the time he does something that will allow for me to get a restraining order it would be too late.

I called upon my skills of extreme alertness, since crazy is never predictable. I decided it would not be wise to continue with the same routine now. If Jacob could show up suddenly at my Starbucks once, he could do it again. I threw away the black jacket I always wore and purchased a white one. I cut my hair short. I changed my parking spot from the cheaper outdoor parking to an indoor parking lot with security. The parking lot had a tunnel that connected to a Starbucks located in the bottom of the Ross building downtown. This way security cameras were present every minute until I decided to head to work. I gave his picture to our building security guards and asked them to alert me if they saw him.

It was a cold, quiet winter and I missed my Starbucks with all its hustle and bustle in the morning. Every time I would say to myself today is the day I am going to head to my Starbucks, my heart would race so fast I would change my mind. Those sixty days passed slowly. I kept looking over my shoulder, afraid he would appear out of nowhere. I dared not even think about what would have happened if he ever found me. It was like every person who turned a corner was him and I was as jumpy as a jack rabbit unless I was in the office or at home.

Finally, at last, the court date arrived. My stepdad came along with the lawyer for an extra layer of protection in case Jacob should decide at the last minute to show up and cause trouble. He didn't show, and the divorce was finalized without a single hiccup. I remember feeling so free again. The judge's decree was mailed to Jacob at the house and upon reading it, he called my lawyer to yell at her, saying, "Tell that bitch that I won't sign them so she can forget about getting married again, I'll drag it out for years until she is old." My lawyer, in all her educated fashion, replied, "Mr. Kawar, that's fine if you don't want to sign the papers, but I want to make it clear that if you don't sign then she will get the house and any other assets that are currently all listed as yours in this divorce decree. If that's what you want it will be up to you. I will be happy to oblige you either way."

He signed the papers and mailed them back but still made a habit of texting me out of the blue with his curse word of the day. I was not willing to block him while the divorce was being finalized since I knew that might cause him to implode, and for the decree to go through without delay depended on him letting it process by leaving it alone. Now that it was done, there was no impediment to blocking his number anymore, but I still didn't block him right away.

When dealing with crazy, the rule I think that works best is to not step on the scorpion since there is a great risk of being stung. Instead, walk around it carefully, ever mindful of its movements. In this case,

Jacob's being able to text me, even if it was obnoxious and getting a response, gave him an outlet for his anger. If that outlet did not exist he would brood until he found another more extreme outlet, such as finding my car and vandalizing it, showing up at my work to create a scene, and hunting me down, but once the divorce decree was final there was no need for me to put up with his messages anymore, but I waited to offer him time for closure.

Jacob: *Hi Sharmota - (means Bitch, Prostitute, and so on)*

Elise: *When your done acting like a small child, when your done using all kinds of words on me that you know I don't deserve then and only then we might talk if you need closure but not before. Your choice. I wish you and your family every happiness in this life. Goodbye Jacob.*

Jacob: *The names don't deserve that because nothing describe you by the way I just got back from Jordan that's why I'm late to respond and thanks for adding me to exs collection what a big mistake I did. GOODBYE ELISE. Enjoy your next future ex.*

I thought it was interesting that he felt the need to explain why his ritual text messaging chain of insults was delayed while he was in Jordan. What I found even more interesting was the fact that someone who could supposedly not afford half the mortgage payment by himself was able to afford a plane ticket and a month-long trip to Jordan. He resumed his routine of sending message followed by message, all ending with a goodbye until I finally replied.

Elise: *Have a good life Yacoub!*

Jacob: *I'm already*

Elise: *Good!*

Jacob: *Fuck off*

Jacob: *Tfee (A sound Arabs make to insinuate that he was spitting on me virtually).*

It always made me wonder why it was that his Arab blood ran so hot that he loved and hated with equally extreme measure. This made an adult relationship following a breakup, like the one I had had with Ata, utterly impossible.

***Jacob**: I say fuck off KHAYNA.*

***Jacob**: Enjoy your full of lies life*

***Elise**: Ok*

***Jacob**: Tfeeee*

***Elise**: Alright since you can't stop, I am going to block you. Goodbye.*

Christmas rolled around. So far, life at my parent's house was not that bad. Noura and I smuggled in wine occasionally. She had become a master at drinking in plain sight, a skill I would have thought was impossible around my stepdad. In her room if she drank from the wine bottle she would pile up this and that to create a kind of camouflage for the bottle, in case my stepdad opened her door without warning. She learned early on that he would normally just stand in the doorway and say whatever he came to say instead of entering so there was no chance of him seeing the bottle. Around the house she had a gold tumbler cup that she filled with whatever she had fancied drinking and she always chose the chair furthest from my stepdad during family movie night. She hid all the bottles in her closet which was so messy you could have hidden a body in there and no one would have been the wiser. She carried the bottles out in her purse and disposed of them when she got to school or work.

I started to go out with my friend Noelle. She was an intern who worked at the Park Cities Newspaper on the second floor of D Magazine. She was Lebanese, sweet, funny, and kind. We would meet after work or on the weekend at our favorite Arabic restaurant, sometimes sitting for hours.

I started to realize that I had spent the last three years in a prison that was Jacob. He never wanted me to go anywhere without him or have anyone over to the house without him. If I was five minutes late getting home or forgot to promptly reply to the message, his response would be to send another message every five to ten minutes. Then there was sure to be a phone call asking where I was and what I was doing. I was the master of my world again at least in part as long as I minded my stepdad.

My office Christmas party came around and I was so excited to be able to attend. I asked Noura if she wanted to go along and be my designated driver. I had taken drinking and driving to heart and if I knew I was going to drive somewhere I would not have even a single beer. My stepdad, upon hearing our plan said, "No drinking. If you want to go you have to drive." "But, it's my Christmas party, come on Baba! I can call an Uber, it's just one night." "No, if you want to go, you have to drive and don't take your sister to such things." I huffed on the inside and agreed to drive. Noura said she would meet me at the office since she always wanted to go to a D Magazine party.

With my divorce to Jacob over and done with, I decided it might be fun to try out some of the new dating apps everyone had been talking about, but I felt like I had no experience in dating at all, so I turned to one of the women in the sales department at work. She seemed to have it down to a science. She was always giggling and sharing stories about this man or that man she met at a party, on the Tinder or Bumble app. I asked, "I wanted to ask you about dating, what are the rules?" "Haven't you ever dated before?" "Well, yes but it's been a while. I mean do you have to sleep with them on the third date, like they say? You all talk about seeing one guy tonight and another tomorrow so I'm a little confused." She placed her arm around me and said, "Well, it's easy. You can date as many guys as you want at once but if you go on more than five dates with one of them you need to put the others on hold until you decide if you like him. For example, I'm dating five guys right now with one I think I like better than the others."

My mind was perplexed. How did she keep all the facts straight? In my mind dating was meant to be about getting to know one person at a time. This way you are giving them your full attention. I wouldn't know the first thing about dating more than one guy at once. Even though technically there was the time I was seeing Firas and Robert but that felt different. She added, "Oh, and if you're not looking for anything serious you can always just enjoy going out." She pointed to one of the other salesgirls saying, "She uses Tinder to get a new date every night and she hasn't paid for dinner in three years." "So, she just lets them take her to dinner and then never calls them back?" "Yup, that's always fun, too, if there is a restaurant in the city you want to try."

My moral compass started to poke me as I thought maybe I had gone to the wrong person for advice. I decided to make up my own rules and take it one day at a time.

My sisters and I kept our dating scenes to weeknights leaving us to appear ever so unattached and boring on the weekends for my stepdad's peace of mind and our ability to live in peace. If one of us was late we would text the other to see where Baba was in the house. In case distraction was needed to slip in without being asked why we were late.

Yasmin's grades started to suffer as she started to think maybe she didn't need a degree after all. She wanted to keep working at the mall and dropout. I went to her room to talk to her. She talked about how she needed money so she could get away from my stepdad's rules and to do that she needed to work. I agreed but said, "It's not long now until you graduate, why not just stick it out. Get your degree and then leave." "I just want to live my life and I need money to do that. I'm tired of sneaking around." There was no consoling her. Noura and I talked it over.

Noura said, "I bet it's the boy she is seeing that is making her this way. Her grades were fine before she met him." "Do you think so? I'm not so sure. I do know that she needs to get that degree even if she doesn't use it. If she drops out she will regret it." "I think we should tell Baba." "Noura. That's crazy, he'll kill her!" "He knows already. If we tell him a little bit maybe he can get her to quit working, stop being a prostitute, and finish her degree." "That's unkind to say!" "Well, she's acting like one." "You have a boyfriend, too." "I'm different …" I gave her my stern stop-being-unkind look and went to bed.

A few days later my stepdad asked me while we were grocery shopping if I had any idea why Yasmin's grades were slipping. There it was, the moment I had dreaded. I knew he knew about the boy so I took a deep breath and figured if he kept digging and she kept failing there was no way of knowing how much unholy terror my stepdad would rain down from the sky.

"I know you already know there is a boy."

"I knew it! I'll chop her up into little pieces and ship her back to Saudi Arabia."

"No, you won't. Calm down, I don't think it's gone very far."

"Then I'll take her back and lock her up until she agrees to give him up. We'll see how long this relationship goes on when she has no access to communications. Then I'll bring her back and she will finish her degree."

"You're being ridiculous. She would bide her time and as soon as you brought her back she would run away. That's if you could even get her to Saudi in the first place."

He was so furious it was as if smoke was coming out of his ears, so I said, "Let me give it a try, there is no need for anything rash. Let me see if I can talk to her. Besides, who cares if she keeps the boy as long as she finishes her degree." He kicked the car. I knew I had to give him something he wanted to hear so I continued, "Besides, doesn't she have to return to work in Saudi for six months after she gets her degree? Isn't that one of the conditions?" He nodded his head and I said, "You see, she will get her degree, keep the boy if she wants and then she will go to Saudi and forget all about him, and that's that. If you make a giant fuss she won't get her degree and she will run away." He grunted and said, "If I don't see her grades go up soon, I'll handle it my way."

I went to see Yasmin that night in her room. I told her she needed to bring her grades up before Baba decides to do something crazy. "He's crazy, he's calm for now, but you need to put working out of your mind and just finish your degree." "Do what? He can't do anything, I'll just run away. I make good money and I don't want the stupid degree." "It's a free degree! If you decide not to use it, fine! Just get the degree then go work in the mall the rest of your life if you want." "I need more money so I can get out of here," she shouted. I took a deep breath and said, "I'll leave you to think about it." I did not broach the subject with her for a while.

Yasmin had a scholarship from the Saudi Government. Women are only allowed to go study abroad if they are accompanied by a male guardian. The government pays all the school fees. They pay for health insurance for both the student and her guardian. And a very nice lump of cash that is paid to the guardian to be used for all her other expenses.

The key factor here is that my stepdad was making money as long as she was in school. If her grades declined too far, the scholarship program would drop her. He was keeping most of the money for himself and giving Yasmin a small amount as spending money, when the money actually belonged to Yasmin. He convinced her that she didn't need that much spending money and placed the bulk of it in a savings account that she could see but not access. While he slowly emptied it out himself. She, like so many women, would never get that money because of a system that was put in place to give male guardians control. Even outside Saudi Arabia today and on a scholarship to become better educated, rules were put in place to make sure these Saudi women came back. Kind of like putting a leash on a dog … "Look, dog! You're outside! Yay! But oops! You don't get the power to decide where you want to go."

Noura had refused to study one of the approved degrees for women by the Saudi Government. Afterall, you can't have women learning just anything... She wanted to study Art, so she went to the Art Institute in Dallas. My stepdad paid part of the tuition, while the rest became student debt. I hated that my stepdad was making money off Yasmin but at least she would get a degree without debt and be able to start her life with a clean slate. I would worry about him trying to take her back to Saudi later. I needed a plan that would get them out from under my stepdad's microscope, but what? It had to be with his blessing since there was no way they could move out without his permission and Yasmin would still need him to do all the paperwork needed by the Saudi Government every term. It was fate that finally threw me a line.

My stepdad's finances were struggling again that year. He had purchased a small party shop for my mother in hopes that it would give her something to do and make some money for the family. But like everything my mother took on, she managed to run it into the ground. Instead of working at the store she used it as a secret hideout to watch her soap operas, play video games and when she got really bored she would pick a fight with her neighboring store owners. My stepdad lost a bunch of money gambling in the currency market as well. He decided that the best solution was for them to take what remained of the cash he had left, have my mother declare bankruptcy and move to a small farm out in the country where life would be less costly and as small towns go, my mom would find it harder to waste money with a lack of shopping options that offered lines of credit.

With Noura and Yasmin both in college it would be difficult for them to move to the country. I suggested that the three of us get an apartment in the city since I had been planning to do so myself eventually. This way we would all have more money to spend since we could split the rent three ways. My stepdad thought it was a great idea since I would be there to watch over them. In his mind I had given up my rebellious ways now, and seen the light: that he knew best....

The only problem with the plan was that Noura and Yasmin had a falling out just as we started to strategize the arrangement. Noura said she would not move into any apartment with Yasmin. As anyone who has grown sisters knows, resolving a fight between sisters is very tricky.

Noura was at fault for starting the silent dagger fight by issuing a blunt low blow to Yasmin in the form of a verbal insult, calling her a prostitute after finding out she had a boyfriend. Noura's Arab blood ran a little thicker than ours, as she refused to admit she was wrong. Yasmin then swore never to speak to her again. Yasmin had the scholarship allowance from the Saudi Government, the portion my stepdad let her have. It would guarantee she would be able to make rent. While Noura was working at Lush, a bath and soap store in the mall, she spent everything she earned on the products she sold. In my mind there was no toss-up. Yasmin was the better roommate but if I chose Yasmin over Noura, I would never hear the end of it. Noura would feel I had betrayed her to the enemy and Noura often held a grudge for a long time. Like our mother, she had inherited the extreme stubbornness of an ox and enjoyed cuddling up to her anger, resentment, jealousy, self-pity, and depression nightly. Finally, there was the Arabs policy where the older should never bow to the younger Arab ... well, now you're cooking with gas!

There was only one way to fix it. That was to get Yasmin to compromise and let Noura know that without Yasmin to pay part of the rent she wouldn't be going either. Try as I might, Noura refused to budge. After two weeks of trying to talk to Noura every night I decided to take her apartment hunting and show her that what the two of us could afford without Yasmin would be far from ideal. Finally, a ray of hope arrived when Noura started talking about how Yasmin didn't acknowledge her. Signaling that finally, she was thinking of letting it go.

That night I texted Yasmin when she was on her way home. "Yasmin, your sister is sewing in the hallway. When you get home, just say hello. I am not asking you to make up or be friends. She was completely wrong but if we're going to move out together this just has to be done." When Yasmin arrived, she stood for a second at the top of the stairs then uttered, "Hey." Noura looked up and said, "Hey," and Yasmin retired to her room. I looked at Noura and said, "We're moving on now, we need to stick together so we can get out of here."

I decided to give the dating apps a try again but with an extra layer of security. This meant that when I went on a first date Noelle and Noura would sit at the bar to make sure the guy wasn't crazy and to help me get out of the date if need be. After a few of these dates I started to realize that maybe not all American males were serial killers. Many of them seemed so lost and confused while trying their best to come off confident and in control. It was hard for me now that I had been married so many times. The list of what a man could do wrong was so long it could have reached a mile to the bottom of the ocean. Which meant despite having a great dinner together, a mistake like forgetting to walk me to my car in a not-so-safe neighborhood meant there would be no second date. I dated now for me, for fun, and with no expectation that anyone would ever meet my very high standards. The freest feeling there is, is to not be afraid to be alone.

THE FRAT–BOY

On the Bumble app, I talked to a very witty and funny physicist who was a few years older than me. He was thoughtful and a lot of fun and as any woman might tell you, making a woman laugh can be very attractive. He came from humble beginnings and obtained his degree after serving in the military. On our first date we went to a car show at a bar called Gas Monkey Bar N' Grill. It was a Saturday mid-day, so I made up plans with Noelle and drove my car to a park near my parent's house and asked James to pick me up there. We sat at the bar, ordered drinks, and he threw out joke after joke. When I got up and left for the bathroom to text Noelle an update, he texted me, "I really like you." It was a cute gesture that made me smile. When I came out I said, "How did you know I would look at my phone?" "That's what girls do when they go to the bathroom, ha-ha!" I giggled. We walked around and saw the cars, had lunch, and then he said, "Do you want to go see a movie?" "What movie?" I asked him. "Well, there is a Superman vs. Batman movie I want to see." "I love Marvel movies, ya, let's do it!" We went to the movie, and he touched my hand a few times. He was sweet. After the movie we went to get something to eat, then to a bowling alley, then to a Starbucks in Frisco, and by this time it was around 10:00 p.m.. We made out a few times along the way and at Starbucks, James started asking if he could come back to my place. "What about your place?" I said. "No, let's go to your place." I thought to myself that's odd, but I can't take him to my place. It's too soon to explain to him about my stepdad and that I lived with my parents. Finally, he said, "Let's get a hotel room." I said, "I don't know, it's late. I should really get home." "It will be fun, come on." I bit my lip and said, "Okay!" Just as we got into his truck my phone rang. I shouted, "Shit! It's my stepdad!" "What is it? What's wrong?" "It's a long story, just stay very silent and don't turn on the car." I answered, "Hey Daddy! So sorry I lost track of the time. I'm at Noelle's parents' house and I was thinking since it's so late and so far to drive, I'll just crash here if that is alright?" "Princess… is everything alright?" "Ya, I'll tell you later. I think she's having a hard time; her parents are fighting, you know. I'm just going to stay the night. I'll be back in the morning." "Okay, Princess, be safe." "Will do!" I exhaled loudly "That was close." James asked no more questions.

We got to the hotel, got a room, went upstairs, and started to fool around. Then James tried to put his penis in my ass, I moved away and said, "Wrong hole and I don't do that." "Sorry, so sorry," and we continued. I woke up in the morning and sat up quickly since as often happens when you're sleeping you forget where you are. I looked at the end of the bed and saw James staring at me. He said, "You're so beautiful." I nodded and started to get dressed. "Do you want to get breakfast before you head back?" "Sure." As we ate breakfast I told him how I had never done something like that and I half expected to find myself without clothes and my purse when I woke up, if not missing a kidney. He laughed and said, "Understandable, but you didn't. When can I see you again?" "I'll text you," I said.

After four or five dates I let him know that if he wanted to date me he would have to date only me. I was not interested in doing the multiple people dance and showing up one day and awkwardly bumping into him and his other girlfriend at a restaurant. I had no expectation that he would say yes. On the contrary, I was resigned for him to say no but now that I dated for me I was going to have things the way I liked them. He loved the idea and so it was then that we started dating exclusively.

One day he texted me out of the blue and told me he needed to talk to me about something and he didn't want me to overreact or feel jealous or anything. I asked what was going on? He said, "It's just that I need to tell you a few things before you come by my place." "Lol okay, I'll call you when I get off work." I drove home and parked at the park as I always did to smoke. I picked up my phone and called him. "What's going on, James, you sound very nervous." "Well, you know I told you

I am divorced, well the truth is I am still in the process of getting a divorce and I have been divorced before and I have an 11-year-old little girl." I let out a chuckle and said, "Well, then I might as well tell you I have no children, but I have been divorced four times." "Wait, what? How did that happen?" I gave him the short version of my story and then he told me about his soon to be ex-wife. The story goes that after ten years of marriage they had agreed to start a family but instead of getting off her birth control she had an IUD inserted, which is a form of long-term birth control. She then went to visit an old high school classmate in another state. Apparently she'd had a crush on him when she was young, but he hadn't given her the time of day. When she returned from that trip, he'd found multiple sex videos and pictures of her and this man on her phone. One thing led to the other and the marriage fell apart. She moved out of the house but left most of her things behind until she found a more permanent solution and filed for divorce.

"James, I don't care that you're going through a divorce but what I need to know, and I need you to ask yourself is, is it over?" "Yes, it's over, there is nothing to worry about." "Well, then I thank you for telling me the truth but now I need to get home. I'll text you tomorrow." The next day a beautiful bouquet of flowers arrived. I finally was invited to his home. It was beautiful, but too big for one person I thought, at about 5,000 sq feet. I rang the doorbell and he said, "It's open!" I walked in and a small bulldog started running towards me. As I reached out my hand to greet the dog I heard James scream, "Don't touch the dog!!!!" as he attempted to beat the dog to the door. I said, "Why?" "Because she, ohhh, it's too late." The dog got so excited she peed all over the floor. As I walked around I noticed all the pictures of him and his ex-wife. I stood for a moment and said, "She's pretty." "Oh, I'm sorry, I just haven't gotten around to taking them down yet, my therapist said I should avoid too much change. I have anxiety sometimes." "I can understand that, I get anxiety sometimes too."

He cooked dinner on the grill outside and we sat up and talked. A part of me, even at that time, felt like I was put in his life to help him through something. He seemed lost, the plan he had in mind for his life fell apart just as he saw it come to life by building his ex-wife the house.

There was a deep sadness in his eyes that I could place but I chose to put off asking him a second time if he was sure it was over.

I started to stop by every day after work and he helped me find an exit off the tollway that was under repair in case my stepdad checked my toll tag records and found out I got off the tollway there every day. Every night I would head home and hangout with my sister, Noura, who was always drinking in my room since hers was always covered in trash and a fabric explosion. Noura thought James was so exciting since he liked to go out, play video games, and he liked Marvel Comics. Like everyone in our household, he was chill, a prankster, and a romantic. The first weekend I slept over at his house when I got into my car in the morning to leave, he had placed post-it notes with little sayings all over my car. When I wasn't looking at a restaurant he would slip small notes into my purse and wait sometimes weeks for me to find them. I found him cute. It made me smile since no one had ever done that for me before. I wondered, "Is this is what it was like to date an American?" I had never dated one before and there were many aspects about him I enjoyed.

He started to call me in the morning while I drank my Starbuck coffee. It became a kind of tradition and after a month he told me that he loved me. As was expected, his ex-wife appeared back on the scene showing up to pick up this and that from the house, James would always text me to tell me when she was coming so that we would not bump into each other. Then on a Wednesday night he invited me to a steak place. As we ate he said, "I need to tell you something about my ex-wife." "What is it?" "Well, my therapist suggested that we go on a date for closure" "A date?" I asked, as I stared blankly at him. I said, "What does that mean exactly?" "Well, I would take her to dinner, and we would talk." "Is that all? I'm all for closure but why are you calling it a date?" He fumbled around and tried to change the subject by saying that he loved me. I did my best to put my feelings aside and understand his side. "Alright, if that is what you need to do." I said.

A week later they were texting back and forth more than normal but I knew that they had a lot of things to work out, so I kept my opinions to myself. Suddenly James said, "I'll be taking her to a concert. We bought the tickets years ago and we both still want to go. Is that okay?" "James, this woman lied to you, cheated on you, and then left you and you're taking her to a concert, what else is going on?" "Well, now that you mention it I had given her one of my guns but I told her she can't take it until she knows how to use it, so I'll be taking her to shooting practice once a week." "Lovely… James, sometimes people come into our lives only to help us through things, and I don't like feeling like I am getting in the way of something so I'll ask you again. How do you feel about her? Is it over and you're just helping her out or is there something else?" "I don't think so, no, I just wanted to go to the concert, and I can't give her the gun if she doesn't know how to use it. That would be dangerous." I stood in disbelief but said, "Alright, if you say so, then it's fine with me."

A few weeks later I suggested that we all go to coffee or dinner with me, him and his ex-wife and the boyfriend she supposedly had. The answer was no that it would be too awkward, and it was too soon. I wondered. I wanted to be civil, since I was in his life, and she obviously was his best friend for ten years. I didn't expect her to go away but I started to feel like the other woman.

Despite his half-a-million-dollar custom home complete with pool table, cinema room, custom furniture and located in a very rich area, it was obvious that he had not been brought up well. There was a crudeness to his mannerisms that both disturbed me and intrigued me all at the same time. His over extravagant romantic nature made up for where his refinement failed. Since I had never gone to a physical college I had never seen a frat-boy, as they call them, up close. Every time we would go out to a bar, he would find a way to chug something, lose his shoes, or fall asleep face first on someone's lawn. The most disturbing thing to me was when he would pretend to go to the bathroom and watch from some obscure corner as men hit on me at the bar. I couldn't figure out if it just turned him on, which was probably the case, or if he was testing me to see if I would cheat on him. It was like watching some strange exotic animal taken from its natural habitat and placed in an upper-class neighborhood.

Sometimes it's nice to experience things that you were sure you didn't like doing if only to assure yourself that you didn't like doing them. We were polar opposites. He enjoyed the outdoors, only dressing up on formal occasions, bar hopping, smoking pot and then playing video games. I was always dressed up in heels and despised eating anywhere that used grease as a form of wallpaper. All that frying over the years seemed to create a kind of grease layering on everything, even the walls. All of this would have made no difference to our relationship until he started to work on changing me, something I took note of very seriously since I was completely happy as I was. He would ask me to dress the way his ex-wife did without saying that was the case, but I knew it was because I saw the pictures of her on the wall. While what turns a man on in one woman can be requested in another, low cut shirts, tight sweatpants and so on is fine, if it's turning the man on it can just be his preference but with James it always felt like it was something else. He missed her. I could see it pop up every once in a while and that made me uncomfortable.

My parents' lease was under my mother's name, so my stepdad packed up the house and broke the lease. Since my mother had declared bankruptcy there was no point in his mind in continuing to pay the rent.

Before the move my sister Noura texted me and said:

> *Here's how I see it. One room: You and Yasmin's sleeping space because that's all you guys will do in the apartment anyways. The other room can be my sleeping space AND! Communal study/workroom. Work there when you choose. Even though I sleep in there, feel free to quietly work on your computer or craft at any time. No loud crafts or work after 10 PM including me. I think you sharing a room with Yasmin shouldn't be a problem and we can get one of those changing dividers like in the old movies for privacy. Fairness achieved.*

I felt a headache coming on as I sat to type out a reply.

> ***Elise****: You don't make enough to even pay your equal portion of the rent, that's first and then you have demands over how much*

space you need. You're texting me like we're American roommates … we're sisters helping each other so we can move out and stand on our feet. I don't mind sharing one room with both of you and making the other room a workspace. My concern, however, is coming home and finding a mess as had been the case in Baba's house (fabric everywhere). I don't want to live like that anymore. I want us to have a cute, clean, fun space for us all to hang out together and relax in. None of us is getting their own room, that is what is fair. Honestly you're overthinking everything way too much you haven't even seen the place yet. Let's talk about this all together, the three of us, and decide together what works best.

***Noura**: Ok*

***Elise**: Honey, we're girls I don't need to have my own room, I don't care. I want to find what works for all of us so everyone is happy. You know that money means nothing to me. I'm sorry about what I said earlier. I would gladly carry you on my shoulders, you're my little sister.*

***Noura**: Well, I don't need to be babied…*

***Elise**: I am not babying you. I am just trying to help, that's what family does. What's going on? Are you ok? It's like someone said something to upset you.*

***Noura**: I'm fine.*

My stepdad helped us move our things and we took some of the furniture from the house to get us started. We got a two-bedroom apartment to save money. I suggested we turn the large room into a closet or communal area. The three of us were the same shoe size and shared everything we could. I suggested the other bedroom be turned into a communal sleeping area. Noura however had other ideas, she wanted a room of her own and argued constantly. After my stepdad moved to Alba, Texas, and was now a two-hour drive away, we were all free to live our lives without him being any the wiser.

Yasmin would commute to Denton and stay with her boyfriend now to be closer to school. I still refused to give Noura her own room citing that even I was not looking to have my own room. "Yasmin is never here unless Baba is coming to check on us, why can't I have my own room?" "No, Noura, it's not fair for any of us to have our own room." "Well, what if I want to have sex?" "Then go to your boyfriend's house, no boys stay over, it's just safer that way for all of us." That was my only rule. Her belongings were like a plague, always inching out of their space and taking over more and more of the house until the closet room looked like an explosion of fabric, sewing supplies, makeup, and clothes. She kept wearing me down until finally the communal room was her workshop and entering could have left you with a needle jabbed in your foot if you did not step very carefully.

If I stayed the weekend with James at his house, I would return to find the living room taken over as well. I was constantly cleaning up and asking her to please respect everyone who lived in the house. "You've already taken over the other room and I said nothing, but come on, Noura. I don't like coming home to a mess. If you use a dish you need to put it in the dishwasher and if you see the trash full you need to take it out, not let it sit there and stink up the whole house." She always nodded and cleaned up. Then like clockwork she would slip back into her natural habits.

James said he was planning to go to Mexico and would love to take me with him. I was flattered but said, "I would love to go but it's just not something I can afford right now. I am just starting to get on my feet." "I'll pay! It's my treat." I smiled and accepted. I went down to Chelsey and requested the time off. Then during our regular calls with my stepdad, I told him my girlfriend and a few other girls were planning a trip to Mexico. He was none the wiser.

We went to Mexico together and it was there that I discovered a whole world I never knew actually existed. The hotel, as it turned out was full of swingers, and at night the restaurant area and all the visible hot tubs were full of naked people. If I was giving advice to someone I would have said get out of there, but it turned out not to be as threatening to my safety as I first thought. James respected that I was only willing to look around and was nowhere near ready to think of participating, or his participating, for that matter. It seemed like I had passed through reality into an Eyes Wide Shut world with James and I the only ones fully clothed. When we returned to Dallas I decided I needed some space. My dreams haunted me night after night. There was no way to unsee what I had seen and If I could have gone back in time I would not have gone to Mexico with him. I made multiple excuses why I couldn't see him for a little while and kept to myself. Finally, I sent him a message (errors retained):

Elise: *I really need you to think about this open relationship thing. I know it's hard for you to make decisions but it's not something I am going to be ok with. I have decided if that lifestyle is something you need then that is something I need to know. If we need to break up so you can go get it out of your system just let me know. I am what I am. You asked me to explore things, I did and I know it's not for me. I know to you monogamy might be dead but I like my bubble and I'm happy in it.*

James: *Where are you?*

Elise: *Drinking and smoking on my balcony. I'm not very good company right now. I have a lot to think about but if you want to come sit with me while I work it through you are welcome to do so.*

James came by with a bottle of wine that had glitter in it, he knew I liked sparkly things. He approached the balcony slowly and sat on the chair beside me. I stayed silent for a bit as I pondered what else I felt like I wanted to say. James said, "Listen, about the whole swinger thing, I really don't have an answer. Right now, I am perfectly satisfied with just you, but I can't guarantee that won't change." "James, I grew up in a world where men can have second wives. I'm not saying I am for it but it's hard wired into me as okay, so I get where you're coming from. But orgies and swingers and couple-swapping, I'm never going to be okay with that. If I was in a monogamous relationship and my partner felt something was lacking then it would depend on how much I wanted him in my life, I don't know what I would do. I might tell him to go get it out of his system. I don't know, James, we haven't been together that long for you to even have that option." James nodded in silence and then said, “I knew I was giving you too much at once. I’m so sorry.” “It’s more than that, it’s your whole ex-wife thing as well.”

He started to speak, and I stopped him and said, “Indulge me for a moment. You gave yourself no time to be truly done with your ex-wife before moving into another serious relationship. You jumped. Let me take you back so you can understand why I am here. Five months ago, my every feeling told me that you weren’t done and so I asked and the reply I got from you was confident and firm that you were done and I believed you. Again, the signs popped up here and there, a look on your face when she called, the sadness in your voice, and I asked and received the same firm answer, “I’m done.” And I believed you still. I’m sure you can understand more than anyone how it feels to see the one you love slipping away somewhere and feeling powerless to stop it. She came back into your life and suddenly I was shelved, you started acting differently. I wasn’t not mad that you texted her or that you took her to a concert or hangout with her, but mainly I was just hurt because I felt like you allowed her to just come back and take space and time that before she came back, was ours, at least in my mind. Our morning calls at Starbucks became her time. Our weekends were cut short if she decided she wanted to spend time with you. You took me to a romantic dinner so you could tell me you were going to take her on a date. Any other girl would have slapped you across the face and left the restaurant immediately. But being caught in a new situation I didn’t know what to believe or do or say. So as is normally the case with me, I tried to understand the other side. Your side. While all the while forgetting about myself. It may not have been the case that you were slipping back to her, maybe you were just lost in a whirlwind of everything, but this is what I felt. For the next four weeks I felt like I was swimming against the current. Most days I would just try and convince myself that everything was fine. Unfortunately, my trust in what you said about her or did regarding her got severely damaged along the way. You started to lie about talking to her. Only telling me you saw her when someone else brought it up. Honestly, I felt stupid for believing you in the first place, like a little fool and that’s the hardest thing to get over. I hate lies. You hid her and that only made things worse. I told someone I loved once that I would never leave him for telling me the truth, that would never be the reason, and I am saying it to you now. When your divorce finally went through I was glad everything was fine, but you didn't give yourself time to put things away. You were depressed and I felt like I was picking up pieces of the man I loved. She still remained in your life, which is fine, but you didn't give us time to move past the damage that happened. Did it ever occur to you to say to her, "Hey, let's take a breather now that the divorce is final, I need to go fix things with Elise." You completely forgot that I had to put aside every uncomfortable feeling I had to help you through your divorce. I think I need to be mad at you for a little while and hurt. I need to see if I can move past it. The longer I avoid being mad at you the deeper the wound becomes, and I don't know what else to do." He apologized again and I said, "I think I have said everything I need to say and I'm going to go to bed soon you should go." It was clear the relationship was on its way out but neither one of us was ready to finish it.

The next morning as I was preparing for the D Magazine huddle, Chelsey asked if I could meet her in the small conference room near her office. Three years before I would have thought for sure I was getting let go but this time I anticipated a promotion to Wick's Executive Assistant / Office Manager. It was known that Chelsey would be moving into another department soon. I walked proudly down to the conference room thinking that finally all my hard work and dedication had paid off. When I sat down Chelsey interlocked her fingers as she often did when she had bad news to deliver. "Elise, you have been doing an amazing job and we all love you here, but they are going to advertise for Wick's new assistant, and I need to ask you not to apply." My mind raced as I asked, "Why?" "It's nothing against your abilities, you're amazing at the front and I know Wick would like to keep you there. So, there is no need to apply. I'll be sure to find you someone that you will get along famously with." "I don't understand, Chelsey, I have been learning and training for this job since I got here, and I can't even apply? You still haven't told me why?" She sighed as they announced it was time for the huddle and she repeated, "Don't apply."

I carried myself to my desk and I managed to not cry in front of anyone. Once the huddle was over I walked into the large conference room and cried. I fixed my face and headed back to my desk. I knew that if I was content to stay in the same role I would have had a job for life. I was the longest sitting Administrative Assistant in the history of the company but apparently I did my job too well to the point that moving me into another role seemed unfathomable. At the end of the day, I headed home where I opened a bottle of wine and sat out on my balcony crying all over poor little Yoshi, who could not understand why I was so sad. When I was done crying I pulled out my computer and applied for ninety-eight jobs that evening.

The next day I seriously contemplated calling in sick but remembered that I had four people coming in to see me and I didn't want to let anyone down. Despite not being even allowed to apply for the job I always wanted, I still loved D Magazine and all the people that had been adopted as my family. If I was going to leave it would not be with anger or resentment but rather with an air of honor and respect. I was ready to grow and there were no possible positions for me at D Magazine except for the one I had and the one I got passed over for.

I often gave tours to visitors, interns, new employees, and media. One by one they all had their tours, all of them praising themselves as we toured, remarking at all times about how it was no surprise that they were selected to be subscriber of the month. Finally, it was time for my final tour of the day.

THE THIRD CULTURE KID

I was standing at my desk when the elevator dinged. As I looked up, a man reached out his hand saying, "Hi, I'm…" and in taking his hand I said, "Daren, yes, it's a pleasure to meet you. I'm Elise." I came around the desk to offer him my full attention. He pulled two small books from his bag saying, "I brought some books for Wick and Christine and this one is for you." I was slightly moved by his kindness and humility as I directed him in the direction we would be heading for his tour. As we passed through the sales department, I began to point out various aspects of the culture, layout, and the history of the magazine.

He interrupted me with a question no guest had ever asked before: "So, where are you from?" I stopped in my tracks, since in three years people, always asked about the magazine and just assumed like most of the staff that I was just another Dallas girl. I turned around and looked at him. I answered, "Well, I'm from California, but I grew up in Saudi Arabia," turning back around to continue with the tour. He said, "That's really cool, you know I grew up in Bangkok, Thailand." I smiled and replied, "Oh, very cool, our brand manager actually went to school there. I'll be happy to introduce you. Let's continue." I tried again to move the conversation back to the tour but department after department brought question after question which normally would have been shut down by a sudden call or meeting that I had to attend but since he was in my charge there was no getting around answering all of his questions.

Once we reached downstairs for his photoshoot he asked if I could take some behind the scenes photos of him having his picture taken by D Magazine. As he handed me his phone he said, "Oh, no, it just died, would you mind using your phone to take some?" "My pleasure," I re-

plied. When the tour was over I called Kate, the employee I'd mentioned to him who had lived in Thailand, to see if she wanted to come say hi. She came out with a few others, and they struck up a conversation. As I tried to slip back from the popular crowd he turned and said, "Elise, would you mind getting a picture of me in front of the big D painting?" "Happy to," I replied. No sooner had I taken the picture that he said, "Would you mind if I got a picture with you?" No guest had ever wanted a picture with me, and he was teetering on the verge of the red boundary line I had drawn for guests. I felt like it was highly inappropriate, but he was the guest, after all, so I decided what was the harm. He seemed excited to be honored as the subscriber of the month and if he wanted a picture with the D Girl, who was I to spoil his dreams?

As he was leaving the office, I asked Daren if he was planning to attend the Best of Big D Party the following night. This was the same question I asked everyone who came and went from the office in the months leading up to our biggest event of the year. "Yes, I have tickets. Will you be there?" "Yes, of course. We look forward to having you."

"Oh, and so sorry to ask for one more thing, but can you send me the pictures?" "Yes, of course I'll get them to you right away." After he left a salesgirl came up to me and said, "Who was the Silver Fox?" "Who?" "The Silver Fox you were showing around?" "Oh, he's a subscriber of the month," I replied, and left it at that. She thought he was charming, and I did too, in a way, but I had not thought of him as dating potential. So much was on my mind that day about whether I would break-up with James and my job search.

An hour later I decided to have another look at his website and what he did since he said he worked in the Company Culture space. With me being the first president of the D Magazine Culture Club, it dawned on me that maybe there was a job offer there. His website was very professional, and I thought I should see if he was looking for an assistant.

The next night was the Best of Big D party and as I was making my rounds, greeting people, and introducing them to my strangely introverted boyfriend, who somehow felt right at home in a crowded swinger resort but so out of place at Best of Big D., I started to really see that I could never fit into James' world, and he could never fit into mine.

A text message came. It was Daren asking if I was here. "Yes, where are you?" "Next to the beer fountain." "Cool, I'll come find you." As I approached the beer fountain I reached out my hand and greeted him warmly. He introduced me to his friend, Ted Hoffman, and I stepped to the side, revealing the cowardly short physicist standing behind me. "This is my boyfriend, James." Silence hit as Daren reached past me to shake James' hand. We chatted for a bit and then as I was leaving I leaned in and said, "Hey, I don't know if you're looking for an Executive Assistant, but I am looking for something else if you are." He leaned back, looked at me, smiled and said, "Actually I am totally looking for an Executive Assistant." I said, "Great, I'll send you my resume tonight when I get home."

I left Best of Big D that evening and went straight to my computer to make sure I sent over my resume as soon as possible. I also suggested we grab coffee together sometime during the following week to talk about the position, to which he responded, "Would you prefer lunch at the Nasher or drinks at St. Ann's after work?" I wanted the job but could never predict my lunch interruptions. I always left an intern at the desk when I went to lunch and if Wick needed something it would send them into a state of panic which would involve calling me every five minutes until they calmed down. I would definitely be interrupted. I agreed to drinks at St. Ann's, which was a small restaurant near D Magazine.

I had planned to leave early to make sure I was on time but as could often happen, Phyllis urgently needed my help with something. I stayed to make sure she was okay. Daren texted to say he was on his way and asked what I would like to drink? I replied, "A glass of white wine." I arrived fifteen minutes late and upon entry he stood up and after handing me my wine, dropped the comment that I was late. "Yes, but I was taking care of my boss, just because I am planning to leave doesn't mean I shouldn't do my job to the best of my ability, while I am still there. I would assume you would appreciate that as a quality in any employee you're thinking of hiring."

He was flabbergasted at my response and asked that we start the interview. We spoke for about an hour. He started the interview with some small talk. He asked about my work at D Magazine and somehow we ended up on the subject of happiness. I related to him that I believe happiness is a choice. He smiled and agreed. I was shocked because before that point no one ever agreed with me on that score. I liked him and I asked myself, "Is he like me?" My mind replied and said, "Brush it off! No one is like you. This is a job interview." We discussed what he was looking for in an assistant and he told me about his past assistants.

When he finished his glass of wine, he inquired if I had eaten, to which I replied, "I have not." "Well would you like to walk over to Mercat Bistro to have dinner?" "Sure," I said. In my head I thought, "YES, the job must be in the bag if he wants to continue the conversation over dinner." As he left to pay the bill, a stranger at the bar said to me, "You know he has been waiting for you for a long time." I didn't know what to reply so I just smiled and said "Oh." As I carried my wine glass he came toward me and insisted on carrying it for me remarking, "A lady should never carry her own wine glass." It was a custom I had never heard of but was nonetheless welcome gentlemanly behavior. Evidently, Daren was so well known at both Saint Ann's and Mercat Bistro that he could walk out of one restaurant with two glasses of wine and right into the next one without anyone saying a word.

I ordered the chicken and picked away at it as I continued to fill him in on my experience as an assistant. He told me about growing up overseas, his children, how he was happy they were all grown up now, indicating he was not interested in having any more, and his work. Suddenly he took a breath and said, "Would you mind if we stopped the job interview for a moment?" I was confused beyond measure. I had no idea what to say. Was he ending the interview because I was not a good fit? What was the problem? During my pause he continued, "Can I just say that when you came over to greet me at the Best of Big D party and told me, "This is my boyfriend," I just went 'Ah.'" He placed his hand on his chest and continued. "You know that I want to date you, right?" I paused and the silence felt almost like it filled the entire area. He added, "How is that relationship going?" I replied, "We're seeing how it goes." His face looked like he was saying, "Yes!" on the inside. He swirled his wine, looked down and said, "Well, will you let me know if that doesn't work out?" I half smiled and said, "Well, hopefully you'll hire me, then I'll never tell." His head moved back as if it was saying, "Well in that case, I'm not going to hire her."

He took a small breath and said, "Let's continue the interview." Relieved to be able to forget and put out of my mind that my potential new employer was hitting on me, I jabbered on until it was time to head home. The valet brought my car around and he opened the car door for me. I drove home.

I walked into the apartment and appeared to my sisters happier than I had been the last few days. Noura asked, "What's going on?" "Oh, I just had the best job interview, I think I'm getting the job with a man who works on culture. How fun is that!" and I spun around like a Disney princess. Noura looked at me for a second and said, "Are you sure that's all?" "Yes!" "Sure?" "Yes, well, he is good looking, very smart, polite and…" Noura giggled a little and said, "Is it time to change boyfriends perhaps?" "Don't be silly, he's going to be my boss and he's probably married," I replied as I headed to the balcony.

As I sat smoking my cigarette I picked up my phone and texted him. My mind was full of ideas for his business. It's amazing how when you talk to the right person they inspire you and excite you, while talking to the wrong person will tire you and drain your energy away.

My life started to get busy and while I thought of him from time to time, I was caught up in all there was to do at work and at home. Once in a while I would get a text from him, and we would message back and forth about work life and so on. Then we would both go on with our busy lives.

My stepdad rarely found time to visit. Yasmin and I took turns driving up to Alba to put his mind at ease that we were behaving. Yasmin's grades went up now that she didn't need to sneak around to see her boyfriend. My stepdad, however, still had a watch on her bank account so she would fill her car with gas before she left for Denton and take all the cash she might need for a few days out so she would not use her card late at night in Denton and alert his attention. She continued to do this almost the entire time she was in college. He only ever asked me about her boyfriend one more time, and now since her grades were up, it was easy to just say, "It didn't work out." He dropped the subject.

When he did decide to pay us a visit, everything contraband by his standards had to be hidden. Noura's pork bacon, our liquor, and anything he might find. He would always enter the apartment, stand for a moment looking around, then pretend he wanted a drink and instead of asking us to get him something like he would have at home, he liked to randomly open the fridge or some cupboard here and there to see what he could find. Yasmin would always rush back from Denton, so it looked like she was living there with us, instead of visiting every once in a while. We were very careful, and I have to say we did it well.

What did he have to control us now? Noura still needed his help with her student loans, Yasmin still needed his signature on documents for her scholarship, and all of us had him as a cosigner on the lease since none of us was qualified on our own. We would need to bide our time for total freedom.

A job offer from Daren never came. Finally, following interview after interview, I accepted an offer from an investment firm in Preston

Center, an area not too far from where my sisters and I lived. The day after I accepted the job offer I went to work and told Chelsey. "When you have a minute I need to talk to you about something." She stopped what she was doing and pointed me in the direction of the conference room. As I sat down with her and told her that I had accepted a position as an office manager at another company. She stood up, hugged me, and said "I'm happy for you!" "Chelsey, of course I'll be here for the next two weeks and if you need me to stay longer I can let them know. I definitely don't want to leave you hanging." "It will all be fine; we will find someone."

The next two weeks I was busy finishing up projects and getting everything in order to handoff to my replacement. My departure was announced by an email to all the staff from Chelsey, It said:

> *As many of you know, the Administrative Assistant position is rarely filled for more than a few months at a time. It's a post that relentlessly challenges your patience, judgement, and faith in the human race. For the last two years, Elise Evans has been an unflinching ray of sunshine at our front desk. She takes on every day with a fearless, positive attitude that would inspire the Dalai Lama. We should all take note.*
>
> *Chelsey*

Daren and I texted every once in a while. I was not about to have my heart stolen by an obvious expert in the craft, but I admired his skill and his confidence. Daren grew up in Bangkok, Thailand. His parents took him there as missionaries when he was three years old. Just as I had gone to Saudi when I was three years old. I wasn't sure if I wanted to date him, but the connection was undeniable. I invited him to my birthday party and thought even if I decided not to date him he was an amazing person that I wanted in my life.

I texted James and asked if we could meet for coffee at the Starbucks near my apartment the next weekend. I wanted time to avoid him for a little while I decided what to do. I find a small break of communication can send a message and help give both parties time to calm down and adjust to the impending breakup. My mind was finally made up.

The morning came and I met him for coffee. As we sat, I said, "James, I love you, you're a wonderful human being but I don't think this is going to work. To be honest you just got out of a ten-year marriage, and I have felt like you were trying to turn me into her. I didn't like the way you teased me for being the best dressed person at every party. How you want me to go camping with you and when I say no, you tease me about that. You tried to dress me like her, and I totally understand that you miss her dearly. I know you don't mean it. I'm not telling you to hurt you but so you can know for your next relationship. Sometimes a person is only meant to come into your life for a short while. To help you get over a hard period in your life. I hope I was able to do that for you. I wish you the best I really do."

Tears filled his eyes as he said, "I love how you dress, I'm sorry, I didn't mean to tease you. I do love you as you are." I nodded and said, "I think you need some time to really find out what you want in a partner. Time to really move on from your past relationship. Time to discover who you are without her. I don't help with that." I kissed his cheek and said goodbye.

The day before my birthday party Daren texted me:

> ***Daren****: Good afternoon! Would you rather me attend your party or take you to dinner to celebrate?*

I put my fingernail in my mouth and bit it a bit with a coy grin on my face every time he texted me and then after reading the message I thought, "Wait a minute, does he have a work trip or did something come up the evening of my birthday party?" I texted back:

> ***Me****: Hahaha what's the scheduling conflict with my party lol, I can't have both hehe.*
>
> ***Daren****: Elise, both sounds like a brilliant plan! ;)*
>
> ***Me****: He is not coming, if that's what you're worried about. I could tell you why but I'm not sure what your intentions are so I will just wait until I see you next time.*
>
> ***Daren****: Wasn't worried about that in the least! My intentions? I believe you know.*

***Me**: We will talk about your intentions next time I see you.*

***Daren**: Are you single now?*

***Me**: You are awful lol yes.*

***Daren**: Well then I want a dinner date!!!*

***Me**: Lol when*

***Daren**: How's Friday night?*

***Me**: I was going to suggest Friday lol done! Adding it to my calendar you can pick me up from my apartment. 7?*

***Daren**: Brilliant! Is it Friday yet?*

***Me**: 5 days away lol*

***Daren**: 😐☹*

I had planned a birthday party for September 2nd at my apartment as a way of seeing everyone I would no longer interact with on a day-to-day basis. I invited everyone at D Magazine that I was close to. I even invited Eddie, the Starbucks Barista who let me into the Starbucks that morning when I crept out of the house as Jacob slept. I would discover that Jacob had stopped by my Starbucks many times that winter when I was hiding at other Starbucks to ask Eddie if he had seen me. Eddie always said, "No, man, I haven't seen her in a long time." He'll probably never know what he did for me that dark morning or the mornings that followed when he sent Jacob packing, but he nonetheless altered a life by saving it.

DAREN MARTIN

To behold he is tall, handsome, and manly. He had piercing blue eyes and silver hair mixed with a bit of brown. His hair is just long enough to curl at the base of his neck. He was born in Louisiana but grew up in Bangkok, Thailand. He went there at the age of three with his parents, and two sisters. He grew up with a father and mother were exceedingly kind to everyone they met. They set an example for him early on. His younger brother was born in Thailand, and they all lived there until it was time for him to attend college. He attended college in Louisiana and met a beautiful girl named Tena. They married and had three children, Jordan, Madison, and Callahan. After he received his Ph.D., he opened a business and supported his family. After the children were almost completely grown, sadly, the marriage fell apart and ended in a divorce twenty years later. Daren got joint custody but that meant that he would only see his kids every other weekend. He and his ex-wife got along well eventually and concentrated on loving the children. Daren and his ex-wife read to their children at a young age and, along with other factors, they all turned out to be extremely smart. All his children went to college on scholarships and exited college debt free. They are one of the greatest accomplishments of his life.

After the divorce his life changed, he was different, and he wanted more. He started consulting and eventually landed a change management consultancy with Holy Frontier that lasted ten years. He got an apartment in downtown Dallas and when he was finally financially ready he bought a two-story condo in Uptown Dallas. The door opened onto a hallway with a small bedroom directly on you right. The rest of the first floor was an open layout with the kitchen, a living room with a

20-foot ceiling and an epic view of Dallas including the ball, Perot museum, the famed Pegasus, and a large balcony. Up the stairs there was a small landing that looked over the living room where he had a small sitting area followed by a hallway that led to a full wall of books upon books, the master bedroom, and a bathroom with a large bathtub and a walk-in closet. It was a milestone in his life and living there in the heart of Dallas changed his life.

In the years after his marriage, he dated multiple girls and accumulated a list of all the others who would visit him when he felt like he wanted company. He had decided, like many bachelors, that he would never marry again and so he kept most of his relationships as casual as possible. So often as it happens, to let people too close is scary after the hurt that comes with a divorce. No one likes to get hurt a second time.

He published his first two books in 2016 and continued to write, read, and grow. He went on to do keynotes all over the world and inspired everyone he would come into contact with, just as his parents had done in Thailand. If you ever meet him, it's not an understatement to say that he would inspire you, change you, and you would feel your greatness amplified.

Thursday rolled around, and I went around finishing up certain tasks and explaining the job duties to the new girl.

That night Daren texted me:

Daren: *"Are you working tomorrow?"*

Elise: *"I'm going in for a little bit but I should be out by noon. Why?"*

Daren: *"Because I thought about moving up our date. You could drive down here and we could go to the Nasher Museum or the Dallas Museum of Art."*

I looked at the message puzzled as to why he wanted to move it up and where was here?

Elise: *"Where is here?"*

Daren: *"My place."*

My head backed away from the phone as I typed out my response.

Elise: *"Listen, I'm not coming to your place. No offense intended but we just met."*

In my mind it sounded like he wanted to play games and maybe he was only looking for a booty call which I was not interested in. He replied,

"Well, what do you want?"

"We can do everything you described, but you need to come pick me up from my place like a gentleman."

I felt sure he would lose interest and to be honest, it was of little concern to me.

He replied, "*Sure*," and the date was moved up to 3:00 p.m. on Friday.

Friday was my last day at D Magazine. I had no plans to come in that day but the new girl looked so lost so I thought it wouldn't bother me to go into the office for a few hours. I recall all the sad goodbyes. I walked around handing out last minute advice to those who needed it the most. I recall all the endless tears and yet all my thoughts turned to the fact that soon I would see him again. I recall the drive home that afternoon, normally I would think about work but there was no more work to concern myself with, so I thought about Daren. What it would be like to see him again. Considering the last time I saw him was technically a job interview .... I got home, went to my balcony, and pondered over all the changes that had taken place recently.

My stepdad was mostly hands off now that he was far away, Yasmin's grades were better, and she lived mostly in Denton. Noura struggled daily with her life, her job, her endless parking and speeding tickets. Yasmin and I carried most of the burden of the apartment costs even though Yasmin was hardly there. In the beginning, the deal was that anything we bought would be split three ways since we all used it. The washer/dryer, the couch, the bills and so on, but Noura was barely able to cover her part of the rent. I thought about my new job and I was nervous about my date with Daren. I had intended to take a nap beforehand but the clock seemed to work against me and as I smoked, the time for my date with Daren came nearer. I changed, got ready and sat down on the couch. I texted him, *"I'm ready"* and just as I did, a knock came at the door.

When I saw him my heart skipped a beat, but I told myself not to be silly, it's just a first date. We went out and I saw his car. I looked at it and smiled, not because it was a sports car but because it was almost exactly like the car I had begged Firas to rent for me after I passed my driving test in Dubai. A small silver convertible. He opened the car door, and I sat inside. As we drove he put some old music on the stereo. He talked about how much music he has and then he said, "I can change it, if you want something else?" I smiled, it was very kind of him, but I said, "No, it's great." I wouldn't have changed a thing. We went to the DMA and then we walked from there to the Nasher. There was a fountain on the way and as I admired it, Daren played like he was going to toss me in. He laughed when I let out a little scream. A part of me didn't think it was funny and a part of me was intrigued by his familiarity and boldness. Then we walked to the Chase building, where people like to go up to the top floor and look out over the city. When we were checking in at the reception Daren asked the man, "It's okay to make out up there, right?" As he looked over at me I rolled my eyes at his confidence. We got up to the top and looked out over the city.

After we left the chase building Daren started to talk about the Cathedral Guadalupe in Downtown Dallas where we would be heading next. As we were crossing the street I stopped and said, "Daren, we don't have to do it all in one day. Can we go sit somewhere? I want to talk and get to know you." The way he looked at me … it was like no one had ever said that to him before. We got back in the car and drove to a restaurant called Savor that was located on the grounds of the Klyde Warren park. I had made numerous reservations for Phyllis at this restaurant, but I had never been to it. We sat and ordered, and I observed how everyone smiled and how they all seemed to adore him. They shared my adoration. We talked about random things and the conversation flowed as if we had known each other for a long time.

We finished eating and got into the car when Daren said, "I live just over here, you want to come up?" I froze for a moment and said, "No." My brain went in a million directions … what was he up to? I wasn't about to go up there so he could put the moves on me! "Especially not on a first date," I said out loud. He looked at me and said, "What do you mean?" "It's just something I don't do, go up to a guy's place on a first date." He looked at me and said, "Nothing is going to happen, one glass of wine, come up." I looked at the apartment building, looked at him, then I said, "Okay," reluctantly.

We entered the condo, and he poured some wine in two glasses as I calculated his every move and kept my physical distance. I thought about what I had in my purse that could be used as a weapon should the need arise … my keys, I thought. We went out to the balcony, sat, and I turned to him and asked what was on my mind. "Why did you and your wife get a divorce?" He laughed and said, "I don't think that's a first date conversation." I replied defensively since I was on edge a little, "I get to ask whatever I want."

Over time people tend to expect certain responses to certain questions and we create preconceived judgements based on those responses. I was waiting for either total avoidance of the question or the usual "she was such a bitch" speech. Neither of those happened, his response was to swirl his wine in his glass and say, "You can ask whatever you want." I was floored. As he replayed the story to me, I admired his honesty and willingness to share with me. We finished our glasses of wine and left. He suggested that we continue the date and go to the Turkish Cafe in Plano, Texas. As we drove I looked at him and thought, wow, he had me in his apartment and didn't try anything? I admired how he kept his word, and I began to admire him more and more. We argued about the distance and the directions. "It's not this far out of the city. I know it's not. Check the GPS." "Yes, it is far out, it is close to where my parents used to live." I pulled up the GPS and showed him. He said, "Oh, I remember it being closer." The way he insisted gave me pause for a moment and reminded me of Firas' endless need to be right, but I brushed it off when he admitted he was mistaken.

As the conversations about Saudi Arabia and Bangkok, Thailand, took on a life of their own, I found myself leaning in a little, begging to be kissed.

He paused the conversation, leaned in, took my head into his hands, and kissed my forehead. It was sweet but my mind suddenly started to reconstruct the puzzle I had been creating since the date started. I thought, "Oh man that sucks! Is he gay? Is that why he was able to keep his hands off me in the apartment and is that why he is so gentlemanly? Had I missed something? What rotten luck!" A few moments later he leaned in and kissed me, and it can only be described as electric. He drove me home and as we drove with the top down that September evening, I felt cold. I said nothing and suddenly he was turning on the heater. The way he paid attention to me was unusual in my experience, but it felt so wonderful. As he walked me to my apartment he kissed me again, this time he placed his arm around my waist and pulled me in. I said goodnight and walked into my apartment as if I was floating on air.

Daren texted me a picture of the view from his balcony and said, "Sweet dreams." I texted back the same. I sighed, then I shook my head and put all thoughts of love out of my mind. I finished my glass of wine and headed to bed.

The next day was the day of my birthday party. Daren texted first thing in the morning saying, "Good morning," and I texted, "Good morning," back. I smiled as I got the house ready for my guests. Daren texted mid-afternoon and said, "What time should I come?" "8:00 p.m.," I said. "What if I come earlier?" he replied. "No, I won't be dressed," I said. He replied, "Is that supposed to detour me?" I laughed and said, "No, come at 8." At the last minute Noura texted me saying she was ill and would be staying at her boyfriend's house so she would not be able to make it. Yasmin and I talked about this and that as we waited for the guests to arrive and she yelled at me for my music playlist saying it was "lame." I laughed.

My gay friends John, his husband, Curtis, and Eddie, the Starbucks barista arrived first. John said, "Tell me about this new man, Honey," and I giggled.

Suddenly there was a knock at the door, I answered and there he was ... the handsome devil! I thought. I wanted to kiss him but feared it would weird everyone out, especially my sister, since we had only been on one date, and I had not had a chance to tell anyone how it had gone. I stepped into the kitchen after introducing him to everyone and offered him a drink. Placing one hand in his pocket and turning side face to look around for a second he looked back at me and said, "Yes, I'll have a glass of red wine, thank you." I smiled and said, "I don't have any red wine, I can't take the risk that someone spills and ruins the carpet. The apartment has big fines for stuff like that." "Well, then, I'll have a glass of white wine if you have it." I poured him a glass. More people arrived and I got busy with my guests, but I was always taking glances of him across the room. I worried if he was okay since the D Magazine people were all so young and some of them tended not to get along with everyone.

The night went on, we opened presents. I opened Daren's last. The first thing I pulled out of the gift bag was his book, *Whiteboard*. My sister and I exchanged glances. She had said before he arrived that if he gave me his book as a gift that would really be tacky. I laughed and said, "We'll see." He also gave me a mug for my morning coffee and a book titled, *The Red Book* by Carl Jung. I hugged the book. Daren was the first to leave. He said, "I'm heading out." I made a face purely out of disappointment that I had not had enough time with him. He said, "What's that face? Someone kept me up late last night." I leaned in and whispered, "Not as late as I could of." "Ya? I feel cheated now. I want to see you tomorrow." I said, "What time?" He laughed and said, "Some absurdly early time, I'll text you." I said, "Okay, I'll walk you out." He kissed me on the stairs, and I headed back to the apartment, smiling.

When I opened the door and closed it behind me everyone jumped on me, "Girl! You have to tell us about this guy!" I smiled and said, "We went on our first date last night and it was amazing." The conversation got cut off because of all the people leaving, so I said goodbye to them. The remaining guests, Callie, John, Curtis, Yasmin, and Michael went out to the balcony. I pulled out my cigarettes and looked at all of them as I said, "Okay, give it to me." Callie was the first to comment saying, "Girl! No, look at the jewelry to hair ratio." Referring to his mid-length hair which I actually really liked and his three Buddhist necklaces and many bracelets he wore. I laughed and said slowly, "o....k." Then Michael, laughing, added, "Dr. Feel Good!" I turned to him and said,

"What the hell, ha-ha." Everyone started to decide that I should not date him. One of them was fueled by a long-hidden jealousy and another fueled by his dreams that one day I would look his way. I listened to them the same way a child hears their mother say candy is bad. It went in one ear and out the other. While they debated John chimed in, "He seems like a nice guy, but I didn't get to talk to him much." The subject shifted to D Magazine, work, life, and then into whatever was bothering John that day. They stayed way past midnight and then everyone headed home.

The next morning, I woke up and cleared away the remaining party remnants and then sat on my balcony to have some coffee. I thought about Daren and wondered what his intentions were and thought about how much I liked him. Daren texted me and asked if I wanted to come over for dinner. Early evening came and I got dressed and headed to his place for dinner. He was heating up a chicken he had bought at a supermarket called Eatzi's along with some vegetables. I looked at the chicken and thought, "Crap, how do I eat this in a ladylike fashion? It's on the bone." In Saudi I avoided eating many kinds of things, so I never had to remove anything from my mouth that had already gone in. Including seeds, watermelon, meat gristle, and so on. Spitting was very unladylike and gnawing on chicken bones was the equivalent. This was not a Saudi tradition for women, just the way my aunt preferred that I ate, so I could always be composed in front of potential mothers looking for a bride for their sons. I turned my attention to the fact that he was basically cooking for me. It was endearing and as I watched him, I smiled.

He turned and said, "Can you put out the placemats?" I paused for a moment. The way he asked, however so sweetly, was interpreted in my brain as an order and not as the kind request it was intended to be. I said, "That's not how this works, aren't you supposed to be wooing me?" He turned around slowly, raised his eyebrows, and said, "Is that how it's supposed to work? Hmmm..." and then he turned back to finish the dinner prep. Needless to say his calm reaction and the word "hmm" made me feel like a brat, so I took the placemats and set the table. As we were eating, he commented a little more on what I had said and asked me to elaborate on my reaction. "Well, it's just because of my experience. I think you should know that I don't cook, I don't clean, and I don't take orders," I nodded my head like a sergeant. Daren took another bite of his food and said, "Hmmm, I see," and changed the subject.

After dinner he brought out a chess set. He had mentioned he liked to play chess on our first date, and I had told him I had never learned. I sat up and paid attention as he explained each piece. I looked at the board and imagined how they moved. I saw them as if they were people and we started playing. He continued to say why he moved certain pieces the way he did, and I watched his moves attentively. Suddenly he looked down and said, "Wait I think you're actually going to beat me, ha-ha how did that happen?" He snapped a picture and posted it on Facebook. Needless to say, I was exceedingly proud of myself. All of a sudden, he moved one of his pawns to the end of the board and turned it into a second queen using the ghost shaped saltshaker that was on the table and just like that, it was checkmate.

We finished our wine, and he took my hand and led me to the couch and started kissing me. Then his hand started to slowly inch down my jeans. It took all my inner strength to reach my hand against his chest, push him back and say, "Look, whatever you think is going to happen is not going to happen. What are your intentions?" He said, "You know." I said, "Do you want to date me or just sleep with me? Because if it's the second that's not going to happen." He brushed back his hair and said, "I want to date you, and do I want to sleep with you? Hell, yes!" I said to myself if this is going to work I might as well tell him before I get too attached. I said, "I have to tell you something you're not going to like." His face slightly moved back, and I said, "Sometimes when I drink, I smoke." There was a pause and then he said, "I don't care about that." Then he said, "What else?" I said, "Well, it's not something you need to decide right now but, if you're going to date me, you're going to date only me. I don't do the whole dating multiple people thing." He looked at me and said, "You date multiple people when you're not really into one person. I actually prefer it that way."

It got late so he said, "Look, you have three options, you can sleep upstairs in the bed, and we won't do anything, you can sleep on the couch, or you can go home." My mind flashed at what sounded like a protest to the fact that I wouldn't put out that night. Puzzled that he would think I would stay when we had only just started dating, I said, "I'm going to go home." I knew I had to go home, I needed to think, reflect, and decide if he was telling the truth. It was hard for me to trust. Over time it got harder and harder for me to trust and I knew people might say things in the moment, but that didn't mean they meant it. Did he really want to date me or was he just way too experienced and I was falling for it? I needed time to process.

Daren was giving a talk on his WSJ bestselling book, *A Company of Owners* in Las Vegas. When I got home one evening I saw he had left me a video message that relayed how happy he was that I had come into his life and how happy he was to be doing life with me. I watched it over and over again, giggling as I smoked that night on my balcony, and then I texted him to thank him. Adding that if that video had been on a VHS tape it would have already been worn out. I had never received anything like it before and the impact was huge. While he was away he invited me to a party at his friend's house the night that he was flying back to Dallas. He asked if I could pick him up from the airport and then we could go straight from there. After I closed the office I took my dress and my makeup that I had brought with me so I could change at work to the ladies' restroom, changed my clothes, refreshed my makeup and headed out to the airport.

I had never picked anyone up at the airport before, people always picked me up, and when they did, they always parked since it is customary to receive guests this way. I parked the car and headed inside the airport to wait for him to exit. When he arrived, he seemed so surprised that I would park the car in order to receive him at the exit. "I thought you would just pull up outside, I didn't expect you to come in." "It's only proper to receive you this way, come on, I'm only parked right around the corner." I held out my arms and he lifted me up into the air. I would like to say he had no idea how much he was stealing my heart with his every breath, but I think he knew all too well.

He said he was tired and had decided he didn't want to go to the party after all, so we picked up Thai food from a place on the way to his condo and had dinner on his balcony as we had always done. We made love and then I gathered my things and headed home again. My sister, Noura, was home and sitting on the couch watching TV. As I entered she asked me how it was going with "my old man." I said, "He's not that old." "He looks old to me, gross, saggy balls, is that what you're into these days?" I gave her a look of disdain for her comment and headed to my balcony to smoke before bed. Noura was very unhappy with her boyfriend and resented that I let James go. She wanted her introverted boyfriend to be more like the party boy James had been and in her mind I was making a mistake, but I had evolved to a place where marriage did not occupy my mind anymore, all that mattered to me was that I was happy. I refused to acknowledge her disdain and I refused to sit with her while she griped and cried over a boy who made her so unhappy and yet she still decided to stay with him.

It might seem cold, but the happiness of others is not our job and even if we thought it was, it is a job we will all fail to do. We can make another person happy for a day or an hour and in that day and that hour there is real happiness, but when that hour is over they will slip back into whatever state they choose to be in ... we must look first to our own contentment, happiness, and success before we even fathom the idea of helping others achieve the same. We all have to walk our own planks and gain our own insight.

The next night Daren invited me to the soft launch opening of a restaurant near his condo. I never liked big crowds and even when I worked at D Magazine, I would leave work at my normal time and not attend the lavish after-work events that always seemed so exciting to all the interns. I kept to myself a lot as I had done most of my life in Saudi and after. Here was a man who threw out the word *friend* like it was rain coming down from the sky and for me the word *friend* is a high honor that involves a sacred trust. Like the pledge a knight would give a king or like the pledge everyone around the king would give the king of Saudi Arabia when he was crowned. Growing up in a world where outsiders were seen as dangerous to our way of life had made me build an invisible wall that only got higher after Jacob. With every failed marriage I became more and more cautious of everyone.

When we entered the restaurant, Daren introduced me to person after person as I stood back and watched how they all reacted to his presence. We headed to the second floor where a band was playing. As I looked at the lead singer, there was Jordan, a man I had gone to his place and had sex with who never called. I again said to Daren, "Hey, let's go see the balcony." "Don't you want to dance?" "No, I'm good." As we exited the room Daren looked at me and said, "Don't you want to go see the band, you look like you know them?" "Ya, I know the singer we went on a few dates a while back." "If he makes you uncomfortable we don't have to go back in." "No, it's not a big deal." Daren took my hand and led me back into the room and we began to dance. The singer looked at us all the while. Daren leaned in, grasped my waist, and pulled me close. He whispered in my ear, "If something makes you uncomfortable, just tell me. I want you to be happy, always. I just want to take care of you." I just about melted when he continued, "You know that I want to date you, right?" "I know." "No, I want to date only you." I lifted my eyes to meet his and smiled.

That night before I headed home Daren said, "You know, you should bring your clothes and stay the weekend." I looked at him and thought, isn't it too soon? Then I said "Okay." Thursday night as I packed to head to Daren's place for the weekend, a text message from Daren came. It said, *"I do, you know"* I looked at my sister Yasmin, since the message was odd. Then I held the phone back for a second and texted back, *"You do what?"* He said, *"I'll tell you soon."* I smiled and headed to bed.

After work I headed to Daren's place. We ordered food and sat all night on the balcony. Talking about the world, sharing old stories, and just enjoying each other. Finally, he looked at me and said, "I do, you know." I said, "What?" with a smile. He said, "I love you." I replied, "I love you, too."

Weeks passed and one night I told Daren if we are going to be in a serious relationship he would need to know about my past. With one ex-husband in town and three more who could pop up at any time to cause trouble, I didn't want to risk losing Daren to a misunderstanding that I had something to hide. I never talked to people about how many times I had been married since it was a topic that was hard for many

Americans to understand without judgment. Not to mention it was a long story. A part of me also felt ashamed and like a failure so I always passed over the most difficult things when I discussed my past. If I was asked why I was in Canada, I would say I went for school and leave it at that. It was the truth just minus the mention of a husband. When people asked what my ex-husband was like, I would call up attributes from all of them, depending on the context of the question.

Women often ask for life examples of how to deal with certain things. Everyone assumed I had only been married once before. It was simpler that way I felt. A man or a woman can have multiple sexual partners throughout their life in the West without judgement but when I would tell someone I had been married four times I often received a look or a comment like, "Oh, you don't take marriage seriously," or, "You're a gold digger, how much did you get each time?" Yes, someone actually asked me, "Did you keep getting married to get material for the book?" I kept my past to myself.

As we sat on the balcony I started to relay my entire story to Daren which had to be stopped and continued for three consecutive nights. He would often stop me and say, "I don't care about your past, I love you," and I would say, "No, you need to know all of it, let me continue." When I was done I felt a sense of relief, since now if the relationship continued, he was aware of what he was getting into. I could now relax if we happened upon Jacob in a restaurant who would surely say all manner of things like, "Did she tell you that she was married four times and that she just uses men!" Now he knew and that was what was important, he had the right to choose to continue or not. My past was a part of me and therefore it came with me.

I waited for him to shame me like Firas did or ask me not to mention my ex-husbands like Jacob did, but he didn't. In fact, he was inquisitive and very interested in my past. He made me feel like I was safe in the ability to see a restaurant or anything, have a memory and be able to share it freely. "Oh, I've been here before with my ex," something I would have never dared utter with any of my ex-husbands for fear it would upset them. Fahad upset Ata, Ata upset Ziyad, Ata and Ziyad upset Firas, and all of them upset Jacob. This is something normal for us in the Middle East. When we move into a new relationship, all the past relationships are banished from our tongues, so we don't create suspicion or jealousy in our new relationship. For example, if a Saudi girl used to speak to men in chat rooms that information would never be uttered to her husband as it would make him question her morality. So, we all learned to pretend and hide our pasts, praying all the while that they would never come back to light.

There was only one piece of information I omitted and that was the history with my stepdad. After Ata, I never wanted to tell anyone again and I felt like it didn't matter, my stepdad would still be in my life as long as Yasmin was still in college and he had his clutches around my youngest sister, Lina. He was living far away now in Alba, Texas, and while I could explain that he was a brute, there was no need now to get Daren riled up. My baggage was heavy enough without adding sexual abuse. Humans can't process as much information at once as people think and often in relationships people forget that it's good to give them the information gradually with time between for them to process it.

I spent every evening Daren was in town at his place before heading home and every weekend I stayed over. Andy, my boss at work, started to make comments like: "How are things with the Doctor?" and "He sounds serious." I always smiled and said, "We'll see how it goes." One evening before we ate dinner Daren sat me down on the couch. He looked at me and asked, "When did we meet?" I smiled and said, "At D Magazine." Thinking he was being silly. He asked again, "When did we meet?" I said, "At D Magazine." He looked at me and said, "We met at Starbucks a year ago." My mind tried to recall as he said, "I used to go on power walks early in the morning and then have a cup of coffee at the Starbucks in the Fairmont Hotel." "Oh my God! I remember you, you looked like a homeless man, ha-ha, that's crazy!" "Yeah, I know, I had a flash this morning. I recall looking at you and thinking you were such a classy classic beauty but every time I would say good morning to you, you would give me a bitchy look like you were saying *Fuck off,* so I decided I had better things to do." "Wow, how crazy." "It's like we were meant to meet but not then." It was as if the universe knew when it was time for us to meet.

We had been dating for a little over two weeks when I came by one day after work and he took me by the hand, and we headed up the stairs. "I need to show you something." As we climbed the stairs he started to talk about the empty side of his closet and how he had emptied it to make space for his partner. My heart began beating at an alarming rate as he said, "I think you should move in." I slowly sat down on the bathroom floor as I said, "It's too soon, too soon." He sat beside me as I started to feel a panic attack coming on. He said, "Okay, it's okay. How about we just say you stay here sometimes, and you can bring some things and just leave them here, but you won't live here. How about that?" I took two deep breaths and said, "Okay, I can stay sometimes, that would be okay." I came to realize later that this was a pretty big deal for Daren. He had never lived with someone outside of his first marriage even though he had some official girlfriends over the years.

After four failed marriages I had become weary of everything. Will it last? I had just accomplished something huge by getting my stepdad to agree to let my sisters and I have an apartment and there was no way they could pay for it on their own. I talked to Yasmin one night about Daren asking me to move in, about how scared I was to leave the apartment only to have him change his mind, and then I would have to start over again. Yasmin suggested I start staying there more and just take it one day at a time. I said, "Of course I won't stop paying my share of the rent as long as you two need the place. I can't do that to you two." Yasmin said, "It's not me that will really have trouble with it, it's Noura. I basically live with Cole full time now. The only other obstacle is Baba." "I know, but I'm not ready to talk to him yet, that will take some careful planning."

Once in a while Yasmin and I would coordinate to drive down to my stepdad's house to pick up Lina to stay with us over for the weekend. One of us would pick her up and the other would drive her back. When I would ask Noura if she was going to come to the apartment that given weekend to see Lina her answer was always, "I have parties to go to."

Our parents' new house, which was really a mobile home without wheels on a large plot of land, was located on the back roads in Alba,

Texas. There were no streetlights so we had to make sure to leave during daylight otherwise we would be stuck sleeping over.

Noura got worse and worse as her boyfriend refused her request for a key to his place. Her reaction was to take his spare and make a copy without him knowing. We told her she was playing with fire, but she just giggled about her secret key. He finally started to insist on space, so she spent more time at the apartment and with neither of us there to object, she moved all our belongings out of the closet and dumped them in the other bedroom and claimed the larger bedroom for herself. The text messages between Yasmin and I went back and forth after we found all our belongings piled in a corner. It was time, I thought, to move in with Daren and so I took a drive down to Alba to see Lina and talk to my stepdad about Daren.

Upon arrival I was nervous and so I asked Lina if Baba had been in a good mood? She said she thought so. I asked my stepdad if he would show me the land. As we walked I said, "So, I wanted to tell you I was seeing someone, I'm not anymore but I thought I would tell you." "I figured when you were staying out a lot there must have been someone. Did anything happen?" Alluding to asking if we had sex. "Oh, nothing happened, we just dated. He was great on paper. He was 36, four years older than me, he had a master's degree in Physics, a good job and was sweet but he still isn't over her ex-wife, and he had an 11-year-old daughter among other things, I just didn't want to deal with it all." He nodded as we walked. I continued, "So, there's this other guy that came along recently and it's in the very early days, but I was thinking about seeing how it goes." I waited to hear his reply. He said, "Tell me about him." "Well, he's older, around 50 I think, has his own business, three kids but they're all grown up. He has a Ph.D. in Psychology, which I find interesting since I got my degree in Psychology, so we find lots of things to talk about." "Well, take it one day at a time, Princess, and see how it goes." I nodded like I wasn't sure I even wanted to date Daren and I was pleased he gave his consent. This would be the first meeting and I planned to talk to him a second time to give him an update. He felt like he was the deciding factor and that kept him calm.

Even when we left Saudi, the control our families and tribes exerted on us remained. We were raised to fear the displeasure of our parents and the wagging tongues of our relatives who have nothing to do with their time but stalk our online profiles for much needed gossip which always results in a phone call to my stepdad about how improper it was for us to have our pictures online. All of us kept our social media profiles private and only friended people we knew we could trust. *Omi* was the worst of all of them, making sure to put our younger cousins to the task of Googling our names on a regular basis. Even this far removed from Saudi society, we were still required to uphold the honor and reputation of the family. The abomination in their minds was to look as though we were sluts running around uncovered in America, since it might have an effect on the marriages of our younger female cousins. It was ridiculous….

Yasmin and I started to brainstorm. Neither of us were happy paying rent so that Noura could party and trash the place. Finally, we came up with a plan and I had to drive down to Alba to convince Baba it was a good idea. My stepdad agreed, based on the videos of how messy the apartment was, that I could move out to my own place. Yasmin could move into an apartment with a female roommate closer to school or a dorm, and Noura could get a female roommate. Yasmin was afraid and rightly so that if she said she had an apartment with a female roommate it would only be a matter of time before Baba showed up in Denton unexpectedly to meet said roommate and find out her roommate was Cole. Neither of us wanted to contemplate what he would do if he knew she was living with a boy. While he might not blow up as he had done in the past, he would have definitely devised a plan that used our knowledge of Saudi Arabia as women against us. He would say something innocent like, "Oh, Yasmin, there is some paperwork I need to file in Saudi at the ministry for your scholarship and you will need to be present." Yasmin would agree to go to Saudi to file the paperwork and never return.

Noura stopped speaking to me, so I had to get my news from Yasmin. Yasmin talked the apartment situation through with Noura and decided she would stay on the lease but move to Denton, this way my stepdad would think she was still living with Noura at least until her degree was done. Noura was hurt because she felt like once again I met a man and abandoned her. Perhaps in a way she was right, but it was my life and I fell in love, and I wanted to see where it would take me. To be honest, looking back I might have taken longer to move in with Daren had our place not been turned upside down and trashed like a crack house by Noura, but I guess we will never know now.

Noura's gay friend, Ale, texted me out of the blue saying he heard I was moving out and that he wanted to move in and to please let him know how soon I could come to the office to sign papers. We decided not to do anything with the lease except take me off it. Adding Ale would surely be reported to my stepdad since he added himself as the financial guarantor. He did that not because we weren't capable like he made us think but so he could hear news of everything and have the right to a key. He was always good at convincing us it was for our own good … in case one of us lost our job we would not lose the apartment and so on. Now it was going to be a set of small moves and waiting until the lease was up before we could officially add Ale. Ale's mother, who said she would pay his rent, was insisting on having him on the lease. Yasmin convinced Noura to convince Ale to keep everything as it was until the lease was up for renewal. By that time Yasmin would have graduated and the apartment management would not need to inform my stepdad of any changes since from his side, the lease just ended. They would then draw up a new lease for Noura and Ale using Ale's mother as a financial guarantor, since neither he nor she were financially stable enough to take on the lease alone.

Daren was wondering why all the back and forth and worry over my stepdad when we were all grown adults, but I explained that it was just how it had to be until Yasmin was officially free. The apartment management agreed that since I had no effect on the lease if I was taken off, there was no need to alert my stepdad and we were all so relieved.

The weekend came and I went to the apartment to move my things. Daren was out of town, so I had to do it myself. I thought it was best since Noura despised Daren for taking me away and I didn't want to deal with any drama. The night before, she had moved every piece of furniture that belonged to me, my books, my clothes, my toiletries, everything, and stacked it in a pile near the front door. I took everything I needed and loaded it in my car and everything else, I placed by the garbage bin outside. It was a new start, and I was not going to have it spoiled by whatever message she was trying to send by piling all my things up that way.

I feel sometimes that I have been trapped in some kind of mental and at times physical cage. A pretty cage most of the time, but still a cage. We all fear flying free, will we survive? Will we be cold? Will we be alone? Will we be able to take care of ourselves? But I feel like one day of freedom is more precious than any beautiful cage without worry. Life is meant to be lived, not waited through.

Daren asked If I could go on a two-week cruise with him through Asia. He had done training for a sales team at Silversea, an elite cruise line, and they had given him a cruise which he had not used because he couldn't find someone he would want to spend that much time with. We would start in Hong Kong, then Vietnam, Thailand, and end in Singapore. I was ecstatic but there were two obstacles. My job and my stepdad, since my cell would be out of touch often overseas and my stepdad would be sure to notice if I went missing. I did not want to be outside the circle of trust with my stepdad again since that would mean I would have no more contact with Lina, who would have been forbidden to talk to me, and I would no longer be able to help my sister navigate life with him.

I decided the easier obstacle to start with would be my job, since if Andy said no, I would not be able to go in any case. As I walked into his office in the morning I said, "Hey, Andy, I was wondering, and I know it's a crazy request since I only just started working here, but I got invited by Daren to go on a two-week cruise through Asia. It's the trip of a lifetime and I know I don't have enough PTO, but would you mind? It's the slow season with Thanksgiving and Christmas around the corner." He turned his head to the large screen which was always on the Golf Network and then looked back at me and said, "This doctor guy, what does he do again?" "He works for himself, travels to present keynotes, and writes bestselling business books. He is really brilliant. Can I go, please?" I said as I put my hands together and bent my knees slightly.

"Well, I guess it will be alright, but your PTO will be in the arrears so don't expect any time off again for a long while." "Yes, of course! Thank you, Andy!" "You better go let HR know that I agreed and make sure the intern knows how to operate the phone." "You got it, Andy." With that I did a little spin on my heels and headed straight to the HR department.

I texted Daren and said, *"Guess what?" "What?" "We're going on a cruise!"* When I got to his place that night, we were celebrating when Daren got a phone call from his mother. They talked about this and that and suddenly Daren's mom said, "You're going with Elise on a two-week cruise? Now, I know you're all grown, but you shouldn't put the honeymoon before the wedding!" Daren let out a loud laugh as he assured her that there was no talk of marriage since neither of us was interested in getting married again. I realized that my stepdad would insist we be married if he knew we were thinking of going on a cruise and it was time to go down to Alba again to see if I could get him to agree.

I called my best friend, Noor, to talk through my plan with her. I had kept her apprised of my relationship with Daren through text messages here and there. While she would have disapproved in the past because Daren wasn't Muslim or Arab, after Jacob she seemed to realize that there was no stopping me from loving whom I pleased. "Honey, he is taking me on a cruise through Asia! The only problem will be getting my stepdad to agree, Honey. He will say we need to be married and Daren doesn't want to get married, neither do I. At the same time, you and I both know he won't want me to marry a Christian or an American. At least those will be his excuses anyway while the truth is he likes to keep me unmarried. As if it makes him my guardian even in America." She huffed and said, "Fuck that Mother Fucker! And stop calling him your dad. His name is Asshole! I hate him more than I hate the devil. He is a vile creature and you let him make you afraid. You're in America, you're American, stop letting him bully you. Go live your life. You don't owe him any explanations." "But my sisters, Honey" "Your sisters are grown, they should do the same." "It's not that simple, Honey!" "Yes, it is!" I lowered my head and let out a sigh. "I know it is, but the truth is I just want it all, like in the movies when you get married and your husband joins the family, you take him home to meet the family, you watch old home movies, your mom brings out the photo album and embarrasses you. Why does it feel like it always has to be a fight, every time I fall in love? Why can't he just let me be happy, married or not?" "Because he is a fucking asshole, he will never change. Ahh, I wish I could kill him! My dad is an asshole, but I have never seen anyone more manipulative and evil like that man you keep calling your dad. He may have raised you, Honey, but he is the fucking devil!"

I knew she was right. I was holding on to a fantasy of a world where my family became the fairy tale version of itself. I knew it would never happen but a part of me never wanted to stop trying. It was what I was raised to expect and the idea that it would never come to life saddened me. It was one of the things I envied about Noor's life. Her mother-in-law was a trial for sure and her dad, too, but at the end of the day after she got married the two families became one and broke bread together. I was always placed in the position to choose to be single and with my own tribe which had all the traditions I loved. Playing Monopoly with my siblings, watching Disney movies as a family, poking fun at my brother, Mohammad, every time he saw a blonde girl. It is life's little details that we find ourselves holding on to time and time again. The smells, the food, the language, and all the flaws my family came with. I had accepted them because they were my tribe, something none of us gets to choose. But the one thing I always wanted no matter how much I tried to obey my stepdad he never granted me that one thing. Harmony.

I texted my stepdad and told him things between me and Daren were evolving, and I wanted to talk to him about a few things. He said I should meet him in Terrell, Texas, which was halfway between Alba and Dallas. Daren was out of town that weekend, so I woke up Saturday morning and started the 45-minute drive to Terrell, Texas. As I drove, I sent Daren a nervous video message telling him to wish me good luck.

When I arrived in Terrell, I parked my car near the restaurant where we would be having breakfast. It was a small rundown diner and the town seemed almost ghost-like in its emptiness. I silenced my cell phone and placed it in my bag, in case Daren called or texted. My stepdad, if I replied to a text, firstly might give away how much in love with Daren I was. But even more frightening was if he were to ask to see our correspondence. Refusing to hand over my phone would give him suspicions. Out of sight out of mind I needed him suspicion free.

My stepdad started the conversation off by saying, "So, tell me what is going on, Princess?" "Well, nothing yet, but I wanted to see what you thought about me going with him on a cruise for two weeks in Asia." "Is that all that is going on?" "Well, he asked me to move in, but I can't do that. Of course, we're not married, and it would be wrong and would set a bad example for my sisters." "Good girl. It's good to see that now that you're older you are thinking about things more clearly." "Tell me more about him," he said. He listened as I prattled on and on about his character, making sure to mention everything I knew my stepdad would like. "Oh, he's like you, Daddy," knowing full well that line would stroke his Saudi ego like he was the example of what I wanted in a future husband.

"He's very polite, he reads a lot like you and it's just so easy to spend time with him. Like I was always used to being in relationships where you feel required to always carry on a conversation but with him we can just be sitting side by side reading and saying nothing and it doesn't feel awkward at all. (Making sure to reference his own comments of how a relationship should be from the email he sent me 12 years earlier, when I was married to Ata). It's like he doesn't invade my space even though he is around all the time."

He said, "You're in love with him, then." I paused and said, "I don't know yet. I know I enjoy his company." My stepdad nodded his head as he took a bite of his breakfast and stared me down to see if I was lying or hiding something. I said, "Tell me what you think, Daddy? I would really love your opinion. I would love for you to meet him and tell me what you think." "You know, when you're in love you glow?" he said. Although the comment would have probably made any daughter smile, it made me extremely uncomfortable. As did anytime he complimented me on an outfit, my hair or anything. He might have been at bay for years now, but I put nothing past him. In this, Noor was always right. He was evil and the most evil people are those who have the patience to wait years and move people around like chess pieces until suddenly unbeknownst to you, you're cornered, trapped and helpless.

It would take me many more years to realize that he was moving me around the chess board with his refusal to meet my husbands, his comments about family, honor, and his emails to me. His slight way of pointing out that Firas, for example, had no right to tell me to cover or not. Thereby silently creating discord. He was creating a false painting whereby I had the illusion of freedom. He knew that because of how he would react every time, I would push forward and yet he was never far away and always happy to pick up the pieces. Divorce by divorce, defiance by defiance in his mind made me realize that he was always right and perhaps I was better off always under his guardianship exactly where he wanted me. As each marriage ended in divorce, I always saw it as a dad who only wanted to help me pick up the pieces of my mistakes.

I said, "No, I'm not in love with him. How could I fall in love with someone I barely know? Besides, even if I was, it would not matter. I'm taking things one step at a time." "Good girl. Well, I think he sounds very nice and mature. As you know, of course, even if I wanted to meet him I cannot until there is a decision." ''What do you mean, Daddy?" He leaned in and said, "A decision." "But what if there is never a decision?" "Then I will never meet with him. You know the rules, Princess." I nodded that I understood. He said, "Now as for the cruise, you know him. If you think it's safe, of course you should go. Asia is beautiful and when you get back if you're still comfortable with him after spending two full weeks in his company every day, then move in with him. As long as your sisters never know." I said, "Really, Daddy?! I can go! Thank you! Thank you!" he smiled as I said, "And I'll keep you updated about how it goes and if I decide to move in once we get back."

I decided to follow my stepdad back to Alba so I could see my sister Lina and hangout with my brothers. As soon as I was in the car alone I took out my phone and called Daren while I was driving to tell him the good news. "Baby! I missed you. Did you see any of my messages? I was worried." "I'm fine. Sorry. I just didn't want to risk having my phone out. He might see a message saying I love you and freak out. I need to give him things gradually. I have seen him overreact before" Daren had no idea how bad his reactions could get. I wanted so much for my stepdad to be on board and for Daren to get along with him so I could have the rosy imaginary picture in my head. Daren said, "Okay, what are you doing now?" "I'm driving down to Alba to spend the night and I won't be able to text you there unless I'm alone, which will be very hard with three siblings, my mom, and my stepdad in a small two-bedroom house. Once they are asleep I'll text you, Baby. The good news is that he said I can go and move in with you! I love you!" "That's great news! I knew he would come round, see there was nothing to worry about. I love you, be safe."

My phone remained in my pocket the entire time at my stepdad's, as it would look suspicious to carry my purse around and I could not leave my phone unattended. There was never any knowing what kind of phone hacking technology my stepdad's idle hands had at his disposal. That night, we played Monopoly, cards, and I taught my little brother how to play chess. We laughed, had dinner and we all sat in the living room to watch a Disney movie. That night after everyone had gone to bed at 9:00 p.m. I took out my phone and texted Daren. "I love you; I'm going to sleep but I wanted to tell you goodnight."

I drove home excited that I would be able to go to Asia with his blessing. I called Yasmin on the way home and Daren to let him know I was safe and sound. I felt like the world was finally going the way it should. I was in a wonderful relationship, and I was going to get to keep my tribe, too.

When Daren got back we sat up at night talking about our upcoming trip, what me and my stepdad talked about and many other things. "I really want to meet him after everything I have heard," Daren said. "He made it clear he won't meet you until there is a decision." "What is the decision?" "It's stupid. He won't meet you because he needs to publicly appear that he disapproves of our living in sin while in fact he obviously doesn't mind." "That's so funny!" "I know, but it's just how he is. He won't change his ways. He allows us to not cover our hair but still observes the public appearance that we do it without his permission. This way when my grandma calls with stories of a picture she found, he can yell and say, 'What! I will punish her,' It's all a big show we are forced to put on, but this is how he is." "I understand," Daren said, "My parents are old fashioned too, my mom even said not to put the honeymoon before the wedding, ha-ha. Our parents are the way they are and there is no changing them." We sat for a good while talking like we always did when suddenly Daren looked at me and said, "Why don't we just do it?" "Do you want to do it?" Daren said, "I never wanted to get married again but if it shuts everyone up, why not!" I smiled and said, "Are you sure you want to get married to me?" Daren said, "Do you want to get married to me?" I said, "I love you; I want to be with you forever, but we don't need to get married just to appease our parents." Daren said, "I know but me meeting your stepdad is important to you and you being able to come with me to see my mother without all her comments, which is important to me so, let's just do it and shock the hell out of them all, ha-ha!" I smiled and said, "Okay, let's do it." We planned that we would get engaged on the ship to make it a romantic memory and then tell everyone.

The next day I texted my stepdad this line: "A decision has been made and he wants to meet you before we leave for Asia." "Are you sure this is what you want, Princess?" "Yes, I think you should meet him." "Okay, tell him to meet me at this location in Terrell on Saturday at 10:00 a.m." "Can't I come along? I can sit at another table. It's so silly that we still do things like we did in the old days." "You know the rules, Princess. The men talk alone." "Okay, Daddy. Thank you." I told Daren the details and that Saturday he headed out.

After Daren left I was a nervous wreck, I had done everything I could to prepare Daren for meeting with my stepdad. So often any man who meets with my stepdad leaves a wreck just like Firas had all those years ago. I made sure Daren took him a gift which was customary for a man asking for his daughter's hand in marriage. As Daren reached the location he called to say he was there. After that, the silence started just as it had been when I was with my stepdad. Thirty minutes turned into an hour and that hour turned into another. I started to worry if my stepdad had scared Daren away or worse thrown him in a ditch somewhere. I paced and smoked as I waited for one of them to call me with an update.

Four hours later my phone rang. It was my stepdad. "Daddy? How did it go?" "If I say I don't want you to marry him, will you still marry him?" I paused and wondered what could have gone wrong? Daren was a wonderful human, and everyone loved him. I gave him all the info he needed to win him over and my stepdad had seemed to like everything he heard. Daren brought him a gift and I'm sure he paid him every respect so what could have happened? "Daddy? What's wrong? What happened?" He only repeated himself, "If I say I don't want you to marry him, will you still marry him? Even if I said no?" I took a deep breath and said, "Well… I guess so. Yes, I'm going to marry him anyway. What's wrong?" "I didn't like him." "Why?" "No matter, you're not my daughter if you marry him even though you know I don't like him." With that he hung up the phone.

I leaned over the table and began to cry. Then I immediately picked up the phone and tried to get a hold of Daren. It rang and rang, and Daren finally picked up. "So sorry I had to fill up gas and I was planning to call you on my way home. It went great, nothing to worry about." "Daren. he just called. and he asked me if I was going to marry you even if he didn't like you and when I said yes, he said I wasn't his daughter and hung up. What happened?" Daren was confused since on his side since everything seemed to go smoothly. "We had a great three-hour conversation. We talked about everything; I really enjoyed our time so I can't think of anything." Just as Daren was speaking my phone started to ring. It was my stepdad. "I have to go, Daren, it's my stepdad calling. Let me call you back."

I accepted the call as soon as I could, afraid if I let it ring too much it would upset him. "Daddy?" " I didn't like him!" "I know, Daddy, but maybe you missed something, he's really a wonderful person." "I didn't like him, Princess." There was a long pause and then he said, "I loved him." I let out a deep breath as I began to cry. "Now go have fun on your trip and let me know once he proposes." I nodded and said, "Thank you, Daddy." With that I hung up the phone and sat down to catch my breath. This was his way. Happiness was a big joke to him and leaving me in my cloud too long was humorous. To him it was dangerous for one person to be so happy; it makes them forget to check for danger. He had to see what would happen if he scratched the layers of my cloud. I suppose a part of him wanted to know that even if I married Daren, my allegiance would always be first to him and the tribe. His success was achieved when I answered, and he heard me crying so he revealed his actual thoughts and left the incident as a warning on my heart that he had the power to change his mind and opinion anytime should I forget to follow his advice.

The worst abuser is the one who breaks you and then convinces you that they were right to do so. I called Daren and told him that he was just messing with me, he loved him, and all was well.

We were on our way to Hong Kong. You learn a lot about people when you travel, and I was pleasantly surprised that Daren was not afraid of flying since all of my previous husbands were. He was courteous, attentive, and sweet, and the long flight to Hong Kong seemed to pass by in the blink of an eye. with one exception. It had been the first time I had taken such a long flight in a long time since I arrived from Geneva and halfway through the flight I was craving a cigarette so badly the only thing I could think of to do to forget about smoking was to sleep. Arriving in Hong Kong we exited the terminal to take the Airport Shuttle Bus. I stood frozen for a moment as I stared at the smokers standing outside in the corner. I wanted a cigarette so badly my mind could think of nothing else. Daren said, "Let's go!" I tensed up and got irritated saying, "I can't walk that fast, slow down," taking hold of my bag and following behind him to the shuttle. Not knowing how to explain to him that I really wanted to smoke.

It's funny how in the beginning of relationships, and for some people forever, we often can't find the words to ask for your needs. As a result, we often penalize our partner for not reading our minds which we forget is impossible. We got off at Mong Kok MTR Station, then we walked around three minutes to our hostel. I was irritated the whole way and Daren kept asking me what was wrong to which I kept saying, "Nothing I'm just tired, let's just get to the hostel." Thinking the whole time once we get to the hostel, I'll be able to smoke.

Arriving at the building where the hostel was, we went up in an elevator that was crammed with people. It was as if there were so many people that almost all the buttons were pushed. When we got to our floor we followed the signs to the office. I had never seen anything like it before. It was a tall square building with a hollow middle. All the balconies were facing the inside of the building facing the center which was a small plot of open sky land jam packed with air conditioner units and their buzzing sounds filled the air. There was not only the hostel in this building there were countless residents, but their laundry also drying on the balconies, the old woman watching TV could be heard and the children playing and running along the open-air halls.

We entered the office and started to check in when the office cleric pointed out our large bag and said, "Umm, I'm not sure your bags will fit." "Fit in the room?" Daren asked. "Well maybe it will fit under the bed," she said as she directed us to the room. When she opened the door we saw what she meant. The door opened up onto a small space only big enough for one person, to the left was the bed and directly in front of the door was the bathroom. In order to save space, the shower was over the toilet meaning you could shower and do your business all at the same time. Daren placed the large bags on the side of the bed, meaning we would have to crawl over them to get out of bed and go the bathroom. There was a mirror behind the bed not for erotic purposes but to make this tiny little room look bigger. Then we closed the door and started to laugh at the size of the room.

Daren reached over and began to kiss me, but I pulled away. Thinking only about how I really wanted to get out of the room and smoke. Daren's mind raced as he said, "What's wrong?" "Nothing!" I finally had to say it, "I just really need to smoke!" Daren laughed and said, "Aha! I forgot you were a smoker. Come on, let's go down." We took the elevator down and crossed the street to the nearby 7/11. I pulled out my cigarettes and lit up as Daren went inside and bought us each a mini bottle of cheap wine. We placed the wine bottle on an electrical box using it as our table and I smoked as we watched all the people walking past. We talked about the size of the room, the strangeness of the city and how he felt like he was almost home. We stayed out there more than three hours before heading up to the room to sleep. That night will forever remain in my memory as one of the most non-conventional dates I have ever heard of, but just like when we were in Dallas, it didn't matter where we were as long as we were in each other's company.

We walked around the rest of the city until finally it was dinner time. We came upon a noodle shop that smelled good and with no access to the Internet we would have to rely on what things looked like and smelled like instead of how many stars they had on Yelp. Once inside we realized that the servers didn't speak English even though the menu was translated into English. There were no pictures on the menu but the dish I ordered said chicken with noodles. Daren ordered something with pork, and we waited. Daren said, "You drink, which is against Islam, so why not eat pork? I think you would really like it." "I have actually tried pork and my sister Noura eats it, but I don't like the taste or the smell. I find it repulsive." "You know that is all in your head, right?" "Perhaps, but it will be hard to shake being told all kinds of scary things about pork my whole life." "Like what?" "Well, my grandma said once that the pig is the only animal who will fornicate with anything while his mate watches and therefore any person who eats pork will turn into a pig that has sex like one..." raising my eyebrows I nodded as Daren laughed. I continued, "It's ridiculous, I know, I can hear it in my head, but it won't leave. My aunt used to say that pigs eat garbage so eating them is like eating garbage. My mom said that the meat is full of parasites and all kinds of other things that will make you sick." "But, you said your sister eats pork, wasn't she raised like you?" "Not really, they are half Saudi, but they left the country when they were in middle school, so they are more American than I am. I grew up there until adulthood and what is drummed into you for a long period of time can continue to beat on long after you decide it is not necessary." "I think you should try it again." "On this front you will lose, I will try anything once but I'm not going to eat pork. Ever!" "We'll see, maybe I'll make it my secret mission to make you like pork, ha-ha."

I half smiled as my mind went over what he meant. The Saudi in me was stubborn and didn't like his blatant disrespect of my choice not to eat pork. What if it had been for religious reasons, what if, what if? Does he think he has the right to change me? I changed my tone and snapped at him a little, "Daren, why is it so important for me to eat pork?" "It's not. I just want to free you from those old superstitions so you can experience things." "I didn't like pork and I'm never going to eat pork; I am happy the way I am and …" He grabbed my hand and said, "Hey, I'm sorry I didn't mean anything by it." I nodded and looked down as I realized that I was overreacting. Like so many who grew up Saudi, we rage against everyone who tries to change us. This is one of the ideologies that will hold the Saudi people back. Change is scary because it can have unknown consequences and as my past had proved with Firas, changing to make him happy bore no fruit. Learn to speak Syrian Arabic, gain weight, walk this way, dress that way and still he never held up his end of the bargain. Maybe that's it, maybe we see modernization and liberties as a change that can head in any direction into the unknown. It's like telling someone something they see as not broken needs fixing.

The next day we woke up more excited than anything. We dressed, headed down to breakfast and were on our way to the ship in a taxi. When we arrived, they asked for our passports. I felt a sense of fear. "Wait, why are they taking our passports, I'd like to keep mine with me." It felt like when my stepdad would keep my passport or when a maid arrives and their guardian keeps their passport, I didn't like feeling like I could leave at any given moment. Daren said, "It's normal, they will need it to apply for all the documentation the ports will need" I reluctantly said. "Oh, well, I guess that's fine as long as they keep it safe."

They said that they could take the bags down to the room if we would like to have some lunch in the main dining room. As I saw the buffet I clasped my hands together and said, "Daren! Have you ever been so excited to see salad!" Daren laughed and said, "No." After two days of not seeing anything that resembled the food we were used to, the sight of the salad was mesmerizing! We grabbed plates and I danced around so excited to be on a cruise ship for the first time. As I walked through the dining room as we headed to our table I let out a short "Hello!" "Hello! "Hello!" while standing up on my toes and leaning in with a smile to every crew member we passed.

The ship was built to support about 220 passengers but due to the season being winter the manifest only had about half that in passengers and just as many crew members. This meant that your glass would magically fill itself if you turned around for a second. Everything was included in the cost of your passage. When we were done eating we headed down to our suite, a good size room with a balcony that looked out over the endless ocean. We were greeted by a crew member who introduced himself. "My name is Joshua, and I will be your personal butler." "Wait, just for us?" Daren asked and I giggled with excitement. "Yes, Sir," Joshua replied as he added, "May I bring you some champagne?" "Yes!" I shouted as I danced around the room in excitement.

As we were drinking the champagne an announcement came over the intercom saying, "All hands-on deck for a safety review before we get underway." We headed out, buzzed on champagne, to the deck where they handed us each a life vest and a whistle. As they talked about the safety procedures and what to do if you fell overboard I would interrupt suddenly and say, "And when do we get to blow the whistle?" "Only in case of emergencies," the crew member replied as he continued with his presentation and then asked if there were any questions. I raised my hand and said, "But can we practice blowing the whistle?" "There is no need," he replied. "But just in case … please, I really want to blow the whistle!" "Alright," he said as he half smiled at my silly behavior. It turns out the entire crew was above us, mesmerized by the bouncy whistle girl!

From that day forward, on the ship I was known by the names Miss Prosecco and the Whistle Girl. The ship to me felt like a world where the rules of society did not exist. There was no proper time to eat, nap, talk, play, swim, dance, skip or everything else. It was a colorful place where every crew member wanted you to be happy at all times. As we toured the small cruise ship we passed a small casino that had a poker table and some slot machines. I asked Daren if he gambled and he said sometimes but not really and asked me, "Do you?" "No, not really, in Islam it is a sin to gamble, but my ex did like scratch cards and once we drove to the casino in Oklahoma." We then passed some gift shops and took the elevator up to the pool deck. Even though it was early December the weather was warm enough to swim.

The butler said we should make a reservation for dinner at one of the five elaborate restaurants on the ship, there was Italian on the lower deck, the large main dining hall that served almost anything, a sizzling steak restaurant on the pool deck where they cooked filet and prawns on a hot rock, the upper deck which only served breakfast and a super private French restaurant with only 6 tables that cost extra if you decided to book it for dinner. We made a reservation for the Italian restaurant and made sure to dress and arrive on time. Upon arrival, however, the number of passengers meant the restaurant was practically empty most of the time. After that we stopped deciding where we planned to eat until we were ready to eat since despite the protocol they were trained with there would definitely be a table … reservation or no reservation. This drove the butler crazy because he only knew how to operate by the handbook and his handbook said he needed to make us a reservation for dinner every night.

The next day we woke up to Bloody Marys by the pool and when we ordered food, I ate the burger as if no one was there to judge me. Daren turned around looked at me and said, "What happened to all that wife training?" I replied out of the side of my full mouth, "What? You never seen anyone having a good time before?" Daren laughed and laughed at my witty reply, and I shocked myself that I was able to let go and just relax like none of the traditions and rules of my past applied to me now. As if the ship was its own free world where no one was judging or gossiping about you.

We stopped in Vietnam, then we reached Bangkok, Thailand, the place where Daren grew up. Daren took me to all his favorite places. He talked about all the adventures he had growing up. I felt so close to him and wished that maybe one day I would be able to take him around where I grew up, but I knew that would be impossible. Even if we could obtain visas to visit Saudi it would not be possible. I was a female Muslim and he was a male Christian and such unions are forbidden under Sharia Law.

We walked into LIYA Indra Jewelry, where Daren's parents had bought so much jewelry, in addition to steering their friends to this respected and dependable store. The amazing Alice, the longtime owner with her husband, John, pulled out many beautiful rings but all of them seemed so normal, white gold with a diamond, yellow gold with a diamond and after having had 5 diamond engagement rings already, I was looking for something unconventional like me. Finally, I saw it. It was a pink and peach colored spinel stone with two small diamonds on either side and a white gold band. There was no one to say, "No, it needs to be bigger! What will people say" or "No, it needs to be a diamond," or "It has to show how much he thinks you're worth." Daren asked if that was the one I wanted and I said yes! We bought it and Daren placed it in his pocket saying, "You can't have it yet." Daren also ordered a ring to be made for him and a band for me. He said he had always wanted a black star sapphire ring and I suggested that we make it his wedding ring. As Alice was ringing up the price of the ring I was online trying to calculate if I had enough money to buy it for him as a wedding gift, but I did not, so I remained silent. Daren did not notice that I was trying to work out how to pay for it as he pulled out his card and paid for everything. He also ordered a white gold diamond band made for me.

I bounced around in a cloud of joy all day knowing soon he might pop the question but when? We visited many dress shops, shopping malls and of course our favorite was the Chatuchak weekend market, which was an outdoor market full of stalls and so vast that it would be impossible to see it all in one day. Finally, as we were finishing up and getting ready to head back to the ship we came across a Thai silk dress shop and there it was, a turquoise dress. It was the same color as the dress Ghadah had worn when she got married. I had always envied her ability to choose the color of the dress she wanted to get married in. I picked it up and tried it on and Daren said, "You should get married in that." I smiled, and we bought the dress. We were so unconventional and yet it was as if we both had been looking for someone who shared our unconventional minds. We were like two trees who looked at all the other trees and decided we would grow differently.

Back on the ship on our way to Singapore we dressed for dinner like we did every night. When we got to the restaurant Daren said, "Oh I forgot my bag, you sit, and I'll just go back to the room and get it." Daren often carried a bag with him everywhere that held a few copies of his WSJ best seller in case he should meet someone he wanted to give a copy to. I sat and Daren arrived, we ate, laughed and at the end of the meal Daren asked for a plate of cheese. I made a face since he really liked this crystalized crunchy cheese they always served at breakfast and the sheer texture repulsed me. The waiter brought out a covered platter and placed it down in front of Daren as usual then suddenly he placed another covered platter down in front of me. I stared at the platter thinking, "Oh man! They brought me cheese, too? Now I'm going to have to eat some to be polite, Yak!" The waiter said, "Bon appétit" and lifted the cover off the platter revealing a pink suede ring box with my engagement ring. I was overjoyed as Daren kneeled down and said, "I've never met anyone who completes me like you do. Will you marry me?" and his eyes welling up with tears. I blushed as he took my hand and I said, "Yes!" I had never been proposed to in such a romantic fashion. The waiter snapped a few pictures of us. Then that evening we made love and Daren started calling me his wife. It felt like the world was just as it should be.

That night Daren posted the pictures on Facebook and announced to everyone that he got engaged. There was a mixture of excitement and sadness for all those who had tried everything to convince him to marry them. Women who had dated him for years, and suddenly I showed up on the scene and he was engaged. The rumor mill started. Was I a gold digger, was he my sugar daddy, and all other manner of thoughts. Our age gap seemed to create quite a stir.

I texted Noor who said, "Congratulations, Honey! I'm so happy for you!" I told her I would tell her more about him when I got back since we only had access to the Internet for one hour each morning unless we wanted to pay for it. Then I texted my stepdad who said, "Good, now go and be happy." Yasmin sent me a dancing emoji and said, "Woohhooo!"

When we docked in Singapore we found a sports bar and ordered a couple of beers while we waited for our plane to take us back to Thailand for a couple of days since we were so close by. I would head back to Dallas and Daren would stay on for a couple more days. I had to get back to work. As we sat Daren was looking at his phone as he asked, "What are you doing on December 22nd?" "Let me check my calendar … I don't have anything that day. Why?" He smiled and said, "Let's get married on the 22nd!" I came around the table and fell into his arms. Daren set up a Facebook invite and started to invite people to a small wedding in his condo. We agreed it would be small since both of us had done the big wedding before. As time went on the number reached more than 70 people; only five of them were people I had met before. Everyone was dying to lay their eyes on the woman who had swooped in and stolen Daren's heart. I invited my stepdad and my mom along with my siblings.

Daren's ex's and past conquests started to act like crabs in a barrel. Climbing over each other to find out when, where and how he was getting married when he had just met me. One night as we were watching TV his phone rang. It was his ex-girlfriend, Heather. She was the first woman he had dated after his divorce 10 years ago. Daren chuckled and said, "You answer it!" I smirked and said, "Okay." Picking up the phone I said, "Hello?" She paused for a moment and said, "Oh! Oh! Hello" as if she just realized who was on the line. "Hey, how are you? I'm Heather. "I'm sorry, Daren is just in the bathroom. He's on his way." "Well, that's okay because I wanted to talk to you to find out, who are you?" "Ummm," I said as I looked over at Daren and said, "He's here!"

handing the phone back to Daren. She prattled on about how excited she was for him all the while probing to find out where I came from, how we met, and secretly, why me and not her. I felt bad for all these women, but pity so often is like butter … at some point you run out and then you have to put something else on your toast. Finally, she asked when we were planning the wedding and Daren told her it would be next week. She freaked out and said, "No, no you can't get married that fast she will need time to find a dress." "Well, actually she got a dress in Thailand and we're doing it in my condo, so we're all set." Daren said goodbye and we both had a good laugh.

There was a never-ending list of strange reactions to our sudden shocking new direction of our relationship. The first day I returned from work, as I walked in, the accountant came out of her office and said, "So? Did you get engaged?" Surprised since I had said nothing to anyone at work, yet I said, "Yes, we did actually!" "Ha! I won the bet!" "What bet?" She turned her head and shouted to the COO, "I win! She got engaged. You owe me breakfast!" then turning to me and saying, "We had a bet that you would get engaged on the cruise and I won!" I smiled and got to work. Midway through the day as she and I were chatting about this and that she said, "So, when's the wedding?" I said, "December 22nd" "Oh nice, next year?" "Next Thursday!" She smiled ever so uncomfortably and then looked at my stomach and said, "Oh I see." I ignored her obvious attempt to infer that I must be pregnant and that was the reason why we were marrying.

Daren invited his children over to have dinner. His middle child, Madison, was as sweet and inquisitive as could be, but Callahan, his youngest, was polite but very reserved. His eldest son, Jordan, could not make it for dinner that night. I expected as much since I could imagine what it was like. They were naturally concerned since they didn't know me at all. Their dad, who had been pretty much single for 10 years, met someone and in the space of less than four months was getting married. He asked them how they felt about it and they both very openly said it felt like it was very sudden. I knew better than to have any input whatsoever this was between them and their dad. He asked them how they would feel about us having children. Callahan folded her arms and said, "It won't be my brother or sister." I paid no mind to it. As they were getting ready to leave they both said, "Dad, will you walk us to the elevator?" Daren walked them to the elevator. They cornered him and said, "Dad, she's been married before. What if she's just after your money? Maybe you're not thinking clearly," Daren laughed and said, "I know what I'm doing."

The next day there was a football game and his friends prescribed caution and said "I wouldn't get married without a prenup. You barely know this girl, I would get one." Daren told me later and I said, "I'm not marrying you for your money so if you want a prenup we can draw one up. I'm happy to sign anything," Daren said, "No, I don't want one. I know you. They were just concerned." "As they should be. I'm glad you have so many people who look out for you."

Thursday morning came and it was the day of our wedding. There were no traditions kept, no societal rules were upheld, and no superstitions given life. He saw my wedding dress when I bought it. There was no need to spend a night apart before the wedding. We slept in the same bed and woke up together the day of the wedding. When 12:00 p.m. rolled around I looked at Andy and said, "May I go?" "You just took two weeks off." "I know, but I'm getting married today and I need to get my hair done." He was clearly irritated, but he said, "Alright, you best get going." I grabbed my purse and jumped out the door.

I got my nails done, then I headed to the hairdresser who put my hair up and secured a bejeweled parrot broach in my hair. It was my ode to Yoshi who was always with me in spirit. I got home around 5:30 p.m., texting Yasmin on the way so she could meet me at the condo. My mother called and said, "I'm trying to come, Honey, but Baba said he has decided he is not coming." "What why?" "I don't know, he just decided he is not coming." I tried to text my stepdad to find out why he was suddenly not coming to my wedding but there was no answer as if he was enjoying adding a little bit of distress to my wedding day. My mom texted saying ,"Can you pick me up?" "Pick you up from where?" "Where else, I only have one home." "Mom, it's 5:30 p.m. and the wedding is at 6:30 p.m. and your home is two hours away." "Okay, I'll manage, thank you."

When I got home I found Daren napping on the bed. I smiled and sat beside him. He opened his eyes, kissed me, and told me how beautiful I looked. As I entered the bathroom I saw a small silk bag and inside was a beautiful opal pendant, I had admired when we were buying the engagement rings. I jumped out of the bathroom and said, "How did you?" "I knew you liked it and so when you went to the bathroom I had her pack it up for me and it's been in my jacket pocket ever since." It was the greatest and most surprising gift I had ever received on a wedding day.

Happy and joyful, Yasmin arrived as I was putting on my makeup. "Honey, do you know why Baba is not coming?" "He's not coming? Didn't he say he liked Daren and he agreed didn't he?" "Yes. Why is he doing this? It's like whenever I'm happy he has to come up with some way to bring me down a notch." "Never mind him, it's your life, not his, and you don't need his approval. Honestly if Cole and I get married, I'm not inviting any of them to my wedding." I nodded and did my best to stop wondering what I had done to upset him. My mother arrived, crying as usual, and there behind her was my stepdad. I hugged him and said, "Thank you for coming," not wanting to ask why he felt the need to play one of his mind games. My stepdad said, "I heard as we were coming in that the wedding is going to be broadcast live on Facebook." "Ya, but you won't be in it not to worry." "We better not be." I looked at Daren and said, "Could you ask your friend not to film my family when it goes live?" "Ya, of course."

It was because my stepdad didn't wish to be in a video that showed my mother without her head cover and my stepdad sitting among people who were drinking. Even though he drank, he never wanted any proof that he did, not to mention appearing to approve of his daughter marrying a Christian. I asked where Lina was but the answer I got was that she was sick … I knew it was because my stepdad didn't want her seeing what was possible and how beautiful a world outside of the world he kept her in was. You can't long for or miss something fully if you've never seen or experienced it. An Amish person, for example, who never saw or heard of a TV would not miss having one.

The condo was packed with people. I could hear all the voices downstairs as I paced back and forth memorizing my vows. We had decided to continue our unconventional approach to love with the writing of our own vows.

I descended the stairs and stood before Daren who said, "I can't say enough about this beautiful, beautiful girl that I am going to marry." I kissed him and hugged his friend, JD Miller, who would be presiding over the ceremony, along with his friend, Kevin, who would officiate the marriage. Daren looked at the crowd and said, "This is going to be a very unconventional wedding by the way, if you haven't already noticed. Also, we're Facebooking live. I don't know if that's ever been done before but if you're wanted by the law best stay away from the camera." My stepdad gave me a look that I pretended not to notice.

JD started off by talking about how we're all here tonight to celebrate love. "You two, like me and my bride, wanted someone to talk about love and just do something spiritual. It's a celebration of finding the person you want to be with in this life and in this journey." Turning to Daren he said, "You and I have talked about this, and I know that if you have chosen this woman to be your bride you don't want to change anything about her. Not only to find a soul mate but to fall in love with them, what a gift." JD then made way for Kevin who said, "I get a text from Southeast Asia that said, "I might get engaged tonight," and I texted back and said, "What do you mean you might? Do you mean you might not ask, or she might not say yes?" I didn't get a response by the next day, my phone started blowing up. With people calling going, "What's going on?" I said, "Well I guess he asked, and she said yes!" and now a couple weeks later here we are. Then I thought, well, if I'm going to stand up here and talk for three minutes, what am I going to say? Because normally I would tell a little bit of your love story. But I don't know it. Then normally I would tell the story of your bride, since no one wants to hear the stories of us catting around as dudes together, but I don't know the story of your bride. So that left me with one thing to talk about and that's marriage. Which is a little dangerous because marriage is being reconsidered and redefined. So, I'm going to tell you what I think it was supposed to be and what it is in this moment. I come from a Christian background and in my faith we believe that everything God made was good. You can read the story that God made the whales and the ocean and the sky and that was good but there was one thing he made that was not good and that was when he made a man and put him in Paradise alone and then he said, "That's not good," because Paradise isn't Paradise if you're alone. So, he makes the woman, and he brings her to the man and at last, Paradise is complete. Daren, your world is full of good things and much of your journey over the last few years has been about gratitude, your beautiful kids, your career, and everything else, but Paradise is not Paradise without that one thing. So, some months ago in an incredible act of grace, God let these two incomplete Paradises intersect. So that at last Paradise could be perfect. I am now going to give you a wish that soon we will turn into a prayer and that wish is that now and forever your Paradise be perfect. Because you have each other. Do you have vows that you would like to exchange?"

Daren said, "Am I going first?" "Yes, you're going first," Kevin said. Daren pulled out his phone and said, "I'm sorry but I've got to read it." I said, "I left mine upstairs, I thought we had to memorize them, ha-ha!" and everyone chuckled. Daren said, "First of all, I do know our story and I do know this girl and we met at D Magazine a few months ago. It was love at first sight for me, I think it was just a job for her. As things progressed I fell madly in love with this girl and then I fell really in love with her on our third date and we sat here at this table, and I taught her how to play chess. Now mind you, I have been playing chess for 35 years and half-way through the game, I looked down and she was about to beat me. A lot of people know her as being bright and bubbly, the biggest compliment I've heard today was from the door man, Simone. I said to him, "Simone, I'm doing it. I'm getting married," and he said, "Oh, Daren, every day she is so happy and it's not a fake happy, it's a real happy." So, beautiful Elise, you entered my life, stole my heart, and fulfilled every want and desire I dreamed about in a lifetime partner. Thank you for showing up at just the right time and for changing my life forever. I commit to loving you, to protecting your heart and doing my best to make you smile every day until your face hurts. I give up nothing and I gain everything by becoming your honored husband. You light up my brain and you are truly my Paradise. The biggest testament to how much I love this girl is that I'm not the least bit hesitant, I'm not the least bit nervous, this is the easiest thing I've done in my life."

I had never written vows before so in the fear that I would never be able to write anything as well as Daren I referred to a romantic comedy called The Vow and crafted my vows from there. My voice was low, since speaking in front of so many people was not something I was used to. "I vow to always hold you with tenderness and have the patience that love demands. To speak when words are needed and to share in the silence when they are not. To agree to disagree on your crystalized crunchy cheese. To live within the warmth of your heart and always call it home." Daren said, "Do I get to kiss her yet?" Everyone laughed as Kevin shook his head no. We exchanged rings and Kevin said a prayer: "We are going to ask God to bless in abundance Daren and Elise. Let their life be infused with joy and peace and we ask it in all faith, Amen. Now, Daren, you may now kiss your bride!" Daren kissed me then leaned back and let out a "Woop!" as Kevin said, "It is my honor to present to you Dr. and Mrs. Daren Martin."

Everyone cheered as Daren introduced his friend, Chart, to give a toast. "Like so much of this I'm unrehearsed. But I probably have a better seat than most to witness you guys fall in love. Considering I live upstairs. I've known Daren now for about five years and I've known Daren to be a man of a lot of wisdom and a man of a lot of faith and what I've seen in his love affair with Elise is that wisdom and is that faith. I think you see that culmination tonight where he's saying that he's not nervous, he's not worried about his decision and he's sure of it. And that's the reflection of the wisdom that he has and his years of experience. Like so many here, I think I regard Daren not so much as a career mentor, but as a spiritual mentor. Someone I look up to as a smart guy and a guy that understands the world in ways that I would like to. In Elise it's been remarkable because she is one of the most worldly but one of the most grounded people I've ever met in my entire life. Someone who grows up in the Middle East but still has a heart that reflects and loves Western civilization but looks back at the Middle East with a sort of reverence. It's remarkable and it's beautiful so I'm more than thrilled for Daren and more than thrilled for Elise and frankly, it's very exciting to be the upstairs neighbor who got to watch them fall in love. So, you all raise a glass to Mr. and Mrs. Daren Martin."

Hearing myself described through the eyes of someone who had only known me a short while, moved me beyond belief and Chart forever became a part of our lives like a very dear brother who could never be replaced.

The guests raised their glasses and the camera panned to show the guests, showing my stepdad and my mom. My stepdad waited for the camera to pass and then promptly got up and issued the order to my mother that it was time to go. Seeing them leaving I came to say goodbye to my stepdad as always uncomfortable with too much happiness, only half smiled and then held out his hand in the direction of the door indicating to my mother, *let's go.* Yasmin stayed for a bit and then headed home. Cole could not attend for fear that my stepdad would recognize him from the picture he had used to scare Yasmin half to death all that time ago.

The number of people was dizzying to me, person after person introducing themselves and saying congratulations. Not unlike any wedding I had attended before, but everyone here was from the West and different somehow. There was happiness in the lack of traditions, customs, and societal restraints. I could smoke when I wanted, drink as I wanted and say whatever I wanted without the concern of judgment or gossip. This time I wasn't just something to create stories to fill time for bored old mothers, I was the queen of the night who could do no wrong.

We moved the party to the Ritz Carlton across the street which continued late into the night then Daren and I came home. In the morning after the cleaning was done and the house was in order I sat on the balcony and thought about how grateful I was that my stepdad agreed for my mother to come to my wedding and that he attended as well. It's hard to explain but this is how we were raised without the tribe's consent, nothing feels complete. You can take the girl out of Saudi Arabia, but it will take a long time if it's possible, to take Saudi Arabia out of the girl. I looked at Daren and said, "We should go visit my family, I want you to meet Lina and my brothers, Mohammad, and Osama. Would you mind a drive to Alba?" "Sure, why not, I would love to meet them." I texted my stepdad and said, "Hey, we were thinking of coming down to see you for lunch. Is tomorrow around noon good?" He replied, "For what purpose?" I was irritated by the question as if I needed a purpose to want to bring my husband to meet the rest of my family. "To see you and the family, Daddy." "I guess that should be fine," he said.

We headed out early and arrived right before noon. As we pulled up and I stepped out of the car, Osama ran towards me saying, "Maha!" I turned to Daren and said, "This is the baby, Osama, but we call him Ozzie." My mother, in her traditional fashion, chose the name because she enjoyed the look of shock on people's faces when she told him his name since he was born only four years after 9/11. We, the siblings, decided it was cruel to name a child something that would get him beat up, so we gave him the nickname Ozzie. Inside, Daren was greeted by Lina, my mom, and my stepdad, who actually rose from his chair to greet Daren. We talked about how the wedding went and everything seemed like some perfect dream as my stepdad pulled up old home movies on the TV of me when I was a girl and, shockingly enough, he even showed old videos of me with my sisters which I could not believe was possible for him. We played chess, Monopoly, and then we went to lunch at a Mexican restaurant. We decided to take one car and piled into my mom's van. Daren asked me as we entered the restaurant quietly if he could order a drink with lunch, I looked at him with the face of someone afraid for their life and shook my head no!

We sat and we talked about normal things like what I was like as a child. When we got back to my parent's house, Daren, as he had always done, got out first to help me out of the car by taking my hand. I kissed him on the cheek and smiled with joy. Was this the happy ending, had I finally managed to have my cake and eat it too? Family and husband, happy.

As it started to get dark we headed back home, I never felt more complete. Arriving home, Daren turned on a documentary we had been watching and I headed to the balcony to smoke since I had not had a cigarette since we left that morning. As I sat in my happy cloud on the balcony a text message came from my stepdad.

***Stepdad**: Please get your car insurance transferred off my policy tomorrow.*

***Me**: Why the hurry? What's wrong?*

***Stepdad**: You're your husbands responsibility now*

***Me**: Ok I get that but why the rush. I am planning to change my name so it will be easier if we just wait until that is done.*

***Stepdad**: Change your name and give up who you are for him… Good luck getting a lawyer to change it back on your next go around. Also, don't come here again and disrespect the rules of this house.*

***Me**: How did I disrespect the rules? I brought my husband to visit my family.*

***Stepdad**: Public displays of affection in front of your siblings is disrespectful even if he is your husband. Also, that man in your wedding referred to me as a Barbarian in his speech. I raised you better than that.*

***Me**: We didn't make out or anything, he just kissed me on the cheek. I don't know what you're going through that is causing you to send me these messages, but I love you daddy and I wish you as much happiness as I have found.*

***Stepdad**: Are you talking about me asking you to stop kissing, touching, and fondling each other in front of your younger siblings and myself, or me seeing history repeat itself and can't do anything to change it? Please explain*

***Me**: Are you okay, Daddy?*

I wondered if he had gone mad or had I finally been able to see it? I didn't want to lose the way I felt watching my siblings meet and hang out with me next to Daren, so I backed down.

***Me**: Look, Daddy, sorry.*

***Stepdad**: You should be, but that in no way change how much I love you and wish you the happiness.*

***Me**: Love you to Daddy will remember to respect your way of life*

Stepdad: *Whatever. I thought I built in you how to sense your surroundings and act in the best way to be as light and grateful as the surroundings needed. I raised you better than this. I am fine, I guess I had great hopes that you learned from your mistakes but oh well, that's life. I'm very happy for you and wish you good life. I've tried not to force my lifestyle on you when you are not around me, all what I'm asking is to respect my lifestyle and do not impose yours on me when I'm around. That should not be hard to figure by a caring person. I don't want to go back and choose isolation as a way of maintaining my lifestyle. Solid foundation of caring between the 2 of you that foundation is the only thing that survives after the fire of love burns out. Unlike what American believe (Which is mainly Movies talk) Love is not everything, caring is. You can never go to a total opposite with caring as you can with love (There is no opposite to caring but to love there is hate) To me love is the higher fluid needed to ignite a good campfire, but caring is the solid wood that will keep burning long after the fluid is gone. But hey what do I know.*

Frustrated and confused. I replied.

Me: *Why are you fighting with me Daddy, I thought we were going to talk to each other not yell at each other over text. I'm sorry that I'm human and in loving and caring for my husband I forgot where I was, I forgot that I need to play along with the way you want to raise the little ones for which you know I am always supportive of how you want them raised. I have always done my best to do everything you ask and sense everything. Sorry again. That being said, I am a 32-year-old woman and I am human. We all need reminders every now and then. I did my best to appease you and that was the best I could do. I don't like this pattern of bringing out all the old wounds and hurting each other. I want us to be past all that. Comparing Daren to anyone who I married before is not fair, saying you are seeing the past repeat itself is not kind. I don't bring up everything I can to hurt you, I just forgive you tell you hey that hurt my feeling and so on, because I love you I don't say things like "Just like always and you did this and* *that" That is not caring Daddy and it's not the relationship I want for us.*

As I walked into the condo with tears in my eyes Daren asked what was wrong. I showed him the messages and Daren picked up his phone and composed a message to my stepdad.

> ***Daren****: Your daughter loves you like crazy. Not sure how we offended you but please stop being an ass to my wife.*

My stepdad texted me right after:

> ***Stepdad****: Please put a leash on your dog, and make sure he barks far away from my phone, I don't speak dogs. I wish you all the happiness in life, and since it got to to this level I think it is best for both of us to stop communicating, or should I say insulting each other.*

He issued an Arabic insult saying, "Put a leash on your dog." My Saudi blood boiled since I knew Daren would not feel the insult as deeply as I did. In calling my husband a dog he was saying that I married a dog, that his children were dogs and that our children would be dogs. Thus is the intricate nature of Arab insults, they usually involve insulting the entire family line. Other examples are *"Kus Ukhtic"* translated literally, it means your sister's pussy but it's real meaning is, I'm going to fuck your sisters pussy even when your sister has nothing to do with it. My favorite one was always the most ridiculous *"Kus Um Illi Nafathic"* Fuck the mother of the person who shot you into life. This one covers insulting three generations at once. If you want to piss off an Arab go after the honor of his family and my stepdad with all the names he had called my past husbands he never employed an Arabic insult as grave as calling my husband a dog.

I texted Yasmin the text messages:

> ***Yasmin****: What the hell, why would he act like that after he gave you the ok that is just ridiculous. Just brush it off, maybe mama got to him and he just bursted. You're happy where you are, don't let him bring you down. I know how it feels when Baba gets like*

that he makes you feel like it's all your fault but it's not. Your 32 for God's sake just be happy in the moment and let him calm down he will warm up to you again. I know he loves you! I guess he just doesn't like seeing any of his girls with other guys. And he's not used to the whole American wedding stuff so that has also pushed his nerves a little. I promise it will be ok in the future but for now ignore it and be happy!! You newlyweds go celebrate and be happy with the one you think is the final one!

As she read the remainder of the messages from my stepdad she sent this:

***Yasmin**: Wait so because you're in a honeymoon phase you're not actually in a caring relationship? I don't understand, and then he does the same thing every time and just shuts you out. That's caring?*

***Me**: I don't even know babes*

***Yasmin**: I'm pretty sure I grew up thinking what's in the movies is love without discussing it or showing it blocking the real world from your kids does not grow them up to make good decisions. He's just very close minded.*

***Me**: I swear I forgot to avoid any contact with Daren, and he seemed fine and then all of a sudden he turned back into himself.*

When Daren saw the message my stepdad sent me he sent him a reply:

***Daren**: I'm so sad for you. That you can't see what you have. That you would dismiss it out of fear. I have a lot of respect for you. Stop being so harsh. Trust me. It will serve you well - The Dog.*

***Stepdad**: Thank you for your "ass"ness, I forgot that you are the bona-fide expert in my life matters, now that you've been in it for a whole long, long, long, long… 3 months. I am so enlightened by these "wise" words my scared merciless "ass" needs room to reflect on them, so why don't you give me some space and don't call for.......ever.*

My stepdad was a snake but every time he shed his skin I thought it meant that he had changed, when the opposite was true. It was time to leave him where he wanted to be. Isolated in the past with his outdated lifestyle.

My stepdad, like many in Saudi Arabia, when he felt that his way of life was being altered or influenced, would retreat into isolation. To him it was like locking all the doors when there was a plague coming and hoping that remaining shut up would prevent the air from entering the house and killing everyone and everything he loved. In reality, it wasn't a plague that was coming at all, just life. A country that can no longer sustain itself on oil revenue alone must change but the biggest battle the Saudi's will face is the concern that what is coming will rip away and kill all that is romantic, all that is beautiful and all that they are accustomed to. The conservative Muslims and the government resisted Satellite TV because they feared it's influence, but they failed to prevent its arrival and its survival. Just like that, they will continue to resist until they wake up and realize that there was never any hope of controlling everything forever. They can resist change, but change will come no matter what and embarrassing it will be much less painful.

I don't know what that change will look like or the future of Saudi Arabia. Will the *Layanrchy* move into a more public figure role? If elections take place and someone from one of the four main regions gets elected, will there be a civil war? Will the *Wahabis* rise up and start fighting a *Jihad* against the modernization they see as leading the people away from the second true coming of Islam that Ibn Abdul Wahab had worked so hard to build. Does the Arab world need a third coming of Islam to lead it's people into a new era of Islam?

All these questions, and many more, swirl in my brain. The biggest question is what questions and fears swirl around in your brain and what good is a question if it is never asked? My hope for the people of Saudi Arabia is simple. Start asking questions. Start allowing your people to have honest and open discussions so you can hear what they really want without repercussions falling down on their heads. I believe that every ruler, leader, or government is responsible for the wellbeing of his people which includes helping them move into the 21st century mentally not just physically. Many of these issues are found at home, for at least three generations still think and live in the past. They think a woman should not be traveling alone, be in mixed company, that our husbands should be chosen based on factors like family, honor, reputation, wealth, and education. I think we need to be left to choose our husbands based on the lifestyle we wish to lead, not just for us, but for our children. I think that we should have better female representation in government and that we should consider one day having a female ruler. Princesses need to be given more credit for their minds and given the right to represent the greater female population musically if you don't want to see all the most brilliant female minds leave the country to perish.

I ask myself questions every day from the simple "Why do I drink coffee? Is it because I like it or is it because society told me that is what you drink in the morning. I asked myself a hundred questions when I left Canada, why do we pray the way we do, why do we cover the way we do, and to find the answers I asked questions and dug through the Islamic library in Abu Dhabi. That is my biggest wish for you, my reader, to remember that through knowledge and the depths of reflection answers can be found and although change is scary it is also a blessing more often than not. It is freedom.

EPILOGUE

Daren and I have been married for seven years now. One night, a year into our marriage, we went to a movie and a rape scene upset me to the point that Daren asked the right questions and I relayed to him everything my stepdad had done to me. I left my job and started working with Daren in his company so I could travel with him to all his fun speaking gigs and we could be together more. It is a rare couple that can spend 24/7 playing, working, traveling, hanging out together and be even more in love five years later. We have joked together that we must have been lovers in a previous lifetime. In 2021 I became the CEO of his company, and I never regretted a single moment.

Noor had another son and, thanks God, she did not have girls. For it provides her one day maybe with a way out, should she find the money and the circumstances to help her carry out her dreams.

I never saw my sister Noura again. She went out into the world and continued as she had always done, spending more than she made, finally turning to online porn to help cover bills. She had more talent in her little finger than any of my siblings and I possessed in our entire bodies.

Yasmin continues to thrive in America. Despite my stepdad's every attempt to get her to come back to Saudi Arabia to complete her required six months of employment in the Kingdom after her scholarship, she has refused to return. She lives with Cole and becomes more and more successful every day. I'm proud of her.

During COVID my stepdad took my mother, my sister Lina, and my two brothers back to Saudi Arabia. I begged Lina to come live with me and not go back, but she did. He isolated her from the world mentally as he had done to me and through that isolation he gained total control.

I hope she is wise enough to navigate the sea she finds herself in and I hope one day she might light up and shine in her homeland.

I never saw my stepdad again, but his words will forever echo in my ears. It is a burden that I carry. Perhaps one day the echoes will turn to nothing but faint whispers on the wind, far away.

Someone asked me recently if I have any regrets and the answer is no. They asked me what I learned from each of my husbands and the question felt difficult to answer at first, but the truth is they all taught me a different degree of one lesson. They taught me how to trust myself.

Ata pushed me the first few steps forward out of the fear of doing things on my own.

Ziyad pushed one bar further when he forced me to find my own accommodations lest I be shipped back to my family in America.

Firas taught me even more through his constant put downs and shaming of my past: that I need no one to validate my worth and that I needed to trust in my own opinions of myself, not those around me.

Jacob taught me that it is okay to be alone after so many years of being raised to believe that without a husband I was incomplete.

Finally, Daren continues to push me further and further out of the rabbit hole that holds all the brainwashing that was my world.

But the real teacher was always me and everyone else was the practical exercises needed to learn these lessons. We are all our own teachers; we just don't know it.

I might never see the place I called home again, Saudi Arabia. But I look back with a great deal of reverence every day. Please see it for me, my dear reader, for despite many things, there is beautiful poetry in that desert, there is wisdom in their coffee, and there is love amongst its people.

CLOSING REMARKS

Even today I still have moments where that shrouded woman who was raised to be silent, docile and submit to men, who is hard to turn down as she nags at me from the back of my mind, whispering, "That's not proper. What will people think. You shouldn't talk about that," and so on. The threads of that covering are a part of me and will never leave me, but I get to decide if I want to take that garment and turn it into something entirely different.

What are your firsts? What will you choose? Where do you want to be? What do you want from your country and what do you want for your daughter?

The choice is yours and always has been. All you need do is reach out and take it. These are my thoughts, and these are my opinions, and this is my journey.

I hope it will inspire you to aspire, experience, breathe, wonder, and succeed in whatever journey you decide to take on the road to whatever your freedom looks like.

I can speak when so many cannot.
- Jamal Khashoggi
(May he rest in peace.)

Elise Evans Martin
– To read more please visit my website Eliseevans.com